Kessinger Publishing's
Rare Mystical Reprints

THOUSANDS OF SCARCE BOOKS ON THESE AND OTHER SUBJECTS:

Freemasonry * Akashic * Alchemy * Alternative Health * Ancient Civilizations * Anthroposophy * Astrology * Astronomy * Aura * Bible Study * Cabalah * Cartomancy * Chakras * Clairvoyance * Comparative Religions * Divination * Druids * Eastern Thought * Egyptology * Esoterism * Essenes * Etheric * ESP * Gnosticism * Great White Brotherhood * Hermetics * Kabalah * Karma * Knights Templar * Kundalini * Magic * Meditation * Mediumship * Mesmerism * Metaphysics * Mithraism * Mystery Schools * Mysticism * Mythology * Numerology * Occultism * Palmistry * Pantheism * Parapsychology * Philosophy * Prosperity * Psychokinesis * Psychology * Pyramids * Qabalah * Reincarnation * Rosicrucian * Sacred Geometry * Secret Rituals * Secret Societies * Spiritism * Symbolism * Tarot * Telepathy * Theosophy * Transcendentalism * Upanishads * Vedanta * Wisdom * Yoga * *Plus Much More!*

DOWNLOAD A FREE CATALOG
AND
SEARCH OUR TITLES AT:

www.kessinger.net

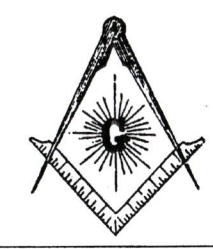

DISCARDED

Geo. W. P. Custis

RECOLLECTIONS

AND

PRIVATE MEMOIRS

OF

WASHINGTON,

BY HIS ADOPTED SON,

GEORGE WASHINGTON PARKE CUSTIS,

WITH

A MEMOIR OF THE AUTHOR,

BY HIS DAUGHTER;

AND

ILLUSTRATIVE AND EXPLANATORY NOTES,

BY

BENSON J. LOSSING.

"First in War, First in Peace, and First in the Hearts of his Countrymen."
Gen. Henry Lee's Oration.

WITH ILLUSTRATIONS

★

First published 1860 by Derby & Jackson
New York.

★

Entered, according to Act of Congress, in the year 1859,
BY MRS. MARY CUSTIS LEE,
in the Clerk's Office of the District Court of the United
States, for the Eastern District of Virginia.

★

INTRODUCTORY REMARKS.

The men and women who were cotemporary with Washington have nearly all passed away, and in a few years every tongue that might now speak of personal recollections of the Father of his Country will be silent, and that for ever.

As we recede from the age of Washington, and history takes the place of verbal traditions in giving a narrative of the events of those days, we become more and more anxious to garner, in memory and in books, the precious seeds of information concerning the men whose names stand prominently on the records of those events. Especially do we desire to know all about Washington, the great central figure of the group of patriots whom we have been taught to revere as the founders of the republic.

We feel confident, therefore, that a work like this, containing the minute details of much of Washington's private life, as well as his public career (which general history does not reveal), and related, too, by a member of Washington's own family — one who lived with him from infancy until his nineteenth year — will be peculiarly acceptable to the American public.

In this work, new phases of Washington's character are displayed. We see him as a private citizen — as a plain farmer — as the head of a family.

The correspondence between Washington and his adopted son, while the latter was in college, first at Princeton and afterward at Annapolis (never before published), will be found deeply interesting, especially to our young men. Washington's letters display the fatherly anxiety and solicitude with which he saw the child of his adoption, sometimes giving promises of great improvement and future usefulness, and at others pursuing a disappointing course, and awakening painful doubts concerning the character of his manhood. These called from Washington words of great wisdom; and the advice contained in his letters to young Custis we would commend to the careful consideration of every young man starting out in life.

The general arrangement of the whole work, and the elaborate explanatory and illustrative notes to the *Recollections*, by the editor, whose familiarity with the subject is well known, so connect and generalize the desultory sketches of the author as to make the work an interesting LIFE OF WASHINGTON. In these notes will be found much rare matter never before presented in a collected form.

The correspondence between Washington and the father of the author of these *Recollections*, during the Revolution (printed in the Appendix, and now for the first time made public), will be found especially interesting. Their letters treat chiefly of private affairs, and give us a vivid picture of Washington's sagacious views in relation to the management of property. They also show the wonderful capacity and adaptation of his mind in giving close and lucid attention to private concerns, while engaged in the most arduous and momentous public duties. Two of Mr. Custis's orations; the famous oration of General Henry Lee on the death of Washington; an interesting account of the presentation of a ring to Lafayette by Custis at the tomb of Washington; a specimen of Washington's care and exactness in the management of his agricultural affairs; and a notice of all the original portraits of Washington, are also printed in the Appendix.

The memoir of Mr. Custis, by his daughter, which properly forms a part of the work, will be found highly interesting, the subject being enriched by the introduction of very curious matter pertaining to the earlier history of the family.

With these few observations, we submit the work to the public, feeling a pride in offering one so intrinsically valuable to every student of our history and lover of his country.

THE PUBLISHERS.

NEW YORK, *August*, 1859.

CONTENTS.

Memoir of George Washington Parke Custis..................PAGE 9
Original Correspondence between Washington and Custis....... 73

RECOLLECTIONS OF WASHINGTON.

Editor's Preface.. 119
Author's Preface... 121

CHAPTER I.
The Mother of Washington....................................... 125

CHAPTER II.
Washington at Mount Vernon..................................... 151

CHAPTER III.
Battle of Princeton and Death of General Mercer................ 179

CHAPTER IV.
Battle of Germantown... 193

CHAPTER V.
The Battle of Monmouth... 211

CHAPTER VI.
The Surrender at Yorktown...................................... 229

CHAPTER VII.
Washington's Life-Guard.. 256

CHAPTER VIII.
The Hunting-Shirt.. 264

CHAPTER IX.
Washington's Headquarters...................................... 273

CHAPTER X.
Mysteries of the Revolution.................................... 289

CHAPTER XI.
The Indian Prophecy.. 300

CHAPTER XII.
Daniel Morgan.. 308

CHAPTER XIII.
Robert Morris.. 323

CHAPTER XIV.
Thomas Nelson.. 333

CHAPTER XV.
Alexander Hamilton... 340

CHAPTER XVI.
Henry Lee.. 354

CONTENTS.

CHAPTER XVII.
Birth-night Balls and the Theatre .... PAGE 364

CHAPTER XVIII.
Life at Mount Vernon 370

CHAPTER XIX.
Washington as a Sportsman 384

CHAPTER XX.
The First Year of the Presidency 393

CHAPTER XXI.
Washington's Home and Household 406

CHAPTER XXII.
The Retired President 433

CHAPTER XXIII.
Outline Life-Pictures 461

CHAPTER XXIV.
Last Hours of Washington 472

CHAPTER XXV.
Personal Appearance of Washington 480

CHAPTER XXVI.
Martha Washington 495

CHAPTER XXVII.
Portraits of Washington 516

APPENDIX.
I. Original Correspondence between General Washington and John Parke Custis 533
II. Oration at the Funeral Solemnities to General James M. Lingan, by G. W. P. Custis 571
III. Address at the Celebration of the Russian Victories over Napoleon, by G. W. P. Custis 585
IV. Presentation of a Ring to General Lafayette, by G. W. P. Custis, at the Tomb of Washington 591
V. Directions for the Management of his Farms, by General Washington 595
VI. Oration on the Death of Washington, delivered before Congress, by General Henry Lee 615
VII. Original Portraits of Washington 624

ILLUSTRATIONS.

George Washington Parke Custis .... Frontispiece
Colonel George Washington .... *Opposite page* 21
Mrs. Eleanor Parke Lewis (Nelly Custis) .... " " 45
Mrs. Martha Washington (Mrs. Custis) .... " " 495
Facsimile of Washington's Account with Miss Custis .. " " 496
Facsimile of Washington's Record of Survey. .... " " 445

MEMOIR

OF

GEORGE WASHINGTON PARKE CUSTIS,

BY HIS DAUGHTER

WITH

THE EPISTOLARY CORRESPONDENCE

BETWEEN

WASHINGTON AND CUSTIS.

MEMOIR

OF

GEORGE WASHINGTON PARKE CUSTIS.

It is with much diffidence that I offer to the public the *Recollections* of my father, in their present unfinished state. They were written by him at intervals of many months, sometimes of a year, during a period of thirty years, and were nearly all first published in the *National Intelligencer*, printed at Washington city, in the District of Columbia. They have been extensively copied by the press throughout the Union, and sometimes quoted by historians, but from the perishable character of the vehicle by which they were conveyed to the public, it is to be doubted whether a perfect copy of the series is preserved, except the one contained in this volume.

For many years my father, influenced by the urgent solicitations of friends in all parts of the Union, entertained a design to arrange and revise his *Recollections*, supply omissions, and have them published in the more durable form of a volume, as a legacy to his countrymen. But this design was never carried out; and now, actuated by filial affection, and a feeling that these recollections of the Father of his Country, by his adopted son, should not be lost—that leaves so precious should not be scattered to the winds—I have undertaken to perform what he left undone.

It seemed to me that a brief memoir of the author of the *Recollections*, and some notices of his family, connected as they have been with stirring scenes in the history of the past, would be acceptable to the public.

The following letter, also, written by an old and esteemed friend, so well expresses the feelings of all who knew my father, and desired the publication of his *Recollections* in permanent form, that I have taken the liberty of inserting it here:—

"WASHINGTON, *October* 6, 1858.

"MY DEAR MADAM: Many causes, unnecessary to mention, have prevented the fulfilment of my cherished purpose to express the pleasure with which I learned your intention of preparing the writings of your venerable father for the press, to be preceded by a notice of his life from the best pen, that of his only child. An intimate and unclouded friendship of more than thirty years with your beloved and lamented parents, gave me advantages for discerning and appreciating those rare and bright virtues which have made Arlington a place of frequent resort to many of the eminent and good of this and other countries.

"Your father was distinguished by talents which would have made him eminent in any profession to which he might have devoted himself; but his ample fortune, extensive and generous hospitality, and the care of large estates, led him rather to agricultural pursuits, general literature, and the indulgence of his taste for the fine arts, than to a profound study of science or philosophy.

"He read much, his memory was quick and retentive, and his knowledge of history and the public affairs of the world was remarkably full and accurate. To the history of his own country he had devoted much time and special attention, and was more familiar with the character of the men and events of the Revolution, than any one I have known.

"Probably no one of his cotemporaries so well understood, or so profoundly admired the retired and less obvious excellences, and the great public virtues and acts of Washington. The glory of that great man ever encompassed him, and inspired him with enthusiasm and eloquence. In his childhood he learned from Washington lessons of patriotism which were never forgotten. Hence, in important political questions he was deeply interested, and amid all the sectional controversies of his day he stood firm to the Union.

"He was warm and constant in friendship, had a high sense of what is due (in conversation) to absent acquaintances, and was ever reluctant to attend to remarks disparaging or injurious to others. He sympathized quickly with distress, and the poor found in him a ready and liberal benefactor.

"Nothing could exceed the easy grace and politeness of his manners, his uniform and benevolent cheerfulness, and the delightful eloquence of his conversation. There was the blending of good humor, cordiality, interest in those whom he addressed, with the riches of a brilliant poetic imagination, throwing light and joy upon all around. Those who visited Arlington immediately found themselves at home. Every want was anticipated by kind attentions, and nothing was omitted which could contribute to their happiness; they seemed to realize the return of the days when Washington himself welcomed his guests at Mount Vernon and presided at the feast.

"The writings you, Madam, are about to publish, will be welcomed by the people of the United States as historical papers of great value; and those containing recollections of Washington, as precious memorials of the life and habits of the Father of his Country in retirement, warm with the love and gratitude of his devoted son, and glowing with his genius. The discourses of your father on the death of General Lingan, and that on the overthrow of Napoleon, were greatly admired at the time they were spoken, and should be preserved as specimens of striking and commanding eloquence.* Your father was an orator, around whom the public ever thronged with delight, and who that ever heard him can forget the vivacity, grace, and interest of his conversation.

"The filial duty in which you so promptly engaged, and which you have so well performed, is a high tribute to the memory of Washington (with which that of your honored father is indissolubly united), and a service to that country which stands the only adequate monument of its great chief. But I will not presume to extend these observations farther, since I can add nothing to your information, and should fill a volume to convey my

---

* These may be found in the Appendix.

own pleasing recollections, or to express adequately my attachment and obligations to your family.

"I have the honor to remain, my dear Madam,
"Most respectfully your friend,
"R. R. GURLEY.

"MRS. MARY CUSTIS LEE, *Arlington.*"

The memoir of one so long known among us as the adopted child of Mount Vernon, whose mind was richly stored with memories of the past, whose heart and home was open to all who loved to hear of our immortal Washington, should be deeply interesting to the world.

The records of his early youth are somewhat imperfect, as those who could have best furnished the details have passed away; nor do we find any letters from his foster-father until the commencement of his collegiate life at Princeton.

Of his paternal ancestry we have accounts gleaned from a chest of old papers, very curious and amusing (though many have mouldered), containing letters, commissions, deeds and patents for land during the reigns of James II., William and Mary, and Queen Anne; and a commission for Major-General John Custis, in 1687, from Johannes, Lord Howard of Effingham, his majesty's lieutenant and governor-general of Virginia, appointing him collector of customs on the Eastern Shore. Mr. Custis had previously been made major-general to command the forces in that quarter during Bacon's rebellion.* He was the

* The episode in Virginia history, known as Bacon's rebellion, occurred in 1675 and 1676. The immediate cause of the outbreak was the dangers threatened by Indians from the north, who had made incursions into the settlements on the James river. It was, however, an outburst of republican feeling, which had long been growing in the colony, and which had become much exasperated by the acts of Governor Berkeley and the aristocracy. Finally, the republicans, under pretence of opposing the Indians, seized their arms, and led on by Nathaniel Bacon, an ener-

owner of a large estate, including several islands. Among these was Smith's island, which is still in possession of the family. General Custis married three wives. In favor of each he made a separate will, providing amply for the comfort of his widow, and even binding his successor in her affections (should she have one) by a heavy forfeit, to maintain the dwelling in the same state in which he left it. He also devised to her, her own wearing apparel, and any stuffs ordered for her that might be *en route* from England. To the last one, Madam Tabitha, who survived him, and married Colonel Hill, he bequeathed a handsome riding horse and accoutrements. His five children, John, Hancock, Henry, Sorrowful Margaret, and Elizabeth, were all apportioned; and legacies in land and money were left to various friends and to his sisters. The eldest son, John, was especially provided with landed property, out of which a hundred pounds were to be expended yearly for the maintainance and education in England of his son, John, the immediate ancestor of the author of the *Recollections*, whose portrait is preserved at Arlington house. In it, his hand grasps a book, near which a *tulip* is placed. The book contained an essay

---

getic young patriot, appeared in formidable array. The movement was without the governor's permission, and he sent troops to arrest the rebel, as he termed Bacon. This led to energetic action. Republicanism had become a power in Virginia, and, at its command, the governor was compelled, on the 4th of July, 1676 (a hundred years before the great Declaration of Independence), to sign a commission, acknowledging Bacon a member of the house of burgesses, to which the people had elected him; and also to give him the commission of a general of a thousand men. Finally, the governor summoned all the loyalists to his standard, declared Bacon a rebel, and received succor from England. Bacon and his troops, hearing of the approach of an overwhelming force, laid old Jamestown in ashes, and fled beyond the York river, where he died of malignant fever. His followers were dispersed, and the civil war ended. Had Bacon been successful, history would have called him a *patriot* instead of a *rebel*.

upon that flower, written by himself. Many works in the library, classical and scientific, with his name prefixed in German text, embellished with many flourishes (for he seems to have prided himself upon his chirography), shows that he was a man of letters, though of an eccentric genius.

This John married at "Queene's creeke," on York river, Frances, the eldest daughter of Colonel Daniel Parke. She and her sister, Lucy (afterward the wife of Colonel William Byrd, of Westover,*) resided there with their mother (whose maiden name was Jane Ludwell) in great seclusion, by the express desire of their father, then seeking his fortunes abroad.† The mother, in many

---

* Colonel William Byrd was a distinguished member of the king's counsel in Virginia, toward the close of the seventeenth century. When, in 1699, about three hundred of the Huguenots, or French Protestants, arrived in Virginia, after fleeing from persecution in their native land, he received them with fatherly affection, and gave them the most liberal assistance. He was generous to the poor around him. He was well educated, and his library was the largest on the western continent. In 1723, he was one of the commissioners for establishing the boundary line between Virginia and North Carolina. He died at an advanced age, in 1743.

† The following letter from Colonel Parke to his daughter, Frances, who married Colonel Custis, is preserved at Arlington House. The orthography of the original is retained:—

"St. James' *October* ye 20th
1697.
"My Dear Fanny—

"I Rec'd y^r first letter, and be shure you be as good as y^t word and mind y^r writing and everything else you have learnt; and doe not learn to Romp, but behave y^{r}selfe soberly and like A Gentlewoman. Mind Reading; and carry y^{r}self so y^t Everyboddy may Respect you. Be Calm and Obligeing to all the servants, and when you speak doe it mildly Even to the poorest slave; if any of the Servants commit small faults y^t are of no consequence, do you hide them. If you understand of any great faults they commit, acquaint y^r mother, but doe not aggravate the fault. l am well, and have sent you everything you desired, and, please God I doe well, I shall see you ere long. Love y^r sister and y^r friends; be dutiful to y^r mother. This' with my blessing is from y^r lo : father
"Danl. Parke.

"Give my Duty to y^r Grandfather, and my love to y^r Mother and Sister and serviss to all friends. My Cosen Brown gives you her serviss, and y^r Aunts and Cousins their love."

long and urgent letters, implored his return, pleading the state of her health as rendering her unequal to guard her treasures from the admiring eyes which pursued them whenever they were seen. Colonel Custis, with his foreign education and great wealth, was no despicable suitor. Colonel Parke gave his approval,* and the haughty beauty yielded. He had been forewarned that he could hope for no complaisance from his bride, whose temper was little calculated to allow happiness in her presence; but with the true spirit of a lover and the gallantry of the age, he professed to feel that to possess her would be heaven enough for him.† Their

---

* The father of young Colonel Custis received the following letter from Colonel Parke on the subject:—

"LONDON, *August* 25, 1705.

"SIR: I received yours relating to your son's desire of marrying my daughter, and your consent if I thought well of it. You may easily inform yourself that my daughter, Frances, will be heiress to all the land my father left, which is not a little, nor the worst. My personal estate is not very small in that country, and I have but two daughters, and there is no likelihood of my having any more, as matters are, I being obliged to be on one side of the ocean, and my wife on the other. I do not know your young gentleman, nor have you or he thought fit to send me an account of his real and personal effects; however, if my daughter likes him, I will give her upon her marriage with him, half as much as he can make appear he is worth.

"I have no one else to give my estate to but my daughters. This is what I think convenient to write at present. My service to you and all friends in Virginia.

"From your humble servant,
"To COLONEL CUSTIS." "DANIEL PARKE.

† The following letter of young Custis to his intended bride a few months before their marriage, in which, according to the custom of the time, he calls her his "Fidelia," is a fair specimen of passionate love-letters in the old colonial days. Its tone is quite different from that which characterizes the inscription upon his tomb, in which he so pointedly, though indirectly affirms, that his life, while he lived with his "Fidelia," was so unhappy that he considered it a blank in his existence:—

"WILLIAMSBURGH, *February* 4, 1705.

"May angels guard my dearest Fidelia and deliver her safe to my arms at our next meeting; and sure they wont refuse their protection to a creature so pure and charming, that it would be easy for them to mistake her for one of themselves. If you could but believe how entirely you possess the empire of my heart, you would easily credit me, when I tell you, that I can neither think nor so much as dream of

connubial enjoyments were of short duration, and in mercy to both, perhaps, after the birth of two children (a son and daughter), the small-pox ended her life at Arlington, on the Eastern Shore. The husband lived many years afterward, and directed in his will that a tomb-stone of white marble (now in existence) should be placed over his grave, inscribed with the following epitaph, to perpetuate his infelicity:—

"UNDER THIS MARBLE TOMB LIES THE BODY
OF THE HON. JOHN CUSTIS, ESQ.,
OF THE CITY OF WILLIAMSBURG,
AND PARISH OF BRUTON.
FORMERLY OF HUNGAR'S PARISH, ON THE
EASTERN SHORE
OF VIRGINIA, AND COUNTY OF NORTHAMPTON,
AGED 71 YEARS, AND YET LIVED BUT SEVEN YEARS,
WHICH WAS THE SPACE OF TIME HE KEPT
A BACHELOR'S HOME AT ARLINGTON,
ON THE EASTERN SHORE OF VIRGINIA."

On the opposite side is the following:—

"THIS INSCRIPTION PUT ON HIS TOMB WAS BY
HIS OWN POSITIVE ORDERS."*

any other subject than the enchanting Fidelia. You will do me wrong if you suspect that there ever was a man created that loved with more tenderness and sincerity than I do, and I should do you wrong if I could imagine there ever was a nymph that deserved it better than you. Take this for granted, and then fancy how uneasy I am like to be under the unhappiness of your absence. Figure to yourself what tumults there will arise in my blood, what a fluttering of the spirits, what a disorder of the pulse, what passionate wishes, what absence of thought, and what crowding of sighs, and then imagine how unfit I shall be for business; but returning to the dear cause of my uneasiness; O the torture of six months' expectation! If it must be so long and necessity will till then interpose betwixt you and my inclinations, I must submit, though it be as unwillingly as pride submits to superior virtue, or envy to superior success. Pray think of me, and believe that Veramour is entirely and eternally yours. ADIEU.

"I beg you write as soon as you receive this, and commit your letter to the same trusty hand that brings you this."

* In his will he directed his son to place this inscription upon his tomb, and provided for his disinheritance in the event of his omitting to do so. The tomb is in the form of a sarcophagus, about five feet high and as many long.

The daughter of Colonel Custis, Fanny Parke, was born in 1710, and married a Captain Dausie, contrary to the wishes of both father and brother, in which she, no doubt, followed the bent of her "own phantasy," as we find many letters extant from her suitors, who were quite eloquent in setting forth their pretensions, especially, in point of property. The old gentleman was over fastidious, and would not listen favorably to any of them; so it ended, as often it happens, in her marrying the least desirable of them all. In his replies, Colonel Custis always remarked, as a reason for his objections: "I have but two children, and they must inherit all I have." Daniel, the son, was the object of very ambitious views. His fine person, large fortune, and irreproachable character, made him quite a desirable match for the fair dames of Virginia, and many negotiations were commenced.* His cousin, Evelyn Byrd of Westover, was proposed, but though Colonel Custis desired earnestly

---

* Mrs. Parke Pepper, wife of a London merchant, and a relative, seems to have desired a matrimonial alliance between the families, as appears by the following letter written by Colonel Custis to her in 1731:—

"It is natural to believe that I must always value a family to whom my two dear pledges are so nearly allied. I do not remember that I expressed anything of matching my daughter to any one. I am sure I had no such thought, so Mr. S. must misapprehend me. Your son may deserve a better match than my daughter, but the distance of place and consanguinity would render such a thing impracticable. She has lately been engaged to a man much against my inclination, and so near, that the wedding-clothes were made, but it is all over now, and she protests she will never marry him or any one else. My son, I believe, is fixed in his affections, only we think both two young as yet. It is an unhappiness that my children's relations by their mother are placed so far distant. I agree with you, that it might do him good to make you a visit and see the world, but I could not spare him so far from me while I live, if he might have the empress of the universe with the whole creation for a fortune. My children are all the comfort I have in the world, for whose sakes I have kept myself single, and am determined so to do as long as it shall please God to continue them to me. I no ways doubt of my young kinswoman's virtues and qualifications, and heartily wish her a husband equal to her merits. I hope Mr.

the connection, he could not be brought to terms; and at length Colonel Byrd, in a very decided letter, in which he tells the wooer how much he regrets his father's impracticability, as he should have preferred him to all others, adds, that he can not trust to such a "phantome as Colonel Custis's generosity."

We rather suspect Daniel was not very earnest in the pursuit, as beautiful Martha Dandridge soon effaced all other impressions from his heart, and was not so readily relinquished.

She was the most attractive belle at the court of Williamsburg,* and won the affections of all by her grace of manner and heartfelt cheerfulness. Governor Gooch† presided over the Old Dominion, and Colonel Custis then held the high office of king's counsellor. Long did he refuse to sanction his son's choice, but at length won over by the report he heard on all sides of the charms and virtues of Miss Dandridge, and especially by a message received from her, he yielded, and we find the following memorandum in his own handwriting: "I give my free consent to the union of

---

Pepper will accept of my best respects. The same salute to you and yours. I am, hon'd madam,   Your most obedient servant,
"JOHN CUSTIS.

"P. S.—If Colonel Parke had lived to see my son, he would have seen his own picture to greater perfection than ever Sir Godfrey Kneller could draw it.—J. C."

This postscript refers to the portrait of Colonel Parke, now at Arlington house, painted by that eminent artist, and to which allusion is made in another part of this memoir.

* Williamsburg was the residence of the royal governors of Virginia until the old war for independence, in 1775. Governor Nicholson made it the capital in 1698. In its palmiest days its population did not exceed twenty-five hundred, yet it was the centre of Virginia's social refinement.

† William Gooch was governor of Virginia from 1727 until 1749, a longer administration than that of any of the royal governors of that province.

my son, Daniel, with Miss Martha Dandridge."* This was a concession he certainly never had cause to regret, as he soon was an admiring witness of their domestic bliss in their pleasant home on the banks of the Pamunkey They had four children, Daniel Parke, Fanny Parke, John Parke (the father of the author of the *Recollections*), and Martha Parke. The two eldest children died very young; and it is said that grief for their loss so preyed upon the mind of the devoted father, who was equally endowed with deep affections, as with manly beauty, that it hastened his death, which occurred at the age of thirty years. He left a young widow with two small children, and a large fortune. His family mourned the loss of a most tender parent, and his numerous servants an indulgent master.†

---

* On that occasion a friend of the suitor wrote to him as follows:—

"DEAR SIR: This comes at last to bring you the news that I believe will be most agreeable to you of any you have ever heard — that you may not be long in suspense I shall tell you at once — I am empowered by your father to let you know that he heartily and willingly consents to your marriage with Miss Dandridge — that he has so good a character of her, that he had rather you should have her than any lady in Virginia — nay, if possible, he is as much enamored with her character as you are with her person, and this is owing chiefly to a prudent speech of her own. Hurry down immediately for fear he should change the strong inclination he has to your marrying directly. I stayed with him all night, and presented Jack with my little Jack's horse, bridle, and saddle, in your name, which was taken as a singular favor. I shall say no more, as I expect to see you soon to-morrow, but conclude what I really am,

"Your most obliged and affectionate humble servant,

"To Colonel DANIEL PARKE CUSTIS, *New Kent.*"   "J. POWER.

The "Jack" referred to in this letter was a small negro boy to whom the old gentleman had taken a most violent fancy; and on one occasion when in great displeasure with his son, Daniel, on account of his refusing to concur in his ambitious views, he made a will, duly recorded, leaving all his fortune to this boy. Through the solicitations of his friends and his own paternal feelings, when the ill-humor had vanished, he destroyed that will, but manumitted the boy with his mother, Alice, and provided them with a most comfortable maintenance.

† Daniel Parke Custis was born at "Queene's creeke," according to the record in a family Bible at Arlington House, on the 15th of October, 1711. There is also a

G. Washington

The circumstances attending the union of Mrs. Custis with Washington are well known, and a narrative of them will be found in the *Recollections*.* Indeed, her life from that time became a matter of history. The death of her only remaining daughter, Martha, at the age of sixteen, threw a cloud of the deepest sorrow over the happiness of the family at Mount Vernon. If we may judge from a miniature taken by the elder Peale, and now in the possession of his son, Rembrandt, and two other portraits, she was endowed with rare beauty, and yet of a complexion so deeply brunette, that she was always called the "dark lady." Her delicate health, or, perhaps her fond affection for the only father she had ever known, so endeared her to the "general," that he knelt at her dying bed, and with a passionate burst of tears, prayed aloud that her life might be spared, unconscious that even then her spirit had departed.

Martha expired at Mount Vernon on the 19th of June, 1773. Washington had been absent at Williamsburg, on public duty, for sometime, and on his return found her in the last stage of consumption. He had arranged to accompany the governor of Virginia (Lord Dunmore) to the western country, but the death of Miss Custis caused him to remain at home a long time to console his wife, and recover from the effects of the blow. In

record there, that "Governor Spottswood, the Honorable William Byrd, Esq., and Mrs. Hannah Ludwell, were godfathers and godmother." There were some portraits of the Custis family at Abington, on the Potomac, which have long since crumbled into dust. One who bore the name of Custis is remembered as being represented as a soldier, in a complete suit of armor; and two now at Arlington, painted by Van Dyke, tradition says came from Holland, where the family originated. The portraits of Daniel Parke Custis, husband of Miss Dandridge (afterward Mrs. Washington), and of his father, are both at Arlington house.

* See sketch of Martha Washington.

testimony of her love for her stepfather, Miss Custis bequeathed to him all of her large fortune, which was entirely in money.

Of Colonel Daniel Parke, already mentioned as one of the ancestors of the present Custis family, and of his eventful career, an interesting volume might be written. This is not the place for even a very extended notice of him; yet some facts and correspondence, having a relation to the family, seem to find here an appropriate position. Besides this, they give us glimpses of character in the olden time, which will not fail to gratify the reader and pardon a digression.

There is a splendid portrait of Colonel Parke at Arlington house, painted by Sir Godfrey Kneller, in which he is represented as arrayed in a coat of crimson velvet embroidered with gold, and which well becomes his fine figure and eminently handsome face. He was born in the colonies, but passed most of his life in England, where he possessed valuable estates, leaving his wife with two daughters in charge of his Virginia property, which was also extensive. She found this charge so burdensome, that in her letters, as we have already observed, she begs to be relieved, and urges his return. She even wrote to his merchant and man of business, Micajah Perry, to use his influence in persuading him to return. But the fascinations of the court prevailed over a sense of duty, and while there he was appointed aid-de-camp to the great Duke of Marlborough, attended him in the battle of Blenheim, and was made the bearer of the following letter to the Duchess of Marlborough:—

"I have not time to say more, but to beg you will give my duty to the queen, and let her know her army has had a glorious victory. M. Tallard and two other generals are in my coach, and I am following the rest. The bearer, my aid-de-camp, Colonel Parke, will give her an account of what has passed. I shall do it in a day or two by another more at large.*   MARLBOROUGH.

"*August* 13, 1704."

It is a high honor to be the bearer of tidings of victory to a monarch, and at that time a reward of £500 was usually given by the sovereigns of England for such services. Colonel Parke, whose estate was ample, requested Queen Anne to give him her portrait instead. The request was granted, and the portrait was painted in miniature, and set with diamonds. Colonel Parke's portrait, painted in 1707, shows this miniature pendant from his neck by a red ribbon, Marlborough's despatch to the queen in his right hand, and the battle of Blenheim in the background. Another portrait of Colonel Parke, painted by Kneller, is still in the possession of William Dillon, Esq., whose late wife was his great-niece.

It appears by the following letter to his daughter, that Colonel Parke went to Flanders as a volunteer, where, doubtless, his gallant conduct won for him his appointment in the staff of Marlborough:—

"ST. JAMES, 1702.

"MY DEAR FANNY: I am going a volunteer under the Duke of Marlborough, to Flanders, where I served also in the last campaign with my Lord Arron, the Duke of

---

* This battle was fought on the 2d of August, 1704, between the English and confederates, commanded by Marlborough, and the French and Bavarians under Marshal Tallard and the Elector of Bavaria. The loss of the latter was twenty-seven thousand killed and thirteen thousand prisoners. The English nation rewarded Marlborough with a large domain, and erected for him one of the finest seats in the kingdom, known as the domain and house of Blenheim.

Ormond's brother, and was in every action. God knows if I may ever see you more, but if I do not, I shall take care to leave you and your sister in very happy circumstances, therefore do not throw yourself away upon the first idle young man that offers if you have a mind to marry. I know it is the desire of all young people to be married, and though very few are as happy after marriage as before, yet every one is willing to make the experiment at their own expense. Consider who you marry is the greatest concern to you in the world. Be kind and good-natured to all your servants. It is much better to have them love you than fear you. My heart is in Virginia, and the greatest pleasure I propose to myself is the seeing you and your sister happy. That you may be ever so, is the earnest desire of your affectionate father,
"Daniel Parke.

"I got some reputation last summer, which I hope I shall not lose this; I am promised the first old regiment that shall fall, being now made a colonel."

Colonel Parke was afterward commissioned a general, and appointed governor of the Leeward islands. An old book in the Arlington library, written by George French, contains an account of his administration there, and of the rebellion in Antigua, by which it seems that he became obnoxious to a seditious faction, was overpowered by numbers, and when there were no hopes of safety showed an undaunted resolution. When he had scarcely a second left, in a personal defence, he defied the whole strength of the rebels, till at last, he received a shot in his thigh, which, though not mortal, disabled him, and he fell into the enemy's hands.

"They had now an opportunity of sending him away to what place and in what manner they think fit," says the account, "but instead thereof, they use him with the utmost contempt and inhumanity. They strip him of his clothes, kick, spurn at, and beat him with the butts of their muskets, by which means, at last, they break his back. They drag him out into the streets by a leg and arm, and his head trails and beats from step to step of the stone stairs at the entrance of his house, and he is dragged on the coarse gravelly street, which raked the skin from his bones.

"These cruelties and tortures force tears from his eyes, and in this condition he is left expiring, exposed to the scorching sun, out of the heat of which he begs to be removed. The good-natured woman, who, at his request, brought him water to quench his thirst, is threatened by one Samuel Watkins to have a sword passed through her for her humanity, and the water is dashed out of her hands. He is insulted and reviled by every scoundrel, in the agonies of death, but makes no other return but these mild expressions: 'Gentlemen, if you have no sense of honor left, pray have some of humanity.' He gratefully owns the kindness of friends, and prays God to reward those who stood by him that day. At last he was removed into the house of one Mr. John Wright, near the place where he lay, and there, recommending his soul to God, with some pious ejaculations, he pays the great debt of nature, and death, less cruel than his enemies, put a period to his sufferings.

"After they had surfeited themselves with cruelties, they plundered the general's house and broke open his store-houses, so that his estate must have suffered by that day in money, plate, jewels, clothes, and household goods, by the most moderate computation, five thousand pounds sterling, for which his executors have obtained no satisfaction to this day. Thus died Colonel Parke, whose brave end shows him sufficiently deserving of the commission he bore, and by his death acquired an honor to his memory, which the base aspersions of his enemies could not overthrow." This tragedy occurred on the 7th of December, 1710.

Colonel Parke's will, in which he devised all of his fortune in the Leeward islands to an illegitimate daughter, on condition that she should take his name and coat-of-arms, naturally gave great offence to his children, and a tedious law-suit was the consequence. His legal descendants are still in possession of much of his property in Virginia, and part of the handsome service of plate presented to him by Queen Anne. His friends maintain that in his public career his life was irreproachable, and that loyalty to the queen was the cause of his destruction; yet his royal mistress forgot her favorite, allowed his murderers to hold his government of Antigua, and never remunerated his heirs for the losses sustained in her cause. The treatment he received is an emphatic example of the wisdom of the injunction, "Put not your trust in princes."

Among the old family papers at Arlington house, I have found many amusing and interesting letters, written by Colonel William Byrd, of Westover (to whom reference has already been made), who as we have observed, married a daughter of Colonel Parke, and was for a long time in London after the death of his father-in-law, attending to the settlement of that gentleman's estate.

As some of these letters have reference to family matters, and are interesting in themselves, I insert a few, believing that they are not out of place here, considering their connection. They are addressed to Colonel John Custis, his brother-in-law.

The following letter, in which reference is made to Colonel Parke, was written in Virginia two years before the tragedy occurred in Antigua:—

"*October*, 1709.

"I have lately been favored with an unusual pleasure from Antigua, in which I find we have not altogether been forgotten. Our Father Parke says his time was very short and he could not write to you *then*, but is much in charity with us all. I give you joy on the blessing you have had of a daughter, and hope she will be an ornament to the sex, and a happiness to her parents. Our son sends you his dutiful respects, and I may venture to say, as much for Miss Evelyn, who has grown a great romp, and enjoys very robust health. How is Madam Dunn? for there goes a prophecy about, that in the eastern parts of Virginia a parson's wife will, in the year of our Lord, 1710, have four children at a birth, one of which will be an admiral, and another Archbishop of Canterbury. What the other two will prove, the sybil can not positively say, but doubtless they will be something extraordinary.

"My choicest compliments to Mrs. Custis, and if Mrs. Dunn be not too demure a prude, now she is related to the church, I would send her my salutes in the best form.

"Your most affectionate humble servant,

W. BYRD.

"To Colonel JOHN CUSTIS."

On the 21st of January, 1715, Colonel Byrd wrote to Colonel Custis, from London, as follows:—

"Tis a singular pleasure to hear by my brigantine of my dear brother's recovery from so sharp and tedious an illness. I long to be with you, for this place, that used to have so many charms is very tasteless, and though my person is here, my heart is in Virginia. My affairs succeed well enough, but all solicitation goes on very slowly by reason that the ministry is taken up with the Rebellion, which is still as flagrant as ever in Scotland, and my patron, the Duke of Argyle, commands there against them.* I am in perfect peace with all concerned in debts due from Colonel Parke. I have paid the most importunate, and allow interest for the bonds I can not yet discharge, and should be very easy if I could get the interest of his customhouse debt remitted, which I do not yet despair of. I wish my dear brother a full confirmation of his health. If he has the courage to venture upon another wife, I hope he will be more easy in his second choice than he was in his first.†

"I am, with most entire affection, dear brother,
    "Your most obedient servant,   W. BYRD."

* King James II., was driven from the English throne in 1688. In 1715 his son, Edward, made an unsuccessful attempt, through the aid of the Scotch, to regain the throne of his father, as his uncle, Charles II., had that of his sire, in 1660. This effort produced quite a serious rebellion. A grandson of King James made another attempt to recover the throne by the aid of the Scotch, in 1745, and a still more serious rebellion was the consequence. The father and son who made these attempts, are known in history as the Old and the Young Pretenders.

† At about this time Colonel Byrd purchased a watch in London for Colonel Custis, and in a letter that accompanied it to Virginia, he said: "I forebode this to be a sort of equipage with which you intend to set out a courting. The misfortune is, that you can not with tolerable decency draw forth your watch in presence of your mistress without giving her some suspicion that you measure the time you spend in her company."

Again, on the 2d of October, 1716, Colonel Byrd wrote from London to Colonel Custis, as follows:—

"It is a great surprise to you as to many others, that Mr. Roscow has been made receiver-general.* I confess, if I had *given* away the place, it is likely Mr. Roscow is not the person in the world I should soonest have given it to, but if you put the case that I *sold* it, you would not wonder that I should dispose of it to so fair a bidder as he was; and, indeed, I fancy there are not many would have given £500 for it. Besides, it is not an easy matter to transfer an office depending upon the treasury; and if I should have taken so much time as to send over to Virginia to treat with any person there, I might have slipt my opportunity and lost my market. This being the case, you will cease to wonder at the matter. The kind visit which my wife has made me will be the occasion of my staying here another winter, that so she may see this town in all its glory; and I am the more content to tarry, because the lieutenant-governor has sent over a spiteful complaint against me and Colonel Ludwell, which it concerns me to answer. I assure you it was not my apprehension of being removed by any complaint that might be formed against me that made me resign; but such an office as that of receiver-general of the king's revenue makes a man liable to be ill-treated by a governor, under the notion of advancing his majesty's interest, by which pious pretence he may

---

* Receiver-general of the colony of Virginia, held by Colonel Byrd at that time. This letter lifts the veil from the secret workings of the old colonial government, when placemen disposed of offices to the highest bidders; for then, as now, there were large opportunities for public plunder. The *people* then had little to say concerning the administration of public affairs, especially by those appointed by the crown.

heap insupportable trouble upon that officer, if he should have the spirit to oppose his will and pleasure—he must either be a slave to his humor, must fawn upon him, and jump over a stick whenever he is bid, or else he must have so much trouble loaded upon him as to make his place uneasy. In short, such a man must be either the governor's dog or his ass; neither of which stations suit in the least with my constitution. For this reason I resolved to make the most of it by surrendering to any one that would come up to my price, well knowing that my interest in the treasury was sufficient to do it, and now I am at full liberty to oppose every design that may seem to be arbitrary or unjust. The current news which you had of my being governor of the Leeward Islands, expresses very naturally the genius of our country for invention. I protest to you it never once entered into my head to sue for that government.

"God in heaven bless you and your two little cherubs, to whom I wish all happiness, being your most affectionate brother,

"W. Byrd."

At this time Colonel Byrd wrote as follows to an unknown female friend:—

"I have been made happy with several of Irene's letters, and at this time stand in need of most diversion to support me under the melancholy I suffer for my dear Fidelia's absence. I fear you are too busy in copying after the wise women that Solomon describes, to spend much of your time upon *how do ye's*. But remember that the consequence of care is early wrinkles, and whatever you may get by it, you will be sure to lose in peace and constitution. They tell me you have been immoderately afflicted for the loss of your 'dear Poppet,' but, by the terms on which it was born, you were to part with it when its Maker pleased. You ought to have reflected that Providence acts by unerring wisdom, and therefore would never had recalled its gifts but because it was better so than the contrary would be. God Almighty is ever contriving for our happiness, and does many things for our good which appear to our short sight to be terrible misfortunes. But by the time the last act of the play comes on, we grow convinced of our mistake, and look back with pleasure to those scenes which at first appeared unfortunate. This is the case in most accidents that are called disasters, misery, and many other terms, which our ignorance gives them. We should imitate the philosopher that we read of, who, when he heard of his son's death, calmly observed, that he was saved from the evil to come; and of the misconduct of his wife, told his friend without any disorder, that he knew he had married a *woman*. This equality of temper would save the world abundance of sighs and complaints, especially that part of it that acknowleges itself in the care of a wise and merciful God.

"Pardon me, dear Irene, for preaching, which is ill-bred, because it supposes that the party stands in need of it. However, I can excuse the rudeness by pleading the infinite inclination I have for your happiness. I would have you without fault, which will suppose you without any misfortune."

Toward the close of the year 1716, Colonel Byrd wrote to Colonel Custis, as follows:—

"My daughter, Evelyn, has arrived safe, thank God, and

I hope I shall manage her in such a manner, that she may be no discredit to her country. I am endeavoring to get something from the treasury for your children and mine, but as the success of it is somewhat doubtful, I will mention no more about it till it shall be determined. I do long to see you, but can hardly persuade myself to return till I can get it decided, whether a governor may hang any man he takes to be his adversary or not. For if it be in his power to appoint me my judges, I am sure I won't come within his reach lest I fall a sacrifice to his resentment. However, I am laboring with all my might to hinder so great a power from being lodged in any bashaw, lest they be too much inclined to make use of it. We have got both the tobacco law and that about the Indian trade repealed, which I hope may not be unacceptable to the country. I wish you, and your dear, pretty children, all health and happiness, being with all my love, dear brother, your most obedient, humble servant. W. BYRD."

Shortly after this, Colonel Byrd conveyed to Colonel Custis very melancholy intelligence, as follows:—

"LONDON, 13th December, 1716.

"When I wrote last I little expected that I should be forced to tell you the very melancholy news of my dear Lucy's death, by the very same, cruel distemper that destroyed her sister. She was taken with an insupportable pain in her head. The doctor soon discovered her ailment to be the small-pox, and we thought it best to tell her the danger.* She received the news without

---

* Two years later than this (1718), Lady Mary Wortley Montagu returned from Constantinople, and introduced the practice of *inoculation* for the small-pox, which she had learned while in that eastern city. *Vaccination* was introduced by Jenner, about the year 1776.

the least fright, and was persuaded she would live until the day she died, which happened in 12 hours from the time she was taken. Gracious God what pains did she take to make a voyage hither to seek a grave. No stranger ever met with more respect in a strange country than she had done here, from many persons of distinction, who all pronounced her an honor to Virginia. Alas! how proud was I of her, and how severely am I punished for it. But I can dwell no longer on so afflicting a subject, much less can I think of anything else, therefore, I can only recommend myself to your pity, and am as much as any one can be, dear brother, your most affectionate and humble servant, W. BYRD."

Returning from this long digression, we will resume the memoir of the author of the *Recollections.*

George Washington Parke Custis was born at Mount Airy, Maryland, on the thirtieth of April, 1781. That was the seat of his maternal grandfather, Benedict Calvert, a descendant of Cecil Calvert, Lord Baltimore.[*] The walls of this venerable mansion are graced with fine portraits of several of the Lords Baltimore, by Vandyke; and one of Eleanor Calvert, the mother of Mr. Custis. It represents a young lady of a romantic and slight figure in a riding costume, with a boy's hat and open jacket. She seems scarcely fifteen, with a bright and hopeful countenance. Such was her temperament, we are told, through all the toils of life. The commencement of her career was brilliant enough. Married at sixteen to John Parke Custis, a youth of nineteen,

---

[*] Cecil Calvert was the second Lord Baltimore, and son of the first of that title, who obtained from Charles the First a charter for a domain in America, which, in honor of his Queen, Henriette Marie (Mary), he called *Maryland.*

the ward and favorite of Washington, the only son of Mrs. Washington, of large fortune, and a most amiable and generous disposition, they passed several years at Abingdon, a country-seat on the Potomac, near Washington city, in the enjoyment of such felicity as rarely falls to the lot of mortals.

After the death of Mrs. Washington's daughter, already mentioned, the hopes of the mother centred in this son, who was then between sixteen and seventeen years of age. She was extremely indulgent to him, and she often pleaded in his behalf, when Washington found it necessary to exercise a wholesome restraint upon him. He was placed under the care of an episcopal clergyman, at Annapolis, in Maryland, to be educated, but the wayward boy was frequently away from his studies, engaged in fox-hunting and other amusements at Mount Vernon. He conceived a strong desire to travel, but Washington opposed a scheme that would interrupt his studies. It was abandoned, but he soon became diverted from his books by a passion stronger than a desire to travel. He became deeply enamored of Eleanor, the second daughter of Benedict Calvert, of Mount Airy, Maryland, and much to the concern of Washington, when he discovered it, they formed a matrimonial engagement. His only objection was their extreme youth; and on the third of April, 1773, he addressed the following letter to Mr. Calvert:—

"MOUNT VERNON, *April* 3rd, 1773.

"DEAR SIR: I am now set down to write to you on a subject of importance, and of no small embarrassment to me. My son-in-law and ward, Mr. Custis, has, as I have been informed, paid his addresses to your second daughter, and, having made some progress in her affections, has solicited her in marriage. How far a union of this sort may be agreeable to you, you best can tell; but I should think myself wanting in candor, were I not to confess, that Miss Nelly's amiable qualities are acknowledged on all hands, and that an alliance with your family will be pleasing to his.

"This acknowledgment being made, you must permit me to add, sir, that at this, or in any short time, his youth, inexperience, and unripened education, are, and will be, insuperable obstacles, in my opinion, to the completion of the marriage. As his guardian, I consider it my indispensable duty to endeavor to carry him through a regular course of education (many branches of which, I am sorry to add, he is totally deficient in), and to guard his youth to a more advanced age, before an event, on which his own peace and the happiness of another are to depend, takes place. Not that I have any doubt of the warmth of his affections, nor, I hope I may add, any fears of a change in them; but at present I do not conceive that he is capable of bestowing that attention to the important consequences of the married state, which is necessary to be given by those who are about to enter into it, and of course I am unwilling he should do it till he is. If the affection which they have avowed for each other is fixed upon a solid basis, it will receive no diminution in the course of two or three years, in which time he may prosecute his studies, and thereby render himself more deserving of the lady, and useful to society. If, unfortunately, as they are both young, there should be an abatement of affection on either side, or both, it had better precede than follow marriage.

"Delivering my sentiments thus freely will not, I hope, lead you into a belief that I am desirous of breaking off the match. To postpone it is all I have in view; for I shall recommend to the young gentleman, with the warmth that becomes a man of honor (notwithstanding he did not vouchsafe to consult either his mother or me on the occasion), to consider himself as much engaged to your daughter as if the indissoluble knot were tied; and, as the surest means of effecting this, to apply himself closely to his studies (and in this advice, I flatter myself, you will join me), by which he will, in a great measure, avoid those little flirtations with other young ladies, that may, by dividing the attention, contribute not a little to divide the affection.

"It may be expected of me, perhaps, to say something of property; but, to descend to particulars, at this time, must seem rather premature. In general, therefore, I shall inform you, that Mr. Custis's estate consists of about fifteen thousand acres of land, a good part of it adjoining the city of Williamsburg, and none of it forty miles from that place; several lots in the said city; between two and three hundred negroes; and about eight or ten thousand pounds upon bond, and in the hands of his merchants. This estate he now holds, independent of his mother's dower, which will be an addition to it at her death; and, upon the whole, it is such an estate as you will readily acknowledge, ought to entitle him to a handsome portion with a wife. But as I should never require a child of my own to make a sacrifice of himself to interest, so neither do I think it incumbent on me to recommend it as a guardian.

At all times when you, Mrs. Calvert, or the young

ladies can make it convenient to favor us with a visit, we should be happy in seeing you at this place. Mrs. Washington and Miss Custis join me in respectful compliments, and,

"I am, dear sir, your most obedient servant."

It was agreed that the youth should pass two years at college, before the marriage could take place. He was sent to King's (now Columbia) college, in New York city, but he remained there only a few months. Love and learning did not move in harmony, and on the third of February, 1774, young Custis was married to Miss Calvert, when the bridegroom was a little more than nineteen years of age.

Four children were the fruits of this union, all born at Abingdon, except George Washington Parke. Elizabeth Parke was born on the twenty-first of August, 1776, and married Mr. Law, nephew of Lord Ellenborough. She was a lady of great beauty and talent. Martha Parke was born on the thirty-first of December, 1777, and was early married to Thomas Peter. She was a woman of fine and dignified appearance. Her husband was a man of wealth, and great excellence of character; and she passed her long life in the conscientous performance of all her domestic duties. Eleanor Parke, born on the twenty-first of March, 1779, married Lawrence Lewis, the favorite nephew of General Washington. George Washington Parke, the youngest child, first saw the light, as we have observed, at Mount Airy, in April, 1781.

Very soon the bright sky that illumined the household of John Parke Custis and his young wife became darkened. He was aid-de-camp to General Washington at the siege of Yorktown. A violent attack of camp-fever obliged him to leave his post for Eltham, a place not far distant. General Washington hastened thither as soon as possible, but was met at the door by Dr. Craik, who informed him that all was over. The chief bowed his head, and in tears gave vent to his deep sorrow; then turning to the weeping mother, he said: "I adopt the two younger children as my own."* Thus, at six months of age, did my father, the subject of this Memoir, become the child of Mount Vernon, the idol of his grandmother, and an object on which was lavished the caresses and attention of the many distinguished guests who thronged that hospitable mansion. His beautiful sister Nelly often observed: "Grandmamma always spoiled Washington." He was "the pride of her heart," while the public duties of the veteran prevented the exercise of his influence in forming the character of the boy, too softly nurtured under his roof, and gifted with talents which, under a sterner discipline, might have been made more available for his own and his country's good.

It was not until he entered the college at Princeton, that the attention of the "father" was particularly drawn to those faults, which should have been corrected at an earlier period. The deep solicitude which these faults occasioned may be estimated, in a measure, by the correspondence between Washington and the son of his adoption, appended to this Memoir.

At the time of the birth of ELEANOR (the eldest of the two children adopted by Washington), her mother was

---

* George Washington Parke Custis, and Eleanor Parke Custis.

very ill, and Mrs. Washington took the child to Mount Vernon, to be nursed by the wife of the steward, a healthy English woman named Anderson, who had lost her infant. She called Mrs. Anderson "mammy," and remembered running with her to meet the General and Lady Washington, on their return from camp in a carriage drawn by six horses. She was then three years old, having remained all that time under the care of Mrs. Lund Washington, the wife of the general's agent. Her young brother, George, was nursed by the same woman.

A daughter of Mrs. Lewis, (formerly Eleanor Parke Custis) informed the writer that their first tutor was Gideon Snow. "I saw him when I was in Boston," she said, "in 1824. He called with a grown daughter to see my mother, and talked of 'little George,' and seemed sincerely attached to both his pupils, and to be himself respected and beloved in Boston."* Their sec-

---

* The following letter, written to Mr. Custis by his old tutor, after the lapse of more than fifty years, possesses much interest:—

"BOSTON, 7*th March*, 1850.

"MY DEAR FRIEND: I am much gratified by receiving your esteemed letter of 3d instant yesterday. You ask a copy of your letter of ancient date. With pleasure I comply with your request. The original has been preserved with care and interest, for the love I bore the writer; but if the writer has a wish to possess it, I shall be gratified to send it to him. I received it enclosed by our mutual friend, Mr. Lear, in a letter, which I can not find, but recollect he informed me it was written at your own request, on a very warm afternoon. When finished you expressed your wish to have it forwarded. Mr. Lear requested me to retain it with care, as it was the first letter you had expressed a wish to write, and the time would come when you would receive pleasure in seeing it should your life be spared.

"I showed you the letter when I had the pleasure of meeting you in Boston, after an absence of more than fifty years. I do not recollect naming the date at any time. I might have done so — the date is 1787, instead of 1785 as named by you.

"In looking over a few of Mr. Lear's letters, which I have retained, I see, under date July 9th, 1787, 'I have a message: Washington sends his love to you, and says you are not a man of your word, for you promised to come down here on Sun-

ond tutor was Mr. Lear, afterward private secretary to General Washington, who lived at the president's house in Philadelphia.

Nelly Custis was considered one of the most beautiful women of the day, to which her portrait, at Arlington house, by Gilbert Stuart, bears testimony. All who knew her can recall the pleasure which they derived from her extensive information, brilliant wit, and boundless generosity. The most tender parent and devoted friend, she lived in the enjoyment of her affections.* She was often urged to write her memoirs, which might even have surpassed, in interest to her countrymen, those of Madame de Sevigné and others of equal note, as her pen gave free utterance to her lively imagination and clear memory. Would that we could recall the many tales of the past we have heard from her lips, but alas! we should fail to give them accurately. One narrative

---

day and did not.'—My inclination was good, but a call to another act prevented. When we met again your interest did not appear diminished. On the 9th January, 1788, 'handsome soft black cloth was purchased for your coat and overalls.' Dec. 18, 1788, I was asked to inquire of Dr. Craik where he procured the Latin grammar for his sons, 'as I am about initiating my young pupil in that language.' These extracts may amuse. From your dear, departed mother I always received maternal kindness. The recollection of her will never pass from me. I passed one Sunday at Hope Park very happily. Your dear mother and your sisters were present. Mrs. Snow requests her respectful remembrance. I thought of you at Richmond with the president. I imagined you happy in the enjoyments of the interesting scene. I thank you for your kind wishes, and sincerely reciprocate them.

"GIDEON SNOW."

The following is the copy of the letter alluded to by Mr. Snow:—

"MOUNT VERNON, *May* 12*th*, 1787.

"DEAR SNOW: I should be very happy to see you here if you can find time to come down. When will you send my waggon to me? For my old one is almost worn out, and I shall have none to get in my harvest with.

I am, dear Snow, your friend, &c.,

Very H'ble Serv't,   G. W. P. CUSTIS."

* She died in Clarke county, Virginia, in 1852, at the age of seventy-four years.

is retained, as it made a strong impression at the time. She said the most perfect harmony always existed "between her grandmamma and the general;" that in all his intercourse with her he was most considerate and tender. She had often seen her when she had something to communicate, or a request to make, at a moment when his mind was entirely abstracted from the present, seize him by the button to command his attention, when he would look down upon her with a most benignant smile, and become at once attentive to her and her wishes, which were never slighted. She also said, the grave dignity which he usually wore did not prevent his keen enjoyment of a joke, and that no one laughed more heartily than he did, when she, herself, a gay, laughing girl, gave one of her saucy descriptions of any scene in which she had taken part, or any one of the merry pranks she then often played; and that he would retire from the room in which her young companions were amusing themselves, because his presence created a reserve which they could not overcome. But he always regretted it exceedingly, as he liked nothing better than to look on at their sports and see them happy. His letter to her on the occasion of her first ball, may be so appropriately introduced here, that we give it entire, precisely as it was written in the original, now before us. Miss Custis was then about sixteen years of age.

"PHILA., *January* 16, 1795.

"Your letter, the receipt of which I am now acknowledging, is written correctly and in fair characters, which is an evidence that you command, when you please, a fair hand. Possessed of these advantages, it will be your own fault if you do not avail yourself of them, and attention being paid to the choice of your subjects, you can have nothing to fear from the malignancy of criticism, as your ideas are lively, and your descriptions agreeable. Let me touch a little now on your Georgetown ball, and happy, thrice happy, for the fair who were assembled on the occasion, that there was a man to spare; for had there been 79 ladies and only 78 gentlemen, there might, in the course of the evening, have been some disorder among the caps; notwithstanding the apathy which *one* of the company entertains for the '*youth*' of the present day, and her determination 'never to give herself a moment's uneasiness on account of any of them.' A hint here; men and women feel the same inclinations to each other *now* that they always have done, and which they will continue to do until there is a new order of things, and *you*, as others have done, may find, perhaps, that the passions of your sex are easier raised than allayed. Do not, therefore, boast too soon or too strongly of your insensibility to, or resistance of, its powers. In the composition of the human frame there is a good deal of inflammable matter, however dormant it may lie for a time, and like an intimate acquaintance of yours, when the torch is put to it, *that* which is *within you* may burst into a blaze; for which reason, and especially too, as 'I have entered upon the chapter of advices, I will read you a lecture drawn from this text.

"Love is said to be an involuntary passion, and it is, therefore, contended that it can not be resisted. This is true in part only, for like all things else, when nourished and supplied plentifully with aliment, it is rapid in its progress; but let these be withdrawn and it may be stifled in its birth or much stinted in its growth. For example, a woman (the same may be said of the other sex) all beautiful and accomplished, will, while her hand and heart are undisposed of, turn the heads and set the circle in which she moves on fire. Let her marry, and what is the consequence. The madness *ceases* and all is quiet again. Why? not because there is any diminution in the charms of the lady, but because there is an end of hope. Hence it follows, that love may and therefore ought to be under the guidance of reason, for although we can not avoid first impressions, we may assuredly place them under guard; and my motives for treating on this subject are to show you, while you remain Eleanor Parke Custis, spinster, and retain the resolution to love with moderation, the propriety of adhering to the latter resolution, at least until you have secured your game, and the way by which it may be accomplished.

"When the fire is beginning to kindle, and your heart growing warm, propound these questions to it. Who is this invader? Have I a competent knowledge of him? Is he a man of good character; a man of sense? For, be assured, a sensible woman can never be happy with a fool. What has been his walk of life? Is he a gambler, a spendthrift, or drunkard? Is his fortune sufficient to maintain me in the manner I have been accustomed to live, and my sisters do live, and is he one to whom my friends can have no reasonable objection? If these interrogatories can be satisfactorily answered, there will remain but one more to be asked, that, however, is an important one. Have I sufficient ground to conclude that his affections are engaged by me? Without this the heart of sensibility will struggle against a passion that is not reciprocated—delicacy, custom, or call it by what epithet you will, having precluded all advances on your part. The declaration, without the *most indirect* invitation of yours, must proceed from the man, to render it permanent and valuable, and nothing short of good sense and an easy unaffected conduct can draw the line between prudery and coquetry. It would be no great departure from truth to say, that it rarely happens otherwise than that a thorough-paced coquette dies in celibacy, as a punishment for her attempts to mislead others, by encouraging looks, words, or actions, given for no other purpose than to draw men on to make overtures that they may be rejected.

"This day, according to our information, gives a husband to your elder sister, and consummates, it is to be presumed, her fondest desires. The dawn with us is bright, and propitious, I hope, of her future happiness, for a full measure of which she and Mr. Law have my earnest wishes. Compliments and congratulations on this occasion, and best regards are presented to your mamma, Dr. Stuart and family; and every blessing, among which, a good husband when you want and deserve one, is bestowed on you by yours, affectionately."*

This beautiful and accomplished lady married Lawrence Lewis, the favorite nephew of Washington, and

---

* Washington wrote many other letters to his sprightly ward and foster-child, but they have been lost or destroyed. These seem to show how his comprehensive mind had moments of thought and action to bestow on all connected with him, and how deeply his affections were interested in the family of his wife, who were cared for as if they had been his own. They were written at a time when the cares of state, as president of the republic, were pressing heavily upon him.

E. N. Lewis.

son of his only sister, Elizabeth, of whose remarkable resemblance to the general, mention is made in the memoir of their mother, given in the *Recollections*. They were married on the twenty-second of February (Washington's birthday), 1799. A month before, Washington wrote to his nephew, as follows:—

"MOUNT VERNON, 23d *January*, 1799.

"DEAR LAWRENCE: Your letter of the 10th instant I received in Alexandria, on Monday, whither I went to become the guardian of Nelly, thereby to authorize a license for your nuptials on the 22d of next month, when, I presume, if your health is restored, there will be no impediment to your union.*

"The letters herewith sent were received two or three days ago; and until your letter of the above date came to hand, I knew not with certainty to what place to direct them. They are put under cover to your brother of Fredericksburgh, to await your arrival at that place.

"I enclose the one to your lieutenant, Mr. Lawrence Washington, for safety, and because it may be necessary that you should have a conference with him respecting the plan for recruiting your troops when the order and the means for doing so are received. All, however, that you, Washington, and Custis, have to do at present, is simply to acknowledge the receipt of the letter from the

---

* The following letter, authorizing the license, is copied from the original, which is addressed "To Captain George Deneale, clerk of Fairfax county court:"—

"MOUNT VERNON, 19th *Feb.* 1799.

"SIR: You will please to grant a license for the marriage of Eleanor Parke Custis with Lawrence Lewis, and this shall be your authority for so doing.

"From sir,
"*Witness*,   "Your very humble servant,
"THOMAS PETER.   "G. WASHINGTON.
"GEORGE W. P. CUSTIS."

secretary of war, to inform him whether you do, or do not accept the appointment, and in either case to request him to thank the president for the honor he has conferred on you in making it.* Perhaps, as this acknowledgment will not be as prompt as might have been expected from you and Custis (for it was supposed that both of you were to be found at Mount Vernon), it would not be amiss if you were to add, that being on an excursion into the upper country is the cause of it. All here, as I presume you will learn from a more pleasing pen, are well; I therefore shall only add, that I am, dear sir, your sincere friend and affectionate uncle,

"GEO. WASHINGTON.

"Mr. LAW. LEWIS."

A few months after this, Washington wrote to his nephew, as follows, in reply to a letter from the young husband concerning a portion of the Mount Vernon estate. Little did any of the parties then suppose, that in less than three months, the hand that penned this letter would be paralyzed by death, and that the will written by that hand, would so soon call for executors:—

"MOUNT VERNON, 20th September, 1799.

"DEAR SIR: From the moment Mrs. Washington and myself adopted the two youngest children of the late

* When, in the summer of 1798, long-pending difficulties with France seemed to be tending toward speedy war, the Congress authorized quite a large standing army, and appointed Washington commander-in-chief, with General Alexander Hamilton as his first lieutenant. Washington consented to accept the appointment, only on condition that General Hamilton should be acting commander-in-chief, unless circumstances should make it necessary for the retired president to take the field. Many young men, especially of families of revolutionary veterans, aspired to military honors at this time. Among others who received commissions, were those alluded to in this letter, namely, Lawrence Lewis, Lawrence Washington, and George Washington Parke Custis. They were never called to the field, as the storm of war passed by without bursting upon the land.

Mr. Custis, it became my intention (if they survived me and conducted themselves to my satisfaction) to consider them in my will when I was about to make a distribution of my property. This determination has undergone no diminution, but is strengthened by the connection one of them has formed with my family.

"The expense at which I live, and the unproductiveness of my estate, will not allow me to lessen my income while I remain in my present situation. On the contrary, were it not for occasional supplies of money in payment for lands sold within the last four or five years, to the amount of upwards of fifty thousand dollars, I should not be able to support the former without involving myself in debt and difficulties.

"But as it has been understood from expressions occasionally dropped from Nelly Custis, now your wife, that it is the wish of you both to settle in this neighborhood, contiguous to her friends, and as it would be inexpedient, as well as expensive, for you to make a purchase of land, when a measure which is in contemplation would place you on more eligible ground, I shall inform you, that in the will which I have made, which I have by me, and have no disposition to alter, that the part of my Mount Vernon tract, which lies north of the public road leading from the Gum spring to Colchester, containing about two thousand acres, with the Dogue-river farm, mill, and distillery, I have left you. Gray's heights is bequeathed to you and her jointly, if you incline to build on it, and few better sites for a house than Gray's hill and that range, are to be found in this country or elsewhere.

"You may also have what is properly Dogue-run farm, the mill, and distillery, on a just and equitable rent; as also the lands belonging thereto, on a reasonable hire, either next year or the year following, it being necessary, in my opinion, that a young man should have objects of employment. Idleness is disreputable under any circumstances, productive of no good, even when unaccompanied by vicious habits, and you might commence building as soon as you please, during the progress of which Mount Vernon might be made your home.

"You may conceive, that building before you have an absolute title to the land is hazardous. To obviate this, I shall only remark, that it is not likely any occurrence will happen, or any change take place that would alter my present intention (if the conduct of yourself and wife is such as to merit a continuance of it); but be this as it may, that you may proceed on sure ground with respect to the buildings, I will agree, and this letter shall be an evidence of it, that if hereafter I should find cause to make any other disposition of the property *here* mentioned, I will pay the actual cost of such buildings to you or yours.

"Although I have not the most distant idea that any event will happen that could effect a change in my present determination, nor any suspicions that you or Nelly could conduct yourselves in such a manner as to incur my serious displeasure, yet, at the same time, that I am inclined to do justice to others, it behooves me to take care of myself, by keeping the staff in my own hands.

"That you may have a more perfect idea of the landed property I have bequeathed to you and Nelly in my will, I transmit a plan of it, every part of which is correctly laid down and accurately measured, showing the number of fields, lots, meadows, &c., with the contents, and relative situation of each, all of which, except the mill and swamp, which has never been considered as a part of Dogue-run farm, and is retained merely for the purpose of putting it into a better state of improvement, you may have on the terms before-mentioned. With every kind wish for you and Nelly, in which your aunt, who is still much indisposed, unites,

"I remain your affectionate uncle,
"GEO. WASHINGTON.
"Mr. LAWRENCE LEWIS."

"MOUNT VERNON, 28th *September*, 1799.

"MY DEAR SIR: The enclosed letter was written agreeably to date, and sent to the postoffice in Alexandria, but owing to an accident it missed the western mail, and was returned to me, since which, Mr. Anderson,* in partnership with his son, John, has discovered an inclination to rent my distillery and mill. I am disposed to let them become the tenants, provided they will give a reasonable rent, and matters in other respects can be adjusted. The reasons are, that although Mr. Anderson is, in my opinion, an honest, sober, and industrious man, understands the management of the plough and the harrow, and how to make meadows, yet he is not a man of arrangement; he wants system and foresight in conducting the business to advantage, is no economist in providing things, and takes little care of them when provided—when, to these defects in his character, are added, his acting too much from the impulse of the moment (which occasions too much doing and undoing), and his high wages and emoluments, I have no hesitation in declaring, that it is my

* Washington's steward.

wish to place my estate in this county on a new establishment, thereby bringing it into so narrow a compass as not only to supersede the necessity of a manager, but to make the management of what I retain in my own hands a healthy and agreeable amusement to look after myself, if I should not be again called in the public service of the country. As the old man is extremely obliging and zealous in my service, I am unwilling, by any act of mine to hurt his feelings, or by discarding him to lessen his respectability in the eyes of the public, but if it should appear to be his own act, both our ends would be answered. I should be lessened so much of my general concerns, and if you take the Dogue-run farm (by odds the best and most productive I possess), I can, if I remain quiet at home, with great ease attend to the other three and the mansion-house, and thereby ease myself of the expense of a manager. You will perceive by my letter of the 20th, herewith enclosed, that the lands therein mentioned are given for the express purpose of accommodating you in a building site, in which case I did not, nor do I now see how you could do without the farm, which is part of the premises, or the hands thereon; and were it not for the reasons which apply to Mr. Anderson, the mill and distillery ought to accompany it as part of the same concern. I shall not go more into details at this time, as I hear from a letter to Nelly that you may be expected shortly. Mr. Anderson, after I had written my letter of the 20th, hinted his desire of renting from me, and was informed I had made the offer to you, and until I received your answer I could say nothing definitely to him on the subject, and so the matter remains. Mrs. Washington has not recovered her health, on the contrary, is at this time weak and low. Mr. and Mrs. Peter (now here) and their children are well. We all unite in best wishes for you, Nelly, and Mr. Carter's family. Your affectionate uncle,

"GEORGE WASHINGTON.

"Mr. LAWRENCE LEWIS."

We have again been led into a digression on a relative subject. Let us now pursue the Memoir to its termination, without further interruption.

Before he had reached his eighteenth year, young Custis was appointed a cornet of horse in the army, as appears by the following letter from the secretary of war:—

"WAR DEPARTMENT, *January* 10*th*, 1799.

"SIR: I have the honor to inform you, that the president, by and with the advice and consent of the senate, has appointed you a cornet in the army of the United States.

"You are requested to inform me as soon as convenient, whether you accept or not the appointment, that I may notify the same to the president.

"To obviate misconception, it is proper to mention, that a want of materials having prevented a complete nomination and appointment of the whole number of officers for the troops to be raised, the president has thought it advisable to reserve the subject of their relative rank for further arrangement.

"I am, sir, with respect, your obedient servant,

JAMES M'HENRY.

"Mr. GEORGE W. P. CUSTIS."

Mr. Custis was soon afterward promoted to the position of aid-de-camp to General Charles Cotesworth Pinck ney, of South Carolina, with the rank of colonel. But he was never called into active service; and a few months afterward he was sorely bereaved by the death of his illustrious foster-father. That event occurred on the fourteenth of December, 1799, and the adopted son became a prospective executor of that great man's will.* Mount Vernon continued to be his home until after the death of his grandmother, when he commenced the erection of a beautiful mansion at Arlington, an estate of a thousand acres, left him by his father, and lying upon the west side of the Potomac, opposite Washington city. There he resided until his death. It is a most lovely spot, overlooking the Potomac; and from the noble portico, that adorns its front, so conspicuous from every point of the federal city and its vicinity, he saw that city grow into its present grand proportions, from a humble and uninteresting village.

At the age of twenty-three, Mr. Custis married Mary Lee Fitzhugh, a lady whose many virtues endeared her to all who came within the circles of her influence, and who will ever live in the memory of her friends. While the pen of filial affection may not be trusted in delineating a character so beloved, it

---

* In the last clause of his will, Washington said: "I constitute and appoint my dearly beloved wife, Martha Washington, my nephews, William Augustine Washington, Bushrod Washington, George Steptoe Washington, Samuel Washington, and Lawrence Lewis, and my ward, George Washington Parke Custis (when he shall have arrived at the age of twenty-one years), executrix and executors of this my last Will and Testament." The will was signed and sealed on the ninth of July, 1799. In it was the following clause: "I give and bequeath to George Washington Parke Custis, the grandson of my wife, and my ward, and to his heirs, the tract I hold on Four-mile run, in the vicinity of Alexandria, containing one thousand and two hundred acres, more or less, and my entire square, No. 21, in the city of Washington."

may be pardoned for transcribing the following testimony of a friend:—

"*To the Editors of the National Intelligencer:*

"Savannah, *May* 16, 1853.

"Gentlemen: Allow me from this distant city to place an humble wreath, bedewed with many tears, on the grave of the best of friends. Since no one living could do justice to the character of that eminent lady, whose decease has spread the gloom of night through all the halls of Arlington, tremblingly I shrink from the attempt to recall and trace out, even faintly, that most rare combination of virtues and graces which, as no modesty or humility could conceal, no language can adequately portray.

"Happy in her descent from the union of Fitzhugh, of Chatham (the friend of Washington), a gentleman unsurpassed for dignity and courtesy of manners by any who enjoyed the society of Mount Vernon, with one of the most beautiful, accomplished, and religious ladies that ever bore the name of Randolph, all the instructions and associations, the habits and studies of her childhood and youth, were suited to nurture those just principles and pure and generous sentiments which ever pervaded and adorned her entire character. Early allied by marriage to a gentleman bred up in Mount Vernon while the spot was the home of the father of his country—a gentleman whose genius, taste, eloquence, and courtesy, have attracted multitudes from this and far distant lands to that mansion, where, alas, he now sits in sorrow and darkness—she dedicated herself to those gentle offices, quiet duties, and daily graceful ministries of love, so becoming to her station and her sex.

"Those who best knew this lamented lady will testify to a charming simplicity and sincerity, expressed in her aspect, manners, and conversation, blended with a majesty of goodness far surpassing the fairest creations of the painter's or the poet's art. Her clear and comprehensive reason, ever submissive as a child to the teachings of its Author; her integrity never wavering and without guile; the purity of all her motives and affections; the energy of purpose with which she applied herself to duty, and that constant cheerfulness which made to her all duty pleasure, rendered her judgment on all moral questions well-nigh infallible, and gave serenity, consistency, and incomparable beauty to her life. For a period of thirty years the writer recollects no instance in which this distinguished Christian lady erred in judgment on any question of taste, propriety, or duty. Her example was a light, never declining, and never eclipsed, which the wise could not hesitate to follow, nor less serious observers to feel and admire. She was familiarly acquainted with the best English literature, and read much, though very careful to select works of unblemished and established reputation, and confining herself mainly, toward the close of her life, to books on practical religion and to Christian biography. But infinitely beyond all the writings of men she valued the word of God. This was her daily companion, study, and guide, and in the law of God was her meditation and delight all the day. She had a remarkably quick perception of beauty and sublimity in composition, art, or nature; and whenever she discerned these qualities, joy lighted up her countenance with a radiance pure and gentle as that shed through the windows of a cathedral from holy fire upon its altar. No member of the Protestant Episcopal church, was more ardently attached to its solemn worship and communion, while she embraced in her affectionate regards the whole company of Christ's disciples, never doubting the unity of his kingdom, or that to his church there is but one Head, and though many members, but one Body.

"Precious to her were all the services of the sanctuary. She loved its very gates; she entered them with joy and thanksgiving; her soul was filled with reverence of the heavenly King in those sacred courts where his honor dwelleth. What disciple present with her in the house of God, what casual observer, what stranger, what child has not been instructed, felt his soul warmed by the manner, the fervor of her heart-penetrating devotion?

"But how can I speak of her as she shone at home, and in the midst of her family and friends? She was a guardian-angel to the objects of her love, and when she left them it was like the going down of the sun for ever. Joy was turned into heaviness, and songs into the voice of them that weep. The fresh flowers of spring seemed to loose their fragrance, to fade and become withered when ceased that beautiful life, more fragrant even in memory than the roses or precious odors, gums and spices of Cashmere, Ceylon, or 'Araby the blest.' Though her life was not short, as was said by Atterbury of Lady Cutts, 'her death was sudden; she was called in haste and without any warning; one day she drooped and the next she died; nor was there the difference of many hours between her being very easy in this world and very happy in another.' Her duties all discharged, the cause of benevolence and religion, aided by habitual and generous gifts and earnest prayers, her work all well done, her lamps well trimmed and brightly burning, she obeyed the summons. Truly was it said in that great hour, a 'purer spirit never left this world for the mansions of heaven.'

"A volume would be insufficient to describe those innumerable acts of courtesy, kindness, and beneficence which adorned and enobled the life of Mrs. Custis; a life retired from general observation, but widely extended in the power of its influence, and, as we doubt not, in the importance of its results. We have read of Lady Russell, the magnanimous daughter of the good Earl of Southampton; of Mrs. Ramsay, the devout and judicious companion of the historian of South Carolina; we have admired the fortitude and genius of Madame Roland; the mystical but sublime piety of Madame Guion, the charming grace and tenderness of Klopstock's wife, and many other touching portraits of female excellence; but in all the elements of a character to be loved, trusted, and imitated, a character to grow brighter by study and time, to be handed down with increasing honors to future ages, and stand in serene beauty among the ruins of the world, we find none in the annals of female biography to surpass that of her on whose dust we lay this poor offering of a sad but grateful heart."*

Mr. and Mrs. Custis had four children, all daughters, only one of whom (Mary Custis, wife of Colonel Robert E. Lee of the United States army) survived the period of infancy. Upon her the fondest affections of both parents were centred. From her father she never

---

* Mrs. Custis died at Arlington on the 23d of April, 1853.

received an unkind word. He was endowed with an even temper and remarkably buoyant spirit; and toward his family, his servants, his friends, and the world, there was a constant outflow of kindly feeling from his warm and generous heart.

Identifying himself with the past, through the power of strong association, he scarcely seemed to live in the present, though deeply interested in the current events of the day. He exercised an unbounded hospitality, and loved to pour forth to his delighted auditors the treasures of his richly-stored mind and wonderful memory. He had a happy faculty for expressing his thoughts by both pen and voice; and this was exercised at a very early period of his life, as is indicated in the following letter from the eminent General Henry Lee, of the revolution, written to him early in the year 1800, when young Custis was not quite nineteen years of age:—

"PHILAD'A, 16 *Feb'y.*

"DEAR SIR: Your polite note, accompanying your feeling address to the youth of America, was duly received. The perusal gave me much pleasure.

"The sentiments which it breathes do honor to your heart; and I ardently pray a similar spirit may pervade the rising generation throughout these states.

"I wished to have sent the paper to the press here; but, referring to your letter, I find no permission of that sort, and therefore have confined my communication of it to my own circle. With best wishes for your welfare, I am your friend and obt. servant,

"HENRY LEE."

The address alluded to was on the subject of the death

of Washington, and its eulogist had recently pronounced an admirable oration on the same subject, before the federal Congress, by invitation of that body.

Possessed of a quick and lively imagination, Mr. Custis sometimes employed a leisure hour in penning poetic effusions; and on several occasions, at the earnest solicitations of friends, he composed dramas, to be acted for a specific purpose. The following letter to his wife, in relation to one of these efforts, exhibits in a remarkable manner the facility with which he could put his thoughts into shape; and also the kindness of his nature. His wife was then on a visit to the family of the now venerable Bishop Meade:—

"ARLINGTON, 12 *Sept'r*, 1833.

"MY DEAREST WIFE: Your letter has been received, giving an account of your pleasurable trip through Fauquier, and safe arrival among your friends in Frederick. Your account of the appearance of the venerable Chief-Justice Marshall is particularly interesting. If you had written a little more in detail, I would have composed a fragment upon it, entitled '*A Scene in Fauquier.*' Dear, glorious old man! I wish he could lay his patriarchal hands upon our boy, and bless him. You know Lafayette's triumph in this country is attributed to his having received a blessing from the 'mother,' on his departure, in 1784.

"I shall hear from my dear Mary and her boy to-day, and, if there is anything to communicate, I will write again in a day or two. If you do not hear from me in *quick* time, you may conclude all are well.

"Remember me kindly and affectionately to the good bishop, and the excellent people around you. Health attend you, dearest wife! *Happiness* I know you have wherever you are.

"Write often, and believe me always yours, &c.,

"G. W. P. CUSTIS.

"P. S.—I have made a great mental effort lately, but 1 am sure you and the bishop will think my energies might have been better employed. I had promised the poor rogues of actors a play for the 12th Sept., the anniversary of the battle of North Point; but, finding myself not *in the vein,* I wrote to them to defer it. On Monday, 9th, the manager came on from Baltimore, and entreated me to prepare something for the 12th, as it would put six or seven hundred dollars in his pocket. On Monday not a line was finished. At five o'clock I commenced, and wrote until twelve; rose the next morning at five, and by seven sent off by the *stages* a two-act piece, with two songs and a finale, called *North Point, or Baltimore Defended,* the whole completed in nine hours. It is to be played to-night. To-morrow I shall hear of its success.

"The principal female character is called Marietta; runs away from her father, disguised as a rifle-boy, &c., &c.

"To Mrs. M. L. CUSTIS,
   "Mountain View, near Millwood,
     "Frederick county, Virginia."

Mr. Custis's private correspondence was written with much ease and grace, and always manifested the vivacity of his temperament. His letters to his family are of a character so purely domestic, that they would have no interest to the public. The following, having relation to another of his literary productions (which appears among the *Recollections*), may with propriety be introduced here:

"ARLINGTON, 19*th July*, 1833.

"MY DEAREST WIFE AND DAUGHTER: Your letter arrived yesterday. It is not in my power to go down to-day; but if nothing occurs, and you remain in your present mind, I will go in the next boat for you, though I can only remain until the following Wednesday. God knows I can be nowhere happier than with my dear children and precious grandson; and, again, the garrison and military matters, the sea-prospect, vessels, &c., all conspire to make a sojourn at the Point a most pleasurable thing to me; but a hard necessity compels me to the constant superintendence of my affairs at home. I hope another year, if I make a tolerable sale of my lands in Stafford and Westmoreland, to be more prosperous.

"I have been requested to write a short biography of my grandmother, to be accompanied by a splendid engraving from one of my originals, for Longacre's work, called *The National Gallery of Portraits,* and have consented to do it. I have written nothing and painted scarcely anything, but have read all the time. I have not been on my farm; go to bed exactly at ten, rise at six, breakfast at seven, and dine at two. I find myself often calling that darling boy in my reveries. Give him grandpa's kiss and blessing; and that God may bless you all, prays your husband and father, G. W. P. CUSTIS.

"To Mrs. M. L. CUSTIS,
    "Old Point Comfort, Virginia.

"P. S.—My Puss has returned, sadly beaten by wild-cats."

Mr. Custis's talent for oratory was brilliant; and, had due attention been paid to its cultivation, he would doubtless have ranked among the first in the land. His speeches, upon many occasions, would fill a volume. One of the earliest of those which have been preserved, was on the occasion of the funeral solemnities held at Georgetown, in the District of Columbia, on the first of September, 1812, in honor of General James M. Lingan, a worthy soldier of the Revolution, who was killed by a political mob, in Baltimore, on the twenty-eighth of July, 1812. This funeral oration was extemporaneous.* Of it a contemporary said: "It riveted the attention of the audience. The solemn stillness which reigned was only interrupted by sighs and tears. We can compare the eloquence of Mr. Custis with nothing but the supposed eloquence of antiquity. His words possess the fire of Demosthenes, and his actions the grace of Cicero. Old warriors, who had almost forgotten how to weep, felt the stream of sympathy stealing down their furrowed cheeks, while their deep, scarred breasts heaved with convulsive sobs. Every period glowed with inspiration."

Not long after this (fifth of June, 1813), he was called to address a large audience at Georgetown, assembled to celebrate the then recent Russian victories over Napoleon.† In that address Mr. Custis displayed, according to his contemporaries, some of the most noble characteristics of true oratory; and it drew from the Russian minister at Washington the following letter:—

"WASHINGTON, *the 7th June*, 1813.

"SIR: In delivering your oration on the occasion of the celebration of the Russian victories, you have been guided by the motives of an enlightened and independent patriot. The subject of it could not fail to be highly interesting to every friend of humanity and virtue; and you must have been highly gratified on perceiving

* See Note ii., p. 571.   † See Note iii, p 585.

the strong impression produced upon your respectable audience by the dignified, touching, and eloquent manner you presented it to their minds. You succeeded in making them fully sympathize with the distresses of my countrymen who have so bravely stemmed the homicidal hurricane raised from the revolutionary den of France, and made them magnanimously rejoice with us for having crushed the most impious attempt against our national independence. You may imagine, sir, what effect it produced upon the hearts of those whose cradles have been burned with their beloved Moscow, and whose tears can only be assuaged by their enemy's blood.

"Permit me to express to you my gratitude, that of my family, and of all my countrymen who shall peruse your oration, for the zeal and interest you have displayed in our cause; and allow me to send you a small medal, with the likeness of Alexander the First, the only one which is now in my possession. I can not give you a greater token of the value I set on your acquaintance.

"I have the honor to be with the most sincere and high consideration,

"Sir, your very humble and obedient servant,

"A. Daschkoff.

"P. S.—You would confer on me a great obligation, if you permit me to take a copy of your oration (should it be not printed), which I would like to send to Russia by the first favorable opportunity."

Mr. Custis was often called upon to speak in public, at every period of his life, nor did age seem to diminish the ardor of his feelings. When in December, 1855, the Amoskeag Veterans of Manchester, New Hampshire, joined their surviving companions in arms during the war of 1812, at Washington city, Mr. Custis was an honored guest among them. He accompanied them, and a large concourse of citizens, to Mount Vernon. The whole company went down from Washington city in steamers. On that occasion, Mr. Custis wore the epaulette which Washington placed upon his shoulder in 1798, as a cornet of horse. "At Alexandria," said the *Washington Evening Star*, "a large concourse of citizens assembled who listened with gratification to the stirring strains of the band. Fort Washington was soon reached, and, landing to the tune of 'Yankee Doodle,' the party took possession of the stronghold, no sentinel appearing to challenge their right.

"As the boat approached the wharf at Mount Vernon, the band played the 'Dead March in Saul,' but on landing, at the especial request of Mr. Custis, the solemn notes were changed into the more inspiring 'Washington's Grand March.' Ascending the hill the long column uncovered, and with reverential tread passed the hallowed spot—

> "'Where rest the ashes of the noblest man,
> That ever freeman mourned since time began;
> Whose lofty virtues in no age surpassed,
> Have blessed our own age and shall bless the last.'

"Countermarching, the battalion repaired to a level space near the tomb, where it was formed in hollow square, and ably addressed by Colonel Potter, who impressed on every mind the privilege in being permitted to gaze on the sacred place, where rest the remains of him, who was 'first in war, first in peace, and first in the hearts of his countrymen.' He dwelt upon his virtues, remarking, that he saw 'no north, no south, no east, no west.' He concluded by introducing the only surviving member of the Washington family, G. W. P. Custis, Esq.

"Loud applause greeted Mr. Custis, who was listened to with deep attention, as he recalled his interesting reminiscences of the illustrious owner of the locality near whose last resting-place they stood. It was an interesting scene to see this living relic of the past surrounded by the veterans, many of them near their last campaign."*

At an early period he became much interested in the improvement of the breed of sheep. Colonel David Humphreys, American minister at Madrid, had recently introduced the fine-wooled Merino sheep into the United States. Mr. Custis saw the great advantages that his country might derive from the cultivation of fine wool, and the establishment of manufactories of cloth, and in 1803 he inaugurated an annual convention for the promotion of agriculture and domestic manufactures, known throughout the country by the title of "Arlington Sheep-Shearing." These gatherings were at Arlington spring, a large fountain of living waters that gushes from

---

* There is no copy of this speech to be found among the papers of Mr. Custis. It was doubtless the immediate and unpremeditated outpourings of his heart. Colonel Potter, in a letter to Mr. Lossing, dated January 10, 1859, alluding to this speech, says:—

"This was among his best, if not the very best of his public speeches. It was on an interesting occasion, and his friends called it his happiest effort. I was in command of the battalion of 'veterans,' and during our whole march from Manchester, N. H., to Mount Vernon, when the best speakers were in requisition at Worcester, Philadelphia, Baltimore, and Washington, I heard no speech that in matter and manner equalled his in true eloquence. Among the hundreds present there was not a dry eye. Men of iron, in my own corps, who probably had never wept since boyhood, were overcome, and shed tears like boys, the drops standing upon their bronzed cheeks like dew in early morning. True, the time and place had its effect, but there was true eloquence in the speech itself."

beneath the shade of a venerable oak, not far from the banks of the Potomac. There, for many years, on the thirtieth of April, the annual shearing took place. A large concourse of people would assemble to participate in or witness the ceremonies. Toasts were drank, speeches were made, and prizes, provided at the sole expense of Mr. Custis, were distributed among those who presented the best specimens of sheep or wool, and domestic manufactures. These were the first prizes ever offered for such objects in America. Under the great war-tent of Washington, yet preserved at Arlington house, many of the noblest men of the land have assembled on these festivals, when they and the entire concourse were entertained in a most generous manner by the host, who usually made a stirring speech appropriate to the occasion. In one of them he said, prophetically: "America shall be great and free, and minister to her own wants by the employment of her own resources. The citizen of my country will proudly appear, when clothed in the produce of his native soil." It must be remembered that, at that time, every yard of broadcloth worn in the United States was imported from Europe.

The following letters to Mr. Custis, from Mr. Madison (then secretary of state, and soon afterward president of the United States), possess an interest in this connection :—

"Mr. Madison has received Mr. Custis's note of the 30th ultimo, with the specimen of fine wool accompanying it. He offers for himself the thanks to which Mr. Custis is entitled, from all his fellow-citizens, for his laudable and encouraging efforts to increase and improve an animal which contributes a material so precious to the independent comfort and prosperity of our country. Mr. Madison wishes that Mr. Custis may be amply gratified in the success of his improving experiments, and that his patriotic example may find as many followers as it merits.

"WASHINGTON, *August* 2, 1807."

"I have been duly favored, dear sir, with yours of the 7th. Not having taken with me to Virginia a sample of the Smith's island wool, which you were so good as to furnish me, I can not judge of its merit by comparison with the fleeces in the part of the country where I dwell. I regret it the more, as I have always considered them as among the best in point of fineness, though not of weight, which the American flocks yield. It gives me pleasure to find your attention to this interesting subject does not relax, and that you are so successfully inviting to it other public-spirited gentlemen.

"I remain, sir, with great respect and esteem,

"Your most obedient humble servant,

"JAMES MADISON.

"WASHINGTON, *October* 10, 1807."

The beautiful flock of fine sheep upon the Arlington farm were preyed upon by thieves and dogs, until their number was reduced to two. These, in the language of the owner, "long ranged over the hills of Arlington in solitary state." Until the close of his life, Mr. Custis took great interest in agricultural affairs, and was for several years previous to that event, an active member, and one of the vice-presidents of the United States Agricultural Society.

In the war of 1812, he served as a volunteer to oppose the British when they penetrated Maryland,

and ascended the Potomac, to attack Washington city. He would never accept any pay for his services; and while assisting the veterans of that war in prosecuting their claims upon the government, he withdrew his own.

When Lafayette came to the United States, in 1824, as the guest of the nation, Mr. Custis was among those who met him at the federal capital as a personal friend. True, his recollection of the illustrious Frenchman, while on his last visit to Mount Vernon in the autumn of 1784, was dim and shadowy, yet the son of that hero and benefactor, who now accompanied him, and who bore the name of GEORGE WASHINGTON, had been the companion of his youthful days at Mount Vernon, when Lafayette was in exile.* Mr. Custis spent much time with the illustrious guest at Arlington and elsewhere. At the tomb of Washington, in the presence of a large number of persons, he presented Lafayette with a ring, in which was some of the hair of the Pater Patriæ. The presentation was accompanied by some touching remarks, to which Lafayette responded in the most feeling manner. An account of the proceedings on that occasion may be found in the Appendix.

After the departure of the illustrious guest from

---

* The following letter written by the younger Lafayette, while in this country, to Mr. Custis, is preserved among others, at Arlington:—

"WASHINGTON CITY, *January the third*, 1825.

"MY DEAR CUSTIS. My father being able to dispose of himself on Wednesday, will do himself the pleasure of going that day to dine at Arlington. It is so long since I wished for that satisfaction myself, that I most sincerely rejoice at the anticipation of it. You know, my friend, how happy I was when we met at Baltimore. Since that day, I felt every day more and more, how much our two hearts were calculated to understand each other. Be pleased, my dear Custis, to present my respectful homage to the ladies, and receive for yourself the expression of my most affectionate and brotherly sentiments.

"G. W. LAFAYETTE."

America, Mr. Custis wrote and published a series of most entertaining articles, entitled, *Conversations with Lafayette*. It was at that time that he conceived the design of committing to paper his own recollections of the private life of Washington, and the first of the series was published in the National Intelligencer in 1826.

One of the principal amusements of Mr. Custis's later years, was painting revolutionary battle-scenes in which Washington participated. Upon these he worked with the greatest enthusiasm. Considering the circumstances under which they were produced — painted without being first composed or drawn in outline, by an entirely self-taught hand more than threescore and ten years old — they are remarkable. In general conception and grouping, they are spirited and original. He was not disposed to devote the time and labor requisite to their careful execution, and therefore, as works of art merely, they have but little merit. Their chief value lies in their truthfulness to history in the delineation of events, incidents, and costumes. They are all at Arlington, six in number, namely, battles of *Trenton, Princeton, Germantown,* and *Monmouth, Washington at Yorktown,* and the *Surrender at Yorktown.*

For some weeks previous to his death, Mr. Custis complained of debility and depression of spirits; but even then, he contemplated, with much pleasure, an excursion to the great West, to attend the agricultural fair at Louisville. Unwillingly was he compelled to relinquish this design; and only for four days did he occupy the bed from which he never arose. His disease was pulmonary pneumonia. Fully impressed with the belief that he could not survive the attack, the terrors of death seemed mercifully withdrawn, and with the gentleness and trust of a child did he await its approach. Regarding his daughter and her children who surrounded him, with touching affection, he often alluded to his "blessed wife," and her unceasing prayers for him. After a night of intense suffering and insensibility, he roused himself, and with that transient gleam. of light that usually precedes dissolution. Solemnly he embraced each member of his family, took leave of an old servant who attended in his room, requested his pastor to be summoned, to whom he avowed his belief and hope in the only atonement offered for sinners, with clasped hands joined in the prayer for the dying, and then gently sunk to rest in the seventy-seventh year of his age.

Thus expired, on the 10th of October, 1857, the last male representative of his family—thus was broken for ever a link between the illustrious Father of his Country and the present generation.

"Palida mors a'quo pulsat pede pauperum tabernas,
Regum-que turres."

The funeral of Mr. Custis took place at Arlington on the 12th. "As was anticipated," said the National Intelligencer, "the solemn event convened a numerous concourse of friends who had long been associated with the venerable man, and who had enjoyed many pleasing hours in listening to and witnessing the feelings of genuine patriotism which inspired him, as he related familiar incidents in the life and character of the illustrious WASHINGTON.

"Besides the family and their particular friends, officers of the army and navy, distinguished gentlemen of the legal profession, residents of Washington, Georgetown, and Alexandria, as well as the neighbors of the deceased for many miles around, thronged the parlors and halls.

"'Mount Vernon Guards of Alexandria,' the 'Association of the Survivors of the War of 1812 of the District of Columbia,' a delegation of the 'Jamestown Society of the District,' field and staff officers of the volunteer-regiment, and the Washington light-infantry, with their banners and fine martial music, and a delegation of the officers of the President's mounted guard, all travelled a distance of six miles to unite in the solemn testimonials of respect.

"The pall-bearers appointed were, William W. Seaton, Philip R. Fendall, Cassius F. Lee, Bushrod W. Hunter, Henry Dangerfield, and William B. Randolph.

"The religious services were conducted in an impressive manner by the Rev. C. B. Dana, of Christ church, Alexandria, according to the usages of the Protestant Episcopal church.

"The interment took place in a beautiful grove a short distance from the mansion, after which all retired in silence. The occasion awakened touching reminiscences of many pleasant days spent at the celebrated 'Spring of Arlington.'"*

---

* The Arlington spring already mentioned, as the place of the annual sheep-shearing, was, for many years, a point of great resort for picnic-parties from Washington, Georgetown, and Alexandria; and a small boat, used for conveying parties thither, was named "G. W. P. CUSTIS." It was estimated that at some seasons, from fifteen to twenty thousand people visited the spring on such occasions. Around the spring is a beautiful shaded lawn; and the generous proprietor, ever ready to give happiness to others, erected a wharf for the public accommodation, a store-room, kitchen, dining-hall sixty feet in length, and a saloon of the same dimensions for dancing in. No spiritous liquors were permitted to be sold there, and visiters were not allowed there on the sabbath. All that he asked in return, was good behavior, and a reciprocation of the kind feeling which made every class of respectable citizens cordially welcome.

The death of Mr. Custis produced a marked sensation throughout the country. He was universally known, beloved, and honored, as the " child of Mount Vernon;" and everywhere the press paid the tribute of most profound respect to his memory. "For several years," said the National Intelligencer, in noticing his death, "he had stood alone in his relations to the Father of his Country, ever anxious, with filial reverence and affection, to illustrate his character, and from the rich stores of his never-failing memory, to bring forward an annual tribute to his immortal worth. Known and honored by his fellow-countrymen, his departure will awaken universally a profound regret.

"Born amid the great events of the Revolution, by the death of his father (Colonel Custis, of the army, and a son of Mrs. Washington by a former marriage), which occurred near the close of the war, he found his home during childhood and youth at Mount Vernon, where his manners were formed after the noblest models; and from the great worthies of that period, frequent guests there, he received impressions of wisdom and patriotism that were never effaced. Under the counsels of Washington he pursued his classical studies at Princeton, and when deprived by death of his great guide and father (and soon after of his revered grandmother), he devoted himself to literary and agricultural pursuits on his ample estate of Arlington.

"Mr. Custis was distinguished by an original genius for eloquence, poetry, and the fine arts; by a knowledge of history, particularly the history of this country; for great powers of conversation, for an ever-ready and generous hospitality, for kindness to the poor, for patriotism, for constancy of friendship, and for a more than filial devotion to the memory and character of Washington. His early speeches on the death of General Lingan and the overthrow of Napoleon were everywhere read and admired, even by those who dissented from the sentiments, for the beauty of their conception and their impassioned eloquence. Those familiar with the columns of this journal will not forget how largely we, and the country, are indebted to the warm and ever-cheerful spirit of the deceased for many invaluable reminiscences of Revolutionary history, of the distinguished men of those times, and especially of the private life of their glorious chief in the retirement of the shades of his home at Mount Vernon.

"Thousands from this country, and from foreign lands, who have visited Arlington to commune with our departed friend, and look upon the touching memorials there treasured up with care, of him who was first in the hearts of his countrymen, will not forget the charm thrown over all by the ease, grace, interest, and vivacity of the manners and conversation of him whose voice, alas! is silent now. The multitudes of our fellow-citizens accustomed, in the heat of summer, to resort to the shades of Arlington, will hereafter miss that old man eloquent, who ever extended to them a warm-hearted welcome and became partaker of their joy."

In stature, Mr. Custis was of medium height, and well-formed; his complexion fair and somewhat florid; his eyes light and expressive of great kindliness of nature; his voice full, rich, and melodious; his deportment graceful and winning; his courtesy to strangers extremely cordial; and his affection for his friends, warm and abiding.

CORRESPONDENCE

BETWEEN

WASHINGTON AND CUSTIS.

PHILADELPHIA, 15*th November* 1796.

DEAR WASHINGTON: Yesterday's mail brought me your letter of the 12th instant, and under cover of this letter you will receive a ten-dollar bill, to purchase a gown, &c., if proper. But as the classes may be distinguished by a different insignia, I advise you not to provide these without first obtaining the approbation of your tutors; otherwise you may be distinguished more by folly, than by the dress.*

It affords me pleasure to hear that you are agreeably fixed; and I receive still more from the assurance you give of attending closely to your studies. It is you yourself who is to derive immediate benefit from these. Your country may do it hereafter. The more knowledge you acquire, the greater will be the probability of your succeeding in both, and the greater will be your thirst for more.

I rejoice to hear you went through your examination

---

* Young Custis, was a student in Princeton college, New Jersey, at that time, and Washington, then president of the United States, was residing in Philadelphia, that being the federal city.

with propriety, and have no doubt but that the president has placed you in the class which he conceived best adapted to the present state of your improvement. The more there are above you, the greater your exertions should be to ascend; but let your promotion result from your own application, and from intrinsic merit, not from the labors of others. The last would prove fallacious, and expose you to the reproach of the daw in borrowed feathers. This would be inexcusable in you, because there is no occasion for it; forasmuch, as you need nothing but the exertion of the talents you possess, with proper directions, to acquire all that is necessary; and the hours allotted for study, if properly improved, will enable you to do this. Although the confinement may feel irksome at first, the advantages resulting from it, to a reflecting mind, will soon overcome it.

Endeavor to conciliate the good will of *all* your fellow-students, rendering them every act of kindness in your power. Be particularly obliging and attentive to your chamber-mate, Mr. Forsyth; who, from the account I have of him, is an admirable young man, and strongly impressed with the importance of a liberal and finished education. But above all, be obedient to your tutors, and in a particular manner respect the president of the seminary, who is both learned and good.

For any particular advantages you may derive from the attention and aid of Mr. Forsyth, I shall have a disposition to reward. One thing more and I will close this letter. Never let an indigent person ask, without receiving *something*, if you have the means; always recollecting in what light the widow's mite was viewed.

Your grandmother, sister, and all here are well, and

feeling a strong interest in your welfare, join most cordially with me in every good wish for it.
Affectionately,
I am your sincere friend,
G. WASHINGTON.

Mr. GEO. WASHINGTON PARKE CUSTIS.

PHILADELPHIA, 28*th November*, 1796.

DEAR WASHINGTON: In a few hasty lines, covering your sister's letter and a comb, on Saturday last, I promised to write more fully to you by the post of this day. I am now in the act of performing that promise.

The assurances you give me of applying diligently to your studies, and fulfilling those obligations which are enjoined by your Creator and due to his creatures, are highly pleasing and satisfactory to me. I rejoice in it on two accounts; first, as it is the sure means of laying the foundation of your own happiness, and rendering you, if it should please God to spare your life, a useful member of society hereafter; and secondly, that I may, if I live to enjoy the pleasure, reflect that I have been, in some degree, instrumental in effecting these purposes.

You are now extending into that stage of life when good or bad habits are formed. When the mind will be turned to things useful and praiseworthy, or to dissipation and vice. Fix on whichever it may, it will stick by you; for you know it has been said, and truly, "that as the twig is bent so it will grow." This, in a strong point of view, shows the propriety of letting your inexperience be directed by maturer advice, and in placing guard upon the avenues which lead to idleness and vice. The latter will approach like a thief, working upon your passions; encouraged, perhaps, by bad examples; the propensity to which will increase in proportion to the practice of it and your yielding. This admonition proceeds from the purest affection for you; but I do not mean by it, that you are to become a stoic, or to deprive yourself in the intervals of study of any recreations or manly exercise which reason approves.

'Tis well to be on good terms with all your fellow-students, and I am pleased to hear you are so, but while a courteous behavior is due to all, select the most deserving only for your friendships, and before this becomes intimate, weigh their dispositions and character *well*. True friendship is a plant of slow growth; to be sincere, there must be a congeniality of temper and pursuits. Virtue and vice can not be allied; nor can idleness and industry; of course, if you resolve to adhere to the two former of these extremes, an intimacy with those who incline to the latter of them, would be extremely embarrassing to you; it would be a stumbling-block in your way, and act like a millstone hung to your neck, for it is the nature of idleness and vice to obtain as many votaries as they can.

I would guard you, too, against imbibing hasty and unfavorable impressions of any one. Let your judgment always balance well, before you decide; and even then, where there is no occasion for expressing an opinion, it is best to be silent, for there is nothing more certain than that it is at all times more easy to make enemies than friends. And besides, to speak evil of any one, unless there is unequivocal proofs of their deserving it, is an injury for which there is no adequate reparation. For, as Shakespeare says, "He that robs me of my good name enriches not himself, but renders me poor indeed," or words to that effect. Keep in mind that scarcely any change would be agreeable to you at *first* from the sudden transition, and from never having been accustomed to shift or rough it. And, moreover, that if you meet with collegiate fare, it will be unmanly to complain. My paper reminds me it is time to conclude.

Affectionately,
Your sincere friend,
G. WASHINGTON.

P. S.—I presume you received my letter covering a ten-dollar bill to pay for your gown, although it is not mentioned. To acknowledge the receipt of letters is always proper, to remove doubts of their miscarriage.

PHILADELPHIA, 19*th December*, 1796.

DEAR WASHINGTON: I am not certain whether I have written to you since the receipt of your letter of the first instant, for, as my private letters are generally despatched in a hurry, and copies not often taken, I have nothing to resort to, to refresh my memory; be this, however, as it may, we are always glad to hear from you, though we do not wish that letter-writing should interfere with your more useful and profitable occupations. The pleasure of hearing you were well, in good spirits, and progressing as we could wish in your studies, was communicated by your letter of the fourteenth instant, to your grandmamma; but what gave me particular satisfaction, was to find that you were going to commence, or had commenced a course of reading with Doctor Smith,[*] of such books as he

---

[*] Samuel Stanhope Smith, then president of Princeton college, was a distinguished Presbyterian clergyman. He was born at Pequea, Pennsylvania, in March, 1750; was educated at his father's academy; entered Princeton college when in his sixteenth year; took the degree of bachelor of arts in 1769, when he was graduated

had chosen for the purpose. The first is very desirable, the other indispensable; for, besides the duty enjoined upon you by the instructions of your preceptors, whilst your own judgment is locked up in immaturity; you now have a peculiar advantage in the attentions of Doctor Smith to you, who, being a man of learning and taste himself, will select such authors and subjects, as will lay the foundation of useful knowledge; let me impress it upon you, therefore, again and again, not only to yield implicit obedience to his choice and instructions in this respect, but to the course of studies also, and that you would pursue both with zeal and steadiness. Light reading (by this, I mean books of little importance) may amuse for the moment, but leaves nothing solid behind.

The same consequences would follow from inconstancy and want of steadiness—for 'tis to close application and constant perseverance, men of letters and science are indebted for their knowledge and usefulness; and you are now at that period of life (as I have observed to you in a former letter) when these are to be acquired, or lost for ever. But as you are well acquainted with my sentiments on this subject, and know how anxious all your friends are

---

and soon afterward became a tutor in the college. There he remained two years, studying theology at the same time, when he became a licensed minister, and entered upon missionary labors in the western counties of Virginia. He was very popular, and was selected to preside over the new college of *Hampden Sidney*, in Prince Edward county, Virginia. He was chosen professor of moral philosophy in Princeton college, in 1779; and after laboring successfully for several years as vice-president, to build up the college, and as a clergymen for the interests of the Presbyterian church, he was chosen, in 1795, president of the college, in place of Doctor Witherspoon, who had died the preceding year. Ill health compelled him to relinquish his charge, in 1812, and in August, 1819, he died, at the age of nearly seventy years. Doctor Smith was distinguished for his great goodness, thorough scholarship, polished manners, eloquence as a preacher, and elegance and perspicuity as a writer.

to see you enter upon the grand theatre of life, with the advantages of a finished education, a highly cultivated mind, and a proper sense of your duties to God and man, I shall only add one sentiment more before I close this letter (which, as I have others to write, will hardly be in time for the mail), and that is, to pay due respect and obedience to your tutors, and affectionate reverence to the president of the college, whose character merits your highest regards. Let no bad example, for such is to be met in all seminaries, have an improper influence upon your conduct. Let this be such, and let it be your pride, to demean yourself in such a manner as to obtain the good will of your superiors, and the love of your fellow-students.

Adieu—I sincerely wish you well, being your attached and affectionate friend,

G. WASHINGTON.

To MR. GEO. WASHINGTON CUSTIS.

PHILADELPHIA, 11*th January*, 1797

DEAR WASHINGTON: I hasten to acknowledge the receipt of your letter, dated the 7th instant, but which did not get to my hands until yesterday, and to express to you the sincere pleasure I feel in finding that I had interpreted some parts of your letters erroneously. As you have the best and most unequivocal evidence the case is susceptible of, that I have no other object in view by extending my cares and advice to you than what will redound to your own respectability, honor, and future happiness in life, so be assured, that while you give me reasons to expect a ready submission to my counsels, and while I hear that you are diligent in pursuing the means which are to acquire these advantages, it will afford me infinite gratification. Your last letter is replete with assurances of this nature—I place entire confidence in them. They have removed all the doubts which were expressed in my last letter to you, and let me repeat it again, have conveyed very pleasing sensations to my mind.

It was not my wish to check your correspondences—very far from it; for with proper characters (and none surely can be more desirable than with your papa and Mr. Lear), and on proper subjects, it will give you a habit of expressing your ideas *upon all occasions* with facility and correctness. I meant no more, by telling you we should be content with hearing from you once a week, than that these correspondences were not to be considered as an injunction or an imposition, thereby interfering with your studies or concerns of a more important nature. So far am I from discountenancing writing of any kind (except upon the principle abovementioned), that I should be pleased to hear, and you yourself might derive advantages from a short diary (recorded in a book) of the occurrences which happen to you within your sphere. Trifling as this may appear at first view, it may become an introduction to more interesting matters. At any rate, by carefully preserving these, it would afford you more satisfaction in a retrospective view, than what you may conceive at present.

Another thing I would recommend to you—not because *I* want to know how *you* spend your money—and that is, to keep an account-book, and enter therein every farthing of your receipts and expenditures. The doing of which would initiate you into a habit, from which considerable advantages would result. Where no account of this sort is kept, there can be no investigation; no correction of errors; no discovery from a recurrence thereto, wherein too much, or too little, has been appropriated to particular uses. From an early attention to these matters, important and lasting benefits may follow.

We are all well, and all unite in best wishes for you; and with sincere affection I am always yours,

G. WASHINGTON.

Mr. G. WASHINGTON CUSTIS.

NASSAU HALL, 25th *March*, 1797.

DEAREST SIR: A letter from my sister this morning, informed me of your safe arrival at Mount Vernon, the ignorance of which event has hitherto prevented me from writing. I congratulate you on a thing so ardently wished for by all those interested in your welfare. The marks of approbation and esteem manifested in the manner of the different states through which you passed, must have have been highly gratifying, and the pleasure felt on reaching the destined haven must have rendered your happiness complete.

The different studies I have passed through during the winter, I am now reviewing; and the evident good effects resulting from an attention to them at first, are now conspicuous. The examination will come on in a fortnight, and immediately after the vacation will commence. The money you were so kind as to transmit for my expenses, I shall receive at my departure, and keep regular accounts of all expenditures. I shall start the next day, and pass through Philadelphia without stopping, so that I can have twenty days to stay at home; my anxiety to attain this end will preponderate against all other considerations. The Roman history I have read, reviewed, and am perfect in. The translating French has become quite familiar, and the great amount of writing attending this exercise has improved my hand. I have read a great many good authors this winter, and have particularly studied *Hume*; have obtained a tolerable idea of geography, and, sir, in justice to myself and my own endeavors, I think I have spent my time in a manner not to be complained of. I must confess I have not made so much progress in arithmetic as I ought, owing to a variety of circumstances, and the superficial manner in which I imbibed the first principles; but in the ensuing summer I shall make up the deficiency, and then hope I shall have nothing to regret. If, sir, by remaining in Philadelphia I could serve you in any way, I will do so with pleasure. For myself, I have no desire to delay a moment. I conclude, by wishing you all health and happiness. Remember me to all the family, and believe me sincerely yours, G. W. P. CUSTIS.

GEORGE WASHINGTON, Esq.

MOUNT VERNON, 3d *April*, 1797.

DEAR WASHINGTON: Your letter of the 25th ultimo has been duly received, and as your grandmamma or sister will write to you by this post, I shall leave it to them to furnish you with the details of our journey, and the occurrences since our arrival.

It gives me singular pleasure to hear that your time has been so well employed during the last winter, and that you are so sensible of the good effects of it yourself. If your improvement in other matters is equal to that which is visible in your writing, it can not but be pleasing to your friends; for the change there, both in the characters and diction is considerably for the better. A perseverance in such a course will redound much to your own benefit and reputation, and will make you at all times a welcome guest at Mount Vernon.

I have nothing to do in which you could be usefully employed in Philadelphia, and approve your determination to delay no time at that or any other place on the road, that you may have the more of it to spend among your friends in this quarter, who are very anxious to see you.

We are all in a litter and dirt, occasioned by joiners, masons, and painters, working in the house, all parts of which, as well as the out-buildings, I find upon examination, to be exceedingly out of repairs.

I am always and affectionately yours,
G. WASHINGTON.

The following letter, as evincing General Washington's deep solicitude for his adopted son, is here inserted, although the occasion that called it forth is unknown, the letter of Dr. Smith not being found among the correspondence:—

MOUNT VERNON, 24th May, 1797.

REVEREND AND DEAR SIR: Your favor of the 18th instant was received by the last post, the contents of which, relative to Mr. Custis, filled my mind (as you naturally supposed it would) with extreme disquietude. From his infancy I have discovered an almost unconquerable disposition to indolence in everything that did not tend to his amusements; and have exhorted him in the most parental and friendly manner often, to devote his time to more useful pursuits. His pride has been stimulated, and his family expectations and wishes have been urged as inducements thereto. In short, I could say nothing to him now by way of admonition, encouragement, or advice, that has not been repeated over and over again.

It is my earnest desire to keep him to his studies as long as I am able, as well on account of the benefits he will derive from them, as for the purpose of excluding him from the company of idle and dissipated young men until his judgment is more matured.

I can but thank you, sir, for your exertions to remove the error of his present thoughts, and I shall hope for your further endeavors to effect it. If you find, however, that the attempt will be in vain, I shall rely on your judgment to employ his time in such studies as you conceive will be most advantageous to him during his continuance with you, and I know of none more likely to prove so than those you have suggested, if his term at college will close with the next vacation. With very great esteem and regard, I am, reverend sir,

Your most obedient and very humble servant,

G. WASHINGTON.

The Reverend Doctor S. SMITH.

Several letters must have been destroyed, as the "error" referred to by Washington is not explained. If we may judge from the following letter, it was *forgiven*.

NASSAU HALL, 29*th May*, 1797.

DEAREST SIR: Words can not express my present sensations; a heart overflowing with joy at the success of conscience over disposition is all I have to give. Dearest sir, did you but know the effect your letter has produced it would give you as consummate pleasure as my former one did pain. My very soul, tortured with the stings of conscience, at length called reason to its aid, and happily for me triumphed. That I shall ever recompense you for the trouble I have occasioned, is beyond my hopes. However, I will now make a grand exertion, and show you that your grandson shall once more deserve your favor. Could you but see how happy I now am, you would soon forget all that is past, and let my future conduct prove the truth of my assertions. Good God, how just your letter! but, alas, we are poor weak creatures, and never believe what we do not feel. Could I hope this would restore your peace of mind my happiness would be complete. My time appears to me now too short. I shall seize the present moments, and God grant I may be a pleasure to my friends, family, and self. I can not say too much on this subject, I wait for your letter which I can already read. That I have abused such goodness is shocking, that I shall ever do so again I will risk my life. Confiding, dearest sir, in your equity and fatherly affection, I subscribe myself, with the sincerest and most heartfelt joy,

G. W. P. Custis.

Mount Vernon, 4th June, 1797.

Your letter of the 29th ultimo, came to hand by the post of Friday, and eased my mind of many unpleasant sensations and reflections on your account. It has, indeed, done more, it has filled it with pleasure more easy to be conceived than expressed; and if your sorrow and repentance for the disquietude occasioned by the preceding letter, your resolution to abandon the ideas which were therein expressed, are sincere, I shall not only heartily forgive, but will forget also, and bury in oblivion all that has passed.

As a testimony of my disposition to do this—of the hope I had conceived that reflection would overcome an indolent habit or bad advice—not a hint respecting this matter has been given to any of your friends in this quarter, although Doctor Stuart* and your mother (with their children) left this on Thursday last, after a stay of a week, and both Mr. Law and Mr. Peter have been here since the receipt of it. In a word, your grandmamma, sister, and myself, are all who were acquainted therewith.

You must not suffer the resolution you have recently entered into, to operate as the mere result of a momentary impulse, occasioned by the letters you have received from hence. This resolution should be founded on sober reflection, and a thorough conviction of your error, otherwise it will be as wavering as the wind, and become the sport of conflicting passions, which will occasion such a lassitude in your exertions as to render your studies of little avail. To insure permanency, think seriously of the advantages which are to be derived, on the one hand, from the steady pursuit of a course of study to be marked out by your preceptor, whose judgment, experience, and acknowledged abilities, enables him to direct them; and, on the other hand, revolve as seriously on the consequences which would inevitably result from an indisposition to this measure, or from an idle habit of hankering after unprofitable amusements at your time of life, before you have acquired that knowledge which would be found beneficial in every situation; I say *before*, because it is not my wish that, having gone through the essentials, you should be deprived of any rational amusement *afterward;*

---

* Doctor Stuart married young Custis's mother not long after her husband's death.

or, lastly, from dissipation in such company as you would most likely meet under such circumstances, who, but too often, mistake ribaldry for wit and rioting, swearing, intoxication, and gambling, for manliness.

These things are not without momentary charms to young minds susceptible of any impression, before the judgment in some measure is formed, and reason begins to preponderate. It is on this ground, as well as on account of the intrinsic advantages that you yourself would experience hereafter from it, that I am desirous of keeping you to your studies. And if such characters as I have described should be found instrumental, either by their advice or example, in giving your mind a wrong bias, shun them as you would a pestilence; for, be assured, it is not with such qualities as these you ought to be allied, or with those who possess them to have any friendship.

These sentiments are dictated by the purest regard for your welfare, and from an earnest desire to promote your *true* happiness, in which all your friends feel an interest, and would be much gratified to see accomplished, while it would contribute in an eminent degree to your respectability in the eyes of others.

Your endeavors to fulfill these reasonable wishes of ours can not fail of restoring all the attentions, protection, and affection, of one who ever has been, and will continue to be, your sincere friend,

G. WASHINGTON.

Mr. GEORGE W. P. CUSTIS.

NASSAU HALL, *June 8th*, 1797.

WITH a heart overflowing with gratitude, love, and joy, I return you thanks for your favor of the 4th ultimo, and could my words do justice to my feelings, I would paint them in their highest tints, but words communicate *ideas* not *sensations*. Your letter, fraught with what reason, prudence, and affection, only can dictate, is engraven on my mind, and has taken root in a soil which I shall cultivate, and which, I hope, may become fruitful; and, dear sir, while I look up to that Providence which has preserved me in my late contest with my passions, and enabled me to act in a way which will redound to my honor, permit me to make this humble confession, that if in any way, or by any means, I depart from your direction and guardianship, I may suffer as such imprudence shall deserve. That your letter and the directions contained therein, were from the purest motives, I can not doubt for one moment, as they are from one to whom I have looked for support on earth, and from whom I have experienced the most unbounded generosity. During my recess from college I was not idle, having with Doctor Smith studied the use of the globes, and got a tolerable insight into geography. We shall pursue, this summer privately, Priestley's Elements of Natural History, and Smith's Constitution. I have, at length, attained a room to myself, and shall take for a room-mate a Mr. Cassius Lee, son of Richard Henry Lee, a young man lately arrived from the eastward, where he has been pursuing his studies privately. He is of an amiable disposition, and very well informed. I shall have an opportunity of giving you better information about him when he has resided with me some time, as yet he is perfectly agreeable and very engaging. My class are now studying the Roman History, with which I am well acquainted, having previously studied it with the doctor. The things you commissioned me to get I have provided, and suppose you have the accounts now for adjustment. They are perfectly suitable, and I hope reasonable. I will now conclude, with expressing, what I have always had nearest my heart, *a desire of your esteem.* Be assured naught shall be wanting on my part to obtain the same; and that the great Parent of the universe may prolong your days, is the sincere prayer of your ever affectionate,

G. W. P. CUSTIS.

NASSAU HALL, *July 1st,* 1797.

DEAREST SIR: Since my last, nothing material has occurred; the weather is excessively sultry, the thermometer being generally at 98°, which makes study and confinement very disagreeable. I have much time to read, which I shall employ to that end, and am studying Priestley's Lectures on History, with the doctor, and reading Smollett and Hume by myself.

We shall commence geography the middle of this month, and devote the remainder of the session to that alone. I have studied the use of the globes and maps during my recess from college.

I have written to my old private tutor to solicit his correspondence, and have received a letter from him expressing his approbation of the measure.

The fourth of July will be celebrated with all possible magnificence; the college will be illuminated and cannon fired; a ball will be held at the tavern in the evening, which I shall not attend, as I do not consider it consistent with *propriety.*

Mr. Cassius Lee, the gentlemen I informed you I had taken as a room-mate, is a remarkably moral and modest young man. I have no doubt we shall live happily together. He is a son of Richard H. Lee, and brother to Ludwell. My room is fitted up very neatly and comfortably, though when the senior class leave college, I may almost have my choice.

Mr. Burwell called on his way to Boston, and informed me you were not very well. I sincerely hope it proceeded merely from cold or fatigue, and will not produce unpleasant consequences.

I now conclude, wishing you health and all the happiness this world can afford. Be assured I remain,
Most sincerely,
Your affectionate,
G. W. P. Custis.

P. S.—Mr. Lee's respectful compliments wait on you, sir. He is happy to inform you he left your nephew well at Andover, Massachusetts.

To George Washington, Esq.

Mount Vernon, 10*th July*, 1797.

Dear Washington: Your letter of the first instant was received by the last mail (on Friday), and your other letter, of the eighth of June, remains unacknowledged, owing principally to engagements without doors in my harvest fields, and to company within, for we have scarcely been alone a day for more than a month, and now have a house full, among whom are your sisters, Law and Peter.

To hear you are in good health, and progressing well in your studies, affords peculiar satisfaction to your friends, and to none more than myself; as it is my earnest desire that you should be accomplished in all the useful and polite branches of literature.

To correspond with men of letters, can not fail of

being serviceable to you, provided it does not interfere with your more important duties, and to hear their sentiments on particular points may not be amiss; but you are not to forget that your course of studies is under the direction of Dr. Smith, who is, at least, equal to any you can correspond with; who knows what you have learned, and what is necessary for you to learn, to be systematical. I enjoin it strongly upon you, therefore, not to suffer any opinion or advice of Mr. Z. Lewis, however well meant they may be, to divert you from the prosecution of any plan which may be marked out by Dr. Smith, or to produce the least hesitation in your mind, for no *good* can come of it, and much *evil* may.

It gives me much pleasure to hear that you have got a chamber-mate that is agreeable to you. We hope he will continue to be so, for your mutual satisfaction and benefit.

The weather has not been intensely hot with us; at no time this summer has the mercury exceeded 90°, and but once, and this was on the twenty-fourth of June, has it been so high.

If it has been usual for the students of Nassau college to go to the balls on the anniversary of the Declaration of Independence, I see no reason why you should have avoided it, as no innocent amusement or reasonable expenditure will ever be withheld from you.

I take it for granted, that your grandmamma and sister Nelly (if no more of the family) are writing to you, and as they detail more than I can the domestic news, I will only subscribe myself,

Your affectionate,   GEO. WASHINGTON

TO MR. G. W. P. CUSTIS.

NASSAU HALL, *July 14th*, 1797.

MOST HONORED SIR: I have just received your kind favor of the tenth ultimo, together with the enclosed, for all of which accept my thanks. I congratulate you upon the enjoyment of your health and prospects of future felicity, which that you may attain and experience is my fervent prayer.

The gentlemen, whose correspondence I have submitted to your inspection, are Messrs. Lewis, Law, Lear, and Dr. Stuart. With respect to your apprehensions of Lewis's advice on subjects which materially affect my conduct, I own they are perfectly just, and am happy you have suggested them, as they will put me on my guard. Our letters are on topics which occasion remarks on both sides, and are improving to me alone, as they tend to correct style and give fluency to expression. I am studying the principles and uses of history in general, in a course of lectures by Priestley, and shall be able to apply them to any history so as to make it easy to be understood and entertaining. I have also much leisure for reading, as the class are studying Roman antiquities, which I have gone through with the doctor. The fourth of July was very grand; we fired three times sixteen rounds from a six-pounder, and had public exhibitions of speaking. At night the whole college was beautifully illuminated. The ball was instituted by the students, and principally attended by them. My ideas of *impropriety* proceeded from a distaste of such things during a recess from them, as I was confident all relish for study would be lost after such enjoyment; for there is a difference between the mind's being entirely taken off from an object, to which it can return with increased vigor, and a momentary relapse, which only whets the appetite that can not be satiated.

The thermometer in the sun is 110°, 98° in the shade. We wear light clothing, and are permitted to appear in morning-gowns. I am at present in want of nothing, and perfectly well. With kind remembrances to all my friends and family, I conclude with wishing you health, peace, and happiness, the only blessings this world can bestow and *man* enjoy, and subscribe myself, with sincere affection and duty,

Yours,
G. W. P. Custis.

George Washington, Esq.

Mount Vernon, 23*d July*, 1797.

Dear Washington: Your letter of the 14th instant has been duly received, and gives us pleasure to hear that you enjoy good health, and are progressing well in your studies.

Far be it from me to discourage your correspondence with Dr. Stuart, Mr. Law, or Mr. Lewis, or indeed with any others, as well-disposed and capable as I believe they are to give you specimens of correct writing, proper subjects, and if it were necessary, good advice.

With respect to your epistolary amusements generally, I had nothing further in view than not to let them interfere with your studies, which were of more interesting concern; and with regard to Mr. Z. Lewis, I only meant that no suggestions of his, if he had proceeded to give them, were to be interposed to the course pointed out by Dr. Smith, or suffered to weaken your confidence therein. Mr. Lewis was educated at Yale college, and as is natural, may be prejudiced in favor of the mode pursued at that seminary; but no college has turned out better scholars, or more estimable characters, than Nassau. Nor is there any one whose president is thought more capable to direct a proper system of education than Dr. Smith; for which reason, if Mr. Lewis, or any other, was to prescribe a different course from the one you are engaged in by the direction of Dr. Smith, it would give me concern. Upon the plan you propose to conduct your correspondence, none of the evils I was fearful of can happen, while advantages may result; for composition, like other things, is made more perfect by practice and attention, and just criticism thereon.

I do not hear you mention anything of geography or mathematics as parts of your study; both these are necessary branches of useful knowledge. Nor ought you to let your knowledge of the Latin language and grammatical rules escape you. And the French language is now so universal, and so necessary with foreigners, or in a foreign country, that I think you would be injudicious not to make yourself master of it.

You certainly do not observe the degree of heat by Farenheit's thermometer, or it must be in a very hot exposure if you do; for at no time this summer has the mercury been above 90°, or at most 91°, at this place; and I should think Princeton must be as cool at least as Mount Vernon, being nearly two degrees north of it.

Your mamma went from here (with your sister Nelly) to Hope Park, on Wednesday, and is as well as usual. Your sister Law and child, were well on that day; and Mr., Mrs., and Eleanor Peter are all well at this place now, and having many others in the house, among whom are Mr. Volney and Mr. William Morris. I shall only add, that I am sincerely and affectionately,

     Yours, G. WASHINGTON.

Mr. G. W. P. CUSTIS.

        NASSAU HALL, *July 30th*, 1797.

DEAREST SIR: It is with pleasure I acknowledge the receipt of your obliging favor of the 23d ultimo, and must congratulate you upon the enjoyment of your health, the preservation of which should always be our aim, and I have no doubt, as long as you are able to take your accustomed exercise that you will be perfectly well.

Mr. Z. Lewis has kept up the correspondence. His letters have generally contained common-place remarks on different subjects. His plans, were he to suggest any, would have very little weight with me, and would not tend to counteract those of Doctor Smith, I assure you. As to the other gentlemen, I am well convinced they would merely suggest, and not pretend to influence me in any pursuit pointed out by him.

With respect to the study of geography, I had forgotten that you were unacquainted with the course of the class, or I should have mentioned it particularly. We are now engaged in geography and English grammar, both of which we shall nearly conclude this session. The senior class will leave college in about a fortnight, when we shall become junior or second class, not in studies, as we do not commence mathematics till next session. The time appears to glide away imperceptibly. This session wants but eight weeks of being out.

It was with heartfelt satisfaction I read that Buonaparte had sued for the liberation of the *marquis*, and sincerely hope poor Mr. Lafayette may have some authentic accounts concerning the same, which will, no doubt, afford him great relief in his present state of suspense.*

The weather has become more moderate. I have no news to tell you, except that Greenleaf is in jail and likely to remain there.

Present my love to the family, and be assured, dearest sir, that bound by ties indissoluble in themselves, and sacred to me, I remain,

Your dutiful and affectionate,

G. W. P. CUSTIS.

MOUNT VERNON, 29*th August*, 1797.

DEAR WASHINGTON: Your letter of the 21st instant, came to hand by the last post, and as usual, gave us pleasure to hear that you enjoyed good health, were progressing well in your studies, and that you were in the road to promotion.

The senior class having left, or being on the point of leaving college, some of them with great *éclat*, ought to provoke strong stimulus to those who remain, to acquire equal reputation, which is no otherwise to be done than by perseverance and close application; in neither of which I hope you will be found deficient.

Not knowing the precise time that the vacation commences, I have put under cover with this letter to Doctor Smith, forty dollars to defray the expenses of your journey; and both your grandmamma and myself desire that you will not think of doing it by water, as the passage

---

* The Marquis de Lafayette suffered much during the storm of the old French Revolution. He was compelled to flee from his country, but being arrested, was for three years in prison in a dungeon at Olmutz, in Germany. His son, George Washington Lafayette, above alluded to, came to America, and found a home in the family of Washington, at Mount Vernon, until his father was set at liberty.

may not only be *very tedious*, but subject to a variety of accidents, to which a journey by land is exempt; and as the yellow fever is announced from authority to be in Philadelphia, we enjoin it on you strictly to pursue the route, and the direction which you may receive from the president of the college, to avoid the inconveniences and consequences which a different conduct might involve you and others in.

Although I persuade myself that there is no occasion for the admonition, yet I exhort you to come with a mind steadfastly resolved to return precisely at the time allotted, that it may be guarded against those ideas and allurements which unbend it from study, and cause reluctance to return to it again. Better remain where you are than suffer impressions of this sort to be imbibed from a visit, however desirous that visit may be to you, and pleasing to your friends, who will prefer infinitely your permanent good, to temporary gratifications; but I shall make all fears of this sort yield to a firm persuasion, that every day convinces you more and more of the propriety and necessity of devoting your youthful days in the acquirement of that knowledge which will be advantageous, grateful, and pleasing to you in maturer years, and may be the foundation of your usefulness here, and happiness hereafter.

Your grandmamma (who is prevented writing to you by General Spotswood and family's being here) has been a good deal indisposed by swelling on one side of her face, but it is now much better. The rest of the family within doors are all well, and all unite in best regards for you, with your sincere friend, and affectionate,

G. WASHINGTON.

Mr. G. WASHINGTON CUSTIS.

The correspondence for the year 1797 here closed. We next find a letter from Washington to Mr. McDowell, president of St. John's college, Annapolis. We know not why Mr. Custis was removed from Princeton.

MOUNT VERNON, *5th March*, 1798.

SIR: Consequent upon a letter received from Mr. George Calvert recently, this letter will be presented to you by Doctor Stuart, who is so obliging as to accompany young Mr. Custis to Annapolis for the purpose of placing him at college under your auspices, and making such arrangements respecting his boarding and the precise line of conduct for him to observe, and such course of studies as you and he (the temper and genius of the youth being considered) shall conceive most eligible for him to pursue.

Mr. Custis possesses competent talents to fit him for any studies, but they are counteracted by an indolence of mind, which renders it difficult to draw them into action. Doctor Stuart having been an attentive observer of this, I shall refer you to him for the development of the causes, while justice from me requires I should add, that I know of no vice to which this inertness can be attributed. From drinking and gaming he is perfectly free, and if he has a propensity to any other impropriety it is hidden from me. He is generous and regardful of truth.

As his family, fortune, and talents (if the latter can be improved), give him just pretensions to become a useful member of society in the councils of his country, his friends, and none more than myself, are extremely desirous that his education should be liberal, polished, and suitable for this end; any suggestions to promote these views will be thankfully received. Whatever is agreed upon by Doctor Stuart in my behalf, with relation to Mr. Custis, will meet the approbation of, and be complied with by, sir, your most obedient humble servant,

G. WASHINGTON.

Mr. McDOWELL,
President of the College at Annapolis.

ANNAPOLIS, *March 12th*, 1798.

DEAREST SIR: I arrived here in due season, after a very agreeable journey, and found all my relations well, and Annapolis a very pleasant place. I visited the principal inhabitants while the doctor was here, and found them all very kind. Mr. McDowell is a very good and agreeable man. He has examined me, and I am now pursuing the study of Natural Philosophy, and hope to distinguish myself in that branch as well as others. Arithmetic I have reviewed, and shall commence French immediately with the professor here. I was so fortunate as to get in with a Mrs. Brice, a remarkably clever woman, with whom I live very well and contented. There are several clever young men boarding in this house, with whom I associate on the most friendly terms. The mail is going out, and I have only to add, that I constantly bear in mind your virtuous precepts, and hope to benefit by them, and am most sincerely and affectionately your dutiful, G. W. P. CUSTIS.

GEORGE WASHINGTON, Esq.

MOUNT VERNON, 19*th March*, 1798.

DEAR WASHINGTON: Your letter of the 12th instant has been received; and it gives me and your friends here much pleasure to find that you are agreeably fixed, and disposed to prosecute your studies with zeal and alacrity.

Let these continue to be your primary objects and pursuits; all other matters at your time of life are of secondary consideration. For it is on a well-grounded knowledge of these, your respectability in maturer age, your usefulness to your country, and, indeed, your own private gratification, when you come seriously to reflect upon the importance of them, will depend. The wise man, you know, has told us (and a more useful lesson never was taught) that there is a *time* for *all things*; and now is the time for laying in such a stock of erudition as will effect the purposes I have mentioned. And above all things, I exhort you to pursue the *course* of studies that Mr. McDowell, of whom every one, as well as yourself, speaks highly, has or shall mark out as the most eligible path to accomplish the end. It is from the experience and knowledge of preceptors that youth is to be advantageously instructed. If the latter are to mark out their own course, there would be little or no occasion for the former, and what would be the consequence it is not difficult to predict.

One or other of the family will expect to receive a letter from you once a fortnight, that we may know how you are in health; in addition to which, I shall expect to hear how you are progressing in your studies, as time advances. All here join in best wishes for you, among whom, your sister Peter is of the number; and you may be assured of the friendship of your affectionate,

G. WASHINGTON.

Mr. G. W. P. CUSTIS.

ANNAPOLIS, *April 2d*, 1798.

DEAREST SIR: Your letter arrived by the ordinary course of mail, which goes by Baltimore, and gave me sincere pleasure hearing you and the family were in good health.

I was somewhat unwell for some time after coming here, owing to the water, but it is entirely removed now. I am going on with the class in college and attending the French master, who is, I believe, very competent. Every week we write dissertations on various subjects, which are both amusing and instructive, and create laudable emulation.

I am very happily situated, perhaps better than many others; and could a repetition of those sentiments I have always avowed express my gratitude and obligations to you, they should be here expressed; but it is sufficient that they are indelibly engraven on my mind, and can never be erased while the principles on which they are grounded exist. These principles are innate. What could be a greater misfortune to me than your displeasure! . What a greater happiness than your confidence!

I find that young M. C. has been at Mount Vernon, and report says, to address my sister. It may be well to subjoin an opinion, which I believe is general in this place, viz., that he is a young man of the strictest probity and morals, discreet without closeness, temperate without excess, and modest without vanity; possessed of those amiable qualities and friendship which are so commendable, and with few of the vices of the age. In short, I think it a most desirable match, and wish that it may take place with all my heart.

I have received every kindness from the citizens of

Annapolis, and could anything heighten my opinion of your character, it would be their expressions of esteem and regard. Adieu, dearest sir, and believe me sincerely and affectionately yours,

G. W. P. Custis.

George Washington, Esq.

Mount Vernon, 15*th April*, 1798.

Dear Washington: Your letter of the 2d instant came duly to hand, and gave us pleasure (as you may naturally conceive from our solicitude for your well-doing) at hearing that you had got over a short indisposition; was happy in your present situation; and going on well in your studies. Prosecute these with diligence and ardor, and you will, sometime hence, be more sensible than now of the rich harvest you will gather from them.

It gave us pleasure, also, to hear that you are kindly treated by the families in Annapolis. Endeavor by a prudent, modest, and discreet conduct, to merit a continuance of it, but do not suffer attentions of this sort to withdraw you from your primary pursuits.

Young Mr. C—— came here about a fortnight ago to dinner, and left us next morning after breakfast. If his object was such as you say has been reported, it was not declared here; and therefore, the less is said upon the subject, particularly by your sister's friends, the more prudent it will be until the subject develops itself more.

The family at this place are much as usual; your sister Peter, and her children are here, and Mr. Peter occasionally so. Dr. Stuart is also here at present, and informs us that your mother and the family (one of your sisters excepted) are very well. Mr. Law has been here, and leaving Mrs. Law at Baltimore, went back for her, and is not returned that we have heard of. This is all the domestic news which occurs to me; and, therefore, with every good wish of those I have enumerated, and particularly the blessings of your grandmamma,

I remain, your sincere friend, and affectionate,

G. WASHINGTON.

To Mr. WASHINGTON CUSTIS.

ANNAPOLIS, *May 5th*, 1798.

DEAREST SIR: Colonel Fitzgerald arrived here about an hour ago, and has politely offered to convey a letter to you. Nothing material has occurred since my last letter, only that we now attend college at six in the morning, which is by no means disagreeable, and conduces to health.

With respect to what I mentioned of Mr. C—— in my last, I had no other foundation but report, which has since been contradicted. All the families in this town in which I visit, express the highest esteem and veneration for your character, which conduces, in great measure, to the satisfaction I feel in their company.

All is well at present. I have found no inconvenience lately from the water, which affected me at first. I attend college regularly, and am determined that nothing shall alienate my attention.

Adieu, dearest sir, may heaven proportion her reward to your merit, is the sincere and ardent prayer of,

GEO. W. P. CUSTIS.

P. S.—I would thank you to inform me to whom I am to apply for money in case of want.

GEO. WASHINGTON, Esq.

MOUNT VERNON, 10*th May*, 1798.

DEAR WASHINGTON: Your letter by Colonel Fitzgerald* has been received, and I shall confine my reply, at present, to the query contained in the postscript, viz., "to whom I am to apply for money in case of need."

This has the appearance of a very early application, when it is considered that you were provided very plentifully, it was conceived, with necessaries of all sorts when you left this (two months ago only); had £4. 6. given to you by me, and £3. 0. 0. by Doctor Stuart, as charged in his account against me (equal together to between 9 and 10 lbs. Maryland currency); had a trunk purchased for you, a quarter's board paid in advance, &c. Except for your washing, and books when necessary, I am at a loss to discover what has given rise to so early a question. Surely you have not conceived that indulgence in dress or other extravagances are matters that were ever contemplated by me as objects of expense; and I hope they are not so by you. As then the distance between this and Annapolis is short, and the communication (by post) easy, regular, and safe, transmit the accounts of such expenses as are necessary, to me, in your letters, and a mode shall be devised for prompt and punctual payment of them. And let me exhort you, in solemn terms, to keep steadily in mind the purposes and the end for which you were sent to the seminary you are now placed at, and not disappoint the hopes which have been entertained from your going thither, by doing which, you will ensure the friendship, &c., of,

G. WASHINGTON.

To Mr. GEO. W. P. CUSTIS.

---

* Colonel Fitzgerald had been one of Washington's favorite aids.

ANNAPOLIS, *May* 26, 1798.

DEAREST SIR: Your last letter arrived safely, and conveyed the pleasing intelligence of your health, a theme always acceptable to my grateful heart. With respect to my expenses I did not mean to insinuate that I was actually in want, but supposed you had placed money in the hands of some one to whom I might apply. I have opened accounts with a shoemaker, tailor, and other persons from whom I might want occasional articles, which shall all be transmitted to you when offered. I got some nankeen and a gingham coat, which, together, with a hat, are all the necessary articles I wanted; the hat might have lasted longer had it not been a worthless one. I have been very careful of my clothes, and frequently revise them myself.

I now enter on a subject which I will endeavor to make plain. Far from being addicted to dress and extravagance, I am not fond of such things, and have not spent money in that way. I confess, that when I have friends at my own house, I like to entertain them with little superfluities, but farther, I sacredly deny any dissipation. I visit of an evening among some families, but never dine out except on Sunday. I have received that attention from the inhabitants of this town which claims my sincere regard, and shall endeavor by my conduct to merit their esteem. General Stone's politeness to me has been particular.

Nothing material has occurred since my last. I attend to my French constantly, with a good teacher, and hope to acquire the pronunciation. Adieu, dear sir, and believe me, ever dutifully and intrinsically yours,

G. W. P. CUSTIS.

GEO. WASHINGTON, Esq.

MOUNT VERNON, 13*th June*, 1798.

DEAR WASHINGTON: It is now near five weeks since any person of this family has heard from you, though you were requested to write once a fortnight. Knowing how apt your grandmamma is to suspect that you are sick, or that some accident has happened to you, how could you omit this?

I have said that none of us have heard from you, but it behooves me to add, that from persons in Alexandria, lately from Annapolis, I have, with much surprise, been informed of your devoting much time, and paying much attention, to a certain young lady of that place. Knowing that conjectures are often substituted for facts, and idle reports are circulated without foundation, we are not disposed to give greater credence to *these* than what arises from a fear that your application to books is not such as it ought to be, and that the hours that might be more profitably employed at your studies are mispent in this manner.

Recollect again the saying of the wise man, "There is a time for all things," and sure I am, this is not a time for a *boy of your age* to enter into engagements which might end in sorrow and repentance.

Yours affectionately,
G. WASHINGTON.

Mr. G. W. P. CUSTIS.

MARLBOROUGH, *June 17th*, 1798.

DEAREST SIR: I received your letter by mamma at this place, where I had come on my uncle's horses, and with Mr. McDowell's permission, in hopes of meeting her. She arrived the same day that I did, and informed me particularly respecting the *subject* of your letter, which appeared to set heavy on your mind. The report, as mamma tells me, of my being *engaged* to the young lady in question, is strictly erroneous. That I gave her reason to believe in my attachment to her, I candidly allow, but that I would *enter into engagements* inconsistent with my duty or situation, I hope your good opinion of me will make you disbelieve. That I stated to her my prospects, duty, and dependance upon the absolute will of my friends, I solemnly affirm. That I solicited her affection, and hoped, with the approbation of my family, to bring about a union at some future day, I likewise allow. The conditions were not accepted, and my youth being alleged by me as an obstacle to the consummation of my wishes at the present time (which was farthest from my thoughts), I withdrew, and that on fair and honorable terms, to the satisfaction of my friends.

Thus the matter ended, and should never have proceeded so far had I not been betrayed by my own feelings. However rash and imprudent I may be, I have always remembered my duty and obligation to you, which is the guide of my actions. It was this which prevented my entering into any engagements which were not entirely conditional.

To my mother I disclosed the whole affair, who is now perfectly satisfied; and I hope this small statement of facts, which I can confirm, either upon oath or the testimony of my friends, will eradicate all uneasiness from your mind.

Let me once more, sir, on the shrine of gratitude, plight my faith to you; let me unclasp the sacred books of morality and lay my duty, nay, my all, at your feet. Your beneficence could not enhance your virtues; on my heart they are engraven as the benefactor, the friend, nay, the more than father of,

G. W. P. CUSTIS.

GEORGE WASHINGTON, Esq.

MOUNT VERNON, 13*th June*, 1798.

SIR: An ardent wish that young Custis should apply closely to his studies, and conduct himself with propriety under your auspices, induces me to give you the trouble of receiving these inquiries, and to know if he is in want of anything that can be provided for him by, sir,

Your obedient and humble servant,

GEO. WASHINGTON.

Mr. McDOWELL.

ANNAPOLIS, *July* 12*th*, 1798.

DEAREST SIR: Not receiving any favor from you in answer to my last, and only a letter from Doctor Stuart, in which he questions but little concerning the affair which caused you so much anxiety, induces me to hope that both my confession of the circumstances of the case, and my error, has obliterated from your mind all unfavorable impressions. Confiding in this hope, I again submit myself to your confidence, and assure you, that though urged by imprudence, I was governed by duty— that duty which I shall hold sacred in all my walks of life; and let the goodness of my heart but cover the imprudence of my actions, and I am contented. My peace of mind, my consciousness of rectitude, will always be to me a sufficient plea for my actions; and be assured, dearest sir, nothing can contribute more to both than your favor.

I have nearly finished the six books of Euclid, and expect that college will adjourn in a fortnight. I can collect and forward all accounts as soon as you shall think fit to call for the same, and I hope that their reasonableness will be acceptable to you.

I need not congratulate you on an appointment* which was always designed by the Creator for one so fully capable of fulfilling it. Let an admiring world again behold a Cincinnatus springing up from rural retirement to the conquest of nations; and the future historian, in erasing so great a name, insert that of the "*Father of his country.*"

Remember me to all, and believe me sincerely, dutifully, and affectionately yours,

GEO. W. P. CUSTIS.

Gen. GEO. WASHINGTON.

The letter immediately preceding the following was not found in the package.

ANNAPOLIS, *July 21st,* 1798.

DEAREST SIR: By the returning mail I heartily acknowledge your last favor, and am sincerely happy in having given you full satisfaction in an affair so interesting, and mutually affecting to both my friends and myself. I this day finish the six books of Euclid, and with that, the course marked out for me while in Annapolis. College breaks up Monday week (the 30th), and I shall always be ready when you may send for me. I shall enclose my accounts by next post, so as to be ready to leave this as soon as convenient. I would thank you to inform me whether I leave it entirely, or not, so that I may pack up accordingly. With sincere affection to all friends I bid you adieu,

G. W. P. CUSTIS.

* As commander-in-chief of the provisional army of the United States.

MOUNT VERNON, 24*th July*, 1798.

DEAR WASHINGTON: Your letter of the 21st was received last night. The question, "I would thank you to inform me whether I leave it entirely, or not, so that I may pack up accordingly," really astonishes me! for it would seem as if *nothing* I could say to you made more than a *momentary* impression. Did I not, before you went to that seminary, and since by letter, endeavor to fix indelibly on your mind, that the object for which you were sent there was to finish a course of education which you yourself were to derive the benefit of hereafter, and for pressing which upon you, you would be the first to thank your friends so soon as reason has its proper sway in the direction of your thoughts?

As there is a regular stage between Annapolis and the federal city, embrace that as the easiest and most convenient way of getting to the latter, from whence Mr. Law or Mr. Peter will, I have no doubt, send you hither; or a horse might meet you there, or at Alexandria, at an appointed time.

The family are well; and I am, as usual, your affectionate,

G. WASHINGTON.

To MR. G. W. P. CUSTIS.

ANNAPOLIS, *July* 23, 1798.

DEAREST SIR: Since my last I have collected all my accounts, which I transmit for your perusal. The only article I apologize for is an umbrella, which I was unavoidably obliged to procure, as I lost one belonging to a gentleman. College breaks up on Saturday, and I shall be ready at any time that you may send. I will look over everything belonging to me and have them adjusted. I am very well, and at variance with no one, so that I shall leave this place just as I first entered it.

Believe me, dearest sir, sincerely and affectionately yours, GEO. W. P. CUSTIS.

GEO. WASHINGTON, Esq.

MOUNT VERNON, 30*th July*, 1798.

SIR: Being very much engaged of late in a manner I little expected, I have not only suffered your favor of the 19th instant to remain unacknowledged, but not attending to the time of the vacation of St. John's college, I have suffered that also to arrive, or to approach too near for the enclosed remittances to defray the expenses of Mr. Custis, before it is probable he left Annapolis.

Allow me the liberty, for this reason, to put the accounts which he has just transmitted to me, under cover to you, with bank-notes of Columbia for one hundred dollars, to discharge and take a receipt thereon, to be returned to me.

The pressure which is upon me at this time will not allow me to say anything relatively to the course of studies marked out for Mr. Custis when he returns to college. I will write more fully to you on this subject at a future time. Sir, I remain, your most obedient,

G. WASHINGTON.

To Mr. MCDOWELL.

MOUNT VERNON, 2*d September*, 1798

SIR: Your favor of the 13th ultimo, with the accounts, came duly to hand, and I thank you for the trouble you have had in paying and taking receipts therefor. The small balance of £„ 3. 5½ may, if you please, be given to Mr. Custis.

It was my intention to have written fully to you by the return of this young gentleman to college, but the debilitated state into which I have been thrown by a fever, with which I was seized on the 18th, and could procure no remission of until the 25th past, renders writing equally irksome and improper.

Were the case otherwise, I should, I confess, be at a loss to point out any precise course of study for Mr. Custis. My views, with respect to him, have already been made known to you, and, therefore, it is not necessary to repeat them on this occasion. It is not merely the best course for him to pursue that requires a consideration, but such an one as he can be induced to pursue, and will contribute to his improvement and the object in view. In directing the first of these objects, a gentleman of your literary discernment and knowledge of the world, would be at no loss, without any suggestions of mine, if there was as good a disposition to receive, as there are talents to acquire knowledge; but as there seems to be in this youth an unconquerable indolence of temper, and a dereliction, in fact, to all study, it must rest with you to *lead* him in the best manner, and by the easiest modes you can devise, to the study of such useful acquirements as may be serviceable to himself, and eventually beneficial to his country.

French, from having become in a manner the universal language, I wish him to be master of, but I do not find, from inquiry, that he has made much progress in the study yet. Some of the practical branches of mathematics, particularly surveying, he ought, possessor as he is of large landed property, to be well acquainted with, as he may have frequent occasion for the exercise of that study.

I have already exceeded the limit I had prescribed to myself when I began this letter, but I will trespass yet a little more, while I earnestly entreat that you will examine him, as often as you can make it convenient, yourself; and admonish him seriously of his omissions and defects; and prevent, as much as it can be done, without too rigid a restraint, a devotion of his time to visitations of the families in Annapolis; which, when carried to excess, or beyond a certain point, can not but tend to divert his mind from study, and lead his thoughts to very different objects. Above all, let me request, if you should perceive any appearance of his attaching himself, by visits or otherwise, to any young lady of that place, that you would admonish him against any such step, on account of his youth and incapability of appreciating all the requisites for a connexion which, in the common course of things, can terminate with the death of one of the parties only; and, if done without effect, to advise me thereof. If, in his reading, he was to make common-place notes, as is usual, copy them fair and show them to you, two good purposes would be answered by it. You would see with what judgment they were done, and it might tend much to improve his hand-writing, which requires nothing but care and attention to render it good. At present, all of his writing that I have seen is a hurried scrawl, as if to get to the end speedily, was the sole object of writing.

With sincerest esteem and regard, I am, sir, your obedient servant,

Geo. Washington.

P. S.—Knowledge of book-keeping is essential to all who are under the necessity of keeping accounts.

Mr. McDowell.

MOUNT VERNON, 16th *September*, 1798.

SIR: The enclosed was written at the time of its date, and, with Mr. Custis, I expected would have left this the next morning for St. John's college; but although he professed his readiness to do whatever was required of him, his unwillingness to return was too apparent to afford any hope that good would result from it in the prosecution of his studies. And, therefore, as I have now a gentleman living with me who has abilities adequate thereto, will have sufficient leisure to attend to it, and has promised to do so accordingly, I thought best, upon the whole, to keep him here.

He returns to Annapolis for the purpose of bringing back with him such articles as he left there, and discharging any accounts which may have remained unpaid. With great esteem and regard, I am, sir, your most obedient servant, G. WASHINGTON.

Mr. MCDOWELL.

MOUNT VERNON, *January* 22, 1799.

DEAR SIR: Washington leaves this to-day on a visit to Hope Park,* which will afford you an opportunity to examine the progress he has made in the studies he was directed to pursue.

I can, and I believe I do, keep him in his room a certain portion of the twenty-four hours, but it will be impossible for me to make him attend to his books, if inclination on his part is wanting; nor while I am out if he chooses to be so, is it in my power to prevent it. I will not say this is the case, nor will I run the hazard of doing him injustice, by saying he does not apply as he ought to what has been prescribed, but no risk will be

---

* The residence of his mother's family.

run, and candor requires I should declare it as my opinion, that he will not derive much benefit in any course which can be marked out for him at this place, without an *able* preceptor always with him.

What is best to be done with him I know not. My opinion always has been, that the university in Massachusetts would have been the most eligible seminary to have sent him to; first, because it is on a larger scale than any other; and, secondly, because I believe that the habits of the youth there, whether from the discipline of the school, or the greater attention of the people generally to morals, and a more regular course of life, are less prone to dissipation and excess than they are at the colleges south of it. It may be asked, if this was my opinion, why did I not send him there? The answer is as short as to me it was weighty: being the only male of his line, and knowing (although it would have been submitted to) that it would have proved a heart-rending stroke to have him at that distance, I was disposed to try a nearer seminary, of good repute, which, from some cause, or combination of causes, has not, after the experiment of a year, been found to answer the end that was contemplated. Whether to send him there now, or, indeed, to any other public school, is, indeed, problematical, and to mispend his time at this place would be disgraceful to himself and me.

If I were to propose to him to go to the university at Cambridge, in Massachusetts, he might, as has been usual for him on like occasions, say, he would go wherever I chose to send him, but if he should go, contrary to his inclination, and without a disposition to apply himself properly, an expense without any benefit would result from the measure. Knowing how much I have been disappointed, and my mind disturbed by his conduct, he would not, I am sure, make a candid disclosure of his sentiments to me on this or any other plan I might propose for the completion of his education, for which reason, I would pray that you (or perhaps Mrs. Stuart could succeed better than any one) would draw from him a frank and explicit disclosure of what his own wishes and views are; for, if they are absolutely fixed, an attempt to counteract them by absolute control would be as idle as the endeavor to stop a rivulet that is constantly running. Its progress, while mound upon mound is erected, may be arrested, but this must have an end, and everything will be swept away by the torrent. The more I think of his entering William and Mary, unless he could be placed in the bishop's family, the more I am convinced of its inutility on many accounts, which had better be the subject of oral communication than by letter. I shall wish to hear from you on the subject of this letter. I believe Washington means well, but has not resolution to act well. Our kind regards to Mrs. Stuart and family, and I am, my dear sir,

Your obedient and affectionate servant,

G. WASHINGTON.

DAVID STUART, Esq.

This is the last letter in the packet from which the foregoing series have been copied. The correspondence exhibits the old story of a youth of genius and fortune disappointing the hopes of his friends while at college; and it presents Washington in a new light, as exercising the tender solicitude of a parent.

RECOLLECTIONS AND PRIVATE MEMOIRS

OF THE

LIFE AND CHARACTER

OF

WASHINGTON.

EDITOR'S PREFACE.

It was the privilege of the writer to enjoy the friendship of Mr. Custis, the author of the following *Recollections of Washington*, for several years, and to experience, on frequent occasions, the hospitalities of Arlington House, his beautiful seat on the Potomac, opposite the federal city. The subject of his *Recollections* was a frequent topic of conversation, and the writer always expressed an earnest desire that Mr. Custis should complete and prepare for publication, in book form, the interesting work begun, many years before, of recording what he knew and remembered concerning the private life of Washington, and some of his compatriots. But his spirit was summoned from earth before that work was completed, and the revision of what was already done was left to other hands.

When invited by the only-surviving child of Mr. Custis to assist her in preparing his imperfect and unfinished *Recollections* for the press, by arranging them properly and adding illustrative and explanatory notes, the writer complied with pleasure, for filial gratitude to the Father of his Country seemed to demand the dedication of whatever labor might be usefully employed in the preservation of precious memorials of that father which had hitherto been left in the perishable form of newspaper articles.

Many of the facts recorded in this volume have already found their way, one by one, into our histories; but the great mass of them will be fresh to every reader, and intrinsically valuable.

The illustrative and explanatory notes have been prepared with the single purpose of *instructing*, not *amusing;* and if, to the well-informed, many of them shall appear unnecessary, let it be remembered that it is only the *few* who *are* well informed, and that the *many* need instruction.

Care has been taken not to alter the text as it flowed from the pen of the author, except in the way of verbal corrections, occasionally, and arrangements of the matter to avoid repetitions as far as practicable — faults which are incident to the production of a series of articles upon a common topic, written at wide intervals, and from memory. The business of the editor has been to arrange and illustrate, according to the dictates of his best judgment, the materials placed in his hands by the family of the author.

A few words concerning the history of these *Recollections* may not be without interest. When Lafayette visited the United States, in 1824 and 1825, as the guest of the nation, Mr. Custis, who had been the intimate companion of the marquis's son, George Washington Lafayette (who accompanied him), when at Mount Vernon, under the care of Washington, in 1797, spent much time with that illustrious man. After his departure, he wrote a series of interesting articles under the title of *Conversations with Lafayette*. These were published in the *Alexandria Gazette*, and attracted much attention. Among those who were specially interested in them, was John F. Watson, Esq., the now venerable annalist of Philadelphia and New York. He wrote to Mr. Custis in September, 1825, urging him to answer publicly a series of questions which he proposed to write, and which would, if fully answered, " go more," as Mr. Watson said, " to develop, as by moral painting, the individual character of General and Mrs. Washington, as they appeared in domestic and every-day life, than all that had ever been published."

Mr. Custis answered Mr. Watson's letter a week afterward, and assured him that as soon as he had completed his *Conversations with Lafayette*, of which the thirteenth number was just then finished, he should commence the publication of *Recollections of Washington* in the *United States Gazette*, printed at Philadelphia — a paper which he had often seen the first president " dry on his knee" as it came fresh from the press. The first number, entitled *The Mother of Washington*, appeared in that paper. The remainder of the series, except two numbers, were first published in the *National Intelligencer*. Such, in brief, is the history of the origin of these *Recollections*, as given to the writer by the venerable annalist above mentioned, in May, 1859.

B. J. L.

POUGHKEEPSIE, *August*, 1859.

AUTHOR'S PREFACE.

It is the public lives of great men that are commonly given to the world; and with all the glare which may dazzle and surprise. It will be the duty of the writer of the following pages to withdraw the curtain, and, in some views of the private life of the most illustrious of men, to develop such truths as shall be acceptable to the mind and heart of every true American.

Much anxiety always has existed, and always will exist, touching the private lives and actions of those who, on the public theatre, have played so many, such various, and such distinguished parts. It is somewhat remarkable, yet such is the fact of history, that when all of the public life and actions of a great man have been published to the world, the world invariably demands the private memoirs. The celebrated Montesquieu once asked an English nobleman respecting Sir Isaac Newton: "Pray, my lord, does the great Newton eat, drink, and sleep like other men?"

The interesting and authentic private memoirs of the Father of his Country, which form this volume, are derived from the relations of those who were the associates of his juvenile years, his comrades in war, and the friends of his fireside in peace. Concerning his domestic habits and manners; the routine of his methodical life; what he said and did, when he retired from public cares and duties, in the evening of his glorious day, *I ought to know much*. Taken from my orphaned cradle to his paternal arms, nourished at his board, cherished in his bosom, from childhood to manhood, I ought to know something of the First President of the United States, and the illustrious Farmer of Mount Vernon.

I write of him who fills so large a space in the best recollections of the world; whose fame, pure, venerable, and time-honored, will descend to the latest posterity, like the ceaseless stream which washes the base of his sepulchre, whose majestic course neither rival currents can disturb, nor the waste of ages can impair.

The first paper in the series of these *Recollections and Private Memoirs of the Life and Character of Washington*, contains a sketch of THE MOTHER OF WASHINGTON — that distinguished woman, whose peculiar cast of character, whose precepts and discipline in the education of her illustrious son, were by himself acknowledged to have been the foundation of his fortune and his fame.

The principal facts I derived from Lawrence and Robin Washington, Esqrs., of Chotank, the associates of the chief in early life, at the maternal mansion on the Rappahannock; and from Bishop, his military servant and humble friend in the war of '55–'56, who helped him to his last horse on the field of Braddock, when death gathered so many sheaves to the garner, and when, in the prophetic words of the Indian commander, in reference to Washington, "the Great Spirit protected that man, that he might become the Chief of Nations."

The veteran Bishop died at Mount Vernon at a very advanced age, having long been settled in the midst of his descendants, and with every possible comfort about him. It was while sitting upon his knee, in the days of my childhood, that I often heard the old man relate the events of the Indian wars, and have seen him raise his withered arm, while his faded eye lighted up, when describing the memorable and heroic achievements of his patron and commander.

From Dr. James Craik, also, whose commission was signed on the same day with that of Washington, as provincial major, I received many and important facts. He and Washington were comrades and fellow-captives at the affair of the Meadows, in '55; were associated in the War of the Revolution, and bosom friends always; and it was the fortune of Craik to receive the Patriot's last sigh at Mount Vernon in 1799, after an affectionate intercourse of almost half a century.

The labor of America's distinguished historians have given to this country and the world the life and actions of Washington, as connected with the age in which he flourished, and the mighty events thereof, in which he bore so prominent and illustrious a part. It has become the honored duty of the author of the *Recollections* to lift the veil that always conceals the private life of a great man from the public gaze, and to show the Pater Patriæ amid the shades of domestic retirement, where, in the bosom of his family, on the farm, and at his fireside, friendship, kindliness, and hospitality shed their benignant lustre upon his latter days.

Long years have elapsed since the first of these *Recollections* were offered to the public. In answer to numerous inquiries why they have not been published in book form, the author begs leave to observe that, having no views as to profit, he was desirous that the Private Memoirs should go to the masses of the people in the cheapest and most diffusible manner practicable.

If it has appeared to any that the *Recollections* have embraced particulars too minute, the author's apology is in various letters, received both from at home and abroad, urging him *to omit no detail, however minute, or deem anything trivial, that related in the smallest degree to the life and character of Washington.*

G W. P. C.

ARLINGTON HOUSE, NEAR ALEXANDRIA, VA., 1856.

RECOLLECTIONS OF WASHINGTON.

CHAPTER I.

THE MOTHER OF WASHINGTON.

THE WASHINGTON FAMILY IN VIRGINIA — WASHINGTON'S EARLY YOUTH — HIS MOTHER'S FAMILY — HER CHARACTER AND INFLUENCE — THE HOME OF WASHINGTON — THE WILD HORSE — YOUNG WASHINGTON'S TRUTHFULNESS — HIS MOTHER AT FREDERICKSBURG — PICTURE OF HER LIFE THERE — AN ALARM IN WASHINGTON'S CAMP — HIS MOTHER'S MANAGEMENT OF AFFAIRS — HER INDUSTRY, ECONOMY, AND CHARITY — HER INDEPENDENCE — HER FEAR OF LIGHTNING — RECEPTION OF WASHINGTON AFTER HIS VICTORY AT YORKTOWN — HIS FILIAL REVERENCE — ADMIRATION OF THE FOREIGN OFFICERS — LAFAYETTE — WASHINGTON'S LAST INTERVIEW WITH HIS MOTHER — HER DEATH — HER MONUMENT.

OF the remote ancestors of the chief, our recollections will, of necessity, be limited. The great-grandfather, John Washington, came from England (from Chester, it is believed) at about the time of the early settlers in the northern neck of Virginia, but the place of his first residence is unknown, though it has been a matter of considerable research to his descendants.*

---

* He came with his brother Lawrence about the year 1657, and settled near the Potomac, between Pope's and Bridge's creeks, in the county of Westmoreland. Having a knowledge of military matters, he was employed, soon after his arrival, in the command of the militia, against the Indians, with the rank of colonel. He was thus employed just previous to the breaking out of the domestic broils in Virginia, known in history as *Bacon's Rebellion*. He married Anne Pope, by whom he had two sons. One of these (Lawrence) married Mildred Warner, of Gloucester county, and had three children. Her second was Augustine, the father of George Washington.

The following letter, translated from the German, contains some interesting particulars respecting a branch of the Washington family. The letter from General

Augustine Washington, the father, we find settled near Pope's creek, a tributary of the Potomac, in the county of Westmoreland, and there the great chief was born, on the

WASHINGTON, to which the writer alludes, may be seen in. Sparks's *Life and Writings of Washington*, vol. xi. p. 393; and other particulars concerning the family in vol. i. p. 554. JAMES WASHINGTON is there mentioned as having been a merchant in Rotterdam:—

"MUNICH, *February* 21, 1844.

"HONORED SIR: It was not till the 17th of this month that I received your favor of December 13th; I could not, therefore, answer it earlier. In compliance with your wish I will, with pleasure, communicate to you some facts relating to my family. The branch from which I am descended has undoubtedly the same ancestor as that from which the American branch descended, which is proved also by the same coat-of-arms.

"The family of Washington is descended from a good old English family, which, in early times, owned considerable possessions in the counties of York and Northampton, and in other places. It became connected, by marriage, with the family of Shirley, Earl Ferrers. Sir Lawrence Washington married Elizabeth, a daughter of the second Earl Ferrers. It was also connected with that of Villiers, duke of Buckingham. A branch of the family, from unknown causes, for they were wealthy, emigrated about the year 1650 to America; and the well-known (one may say with truth the universally famous) General and President George Washington was descended from it.

"My great-grandfather, James Washington, was so deeply implicated in the unfortunate affair of the duke of Monmouth, in the time of Charles II., 1683 and 1684, that he was obliged to fly from England, and, after losing by shipwreck on the coast of Portugal everything of his personal property that he had been able to carry away from England, he came to Holland. While there, he was frequently demanded on the part of England by its ambassador, and his delivery insisted upon; but the States-General did not consent; and thus he became the founder of that branch which then began to flourish in Holland, and is still in existence in the persons of two individuals, cousins, lieutenants in the army and navy.

"I possess an autograph letter of the great man, George Washington, from Mount Vernon, January 20, 1799, in which, among other things, it is said: 'There can be but little doubt, sir, of our descending from the same stock, as the branches of it proceeded from the same country; at what time your ancestors left England is not mentioned; mine came to America nearly one hundred and fifty years ago.'

"At the age of sixteen I received, in 1794, a commission in the Dutch service, but was unwilling to serve the Bavarian republic founded in 1795; and, being a faithful follower of the house of Orange, I emigrated. At the formation of the Dutch brigade of the Prince of Orange in the English service in 1799, I was appointed lieutenant in that brigade, until the disbanding of the latter, after the peace of Amiens, in 1802. A few months later I had the good fortune to enter the Bavarian service.

eleventh of February (Old style), 1732. This interesting spot is now marked by a stone, placed there by the hand of filial affection and gratitude in 1815.*

Since then, nearly forty-two years have passed, of which I have been attached no less than thirty-seven years to the most high person of the king, partly as marshal of the court, and partly as aid-de-camp.

"I have also planted a stock in Bavaria, which, if God will, is some time to bear good fruit to the king and country. I have three sons: the eldest, Ludwig, sixteen years old, is a page of his majesty the king; the second, Max, fourteen years old, is pupil in the royal corps of cadets; and the third, Karl, ten years old, frequents the public school. By my two marriages with daughters of families of the highest nobility in the land, my children are placed in agreeable circumstances, even when I shall be no more; and, in this manner, this branch of the family in this new country may flourish. God give his blessing to it!

"It would lead me too far to enter into details of my biography; for, being in earlier years frequently exposed to the storms of fate, brought on chiefly by revolutions, and at a later period in important offices and other relations, I could not do it without being very long; and, since this letter has already attained a considerable extent, that which has been said will, I hope, satisfy you. I will only add, in order that you may become altogether acquainted with my situation here, that I will subjoin to the signature of my name what is otherwise not usual; but in this case, I think, may make an exception, because it forms in a manner a part of my biography.

"Thanking you for the literary production transmitted to me, which possesses, by the preface of the renowned Professor Herman, an enhanced value, I remain, with sentiments of perfect esteem, your devoted,

"BARON VON WASHINGTON.

"*Royal Bavarian Chamberlain, Lieutenant-General and Aid-de-Camp to his Majesty the King, Commander of the Order of Civil Merit of the Bavarian Crown, of the Greek Order of the Saviour, of the British Military Order of the Bath, Knight of the Royal French Order of the Legion of Honor, and Lord of Notzing.*

"To Dr. J. G. FLUZEL,
    "*Consul of the U. S. of N. America, in Leipsic.*"

* In a letter to the editor of the *Alexandria Gazette*, dated Arlington house, April 14, 1851, Mr. Custis gave the following interesting account of the placing of that memorial stone, with his own hands, upon the spot where stood the birthplace of Washington:—

"Observing in your valuable journal, of a late date, the notice of a stone placed on the ruins of the house in which the beloved Washington first saw the light, permit me to offer to you a brief account of that interesting event, as it occured six-and-thirty years ago.

"In June, 1815, I sailed on my own vessel, the 'Lady of the Lake,' a fine topsail schooner of ninety tons, accompanied by two gentlemen, Messrs. Lewis and

Upon the father becoming engaged in the agency of the Principe iron-works, and after the conflagration of his

Grimes, bound to Pope's creek, in the county of Westmoreland, carrying with us a slab of freestone, having the following inscription :*—

HERE
THE 11TH OF FEBRUARY, 1732, (Old Style,)
GEORGE WASHINGTON
WAS BORN.

Our pilot approached the Westmoreland shore cautiously (as our vessel drew nearly eight feet of water), and he was but indifferently acquainted with so unfrequented a navigation.

"We anchored some distance from the land, and, taking to our boats, we soon reached the mouth of Pope's or Bridge's creek, and proceeding upward we fell in with McKenzie Beverly, Esq., and several gentlemen composing a fishing party, and also with the overseer of the property that formed the object of our visit. We were kindly received by these individuals, and escorted to the spot, where a few scattered bricks alone marked the birthplace of the chief.

"Desirous of making the ceremonial of depositing the stone as imposing as circumstances would permit, we enveloped it in the 'star-spangled banner' of our country, and it was borne to its resting-place in the arms of the descendants of four revolutionary patriots and soldiers — SAMUEL LEWIS, son of George Lewis, a captain in Baylor's regiment of horse, and nephew of Washington; WILLIAM GRYMES, the son of Benjamin Grymes, a gallant and distinguished officer of the life-guard; the CAPTAIN of the vessel, the son of a brave soldier wounded in the battle of Guilford; and GEORGE W. P. CUSTIS, the son of John Parke Custis, aid-de-camp to the commander-in-chief before Cambridge and Yorktown.

"We gathered together the bricks of an ancient chimney that once formed the hearth around which Washington in his infancy had played, and constructed a rude kind of pedestal, on which we reverently placed the FIRST STONE, commending it to the respect and protection of the American people in general, and the citizens of Westmoreland in particular.

"Bidding adieu to those who had received us so kindly, we re-embarked, and hoisted our colors, and being provided with a piece of cannon and suitable amunition, we fired a salute, awakening the echoes that had slept for ages around the hallowed spot; and while the smoke of our martial tribute to the birthplace of the Pater Patriæ still lingered on the bosom of the Potomac, we spread our sails to a favoring breeze, and sped joyously to our homes.

"Such was an act of filial love and gratitude, performed more than a third of a century ago; such is the history of the FIRST STONE TO THE MEMORY OF WASHINGTON.

"Health and respect, my dear sir,

"GEORGE W. P. CUSTIS."

---

* A drawing of this stone, with the inscription, may be found in Lossing's *Field Book of the Revolution.*

seat in Westmoreland, he removed, with his family, to a situation near the village of Fredericksburg,* where he died about middle age, universally esteemed as a man of worth and honor, and as a useful member of society. He is described as having been of fair complexion, tall stature, and manly proportions.

At the time of his father's death, George Washington was between eleven and twelve years of age. He has been heard to say, that he knew little of his father, other than a remembrance of his person, and of his parental fondness. Of the mother, that distinguished woman, to whose peculiar cast of character, and more than ancient discipline in the education of her illustrious son, himself ascribed the origin of his fortunes and his fame, we have much to say.

She was descended from the very respectable family of Ball, who settled as English colonists, on the banks of the Potomac.† Bred in those domestic and independent habits, which graced the Virginia matrons in the olden days, this lady, by the death of her husband, became involved in the cares of a young family, at a period when

---

* A picture of this dwelling of the Washington family may be found in Lossing's *Field-Book of the Revolution.*

† Bishop Meade in his *History of Old Churches, Ministers, and Families of Virginia,* gives a description of a picture of armorial bearings that he had seen, on which is a lion rampant with a globe in his paws; a helmet, and shield, and vizor; a coat-of-mail, and other things betokening strength and courage; and for a motto words from a line of Ovid — CŒLUMQUE TUERI. On the back of the picture is written — "The coat-of-arms of Colonel William Ball, who came from England with his family about the year 1650, and settled at the mouth of Corotoman river, in Lancaster county, Virginia, and died in 1669, leaving two sons, William and Joseph, and one daughter, Hannah, who married Daniel Fox. William left eight sons (and one daughter) five of whom have now (Anno Domini, 1779) male issue. Joseph's male issue is extinct. General George Washington is his grandson, by his youngest daughter, Mary."

these responsibilities seem more especially to claim the aid and control of the stronger sex; and it was left for this remarkable woman, by a method the most rare, by an education and discipline the most peculiar and imposing, to form in the youth-time of her son those great and essential qualities which led him on to the glories of his after-life. If the school savored more of the Spartan than the Persian character, it was a fitter one in which to form a hero, destined to be the ornament of the time in which he flourished, and a standard of excellence for ages yet to come.

It was said by the ancients that the mother always gave the tone to the character of the child; and we may be permitted to say, that since the days of antiquity, a mother has not lived, better fitted to give the tone and character of real greatness to her child, than her, whose life and actions this reminiscence will endeavor to illustrate.

The mother of Washington, in forming him for those distinguished parts he was destined to perform, first taught him the duties of obedience, the better to prepare him for those of command. In the well-ordered domicil, where his early years were passed, the levity and indulgence, common to youth, was tempered by a deference and well-regulated restraint, which, while it curtailed or suppressed no rational enjoyment, usual in the spring-time of life, prescribed those enjoyments within the bounds of moderation and propriety.

The matron held in reserve an authority, which never departed from her; not even when her son had become the most illustrious of men. It seemed to say, "I am your mother, the being who gave you life, the guide who directed your steps when they needed the guidance of age and wisdom, the parental affection which claimed your love, the parental authority which commanded your obedience; whatever may be your success, whatever your renown, next to your God you owe them most to me." Nor did the chief dissent from these truths, but to the last moments of the life of his venerable parent, he yielded to her will the most dutiful and implicit obedience, and felt for her person and character the most holy reverence and attachment.

This lady possessed not the ambition which is common to lesser minds; and the peculiar plainness, yet dignity of her habits and manners, became in nowise altered, when the sun of glory rose upon her house, in the character of her child. The late Lawrence Washington, Esq., of Chotank, one of the associates of the juvenile years of the chief, and remembered by him in his will, thus describes the home of the mother:—

"I was often there with George, his playmate, schoolmate, and young man's companion. Of the mother I was ten times more afraid than I ever was of my own parents. She awed me in the midst of her kindness, for she was, indeed, truly kind. I have often been present with her sons, proper tall fellows too, and we were all as mute as mice; and even now, when time has whitened my locks, and I am the grand-parent of a second generation, I could not behold that remarkable woman without feelings it is impossible to describe. Whoever has seen that awe-inspiring air and manner so characteristic in the Father of his Country, will remember the matron as she appeared when the presiding genius of her well-ordered household, commanding and being obeyed."

Of the many anecdotes touching the early life of the chief, we shall present our readers with one of no ordinary interest and character.

The blooded horse was the Virginian favorite of those days as well as these. Washington's mother, fond of the animal to which her deceased husband had been particularly attached, had preserved the race in its greatest purity, and at the time of our story possessed several young horses of superior promise.

One there was, a sorrel, destined to be as famous (and for much better reason) as the horse, which the brutal emperor raised to the dignity of consul. This sorrel was of a fierce and ungovernable nature, and resisted all attempts to subject him to the rein. He had reached his fullest size and vigor, unconscious of a rider; he ranged free in the air, which he snuffed in triumph, tossing his mane to the winds, and spurning the earth in the pride of his freedom. It was a matter of common remark, that a man never would be found hardy enough to back and ride this vicious horse. Several had essayed, but deterred by the fury of the animal, they had desisted from their attempts, and the steed remained unbroken.

The young Washington proposed to his companions, that if they would assist him in confining the steed, so that a bridle could be placed in his mouth, he would engage to tame this terror of the parish. Accordingly, early the ensuing morning, the associates decoyed the horse into an inclosure, where they secured him, and forced a bit into his mouth. Bold, vigorous, and young, the daring youth sprang to his unenvied seat, and bidding his comrades remove their tackle, the indignant courser rushed to the plain.

As if disdaining his burden, he at first attempted to fly, but soon felt the power of an arm which could have tamed his Arab grandsires, in their wildest course on their native deserts. The struggle now became terrific to the beholders, who almost wished that they had not joined in an enterprise, so likely to be fatal to their daring associate. But the youthful hero, that "spirit-protected man,"* clung to the furious steed, till centaur-like, he appeared to make part of the animal itself. Long was the conflict, and the fears of the associates became more relieved as, with matchless skill the rider preserved his seat, and with unyielding force controlled the courser's rage, when the gallant horse, summoning all his powers to one mighty effort, reared, and plunged with tremendous violence, burst his noble heart, and died in an instant.

The rider, "alive, unharmed, and without a wound," was joined by the youthful group, and all gazed upon the generous steed, which now prostrate, "trailed in dust the honors of his mane," while from distended nostrils gushed in torrents the life-blood that a moment before had swollen in his veins.

The first surprise was scarcely over, With a what's to be done? Who shall tell this tale? when the party were summoned to the morning's meal. A conversation, the most *mal à propos* to the youthful culprits, became introduced by the matron's asking, "Pray, young gentlemen, have you seen my blooded colts in your rambles? I hope they are well taken care of; my favorite, I am told, is as large as his sire." Considerable embarrassment being

---

* This refers to a remarkable Indian prophecy, given in a future chapter of this work.

observable, the lady repeated her question, when George Washington replied, "Your favorite, the sorrel, is dead, madam." "Dead," exclaimed the lady; "why, how has this happened?" Nothing dismayed, the youth continued, "That sorrel horse has long been considered ungovernable, and beyond the power of man to back or ride him; this morning, aided by my friends, we forced a bit into his mouth; I backed him, I rode him, and in a desperate struggle for the mastery, he fell under me and died upon the spot." The hectic of a moment was observed to flush on the matron's cheek, but like a summer cloud, it soon passed away, and all was serene and tranquil, when she remarked: "It is well; but while I regret the loss of my favorite, *I rejoice in my son, who always speaks the truth.*"

At the time of this occurrence, the figure of the lad is described by his contemporaries as being that of the athletæ of the games. Although of manners somewhat grave and reserved, he indulged in the gayeties common to the youth at that period. He particularly excelled in all the manly exercises, sought the companionship of the intelligent and deserving, and was beloved and admired by all who knew him.

Upon his appointment to the office of commander-in-chief of the American armies,* General Washington, pre-

---

* Washington was appointed commander-in-chief of all the forces raised, or to be raised, for the defence of the colonies, on the fifteenth of June, 1775. John Adams has left on record the following interesting particulars concerning that appointment:—

"Every post brought me letters from my friends, Dr. Winthrop, Dr. Cooper, General James Warren, and sometimes from General Ward and his aids, and General Heath and many others, urging, in pathetic terms, the impossibility of keeping their men together without the assistance of Congress. I was daily urging all these things, but we were embarrassed with more than one difficulty, not only with the party in favor of the petition to the king, and the party who were jealous of inde-

viously to his joining the forces at Cambridge [July 3, 1775], removed his mother from her country residence to the village of Fredericksburg, a situation remote from danger, and contiguous to her friends and relatives.

pendence, but a third party, which was a southern party against a northern, and a jealousy against a New-England army under the command of a New-England general. Whether this jealousy was sincere, or whether it was mere pride and a haughty ambition of furnishing a southern general to command the northern army, I can not say; but the intention was very visible to me that Colonel Washington was their object, and so many of our stanchest men were in the plan that we could carry nothing without conceding to it. Another embarrassment, which was never publicly known, and which was carefully concealed by those who knew it, the Massachusetts and other New-England delegates were divided. Mr. Hancock and Mr. Cushing hung back, Mr. Paine did not come forward, and even Mr. Samuel Adams was irresolute. Mr. Hancock himself had an ambition to be appointed commander-in-chief Whether he thought an election a compliment due to him, and intended to have the honor of declining it, or whether he would have accepted it, I know not. To the compliment he had some pretensions; for, at that time, his exertions, sacrifices, and general merits in the cause of his country, had been incomparably greater than those of Colonel Washington. But the delicacy of his health, and his entire want of experience in actual service, though an excellent militia officer, were decisive objections to him in my mind. In canvassing this subject out of doors, I found, too, that even among the delegates of Virginia there were difficulties. The apostolical reasonings among themselves which should be the greatest were not less energetic among the saints of the Ancient Dominion than they were among us of New England. In several conversations I found more than one very cool about the appointment of Washington, and particularly Mr. Pendleton was very clear and full against it.

"Full of anxieties concerning these confusions, and apprehending daily that we should hear very distressing news from Boston, I walked with Mr. Samuel Adams in the statehouse-yard for a little exercise and fresh air before the hour of Congress, and there represented to him the various dangers that surrounded us. He agreed to them all, but said, 'What shall we do?' I answered him that he knew I had taken great pains to get our colleagues to agree upon some plan, that we might be unanimous; but he knew that they would pledge themselves to nothing; but I was determined to take a step which should compel them and all the other members of Congress to declare themselves for or against something. 'I am determined this morning to make a direct motion that Congress should adopt the army before Boston, and appoint Colonel Washington commander of it.' Mr. Adams seemed to think very seriously of it, but said nothing.

"Accordingly, when Congress had assembled, I rose in my place, and in as short a speech as the subject would admit, represented the state of the colonies, the uncertainty in the minds of the people, their great expectation and anxiety, the distresses

It was there the matron remained during nearly the whole of the trying period of the Revolution. Directly in the way of the news, as it passed from north to south, one courier would bring intelligence of success to our arms, another "swiftly coursing at his heels," the saddening tale of disaster and defeat. While thus ebbed and

of the army, the danger of its dissolution, the difficulty of collecting another; and the probability that the British army would take advantage of our delays, march out of Boston, and spread desolation as far as they could go. I concluded with a motion, in form, that Congress would adopt the army at Cambridge, and appoint a general; that though this was not the proper time to nominate a general, yet, as I had reason to believe this was a point of the greatest difficulty, I had no hesitation to declare that I had but one gentleman in my mind for that important command, and that was a gentleman from Virginia, who was among us, and very well known to all of us; a gentleman whose skill and experience as an officer, whose independent fortune, great talents, and excellent universal character would command the approbation of all America, and unite the cordial exertions of all the colonies better than any other person in the Union. Mr. Washington, who happened to sit near the door, as soon as he heard me allude to him, from his usual modesty, darted into the library room. Mr. Hancock, who was our president, which gave me an opportunity to observe his countenance while I was speaking on the state of the colonies, the army at Cambridge, and the enemy, heard me with visible pleasure; but when I came to describe Washington for the commander, I never remarked a more sudden and striking change of countenance. Mortification and resentment were expressed as forcibly as his face could exhibit them. Mr. Samuel Adams seconded the motion, and that did not soften the president's physiognomy at all. The subject came under debate, and several gentlemen declared themselves against the appointment of Mr. Washington, not on account of any personal objection against him, but because the army were all from New England, had a general of their own, appeared to be satisfied with him, and had proved themselves able to imprison the British army in Boston, which was all they expected or desired at that time.

"Mr. Pendleton, of Virginia, Mr. Sherman, of Connecticut, were very explicit in declaring this opinion. Mr. Cushing and several others more faintly expressed their opposition, and their fears of discontent in the army and in New England. Mr. Paine expressed a great opinion of General Ward, and a strong friendship for him, having been his classmate at college, or, at least, his contemporary; but gave no opinion on the question. The subject was postponed to a future day. In the meantime, pains were taken out of doors to obtain a unanimity, and the voices were generally so clearly in favor of Washington, that the dissenting members were persuaded to withdraw their opposition, and Mr. Washington was nominated, I believe, by Mr. Thomas Johnson, of Maryland, unanimously elected, and the army adopted "— *Life and Works of John Adams*, ii. 415 to 418, inclusive.

flowed the fortunes of our cause, the mother, trusting to the wisdom and protection of Divine Providence, preserved the even tenor of her life, affording an example to those matrons whose sons were alike engaged in the arduous contest; and showing that unavailing anxieties, however belonging to human nature, were unworthy of mothers whose sons were combatting for the inestimable rights of mankind, and the freedom and happiness of unborn ages.

When the comforting and glorious intelligence arrived of the passage of the Delaware (Dec. '76*), an event which restored our hopes from the very brink of despair, a number of her friends waited upon the mother with congratulations. She received them with calmness; observed that it was most pleasurable news, and that George appeared to have deserved well of his country for such signal service; and continued, in reply to the gratulating patriots (most of whom held letters in their hands, from which they read extracts, for gazettes were not so plenty then as now), "but, my good sirs, here is too much flattery; still George will not forget the lessons I early taught him—he will not forget himself, though he is the subject of so much praise."

Here I will speak of the absurdity of an idea which, from some strange cause or other, has been suggested, though certainly never believed, that the mother of Washington was disposed to favor the royal cause. Not the slightest foundation has such a surmise in truth. Like many others, whose days of enthusiasm were in the wane, that lady doubted the prospects of success in the outset of the war, and long during its continuance

---

* See notes on the battle of Princeton.

feared that our means would be found inadequate to a successful contest with so formidable a power as Britain; and that our soldiers, brave, but undisciplined and ill provided, would be unequal to cope with the veteran and well-appointed troops of the king. Doubts like these were by no means confined to this Virginia matron, but were both entertained and expressed by the stanchest of patriots and the most determined of men. When that mother, who had been removed to the county of Frederick, on the invasion of Virginia, in 1781, was informed by express of the surrender of Cornwallis, she raised her hands to heaven, and exclaimed, "Thank God, war will now be ended, and peace, independence, and happiness, bless our country."

The commander-in-chief was absent from his native state from the spring of '75 to the fall of '81, a period of nearly seven years. It was his habit to send for Mrs. Washington at the close of a campaign, and to return her to Mount Vernon on the opening of an ensuing one. This estimable lady used to observe, that she always heard the first cannon on the opening, and the last at the close of the campaigns of the Revolutionary war.

It happened that while remaining later than usual in the camp on the Hudson, an alarm was given of the approach of the enemy from New York. The aids-de-camp proposed that the ladies (these being the wives of Generals Greene and Knox, and others at headquarters) should be sent off under an escort. This the chief refused, remarking, the presence of our wives will the better encourage us to a brave defence. On a dark night, the words of command from the officers, the marching of the troops, the dragging of artillery into the yard, the taking out of the windows of the house, and the filling of the house itself with soldiers, "all gave dreadful note of preparation," when the enemy finding themselves mistaken in their hopes of surprise, withdrew without coming to blows.*

During the war, and indeed during her useful life, and until within three years of her death, when an afflictive disease prevented exertion, the mother of Washington set a most valuable example in the management of her domestic concerns, carrying her own keys, bustling in her household affairs, providing for her own wants, and living and moving in all the pride of independence. There are some of the aged inhabitants of Fredericksburg who well remember the matron as, seated in an old-fashioned open chaise, she was in the habit of almost

---

* This little episode, so abruptly introduced here, is doubtless one of a series of similar events which took place while the American army lay at Morristown, in New Jersey, during the winter and spring of 1779 and 1780. The main body of the army was encamped upon the southern slope of a mountain near that village, and until the middle of February occupied tents. Then they were received into comfortable huts, which they occupied until the breaking up of the camp in the spring. The camp extended from the headquarters in the Ford mansion, about a quarter of a mile from the village of Morristown, westward for several miles. During that winter, the proximity of the army to the enemy in New York caused frequent alarms, which usually set the whole camp in motion. Sentinels were set at intervals between the camp and headquarters, and pickets were planted at distant points toward the Raritan and Hudson, with intervening sentinels. Sometimes an alarm would commence by the firing of a gun at some distant point. This would be responded to by the sentinels all along the line to headquarters, when the general's life-guard would rush to the house of the chief, barricade the doors and throw up the windows. At each window five soldiers, with their muskets cocked and brought to a charge, would generally be placed, and there remain until the troops from the camp marched to headquarters, and the cause of the alarm was ascertained. These occasions were very annoying to the ladies of the household; for, as I was informed by the late Judge Ford (then a boy fourteen years of age, and living there), Mrs. Washington and his mother were obliged to lie in bed, sometimes for hours, with their room full of soldiers, and the keen winter air from the open windows piercing through their drawn curtains.

daily visiting her little farm in the vicinity of the town. When there, she would ride about her fields, giving her orders, and seeing that they were obeyed. On one occasion an agent to whom she had given directions as to a particular piece of work, varied from his instructions in its execution. The lady, whose *coup d'œil* was as perfect in rural affairs as that of her son in war, pointed out the error. The agent excused himself by saying, that "in his judgment the work was done to more advantage than it would have been by his first directions." Mrs. Washington replied, "And pray, who gave you any exercise of judgment in the matter? I command you, sir; there is nothing left for you but to obey."

Her great industry, with the well-regulated economy of all her concerns, enabled the matron to dispense considerable charities to the poor, although her own circumstances were always far from rich. All manner of domestic economics, so useful in those times of privation and trouble, received her zealous attention; while everything about her household bore marks of her care and management, and very many things the impress of her own hands.

In a very humble dwelling, at the advanced age of eighty-two, and suffering under an excruciating disease (cancer of the breast), thus lived this mother of the first of men, preserving unchanged her peculiar nobleness and independence of character. She was continually visited and solaced by her children and numerous grandchildren, particularly her daughter, Mrs. Lewis. To the repeated and earnest solicitations of this lady, that she would remove to her house and pass the remainder of her days; to the pressing entreaties of her son that she would make Mount Vernon the home of her old age, the matron replied; "I thank you for your affectionate and dutiful offers, but my wants are few in this world, and I feel perfectly competent to take care of myself." Upon her son-in-law, Colonel Fielding Lewis proposing that he should relieve her in the direction of her affairs, she observed; "Do you, Fielding, keep my books in order, for your eyesight is better than mine, but leave the executive management to me."

One weakness alone belonged to this lofty-minded and intrepid woman, and that proceeded from a most affecting cause. It was a fear of lightning. In early life, a female friend had been killed at her side, while sitting at the table, the knife and fork in the hands of the unfortunate being melted by the electric fluid. The matron never recovered from the shock occasioned by this distressing incident. On the approach of a thunder-cloud, she would retire to her chamber, and not leave it again till the storm had passed over.

Always pious, in her latter days her devotions were performed in private. She was in the habit of repairing every day to a secluded spot, formed by rocks and trees near to her dwelling, where, abstracted from the world and worldly things, she communed with her Creator in humiliation and prayer.

Late in the year 1781, on the return of the combined armies from Yorktown, the mother of Washington was permitted again to see and embrace her illustrious son, the first time in almost seven years. As soon as he had dismounted, in the midst of a numerous and brilliant suite, after reaching Fredericksburg, he sent to apprize her of his arrival, and to know when it would be her pleasure to receive him. And now, reader, mark the force of early education and habits, and the superiority of the Spartan over the Persian school, in this interview of the Great Washington with his admirable parent and instructor. No pageantry of war proclaimed his coming, no trumpets sounded, no banners waved. Alone and on foot, the general-in-chief of the combined armies of France and America, the deliverer of his country, the hero of the age, repaired to pay his humble duty to her whom he venerated as the author of his being—the founder of his fortunes and his fame; for full well he knew that the matron was made of sterner stuff than to be moved by all the pride that glory ever gave, and all "the pomp and circumstance" of power.

She was alone, her aged hands employed in the works of domestic industry, when the good news was announced, and it was further told, that the victor-chief was in waiting at the threshold. She bid him welcome by a warm embrace, and by the well-remembered and endearing name of George—the familiar name of his childhood; she inquired as to his health, remarked the lines which mighty cares and many toils had made in his manly countenance, spoke much of old times and old friends, but of his glory not one word.

Meantime, in the village of Fredericksburg, all was joy and revelry; the town was crowded with the officers of the French and American armies, and with gentlemen for many miles around, who hastened to welcome the conquerors of Cornwallis.* The citizens got up a splendid ball, to which the matron was specially invited. She observed, that although her dancing days were pretty

* See account of the victory at Yorktown in Chapter vi.

well over, she should feel happy in contributing to the general festivity, and consented to attend.

The foreign officers were anxious to see the mother of their chief. They had heard indistinct rumors touching her remarkable life and character, but forming their judgments from European examples, they were prepared to expect in the mother, that glitter and show which would have been attached to the parents of the great, in the countries of the old world. How were they surprised, when leaning on the arm of her son, she entered the room, dressed in the very plain, yet becoming garb, worn by the Virginia lady of the old time. Her address always dignified and imposing, was courteous, though reserved. She received the complimentary attentions which were paid to her without evincing the slightest elevation, and at an early hour, wishing the company much enjoyment of their pleasures, observed, that it was high time for old folks to be in bed, and retired, leaning as before on the arm of her son.

The foreign officers were amazed in beholding one whom so many causes conspired to elevate, preserving the even tenor of her life, while such a blaze of glory shone upon her name and offspring. It was a moral spectacle such as the European world had furnished no examples. Names of ancient lore were heard to escape from their lips; and they declared, "if such are the matrons in America, well may she boast of illustrious sons."

It was on this festive occasion, that General Washington danced a minuet with Mrs. Willis. It closed his dancing days. The minuet was much in vogue at that period, and was peculiarly calculated for the display of the splendid figure of the chief, and his natural grace and elegance of air and manner. The gallant Frenchmen who were present, of which fine people it may be said that dancing forms one of the elements of their existence, so much admired the American performance, as to admit that a Parisian education could not have improved it. As the evening advanced, the commander-in-chief yielding to the general gayety of the scene, went down some dozen couple in the contre dance with great spirit and satisfaction.*

Previous to his departure for Europe, in the fall of 1784, the Marquis de Lafayette† repaired to Fredericksburg to pay his parting respects to the mother, and to ask her blessing.

Conducted by one of her grandsons, he approached the house, when the young gentleman observing, "There, sir, is my grandmother;" the marquis beheld, working in her garden, clad in domestic-made clothes, and her gray head covered by a plain straw hat, the mother of "his hero, his friend, and a country's preserver." The lady saluted him kindly, observing, "Ah, marquis, you see an old woman; but come, I can make you welcome to my poor dwelling, without the parade of changing my dress."

Much as Lafayette had seen and heard of the matron

---

* The venerable widow of General Alexander Hamilton, informed me, that Washington was never known to dance after the close of the Revolutionary war. She was present at many balls where he attended. He would sometimes *walk* through a figure or two with ladies, during the evening, but never took the steps of the dance.

† Lafayette revisited the United States in 1784, and with eager steps he made his way to Mount Vernon as quickly as possible, after reaching our shores. He was twice a guest with Washington during that year; the first time in July, and the last in November. An account of these visits will be found in another part of this volume.

before, on this interesting interview he was at once charmed, and struck with wonder. When he considered her great age, the transcendant elevation of her son, who, surpassing all rivals in the race of glory, "bore the palm alone," and at the same time discovered no change in her plain, yet dignified life and manners, he became assured that nature had not cast this distinguished woman in an ordinary mould, and that the Roman matron could flourish in the modern day.

The marquis discoursed of the happy effects of the Revolution, and the goodly prospects which opened upon regenerated America; spoke of his speedy departure for his native land; paid the tribute of his heart, in his love and admiration of her illustrious son; and concluded, by asking her blessing. She gave it to him, and to the encomiums which he had lavished upon his hero and paternal chief, she replied in these words, "I am not surprised at what George has done, for he was always a very good boy."

Immediately after the organization of the present government,* the chief magistrate repaired to Fredericksburg, to pay his humble duty to his mother, preparatory to his departure for New York. An affecting scene ensued. The son feelingly remarked the ravages which a torturing disease had made upon the aged frame of the mother, and addressed her with these words: "The people, madam, have been pleased, with the most flattering unanimity, to elect me to the chief magistracy of these United States, but before I can assume the functions of my office, I have come to bid you an affectionate farewell. So soon as the weight of public business, which

* In the spring of 1789

must necessarily attend the outset of a new government, can be disposed of, I shall hasten to Virginia, and"—Here the matron interrupted with—" and you will see me no more; my great age, and the disease which is fast approaching my vitals, warn me that I shall not be long in this world; I trust in God that I may be somewhat prepared for a better. But go, George, fulfil the the high destinies which Heaven appears to have intended you for; go, my son, and may that Heaven's and a mother's blessing be with you always."

The president was deeply affected. His head rested upon the shoulder of his parent, whose aged arm feebly, yet fondly encircled his neck. That brow on which fame had wreathed the purest laurel virtue ever gave to created man, relaxed from its lofty bearing. That look which could have awed a Roman senate in its Fabrician day, was bent in filial tenderness upon the time-worn features of the aged matron. He wept. A thousand recollections crowded upon his mind, as memory retracing scenes long passed, carried him back to the maternal mansion and the days of juvenility, where he beheld that mother, whose care, education, and discipline, caused him to reach the topmost height of laudable ambition. Yet, how were his glories forgotten, while he gazed upon her whom, wasted by time and malady, he should part with to meet no more. Her predictions were but too true. The disease which so long had preyed upon her frame, completed its triumph, and she expired at the age of eighty-five, rejoicing in the consciousness of a life well spent, and confiding in the belief of a blessed immortality.

In her person, the matron was of the middle size, and

well proportioned; her features pleasing, yet strongly marked. It is not the happiness of the author to remember her, having only seen her with infant eyes. The sister of the chief he perfectly well remembers. She was a most majestic-looking woman, and so strikingly like the brother, that it was a matter of frolic to throw a cloak around her, and placing a military hat on her head, such was her amazing resemblance, that on her appearance, battalions would have presented arms, and senates risen to do homage to the chief.*

In her latter days, the matron often spoke of her own good boy; of the merits of his early life; of his love and duty; but of the deliverer of his country—the chief magistrate of the great republic, never. Call you this insensibility? call you it want of ambition? Oh, no; her ambition had been gratified to overflowing. In her Spartan school she had taught him to be good—that he became great, was a consequence, not the cause.

Thus lived and died this distinguished woman. Had she been of the olden time, statues would have been erected to her memory in the capitol, and she would have been called the Mother of Romans. When another century shall have elapsed, and our descendants shall have learned the true value of liberty, how will the fame of the paternal chief be cherished in story and in song, nor will be forgotten her, who first "bent the twig" to "incline the tree" to glory.

Then, and not till then, will youth and age, maid and matron, aye, and bearded men, with pilgrim step, repair

---

* This was the mother of Lawrence Lewis, the favorite nephew of Washington, who married Eleanor Parke Custis, mentioned in the preceding Memoir of the author of these *Recollections*.

to the now neglected grave of the mother of Washington.*

* It is yet a neglected grave. This Memoir was written more than thirty years ago. It was first published in the *National Gazette*, on the 13th of May, 1826. It attracted a great deal of attention at the time, and a project was set on foot for the re-entombment of the remains of the matron, and the erection of a monument over them. This movement was by no means confined to the people of Virginia. It elicited the public sympathy throughout the Union. The press, as usual, discussed the subject, and a New York paper proposed that the whole matter of raising the moderate sum of two thousand dollars, for the erection of the monument, should be left entirely in the hands of "the American Maids and Matrons." Mr. Gordon, the proprietor of the estate on which was the matron's grave, had some correspondence with Mr. Custis on the subject, and the inhabitants of Fredericksburg got up a memorial. But the whole project slumbered for several years.

Finally, in 1833, Silas E. Burrows, Esq., of the city of New York, undertook to erect a monument to the memory of the mother of Washington, at his own expense. The corner-stone was laid with appropriate ceremonies, very near her grave, a spot which she herself had selected for burial, on the land of her son-in-law, Colonel Fielding Lewis, near the ledge of rocks where she used to retire for meditation and devotion. It was placed by Andrew Jackson, then president of the United States, on the seventh of May, 1833, in the presence of a great concourse of people. He went down the Potomac from Washington city, on the sixth, and was met at Potomac creek, nine miles from Fredericksburg, by the monument committee of that city. He was received by a military escort, by whom he was conducted to the residence of Doctor Wallace, in Fredericksburg, where he was entertained until the following day, when a large military and civic procession was formed, proceeded to the grave, and there engaged in imposing ceremonies.

The procession was formed in the following order:—

1. A detachment of cavalry.

2. The chief architect and masonic societies. In this division, Silas E. Burrows, of New York, was assigned a conspicuous and honorable station.

3. The president of the United States in an open carriage, with the heads of departments, and his private secretary (Major Donelson), accompanied by the monument committee.

4. The clergy, and relatives of Washington.

5. The mayor and common council of Fredericksburg.

6. A handsome company of small boys, in complete uniform, with wooden guns.

7. The officers of the army and navy of the United States, and the invited strangers.

8. A battalion of volunteers under the command of Major Patten, and several companies of infantry from Washington and Alexandria, with the marine band.

9. Strangers and citizens, six abreast.

It was estimated that at least fifteen thousand persons were present on the occasion. After an appropriate prayer by the Reverend E. C. M'Guire (since author of a volume on the Religious Character of Washington), Mr. Bassett, one of the members of the monument committee, delivered an eloquent address to the president on the character of her whom they sought to honor. The president made a most touching reply, and as he deposited an inscribed plate in the corner stone, he said, "Fellow-citizens, at your request, and in your name, I now deposite this plate in the spot destined for it; and when the American pilgrim shall, in after ages, come up to this high and holy place, and lay his hand upon this sacred column, may he recall the virtues of her who sleeps beneath, and depart with his affections purified, and his piety strengthened, while he invokes blessings upon the memory of the mother of Washington."

Mrs. Sigourney thus wrote, in reference to this event :—

"Long hast thou slept unnoticed. Nature stole
  In her soft minstrelsy around thy bed,
  Spreading her vernal tissue, violet-gemmed,
    And pearled with dews.
        She bade bright summer bring
Gifts of frankincense, with sweet song of birds,
And autumn cast his reaper's coronet
Down at thy feet, and stormy winter speak
Sternly of man's neglect. But now we come
To do thee homage — Mother of our chief! —
Fit homage, such as honoreth him who pays.
Methinks we see thee, as in olden time —
Simple in garb, majestic, and serene;
Unmoved by pomp or circumstances; in truth
Inflexible; and, with a Spartan zeal,
Repressing vice and making folly grave.
Thou didst not deem it woman's part to waste
Life in inglorious sloth — to sport a while
Amid the flowers, or on the summer wave,
Then, fleet like the Ephemeron, away,
Building no temple in her children's hearts,
Save to the vanity and pride of life
Which she had worshipped.
        For the might that clothed
The "Pater Patriæ" — for the glorious deeds
That make Mount Vernon's tomb a Mecca shrine
For all the earth, what thanks to thee are due,
Who, 'mid his elements of being wrought,
  We know not — Heaven can tell."

The monument thus commenced, was never finished. Everything was completed but the obelisk with which it was to be surmounted, and the inscription. Commercial reverses soon afterward befel the noble inceptor and designer, and he was compelled to abandon his patriotic work. And with shame be it spoken, the citizens of

Virginia have left the unfinished monument to crumble into dust, and the mother of Washington to remain unhonored. Yet there is a ray of light. A correspondent of the *New Hampshire Patriot*, writing from Whampoa, in China, under date of December 20, 1858, speaks thus of Mr. Burrows and the monument:—

"I supposed he was long since dead, and that his monument and memory would perish together. But he still lives; and though his great object is suspended, it is not abandoned, but only adjourned till he can recuperate his fortunes. I met with him in Hong Kong, where, with two sons, he is conducting commercial enterprises, and sails back and forward between China and California with as little thought as you in taking the railroad for Boston. An old man and lame, on the other side of the globe, so far from his monument, and forgotten around the monument, even, as well as at home, it was touching to the heart to find him here, with one object, one thought, one last effort, remembering the 'Mother of Washington,' when he himself had passed from the memory of the living."

I visited that unfinished monument near the close of 1848, when the huge obelisk of white marble, ready for the sculptor's hand lay there, broken and defaced. The monument is also of white marble, and even in its unfinished state, had an imposing appearance. The years of more than a quarter of a century have now passed by since that corner-stone was laid, with so much pomp and promise, to the memory of her, of whom it was said by a distingushed gentleman in the city of modern Rome, that she was "the most fortunate of American matrons, in having given to her country and to the world, a hero without ambition, and a patriot without reproach;" and yet the monument is unfinished. It stands there silently appealing to national patriotism and local pride to sculpture its ornaments and seat its obelisk. It does more; it rebukes the insensibility of the sons and daughters of Virginia, to the memory of the most honored woman of the land. Year after year the dust of the plain has lodged upon the top of the half-finished pile, and the winds have planted the seeds of flowers and weeds wild there; and upon the base where that noble obelisk should stand, the sun, the rain, and the dew, annually weave green garlands and festoons, as if rebuking the indolence or avarice of insensate man. Even the marble tablet upon which was to be inscribed the simple words,

MARY, THE MOTHER OF WASHINGTON,

is covered with green moss; and there is nothing to tell the stranger that near him lie the mortal remains of her who gave birth to the FATHER OF HIS COUNTRY.

A picture of this unfinished monument may be found in *Lossing's Field-Book of the Revolution.*

CHAPTER II.

WASHINGTON AT MOUNT VERNON.

Mrs. Washington's Miniature — Washington's Letter to Her on accepting the Command of the Army — Member of the Virginia House of Burgesses — His Personal Attractions — Mansion-House at Mount Vernon — The Chase — His Company — A Master of Slaves — Billy — Bishop — The Military Hat and War Sword — Billy at Mount Vernon — Washington's Exemption from Disease — An Early Riser — His Habits in Private and Public — His Costume — His War Horse — His Guests and His Duties — Tour of His Farms — A Description of Him — Use of the Umbrella — Toasts — Washington's Evenings — His Habit in Winter — His Exercise — Partiality to Children — Washington an Observer of the Sabbath.

Forty years a husband, General Washington retained an old-fashioned habit of husbands, as he always did the ease and elegance of old-fashioned manners.* From the time of his marriage, until he ceased to live in nature, he wore suspended from his neck, by a gold chain, and resting on his bosom, the miniature portrait of his wife. The letter which he wrote to her, upon his acceptance of the command of the American army,† is a proof, both of his

---

* Washington was married in January 1759, and died in December 1799.

† The following is a copy of the letter, transcribed from the autograph preserved at Arlington house. It is the only letter from Washington to his wife known to be in existence:—

"Philadelphia, *June* 18, 1775.

"My Dearest: I am now sit down to write you on a subject which fills me with inexpressible concern, and this concern is greatly aggravated and increased when I reflect upon the uneasiness I know it will give you. It has been determined in Congress that the whole army raised for the defence of the American cause shall be put under my care, and that it is necessary for me to proceed immediately to Boston to take upon me the command of it.

"You may believe me, my dear Patsy, when I assure you in the most solemn manner, that, so far from seeking this appointment, I have used every endeavor in my power to avoid it, not only from my unwillingness to part with you and the family

conjugal tenderness, and diffidence in receiving so important a commission; also, of the purity of his heart, and of the generous and nobly disinterested motives which governed his life and actions.

Soon after his marriage, Colonel Washington became settled at Mount Vernon,* and was elected frequently

but from a consciousness of its being a trust too great for my capacity, and that I should enjoy more real happiness in one month with you at home than I have the most distant prospect of finding abroad, if my stay were to be seven times seven years. But as it has been a kind of destiny that has thrown me upon this service, I shall hope that my undertaking it is designed to answer some good purpose. You might, and I suppose did perceive, from the tenor of my letters, that I was apprehensive I could not avoid this appointment, as I did not pretend to intimate when I should return. That was the case. It was utterly out of my power to refuse this appointment without exposing my character to such censures as would have reflected dishonor upon myself and given pain to my friends. This I am sure could not, and ought not, to be pleasing to you, and must have lessened me considerably in my own esteem. I shall rely, therefore, confidently on that Providence which has heretofore preserved and been bountiful to me, not doubting but that I shall return safe to you in the fall. I shall feel no pain from the toil or the danger of the campaign; my unhappiness will flow from the uneasiness I know you will feel from being left alone. I therefore beg that you will summon your whole fortitude, and pass your time as agreeably as possible. Nothing will give me so much sincere satisfaction as to hear this, and to hear it from your own pen. My earnest and ardent desire is, that you would pursue any plan that is most likely to produce content and a tolerable degree of tranquillity; and it must add greatly to my uneasy feelings to hear that you are dissatisfied or complaining at what I really could not avoid.

"As life is always uncertain, and common prudence dictates to every man the necessity of settling his temporal concerns, while it is in his power, and while the mind is calm and undisturbed, I have, since I came to this place (for I had not time to do it before I left home), got Colonel Pendleton to draft a will for me, by the directions I gave him, which will I now enclose. The provision made for you in case of my death will, I hope, be agreeable.

"I shall add nothing more, as I have several letters to write, but to desire that you will remember me to your friends, and to assure you that I am, with the most unfeigned regard, my dear Patsy, your affectionate, &c."

* The eminence which gave name to the whole estate on the Potomac, owned by Washington, and on which the mansion was built, was called Mount Vernon in honor of Admiral Vernon of the British navy. Lawrence Washington, half-brother of George, and owner of the estate at that time, had served in the British army before Carthagena, where Vernon was the naval commander. Lawrence died in July 1752,

from the county of Fairfax to the house of burgesses.* During the reigns of the provincial governors, Bote-

at the early age of thirty-four years, leaving a wife and infant daughter. The Mount Vernon estate was bequeathed to that daughter, and in the event of her decease without issue, the property was to pass into the absolute possession of George, to whom, in his will, Lawrence had entrusted the chief care of his affairs, although he was the youngest executor. He was then only twenty years of age. The daughter did not long survive her father, and Mount Vernon became the property of George Washington. In a letter to a friend in London, soon after his marriage, Washington wrote concerning his home: "No estate in United America is more pleasantly situated. In a high and healthy country; in a latitude between the extremes of heat and cold; on one of the finest rivers in the world—a river well stock with various kinds of fish at all seasons of the year, and in the spring with shad, herring, bass, carp, sturgeon, &c., in great abundance. The borders of the estate are washed by more than ten miles of tide-water; several valuable fisheries appertain to it; the whole shore, in fact, is one entire fishery."

* While engaged in the campaign of 1758, Colonel Washington was elected a representative of Frederick county, in the Virginia house of burgesses. Just previous to the election, his friends urged him to leave the army for a few days, and give the weight of his personal presence in favor of himself, as a candidate. The public good required him to remain with the army, and as that always outweighed every private consideration, he refused to leave. There were four candidates, and he was chosen by a large majority over all his competitors. "Your friends," wrote one of his correspondents, "have been very sincere, so that you have received more votes than any other candidate. Colonel Ward sat on the bench and represented you, and he was carried round the town in the midst of a general applause, and huzzaing for Colonel Washington." This was a gratifying result for the young commander, for he had received the support of the people among whom, in the most trying times, he had been compelled to exercise strong military restraint.

This election cost Colonel Washington thirty-nine pounds and six shillings, Virginia currency. "Among the items of charge which have been preserved," says Sparks, "are a hogshead and a barrel of punch, thirty-five gallons of wine, forty-three gallons of strong beer, cider, and dinner for his friends."

Colonel Washington was a member of the house of burgesses for about fifteen years. Soon after the meeting of that body, in January 1757, when Washington appeared there as a member for the first time, it was resolved to return thanks to him for the distinguished service he had rendered his country in the field. Upon Speaker Robinson devolved the pleasing duty. "As soon as Colonel Washington took his seat," says Mr. Wirt, "Mr. Robinson, in obedience to the order, and following the impulse of his own generous and grateful heart, discharged the duty with great dignity, but with such warmth of coloring, and strength of expression, as entirely to confound the young hero. He rose to express his acknowledgments for the honor, but such was his trepidation and confusion, that he could not give distinct utterance to a single syllable. He blushed, stammered, and trembled for a

tourt* and Eden,† the courts of Williamsburg‡ and Annapolis§ displayed as much of the polish of high life as was

second; when the speaker relieved him by a stroke of address that would have done honor to Louis the Fourteenth in his proudest and happiest moment. 'Sit down Mr. Washington,' said he, with a conciliatory smile, 'your modesty is equal to your valor, and that surpasses the power of any language that I possess.'"

* Lord Botetourt, one of the king's lords of the bedchamber, arrived in Virginia as governor of the colony, in the autumn of 1768. He was the successor of Governor Fauquier. He was an Englishman; upright, honorable, benevolent and accomplished. When asked by the king, on receiving his appointment, "When will you be ready to go?" he promptly replied, "To-night." His manners were very conciliatory. For this reason Junius described him as a "cringing, bowing, fawning, and sword-bearing courtier;" and Horace Walpole said, on his departure, "if his graces don't captivate the Virginians, he will enrage them to fury; for I take all his *douceur* to be enamelled on iron." Like others of his class, Lord Botetourt had underrated the people he had consented to govern; and his ostentatious display of vice-regal pomp, when proceeding to open the Virginia assembly, for the first time, disgusted them. He was, on the whole, one of the best of the royal governors ever vouchsafed to Virginia, and his memory is cherished with affection in the Old Dominion. On the green, in front of William and Mary College, at Williamsburg, is a statue of Lord Botetourt. He died in 1771, and was succeeded by Lord Dunmore.

† Sir Robert Eden was the last of the royal governors of Maryland, and succeeded Governor Sharpe in 1768. He was a very amiable gentleman, and at the commencement of revolutionary movements against royal authority, he was disposed to be very conciliatory toward the people of Maryland. But, as royal governor, he was compelled to obey the commands of his king and his ministers, and in so doing, he offended the republican sentiment of his colony, and was obliged to abdicate. He returned after the war to recover his estates, and died at Annapolis, in September 1784. His wife was sister to Lord Baltimore.

‡ Williamsburg, as we have elsewhere remarked, was made the capital of Virginia at an early day, and the governors held courts there in a style approaching that of royalty itself, only on a smaller scale. The remains of the "palace" of Lord Dunmore may yet be seen. These consist of the two wings. The whole was constructed of brick. The centre portion was accidentally destroyed by fire, while occupied by the French troops, immediately after the surrender of Cornwallis, at Yorktown. It was seventy-four feet long and sixty-eight feet wide, and occupied the site of the old palace of Governor Spottswood, at the beginning of the eighteenth century. Attached to the palace were three hundred and sixty acres of land, beautifully laid out in gardens, parks, carriage-ways, and a bowling-green.

§ Annapolis, on the Chesapeake, at the mouth of the Severn, became the seat of the government of Maryland in the year 1694, when all the records and offices were moved there from St. Marys, the first capital. There, as at Williamsburg, was found the most polished society; and of so much importance were these two places

to be found in the larger cities of Europe, with far less of their corruptions and debaucheries. It was the custom for gentlemen of fortune to have their town houses during the sessions of the legislature, where they lived in great splendor and hospitality. Colonel Washington was of this number. His personal attractions, not less than his early renown in arms, made him a subject of much interest to the Europeans, who were frequent visitors to the capitals of Virginia and Maryland. Straight as an Indian arrow, he was easily distinguished in the gay crowds which appeared at the palaces of the vice-kings, by a something in his air and manner which bespoke no ordinary man. His lower limbs, being formed mathematically straight, he walked, as it were, on parallel lines, while his mode of placing and taking up his feet resembled the step of precision and care so remarkable in the aboriginal children of the forest. He might be termed rather a silent than a speaking member of the house of burgesses, although he sometimes addressed the chair, and was listened to with attention and respect, while the excellence of his judgment was put in requisition on all committees, either of important general or local policy.*

considered, in point of social character, that the first theatrical performances ever given in America, by a regular company, were at those two places. The toleration extended to such amusements by the Anglican church, then the established church in Virginia and Maryland, may have had some influence in causing Hallam and his company first to try their fortunes there. It was in 1752 and 1753 that the performances were first presented in those two cities; and it is on record, that Washington, who was very fond of dramatic entertainments, attended them at both places.

* So in the continental Congress, of which Washington was a member in 1774 and 1775. He had no ability for an extemporary speaker, and did not there engage in the public debates. He was an excellent counsellor, and was assiduous in his attendance at Carpenter's hall whenever the Congress was in session. Patrick Henry, when asked, on his return home from the Congress, whom he considered the greatest

When Colonel Washington first resided at Mount Vernon, both the mansion-house and estate were inconsiderable. All the embellishments of the house and grounds are owing to his creative hand. Prior to the War for Independence, he was much attached to the pleasures of the chase, and is described as a bold and fearless rider. He kept hounds for a short time after the Revolution, but declined hunting altogether about 1787 or '88.

He was never disposed to conviviality, but liked the cheerful converse of the social board. He indulged in no games of chance, except in the olden times, when required to make up a party at whist, in playing for a trifle; although, for many years, play of all kinds was unknown in his household.* After his retirement from public life, all the time which he could spare from his library, was devoted to the improvement of his estates, and the elegant and tasteful arrangement of his house and grounds. He was his own surveyor,† and the dis-

---

man in that body, replied: "If you speak of eloquence, Mr. Rutledge, of South Carolina, is by far the greatest orator; but if you speak of solid information and sound judgment, Colonel Washington is unquestionably the greatest man on that floor."

* During his younger married life, Washington indulged in all lawful amusements. His home was a gay one, and almost every day he had company at dinner. "Would any person believe," he says in his diary, in 1768, "that, with *a hundred and one cows* actually reported at a late enumeration of the cattle, I should still be obliged to buy butter for my family?" The hunting days, which occurred frequently, generally ended in a dinner at Belvoir, the seat of the Fairfaxes, a little lower on the Potomac, or at Mount Vernon—more frequently at the latter. The company usually staid all night, and bad weather might keep them there. Washington was indifferent to games, but on such occasions he resorted to them to amuse his guests. On one of these, he records in his diary: "At home all day at cards; it snowing."

† A facsimile of the record of one of the latest of his surveys, is presented in this work. Surveying was Washington's earliest occupation for gain, he having been employed in that business by Lord Fairfax, who owned immense tracts of land in the valleys beyond the Blue Ridge. Washington set out on his first surveying expedition, on account of Lord Fairfax, in March, 1748, just one month from the

position and appearance of his farms, gave evident proofs that the genius of useful improvement had directed its energies with beneficial, as well as ornamental effects.

As a master of slaves, General Washington was con sistent, as in every other relation of his meritorious life They were comfortably lodged, fed, and clothed; required to do a full and fair share of duty; well cared for in sickness and old age, and kept in strict and proper discipline. These, we humbly conceive, comprise all the charities of slavery. To his old servants, where long and faithful services rendered them worthy of attachment and esteem, he was most kind. His huntsman and Revolutionary attendant, Will Lee, commonly called Billy, was specially provided for, and survived his master a good many years. Will had been a stout active man, and a famous horseman, but, from accident, was a cripple for many years before his death, which occurred at a very advanced age.* This ancient follower, both in the chase and war, formed a most interesting relic of the chief, and received considerable largesses from the numerous visiters to Mount Vernon. The slaves were left to be emancipated at the

---

day on which he was sixteen years of age. I have before me his original drawings of the plan for laying out the grounds around the Mount Vernon mansion, made after his return from the army and retirement to private life, in 1784. A particular account of these may be found in a volume entitled, "*Mount Vernon, and its Associations*," published in 1859, by W. A. Townsend & Company, New York.

* I visited Mount Vernon in October, 1858, where I saw an old mulatto, named Westford, who had been a resident there since August, 1801. He was raised in the family of Judge Bushrod Washington, who came into possession of Mount Vernon, by inheritance, after the death of Mrs. Washington. Westford knew Billy well. His master having left him a house, and a pension of one hundred and fifty dollars a year, Billy became a spoiled child of fortune. He was quite intemperate at times, and finally *delirium tremens*, with all its horrors, seized him. Westford frequently relieved him on such occasions, by bleeding him. One morning, a little more than thirty years ago, Westford was sent for to bring Billy out of a fit. The blood would not flow. Billy was dead!

death of Mrs. Washington; but it was found necessary (for *prudential* reasons) to give them their freedom in one year after the general's decease. Although many of them, with a view to their liberation, had been instructed in mechanic trades, yet they succeeded very badly as freemen: so true is the axiom, " that the hour which makes man a slave, takes half his worth away."

Bishop, an English soldier, formed an interesting reminiscence of the war of '55. He belonged to Braddock's own regiment; and, on account of possessing superior intelligence, was detailed as a body-servant, to accompany that ill-fated commander on the expedition to Fort du Quesne.* Bishop firmly believed in the Providence which shielded the provincial colonel, in the memorable battle of Monongahela, and observed, he was the only mounted officer left. The enemy knew him well, from their having felt him severely, the year be-

* On account of boundary disputes, at about the middle of the last century, the French and English in America, engaged in a war, and finally hostilities between the two nations were officially declared. The war commenced in the Ohio region. Englishmen attempted to build a fort at the forks of the Ohio, upon territory claimed by the French. The latter, aided by Indians, drove the English off, finished the fort, and named it Du Quesne, in honor of the governor-general of Canada. Against this fort General Braddock, an Irish officer of considerable military renown, led an expedition in the year 1755. After much toil and difficulty he reached the Monongahela early in the month of July. Washington, with the rank of colonel, accompanied him as aid. On the ninth, they suddenly fell into an Indian ambush, and a terrible encounter ensued between French and Indians on one side, and English and provincial soldiers on the other. Washington urged Braddock to fight, as the Indians did, or rather, as the provincials were accustomed to, but that general would not swerve from the rules of European tactics. The consequence was, a terrible slaughter of his troops, and a defeat. Braddock himself was mortally wounded, and the remnant of his army was saved by the skill and gallant conduct of Colonel Washington. He was the only mounted officer who, on that day, was not wounded. He had two horses shot under him, and four bullets passed through his coat. "By the all-powerful dispensations of Providence," he wrote to his brother, "I have been protected beyond all human probability or expectation."

fore at the affair of the Meadows;* and the provincial military being far more obnoxious to the French and Indians than the European troops, from the marksmanship of the rangers, and their intimate knowledge of the modes of forest warfare, the fire of the enemy became particularly directed against the devoted young warrior, whom they afterward termed " the spirit-protected man," destined to " become the chief of nations," and who " could not die in battle." The hat worn on that eventful day, and which was pierced by two balls, was at Mount Vernon, and both seen and handled by several persons, long within our remembrance; yet, strange to say, it was no where to be found on the demise of the chief. Another and invaluable relict was also missing; we mean the sword of service which was worn in action in the War for Independence. It was described to us, by one who had often buckled it to the hero's side, as being a kind of hanger; and we have an indistinct recollection of having been told in the family, that it was given to General Greene at the close of the war. If so, it surely could not have been more worthily bestowed. Upon mentioning these circumstances to General Andrew Jackson, he was pleased to say that he would make inquiry among the descendants of Greene, who, if they

* When, by order of Governor Dinwiddie, Major Washington, in 1754, was marching toward the forks of the Ohio, he was informed that the French had driven the English away, and that a strong force of French and Indians were on their march to attack him. He prudently wheeled, marched back to a place called the Great Meadows, and there hastily erected a stockade, and called it Fort Necessity. Again, on the death of the leader of the expedition, when the whole command devolved on Major Washington, he advanced with four hundred men. He was soon advised of the approach of a much larger number of the enemy, and he fell back to Fort Necessity at the Great Meadows. There, on the third of July, he was besieged by about fifteen hundred foes, and on the morning of the fourth surrendered. It was upon honorable terms; and Washington and his troops were allowed to return to Virginia.

possess, will, no doubt, most dearly prize so valued a gift as the *Sword of the Revolution.**

* This was written in February, 1827. That sword, with Franklin's staff, is preserved in a glass case, with other personal mementoes of Washington, in the model-hall of the patent-office at Washington city. The handle is of ivory, colored a pale green, and wound spirally at wide intervals with silver wire. It was manufactured by J. Bailey, Fishkill, Duchess county, New York, and has the maker's name engraven upon the hilt. The belt is of white leather, silver mounted, and was in the old French and Indian war. It bears a silver plate, on which is engraved, "1757."

The long black staff grouped with the sword, was bequeathed to Washington by Doctor Franklin, in the following clause of the codicil to his will:—

"My fine crab-tree walking-stick, with a gold head curiously wrought in the form of the cap of liberty, I give to my friend, and the friend of mankind, *General Washington*. If it were a sceptre, he has merited it, and would become it. It was a present to me from that excellent woman, Madame De Forbach, the dowager-duchess of Deux-Ponts, connected with some verses which should go with it."

Of these relics, our lyric poet, George P. Morris, has sweetly sung in the following ode, called "*The Sword and the Staff*."

> "The sword of the Hero!
>   The staff of the Sage!
> Whose valor and wisdom
>   Are stamped on the age!
> Time-hallowed mementoes
>   Of those who have riven
> The sceptre from tyrants,
>   'The lightning from heaven.
>
> "This weapon, O Freedom!
>   Was drawn by thy son,
> And it never was sheathed
>   Till the battle was won!
> No stain of dishonor
>   Upon it we see!
> 'T was never surrendered—
>   Except to the free!
>
> "While Fame claims the hero
>   And patriot sage,
> Their names to emblazon
>   On History's page,
> No holier relics
>   Will Liberty hoard,
> Than FRANKLIN'S staff, guarded
>   By WASHINGTON'S sword."

At the commencement of hostilities, in 1775, Bishop being too old for active service, was left at home in charge of the manufacturing establishments of the household, wherein the veteran would flourish his cane, exacting as perfect obedience as though he had been a commanding officer on parade. A comfortable house had been built for him; he had married; and, looking no more toward his native land, he was contented to pass the remainder of his days on the domain of his patron, where he rested from labor, in the enjoyment of every possible ease and indulgence—the reward of his long and faithful services. In his comfortable homestead, and hoary with age, he would delight the young with tales of fearful interest of the Indian war; while, his own conflicts ended, and himself at peace with all the world, he feebly trimmed the lamp of life, which, having burned for more than eighty years, could but for a little while longer be kept from expiring.

Notwithstanding his perfect reverence for his patron, this old soldier would sometimes, presuming on the privilege of age and long services, chafe his protector on points of expediency, though never on those of obedience. The general would assume a lofty tone, saying, "It is very well, sir; if you are at length tired of my service, you are at perfect liberty to depart." The ancient follower of Braddock, however, knew his man, and knew exactly what best to do; so he would wisely become silent, and the storm which appeared to be brooding would quickly pass away, then returning sunshine, cheered with the warmth of its kindness the veteran of '55.*

* See note on page 158. Braddock had five horses shot under him before receiving his mortal wound. Bishop was in close attendance upon his master all

The Washington family were subject to hereditary gout. The chief never experienced a pang. His temperance, and the energetic employment of both his body and mind, seemed to forbid the approach of a disease, which severely afflicted several of his nearest kindred. His illnesses were of rare occurrence, but were particularly severe. His aversion to the use of medicine was extreme; and, even when in great suffering, it was only by the entreaties of his lady, and the respectful, yet beseeching look of his oldest friend and companion in arms (Doctor James Craik), that he could be prevailed upon to take the slightest preparation of medicine.*

General Washington, during the whole of both his public and private life, was a very early riser; indeed,

---

the while, and assisted in carrying the wounded general from the field. He was conveyed, first in a tumbrel, then on horseback, and finally by his soldiers on a litter, in the flight toward Fort Cumberland. He was attended by Dr. James Craik, the life-long friend of Washington, and also by Colonel Washington himself. Braddock died on the night of the fifteenth. Just before his death, he commended Bishop, who had served him faithfully, to the protection of Colonel Washington, who, two hours afterward, read the impressive funeral service of the Anglican church over his grave, by the light of torches. It was a little past midnight when they laid their commander in a grave, dug in the middle of the road, to prevent his body being discovered and treated with indignity by the Indians.

* Colonel Washington's health suffered much during the campaigns of 1757 and 1758. Late in the autumn of 1757, he was compelled to leave his command and go home, severely suffering from dysentery. His malady, which had been wearing upon him for some time, increased, and Doctor Craik warned him that his life was in danger. He went home to Mount Vernon, where his disease settled into a fever, from which he did not recover in less than four months. He endeavored to go to Williamsburg on urgent business, in February following, but could not; and toward the close of that month he wrote to Colonel Stanwix, saying, "I have never been able to return to my command, since I wrote to you last, my disorder, at times, returning obstinately upon me, in spite of the efforts of all the sons of Æsculapius, whom I have hitherto consulted. At certain periods I have been reduced to great extremity, and have now too much reason to apprehend my approaching decay [consumption], being visited with several symptoms of such disease." He was then twenty-six years of age. As we shall hereafter observe, he was very dangerously ill while president of the republic.

in the maternal mansion, at which his first habits were formed, the character of a sluggard was abhorred. Whether as chief magistrate, or the retired citizen, we find this man of method and labor seated in his library from one to two hours before day, in winter, and at daybreak in summer. We wonder at the amazing amount of work which he performed. Nothing but a method the most remarkable and exemplary, could have enabled him to accomplish such a world of labor, an amount which might have given pretty full employment to half a dozen ordinary, and not idle men, all their lives. When we consider the volume of his official papers—his vast foreign, public, and private correspondence—we are scarcely able to believe that the space of one man's life should have comprehended the doing of so many things, and doing them so well.

His toilette was soon made. A single servant prepared his clothes, and laid them in readiness. He also combed and tied his hair.* He shaved and dressed himself, but giving very little of his precious time to matters of that sort, though remarkable for the neatness and propriety of his apparel. His clothes were made after the old-fashioned cut, of the best, though plainest materials.†

---

* In those days the hair was left to grow long, and was tied up in a long bunch with a ribbon, behind, in a form called a *queue*. It was the universal fashion. Powder was also used for the hair, which gave it a frosted appearance. This was put on with a puff-ball, usually made of cotton yarn, which, with the powder, was carried in a dressed buckskin pouch.

† It was the practice in Virginia, previous to the Revolution, for the planters to send to London for all articles in common use, that could not be manufactured as well at home, such as agricultural implements, saddles, bridles, harness, and wearing apparel. Washington was in the habit of sending to his agent in London lists of articles that he desired for himself and family. He gave the names, ages, sizes, and general description of those for whom wearing apparel was needed. In an order sent to Richard Washington, in 1761, he says, after referring to an invoice of clothes

When president of the United States, the style of his household and equipage corresponded with the dignity of his exalted station, though avoiding as much as was possible everything like show or parade. The expenses of his presidency, over and above the salary of government, absorbed the proceeds of the sale of a very considerable estate.*

already sent: "As they are designed for wearing apparel for myself, I have committed the choice of them to your fancy, having the best opinion of your taste. I want neither lace nor embroidery. Plain clothes, with gold, or silver buttons, if worn in genteel dress, are all that I desire. Whether it be the fault of the tailor or of the measure sent, I can not say, but, certain it is, my clothes have never fitted me well. I enclose a measure, and, for a further direction, I think it not amiss to add, that my stature is six feet; otherwise rather slender than corpulent." He was six feet two inches in height, according to the best authorities.

Although Washington and his family were plain in their persons, they lived at home, and appeared abroad, not unlike the English aristocracy at that time. When abroad, he always appeared on horseback, with fine equipments, accompanied by Bishop. His stable was well furnished with thoroughbred horses; and for Mrs. Washington and her lady-visiters, he kept a chariot and four horses, with black postillions in livery, and these frequently excited the admiration of travellers and dwellers upon the road from Mount Vernon to Alexandria, or to the neighboring estates.

The following order, sent to his London agent for out-of-door equipage, will give an idea of the appearance of Washington when on the road:—

"1 Man's riding saddle, hogskin seat, large plated stirrups, and everything complete. Double-reined bridle and Pelham bit, plated.

"A very neat and fashionable Newmarket saddle-cloth.

"A large and best portmanteau, saddle, bridle, and pillion.

"Cloak-bag; surcingle; checked saddle-cloth, holsters, &c.

"A riding-frock of a handsome drab-colored broadcloth, with plain double-gilt buttons.

"A riding waistcoat of superfine scarlet cloth and gold lace, with buttons like those of the coat.

"A blue surtout-coat.

"A neat switch-whip, silver cap.

"Black velvet cap for servant."

The ladies in those days rode much on horseback (usually upon ponies), followed by black servants. The gayest of them wore scarlet cloth riding-habits.

* The salary of the president was then, as now, twenty-five thousand dollars per annum. The sale of that "considerable estate," which was chiefly wild land, is alluded to in Washington's letter to Lawrence Lewis, printed in the Memoir of the author of these *Recollections, ante,* page 47.

The president never appeared in military costume, unless to receive his brethren of the Cincinnati, or at reviews.* He then wore the old opposition colors of England, and the regimental dress of the volunteer corps which he commanded prior to the Revolution.† With the exception of the brilliant epaulettes (we believe a present from General Lafayette), and the diamond order of the Cincinnati, presented by the seamen of the French fleet, our allies in the War for Independence,‡ the uniform of the commander-in-chief of the army and navy, under the Constitution, was as plain as blue and buff could make it. The cocked hat, with the black ribbon cockade, was the only type of the heroic time which appended to the chief during his civil magistracy; in all other respects, he seemed studiously to merge the military into the civil characteristics of his public life.

About sunrise, General Washington invariably visited and inspected his stables. He was very fond of horses,

---

* A full account of the *Society of the Cincinnati*, of which Washington was the first president-general, may be found in another part of this work.

† When the sessions of the first continental Congress closed, the whole country, alive to the apprehension that war would soon be kindled, was filled with military preparations. When Washington returned to Mount Vernon, he found the independent companies throughout the province waiting for the voice of his experience, to teach them how to prepare for the conflict. He coveted the sweets of rural and domestic life, but duty bade him relinquish all for the good of his country. A few days after his arrival home, the *Independent Company of Cadets* of Prince William county, a well-equipped corps, whose motto was *Aut liber aut nullus*, solicited him to take command of them, as a field-officer. They had appointed a committee to wait on him with the invitation, and to request him to "direct the fashion of their uniform, and that they also acquaint him with the motto of their company, which is to be fixed on their colors." Other companies offered him the same honor. He yielded, and reviewed the volunteer corps, which assembled at various places, always wearing, on such occasions, the costume of a Virginia colonel of the period. It was in that costume that the elder Peale painted him, in the picture now at Arlington house, a copy of which is given in this volume.

‡ See chapter containing an account of the "Surrender of Yorktown."

and his equipages were always of a superior order. The horses which he rode, in the War for Independence, were said to be superb. We have a perfect remembrance of the charger which bore him in the greatest of his triumphs, when he received the sword of the vanquished, on the ever-memorable nineteenth October, 1781.* It was a chestnut, with a white face and legs, and was called *Nelson*, after the patriotic governor of Virginia.† Far different was the fate of this favorite horse of Washington, from that of "the high-mettled racer." When the chief had relinquished his seat upon its back, after the war was over, it was never mounted more, but cropped the herbage in summer, was housed and well cared for in winter, often caressed by the master's hand, and died of old age at Mount Vernon, many years after the Revolution.

The library and a visit to the stables occupied the morning till the hour of breakfast. This meal was without change to him, whose habits were regular, even to matters which others are so apt to indulge themselves in to endless variety. Indian cakes, honey, and tea, formed this temperate repast.‡ On rising from the table,

---

* See chapter on the "Surrender of Yorktown."

† See a sketch of the life and services of this gentleman in a future chapter.

‡ This abstemiousness appears to have been a marked exception to a general rule. The Reverend Andrew Burnaby, who travelled quite extensively in America, in the years 1759 and 1760, and visited Mount Vernon two or three times during the first year of Washington's married life, says in a note, "In several parts of Virginia, the ancient custom of eating meat at breakfast still continues. At the top of the table, where the lady of the house presides, there is constantly tea and coffee; but the rest of the table is garnished out with roast fowls, ham, venison, game, and other dainties. Even at Williamsburg, it is the custom to have a plate of cold ham upon the table; and there is scarcely a Virginian lady who breakfasts without it."

Speaking of Mount Vernon, Mr. Burnaby says: "This place is the property of Colonel Washington, and truly deserving of its owner. The house is most beauti

if there were guests (and it was seldom otherwise), books and papers were offered for their amusement; they were requested to take good care of themselves, and the illustrious farmer proceeded to the daily tour of his agricultural concerns.* He rode upon his farms entirely unattended, opening his gates, pulling down and putting up his fences, as he passed, visiting his laborers at their work, inspecting all the operations of his extensive agricultural establishments with a careful eye, directing useful improvements, and superintending them in their progress. He introduced many and valuable foreign as well as domestic modes of improved husbandry, showing, by experiment, their practical utility, and peculiar adaptation to our system of rural affairs; and, by his zeal and ability, "gave a speed to the plough," and a generous impulse to the cause of agricultural and domestic economy — those important sources of national wealth, industry, and independence.†

fully situated upon a very high hill on the banks of the Potomac, and commands a noble prospect of water, of cliffs, of woods, and plantations. The river is near two miles broad, though two hundred from the mouth, and divides the dominions of Virginia from Maryland."

* Never was hospitality dispensed with a more generous and kindly spirit. The translator of De Chastellux's travels in North America, at the close of the Revolution, writing of the mistress of that mansion, says: "Your apartments were your house; the servants of the house were yours; and, while every inducement was held out to bring you into the general society of the drawing-room, or at the table, it rested with yourself to be served or not with everything in your own chamber."

† Washington raised large quantities of tobacco, wheat, and Indian corn; and he aimed to have everything upon his estates of the best quality. So noted for excellence was everything bearing his brand, that a barrel of flour stamped "*George Washington*, Mount Vernon," was exempted from the customary inspection in the West India ports. In his Diary, under date of twenty-second January, 1790, while he was president of the United States, and residing in New York, is the following entry. "Called in my ride on the Baron de Poellnitz, to see the operation of his (Winlaw's) thrashing-machine. The effect was, the heads of the wheat being separated from the straw, as much of the first was run through the mill in 15 minutes as made half

The tour of the farms might average from ten to fifteen miles per day. An anecdote occurs to us at this moment, which, as it embraces a Revolutionary worthy, a long-tried and valued friend of the chief, and is descriptive of *Washington on his farm*, we shall, without apology, present it to our readers.

We were accosted, while hunting, by an elderly stranger, who inquired whether the general was to be found at the mansion house, or whether he had gone to visit his estate. We replied, that he was abroad, and gave directions as to the route the stranger was to pursue, observing, at the same time, " You will meet, sir, with *an old gentleman riding alone, in plain drab clothes, a broad-brimmed white hat, a hickory switch in his hand, and carrying an umbrella with a long staff, which is attached to his saddle-bow—that person, sir, is General Washington!*" The stranger, much amused at our description, observed, with a good humored smile:—

a bushel of clean wheat. Allowing 8 working hours in the 24, this would yield 16 bushels per day. Two boys are sufficient to turn the wheel, feed the mill, and remove the thrashed grain after it has passed through it. Two men were unable, by winnowing, to clear the wheat as it passed through the mill, but a common Dutch fan, with the usual attendance, would be *more* than sufficient to do it. The grain passes through without bruising, and is well separated from the chaff. Women, or boys of 12 or 14 years of age, are fully adequate to the management of the mill or thrashing-machine. Upon the whole, it appears to be an easier, more expeditious, and much cleaner way of getting out grain than by the usual mode of thrashing; and vastly to be preferred to treading, which is hurtful to horses, filthy to the wheat, and not more expeditious, considering the numbers that are employed in the process from the time the head is begun to be formed until the grain has passed finally through the fan."

In December previous, Washington, in a letter to the Baron de Poellnitz (who was the inventor of several agricultural machines, and had a small farm on York island, in the vicinity of Murray hill), had proposed to take some occasion of " seeing the manner in which the thrashing-machine operated." This was the occasion noted in his Diary. From some intimations elsewhere, it is quite certain that he sent one of these machines to his general overseer at Mount Vernon.

"Thank ye, thank ye, young gentleman; I think, if I fall in with the general, I shall be apt to know him."

At dinner, we had the pleasure of being introduced to Colonel Meade,* who had been aid-de-camp to the commander-in-chief in the war of the Revolution. The umbrella was not used by Washington as an article of luxury, for luxuries were to him known only by name. Being naturally of a very fair complexion, his skin was liable to be affected by the influence of the sun. This umbrella, just as it was when last he laid it down, never again to require its friendly shade, we have had the good fortune to preserve for a quarter of a century,† and also the happiness to present it the patriarch of La Grange, in whose possession it will long be treasured as the relique of his paternal chief, and as an appropriate memorial of the modern Cincinnatus.‡

Precisely at a quarter before three, the industrious farmer always returned, dressed, and dined at three o'clock. At this meal he ate heartily, but was not particular in his diet, with the exception of fish, of which he was excessively fond. He partook sparingly of desert, drank a home-made beverage, and from four to five glasses of Madeira wine. When the cloth was removed, with old-fashioned courtesy, he drank to the health of every person present, and then gave his toast, his only toast—"*All our friends*"—than which a nobler or a kindlier sentiment never was pledged at the board of social friendship, or "brayed out with the trumpet's triumphs," at the carousals of a king.

* Colonel Richard K. Meade, father of Bishop Meade, of Virginia.
† This written on the twenty-second of February, 1827.
‡ Mr. Custis presented the umbrella to General Lafayette when he was in this country as the nation's guest, in the years 1824 and '25.

While on the subject of toasts, we will mention another. The late Colonel Cropper, of Accomac, was a captain in the ninth Virginia regiment of the line, which formed part of the southern division, under Greene, and covered the retreat of our discomfitted army at the battle of Brandywine. On the evening of that hard-fought day, Cropper marched the remains of his company into Chester, having his handkerchief fastened to a ramrod, in place of a flag.* After serving his country with fidelity and distinction, Colonel Cropper retired to his estate on the Eastern shore, where he lived to an advanced age. This worthy veteran, like his general, had but one toast, which he gave every day, and to all companies; it was, " God bless General Washington." Toasts are supposed to convey the feelings and wishes of our hearts; and if ever an aspiration, warm and direct from the heart, deserved to find favor with "heaven's chancery" on high, it was when, with pious fervor, this old soldier's prayer implored a blessing upon his revered commander.

The afternoon was usually devoted to the library. At

* A British army, under General Sir William Howe, landed from a British fleet commanded by his brother, Richard Earl Howe, a few miles below Elkton, on the shores of Chesapeake bay, toward the close of August, 1777. Washington, with the American army, marched southward from Philadelphia to oppose Howe's progress into the country, and advanced some distance beyond the Brandywine creek. When the British approached, he was compelled to fall back to the eastern side of that stream, and near Chad's ford, he made a disposition of his forces to oppose the passage of the enemy. Philadelphia was the prize for which Howe was pressing, and Washington resolved to do all in his power to keep it out of his hands. By a stealthy movement, Cornwallis, under cover of a fog, marched up the west side of the Brandywine with a large force, crossed, and fell suddenly upon the right wing of the American army, under General Sullivan. A severe contest ensued. Soon afterward, Knyphausen, the Hessian general, crossed Chad's ford and attacked the American centre, and after a hot battle, the republicans were driven from the field, and fled to Chester that night. The next morning they continued their retreat toward Philadelphia, and encamped near Germantown, where, soon afterward, a severe engagement occurred, which is described in another chapter.

night, his labors over, the venerated citizen would join his family and friends at the tea-table, and enjoy their society for several hours. He took no supper, and about nine o'clock retired to bed. When without company, he frequently read to his family extracts from the new publications of the day; and, on Sunday, sermons and other sacred writings.* He read with distinctness and precision, though with a voice, the tones of which had been considerably broken by a pulmonary affection in early life, and which, when greatly excited, produced a laboring of the chest. He would frequently, when sitting with his family, appear absent; his lips would move, his hand be raised, and he would evidently seem under the influence of thoughts, which had nothing to do with the quiet scene around him. This peculiarity is readily accounted for, since it must be no very easy matter for one who so long had borne the cares of public life, at once to lay aside all thoughts for others, and become content with individual concerns.

In winter, when stress of weather prevented his taking his usual exercise, he was in the habit of walking for an hour in the eastern portico of the mansion, before retiring to rest. As that portico is more than ninety feet in length, this walk would comprise several miles.†

---

* In the library at Mount Vernon, there are several volumes of sermons, and other religious books, written by old English divines. In one of these, written by Sir Matthew Hale, are the autographs of the two wives of Washington's father, Jane Washington and Mary Washington — the latter (the mother of the general) written under the former.

† In a letter to Mr. Rumney (a gentleman about to depart for England), in which Washington desires him to make some inquiries there about certain kinds of marble, with which he would like to pave the floor of the portico, he says: "The piazza, or colonade, for which this is wanted as a floor, is ninety-two feet eight inches, by twelve feet eight inches, within the margin or border that surrounds it"

Thus, in the seldom-varied routine of useful industry, temperate enjoyment, and the heartfelt gratifications of domestic felicity, sped the latter days of the Father of his Country; and oh! it was delightful to behold this "time-honored man," the race of whose glory was run, who had reached the goal of all his most earnest desires, and obtained a reward for all his toils, in the contemplation of the freedom and happiness of a rising empire, resting from his mighty labors, amid the tranquil retirement of Mount Vernon.

The sedentary occupations of a president of the United States necessarily limited the opportunities for active exercise. These were principally enjoyed in occasional rides to the country, and in frequent walks to his watchmaker's, in Second street, for the purpose of regulating his watch by the time-keeper.* As he passed along, often would mothers bring their children to look on the paternal chief, yet not a word was heard of president of the United States: the little innocents were alone "taught to lisp the name of WASHINGTON." He was rather partial to children; their infantine playfulness appeared to please him, and many are the parents who at this day rejoice that his patriarchal hands have touched their offspring.†

---

* This was while he resided in Philadelphia.

† Thousands of children have since borne the name, given them at baptism, of George Washington. In the *Londonderry* (Ireland) *Journal*, February 30, 1783, is the following item: "Whereas, on February 14, 1783, it pleased kind Providence to confer on Mathew Neely, of Burnally, parish of Tamlaghtsinlagan, and county of Londonderry, a man-child, whose appearance is promising and amiable, and hopes the Being who first caused him to exist will grant him grace.

"Also, in consideration and in remembrance of the many heroic deeds done by that universally-renowned patriot, General Washington, the said Mathew Neely hath done himself the honor of calling the said man-child by the name of *George Washington Neely*, he being the first child known, or so called, in this kingdom, by the

General Washington was always a strict and decorous observer of the sabbath. He invariably attended divine service once a day, when within reach of a place of worship.* His respect for the clergy, as a body, was shown by public entertainments to them, the same as to the corps legislative and diplomatic; and among his bosom friends were the present venerable bishop of Pennsylvania,† and the late excellent prelate and ardent friend of American liberty, Doctor Carroll, archbishop of Baltimore.‡

name of Washington, that brilliant western star." See *Massachusetts Magazine*, i., 62, January, 1789. It would be very difficult to ascertain who was the first person so named in this country.

* Washington was a member, in full communion, of the Protestant Episcopal church, and was for many years before and after the Revolution, a vestryman in Truro parish, whose church (Pohick) built under his supervision, is yet standing. I have before me the original drawing of the ground-plan and elevation of that church, made by Washington himself. He was also a vestryman previous to the Revolution, in Fairfax parish, whose church, wherein he frequently worshipped, is yet standing, in the city of Alexandria. While president of the United States, and residing in New York, he attended Saint Paul's church; in Philadelphia, Christ church. He seldom went to the sanctuary in the afternoon, according to his own diary.

† Right Reverend William White, D. D., the first American bishop in the Protestant Episcopal church. He was a son of a Philadelphia lawyer, and was born in that city, on the fourth of April, 1748. The preaching of Whitefield greatly deepened his habitual and religious feelings, and on graduating at the college in Philadelphia, at the age of fifteen years, he commenced the study of theology. He was ordained a deacon in London in 1770, and before he returned, in 1772, he received priest's orders. He was first an assistant minister of Christ church, Philadelphia; and he was a faithful pastor in that parish for sixty-four years. He was chaplain to the continental Congress a short time in 1777; and in 1787 he and Doctor Provoost, of New York, were consecrated bishops. He was chiefly instrumental in framing the constitution of the church in America, and compiled its liturgy and canons. Among his last official labors was the preparation of instructions for missionaries going to China. That was in 1835, when he was eighty-eight years of age. He preached his last sermon in June, 1836, and on the seventeenth of the following month he expired, when little more than eighty-nine years old.

‡ Right Reverend John Carroll, D. D, the first bishop of the Roman Catholic church in the United States. He was born at Upper Marlborough, Maryland, on the eighth of January, 1735. At the age of thirteen years he was sent to the college of St. Omer, in French Flanders, where he remained until he was transferred to the Jes-

On Sunday no visiters were admitted to the president's house, save the immediate relatives of the family, with only one exception: Mr. Speaker Trumbull, since governor of Connecticut, and who had been confidential secretary to the chief in the War of the Revolution, was in the habit of spending an hour with the president, on Sunday evenings.* Trumbull practised the lesson of punctuality, which he learned in the service of the olden time, with such accuracy, that the porter, by consulting his clock, could tell when to stand ready to open to the *Speaker's Bell*, as it was called in the family, from the circumstance of no hand, other than the speaker's, touching the bell on the evenings of the sabbath.

---

uits' college at Liege, six years afterward. He was ordained a Jesuit priest in 1769, became a teacher in the college of Liege, and in 1773, when the Jesuits were expelled from France, he was obliged to abandon a professorship at Bruges, to which he had lately been appointed, and retire to England. He travelled much, and returned to his native country in 1775. He accompanied a committee of the continental Congress, on a political mission to Canada in the spring of the following year, and throughout the War for Independence, he was attached to the patriot cause. In 1786 he was appointed vicar-general of the Roman Catholic church in America. In 1790 he was consecrated a bishop, and the following year founded the college at Georgetown. On the invitation of Congress, he delivered a eulogy on Washington, in St. Peter's church, Baltimore, on the twenty-second of February, 1800. In 1808, Doctor Carroll was made archbishop, with four suffragan bishops. With every additional duty, his zeal for his Zion seemed to increase, and he labored faithfully until his death, which occurred at Baltimore, on the third of December, 1815, when he was eighty years of age.

* Jonathan Trumbull, son of the patriotic governor of Connecticut, of the same name. He was born at Lebanon, in March 1740, and graduated at Harvard college in 1759. From 1775 to the close of the campaign in 1778, he was paymaster to the army in the northern department. In 1780, he was appointed secretary and aid to General Washington, and in that situation he remained until the end of the war, in the enjoyment of the perfect confidence of the commander-in-chief. He was chosen a representative in the first Congress under the federal constitution, and in 1791 became speaker of the house of representatives. He was elevated to the senate in 1794, and in 1798 succeeded Oliver Wolcott as governor of his native state. He remained in office until his death, a period of eleven years. He died at Lebanon, on the seventh of August, 1809, at the age of sixty-nine years

The remarkable degree of admiration and awe that was felt by every one, upon the first approach to Washington, evidences the imposing power and sublimity which belongs to real greatness. Even the frequenters of the courts of princes were sensible of this exalted feeling, when in the presence of the hero, who, formed for the highest destinies, bore an impress from nature, which declared him to be one among the noblest of her works.*

Those who have only seen him as the leader of armies and the chief magistrate of the republic, can have but an imperfect idea of him when merged into the retired citizen, embosomed among his family and friends, cultivating the social and domestic virtues, and dispensing pleasure and happiness to all around him.

Persons in general have been in error, in supposing that there belonged to this dignified man nothing of the gentler sort—"no tear for pity." In the master-spirit in the direction of those vast events which gave a new empire to the world, the austerity of command could never destroy those kindlier feelings in which he delighted to indulge himself, and to inspire them in others. Stern he was, to all whom he deemed wanting in those high moral requisites, which dignify and adorn our natures—stern he was, to the disturbers of the repose of society, the violators of those institutions which promote peace and good will among men; but he was for-

* It is related of the Honorable Gouverneur Morris, who was remarkable for his freedom of deportment toward his friends, that on one occasion he offered a wager that he could treat General Washington with the same familiarity as he did others. This challenge was accepted, and the performance tried. Mr. Morris slapped Washington familiarly on the shoulder, and said, "How are you, this morning, general?" Washington made no reply, but turned his eyes upon Mr. Morris with a glance that fairly withered him. He afterward acknowledged, that nothing could induce him to attempt the same thing again

bearing toward the imperfections of human kind, where they arose from the passions only, and not from the depravity of the heart.

He was reserved toward the many; but there were a chosen few, who, having passed that barrier, were wooed by his kindly friendship to push their fortunes, till they finally gained footing in the citadel of his esteem.

He was tender, compassionate, and sympathizing. We have seen him shed tears of parental solicitude over the manifold errors and follies of our unworthy youth.* He shed a tear of sorrow for his suffering country in the dark hour of her destiny; and a tear of joy and gratitude to heaven for her deliverance, when, in 1789, he crossed the *bridge of Trenton*, where the hands of freemen " reared for him triumphal bowers," while a choir of innocents, with seraph chant, " welcomed the mighty chief once more," and " virgins fair, and matrons grave, strewed the hero's way with flowers."†

The journey of the first president to the seat of government was one continued triumph; but nowhere was it of so feeling a character as at the bridge of Trenton. That was, indeed, a classic ground. It was there, on a frozen surface, that, in 1776, was achieved the glorious event which restored the fast-failing fortunes of liberty, and gave to her drooping eagles a renewed and bolder flight. What a contrast to the chief must have been this spot in 1789, when no longer " a mercenary foe aimed against him the fatal blow;" when no more was heard

---

* See the correspondence between Washington and young Custis during the collegiate days of the latter, appended to the *Memoir*.

† A more minute account of Washington's reception at Trenton, when on his way to New York, in the spring of 1789, to be inaugurated the first president of the United States, will be found in another chapter.

the roar of combat, the shouts of the victors, the groans of the dying—but the welcome of thousands to liberty's great defender—the heartfelt homage of freemen to the deliverer of his country. The president alighted from his carriage, and approached the bridge uncovered. As he passed under the triumphal arch, a cherub, in the form of a young girl, perched amid the foliage that covered it, crowned him with laurel which will never fade, while the sweetest minstrelsy from human lips filled the air, as the hero trod on his way of flowers. Washington then shed tears—tears of the deepest emotion.

The merit of these appropriate and classical decorations is due to the late Mrs. Stockton, of Princeton, a lady of superior literary acquirements and refined taste. She was familiarly called *duchess*, from her elegance and dignity of manners. She was a most ardent patriot during the War of the Revolution, and, with the Stockton family, was marked for persecution on the ruthless invasion of the Jerseys.* This distinguished lady was the

---

* Like others of the signers of the great Declaration, Mr. Stockton was marked for peculiar vengeance by the enemy. So suddenly did the flying Americans pass by Princeton, in the autumn of 1776, and so soon were the Hessian vultures and their British companions on the trail, that he had barely time to remove his family to a place of safety before his beautiful mansion was filled with rude soldiery. The house was pillaged; the horses and stock were driven away; the furniture was converted into fuel; the choice old wines in the cellar were drunk; the valuable library and all the papers of Mr. Stockton were committed to the flames, and the estate was laid waste. The plate had been hastily buried in the woods, in boxes. A treacherous servant revealed their place of concealment, and two of the boxes were disinterred and rifled of their contents; the other was saved. Mr. Stockton and family took refuge with a friend in Monmouth county. His place of concealment was discovered by a party of refugee loyalists, who entered the house at night, dragged him from his bed, and treating him with every indignity which malice could invent, hurried him to Amboy, and from thence to New York, where he was confined in the loathsome provost jail. There he suffered dreadfully; and when, through the interposition of

grandmother of Mr. Secretary Rush, who is "doubly blessed" in his Revolutionary ancestry; both his father and grandfather having signed the Declaration of Independence—a most honored distinction, and, we believe, enjoyed by no other citizen of our extensive American empire.*

Congress, he was released, his constitution was hopelessly shattered, and he did not live to see the independence of his country achieved. He died at *Morven*, his seat at Princeton, in February, 1781, blessed to the last with the tender and affectionate attentions of his Annis, whom he called "the best of women." Night and day she was at his bedside, and when his spirit was about to depart, she wrote, impromptu, several verses, of which the following is indicative of her feelings:—

"Oh, could I take the fate to him assigned,
And leave the helpless family their head,
How pleased, how peaceful to my lot resigned,
I'd quit the nurse's station for the bed!"

Lossing's Field-Book of the Revolution.

Mrs. Ellet, in her *Women of the Revolution*, has given an interesting biography of Mrs. Annis Stockton. She relates, that when that excellent lady heard of the destruction of the library, she remarked, that "there were two books in it she would like to have saved—the Bible and Young's Night Thoughts." Tradition says, that these two books were the only ones left.

* Honorable Richard Rush, of Philadelphia. When Mr. Custis wrote, he was in the cabinet of President Adams, as secretary of the treasury, and in the prime of life, being about forty-seven years of age. He was graduated at Princeton college in 1797, became a lawyer, and in 1811 was appointed attorney-general of Pennsylvania. He became the United States attorney-general in 1814. He was secretary of state under President Monroe, and then succeeded John Quincy Adams as minister at the court of St. James. There he remained over seven years, when Mr. Adams called him into his cabinet. During that time he negotiated some very important treaties. At the request of President Jackson, Mr. Rush went to London, in 1836, to obtain Mr. Smithson's legacy to the United States, out of the English court of chancery. In August, 1838, he returned with the entire sum. In 1847, President Polk appointed him minister to France. After his return he remained in private life, at his beautiful seat of Sydenham, near Philadelphia, where, on the verge of octogenarian honors (having been born in 1780) he died on the 1st. of August, 1859. In 1857, Mr. Rush prepared and published a valuable little volume, entitled, *Washington in Domestic Life,* from original letters and manuscripts then in his possession.

CHAPTER III.

BATTLE OF PRINCETON AND DEATH OF GENERAL MERCER.

Errors of History — Manner of Mercer's Fall and Reception of Death-Wounds — Taken to Clark's House, near the Battle-Field — Major Lewis sent to take Care of Him — His accurate Knowledge of his Situation — His Explanation of his Wounds — His Death — His Burial-Place — Anecdote of his Early Patriotism — Death of Captain Leslie — Doctor Rush — The Seventeenth British Regiment — Composition of the American Army — The Die cast at Princeton — Washington on the Battle-Field there — Colonel Fitzgerald, his Aid-de-Camp.

There has always been an erroneous impression on the public mind, concerning the death of General Mercer, who fell at the battle of Princeton, January 3, 1777.*

* The battle at Princeton occurred a few days after Washington's triumph at Trenton, on the morning of the twenty-sixth of December, 1776, and was the close of a melancholy, yet brilliant chapter in the history of the old War for Independence. A little while before, Washington and his army had been expelled from the east side of the Hudson river, and for the space of three weeks were flying across New Jersey before a victorious pursuer, who was so close upon him at times, that each could hear the martial music of the other. The flight ended and repose came only when the Americans had crossed the Delaware, taken all the boats with them, and placed a broad and rapid stream filled with ice, between themselves and the foe.

The British formed small encampments along the Jersey side of the Delaware, from Trenton to Burlington, and below. At Trenton were a thousand Hessian and some British cavalry. On Christmas night, Washington with his refreshed troops recrossed the Delaware, eight miles above Trenton, and early in the morning, fell upon and captured those hirelings, and, with his prisoners, went back to the Pennsylvania shore.

Once more Washington recrossed the Delaware, and with five thousand soldiers, encamped there. On the second of January Cornwallis, with veteran British troops, came from Princeton to attack him. There was some fighting at Trenton just at evening, when the British general, feeling sure that he could capture the whole American army in the morning, took rest for the night. The Americans were in great peril. They could not retreat across the river, and were too feeble to fight so large an army as that before them, with any chance for success. So, at midnight,

We offer the homage of our veneration for this martyr's memory, by giving to his adopted country and the world authentic particulars of the heroism and devotion that attended his fall. Our authority is derived from the late Major George Lewis, the nephew of the commander-in-chief, and captain of his Guard, and who was sent in with a flag to afford to the wounded general every possible comfort and assistance.

It was immediately after the sharp conflict at the fence* between the advanced guard of the American army, led by General Mercer, and the British seventeenth regiment, and the retreat of the Americans through the orchard near to Clark's house and barn, that General Mercer, while exerting himself to rally his

---

the ground having frozen so as to allow them to roll away their cannon, the whole army decamped, by an unfrequented road, toward Princeton, leaving their camp-fires burning, to deceive the British. In the morning Cornwallis was mortified to find his expected prey had escaped; and the first intimation that he had of the direction in which he had fled, was the booming of cannon at Princeton, just at sunrise, which, though a clear morning, and in midwinter, he mistook for distant thunder. Then commenced the battle of Princeton between a part of Washington's army, under General Mercer, and some British troops that had just begun their march to join Cornwallis at Princeton. In that battle the Americans were victorious, and going into winter-quarters among the hills near Morristown immediately afterward, Washington, by sending out detachments and otherwise, drove the enemy out of New Jersey, except at Brunswick and Amboy.

* When the British brigade, under Lieutenant-Colonel Mawhood, first discovered the Americans, under Mercer, near Princeton, they wheeled, and both parties rushed forward to cross Stony brook, then a full and frozen stream, at Worth's mills, in order to gain the high and advantageous ground beyond, toward Princeton. The British crossed first, but Mercer and his troops soon reached the house and orchards of William Clark, eastward of the present turnpike from Princeton to Trenton. Mercer there perceived the British line approaching from the opposite side of the height, and pushed through the orchard to a hedge-fence, from behind which his riflemen discharged a deadly volley. It was quickly returned by the enemy, who instantly charged. The Americans, armed only with rifles and muskets, could not withstand the furious attack of the British bayonets. After the third fire they abandoned the fence and fled in great disorder.

broken troops, was brought to the ground by a blow from the butt of a musket. He was on foot at this time—the gray horse he rode at the beginning of the action having been disabled by a ball in the fore-leg The British soldiers were not at first aware of the general's rank, for, the morning being very cold, he wore a surtout over his uniform. So soon as they discovered that he was a general officer, they shouted that they had got the rebel general, and cried, "Call for quarters you d—d rebel!" Mercer to the most undaunted courage united a quick and ardent temperament: he replied with indignation to his enemies, while their bayonets were at his bosom, that he deserved not the name of rebel; and, determining to die as he had lived, a true and honored soldier of liberty, lunged with his sword at the nearest man. They then bayoneted him, and left him for dead.

Upon the retreat of the enemy, the wounded general was conveyed to Clark's house, immediately adjoining the field of battle.* The information that the commander-in-chief first received of the fall of his old companion in arms of the war of 1755, and beloved officer, was that he had expired under his numerous wounds; and it was not until the American army was in full march for Morristown that the chief was undeceived, and learned, to his great gratification, that Mercer, though fearfully wounded, was yet alive.† Upon the first halt

---

* This was then a new house, owned by Thomas Clark, a member of the Society of Friends, or Quakers. It is yet [1859] standing, and in possession of a member of the Clark family. There General Mercer was nursed by Sarah Clark and a colored woman belonging to the family. The house stands on the south side of the battlefield, and about a mile and a quarter south of Princeton.

† Washington wrote to the president of Congress on the fifth of January, 1777, from Pluckemin, New Jersey, giving an account of events in which he had been engaged since his communication from Trenton, on the first of the month, and men-

at Somerset courthouse, Washington despatched Major George Lewis with a flag and a letter to Lord Cornwallis, requesting that every possible attention might be shown to the wounded general, and permission that

tioned the death of General Mercer. Two days afterward he wrote: "I am happy to inform you, that the account of General Mercer's death, transmitted in my last, was premature, though it was mentioned as certain by many who saw him after he was wounded. By intelligence from Princeton yesterday evening, he was alive, and seemed as if he would do well. Unhappily he is a prisoner. Had it not been for the information of his death, I would have tried to bring him away, though I believe it could not have been effected."

General Mercer died on the twelfth, at Clark's house, and was buried there, but two days afterward his remains were removed to Philadelphia, and interred with military honors, in Christ churchyard. A committee of the Congress was appointed to consider what honor should be paid to the memories of General Warren, killed on Breed's hill on the seventeenth of June, 1775, and to General Mercer. The committee reported on the eighth of April, recommending the erection of a monument in Boston, with suitable inscriptions, in honor of Warren, and another at Fredericksburg, in Virginia, in honor of Mercer, with the following inscription:—

'SACRED TO THE MEMORY OF
HUGH MERCER,
BRIGADIER-GENERAL IN THE ARMY OF
THE UNITED STATES.
HE DIED ON THE 12TH OF JANUARY, 1777, OF THE
WOUNDS HE RECEIVED ON THE 3D OF THE SAME MONTH,
NEAR PRINCETON, IN NEW JERSEY,
BRAVELY DEFENDING THE
LIBERTIES OF AMERICA.
THE CONGRESS OF THE UNITED STATES,
IN TESTIMONY OF HIS VIRTUES, AND THEIR GRATITUDE,
HAVE CAUSED THIS MONUMENT TO BE ERECTED."

They also resolved, that "the eldest son of General Warren, and the youngest son of General Mercer, be educated, from this time, at the expense of the United States." Neither monument was ever erected, but the children were educated at the expense of the government. General Mercer's son (the late Colonel Hugh Mercer, of Fredericksburg, Virginia), was then about six months old, having been born in July, 1776. He was educated at William and Mary college, in Virginia, when Bishop Madison was its president. He was for many years colonel of the militia of his native county, and an active magistrate. For five consecutive years he was a member of the Virginia legislature, and for many years was president of the Branch Bank of Virginia, at Fredericksburg. He died at his seat, called *The Sentry-Box*, in 1855, at the age of seventy-nine years. A portrait of this "Child of the Republic" may be found in Lossing's *Field-Book of the Revolution*.

BATTLE OF PRINCETON AND DEATH OF MERCER. 183

Lewis should remain with him to minister to his wants. To both requests his lordship yielded a willing assent, and ordered his staff-surgeon to attend upon General Mercer. Upon an examination of the wounds, the British surgeon remarked, that although they were many and severe, he was disposed to believe that they would not prove dangerous. Mercer, bred to the profession of an army-surgeon in Europe,* said to young Lewis, "Raise up my right arm, George, and this gentleman will there discover the smallest of my wounds, but which will prove the most fatal. Yes sir, that is a fellow that will very soon do my business." He languished till the twelfth, and expired in the arms of Lewis, admired and lamented by the whole army. During the period that he lay on the couch of suffering, he exonerated his enemies from the foul accusation which they bore, not only in 1777 but for half a century since, viz., of their having bayoneted a general officer after he had surrendered his sword, and become a prisoner-of-war—declaring that he only relinquished his sword when his arm had become powerless to wield it.† He paid the homage of his whole heart

---

* He was a native of Scotland, and was an assistant-surgeon in the battle of Culloden, which decided the fate of Charles Edward, the Young Scotch Pretender to the throne of England, as the lineal representative of the Stuart family, who were expelled in the person of James II., in 1688. Soon after that battle Mercer came to America, took up his residence at Fredericksburg, and was engaged in the practice of medicine and the business of an apothecary there, when the War for Independence broke out. He espoused the cause, left his profession, took the command of three regiments of minute-men in 1775, and, in 1776, organized and drilled a large body of Virginia militia. Congress gave him the commission of a brigadier on the fifth of June, 1775, and appointed him to the command of the flying camp of ten thousand men, authorized to be raised in the middle states.

† "Lewis," says Mr. Custis, elsewhere, "mentioned to General Mercer the extreme indignation which prevailed in the American army, together with threats of retaliation at the inhuman treatment it was supposed the general had received from the enemy, viz., that he had been bayoneted after having surrendered and asked for

to the person and character of the commander-in-chief, rejoiced with true soldierly pride in the triumphs of Trenton and Princeton, in both of which he had borne a conspicuous part, and offered up his fervent prayers for the final success of the cause of American Independence.

Thus lived and died Hugh Mercer, a name that will for ever be associated with momentous events in the history of the War of the Revolution. When a grateful posterity shall bid the trophied memorial rise to the martyrs who sealed with their blood the charter of an empire's liberties, there will not be wanting a monument to him whom Washington mourned as "the worthy and brave General Mercer."

General Mercer lies buried, in Philadelphia, where a plain slab, with the initials H. M., denotes the last earthly dwelling of the patriot brave,

> "Who sunk to rest,
> With his country's wishes blest."*

quarter: when the magnanimous Mercer observed, "The tale which you have heard, George, is untrue. My death is owing to myself. I was on foot, endeavoring to rally my men, who had given way before the superior discipline of the enemy, when I was brought to the ground by a blow from a musket. At the same moment the enemy discovered my rank, exulted in their having taken the rebel general, as they termed me, and bid me ask for quarters. I felt that I deserved not so opprobrious an epithet, and determined to die, as I had lived, an honored soldier in a just and righteous cause; and without begging my life or making reply, I lunged with my sword at the nearest man. They then bayoneted and left me."

* This was written in October, 1839. A plain marble slab was afterward placed at the head of his grave, with the simple inscription: "*In Memory of General Hugh Mercer, who fell at Princeton, Jan. 3d, 1777.*" There his remains lay until 1840, when his countrymen, of the St. Andrew's, and the Thistle societies, removed them to Laurel Hill cemetery, and erected a fine white marble monument over them, near the chapel. The monument bears the following inscriptions, which give the most important incidents of his public life. *East side*, or principal front: "Dedicated to the Memory of GENERAL HUGH MERCER, who fell for the Sacred Cause of Human Liberty, and American Independence, in the Battle of Princeton. He poured out his blood for a Generous Principle." *West side:* "GENERAL MERCER, a Physician

We shall give a single anecdote of the subject of the foregoing memoir, to show the pure and high-souled principles that actuated the patriots and soldiers of the days of our country's trial.

Virginia at first organized two regiments for the common cause. When it was determined to raise a third, there were numerous applications for commissions; and these being mostly from men of fortune and family interest, there was scarcely an application for a rank less than a field officer. During the sitting of the house of burgesses upon this important motion, a plain but soldierly-looking individual handed up to the speaker's chair a scrap of paper, on which was written, "Hugh Mercer will serve his adopted country and the cause of liberty *in any rank or station* to which he may be appointed." This, from a veteran soldier, bred in European camps,

---

of Fredericksburg, in Virginia, was distinguished for his skill and learning, his gentleness and decision, his refinement and humanity, his elevated honor, and his devotion to the great cause of Civil and Religious Liberty." *North side:* "GENERAL MERCER, a native of Scotland, was an assistant-surgeon in the Battle of Culloden, and the companion of WASHINGTON in the Indian Wars of 1755 and 1756. He received a *Medal* from the Corporation of Philadelphia, for his courage and conduct in the Expedition against the Indian Settlement of Kittanning." *South side:* "The St. Andrew's Society of Philadelphia offer this humble tribute to the memory of an illustrious BROTHER. When a grateful posterity shall bid the trophied memorial rise to the martyrs who sealed with their blood the charter of an Empire's liberties, there shall not be wanted a monument to him whom WASHINGTON mourned as the worthy and brave MERCER." General Mercer was about fifty-six years of age when he was slain.

The funeral ceremonies on the occasion of the re-interment of the remains of General Mercer, were very imposing. They took place on the twenty-ninth of November, 1840. The pall was borne by Commodores Read, Biddle, and Stewart, and Colonel Miller. The first troop of city cavalry, whose predecessors took part in the battle in which Mercer was mortally wounded, composed the guard of honor (there being at that time, not a single survivor of the original corps); and William B. Reed, Esq., grandson of General Joseph Reed, of the Revolution, pronounced an eloquent oration.

the associate of Washington in the war of 1755,* and known to stand high in his confidence and esteem, was all-sufficient for a body of patriots and statesmen such as composed the Virginia house of burgesses in the days of the Revolution. The appointment of Mercer to the command of the third Virginia regiment was carried instanter.

It was while the commander-in-chief reined up his horse, upon approaching the spot in a ploughed field where lay the gallant Colonel Haslet† mortally wounded, that he perceived some British soldiers supporting an officer, and upon inquiring his name and rank, was answered, Captain Leslie. Doctor Benjamin Rush,‡ who formed a part of the general's suite, earnestly asked, "A son of the Earl of Levin?" to which the soldiers replied in the affirmative. The doctor then addressed the general-in-chief: "I beg your excellency to permit this wounded officer to be placed under my especial care, that I may return, in however small a degree, a part of

* Mercer was with Washington on the Virginia frontier in the French and Indian war.

† Colonel Haslet was in command of Delaware troops, and had done noble service on Long Island and at White Plains. In the engagement, at the latter place, he was the first to take post on Chatterton's hill, where the principal battle was fought, with his own and some Maryland troops and militia, in all about sixteen hundred men.

‡ Benjamin Rush was born near Philadelphia, on the fifth of January, 1745. He graduated at Princeton college, in 1760, commenced the study of medicine the next year, and in 1766 went to Edinburgh, where, two years afterward, he received the degree of M.D. He returned to Philadelphia in 1769, where he commenced the practice of medicine, and was soon afterward elected professor of chemistry in the College of Pennsylvania. He was chosen a member of the continental Congress in 1776, and in April, 1777, he was appointed surgeon-general of the military hospitals of the middle department. From that period until his death he took an active part in public affairs—politics, science, and general literature. He stands in the highest rank of American physicians and philosophers. Doctor Rush died on the eighteenth of April, 1813, in the sixty-ninth year of his age.

of the obligations I owe to his worthy father for the many kindnesses received at his hands while I was a student in Edinburgh." The request was immediately granted; but, alas! poor Leslie was soon "past all surgery." He died the same evening, after receiving every possible kindness and attention, and was buried the next day at Pluckemin with the honors of war; his companions, as they lowered his remains to the soldier's last rest, shedding tears over the grave of a much-loved commander.

The battle of Princeton, for the time it lasted and the numbers engaged, was the most fatal to our officers of any action during the whole of the Revolutionary war— the Americans losing one general, two colonels, one major, and three captains, killed*—while the martial prowess of our enemy shone not with more brilliant lustre, in any one of their combats during their long career, of arms than did the courage and discipline of the 17th British regiment on the third of January, 1777.† Indeed, Washington himself, during the height of the conflict, pointed out this gallant corps to his officers, exclaiming, "See how those noble fellows fight! Ah! gentlemen, when shall we be able to keep an army long enough together to display a discipline equal to our enemies."‡

* These were General Mercer, Colonels Haslet and Potter, Major Morris, and Captains Shippen, Fleming, and Neal.

† This was Colonel Mawhood's regiment, and the one that drove the Americans from the hedge fence, at the point of the bayonet.

‡ During the whole of the year 1776, Washington frequently pressed upon the attention of Congress, the necessity for establishing a system of long enlistments in the army, for every day the evils of short enlistments were felt. Up to the close of 1776, the chief dependence of the army was upon the militia. "Who," Washington said in a letter to the president of Congress, toward the close of December,

The regular troops that constituted the grand army at the close of the campaign of '76 were the fragments of many regiments, worn down by constant and toilsome marches, and suffering of every sort, in the depth of

"come in, you can not tell how; go, you can not tell when; and act, you can not tell where; consume your provisions, exhaust your stores, and leave you at a critical moment." He then urged the establishment of a standing army, sufficient for the exigencies of the case, and said: "In my judgment this is not a time to stand upon expense; our funds are not the only object of consideration." He then informed the Congress that he had taken the responsibility of offering to regiment recruits, and to place them on the continental establishment as to rank and pay, and added: "It may be thought that I am going a good deal out of the line of my duty to adopt these measures, or to advise thus freely. A character to lose, an estate to forfeit, the inestimable blessings of liberty at stake, and a life devoted, must be my excuse."

The Congress had already resolved to establish a grand army of eighty-eight battalions of seven hundred and fifty men each, to be raised in the several states; and their confidence in Washington was manifested by their clothing him with the absolute powers of a military dictator, for six months. And a week after the foregoing letter to the Congress was written, they authorized the raising of sixteen additional battalions, and at the same time thus defined by resolution, the extraordinary powers which they had given to the commander-in-chief:—

"This Congress, having maturely considered the present crisis, and having perfect reliance on the wisdom, vigor, and uprightness of General Washington, do hereby—

"Resolve, That General Washington shall be, and he is hereby, vested with full, ample, and complete powers to raise and collect together, in the most speedy and effectual manner, from any or all of these United States, sixteen battalions of infantry, in addition to those already voted by Congress; to appoint officers for the said battalions of infantry; to raise, officer, and equip three thousand light-horse, three regiments of artillery, and a corps of engineers, and to establish their pay; to apply to any of the states for such aid of the militia as he shall judge necessary; to form such magazines, and in such places, as he shall think proper; to displace and appoint all officers under the rank of brigadier-general, and to fill up all vacancies in every other department in the American army; to take, wherever he may be, whatever he may want for the use of the army, if the inhabitants will not sell it, allowing a reasonable price for the same; to arrest and confine persons who refuse to take the continental currency, or are otherwise disaffected to the American cause, and return to the states of which they are citizens their names, and the nature of their offences, together with the witnesses to prove them.

"That the foregoing powers be vested in General Washington for and during the term of six months from the date hereof, unless sooner determined by Congress."
Journals of Congress, December 27, 1776.

winter. The fine regiment of Smallwood, composed of the flower of the Maryland youth, and which in the June preceding, marched into Philadelphia eleven hundred strong, was, on the third of January, reduced to scarcely sixty men, and commanded by a captain.* In fact, the bulk of what was then called the grand army consisted of the Pennsylvania militia and volunteers—citizen-soldiers who had left their comfortable homes at the call of their country, and were enduring the rigors of a winter campaign. On the morning of the battle of Princeton, they had been eighteen hours under arms, and harassed by a long night's march. Was it then to be wondered at that they should have given way before the veteran bayonets of their fresh and well-appointed foe?

The heroic devotion of Washington was not wanting in the exigencies of this memorable day. He was aware that his hour was come to redeem the pledge he had laid on the altar of his country when first he took up arms in her cause: to win her liberties or perish in the attempt. Defeat at Princeton would have amounted to the annihilation of America's last hope; for, independent of the enemy's forces in front, Cornwallis, with the flower of the British army, eight thousand strong, was already panting close on the rear.† It was, indeed, the very

---

* Colonel Smallwood's battalion was one of the finest in the army, in dress, equipment, and discipline. Their scarlet-and-buff uniforms, and well-burnished arms, contrasted strongly with those of the New England troops, and were "distinguished at this time," says Graydon, "by the most fashionable-cut coat, the most *macaroni* cocked hat, and hottest blood, in the Union." In the battle on Long Island, at the close of the previous August, this fine corps had been dreadfully decimated. Full two hundred and fifty of them perished in the last deadly struggle between Stirling and Cornwallis, near the shores of Gowanus creek.

† When Cornwallis heard the firing at Princeton, on the morning of the third of January, he hastened in that direction with his whole force, for he considered his valuable stores at Brunswick in danger. He reached Princeton just as the Ameri-

crisis of the struggle. In the hurried and imposing events of little more than one short week, liberty endured her greatest agony. What, then, is due to the fame and memories of that sacred band who, with the master of liberty at their head, breasted the storm at this fearful crisis of their country's destiny?*

The heroism of Washington on the field of Princeton is matter of history. We have often enjoyed a touching reminiscence of that ever-memorable event from the late Colonel Fitzgerald, who was aid to the chief, and who never related the story of his general's danger and almost miraculous preservation, without adding to his tale the homage of a tear.

The aid-de-camp had been ordered to bring up the troops from the rear of the column, when the band under General Mercer became engaged. Upon returning to

---

cans had secured their victory, who, though wearied and worn with fatigue and want of sleep, were in pursuit of the fugitive British soldiers who had fled from Princeton toward Brunswick. Cornwallis pursued Washington as far as the Millstone river, when he gave up the chase.

* "Achievements so stirring," says the eloquent Charles Botta, "gained for the American commander a very great reputation, and were regarded with wonder by all nations, as well as by the Americans. The prudence, constancy, and noble intrepidity of Washington, were admired and applauded by all. By unanimous consent, he was declared to be the savior of his country; all proclaimed him equal to the most renowned commanders of antiquity, and especially distinguished him by the name of the AMERICAN FABIUS. His name was in the mouths of all; he was celebrated by the pens of the most distinguished writers. The most illustrious personages of Europe lavished upon him their praises and their congratulations. The American general, therefore, wanted neither a cause full of grandeur to defend, nor occasion for the acquisition of glory, nor genius to avail himself of it, nor the renown due to his triumphs, nor an entire generation of men perfectly well disposed to render him homage."

It is said Frederick the Great of Prussia declared, that the achievements of Washington and his little band of compatriots, between the twenty-fifth of December, 1776, and the fourth of January, 1777, a space of ten days, were the most brilliant of any in the annals of military achievements.

the spot where he had left the commander-in-chief, he was no longer there, and, upon looking around, the aid discovered him endeavoring to rally the line which had been thrown into disorder by a rapid on-set of the foe.* Washington, after several ineffectual efforts to restore the fortunes of the fight, is seen to rein up his horse, with his head to the enemy, and in that position to become immovable. It was a last appeal to his soldiers, and seemed to say, Will you give up your general to the foe? Such an appeal was not made in vain. The discomfitted Americans rally on the instant, and form into line; the enemy halt, and dress their line; the American chief is between the adverse posts, as though he had been placed there, a target for both. The arms of both lines are levelled. Can escape from death be possible? Fitzgerald, horror-struck at the danger of his beloved commander, dropped the reins upon his horse's neck, and drew his hat over his face, that he might not see him die. A roar of musketry succeeds, and then a shout. It is the shout of victory. The aid-de-camp ventures to raise his eyes, and O, glorious sight! the enemy are broken and flying, while dimly amidst the glimpses of the smoke is seen the chief, "alive, unharmed, and with-

---

* Mawhood and his regiment pressed forward in vigorous pursuit of the scattered Americans, and it was while endeavoring to rally them that Mercer fell. The British were soon checked by Washington, who was advancing over a hill at the head of a column of regulars and Pennsylvania militia. Perceiving at a glance the desperate state of affairs, Washington ordered Captain Moulder to form his field-battery for immediate action, while the chief, in person, should attempt to rally the Americans. His stately form was seen by Mawhood, as he rode backward and forward, and by word and action called upon the panic-stricken troops to turn upon the foe. He ordered a halt, in battle line, and drew up his artillery with the intention of charging upon Moulder to capture his battery. This was the movement alluded to in the text.

out a wound," waving his hat, and cheering his comrades to the pursuit.

Colonel Fitzgerald, celebrated as one of the finest horsemen in the American army, now dashed his rowels in his charger's flanks, and, heedless of the dead and dying in his way, flew to the side of his chief, exclaiming, "Thank God! your excellency is safe!" The favorite aid, a gallant and warm-hearted son of Erin, a man of thews and sinews, and "albeit unused to the melting mood," now gave loose rein to his feelings, and wept like a child, for joy.

Washington, ever calm amid scenes of the greatest excitement, affectionately grasped the hand of his aid and friend, and then ordered—"Away, my dear colonel, and bring up the troops—the day is our own!"*

---

* Being severely galled by the grape-shot of the Americans, and perceiving Hitchcock's and another continental regiment advancing from behind the republican column, Mawhood wheeled and retreated toward the high ground in the rear, leaving his artillery upon the field. They fled to the Trenton road in confusion, crossed the bridge over Stony Brook, and hastened to join Cornwallis, then on his march from Trenton.

CHAPTER IV.

BATTLE OF GERMANTOWN.*

Washington undismayed by Defeat—Position of the British Army—March of the Americans upon Germantown—Anecdote of Pulaski—An Intoxicated General Officer—Surprise of the Enemy—Retreat into Chew's House—Attempt to Dislodge the British—A Council of War—Intense Fog—Alarm and Panic among the Americans—Washington in Danger—Result of the Battle—General Nash Mortally Wounded—His Presence of Mind—His Death—The Undisciplined Americans—Congress Complimentary—How near the Americans were Victorious—Remarks of the French Minister on the Battle of Germantown—March of the Army to Valley Forge—Washington's Compassion.

Undismayed by his defeat at the battle of the Brandywine, Washington hovered on the march of his enemy; not with the hope of saving Philadelphia, but with the determination to strike yet another blow before the conclusion of the campaign of 1777. Charmed with the courage displayed by his undisciplined soldiers, when opposed to a superior army of veterans, in the combat at Chad's ford, the American general anxiously watched for an opportunity of again measuring his sword with that of his skilful and far better appointed adversary, though vast were the advantages in favor of the latter.†

---

* Written, and published in the *National Intelligencer*, on the twenty-second February, 1841.

† The retreat of the Americans after the disastrous contests near the Brandywine creek, in Chester county, Pennsylvania, on the eleventh of September, 1777, was precipitate, and at first confused. Lafayette, who had been severely wounded, has left a vivid picture of the scene. Chester road, he said, was crowded with the flying fugitives, cannon, baggage-carts, and everything else pertaining to an army, even before the combats had entirely ceased; and the confusion of the scene was enhanced by the roar of cannon and the rattle of musketry in the rear. On the banks of a

Sir William Howe,* flushed with his victory over the American grand army, and the occupation of the then capital of the American Union, and presuming that his foe was sufficiently subdued to give him no further molestation for the remainder of the campaign, quartered a large portion of his troops in the village of Germantown, about seven miles from the city of Philadelphia, while he despatched considerable detachments toward the positions still held by the American forces on the Delaware.†

Washington promptly embraced the opportunity thus offered of striking at his powerful adversary with fair hopes of success. Gathering together all the troops within his reach, and having received some reinforce-

stream, near Chester, twelve miles from the battlefield, the flight of the fugitives was checked by their own officers, and Washington coming up toward midnight, restored order. The next morning they continued their retreat toward Chester; while Howe, as usual, neglecting to follow up a capital advantage, remained two or three days near the scene of the conflict.

Washington and his broken army halted at Germantown, rested there one day, and then recrossed the Schuylkill, to attack the advancing foe. Both parties were prepared for action, when a heavy rain so interferred, that it was indefinitely postponed. Then commenced a series of marches and counter-marches. Sir William Howe endeavoring to take possession of Philadelphia, and Washington doing all in his power to keep him on the lower side of the Schuylkill. Howe succeeded, and Washington took post within about fourteen miles of Germantown, from which point he advanced to the engagement delineated in the text.

* General William Howe had been commander-in-chief of the British forces in America since the retirement of General Gage, in the autumn of 1775. In the summer of 1776, a British fleet, commanded by his brother, Admiral Lord Howe, came upon the American coast, and at this time was co-operating with the land forces. After the battle on Long Island, at the close of August, 1776, in which the British were victorious, General Howe was knighted, and created a baronet. From that time he was called Sir William Howe.

† These positions were Billingsport, Fort Mercer, at Red Bank, on the Jersey shore, and Fort Mifflin, upon Mud island, near the Pennsylvania shore, below Philadelphia. The channel of the river was obstructed by *chevaux de frise*, constructed by the Americans upon a plan said to have been suggested by Doctor Franklin.

ments, although they consisted mostly of new levies, the American army broke up its encampment, about fifteen miles from Germantown, on the night of the third of October, and advanced upon the enemy in three columns, in order of battle.

During the night march, several incidents occurred that might be deemed ominous of the fortunes of the coming day. The celebrated Count Pulaski, who was charged with the service of watching the enemy and gaining intelligence, was said to have been found asleep in a farm-house. But although the gallant Pole might have been overtaken by slumber, from the great fatigue growing out of the duties of the advanced guard, yet no soldier was more wide awake in the moment of combat than the intrepid and chivalric Count Pulaski.*

---

* Count Casimir Pulaski was a native of Lithuania, in Poland. He was educated for the law, but stirring military events had their influence upon his mind, and he entered the army. With his father, the old Count Pulaski, he was engaged in the rebellion against Stanislaus, king of Poland, in 1769. The old count was taken prisoner, and put to death. In 1770, the young Count Casimir was elected commander-in-chief of the insurgents, but was not able to collect a competent force to act efficiently, for a pestilence had swept off 250,000 Poles the previous year. In 1771, himself and thirty-nine others entered Warsaw, disguised as peasants, for the purpose of seizing the king. The object was to place him at the head of the army, force him to act in that position, and call around him the Poles to beat back the Russian forces which Catharine had sent against them. They succeeded in taking him from his carriage in the streets, and carrying him out of the city; but were obliged to leave him, not far from the walls, to effect their own escape. Pulaski's little army was soon afterward defeated, and he entered the service of the Turks, who were fighting the Russians. His estates were confiscated, and himself outlawed. He went to Paris, had an interview there with Doctor Franklin, and came to America in 1777. He joined the army under Washington, and, on the fifteenth of September, 1777 (four days after the battle of Brandywine, in which he behaved gallantly), he was appointed to the command of a troop of cavalry. His legion did good service at the North. Early in the spring of 1778 he was ordered to Little Egg Harbor, on the New Jersey coast. His force consisted of cavalry and infantry, with a single field-piece from Proctor's artillery. While on his way from Trenton to Little Egg Harbor, and when within eight miles of the coast, he was surprised by a

The delay in the arrival of the ammunition-wagons was productive of the most serious consequences in the action of the succeeding day. The general officer to whom the blame of this delay was attached was afterward discovered in a state of intoxication, lying in the corner of a fence. Lieutenant Benjamin Grymes, of the Life-Guard,* grasping the delinquent by the collar, placed him on his legs, and bade him go and do his duty. This bold proceeding on the part of a subaltern toward a general officer was certainly at variance with all rules or orders of discipline; but the exigency of the moment, and the degraded spectacle that an officer of high rank had presented to the eyes of the soldiery, would seem to have warranted a proceeding that, under different circumstances, must be considered as subversive of all military discipline. Grymes was a bold, brave soldier, enthusiastically attached to the cause of his country, and foremost among the asserters of her liberties. The general officer of whom we have spoken was brought to a court-martial and cashiered.†

party of British, and a large portion of the infantry were bayoneted. Julien, a deserter from his corps, had given information of his position; the surprise was complete. His loss was forty men, among them Lieutenant-Colonel Baron de Botzen. Pulaski was ordered to the South in February, 1779, and was in active service under Lincoln until the siege of Savannah, in October of that year, where he was mortally wounded. His banner, made of crimson silk, and beautifully embroidered by the Moravian sisters of Bethlehem, was preserved, and carried to Baltimore. He was taken to the United States brig *Wasp*, where he died. He was buried under a large tree on St. Helen's island, about fifty miles from Savannah, by his first lieutenant and personal friend, Charles Litomiski. Funeral honors were paid to his memory at Charleston; and, on the 29th of November, Congress voted the erection of a monument to his memory. Like other monuments ordered by the continental Congress, the stone for Pulaski's is yet in the quarry. The citizens of Savannah have reared a fine marble obelisk, upon a granite base, in commemoration of the services of General Greene and Count Pulaski.

* A notice of Washington's Life-Guard is given in another chapter.

† The officer here alluded to, was General Adam Stephen of the Virginia line,

BATTLE OF GERMANTOWN.

The surprise was complete. Between daybreak and sunrise the British pickets were forced, and the light-infantry, routed in their camp, fled in confusion, leaving their camp standing.* So complete was the surprise,

and a companion-in-arms of Washington, during the French and Indian war. He was a captain in the Ohio expedition in 1754, conducted by Colonel Washington. Afterward raised to the rank of lieutenant-colonel, he was intrusted with the command of Fort Cumberland. He was left in the command of the Virginia forces while Washington went to Boston, on an official errand to Governor Shirley, in 1755, and was afterward despatched to South Carolina, to oppose the Creek Indians. On his return, he was placed at the head of troops for the defence of the Virginia frontier, and was commissioned a brigadier. Congress appointed him a major-general, early in 1777, and he behaved well in the battle of Brandywine. Yielding to a bad habit, he fell into disgrace at Germantown. His troops, it can scarcely be said, were in the action at all. He was accused of "unofficer-like-conduct" during the action and the retreat, was found guilty of being intoxicated, and was dismissed from the army, much to the chagrin of many of the officers, for he was a pleasant, companionable man. On the third of December, 1777, the Marquis de Lafayette was appointed to the command of General Stephen's division. This was the first time that the marquis had been honored with a leadership appropriate to his rank since he joined the army.

* Washington arranged the following order of march against the enemy at Germantown:—

"The divisions of Sullivan and Wayne, flanked by Conway's brigade, were to enter the town by way of Chestnut hill; while General Armstrong, with the Pennsylvania militia, should fall down the Manatawny road by Vandeering's mill, and get upon the enemy's left and rear. The divisions of Green and Stephen, flanked by M'Dougall's brigade, were to enter by taking a circuit by way of the Lime-Kiln road, at the market-house, and attack their right wing; and the militia of Maryland and Jersey, under Generals Smallwood and Forman, were to march by the old York road, and fall upon the rear of their right. Lord Stirling, with Nash's and Maxwell's brigade was to form a *corps de reserve*."—*Washington's letter to the president of Congress, 5th October,* 1777.

To understand this march, it is necessary to define the location of the four several roads mentioned. The Skippack or main road over Chestnut hill and Mount Airy, passed through the village and on to Philadelphia, forming the principal street of Germantown. The Manatawny or Ridge road, parallel with this, was nearer the Schuylkill, and entered the main road below the village. Eastward of the village was the Lime-Kiln road, which entered at the market-place, and still farther eastward, was the old York road, which fell into the main road, some distance below the village. The main British army lay encamped across the lower part of the village. The right, commanded by General Grant, lay eastward of the village—

that the officer's watches were found hanging up in their marquees, together with their portmanteaus and trunks of clothes, the latter affording a most seasonable booty to the American soldiery. Many of the tents and marquees were burnt, owing to a want of vehicles to carry them away. Although completely routed in the onset, the British light-infantry rallied under their officers, and annoyed their enemy from every house, enclosure, or other defensible position that offered in the line of their retreat; thus showing the mighty power of discipline over broken troops, and its invaluable influences amid the greatest emergencies of war.

Six companies of the fortieth regiment, under their lieutenant-colonel,† being hard pressed by the advancing columns of the Americans, threw themselves into Chew's house, a strongly-constructed stone building, and barricading the lower windows, opened a destructive fire from the cellars and upper windows. The Americans, finding their musketry made no impression, were in the act of dragging up their cannon to batter the walls, when a *ruse de guerre* was attempted, which, however, failed of success. An officer galloped up from the house, and cried out, "What are you about; you will fire upon your

---

each wing covered by strong detachments, and guarded by cavalry. Howe's headquarters was in the rear of the centre. About two miles in advance was a battalion of British infantry, with a train of artillery; and an out-lying picket with two six-pounders, was at Mount Airy. It was this picket and light-infantry which are referred to in the text. The attack was led by General Wayne, whose men remembered the massacre of their companions-in-arms at Paoli, on the night of the twentieth of September. "They pushed in with the bayonet," says Wayne, "and took ample vengeance for that night's work."

* Lieutenant-Colonel Musgrave. He lay encamped in a field west of the main road, opposite the heavy stone-house of Chief-Justice Chew, which is yet standing at Germantown.

own people." The artillery opened, but, after fifteen or twenty rounds, the pieces were found to be of too small caliber to make a serious impression, and were withdrawn.

A most daring and chivalric attempt was now made to fire the building. Lieutenant-Colonel Laurens, aid-de-camp to the commander-in-chief, with a few volunteers, rushed up to the house under cover of the smoke, and applied a burning brand to the principal door, at the same time exchanging passes with his sword with the enemy on the inside. By almost a miracle, this gallant and accomplished officer escaped unharmed, although his clothes were repeatedly torn by the enemy's shot. Another and equally daring attempt was made by Major White, aid-de-camp to General Sullivan, but without as fortunate a result. The major, while in the act of firing one of the cellar windows, was mortally wounded, and died soon afterward.*

Washington accompanied the leading division under Major-General Sullivan, and cheered his soldiers in their brilliant onset, as they drove the enemy from point to

---

* I visited "Chew's house" in the autumn of 1848, when the venerable daughter-in-law of Judge Chew was yet living there. She informed me that, several years after the war, and soon after her marriage, while a young man named White was visiting her father-in-law, the old gentleman, in relating incidents of the battle in Germantown, mentioned the circumstance that a Major White, an aid of General Sullivan, and one of the handsomest men in the continental army, attempted to fire the house for the purpose of driving out the British. He ran under a window with a fire-brand, where shots from the building could not touch him. He was discovered, and a British soldier, running into the cellar, shot him dead from a basement window. The young man was much affected by the recital, and said to Judge Chew, "That Major White, sir, was my father." Mrs. Chew pointed out to me the window, near the northwest corner of the house, from which the shot was fired. The Marquis de Chastellux, in his Journal (i. 212) says, that M. Manduit, a meritorious officer in the continental service, tried to fire the house with burning straw.

point. Arrived in the vicinity of Chew's house, the commander-in-chief halted to consult his officers as to the best course to be pursued toward this fortress that had so suddenly and unexpectedly sprung up in their way. The younger officers who were immediately attached to the person of the chief, and among the choicest spirits of the Revolution, including the high and honored names of Hamilton, of Reed, of Pinckney, of Laurens, and of Lee, were for leaving Chew's house to itself, or of turning the siege into a blockade, by stationing in its vicinity a body of troops to watch the movements of the garrison, and pressing on with the column in pursuit of the flying enemy. But the sages of the army, at the head of whom was Major-General Knox, repulsed at once the idea of leaving a fortified enemy in the rear, as contrary to the usages of war, and the most approved military authorities.*

At this period of the action the fog had become so dense that objects could scarcely be distinguished at a few yards distance. The Americans had penetrated the enemy's camp even to their second line, which was drawn up to receive them about the centre of Germantown. The ammunition of the right wing, including the

* "What!" exclaimed Reed, when Knox spoke of Chew's house as a fort, "call this a fort, and lose the happy moment!" They then sought Conway to decide the point, but he was not to be found. The author is evidently in error, in supposing Washington to have been engaged in this consultation. He had not yet arrived to that point of the conflict. Knox's opinion prevailed, and pursuit was abandoned. Wayne heartily condemned the attack upon Chew's house, and attributed the loss of the day chiefly to the delay and confusion which it caused. "A *windmill* attack," he said, "was made upon a house into which six light companies had thrown themselves to avoid our bayonets. Our troops were deceived by this attack, thinking it something formidable. They fell back to assist — the enemy believing it to be a retreat, followed — confusion ensued, and we ran away from the arms of victory open to receive us."

Maryland brigades, became exhausted, the soldiers holding up their empty cartridge-boxes, when their officers called on them to rally and face the enemy. The extended line of operations, which embraced nearly two miles; the unfavorable nature of the ground in the environs of Germantown for the operation of troops (a large portion of whom were undisciplined), the ground being much cut up, and intersected by stone-fences and enclosures of various sorts; the delay of the left wing under Greene in getting into action*—all these causes, combined with an atmosphere so dense from fog and smoke as to make it impossible to distinguish friend from foe, produced a retreat in the American army at the moment when victory seemed to be within its grasp.

Washington was among the foremost in his endeavors to restore the fortunes of the day, and while exerting himself to rally his broken columns, the exposure of his person became so imminent, that his officers, after affectionately remonstrating with him in vain, seized the bridle of his horse.†

* The divisions of Greene and Stephen having to make a circuit, were quite late in coming into action. They became separated, part of Stephen's division having been arrested by the fire from Chew's house; and the fog prevented a knowledge of their relative position. Greene had attacked and routed a battalion of light-infantry and the Queen's rangers, under Lieutenant-Colonel Simcoe; and believing that the Pennsylvania militia on the right, under General Armstrong, and those of Maryland and New Jersey on the left, under Smallwood, would carry out the order of the commander-in-chief, by attacking and turning the first left and second right flank of the enemy, he pressed forward with the brigades of Muhlenburg and Scott, drove an advanced regiment of light-infantry before him, took a number of prisoners, and made his way to the market-house, near the centre of the town, where he came full upon the British right wing, drawn up in battle order. The British were amazed at the vigor of the republicans, and, as was afterward ascertained, were on the point of retreating, when a panic, caused by a false alarm, and the total ignorance of each corps, of the position of the other, on account of the fog, put everything into confusion, and a retreat ensued.

† "I saw our brave commander-in-chief," wrote General Sullivan, "exposing him-

The retreat, under all circumstances, was quite as favorable as could be expected. The whole of the artillery was saved, and as many of the wounded as could be removed. The ninth Virginia regiment, under Colonel Matthews, having penetrated so far as to be without support, after a desperate resistance, surrendered its remnant of a hundred men, including its gallant colonel, who had received several bayonet wounds. The British pursued but two or three miles, making prisoners of the worn-out soldiers, who, after a night-march of fifteen miles, and an action of three hours, were found exhausted and asleep in the fields and along the roads.

While gallantly leading the North Carolina brigade, that formed part of the reserve, into action, General Nash was mortally wounded. A round-shot from the British artillery striking a sign-post in Germantown, glanced therefrom, and, passing through his horse, shattered the general's thigh on the opposite side. The fall of the animal hurled its unfortunate rider with considerable force to the ground. With surpassing courage and presence of mind, General Nash, covering his wound with both of his hands, gayly called to his men, "Never mind me, I have had a devil of a tumble; rush on, my boys, rush on the enemy, I'll be after you presently." Human nature could do no more. Faint from loss of blood, and the intense agony of his wound, the sufferer was borne to a house hard by, and attended by Doctor Craik, by special order of the commander-in-chief. The doctor gave his patient but feeble hopes of recovery, even with

self to the hottest fire of the enemy in such a manner, that regard for my country obliged me to ride to him and beg him to retire. He, to gratify me and some others, withdrew to a small distance, but his anxiety for the fate of the day soon brought him up again, where he remained till our troops had retreated."

the chances of amputation, when Nash observed, "It may be considered unmanly to complain, but my agony is too great for human nature to bear. I am aware that my days, perhaps hours, are numbered, but I do not repine at my fate. I have fallen on the field of honor while leading my brave Carolinians to the assault of the enemy. I have a last request to make of his excellency the commander-in-chief, that he will permit you, my dear doctor, to remain with me, to protect me while I live, and my remains from insult."

Dr. Craik assured the general that he had nothing to fear from the enemy; it was impossible that they would harm him while living, or offer an insult to his remains; that Lord Cornwallis was by this time in the field,* and that, under his auspices, a wounded officer would be treated with humanity and respect. The dying patriot and hero then uttered these memorable words: "I have no favors to expect from the enemy. I have been consistent in my principles and conduct since the commencement of the troubles. From the very first dawn of the Revolution I have ever been on the side of liberty and my country."

He lingered in extreme torture between two and three days, and died, admired by his enemies—admired and lamented by his companions-in-arms. On Thursday, the

---

* General Gray, with the British left wing, was just pressing hard upon the Americans in their flight, when Cornwallis arrived from Philadelphia, with a squadron of light-horse, and joined in the pursuit. Through the skilful management of Greene, the retreat was well conducted, after the first paroxysm of the panic had subsided; and Wayne, on gaining an eminence near White Marsh, turned his cannon upon the pursuers, and effectually checked them. There were about one thousand Americans lost in that battle, killed, wounded, and missing. According to Howe's official account, the British loss from the same cause, was five hundred and thirty-five.

ninth of October, the whole American army was paraded by order of the commander-in-chief, to perform the funeral obsequies of General Nash, and never did the warrior's last tribute peal the requiem of a braver soldier or nobler patriot than that of the illustrious son of North Carolina.

Taking rank with the chiefs who had fallen in the high and holy cause of a Nation's Independence, the name of Nash will be associated with the martyr names of Warren, Montgomery, Wooster, and Mercer, while the epitaph to be graven on his monumental marble should be the memorable words of the patriot and hero on the field of his fame: *From the very first dawn of the Revolution, I have ever been on the side of liberty and my country.**

---

* Francis Nash was a captain in North Carolina, in 1771, and was distinguished in the movements in the western parts of this province, known as the *Regulator War*. He was commissioned a colonel by the convention of North Carolina, at the commencement of the war, and in February, 1777, the continental Congress commissioned him a brigadier in the grand army. The ball that wounded him at Germantown, killed his aid, Major Witherspoon, son of Doctor Witherspoon, president of Princeton college. Nash's remains were conveyed to Kulpsville, and buried in the Mennonist burrying-ground there, about twenty-six miles from Philadelphia. On receiving intelligence of his death, the Congress resolved to request Governor Caswell, of North Carolina, "to erect a monument of the value of five hundred dollars, at the expense of the United States," in honor of his memory.

That proposed monument has not been erected. Private patriotism has been more faithful. Through the efforts of John F. Watson, Esq., the annalist of Philadelphia and New York, the citizens of Germantown and Norristown have erected a neat marble monument to the memory of the gallant Nash, upon which is the following inscription:—

VOTA VIA MEA JUS PATRIÆ.
IN MEMORY OF
GENERAL NASH, OF NORTH CAROLINA,
MORTALLY WOUNDED AT THE BATTLE OF GERMANTOWN,
HERE INTERRED, OCTOBER 17TH, 1777,
IN PRESENCE OF THE ARMY HERE ENCAMPED.—J. F. W.

Among the British officers killed on that occasion, were Brigadier-General James Agnew, and Lieutenant Bird. These were inhumed in the South burying-ground at Germantown, and over their graves also Mr. Watson has erected a neat marble slab. In the North burying-ground, the same patriotic gentleman has set up com-

It was not the halt at Chew's house, it was not the denseness of the fog, that produced the unfortunate ter-

memorative slabs at the head of the graves of Captain Turner, of North Carolina, Major Irvine, and six private soldiers of the American army, who were killed in the battle, and there buried together.

We insert the following letter to the author of the *Recollections*, from a gentleman of Washington city, because it is a tribute to a brave officer, whose merits have not been recorded in history:—

"WASHINGTON, *February 24th*, 1841.

"DEAR SIR: I was much gratified at the publication in the Intelligencer, on the 22d instant, of your reminiscences of the battle of Germantown, but regret that your information was not sufficient to embrace Colonel John H. Stone, of the Maryland brigade. This patriotic and gallant soldier was conspicuous in the battles of Long Island, White Plains, Trenton, Princeton, and Brandywine, in all of which his conduct commanded the high admiration and warm approbation of his commander-in-chief, General Washington. In the latter battle the duty assigned him was, with his men, to cover and protect the American artillery, which he did — the corps, however, under his command suffering immensely, as was expected. When the order for retreat was given, in wheeling, his horse was killed and he slightly wounded, but in the confusion, dropped behind a bush exhausted with fatigue; he was discovered by one of his men, whom he begged to pass on and make his escape, as he (Stone) was exhausted, wounded, and must inevitably be taken prisoner; he was prepared to meet his fate, whatever it might be; the soldier, however, could not be persuaded to leave him; he raised him from the ground, took off his boots, threw out the sand and pebbles, and finally they succeeded in making their escape under cover of the wood.

"At the battle of Germantown he was again found at the head of his men, and in the midst of that disastrous action had his leg shattered by a musket-ball, when his brother-officers implored him to allow himself to be taken from the field; his reply was, 'No, never while I can wield a sword, will I desert my corps and colors in the face of an enemy.' He soon, however, became faint from the loss of blood and anguish of the wound (the bone being shattered in a thousand pieces), when, to all appearance in a dying state, three of his faithful soldiers bore him off the field. He was taken five or six miles on a litter and placed in a farm-house. When General Washington heard of it, he despatched Doctor Craik, his family surgeon, and Doctor Rush, the physician-general to the army, bidding them be kind and attentive, and leave nothing undone which was in the power of man, or skill of physcans, to save his life. They immediately advised amputation, but he refused, and was on the next day returned as mortally wounded. After lingering some time in great torture, and suffering from a severe attack of tetanus, he recovered so far as to be able to be taken on a litter to Annapolis, where he lingered out some fifteen or twenty years a suffering cripple, and at length fell a victim to the irritation of his wounded condition. After death several buckshot were taken from his groin."

mination of the battle of the fourth of October. Time that sheds the sober and enduring colors of truth over the events of the world, has determined that the misfortunes of the battle of Germantown are rather to be ascribed to the undisciplined character of a large proportion of the American troops, than to all other causes combined. Washington's oldest continental regiments were of but little more than a year's standing, while many of his troops had seen but a few months' and some but a few weeks' service. With all these disadvantages, the plan of the surprise of Germantown was ably conceived and gallantly executed in the outset, and failed of complete success only from circumstances beyond all human control.

Congress passed a unanimous resolution, conciliatory to the feelings of the commander-in-chief, his officers and soldiers, under their disappointment, intimating "that it was not in nature to command success," but their brave army "had done more; it had deserved it."*

The effects resulting from the battle of Germantown were most happy both at home and abroad. The enemy were taught to respect American troops which they had affected to despise; and Sir William Howe deemed it prudent to draw in all his outposts, and shelter himself in Philadelphia, which proved a great relief to a large and valuable portion of the adjacent country. Indeed, it becomes the duty of the historian to declare that matters might have been much worse on the fourth of October. When the Americans retreated, the second line of the enemy was in great force, having been but little impaired

* See Journals of Congress, October 8, 1777. A medal was also ordered to be struck in commemoration of that event, and presented to Washington.

in the action, while the reserve, consisting of the grenadiers, were close at hand to sustain their comrades, those chosen fellows having, at the first alarm, seized their arms, and ran, without halting, from the commons of Philadelphia to Germantown. Howe's army in 1777, without disparagement of the British service before or since that time, may be considered as the finest body of troops that ever embarked from the British dominions; yet such was the alarm and confusion into which these veterans were thrown by the masterly surprise at Germantown, and such the courage and vigor displayed by the Americans in their attacks in the early part of the day, that a rendezvous at Chester became a measure of serious contemplation among the commanders of the British army.*

But the most happy and imposing influences upon

---

*In a letter to the president of Congress, written three days after the battle, Washington says:—

"It is with much chagrin and mortification I add, that every account confirms the opinion I at first entertained, that our troops retreated at the instant when victory was declaring herself in our favor. The tumult, disorder, and even despair, which, it seems, had taken place in the British army, were scarcely to be paralleled; and, it is said, so strongly did the idea of a retreat prevail, that Chester was fixed on as a place of rendezvous. I can discover no other cause for not improving this happy opportunity than the extreme haziness of the weather." Writing, at the same time, to Governor Trumbull, of Connecticut, Washington said: "But the morning was so excessively foggy, that we could not see the confusion the enemy were in, and the advantage we had gained; and fearing to push too far through a strong village, we retired, after an engagement of two hours, bringing off all our artillery with us. We did not know until after the affair was over how near we were to gaining a complete victory." Captain William Heth, a Virginia officer, in a letter to Colonel John Lamb, of the artillery, asserted, that Chester had been fixed upon as a place of rendezvous, and that "upwards of two thousand Hessians had actually crossed the Schuylkill for that purpose." He also stated, that the tories in Philadelphia were in great distress, and commenced moving out of the city; and that in the pursuit, the republicans passed "upward of twenty pieces of cannon, and their tents standing, filled with their choicest baggage."

America and her cause, resulting from the battle of Germantown, were experienced abroad. "Eh, mon Dieu," exclaimed the Count de Vergennes, the French minister of foreign affairs, to the American commissioners in Paris, "what is this you tell me, Messieurs; another battle, and the British grand army surprised in its camp at Germantown, Sir William and his veterans routed and flying for two hours, and a great victory only denied to Washington by a tissue of accidents beyond all human control. Ah, ah, these Americans are an elastic people. Press them down to-day, they rise to-morrow. And then, my dear sirs, these military wonders to be achieved by an army raised within a single year, opposed to the skill, discipline, and experience of European troops commanded by generals grown gray in war. The brave Americans, they are worthy of the aid of France. They will succeed at last."*

The winter of 1777 set in early, and with unusual severity. The military operations of both armies had ceased, when a detachment of the southern troops were seen plodding their weary way to winter quarters at the Valley Forge.†

---

* When intelligence of these bold and vigorous movements, and the victory of the republicans at Saratoga, reached Europe, the most timid friend of the Americans took courage. At the French court the most active sympathy for them was professed. "Surely such a people possess the elements of success, and will achieve it. We may now safely strike England a severe blow, by acknowledging the independence, and forming an alliance with her revolted colonies," argued the French government; and so, with more of a desire to injure the old enemy of France than to help a people struggling for freedom, the French court speedily acknowledged the independence of the United States, and formed a treaty of friendship and alliance with them.

† On the west side of the Schuylkill, in Montgomery county, Pennsylvania, about twenty miles from Philadelphia, is a deep rugged gorge, scooped from a slope stretching from high land down to the river, and through which runs a considerable stream. There, Isaac Potts, in whose house Washington kept his headquarters in the winter of 1777, '78, erected iron-works and a forge, and the place became known

The appearance of the horse-guard announced the approach of the commander-in-chief. The officer commanding the detachment, choosing the most favorable ground, paraded his men to pay their general the honors of the passing salute. As Washington rode slowly up, he was observed to be eying very earnestly something that attracted his attention on the frozen surface of the road. Having returned the salute with that native grace, that dignified air and manner, that won the admiration of the soldiery of the old Revolutionary day, the chief reined up his charger, and, ordering the commanding officer of the detachment to his side, addressed him as follows: "How comes it, sir, that I have tracked the march of your troops by the blood-stains of their feet upon the frozen ground? Were there no shoes in the commissary's stores, that this sad spectacle is to be seen along the public highways?" The officer replied: "Your excellency may rest assured that this sight is as painful to my feelings as it can be to yours; but there is no remedy within our reach. When the shoes were issued, the different regiments were served in turn; it was our misfortune to be among the last to be served, and the stores became exhausted before we could obtain even the smallest supply."

The general was observed to be deeply affected by his officer's description of the soldiers' privations and sufferings. His compressed lips, the heaving of his manly chest, betokened the powerful emotions that were struggling in his bosom, when, turning toward the troops with

as Valley Forge. After the retreat from Germantown the Americans encamped at White Marsh, but the weather becoming too severe for them to remain in tents, Washington broke up his camp and moved his troops to Valley Forge, where they constructed huts and remained during the severe winter that ensued.

a voice tremulous yet kindly, Washington exclaimed, "*Poor fellows;*" then giving rein to his charger, rode away.

During this touching interview, every eye was bent upon the chief, every ear was attentive to catch his words; and when those words reached the soldiers, warm from the heart of their beloved commander, and in tones of sorrow and commiseration for their sufferings, a grateful but subdued expression burst from every lip, of "God bless your excellency, your poor soldiers' friend."

In this interesting event in the life and actions of Washington, he appears in a new light. He is no longer the grave, the dignified, the awe-inspiring and unapproachable general-in-chief of the armies of his country. All these characteristics have vanished, and the Pater Patriæ appears amid his companions in arms, in all his moral grandeur, giving vent to his native goodness of heart.*

---

* Doctor Gordon, the earliest historian of the war, says, that "while at Washington's table, in 1784, the chief informed him that bloody foot-prints were everywhere visible in the course of their march of nineteen miles from Whitemarsh to Valley Forge." The commissary and quartermaster's department had been so much deranged by the interference of Congress and the neglect of officers, that while there was an ample supply of shoes, which had been provided for the army, they were not where they should have been when wanted. Gordon asserts, on good authority, that at that very time, "hogsheads of shoes, stockings, and clothing, were lying at different places on the roads, and in the woods, perishing for want of teams, or of money to pay the teamsters."

CHAPTER V.

THE BATTLE OF MONMOUTH.*

Approach of the Americans toward Monmouth Courthouse—Decision of a Council of War—Washington assumes Great Responsibility—He Determines to Fight the Enemy—Notice of Jefferson's Opinion of Washington—Washington meets the Flying American Army—Anecdote of Colonel Hamilton—Washington restores the Fortunes of the Day—His Horses—Lafayette's Account of Washington's Appearance—Death of Colonel Monckton—Captain Fauntleroy—Proposed Memorial to Washington concerning Exposure of Himself in Battle—Remarks of Doctor Craik—The Indian Prophecy—Baron Steuben—The Valets Cannonaded—Captain Molly—Washington on the Night of the Battle—Retreat of the British—Vote of Thanks by the Congress.

The commander-in-chief having completed his arrangements for bringing the enemy to a general action, proceeded slowly toward Monmouth courthouse, early on the morning of the twenty-eighth of June, 1778.†

---

* Published in the *National Intelligencer*, February 22, 1840.

† Toward the close of May, 1778, General Sir Henry Clinton succeeded General Sir William Howe in the command of the British forces in America. Perceiving the dangers to be apprehended from the co-operation of a French fleet under Count D'Estaing, with the republican armies, Sir Henry determined to concentrate his forces at New York, the most eligible point for acting efficiently against the "rebels." Accordingly, on the eighteenth of June, he evacuated Philadelphia, pursuant to an order of the British ministry. His whole army crossed the Delaware, into New Jersey, eleven thousand strong, with an immense baggage and provision train, and marched for New York by way of New Brunswick and Amboy.

Washington, meanwhile, had been led to suspect some movement of this kind, and was on the alert. He broke up his encampment at Valley Forge, and moved toward the Delaware, and when he ascertained that Clinton had passed over into New Jersey, he crossed also, at a point some distance above Philadelphia, and commenced a series of manœuvres to compel Clinton to change his course in the direction of Sandy Hook. This he effected, having with him a force equal to the enemy, and Sir Henry marched toward Monmouth courthouse.

In the council of war there were but two voices for risking a general engagement, Cadwalader,* a gallant fellow, and devoted in his attachment to the chief, and Anthony Wayne, who always said aye when fighting was to be had on any terms.†

Washington certainly assumed a great responsibility in risking an engagement, contrary to the opinions of a large majority of his generals, and notwithstanding the vast disparity of his forces when compared with those of his adversary—the disparity consisting more in the materiel of which the respective armies was composed than in their numerical estimates. But it is to be remembered

---

* General John Cadwalader. He was a native of Philadelphia, and in 1775, was a member of the Pennsylvania convention. He entered the army, and was appointed brigadier by Congress in February, 1777, and also in 1778, as commander of cavalry, but declined the appointment on both occasions. He participated in the battles of Princeton, Brandywine, Germantown, and Monmouth. On the fourth of July, 1778, he fought a duel with General Conway, the quarrel which led to it growing out of the intrigue of that officer with Gates and others against Washington. Conway was badly, but not mortally, wounded. Cadwalader removed to Maryland after the war, and became a member of its state legislature. He died on the tenth of February, 1786, aged forty-three years. He was a gentleman of large fortune, and dispensed its blessings with a liberal hand. Many of his descendants yet reside in Philadelphia and vicinity.

† Washington held a council of war at Valley Forge, on the seventeenth of June, when a proposition was submitted, whether it would be advisable, in case an opportunity offered, to hazard a general engagement with the enemy, in New Jersey. The decision was a negative; but it was recommended to send out detachments to harass the enemy. Of the nine general officers in that council, only four (not two only, as asserted by the author of the *Recollections*) were in favor of a general engagement. These were the chief's four best officers — Greene, Lafayette, Wayne, and Cadwalader. At Hopewell, in New Jersey, he called another council, submitted a similar question, and obtained the same result. Cadwalader was not present; Greene, Lafayette, and Wayne, adhered to their former opinion. General Lee, who had lately been exchanged for Prescott, and had joined the army as Washington's second in command, opposed the measure with warmth, as before. At first, Washington was embarrassed by their divided opinions; but, relying upon his own judgment, which was strongly in favor of an engagement, he asked no further advice, and proceeded to make arrangements for battle.

that the two principal actions of the grand army in the preceding campaign, though bravely contested, had resulted unfortunately.* Since the close of the campaign of '77, an alliance had been formed with France, whose fleets and armies were hourly expected on our coasts, while the demands of the people, and those often loudly expressed, were for battles.† Urged by these considerations, the American chief determined, happen what would, to fight Sir Henry Clinton, so that he should not evacuate Philadelphia, and reach his stronghold in New York unscathed. Crossing the Delaware, the American approached his formidable foe, who, trusting in his superiority of numbers, discipline, and appointment, was leisurely wending his way toward Staten Island, the place of embarkation for New York.

As a soldier, Washington was by nature the very soul of enterprise; but, fortunately for his fame and for his country, this daring spirit was tempered by a judgment and prudence the most happy in their characters and effects. And yet an illustrious patriot and statesman of the Revolution, and most accomplished writer (Mr. Jefferson), has said that the Pater Patriæ was rather the Fabius than the Marcellus of war, his extreme caution fitting him better for the cool and methodical operations of sieges than for the daring strategy of surprise, or the

---

* Brandywine and Germantown.

† The first movement of the French government, in compliance with the provisions of the treaty of friendship and alliance made with the Americans, was to despatch a squadron, consisting of twelve ships of the line and four large frigates, under Count D'Estaing, to blockade the British fleet in the Delaware. Fortunately for Admiral Howe, he received from the British ministry timely notice of the fitting out of this armament, and left the Delaware in time to escape the blockade, and took post, with his fleet, in the bay between Staten Island and Sandy Hook. D'Estaing arrived off the capes of the Delaware, on the eighth of July, 1778.

close and stubborn conflict of the field.* Never was there such a misconception of a great soldier's attributes.

* The following interesting sketch of the character of Washington was drawn by the pen of Jefferson, at Monticello, his seat in Virginia, on the second of January, 1814, in a letter to Doctor Walter Jones of Virginia, who had written an able letter to the venerable statesman, on parties in the United States, and proposed to prepare another. In his letter, Doctor Jones had expressed some doubt concerning Washington as a topic, to which Jefferson replied, as follows:—

"You say that in taking General Washington on your shoulders, to bear him harmless through the federal coalition, you encounter a perilous topic. I do not think so; you have given the genuine history of the course of his mind through the trying scenes in which it was engaged, and of the seductions by which it was deceived, but not depraved. I think I knew General Washington intimately and thoroughly; and were I called on to delineate his character, it should be in terms like these.

"His mind was great and powerful, without being of the very first order; his penetration strong, though not so acute as that of a Newton, Bacon, or Locke; and as far as he saw, no judgment was ever sounder. It was slow in operation, being little aided by invention or imagination, but sure in conclusion. Hence the common remark of his officers, of the advantage he derived from councils of war, where hearing all suggestions, he selected whatever was best; and certainly no general ever planned his battles more judiciously. But if deranged during the course of the action, if any member of his plan was dislocated by sudden circumstances, he was slow in re-adjustment. The consequence was that he often failed in the field, and rarely against an enemy in station, as at Boston and York. He was incapable of fear, meeting personal dangers with the calmest unconcern. Perhaps the strongest feature in his character was prudence, never acting until every circumstance, every consideration was maturely weighed; refraining if he saw a doubt, but, when once decided, going through with his purpose whatever obstacles opposed. His integrity was most pure, his justice the most inflexible I have ever known, no motives of interest or consanguinity, of friendship or hatred, being able to bias his decision. He was indeed, in every sense of the word, a wise, a good, and a great man. His temper was naturally irritable and high-toned; but reflection and resolution had obtained a firm and habitual ascendency over it. If ever, however, it broke its bonds, he was most tremendous in his wrath. In his expenses he was honorable, but exact; liberal in contributions to whatever promised utility; but frowning and unyielding on all visionary projects and all unworthy calls on his charity. His heart was not warm in its affections; but he exactly calculated every man's value, and gave him a solid esteem proportioned to it. His person, you know, was fine, his stature exactly what one would wish, his deportment easy, erect, and noble; the best horseman of his age, and the most graceful figure that could be seen on horseback. Although, in the circle of his friends, where he might be unreserved with safety, he took a free share in conversation, his colloquial talents were not above

Did not this modern Fabius, in the very depth of winter, and after overcoming mighty obstacles, surprise his ene-

mediocrity, possessing neither copiousness of ideas, nor fluency of words. In public, when called on for a sudden opinion, he was unready, short, and embarrassed. Yet he wrote readily, rather diffusely, in an easy and correct style. This he had acquired by conversation with the world, for his education was merely reading, writing, and common arithmetic, to which he added surveying at a later day. His time was employed in action chiefly, reading little, and that only in agriculture and English history. His correspondence became necessarily extensive, and, with journalizing his agricultural proceedings, occupied most of his leisure hours within doors.

"On the whole, his character was, in its mass, perfect, in nothing bad, in few points indifferent; and it may truly be said that never did nature and fortune combine more perfectly to make a man great, and to place him in the same constellation with whatever worthies have merited from man an everlasting remembrance. For his was the singular destiny and merit of leading the armies of his country successfully through an arduous war, for the establishment of its independence; of conducting its councils through the birth of a government new in its forms and principles, until it had settled down into a quiet and orderly train; and of scrupulously obeying the laws through the whole of his career, civil and military, of which the history of the world furnishes no other example. How then can it be perilous for you to take such a man on your shoulders? I am satisfied the great body of republicans think of him as I do—we were indeed dissatisfied with him on his ratification of the British treaty, but this was short-lived. We knew his honesty, the wiles with which he was encompassed, and that age had already begun to relax the firmness of his purposes: and I am convinced he is more deeply seated in the love and gratitude of the republicans, than in the pharisaical homage of the federal monarchists. For he was no monarchist from preference of his judgment. The soundness of that gave him correct views of the rights of man, and his severe justice devoted him to them. He has often declared to me that he considered our new constitution as an experiment on the practicability of republican government, and with what dose of liberty man could be trusted for his own good: that he was determined the experiment should have a fair trial, and would lose the last drop of his blood in support of it. And these declarations he repeated to me the oftener, and the more pointedly, because he knew my suspicions of Colonel Hamilton's views, and probably had heard from him the same declarations which I had, to wit: 'That the British constitution, with its unequal representation, corruption, and other existing abuses, was the most perfect government which had ever been established on earth, and that a reformation of those abuses would make it an impracticable government.' I do believe that General Washington had not a firm confidence in the durability of our government He was naturally distrustful of men, and inclined to gloomy apprehensions; and I was ever persuaded that a belief that we must at length end in something like a British constitution, had some weight in his adoption of the ceremonies of levees, birth-days, pompous meetings with Congress, and other forms of the same character,

my at Trenton, and recall Victory to his standard, when Hope was almost sinking in despair? Did he not, by a masterly manœuvre and midnight march, surprise his enemy in Princeton, and add yet another laurel to the one acquired by the capture of the Hessians? Did he not, with an army hastily raised, and defeated at Brandywine, in twenty-three days thereafter, surprise the enemy at Germantown? And though victory was denied him by a force of circumstances no human power could have controlled, yet the boldness of the enterprise, and the success attending it in the outset, produced such a confidence abroad in our courage and resources, as to lead to our alliance with a powerful nation. Did he not surprise the enemy at Monmouth? And, although untoward events served to cripple the operations of the early part of the day, yet the setting-sun shone upon the battlefield in possession of the Americans, the enemy retreat-

calculated to prepare us gradually for a change which he believed possible, and to let it come on with as little shock as might be to the public mind. These are my opinions of General Washington, which I would vouch at the judgment seat of God, having been formed on an acquaintance of thirty years. I served with him in the Virginia legislature from 1769 to the Revolutionary war, and again a short time in Congress, until he left us to take command of the army. During the war, and after it, we corresponded occasionally, and in the four years of my continuance in the office of secretary of state, our intercourse was daily, confidential, and cordial After I retired from that office great and malignant pains were taken by our federal monarchists, and not entirely without effect, to make him view me as a theorist, holding French principles of government which would lead infallibly to licentiousness and anarchy. And to this he listened the more easily from my known disapprobation of the British treaty. I never saw him afterwards, or these malignant insinuations should have been dissipated before his just judgment as mists before the sun. I felt, on his death, with my countrymen, that 'verily a great man hath fallen this day in Israel.'

"More time and recollection would enable me to add many other traits of his character; but why add them to you who know him well? and I can not justify to myself a longer detention of your paper.

"*Vale, proprieque tuum, me esse tibi persuadeas.*

"TH. JEFFERSON."

ing, and their dead and wounded left as trophies to the victors. Such were the memorable instances in which Washington, with troops newly raised, and badly provided with every necessary of war, struck at his veteran and well-appointed foe when least expected, producing the happiest influences upon the American cause, both at home and abroad; for it is perfectly well known that the battle of Germantown decided the ministry of France to form the alliance that so materially contributed to the conclusion of the war and the consummation of our independence.*

As the commander-in-chief, accompanied by a numerous suite, approached the vicinity of Monmouth courthouse,† he was met by a little fifer-boy, who archly observed, "They are all coming this way, your honor." "Who are coming, my little man," asked General Knox. "Why, our boys, your honor, our boys, and the British right after them," replied the little musician. "Impossible," exclaimed Washington! And giving the spur to his charger, proceeded at full gallop to an eminence a short distance ahead. There, to his extreme pain and mortification, it was discovered that the boy's intelligence was but too true. The very *élite* of the American army,

---

* This battle had a powerful influence, no doubt, but the conquest over the army of Burgoyne, it must be acknowledged, was far more potent. That conquest, and the general failure of the campaign of 1777, produced a marked sensation upon the legislature and the common mind of Great Britain, and a great majority of the people and a powerful minority in Parliament, were clamorous for peace and reconciliation. Even Lord North, who had so long, as prime minister of England, treated the Americans with scorn, proposed, soon after hearing of the surrender of Burgoyne, a repeal of all the acts of Parliament obnoxious to the Americans, which had been enacted since 1763! But in this the minister was not sincere, and these propositions were called "deceptionary bills," in America.

† This was situated at the present village of Freehold, the capital of Monmouth county, New Jersey.

five thousand picked officers and men, were in full retreat, closely pursued by the enemy.* The first inquiry

* General Clinton lay near Monmouth courthouse, on the night of the twenty-seventh of June. The next day he would reach the heights of Middletown, when his strength would thereby be greatly increased. Washington determined to attack him the moment he should commence his march. Lafayette was then at Englishtown, a few miles in the rear of the enemy, to watch Sir Henry's movements. General Lee was sent with two brigades to join Lafayette, and, as senior officer, to take the general command of the whole division designed for making the first attack. At the same time, the main body, under Washington, encamped within three miles of Englishtown. Lee was ordered to make an attack when Sir Henry should attempt to move.

Before daylight, on the morning of the twenty-eighth of June, several other American corps were in motion toward the flank and rear of the enemy, and by eight o'clock, the whole British army had taken up its line of march. Lee, with four thousand troops, exclusive of Morgan's riflemen, and the Jersey militia, pressed forward under cover of a forest to an open field, and formed his line for action, while Wayne was detailed with seven hundred men and two pieces of artillery, to attack the covering parties in the rear of the enemy. A little after nine, while Wayne was prosecuting his attack with vigor, he received an order from Lee to make only a feigned attack, and not push on too precipitately. Wayne was disappointed, irritated, and chagrined, for he felt that his commander had plucked the palm of victory from his hand; but, like a true soldier, he obeyed, hoping Lee would recover what he had evidently lost. But in this, too, he was disappointed. Clinton had changed front, and a large body of his cavalry approached cautiously toward the right of Lee's troops. Lafayette thought this a fine opportunity to gain the rear of Clinton's division, and riding quickly up to Lee, asked permission to make the attempt. "Sir," replied Lee, "you do not know British soldiers; we can not stand against them; we shall certainly be driven back at first, and we must be cautious." Lafayette was disposed to make the trial, and Lee partially complied. He then weakened Wayne's division by drawing off three companies to the support of the right. Soon after this, by Lee's order, a general retreat commenced, without any apparent cause. The British pursued; a panic seized the Americans, and they fled in great confusion. These were the fugitives met by Washington. The chief was surprised and exasperated, and on this occasion, his feelings completely controlled his judgment for a moment. When he met Lee, he exclaimed in fierce tones, "What is the meaning of all this, sir?"

Lee hesitated a moment, when, according to Lafayette, the aspect of Washington became terrible, and he again demanded — "I desire to know the meaning of this disorder and confusion!"

The fiery Lee, stung by Washington's manner, made an angry reply, when the chief, unable to control himself, called him "a damned poltroon." "This," said Lafayette, when relating the circumstance to Governor Tompkins, in 1824, while on his visit to this country, "was the only time I ever heard General Washington swear."

Lee attempted a hurried explanation, and after a few more angry words between

of the chief was for Major-General Lee, who commanded the advance, and who soon appeared, when a warm conversation ensued, that ended by the major-general being ordered to the rear. During this interview, an inciden of rare and chivalric interest occurred. Lieutenant Colonel Hamilton, aid to the general-in-chief, leaped from his horse, and, drawing his sword, addressed the general with—"We are betrayed; your excellency and the army are betrayed, and the moment has arrived when every true friend of America and her cause must be ready to die in their defence."* Washington, charmed with the generous enthusiasm of his favorite aid, yet deemed the same ill-timed, and pointing to the colonel's horse that was cropping the herbage, unconscious of the great scene enacting around him, calmly observed, " Colonel Hamilton, you will take your horse."

The general-in-chief now set himself in earnest about restoring the fortunes of the day. He ordered Colonel Stewart and Lieutenant-Colonel Ramsay, with their regiments, to check the advance of the enemy, which service was gallantly performed; while the general, in person, proceeded to form his second line. He rode, on the morning of the twenty-eighth of June, and for that time

them, Washington departed to form his line. Then riding back to Lee in calmer mind, he said, "Will you retain the command on this height or not? If you will, I will return to the main body, and have it formed on the next height."

Lee replied, "It is equal to me where I command."

"I expect you will take proper means for checking the enemy," said Washington.

"Your orders shall be obeyed," rejoined Lee; "and I shall not be the first to leave the ground."

After the battle, Lee wrote insulting letters to Washington. He was arraigned before a court-martial, because of his conduct on the twenty-eighth, and was suspended from all command, for one year.

* This is explained in a future chapter of these *Recollections*, which is entitled, Mysteries of the Revolution."

only during the war, a white charger, that had been presented to him.* From the over-powering heat of the day, and the deep and sandy nature of the soil, the spirited horse sank under his rider, and expired on the spot. The chief was instantly remounted upon a chestnut blood-mare, with a flowing mane and tail, of Arabian breed, which his servant Billy was leading. It was upon this beautiful animal, covered with foam, that the American general flew along the line, cheering the soldiers in the familiar and endearing language ever used by the officer to the soldier of the Revolution, of "Stand fast, *my boys*, and receive your enemy; the southern troops are advancing to support you."

The person of Washington, always graceful, dignified, and commanding, showed to peculiar advantage when mounted; it exhibited, indeed, the very *beau ideal* of a perfect cavalier. The good Lafayette, during his last visit to America, delighted to discourse of the "times that tried men's souls."† From the venerated friend of our country we derived a most graphic description of Washington and the field of battle. Lafayette said, "At Monmouth I commanded a division, and, it may be supposed, I was pretty well occupied; still I took time, amid the roar and confusion of the conflict, to admire our beloved chief, who, mounted on a splendid charger, rode along the ranks amid the shouts of the soldiers,

---

* This fine horse was presented to Washington, by Governor William Livingston, of New Jersey, after the chief had crossed the Delaware into his state.

† This now trite expression, originated with Thomas Paine, author of *Common Sense, The Crisis*, etc. He commenced his second number of *The Crisis*, written in December, 1776, as follows: "THESE ARE THE TIMES THAT TRY MEN'S SOULS. The summer soldier and the sunshine patriot will, in this crisis, shrink from the service of his country; but he that stands it *now*, deserves the thanks of man and woman."

cheering them by his voice and example, and restoring to our standard the fortunes of the fight. I thought then as now," continued Lafayette, "that never had I beheld so *superb a man.*"

Among the incidents of this memorable day may be considered, on the part of the British, the death of the Honorable Colonel Monckton, a brother of Earl Galway. It is said this gallant and accomplished officer had greatly injured his fortune by the dissipations incident to a long sojourn in city quarters, and that, in consequence, he exposed himself recklessly on the twenty-eighth of June. He was much regretted in the British army.*

On the part of the Americans, the fate of the young and brave Captain Fauntleroy, of the Virginia line, was

---

* The flying Americans were checked by Washington, and were soon formed into battle order, and led into action. The battle became general. It was one of the hottest days on record, and many, on both sides, died from the effects of the heat. The British grenadiers, the finest corps in the army, were commanded by Colonel Monckton. They had been repulsed several times by Wayne, and Monckton determined to drive him from his strong position. He advanced silently, and when near enough for the purpose, he waved his sword, shouting, "On my brave grenadiers to the charge!" and at their head rushed forward with impetuosity. A terrible volley from Wayne's artillery swept the ranks of the foe, and Monckton fell, mortally wounded. Over his body the warriors fought desperately, until the Americans secured it and bore it to the rear.

Monckton was a gallant officer. He was a lieutenant-colonel in the battle of Long Island, where he was shot through the body. On the day after the battle at Monmouth, his remains were deposited in the burial-ground of the Freehold meetinghouse, near the west end of the building. The only monument that marked his grave a few years ago, when I visited the spot, was a plain board, painted red, on which were drawn, in black letters, the words:—

"HIC JACET.
COL. MONCKTON,
KILLED, 28 JUNE,
1778.
W. R. W."

This was erected by a worthy Scotch schoolmaster, named William R. Wilson An engraving of it, and also of the meetinghouse, may be found in Lossing's *Field-Book of the Revolution.*

remarkable. He was on horseback, at a well near a farmhouse, waiving his turn, while the fainting soldiers, consumed by a thirst arising from their exertions on the hottest day supposed ever to have occurred in America, were rushing with frantic cries, to the well, imploring for water. The captain, with the point of his sword resting on his boot, his arm leaning on the pommel, continued to waive his turn, when a cannon-shot, bounding down the lane that led to the farmhouse, struck the unfortunate officer near the hip, and hurled him to the ground a lifeless corse. The lamented Fauntleroy was descended from one of the old and highly-respected families of Virginia. Leaving the comforts of home and the delights of a large circle of friends, this gallant young soldier repaired to the standard of his country early in the campaign of 1776. He was greatly respected in his grade, and his untimely fate was deeply mourned in the American army.

Heedless of the remonstrances and entreaties of his officers, the commander-in-chief exposed his person to every danger throughout the action of the twenty-eighth of June. The night before the battle of Monmouth, a party of the general officers assembled, and resolved upon a memorial to the chief, praying that he would not expose his person in the approaching conflict. His high and chivalric daring and contempt for danger at the battle of Princeton, and again at Germantown, where his officers seized the bridle of his horse, made his friends the more anxious for the preservation of a life so dear to all, and so truly important to the success of the common cause. It was determined that the memorial should be presented by Doctor Craik, the companion-in-arms of

Colonel Washington in the war of 1755; but Craik at once assured the memorialists that, while their petition would be received as a proof of their affectionate regard for their general's safety, it would not weigh a feather in preventing the exposure of his person, should the day go against them, and the presence of the chief become important at the post of danger. Doctor Craik then related the romantic and imposing incident of the old Indian's prophecy, as it occurred on the banks of the Ohio in 1770, observing that, bred, as he himself was, in the rigid discipline of the Kirk of Scotland, he possessed as little superstition as any one, but that really there was a something in the air and manner of an old savage chief delivering his oracle amid the depths of the forest, that time or circumstance would never erase from his memory, and that he believed with the tawny prophet of the wilderness, that their beloved Washington was the spirit-protected being described by the savage, that the enemy could not kill him, and that while he lived the glorious cause of American Independence would never die.*

On the following day, while the commander-in-chief, attended by his officers, were reconnoitring the enemy from an elevated part of the field, a round-shot from the British artillery struck but a little way from his horse's feet, throwing up the earth over his person, and then bounding harmlessly away. The Baron Steuben, shrugging up his shoulders, exclaimed, "Dat wash very near," while Doctor Craik, pleased with this confirmation of his faith in the Indian's prophecy, nodded to the officers who composed the party of the preceding evening, and then,

* See chapter entitled, "Indian Prophecy."

pointing to Heaven, seemed to say, in the words of the savage prophet, "The Great Spirit protects him; he can not die in battle."

A ludicrous occurrence varied the incidents of the twenty-eighth of June. The servants of the general officers were usually well-armed and mounted. Will Lee, or Billy, the former huntsman, and favorite body-servant of the chief, a square muscular figure, and capital horseman, paraded a corps of valets, and, riding pompously at their head, proceeded to an eminence crowned by a large sycamore-tree, from whence could be seen an extensive portion of the field of battle. Here Billy halted, and, having unslung the large telescope that he always carried in a leathern case, with a martial air applied it to his eye, and reconnoitred the enemy.* Washington having observed these manœuvres of the corps of valets, pointed them out to his officers, observing, "See those fellows collecting on yonder height; the enemy will fire on them to a certainty." Meanwhile the British were not unmindful of the assemblage on the height, and perceiving a burly figure well-mounted, and with a telescope in hand, they determined to pay their respects to the group. A shot from a six-pounder passed through the tree, cutting away the limbs, and producing a scampering among the corps of valets, that caused even the grave countenance of the general-in-chief to relax into a smile.

Nor must we omit, among our incidents of the battle of Monmouth, to mention the achievement of the famed Captain Molly, a *nom de guerre* given to the wife of a

* The telescope is in possession (1859) of the Washington family, and has always been a conspicuous object upon the wall of the great passage at Mount Vernon.

matross in Proctor's artillery. At one of the guns of Proctor's battery, six men had been killed or wounded. It was deemed an unlucky gun, and murmurs arose that it should be drawn back and abandoned. At this juncture, while Captain Molly was serving some water for the refreshment of the men, her husband received a shot in the head, and fell lifeless under the wheels of the piece. The heroine threw down the pail of water, and crying to her dead consort, "Lie there my darling while I revenge ye," grasped the ramrod the lifeless hand of the poor fellow had just relinquished, sent home the charge, and called to the matrosses to prime and fire. It was done. Then entering the sponge into the smoking muzzle of the cannon, the heroine performed to admiration the duties of the most expert artilleryman, while loud shouts from the soldiers rang along the line. The doomed gun was no longer deemed unlucky, and the fire of the battery became more vivid than ever. The Amazonian fair one kept to her post till night closed the action, when she was introduced to General Greene, who, complimenting her upon her courage and conduct, the next morning presented her to the commander-in-chief. Washington received her graciously, gave her a piece of gold, and assured her that her services should not be forgotten.

This remarkable and intrepid woman survived the Revolution, never for an instant laying aside the appellation she had so nobly won, and levying contributions upon both civil and military, whenever she recounted the tale of the doomed gun, and the famed Captain Molly at the battle of Monmouth.*

* Molly was a sturdy young camp-follower, only twenty-two years of age, and, in devotion to her husband, she illustrated the character of her countrywomen of "the

On the night of the memorable conflict, Washington laid down in his cloak under a tree, in the midst of his brave soldiers. About midnight, an officer approached cautiously, fearful of awakening him, when the chief called out, "Advance, sir, and deliver your errand. I lie here *to think and not to sleep.*"

In the morning the American army prepared to renew the conflict, but the enemy had retired during the night, leaving their dead and many of their wounded to the care of the victors.* Morgan's mountaineers pursued on

---

Emerald isle." When her husband fell, and there appeared to be no one to take his place at the gun, the officer in command ordered it to be removed. Then she took her husband's place, as related in the text. Washington conferred upon her the commission of a sergeant, which her husband held, and by his recommendation her name was placed upon the list of half-pay officers, for life. Sergeant Molly left the army soon after the battle of Monmouth, and made her abode in the Hudson Highlands, near Fort Clinton, where, during the attack upon that fortress the previous autumn, she had displayed her heroism. She was there with her husband. When the British scaled the ramparts, he dropped his match and fled. Molly caught it up, touched off the piece, and then scampered away with the rest of the garrison. She fired the last gun at Fort Clinton. The venerable widow of General Hamilton told me that she had often seen Sergeant Molly, who was generally called captain. She described her as a stout, red-haired, freckled faced young Irish woman, with a handsome, piercing eye. The French officers, charmed with the story of her bravery, made her many presents. She would sometimes pass along the French lines, when they were in Westchester county, with her cocked hat, and get it almost filled with silver crowns. She wore a hybrid costume after the war — the petticoat of her sex, with an artilleryman's uniform over it. This woman died near Fort Montgomery, a victim to the indulgence of licentiousness. Art and Romance have confounded her with another character, Moll Pitcher.

* Sir Henry Clinton dared not risk another engagement. Both parties lay upon their arms during the evening after the battle. The Americans slept until morning; but the British commenced moving silently away from the field at midnight. Sir Henry Clinton was unwilling to give the impression that he made the movement by stealth, so he wrote to the ministry, saying, "Having reposed the troops until ten at night, to avoid the excessive heat of the day, *I took advantage of the moonlight* to rejoin General Knyphausen, who had advanced to Nut swamp, near Middletown." This assertion caused much merriment in America, because, according to Poor Will's Almanac, published in Philadelphia by Joseph Cruikshank, it was new moon on the twenty-fourth of June, and on the night of the battle was only four days old

their trail, and made some captures, particularly the coach of a general officer.

The British grand army embarked for Staten Island. The number, order, and regularity of the boats, and the splendid appearance of the troops, rendered this embarkation one of the most brilliant and imposing spectacles of the Revolutionary war.*

Congress passed a unanimous vote of thanks to the general-in-chief, his officers and soldiers, for the prompt-

---

and set at fifty-five minutes past ten. Trumbull, in his *M'Fingal*, thus alludes to the circumstance:—

> "He forms his camp with great parade,
> While evening spreads the world in shade,
> Then still, like some endangered spark,
> Steals off on tiptoe in the dark;
> Yet writes his king in boasting tone,
> How grand he marched by light of moon!
> . . . .
> Go on, great general, nor regard
> The scoffs of every scribbling bard,
> Who sings how gods, that fearful night,
> Aided, by miracle, your flight;
> As once they used in Homer's day,
> To help weak heroes run away;
> Tells how the hours, at this sad trial,
> Went back, as erst on Ahaz's dial,
> While British Joshua stayed the moon
> On Monmouth's plain for Ajalon.
> Heed not their sneers or gibes so arch,
> Because she set before your march."

* The Americans were ignorant of the departure of the enemy until dawn, when they were three hours on their way toward the shore. Washington considered pursuit to be fruitless, for his men were greatly fatigued, the heat was excessive, the soil was loose sand, and very little water could be found. Earl Howe's fleet was then lying in the waters between Staten Island and Sandy Hook, and on board of these vessels Sir Henry's troops were conveyed in boats from the latter port, on the thirtieth, and he escaped to New York. Washington marched his army to Brunswick, and thence to the Hudson river, which he crossed at King's ferry, just below the Highlands, and encamped near White Plains, in Westchester county.

ness of their march from Valley Forge, and their surprise and defeat of the enemy; and a *feu de joie* was fired by the whole American army for the victory of Monmouth.*

---

* On the seventh of July, the continental Congress adopted the following resolutions:—

"*Resolved unanimously*, That the thanks of Congress be given to General Washington for the activity with which he marched from the camp at Valley Forge in pursuit of the enemy; for his distinguished exertions in forming the line of battle; and for his great good conduct in leading on the attack and gaining the important victory of Monmouth over the British grand army, under the command of General Sir Henry Clinton, in their march from Philadelphia to New York.

"*Resolved*, That General Washington be directed to signify the thanks of Congress to the gallant officers and men under his command, who distinguished themselves by their conduct and valor at the battle of Monmouth."

CHAPTER VI.

THE SURRENDER AT YORKTOWN.

DE GRASSE EXPECTED FROM THE WEST INDIES — INTENDED ATTACK UPON NEW YORK — THE ENTERPRISE ABANDONED — MARCH OF THE ALLIED ARMIES FOR VIRGINIA — SIR HENRY CLINTON AND LORD CORNWALLIS — WASHINGTON'S INTERCEPTED LETTER — ARRIVAL OF COUNT DE GRASSE — LAFAYETTE'S GENEROSITY — WASHINGTON AND COUNT DE ROCHAMBEAU IN VIRGINIA — VISIT TO THE VILLE DE PARIS — ANECDOTE — ANTICIPATED TROUBLE — NAVAL BATTLE — APPROACH OF ALLIED TROOPS TO YORKTOWN — THE SIEGE OF YORKTOWN — INCIDENTS OF THE SIEGE — WASHINGTON EXPOSED TO DANGER — A SOLDIER'S APPEAL — PATRIOTISM OF GOVERNOR NELSON — CORNWALLIS'S HEADQUARTERS — FOOLISH DARING OF AN OFFICER — NEWS OF THE SURRENDER OF CORNWALLIS — CORNWALLIS'S ATTEMPT TO ESCAPE — THE SURRENDER OF THE BRITISH ARMY — WASHINGTON'S WAR-HORSE — CORNWALLIS AT WASHINGTON'S TABLE — COLONEL TARLETON HUMILIATED — SICKNESS AT YORKTOWN — DEATH OF JOHN PARKE CUSTIS — WASHINGTON'S GRIEF AND KINDNESS.*

THE campaign of 1781 was considerably advanced, without any decided advantages to the combined armies, when the chevalier de Barras, the commander of the French naval forces at Rhode Island,* announced to Gen-

---

* This chapter was first published in the *National Intelligencer*, on the nineteenth of October, 1840.

† On the sixth of February, 1778, France formally acknowledged the Independence of the United States, and entered into an alliance with them by solemn treaty. A French fleet was immediately fitted out at Toulon, and sent to aid the Americans, under the command of the Count D'Estaing. His performances on our coasts disappointed the Americans. The Marquis de Lafayette, then serving in the armies of the United States, procured leave of absence for one year, returned to France, and by great personal efforts, induced the king to send a much more powerful and substantial aid to the Americans, in the form of a strong naval and military force, arms, ammunition, and money. Admiral de Ternay was appointed commander of the fleet, and the Count de Rochambeau the leader of the land forces. The French fleet appeared off the coasts of Virginia, on the fourth of July, 1780, and on the evening of the tenth entered Newport harbor. There the fleet and army retained their headquarters until the following year, and were comparatively inactive. Admiral Ternay

eral Washington that the Count de Grasse would sail from the West Indies, with a powerful fleet and three thousand troops, on the third of August, and might be expected in the Chesapeake about the first of September. Upon the receipt of this agreeable intelligence, the allies lost no time in preparing for the investiture of New York; the Americans approaching gradually toward the city, and the French from Newport, the two armies forming a junction at Dobbs's ferry, on the Hudson.* Large bodies of troops were moved toward Staten Island, the first object of attack;† extensive magazines were collected, ovens built,‡ and everything indicating that the fleet alone was wanting to commence the siege in earnest, when, in the midst of these demonstrations, the combined armies suddenly decamped, and masking New York, proceeded in full march for the South.

The reasons that induced Washington thus to change the scene of his operations were, some of them, governed

---

had died soon after its arrival, and was buried with distinguished honors in Trinity churchyard, at Newport, and Admiral de Barras, mentioned in the text, became his successor in the command, the following spring.

* Dobbs's ferry is about twenty-two miles from the city of New York. There the combined armies of the United States and France first met. Washington, hoping to secure the co-operation of the Count de Grasse, with a French fleet then in the West Indies, had conceived a plan for attacking the headquarters of the British army at New York. He held an interview with Rochambeau, at Hartford, late in May, and an arrangement was made for the French army to march to Hudson's river as speedily as possible, and form a junction with the Americans encamped there. Four thousand fresh troops were soon in motion, and reached the Hudson, near Dobbs's ferry, early in July.

† Staten Island, between which and the city of New York, is the fine bay and harbor of New York, was an important point in the programme of operations against the enemy. There many of the British troops were encamped, and its heights commanded every opening to the sea.

‡ The remains of these ovens were to be seen in some places in that vicinity; until within a very recent period.

by circumstances beyond his control, especially as regarded the co-operation of the French naval forces. The Count de Grasse preferred the Chesapeake to the bay of New York, as being better suited to his large vessels, while the admiral, being limited in his remaining in the American waters to a certain and an early day, could most conveniently render his assistance in the South.* This, together with other and imposing considerations, induced the American general, while continuing to threaten Sir Henry Clinton, to strike at Cornwallis in Virginia.*

Sir Henry Clinton, aware that a powerful French fleet was destined for the American coast, and presuming that, upon its arrival, a combined attack would be made upon New York, ordered Earl Cornwallis, then pursuing his victorious career in Virginia, to fall down upon the tidewater, and, after selecting a spot where he could conveniently embark a part of his troops to reinforce his

* When the determination of the Count de Grasse was made known to Washington, he was sorely disappointed, for the recapture of New York seemed to be certainly promised, if the admiral's co-operation could be had. Washington was then at the house of Van Brugh Livingston, at Dobbs's ferry, and Robert Morris, then superintendent of finance, and Richard Peters, secretary of the board of war, were present. The cloud of disappointment upon Washington's brow remained only for a moment. He received the despatch from De Barras, mentioned in the first paragraph of this chapter, and he instantly conceived an expedition against Cornwallis, in Virginia. Turning to Peters, he asked, "What can you do for me?"—"With money, everything, without it nothing," was his brief reply, at the same time turning an anxious look toward Morris. "Let me know the sum you desire," said the patriotic financier, comprehending the expression of his eye. Before noon Washington had completed his estimates, and arrangements were made with Morris for the funds. Twenty thousand hard dollars were loaned from Count de Rochambeau, which Mr. Morris agreed to replace by the first of October. The arrival of Colonel Laurens from France, on the twenty-fifth of August, with two millions and a half of livres, a part of a donation of six millions by Louis XIV. to the United States, enabled the superintendent of finance to fulfil his engagement, without difficulty.

commander-in-chief, to entrench the remainder, and await further orders.* But the sudden and unexpected march of the combined armies to the South entirely changed the aspects of military affairs. It was now the earl, and not Sir Henry, that required reinforcement, and Sir Henry again writing to his lordship, bade him strengthen his position at Yorktown, promising him the immediate aid of both land and naval forces.†

Meantime, Washington had written a letter to the Marquis de Lafayette, then in Virginia, which he caused

---

* At the close of 1780, Benedict Arnold, the traitor, was in the service of his royal purchaser; and at the commencement of 1781, he invaded lower Virginia with about sixteen hundred British and Tory troops. He penetrated as far as Petersburgh, where he was joined by Lord Cornwallis, in May. The earl took command of all the British forces then in Virginia, who were opposed by a considerable army under Lafayette. He attempted the subjugation of the state, and penetrated the country into Hanover county, beyond Richmond, marking his pathway with the destruction of an immense amount of property, public and private. Two other commanders soon appeared in the field against him — General Wayne, who came from victorious fields in Georgia, and the Baron von Steuben. Cornwallis soon found himself in peril, and moved slowly down the peninsula, between the York and James rivers, followed by Lafayette, Wayne, and Steuben.

At Williamsburg, Cornwallis received the order from Sir Henry Clinton alluded to in the text, and, aware that he would be too weak after complying with it, to withstand the Americans, he crossed the James river, at old Jamestown, after a skirmish with the republicans under Wayne, and proceeded to Portsmouth, opposite Norfolk. Disliking that situation, he went to Yorktown, on the York river, and commenced fortifying that place, and Gloucester Point, opposite.

† The combined armies, after remaining about six weeks at Dobbs's ferry, crossed the Hudson at Verplanck's point, and under the general command of Lincoln, marched by different routes toward Trenton. By deceptive military movements, and letters that were intended to be intercepted, Washington misled Sir Henry Clinton with the belief that an attack upon New York was still in contemplation; and the British commander was not undeceived until the allied armies had crossed the Delaware, and were far on their way toward the Head of Elk. Clinton endeavored to recall the republican armies, by sending Arnold to ravage the New England coasts, and other forces to menace New Jersey and the Hudson Highlands, but in vain. The allies made their way rapidly toward Virginia, and the earl implored aid from Sir Henry.

to be intercepted. In the letter he remarked that he was pleased with the probability that Earl Cornwallis would fortify either Portsmouth or Old Point Comfort, *for, were he to fix upon Yorktown,* from its great capabilities of defence, he might remain there snugly and unharmed, until a superior British fleet would relieve him with strong reinforcements, or embark him altogether.

This fated letter quieted the apprehensions of the British commander-in-chief as to the danger of his lieutenant, and produced those delays in the operations of Sir Henry that tended materially to the success of the allies and the surrender of Yorktown.*

The fleet of the Count de Grasse, consisting of twenty-eight sail of the line, and a due proportion of frigates, containing three thousand veteran troops under the Marquis de St. Simon, anchored in the Chesapeake on the thirtieth of August.† The frigates were immediately

---

* Washington wrote other similar letters. The bearer of one of these was a young Baptist clergyman, named Montagnie, an ardent whig, who was directed by Washington to carry a despatch to Morristown. He directed the messenger to cross the river at King's ferry, proceed by Haverstraw to the Ramapo clove, and through the pass to Morristown. Montagnie, knowing the Ramapo pass to be in possession of the cow-boys and other friends of the enemy, ventured to suggest to the commander-in-chief that the upper road would be the safest. "I shall be taken," he said, "if I go through the clove." "Your duty, young man, is not to talk, but to obey!" replied Washington, sternly, enforcing his words by a vigorous stamp of his foot. Montagnie proceeded as directed, and, near the Ramapo pass, was caught. A few days afterward he was sent to New York, where he was confined in the Sugar-House, one of the famous provost prisons in the city. The day after his arrival, the contents of the despatches taken from him were published in *Rivington's Gazette* with great parade, for they indicated a plan of an attack upon the city. The enemy was alarmed thereby, and active preparations were put in motion for receiving the besiegers. Montagnie now perceived why he was so positively instructed to go through the Ramapo pass, where himself and despatches were quite sure to be seized.—Lossing's *Field-Book of the Revolution,* i. 781, note.

† François Joseph Paul, Count de Grasse, a native of France, was born in 1723. He was appointed to command a French fleet, to co-operate with the Americans at the beginning of 1781. Although he was the junior, in service, of Count de Barras,

employed in conveying the troops up the James river, where they were landed, and reinforced the army of Lafayette, who then commanded in Virginia. An instance of virtue and magnanimity that occurred at this period of our narrative adorns the fame and memory of Lafayette.

Upon the arrival of the French land and naval forces in our waters, their commanders said to Lafayette: " Now, marquis, now is your time; a wreath of never-fading laurel is within your grasp! Fame bids you seize it. With the veteran regiments of St. Simon, and your own continentals, you have five thousand; to these add a thousand marines, and a thousand seamen, to be landed from the fleet, making seven thousand good soldiers, which, with your militia, give you an aggregate exceeding ten thousand men. With these, storm the enemy's works while they are yet in an unfinished state, and before the arrival of the combined armies you will end the war, and acquire an immortal renown."—" Believe me, my dear sir," said the good Lafayette, during his visit in America, " this was a most tempting proposal to a young general of twenty-four, and who was not unambitious of

---

he was made his superior in command, with the title of lieutenant-general. His co operation was much more valuable to the Americans than that of D'Estaing; and in the capture of Cornwallis and his army at Yorktown, he played a very important part. His domestic relations seem to have been very unhappy, his second wife, whom he married after leaving America, proving a very unworthy woman. His life was a burden to him, particularly after losing the favor of his king in consequence of an unfortunate military movement. He died early in 1788, at the age of sixty-five years. Alluding to the unhappiness of his latter days, Washington, in a letter to Rochambeau, April, 1788, on hearing of the death of De Grasse, said, " His frailties should now be buried in the grave with him, while his name will be long deservedly dear to this country, on account of his successful co-operation in the glorious campaign of 1781. The Cincinnati in some of the states have gone into mourning for him."

fame by honest means; but insuperable reasons forbade me from listening to the proposal for a single moment. Our beloved general had intrusted to me a command far above my deserts, my age, or experience in war. From the time of my first landing in America, up to the campaign of 1781, I had enjoyed the attachment, nay, parental regards of the matchless chief. Could I then dare to attempt to pluck a leaf from the laurel that was soon to bind his honored brow — the well-earned reward of long years of toils, anxieties, and battles? And lastly, could I have been assured of success in my attack, from the known courage and discipline of the foe, that success must have been attended by a vast effusion of human blood."

The commander-in-chief, accompanied by the Count de Rochambeau, arrived at Williamsburg,* the head-quarters of Lafayette, on the fourteenth of September. The general, attended by a numerous suite of American and French officers, repaired to Hampton,† and thence on board the *Ville de Paris*, the French admiral's ship, lying at anchor in the chops of the Capes, to pay their

---

* The allied armies made their way slowly southward. For want of sufficient vessels at the Head of Elk, where they expected to embark for a voyage down the Chesapeake, a greater portion of the troops proceeded by land to Baltimore and Annapolis. Washington and his suite, accompanied by the Count de Rochambeau, and the Marquis de Chastellux, reached Baltimore on the eighth, Mount Vernon on the tenth, and Williamsburg on the evening of the fourteenth. That brief visit was the first that Washington had made to Mount Vernon since the spring of 1775, when he left for Philadelphia, as a delegate to the continental Congress.

† Hampton is near Old Point Comfort, at the mouth of the James river, having in front one of the finest harbors in the world, called Hampton roads, which opens to the Chesapeake bay. Washington and his party, consisting of Lafayette, Rochambeau, Knox, Harrison, Hamilton, and others, sailed for the *Ville de Paris*, in a small vessel called the *Queen Charlotte*, and arrived on board on the eighteenth of September. They were greeted with a salute of thirteen guns, and welcomed to an entertainment prepared in haste, but with great taste.

respects to the Count de Grasse, and consult with him as to their future operations.

On the American chief's reaching the quarter-deck, the admiral flew to embrace him, imprinting the French salute upon each cheek. Hugging him in his arms, he exclaimed, "*My dear little general!*" De Grasse was of lofty stature; but the term *petit*, or small, when applied to the majestic and commanding person of Washington, produced an effect upon the risible faculties of all present not to be described. The Frenchmen, governed by the rigid etiquette of the *ancien régime*, controlled their mirth as best they could; but our own jolly Knox, heedless of all rules, laughed, and that aloud, till his fat sides shook again.

Washington returned from this conference by no means satisfied with its result. The admiral was extremely restless at anchor while his enemy's fleet kept the sea; and having orders limiting his stay in the American waters to a certain and that not distant day, he was desirous of putting to sea to block up the enemy's fleet in the basin of New York, rather than to run the risk of being himself blockaded in the bay of the Chesapeake.

Washington urged De Grasse to remain, because his departure, he said, " by affording an opening for the succor of York, which the enemy would instantly avail themselves of, would frustrate our brilliant prospects; and the consequence would be, not only the disgrace and loss of renouncing an enterprise, upon which the fairest expectations of the allies have been founded, after the most expensive preparations, but perhaps disbanding the whole army for want of provisions."

Washington now despatched Lafayette on a secret

mission to the count; and never, in the whole course of the Revolutionary contest, were the services of that friend of America of more value to her cause than in the present instance.

The all-commanding influence of Lafayette at this period, not only with the French court, of which he was the idol, but with the whole people of France; his powerful family connections with the high *noblesse*, particularly the distinguished family of De Noailles;* all these considerations enabled Lafayette to throw himself as a shield between the Count de Grasse and any blame that might be attached to him at home for yielding to the views and wishes of the American chief.

The marquis prevailed, and he soon returned to headquarters with the gratifying intelligence that the admiral had consented to remain at his anchors (unless a British fleet should appear off the capes), and would send a part of his vessels higher up the bay, the better to complete the investiture of Yorktown.

The fate of De Grasse and the *Ville de Paris* is well known to history. That magnificent ship was a present from the city of Paris to the French king. She rated one hundred and ten guns, and thirteen hundred men. It is said that on her arrival in the Chesapeake, flowers and tropical plants were interspersed upon her quarter-deck, amid the engines of war; while her sides, covered with bright varnish, gave to this superb vessel a most brilliant and imposing appearance. On the memorable twelfth of April, 1782, De Grasse, deserted by some

* Lafayette married the Countesse Anastasie de Noailles, daughter of the Duke de Noailles, a young lady possessed of an immense fortune in her own right. The Duke de Noailles was a member of one of the oldest and most influential families in France.

of his captains, his own ship totally dismasted, a large proportion of his officers and crew killed or wounded, nobly maintained the unequal contest, and refused to yield to any ship carrying less than an admiral's flag.* At length the *Barfleur* of ninety-eight guns, Sir Samuel Hood, ranging alongside, the colors of France were lowered on the poop of as bravely-defended a vessel as hath adorned the annals of the French marine, either before or since. Let those who would put their trust in princes, mark the fate of gallant De Grasse. When he struck, but three men remained alive on the quarter-deck of the *Ville de Paris*, one of whom was the admiral; yet, on his return to his native country, the king, whose colors he had so nobly defended, turned with coldness from the unfortunate brave, leaving him to languish in retirement and disgrace. How different was the conduct of the enemies of De Grasse, the English sailors, who, on the arrival of their prisoner at Portsmouth, *hoisted him on their shoulders*, and honoring high courage in misfortune, *carried him in triumph* to his lodgings, bidding him adieu, with three hearty cheers. It is thus the brave should honor the brave.

On the fifth of September, Admiral Graves, with nineteen sail-of-the-line, appeared off the capes of Virginia.†

---

* The *Ville de Paris* had been reduced to almost a wreck by the *Canada*, commanded by Captain Cornwallis, brother of Lord Cornwallis, who seemed determined to avenge his kinsman's fate at Yorktown. This severe naval battle, under the general command of Admiral Rodney, occurred in the West Indies. The English were victorious. But several of their prizes were lost in hurricanes that ensued. Four of the French ships captured on the twelfth of April, namely, the *Ville de Paris*, *Centaur*, *Glorieux*, and *Hector*, and an English-built ship-of-the-line, the *Ramillies*, all foundered at sea while employed in giving convoy to a great fleet of West Indiamen.

† Admiral Rodney, commander of the British fleet in the West Indies, aware that De Grasse had sailed for the American coast, sent Sir Samuel Hood after him with only fourteen sail, not suspecting that the French admiral had taken his whole fleet

Count de Grasse immediately slipped his cables, and put to sea with twenty-four line-of-battle ships. An engagement ensued, without material results to either side, and, after four days of manœuvring, the French fleet returned to its former anchorage, the British bearing away for New York.*

Meantime, the Chevalier de Barras had arrived, with eight sail-of-the-line, bringing a battering-train, and an ample supply of all the munitions necessary for the siege. These were speedily landed up the James river, and many delays and disappointments occurred in their transportation to the lines before Yorktown, a distance of six miles. Long trains of the small oxen of the country tugged at a single gun, and it was not until the arrival of the better teams of the grand army that much progress could be made.†

The combined armies, arriving at the Head of Elk,‡ embarked a portion of the troops in transports; another

---

to the shores of the neighboring continent. Hood arrived at Sandy Hook at the close of August, and gave Admiral Graves, then lying in the harbor of New York, with five ships-of-the-line prepared for service, notice of the destination of De Grasse's fleet. On the same day information reached Sir Henry Clinton, that Admiral de Barras had sailed from Newport for the Chesapeake, with a considerable squadron. Graves, with nineteen sail, departed for the same waters, as speedily as possible.

* This naval engagement took place outside the capes of Virginia, upon the bosom of the broad Atlantic. The engagement was partial. The hostile fleets were within sight of each other for five successive days. The French lost in the action two hundred and twenty men, and four officers, killed and wounded. The loss of the English was ninety killed and two hundred and forty-six wounded.

† Within the state-arsenal, at Richmond, Virginia, there are several French cannon, long, and highly wrought, and some of them a hundred years old; also two or three howitzers. How they came there no one can tell. Old people remember to have seen them on the grounds of the capitol fifty years ago, but knew not how they came there. They were probably left by the French at the siege of Yorktown, and afterward taken up the river to Richmond.

‡ The narrow part of the Chesapeake bay, at it head, is called Elk river, and where Elkton now stands, was known, at that time, as *Head of Elk*.

portion were embarked at Baltimore; while the remainder pursued the route by land to Virginia—the whole rendezvousing at Williamsburg.*

On the twenty-eighth of September the allies moved in four columns, in order of battle, and, the outposts of the enemy being driven in, the first parallel was commenced. The work continued with such diligence that the batteries opened on the night of the ninth of October, and a tremendous fire of shot and shells continued without interruption. A red-hot shot from the French, who were on the left, fell upon the *Gaudaloupe* and *Charon*, two British frigates. The latter, of forty-four guns, was consumed together with three transports.†

The defences of the town were hourly sinking under the effects of the cannonade from the American and French batteries, when, on the night of the fourteenth, it was determined to carry the two British redoubts on the south, by the bayonet. For this service, detachments were detailed from both the American and French armies—the former under the command of Lieutenant-Colonel Hamilton, long the favorite aid of the commander-

---

* When Washington arrived at Williamsburg, and found both the French fleets in Chesapeake bay, he sent ten transports of De Barras's squadron to bring on the allied forces from Maryland. The last division of the allied troops reached Williamsburg on the twenty-fifth of September.

† The first heavy cannonade and bombardment by the allied forces occurred on the tenth of October. On that evening the vessels mentioned in the text, were set on fire. Three large transports were consumed at the same time. Doctor Thacher in his journal, page 274, says, "From the bank of the river I had a fine view of this splendid conflagration. The ships were enwrapped in a torrent of fire, which, spreading with vivid brightness among the combustible rigging, and running with amazing rapidity to the tops of the several masts, while all around was thunder and lightning from our numerous cannons and mortars, and in the darkness of night, presented one of the most sublime and magnificent spectacles which can be imagined. Some of our shells over-reaching the town, were seen to fall into the river, and bursting, threw up columns of water like the spouting of the monsters of the deep."

in-chief, but now restored to his rank and duty in the line,* and the latter under the Baron de Viomenil.

At a given signal the detachments advanced to the assault. As the Americans were mounting the redoubt, Lieutenant-Colonel Laurens,† aid-de-camp to the commander-in-chief, appeared suddenly on their flank, at the head of two companies. Upon Major Fish‡ hailing him with, "Why, Laurens, what brought you here?" the hero replied, "I had nothing to do at headquarters, and so came here to see what you all were about." Bravest among the brave, this Bayard of his age and country rushed with the foremost into the works, making with his own hand, Major Campbell, the British commandant, a prisoner-of-war.§ The cry of the Americans as they mounted to the assault was, "Remember New London." But here, as at Stony Point, notwithstanding the provocation to retaliate was justified by the inhuman massa-

* In the preceding February a misunderstanding occurred between Washington and Hamilton. The latter, feeling aggrieved at some words of censure spoken by his general, promptly proposed a separation. "Very well, sir," said Washington, "if it be your choice." But within an hour he sent an aid to offer Hamilton the olive-branch of reconciliation. But the young officer, who, for some time, had been anxious to hold a more independent and distinguished part in the army, would not listen to the generous overture, and from that time he was separated from the general's military family, but not from his friendship.

† John Laurens, son of Henry Laurens, who was president of the continental Congress in 1777. He was one of the most gallant young men in the army. He was sent on a special mission to France early in 1782, to solicit a loan of money and to procure arms. He was successful, and received the thanks of Congress. He did good service in the South under General Greene, and was killed on the bank of the Combahee, while opposing marauding parties of the British, on the twenty-seventh of August, 1782, at the age of twenty-nine years.

‡ Major Nicholas Fish, of the New York line, and father of Honorable Hamilton Fish, late governor of the state of New York.

§ Major Campbell, several inferior officers, and seventeen privates, were made prisoners. This redoubt was on the bank of the York river. The mounds were quite prominent when I visited the spot in the winter of 1848-9.

cres of Paoli and Fort Griswold, mercy, divine mercy, perched triumphant on our country's colors.*

Washington, during the whole of the siege, continued to expose himself to every danger. It was in vain his officers remonstrated. It was in vain that Colonel Cobb, his aid-de-camp, entreated him to come down from a parapet, whence he was reconnoitring the enemy's works, the shot and shells flying thickly around, and an officer of the New England line killed within a very few yards. During one of his visits to the main battery, a soldier of Colonel Lamb's artillery† had his leg shattered by the

---

* We have already observed that Arnold was sent to ravage the New England coasts, in order to draw the combined armies back from their march toward Virginia. On the morning of the sixth of September, 1781, Arnold, with a considerable force, consisting mostly of tories and Hessians, landed upon the shores of the Thames, below New London. They landed in two divisions, the one on the New London side being commanded by Arnold in person. He proceeded to lay New London in ashes, while, Nero-like, he stood in the belfry of a church and watched the conflagration; and from that elevated point he could almost see his own birthplace, at Norwich, at the head of the river. The other division, under one of Arnold's subordinates, attacked Fort Griswold, at Groton, on the opposite shore, and murdered Colonel Ledyard and most of the garrison under him, in cold blood. It was to these atrocities that the war-cry alluded to referred. Gordon asserts, that Lafayette, with the sanction of Washington, ordered the assailants to *remember Fort Griswold,* and put every man of the redoubt to death. This order, so repugnant to the character of both Washington and Lafayette, could never have been issued. Colonel Hamilton afterward publicly denied the truth of the allegation; so also did Lafayette.

† Colonel John Lamb was one of the most meritorious of the officers of the artillery department. He was then fifty years of age, and had been one of the earliest of the opposers of the British government in New York, who bore the name of Liberty Boys. He was a good writer and fluent speaker, both of which accomplishments he brought into useful requisition when the troubles with Great Britain began. In all the commotions in his native city (New York), previous to the breaking out of the Revolution, he was very active; and in 1775, he received a captain's commission in a New York artillery corps. He accompanied Montgomery to Quebec, where, in the siege of that city, at the close of 1775, he was severely wounded and made prisoner. He returned to New York the ensuing summer, was promoted to major, and became attached to the artillery regiment under Knox. From that time until the close of the war he was in active service, when the army was in the field. He

explosion of a shell. As they were bearing him to the rear, he recognised the chief, and cried out, "God bless your excellency, save me if you can, for I have been a good soldier, and served under you during the whole war." Sensibly affected by the brave fellow's appeal, the general immediately ordered him to the particular care of Doctor Craik. It was too late; death terminated his sufferings after an amputation was performed.

At this period of the siege occurred that sublime instance of patriotism which we have recorded in another chapter, when Governor Nelson directed the heavy shot and bomb-shells of the Americans to be cast upon his own fine house, in order to dislodge British officers who had their quarters there.

And yet how many and how endearing recollections must have crowded upon the patriot's mind as he thus consigned his ancient domicil to destruction. Erected by his forefathers, it was around its hearths that, in his childhood, he had played.* Beneath its roof he had reared a numerous and interesting family, and passed his better days in dispensing the most liberal hospitality to a large and estimable circle of relatives and friends; all, all were forgotten as, with Roman heroism, he bade the batteries direct their thunders against the seat of his happiness and his home.

---

afterward became a legislator in his native State; and Washington, when he became president of the United States, appointed him collector of customs at the port of New York. He held that office until his death, on the thirty-first of May, 1800.

* In an old burial-ground at Yorktown, are the remains of several of the Nelson family, covered by fine marble monuments, one of them quite costly. And the stone house, battered by the cannon balls during the siege, is yet standing. See biographical sketch of Governor Nelson in another chapter.

The first headquarters of Earl Cornwallis were in the house of Mr. Secretary Nelson, a relative of the governor, and a gentleman attached to the royal cause. It was a very large and splendid brick mansion, and towering above the ramparts, afforded a fine mark for the American artillery, that soon riddled it, having learned from a deserter that it contained the British headquarters. His lordship remained in the house until his steward was killed by a cannon-ball while carrying a tureen of soup to his master's table.

The British general then removed his headquarters to the house of Governor Nelson, and finally to apartments excavated in the bank on the southern extremity of the town, where two rooms were wainscotted with boards, and lined with baize, for his accommodation.* It was in that cavernous abode that the earl received his last letter from Sir Henry Clinton. It was brought by the honorable Colonel Cochran, who, landing from an English cutter on Cape Charles, procured an open boat, and threading his way, under cover of a fog, through the French fleet, arrived safely, and delivered his despatches. They contained orders for the earl to hold out to the last extremity, assuring him that a force of seven thousand men would be immediately embarked for his relief.†

---

* No traces of this retreat can now be found. It was excavated in the bank of rock-marl upon which the village of Yorktown stands, but has disappeared long ago. Full a quarter of a mile above the spot, there is an excavation in the same bank, to which strangers were directed, when I visited Yorktown a few years ago, as the veritable council-chamber of Cornwallis; but I was informed, by good authority, that the cave I visited was made, at or before the siege, to hide valuables in. I saw the remains of a house that had stood directly in front of it, and which must have concealed the entrance to the cavern.

† From the first, Cornwallis appears to have doubted his ability to maintain his position long. When he first saw perils gathering thick around him, the French fleet

While taking wine with his lordship after dinner, the gallant colonel proposed that he should go up to the ramparts and take a look at the Yankees, and upon his return give Washington's health in a bumper. He was dissuaded from so rash a proceeding by every one at the table, the whole of the works being at that time in so ruinous a state that shelter could be had nowhere. The colonel however persisted, and gayly observing that he would leave his glass as his representative till his return, which would be quickly, away he went. Poor fellow, he did return, and that quickly, but he was borne in the arms of the soldiers, not to his glass, but his grave.

For a great distance around Yorktown the earth trembled under the cannonade, while many an anxious and midnight watcher ascended to the housetops to listen to the sound, and to look upon the horizon, lighted up by the blaze of the batteries, the explosions of the shells, and the flames from the burning vessels in the harbor.

At length, on the morning of the seventeenth, the thundering ceased, hour after hour passed away, and the most attentive ear could not catch another sound. What had happened? Can Cornwallis have escaped? To suppose he had fallen, was almost too much to hope for. And now an intense anxiety prevails: every eye is

approaching on one hand, and the allied armies on the other, he conceived a plan of escaping into North Carolina; but the vigilant Lafayette prevented his flight. He at once sent a message to Clinton for aid, and received the reply alluded to in the text. He used every endeavor to delay, first his offer to capitulate, and then the signing of the capitulation, hoping for aid. Washington, suspecting the reason, would suffer no delay, and on the very day when the capitulation was signed, Clinton, with seven thousand men, left New York for the Chesapeake, convoyed by twenty-six ships of the line, under Admiral Digby. This armament appeared off the capes of Virginia, on the twenty-fourth of October; but receiving unquestionable intelligence of the capitulation at Yorktown, Clinton returned to New York.

turned toward the great southern road, and "the express! the express!" is upon every lip. Each hamlet and homestead pours forth its inmates. Age is seen leaning on his staff; women with infants at the breast; children with wondering eyes, and tiny hands outstretched—all, all, with breathless hopes and fears, await the courier's coming. Ay, and the courier rode with a red spur that day; but had he been mounted on the wings of the wind, he could scarcely have kept pace with the general anxiety.

At length there is a cry—"He comes! he comes!" and merging from a cloud of dust, a horseman is seen at headlong speed. He plies the lash and spur; covered with foam, with throbbing flank, and nostril dilated to catch the breeze, the generous horse devours the road, while ever and anon the rider waves his cap, and shouts to the eager groups that crowd his way, "Cornwallis is taken!"*

And now arose a joyous cry that made the very welkin tremble. The tories, amazed and confounded, shrunk away to their holes and hiding-places, while the patriotic whigs rushed into each other's arms, and wept for gladness. And oh! on that day of general thanksgiving and

* The accomplished Lieutenant-Colonel Tilghman, one of Washington's aids, was sent to Philadelphia by the chief, with despatches to the Congress, announcing the surrender of Cornwallis. He arrived there in the night, and soon the watchmen of the city were calling the hours, with the suffix, "*and Cornwallis is taken!*" That annunciation ringing out on the frosty night-air, aroused thousands from their slumbers. Lights were soon seen moving in almost every house; and presently the streets were thronged with men and women, all eager to hear the details. It was a joyous night for Philadelphia. The old state-house bell rang out its jubilant notes more than an hour before dawn, and the first blush of morning was greeted with the booming of cannon. The Congress assembled at an early hour, when Charles Thomson read Washington's despatch, and then they resolved to go in procession at two o'clock the same day, to a temple of worship, "and return thanks to Almighty God for crowning the allied armies of the United States and France with success."

praise, how many an aspiration ascended to the Most High, imploring blessings on him whom all time will consecrate as the FATHER OF HIS COUNTRY. That event was indeed the crowning glory of the war of the Revolution; hostilities languished thereafter, while Independence and empire dawned upon the destinies of America, from the surrender at Yorktown.

After a fruitless attempt to escape, in which the elements, as at Long Island, were on the side of America and her cause,* on the morning of the seventeenth Cornwallis beat a parley. Terms were arranged, and, on the nineteenth, the British army laid down its arms.†

The imposing ceremony took place at two o'clock. The American troops were drawn up on the right, and the French on the left, of the high road leading to Hampton. A vast crowd of persons from the adjoining country attended to witness the ceremony.‡

The captive army, in perfect order, marched in stern

---

* This has reference to the fog on the East river that allowed the Americans to retreat from Brooklyn, unperceived by the enemy, after the disastrous battle near there on the twenty-ninth of August, 1776. On the present occasion, a storm suddenly arose, and prevented Cornwallis and his troops from crossing the York river to Gloucester, in boats which had been prepared for the purpose. His plan was to withdraw in that way from Yorktown, in the night, by rapid marches gain the forks of the Rappahannock and Potomac, and forcing his way through Maryland, Pennsylvania, and New Jersey, form a junction with the British army under Clinton, in New York.

† The siege had continued thirteen days. The British lost during the siege one hundred and fifty-six killed, three hundred and twenty-six wounded, and seventy missing. The whole number surrendered by capitulation was a little more than seven thousand. Besides these, there were sailors, negroes, and tories, who became prisoners, making the whole number between eleven and twelve thousand.

‡ It has been estimated that the number of spectators of the ceremony of surrender, was quite equal to that of the military. Universal silence prevailed as the vanquished troops slowly marched out of their intrenchments, with their colors cased and their drums beating a British tune, and passed between the columns of the combined armies.

and solemn silence between the lines. All eyes were turned toward the head of the advancing column. Cornwallis, the renowned, the dreaded Cornwallis, was the object that thousands longed to behold. He did not appear, but sent his sword by General O'Hara, with an apology for his non-appearance on account of indisposition. It was remarked that the British soldiers looked only toward the French army on the left, whose appearance was assuredly more brilliant than that of the Americans, though the latter were respectable in both their clothing and appointments, while their admirable discipline and the hardy and veteran appearance of both officers and men showed they were no "carpet knights," but soldiers who had seen service and were inured to war.

Lafayette, at the head of his division, observing that the captives confined their admiration exclusively to the French army, neglecting his darling light-infantry, the very apple of his eye and pride of his heart, determined to bring "eyes to the right." He ordered his music to strike up Yankee Doodle: "Then," said the good general, "they did look at us, my dear sir, but were not very well pleased."

When ordered to ground arms, the Hessian was content. He was tired of the war; his pipe and his patience pretty well exhausted, he longed to bid adieu to toilsome marches, battles, and the heat of the climate that consumed him. Not so the British soldier; many threw their arms to the ground in sullen despair. One fine veteran fellow displayed a soldierly feeling that excited the admiration of all around. He hugged his musket to his osom, gazed tenderly on it, pressed it to his lips,

SURRENDER AT YORKTOWN.

then threw it from him, and marched away dissolved in tears.*

On the day of the surrender, the commander-in-chief rode his favorite and splendid charger, named Nelson, a light sorrel, sixteen hands high, with white face and legs, and remarkable as being the first nicked horse seen in America. This famous charger died at Mount Vernon many years after the Revolution, at a very advanced age. After the chief had ceased to mount him, he was never ridden, but grazed in a paddock in summer, and was well cared for in winter; and as often as the retired farmer of Mount Vernon would be making a tour of his grounds, he would halt at the paddock, when the old war-horse would run, neighing, to the fence, proud to be caressed by the great master's hands.

The day after the surrender, Earl Cornwallis repaired to headquarters to pay his respects to General Washington and await his orders. The captive chief was received with all the courtesy due to a gallant and unfortunate foe. The elegant manners, together with the manly, frank, and soldierly bearing of Cornwallis, soon made him a prime favorite at headquarters, and he often formed part of the suite of the commander-in-chief in his rides to inspect the levelling of the works previous to

* The delivering of the colors was one of the most painful events of the surrender, to the captives. There were twenty-eight of them. For this purpose, twenty-eight British captains, each bearing a flag in a case, were drawn up in line. Opposite to them, at a distance of six paces, twenty-eight American sergeants were placed to receive the colors, and an ensign was appointed by Colonel Hamilton, the officer of the day, to conduct the ceremony. When the ensign gave an order for the captains to advance two paces, and the American sergeants to advance two paces, the former hesitated, saying they were unwilling to surrender their flags to non-commissioned officers. Hamilton, sitting upon his horse at a distance, observed this hesitation. He rode up, and when informed of the difficulty, ordered the ensign to receive them all and hand them over to the sergeants.

the retirement of the combined armies from before Yorktown.*

At the grand dinner given at the headquarters to the officers of the three armies, Washington filled his glass, and, after his invariable toast, whether in peace or war, of "*All our friends*," gave "The British Army," with some complimentary remarks upon its chief, his proud career in arms, and his gallant defence of Yorktown. When it came to Cornwallis's turn, he prefaced his toast by saying that the war was virtually at an end, and the contending parties would soon embrace as friends; there might be affairs of posts, but nothing on a more enlarged scale, as it was scarcely to be expected that the ministry would send another army to America.† Then turning to Wash-

---

* Yorktown was evacuated by conquerors and captives, within a fortnight after the surrender. Some of the prisoners were marched to Winchester, in Virginia, and some to Fort Frederick and Fredericktown, in Maryland. The latter were finally removed to Lancaster, in Pennsylvania, and guarded by continental troops. Cornwallis and other British officers went by sea to New York, on parole. Finally, they were all exchanged.

† The fall of Cornwallis was a severe blow to the British ministry. Sir N. W. Wraxall, in his *Historical Memoirs of his Own Times* (page 246), has left an interesting record of the effect of the news of the surrender of Cornwallis upon the minds of Lord North and the king. The intelligence reached the cabinet on Sunday, the twenty-fifth of November, at noon. Wraxall asked Lord George Germain how North "took the communication?"—"As he would have taken a cannon-ball in his breast," replied Lord George; "for he opened his arms, exclaiming wildly, as he paced up and down the apartment during a few minutes, 'Oh! God, it is all over!' words which he repeated many times, under emotions of the deepest consternation and distress." Lord George Germain sent off a despatch to the king, who was then at Kew. The king wrote a calm letter in reply, but it was remarked, as evidence of unusual emotion, that he had omitted to mark the hour and minute of his writing, which he was always accustomed to do with scrupulous precision. Yet the handwriting evinced composure of mind.

Parliament assembled on the twenty-seventh of November, and its first business was the consideration of events in America. Violent debates ensued, in which Edmund Burke, Charles James Fox, General Conway, and the younger Pitt, engaged on the side of the opposition. Parliament adjourned until after the holydays, with-

ington, his lordship continued: "And when the illustrious part that your excellency has borne in this long and arduous contest becomes matter of history, fame will gather your brightest laurels rather from the banks of the Delaware than from those of the Chesapeake." In this his lordship alluded to the memorable midnight march made by Washington with the shattered remains of the grand army, aided by the Pennsylvania militia, on the night of the second of January, 1777, which resulted in the surprise of the enemy in his rear, and the victory of Princeton, restoring hope to the American cause when it was almost sinking in despair.

Colonel Tarleton, alone of all the British officers of rank, was left out in the invitations to headquarters. Gallant and high-spirited, the colonel applied to the Marquis de Lafayette to know whether the neglect might not have been accidental? Lafayette well knew that accident had nothing to do with the matter, but referred the applicant to Lieutenant-Colonel Laurens, who, as aid-de-camp to the commander-in-chief, must of course be able to give the requisite explanation. Laurens at once said, "No, Colonel Tarleton, no accident at all; intentional, I can assure you, and meant as a reproof for

out taking any definite action in the matter. On reassembling, the subject was again brought up, when General Conway offered a resolution preliminary to the enactment of a decree for commanding the cessation of all hostilities. It was lost by only one vote. The opposition were encouraged, and again pressed the matter, and finally, on the fourth of March, 1782, a resolution was offered by Conway, "That the house of commons and the nation would consider as enemies to his majesty and the country, all those who should advise, or by any means attempt, the further prosecution of offensive war on the continent of North America." The ministry were signally defeated in the vote on this resolution, and Lord North, after an administration as prime minister, of twelve years, resigned the seals of office; and soon a decree to cease hostilities, was furnished to the British commanders in America.

certain cruelties practised by the troops under your command in the campaigns of the Carolinas."—"What, sir," haughtily rejoined Tarleton, "and is it for severities inseparable from war, which you are pleased to term cruelties, that I am to be disgraced before junior officers? Is it, sir, for a faithful discharge of my duty to my king and my country, that I am thus humiliated in the eyes of three armies?"—"Pardon me," continued Colonel Laurens, "there are modes, sir, of discharging a soldier's duty, and where mercy has a share in the mode, it renders the duty the more acceptable to both friends and foes." Tarleton stalked gloomily away to his quarters, which he seldom left until his departure from Virginia.*

* Banastre Tarleton was born in Liverpool, England, in 1754. He had commenced the study of law when the American war broke out. He then joined the army and came over with Cornwallis. He was with that officer in all his campaigns in this country, was an active leader of cavalry at the South, and ended his military career at Yorktown. He seemed innately cruel while in this country. On his return to England, the inhabitants of Liverpool elected him their representative in the house of commons. He married the daughter of the duke of Ancaster in 1798, and in 1817 became a major-general in the British army. When George IV. was crowned, he was created a baronet. He died in 1833.

In a personal rencounter with Colonel William Washington, at the battle of the Cowpens, Colonel Tarleton was severely wounded in the hand. According to Mrs. Ellet's "Women of the Revolution," this wound was twice made the point of severe wit by two American ladies, who were daughters of Colonel Montfort, of Halifax, North Carolina. Because of his cruel and resentful disposition, he was most heartily despised by the republicans. The occasions were as follows: When Cornwallis and his army were at Halifax, on their way to Virginia, Tarleton was at the house of an American. In the presence of Mrs. Willie Jones (one of these sisters), Tarleton spoke of Colonel Washington as an illiterate fellow, hardly able to write his name. 'Ah, colonel," said Mrs. Jones, "you ought to know better, for you bear on your erson proof that he knows very well *how to make his mark!*" At another time, Tarleton was speaking sarcastically of Washington, in the presence of her sister, Mrs. Ashe. "I would be happy to see Colonel Washington," he said, with a sneer. Mrs. Ashe instantly replied, "If you had looked behind you, Colonel Tarleton, at the battle of the Cowpens, you would have enjoyed that pleasure." Stung with this keen wit, Tarleton placed his hand on his sword. General Leslie, who was present, remarked, "Say what you please, Mrs. Ashe, Colonel Tarleton knows better than to insult a lady in my presence."

Upon the surrender of the post of Gloucester, Colonel Tarleton, knowing himself to be particularly obnoxious to the Americans from his conduct in the South, requested a guard for his person. This was afterward dispensed with, but he was destined to be sadly humiliated upon his arrival in Yorktown, being dismounted in the street from a beautiful blood-horse that was claimed by a Virginian gentleman as his property. The colonel was on his way to dine with the Baron de Viomenil, and but for a French officer who was passing, dismounting an orderly, and giving his steed to the unfortunate colonel, this celebrated cavalier, badly calculated for a pedestrian, from a defect in one of his feet, must have trudged it to the baron's quarters, a distance of more than a mile.

The weather during the siege of Yorktown was propitious in the extreme, being, with the exception of the squall on the night of the sixteenth,[*] the fine autumnal weather of the South, commonly called the Indian summer, which greatly facilitated the military operations. Washington's headquarters were under canvass the whole time.[†]

The situation of Yorktown, after the surrender, was pestilential. Numbers of wretched negroes who had either been taken from the plantations, or had of themselves followed the fortunes of the British army, had died of the small-pox, which, with the camp-fever, was raging in the place, and remained unburied in the streets.

[*] The night when Cornwallis attempted to escape.

[†] The place where the commissioners met to agree upon terms of capitulation was Moore's house, near the banks of the York river. It has sometimes been erroneously called Washington's headquarters. That building is yet standing, in the midst of a beautiful lawn and a pleasant surrounding country. I visited it on the twenty-first of December, 1848, when so mild was the weather, that, by permission of the occupant, I plucked a full-blown rose that was blooming near a verandah.

When all hope of escape was given up, the horses of the British legion were led to the margin of the river, shot, and then thrown into the stream. The carcasses, floating with the tide, lodged on the adjacent shores and flats, producing an effluvium that affected the atmosphere for miles around. Indeed, it was many months before Yorktown and its environs became sufficiently purified to be habitable with any degree of comfort.

A domestic affliction threw a shade over Washington's happiness, while his camp still rang with shouts of triumph for the surrender of Yorktown. His step-son* (to whom he had been a parent and protector, and to whom he was fondly attached), who had acccompanied him to the camp at Cambridge, and was among the first of his aids in the dawn of the Revolution, sickened while on duty as extra aid to the commander-in-chief in the trenches before Yorktown. Aware that his disease (the camp-fever), would be mortal, the sufferer had yet one last lingering wish to be gratified, and he would die content. It was to behold the surrender of the sword of Cornwallis. He was supported to the ground, and witnessed the admired spectacle, and was then removed to Eltham, a distance of thirty miles from camp.†

An express from Dr. Craik announced that there was no longer hope, when Washington, attended by a single officer, and a groom, left the headquarters at midnight, and rode with all speed for Eltham.

The anxious watchers by the couch of the dying were, in the gray of the twilight, aroused by a trampling of

---

* John Parke Custis, the only son of Mrs. Washington, and father of the author of these *Recollections*.

† The residence of Colonel Basset, who married Mrs. Washington's sister.

horse, and, looking out, discovered the commander-in-chief alighting from a jaded charger in the courtyard. He immediately summoned Doctor Craik, and to the eager inquiry, "Is there any hope?" Craik mournfully shook his head. The general retired to a room to indulge his grief, requesting to be left alone. In a little while the poor sufferer expired. Washington, tenderly embracing the bereaved wife and mother, observed to the weeping group around the remains of him he so dearly loved, "From this moment I adopt his two youngest children as my own."* Absorbed in grief, he then waived with his hand a melancholy adieu, and, fresh horses being ready, without rest or refreshment, he remounted and returned to the camp.

* These were Eleanor Parke Custis, who married Lawrence Lewis, the favorite nephew of General Washington, and George Washington Parke Custis — the latter, the author of these *Recollections*.

NOTE.—After the foregoing chapter was in type, I found in the Philadelphia *Sunday Despatch*, in one of a series of articles on the *History of Chestnut street*, from the pen of one of the editors, the following extract from an old paper, entitled the *Allied Mercury or Independent Intelligencer*, of the date of fifth November, 1781 which relates to the British banners surrendered at Yorktown, mentioned in a note on page 249 of these *Recollections* :—

"On Saturday last (November 3, 1781), between three and four o'clock in the afternoon, arrived here twenty-four standards of colors taken with the British army under the command of Earl Cornwallis. The volunteer cavalry of this city received these trophies of victory at Schuylkill, from whence they escorted and ushered them into town amidst the acclamations of a numerous concourse of people. Continental and French colors, at a distance, preceded the British, and thus they were paraded down Market street to the state-house. They were then carried into Congress and laid at their feet.

> The crowd exulting fills with shouts the sky,
> The walls, the woods, and long canals reply:
> Base Britons! Tyrant Britons — knock under,
> Taken 's your earl, soldiers and plunder.
> Huzza! what colors of the bloody foe,
> Twenty-four in number, at the State-House door;
> Look: they are British standards, how they fall
> At the president's feet, Congress and all."

CHAPTER VII.

WASHINGTON'S LIFE-GUARD.

NUMBER AND UNIFORM OF THE GUARD—THEIR APPEARANCE AND DISCIPLINE—THE FAITHLESS GUARDSMAN—GUARD BORROWED FOR IMPORTANT EXPEDITIONS—THE AFFAIR AT BARREN HILL—LAFAYETTE IN PERIL—ALLEN M'LANE—ESCAPE OF THE REPUBLICANS—PASSAGE OF THE SCHUYLKILL—THE LIFE-GUARD AT MONMOUTH—MORGAN'S MERRIMENT—LAST SURVIVOR OF THE GUARD.

THE Life-Guard was a select corps, composed of a major's command, or about one hundred and fifty men.* Caleb

* Among the Connecticut troops who were engaged in the battle of Bunker's Hill, was a company under Captain Thomas Knowlton, who was mortally wounded in a skirmish on Harlem plains, on the sixteenth of September, 1776. His was one of the best-disciplined companies in the crude army that gathered so suddenly near Boston, after the bloodshed at Lexington and Concord became known. This company and others were formed into a battalion known as the Connecticut rangers, to the command of which Knowlton was appointed, with the rank of Lieutenant-Colonel. It formed a part of the central division of the army at Cambridge, after Washington had taken the chief command, and was under his immediate control. The corps soon held the same enviable position, as to discipline and soldierly deportment, as Captain Knowlton's *company* had done; and the commander, proud of his battalion, made it a sort of voluntary body-guard to the general-in-chief, and called it *Congress's own*."

This appellation produced some jealousy in the army, which Washington perceived; and, on the eleventh of March, 1776 (a few days before the termination of the siege of Boston), he ordered a corps to be formed, of *reliable* men, as guard for himself, baggage, &c. He directed them to be chosen from various regiments, specifying their height to be "from five feet nine inches, to five feet ten inches, and to be handsomely and well made." It consisted of a major's command—one hundred and eighty men. Caleb Gibbs, of Rhode Island, was its first chief, and bore the title of captain-commandant, having three lieutenants. When this corps was formed, that of Knowlton was no longer regarded with jealousy, as a special favorite, although it continued to be so in the estimation of Washington.

The Life-Guard appear to have been quite popular. Captain Harding, of Fair-

Gibbs was the first captain-commandant, and was ably seconded by brave and gallant young officers. Their uniform consisted of a blue coat, with white facings; white waistcoat and breeches; black stock and black half-gaiters, and a round hat with blue and white feather.*

field, Connecticut, writing to Governor Trumbull, on the twentieth of May, 1776, said: "I am now about fitting out another small sloop [privateersman], that was taken from a tory, that I have called the *Life-Guard*, to be commanded by Mr. Smedley, to cruise to the eastward," &c., &c. On the sixteenth of the same month, Washington, then in New York, issued the following order: "Any orders delivered by Caleb Gibbs and George Lewis, Esqrs., [officers of the general's Guard], are to be attended to in the same manner as if sent by an aid-de-camp."

We find no further mention of the Guard until in June following, when members of it were suspected of being engaged in an alleged conspiracy to assassinate Washington and his staff. This conspiracy was concocted by Governor Tryon, then a refugee on board of a British man-of-war in the harbor of New York, and the tories in the city and vicinity, at the head of whom was Matthews the mayor. They were made bold by the expected speedy arrival of a strong British land and naval force. It was arranged, that on the arrival of these forces, the tories were to rise, full-armed, to co-operate with them; that Kingsbridge, at the upper end of York island should be destroyed, so as to cut of all communication with the main land; that the magazines should be fired, and Washington and his staff be murdered, or seized and given up to the enemy. The plan was hinted at by the voice of rumor, and suspicion of complicity rested upon one or two of the Life-Guard. One, named Hickey, was proved to have made arrangements to have poison placed in some green peas of which Washington was about to partake. He was hanged on the twenty-eighth of June, 1776. It is a singular fact, that the victim of this, the first military execution in the continental army, was a member of the body-guard of the commander-in-chief, who were chosen for their trustworthiness.

* This description exactly corresponds with the device on a flag that belonged to the cavalry of the Guard, which is preserved in the museum at Alexandria, and of which I have a drawing. The flag is made of white silk, on which the device is neatly painted. One of the Guard is seen holding a horse, and is in the act of receiving a flag from the genius of liberty, who is personified as a woman leaning upon the Union shield, near which is the American eagle. The motto of the corps, "CONQUER OR DIE," is upon a ribbon. Care was always taken to have each state, from which the continental army was supplied with troops, represented by members of this corps. It was the duty of the infantry portion to guard the headquarters, and to insure the safe-keeping of the papers and effects of the commander-in-chief, as well as the safety of his person. The mounted portion accompanied the general in his marches and in reconnoitering, or other like movements. They were employed as patrols, videttes, and bearers of the general's orders to various military posts; and they were never spared in battle.

The cavalry of the Guard was detailed from various corps during the contest.* In the earlier campaigns,

---

* A new organization of the Guard took place at the close of April, 1777, when Washington was at Morristown, in New Jersey. On the thirtieth of that month, he issued the following circular to the colonels of regiments stationed there:—

"SIR: I want to form a company for my guard. In doing this, I wish to be extremely cautious, because it is more than probable that, in the course of the campaign, my baggage, papers, and other matters of great public import, may be committed to the sole care of these men. This being premised, in order to impress you with proper attention in the choice, I have to request that you will immediately furnish me with four men of your regiment; and, as it is my farther wish that this company should look well, and be nearly of a size, I desire that none of the men may exceed in stature five feet ten inches, nor fall short of five feet nine inches—sober, young, active, and well made. When I recommend care in your choice, I would be understood to mean, of good character, in the regiment—that possess the pride of appearing clean and soldierlike. I am satisfied there can be no absolute security for the fidelity of this class of people; but yet I think it most likely to be found in those who have family connections in the country. You will, therefore, send me none but natives. I must insist that, in making this choice, you give no intimation of my preference of natives, as I do not want to create any invidious distinction between them and the foreigners."

A few days before making this requisition, Washington wrote as follows to the captain-commandant of his Guard — Caleb Gibbs:—

"MORRISTOWN, April 22, 1777.

"DEAR SIR: I forgot before you left this place to desire you to provide clothing for the men that are to compose my Guard—but now desire that you will apply to the clothier-general, and have them forwarded to this place, or headquarters, as soon as possible.

"Provide for four sergeants, four corporals, a drum and fife, and fifty rank and file. If blue and buff can be had, I should prefer that uniform, as it is the one I wear myself. If it can not, Mr. Mease and you may fix upon any other, red excepted. I shall get men from five feet nine to five feet ten, for the Guard; for such sized men, therefore make your clothing. You may get a small round hat, or a cocked one, as you please.

"In getting these clothes no mention need be made for what purpose they are intended; for though no extraordinary expense will attend it, and the Guard which is absolutely necessary for the security of my baggage and papers, &c., may as well be in uniform; yet the report of making a uniform (or if already made, of providing uniform) for the Guards, creates an idea of expense which I would not wish should go forth.

"That your arms may also be of a piece, I herewith enclose you an order on the com'y of stores for fifty muskets. I am, dear sir, your most obe'dt,

"GEO. WASHINGTON."

from Baylor's regiment, which was called *Lady Washington's Dragoons* — uniform white, with blue facings, &c.* The Life-Guard, always attached to the headquarters, was admired as well for its superior appearance as for its high state of discipline; it being considered, in the olden time, a matter of distinction to serve in the Guard of the commander-in-chief.†

* Lieutenant-Colonel Baylor's corps was one of the finest in the army. While lying at Old Tappan, near the Hudson, with his regiment, in fancied security, toward the close of September, 1778, he was surprised by General Grey (father of Earl Grey, late premier of England), of Cornwallis's army, and a large number of his men were brutally bayoneted while imploring quarter. Out of one hundred and sixty-four men, sixty-seven were killed or wounded. Lieutenant-Colonel Baylor was taken prisoner; and seventy horses belonging to the corps were butchered.

† After the reorganization of the Guard, in the spring of 1777, the number was considerably increased. In the spring of 1778, the Baron von Steuben arrived at the camp at Valley Forge, and assumed the office of inspector-general of the army. He selected one hundred and twenty men from the line, whom he formed into a special guard for the general-in-chief. He made them his military school, drilled them twice a-day, and thus commenced that admirable system of discipline by which he rendered most important service to the American cause.

Caleb Gibbs was still captain-commandant, and remained in that position until near the close of 1779, when he was succeeded by William Colfax, one of his three lieutenants, the other two being Henry P. Livingston, of New York, and Benjamin Grymes, of Virginia. Colfax became commandant while Washington was stationed at Morristown, and when the number of the corps was greater than at any other period during the war. He was born in Connecticut, in the year 1760, and at the age of seventeen he was commissioned as lieutenant of the continental army. He was in the battle at White Plains, where he was shot through the body. When he became the leader of the general's Guard, a strong attachment was formed between the commander-in-chief and the young subaltern. Washington often shared his tent and his table with him; and he gave the young man many tokens of his esteem. One of these the family of General Colfax yet possesses. It is a silver stock-buckle, set with paste brilliants. Colfax was at the surrender of Cornwallis at Yorktown, and he remained with the army until it was disbanded late in 1783. He then settled at Pompton, New Jersey, where he married Hester Schuyler, a cousin of General Philip Schuyler. In 1793, he was commissioned by Governor Howell, general and commander-in-chief of the militia of New Jersey. He was a presidential elector in 1798; and in 1810 he was commissioned a brigadier-general of the Jersey Blues, and was active during the earlier period of the war of 1812. He was appointed a judge of the Common Pleas of Bergen county, which office he

The Life-Guard was borrowed by favorite officers for several important expeditions. In the affair of Barren Hill, in May '78,* the Life-Guard formed a part of the troops under the Marquis de Lafayette, who, recovered of the wound he received in the preceding campaign,† in '78 made his debut in arms as a general officer. The position at Barren hill becoming extremely hazardous, on account of two heavy columns of the enemy that were marching to intercept the communication of the marquis with the main army at Valley Forge, the young general determined, by a gallant dash between the advancing columns, to reach the ford on the Schuylkill, and thus secure his retreat to the main army. Here let our narration pause, while we pay a well-merited tribute to the memory and services of Allen M'Lane, to whose untiring vigilance in watching the stealthy approach of the enemy's columns toward Barren hill, and promptness in attacking them on their route, the marquis was mainly indebted for success in the celebrated retreat that shed such lustre on his first command.

In Allen M'Lane, we have the recollection of a partisan who, with genius to conceive, possessed a courage even to chivalry to execute the most daring enterprises;

---

held until his death, which occurred in 1838, when he was seventy-eight years of age. He was then buried with military honors.

* When rumors reached Washington, in his camp at Valley Forge, that the British were about to evacuate Philadelphia, he detached Lafayette, with little over a thousand chosen men, and five pieces of cannon, to take position eastward of the Schuylkill, nearer Philadelphia, to watch their movements. He took post upon Barren hill, about half way between Valley Forge and Philadelphia, on the eighteenth of May.

† Lafayette was severely wounded in his leg, by a musket ball, at the battle of Brandywine, on the eleventh of September, 1777. He tarried, during his disability among the Moravians, at Bethlehem, in Pennsylvania.

who ever ranked with the foremost in the esteem of the chief, and was considered by the whole army as one of the most intrepid and distinguished officers of the war of the Revolution.

When the retiring Americans reached the ford of the Schuylkill,* they hesitated in attempting the passage. Lafayette sprang from his horse, and rushed into the water waist deep, calling on his comrades to follow. Animated by the example of their youthful general, the soldiers entered the river, the taller men sustaining the shorter, and after a severe struggle gained the southern or friendly shore, having suffered but inconsiderable loss.

Meanwhile, the enemy were in close pursuit, and the commander-in-chief, fearing for the detachment, which consisted of his choicest troops, including the Life-Guard, dragged his artillery to the rocky heights that commanded the ford, and opened upon the enemy's advance, checking them so far as to enable the marquis the better to secure his retreat. There was one feature in the martial spectacle of the passage of the Schuylkill of rare and imposing interest: it was the admired form of Washington, at times obscured, and then beheld amid the smoke of the cannonade, as, attended by his generals and staff, he would waive his hat to encourage the soldiers in their perilous passage of the stream.

On the morning of the battle of Monmouth, June, '78, a detachment from the Life-Guard, and one from Mor-

* Matson's ford, a few miles below Norristown. Through lack of vigilance on the part of some militia, Lafayette came very near being surrounded at Barren hill by General Grant, with five thousand men. With perfect presence of mind, the marquis threw out small parties so judiciously, that Grant, supposing he was preparing for an attack, halted his column to make similar preparations. This gave Lafayette an opportunity to escape.

gan's riflemen, led by Morgan's favorite, Captain Gabriel Long, made a brilliant dash at a party of the enemy which they surprised while washing at a brook that ran through an extensive meadow. Seventeen grenadiers were made prisoners, and borne off in the very face of the British light-infantry, who fired upon their daring assailants, and immediately commenced a hot pursuit; yet Long displayed such consummate ability as well as courage, that he brought off his party, prisoners and all, with only the loss of one sergeant wounded.

Morgan was in waiting, at the out-post, to receive the detachment on their return, having listened, with much anxiety, to the heavy fire of the pursuing enemy. Charmed with the success of the enterprise, in the return of the troops almost unharmed, and in the prisoners taken, Morgan wrung the favorite captain by the hand, and paid his compliments to the officers and men of his own corps, and of the Life-Guard. Then the famed Leader of the Woodsmen indulged himself in a stentorian laugh that made all ring again, at the bespattered condition of the *gentlemen*, as he was pleased to term the Life-Guard, and who, in their precipitate retreat, having to pass through certain swamps that abound in the portion of New Jersey then the seat of war, presented a most soiled appearance for troops who might be termed the martinets of sixty years ago.

It is believed that the late Colonel John Nicholas, of Virginia, was *the last of the Life-Guard.**

---

* This was first published in the *National Intelligencer*, on the thirtieth of January, 1838. One of the Life-Guard, and doubtless the *very last* survivor, lived until early in 1856, eighteen years after the text of this chapter was published. His name was Uzal Knapp, and at the time of his death, was a resident of New Windsor, Orange county, New York. He was a native of Stamford, Connecticut, where he

was born in October, 1758. At the age of eighteen years he enlisted in the continental army, as a common soldier, to serve "for and during the war;" and he was continually on duty from that time until his discharge in June, 1783. His first active service was at White Plains, in the autumn of 1776. He was with Wooster at Ridgefield; and was at Peekskill when Forts Clinton and Montgomery were stormed and taken by the British, in the autumn of 1777. He passed the following winter among the snows of Valley Forge, and in May he joined the light-infantry of Lafayette, at Barren hill. He was with him in the battle of Monmouth, in June; and in the winter of 1780, when the number of the Life-Guard was augmented, he entered that corps at Morristown, and received from the hands of Washington the commission of sergeant. At the time of his discharge, he received from the commander-in-chief the *Badge of Military Merit,* for six years' faithful service. This honorary badge of distinction was established by Washington, in August, 1781, and was conferred upon non-commissioned officers and soldiers who had served three years with bravery, fidelity, and good conduct, and upon every one who should perform any singularly meritorious action. The badge entitled the recipient "to pass and repass all guards and military posts as fully and amply as any commissioned officer whatever." It was the order of the American "Legion of Honor."

After the war, Sergeant Knapp settled in New Windsor, near Newburgh; and there he lived the quiet life of a farmer until his death, which occurred on the eleventh of January, 1856, when he was little more than ninety-six years of age. His body was taken to Newburgh, and there lay in state for three days, in the centre of the reception-room in Washington's headquarters, so well preserved as the property of the state. On Wednesday, the sixteenth of January, attended by a civic and military pageant, and a vast assemblage of people, it was buried at the foot of the flag-staff, on the slope near that venerated building around which cluster so many memories of Washington and the continental army. It is a most appropriate burial-place for the mortal remains of the veteran guardsman.

CHAPTER VIII.

THE HUNTING-SHIRT.

Major Adlum's Letter—Account of Smallwood's Regiment in Philadelphia—Their Attire—Character of the Members—The Regiment on Long Island—Its Wreck—Remarks by Mr. Custis—Morgan's Riflemen at Quebec—Their Appearance—Anecdote of a Yankee Captain—A British Admiral Outwitted—Fear of Morgan's Riflemen—Their Attachment to their Leader—The Highland Costume—A Plea for the Hunting-shirt.

In the National Intelligencer, on the twelfth of October, 1833, the editor remarked:—

"The following interesting reminiscence of the days of trial, with a graphic description of a corps, that was composed of the chivalry of Maryland, and formed the very *élite* of the army of independence, in the memorable campaign of 1776, will, we are assured, be read with gratification by all the Americans.

"These details are selected from among a series of papers, furnished by our venerable neighbor, and Revolutionary veteran, Major Adlum, to Mr. Custis, of Arlington, for the latter gentleman's work, 'The Private Memoirs of Washington.'

"'Smallwood's regiment arrived in Philadelphia about the middle of July, 1776, the day after the militia of Yorktown* got there. I happened to be in Market street when the regiment was marching down it. They turned up Front street, till they reached the Quaker meeting-

---

* York, Pennsylvania.

house, called the Bank meeting, where they halted for some time, which I presumed was owing to a delicacy on the part of the officers, seeing they were about to be quartered in a place of worship. After a time, they moved forward to the door, where the officers halted, and their platoons came up, and stood with their hats off, while the soldiers with recovered arms, marched into the meeting-house. The officers then retired, and sought quarters elsewhere.

"'The regiment was then said to be eleven hundred strong; and never did a finer, more dignified, and braver body of men, face an enemy. They were composed of the flower of Maryland, being young gentlemen, the sons of opulent planters, farmers, and mechanics. From the colonel to the private, all were attired in *hunting-shirts*. I afterward saw this fine corps on their march to join General Washington.*

"'In the battle of Long Island,† Smallwood's regiment, when engaged with an enemy of overwhelmingly superior force, displayed a courage and discipline, that sheds upon its memory an undying lustre, while it was

* They joined the American army under Washington, at New York, at the close of July, and presented a strong contrast to the irregularly-dressed troops from New England.

† British and German troops, to the number of about thirty thousand, arrived at Staten Island, before New York, at the close of July, 1776. Washington, with an army of about seventeen thousand men, mostly militia, lay intrenched in New York and vicinity, waiting for the expected foe. In that relative position the two armies lay until the morning of the twenty-second of August, when ten thousand of the enemy landed upon the west end of Long Island. Meanwhile, Washington had formed a fortified camp on high ground near Brooklyn, on Long Island, opposite New York, and in that vicinity a severe battle was fought, on the twenty-seventh of August, in which the British were victorious, the Americans losing in killed, wounded, and prisoners, about sixteen hundred men. These were soon made to feel the horrible sufferings which gave the name of *hells* to the prison-ships in the harbor of New York and the jails in the city.

so cut to pieces, that in the October following, when I again saw the regiment, its remains did not exceed a hundred men.*

"'Captain Edward de Courcy, Captain Herbert, a captain, and a Doctor Stuart, of Smallwood's, were among the prisoners taken at Long Island, with whom I became acquainted, while I was a prisoner in New York.

"'The wreck of the once superb regiment of Smallwood fought in the battles of the White Plains and the subsequent actions in the Jerseys, and in the memorable campaign of 1776, terminating with the battle of Princeton, January, 1777, where the remains of the regiment, reduced to little more than a company, were commanded by Captain, afterward Governor Stone of Maryland.'"

To the above communication Mr. Custis added the following remarks:—

The hunting-shirt, the emblem of the Revolution, is banished from the national military, but still lingers among the hunters and pioneers of the Far West. This national costume, properly so called, was adopted in the outset of the Revolution, and was recommended by Washington to his army,† in the most eventful period of

---

* In a severe conflict between the divisions of Lord Stirling, of the republican army, and Lord Cornwallis, of the British army, Smallwood's regiment lost two hundred and fifty-nine of its members.

† Washington was an early advocate for the hunting-shirt, in imitation of the Indian costume. While on the march for Fort du Quesne, in July 1758, he wrote to Colonel Boquet, saying: "My men are very bare of regimental clothing, and I have no prospect of a supply. So far from regretting this want during the present campaign, if I were left to pursue my own inclination, I would not only order the men to adopt the Indian dress, but cause the officers to do it also, and be the first to set the example myself. Nothing but the uncertainty of obtaining the general approbation causes me to hesitate a moment to leave my regimentals at this place [camp near Fort Cumberland], and proceed as light as any Indian in the woods. It is an unbecoming dress, I own, for an officer; but convenience, rather than show, should

the War for Independence. It was a favorite garb with many of the officers of the line, particularly by the gallant Colonel Josiah Parker.

When Morgan's riflemen, made prisoners at the assault on Quebec, in 1775,* were returning to the South to be exchanged, the British garrisons on the route beheld with wonder these sons of the mountain and the forest. Their hardy looks, their tall athletic forms, their marching always in Indian file, with the light and noiseless step peculiar to their pursuit of woodland game; but, above all, to European eyes, their singular and picturesque costume, the hunting-shirt, with its fringes, the wampum belts, leggins, and moccasins, richly worked with the Indian ornaments of beads and porcupine quills of brilliant and varied dyes, the tomahawk and knife; these, with the well known death-dealing aim of those matchless marksmen, created in the European military a degree of

---

be consulted. The reduction of bat-horses alone would be sufficient to recommend it, for nothing is more certain than that less baggage would be required, and the public benefited in proportion."

Boquet, like a sensible man, gave a sympathetic response to Washington's suggestions, but the remainder of the regular officers opposed it. Washington tried the experiment, and it was eminently successful. He equipped two companies in that way and sent them to headquarters. The weather was then extremely hot, and the light costume pleased all wearers. Colonel Boquet wrote to Washington: "The dress takes very well here, and, thank God, we see nothing but shirts and blankets." Such was the origin of the hunting-shirt, or costume of the American riflemen.

* Morgan, at the head of a rifle corps, accompanied General Arnold in the expedition across the country from the Atlantic to the St. Lawrence, in the autumn of 1775. That expedition, emerging from the wilderness, appeared at Point Levi, opposite Quebec, in the midst of falling snow, in November. The apparition startled the Quebec people, and by the mistake of a single word, their fears were greatly increased. Morgan's men had the linen hunting-shirt over their thick clothing, and those who first saw them, reported that they were *vêtu en toile*—clothed in linen clothes. The word *toile* was mistaken for *tole*, iron plate, and the news spread that they were clad in *sheet iron!* In the siege that afterward followed, Morgan and his brave men were made prisoners by the British.

awe and respect for the hunting-shirt, which lasted with the War of the Revolution.*

That the fame of the prowess of American woodsmen had not been effaced by time, let me instance the "*ruse de guerre*" most happily played off by a Yankee captain upon a British admiral during the last war.

A Captain G—— had been taken by one of the vessels composing the Chesapeake squadron,† and was carried on board the admiral's ship, who, after civilly treating his prisoner, one day observed, "Pray, Captain G——, if I should determine to make a reconnoissance up the Potomac, toward your seat of government, how many riflemen may I expect to find on the banks of the river, as my pilots tell me the channel-way in some places runs very near the land? I do not mean your regulars, but those hunting-shirt fellows, from the woods, who can hit any button on my coat, when they are in the humor of sharp-shooting." Here the Yankee, being wide awake to the importance of the question, as regarding his country's interests, went right to windward of the admiral at once. He looked grave, and began to reckon deliberately on his fingers; after a time, he replied, with perfect composure, "Why, I guess somewhere about ten or eleven thousand, sir." The Briton, in his turn, looked grave,

* General Gates bore testimony to the fact, that Morgan's corps inspired the British with fear. Washington had sent that fine corps to assist Gates in opposing Burgoyne. After the battle near Stillwater, on the nineteenth of September, 1777, he wrote to Gates to send them back again if he could possibly spare them. Gates received the letter just before the decisive engagement of the seventh of October, and in reply, after stating that he could not then part with any of his troops, he remarked, "In this situation your excellency would not wish me to part with *the corps* the army of General Burgoyne are most afraid of."

† Under Admiral Cockburn, who engaged in an amphibious marauding warfare on the shores of that bay.

and turning to his officers, observed, "I believe we will not go up at this time."

Not a long rifle, that is, such as a hunting-shirt would use (for a genuine Tomahawk would not pick up in the street a short, or jager piece), was at the time within a hundred miles of the Potomac, and the Yankee well knew it; but finding that he had an opportunity of protecting an important portion of his country by hoaxing a British admiral, he thought that the end justified the means, as to take advantage is the true morality of war. The Yankee so played his part, and famously too.

General Morgan frequently observed, "The very sight of my riflemen was always enough for a Hessian piquet. They would scamper into their lines as if the d—l drove them, shouting in all the English they knew, 'Rebel in de bush! rebel in de bush!'"*

The famed corps of Morgan was raised in the Shenandoah valley and the mountains circumjacent. The drum and fife, and even the sergeant's *hard dollars* on the drumhead, would not have enlisted a man of this corps. It was like the devotion of a Highland clan to its chief. Morgan was the chief—Morgan, with whom those hardy fellows had wrestled and fought, and kicked up all sorts

---

* In the autumn of 1775, the British ministry concluded a bargain with some of the petty German princes for the use of seventeen thousand troops in America. The landgrave of Hesse Cassel, having furnished the most considerable portion of these mercenaries, all that came over in the spring of 1776, were called by the general name of *Hessians*. Many of them ignorant, brutal, and blood-thirsty, were hated by the patriots, and despised even by the regular English army. They were always employed at posts of greatest danger, or in expeditions least creditable. These troops cost the British government eight hundred thousand dollars, besides the necessity, according to the contract, of defending the little principalities thus stripped, against their foes. A large portion of them were pressed into the service, and dragged away from their families; and great numbers of them deserted before the close of the war.

of a dust for a long time. When Morgan cried, with his martial inspiration, "Come, boys, who's for the camp before Cambridge," the mountaineers turned out to a man. Short was their "note of preparation." The blanket buckled to their backs, their baggage, a supply of food in their pouches, scanty as an Aborigine would take for a long march, their commissariat—they grasped their rifles, and strode away to the North, a band of young giants, for the combats of liberty.

The Americans may be said at this time to have no national costume—all borrowed from abroad. They "order things" better in Scotland. There the Gael adheres to the martial habiliments of his ancestors, proud of their renowned recollections, and jealous of the peculiar colors of his tartan. Amid the cruel persecutions of Forty-five,* was the proscription of the Highland costume; which is, in truth, the only relic of the ancient Roman dress. What British ministry would proscribe it now. They hail with joy the philebeg and hose, whose warriors have covered their arms with glory in every quarter of the world. From the time that the old Highland watch, the renowned "Fortie-twa,"† first embarked for

---

* This has reference to the action of the British government after the rising of the Scotch in 1745, in favor of Charles Edward, grandson of James II. of England, who claimed a right to the British throne. They were put down in 1746, and many suffered punishments.

† The celebrated forty-second regiment of the British infantry, known as the Royal Highlanders. It was organized in May, 1740. It was embodied in Perthshire, Scotland, in 1730, as a local corps, and was widely known as the "Black Watch," the privates even, being gentlemen by birth and fortune. It was first called the forty-third regiment, and was then numbered as the forty-second in 1749. It was made "royal" in 1758, by George II., as a testimony of his approbation of the "extraordinary courage and exemplary conduct of the Highland regiment."

This gallant corps has been abroad on active service more than sixty-four years, and in England and Ireland thirty-five — only thirteen years being spent in Scot-

foreign service, down to the present hour, in every action where they have been engaged, in every quarter of the world, the friend and the foeman have alike awarded glory to the kilts. But suppose, for a moment, yielding to the "march of intellect," you disrobe Donald of his trews, and fit him with "braw breeks," in their stead — adieu, then, adieu to the magic influence of the soul-stirring pipes; no longer will the awful cry of Claymore drive him headlong into the ranks of the foe; and soon,

land. It has served in twenty-nine expeditions and campaigns, and has been engaged in more than fifty battles, sieges, and skirmishes. The following is a list of the principal campaigns and actions of note in which it has distinguished itself:—

At the bloody battle of Fontenoy, in 1745; the descent on the coast of France and the siege of L'Orient, in 1746; the raising of the siege of Hulse, and the campaign in South Beveland, in 1747; the attack on Ticonderoga, in 1758; that on Martinique and the capture of Guadaloupe; the expedition to Lakes George and Champlain, under General Amherst, including the surrender by the French of Crown Point and Ticonderoga, in 1759; the surrender of Montreal, in 1760; the capture of Martinique, siege of the Moro castle and capture of Havana, in 1762; the campaigns against the North American Indians in 1763, 1764, and 1765.

During our War for Independence the forty-second was present at the battles of Brooklyn and Long Island, and the capture of Fort Washington, in 1776; Brandywine and Germantown, 1777; Monmouth, 1778; Elizabethtown, 1779; siege of Charleston, 1780, and many minor affairs.

During the war of the first French Revolution, the forty-second was engaged in the battles of Nieuport, 1793; Gildermaison, 1795; the capture of St. Lucia and St. Vincent, 1796, and Minorca, 1798. In Egypt, it was present in the several actions under Abercrombie, and gained the red-feather as a particular mark of distinction for its gallantry there. The regiment was also in Moore's campaign in Portugal and Spain, the disastrous retreat to Corunna and the fierce fight there, in 1808-9. It was in the unfortunate Walcheren expedition; fought in the battle of Salamanca; was at the siege of and retreat from Burgos, and in the battles in and near the Pyrenees — Nivelle, Nive, Orthes, and finally at Thoulouse — which terminated Wellington's campaigns in Spain and the occupation of that country by the French armies. The regiment was in the bloody battle of Quatre Bras, and distinguished itself a few days after in the awful struggle at Waterloo. Since then they have maintained their well-earned reputation in the Crimea and in India.

The forty-second is one of the oldest of all the Scotch regiments now in the British army; the others are the seventy-first, seventy-second, seventy-third, seventy-fourth, seventy-fifth, seventy-sixth, seventy-eighth, ninety-first, ninety-second, and ninety-third.

very soon, would there be a farewell to the glories of the "forty-twa."

And should not Americans feel proud of the garb, and hail it as national, in which their fathers endured such toil and privation, in the mighty struggle for Independence, which is associated with so many and imposing events of the days of trial—the march across the frozen wilderness, the assault on Quebec,* the triumphs of Saratoga† and the King's mountain?‡ But a little while, and of a truth, the hunting-shirt, the venerable emblem of the Revolution, will have disappeared from among the Americans, and only to be found in museums, like ancient armor, exposed to the gaze of the curious.

* Arnold's expedition in the autumn of 1775, and the siege of Quebec, where they were made prisoners. See page 267.

† When General Burgoyne, with a large invading army that had penetrated from Canada, was obliged to surrender to the republicans, under General Gates.

‡ Early in the autumn of 1780, Cornwallis, who held South Carolina in subjection, resolved to invade the North State. As a part of his plan, he sent Major Patrick Ferguson to embody the tories among the mountains, west of the Broad river. Early in October he crossed that stream with a considerable force, and encamped among the hills of King's mountain. There he was attacked on the seventh by several corps of whig militia. A bloody contest ensued, and the republicans were victorious. Ferguson was slain, and three hundred of his men were killed and wounded. Eight hundred of them were made prisoners. There were many hunting-shirts in the republican ranks on that day.

CHAPTER IX.

WASHINGTON'S HEADQUARTERS.

HEADQUARTERS AT MORRISTOWN — VALLEY FORGE AND ITS ASSOCIATIONS — PRIVATIONS THERE — CONWAY'S CABAL — ALLIANCE WITH FRANCE PROCLAIMED — HEADQUARTERS UNDER CANVASS — BANQUETING AND SLEEPING MARQUEES — WASHINGTON WITHIN THEM — THE MAKER OF THE MARQUEES — THE LIFE-GUARD — GOVERNOR TRUMBULL — PUTNAM STARTING FOR THE CAMP — WASHINGTON'S APPEAL FOR ASSISTANCE — SCENE IN GOVERNOR TRUMBULL'S PRESENCE — THE GOVERNOR'S PATRIOTISM — SUPPLIES PROMISED — JOY ON THEIR ARRIVAL — TRUMBULL'S TWO SONS — CAPTAIN MOLLY AND THE COMMANDER-IN-CHIEF — OLD SOLDIERS AT THE PRESIDENTIAL MANSION — REVERENCE FOR HEADQUARTERS.

MANY of the establishments that constituted the headquarters during the Revolution yet remain for the veneration of the Americans.* At Cambridge,† Morristown,‡

---

* This chapter was first published in the *National Intelligencer*, on the twenty-third of February, 1843.

† Washington's residence during the time a portion of the American army occupied Cambridge, near Boston, from the spring of 1775 until that of 1776, is yet standing, and is well preserved. It was known as the *Cragie House*, and has been for many years the property and residence of Professor Henry Wadsworth Longfellow, the poet. It is a spacious building, standing at the upper of two terraces, which are ascended by five stone steps. At each front of the house is a lofty elm, mere saplings when Washington was there. Everything within is sacredly preserved in its ancient style, for the hand of the iconoclast, Improvement, has not been allowed to strike a single blow there.

‡ The house in which Washington resided at Morristown is well preserved. It is about a quarter of a mile eastward of the village green. Washington first occupied it in the winter of 1777, after his brilliant achievements at Trenton and Princeton. He was again there during the winter of 1779-'80. During the war it was the residence of Widow Ford, mother of the late Judge Gabriel Ford, who lived there until his death, which occurred a few years ago. It, too, is quite a spacious mansion, pleasantly situated near the highway. There in the autumn of 1848, while Judge Ford was yet living, I passed a night, and slept in the room occupied by General Washington and his lady. The carpet and some of the furniture were the same that belonged to the room when that illustrious couple occupied it.

Newburgh,* New Windsor,† West Point,‡ and other places, the buildings are still preserved; but of the

* The headquarters at Newburgh presents a point of great attraction to tourists on the Hudson during the summer season. It is a rather small, old-fashioned Dutch house, fronting the river, and now belongs to the state of New York, it having come into its possession by foreclosure of a mortgage. It is in charge of the public authorities at Newburgh, and has been thoroughly repaired, care having been taken to preserve the ancient form of every part that was renewed. It was dedicated to the public service with appropriate ceremonies, on the fourth of July, 1850, when Major-General Winfield Scott, who was present, hoisted the American flag upon a lofty staff that had just been erected near. At the foot of that flag-staff, as we have already observed, the last survivor of Washington's Life-Guard lies buried.

The front door of this mansion opens into a large square room, which was used by Washington for his public audiences, and as a dining hall. It is remarkable as having seven doors, and only one window. In the December number of the New York Mirror for 1834, is an interesting account of this old building, by Gulian C. Verplanck, Esq. He relates the following anecdote connected with this room, which he received from Colonel Nicholas Fish, father of the late governor of the state of New York. Just before Lafayette's death, himself and the American minister, with several of his countrymen, were invited to dine at the house of the distinguished Frenchman, Marbois, who was the French secretary of legation here during the Revolution. At the supper hour the company were shown into a room which contrasted quite oddly with the Parisian elegance of the other apartments where they had spent the evening. A low boarded, painted ceiling, with large beams, a single small, uncurtained window, with numerous small doors, as well as the general style of the whole, gave, at first, the idea of the kitchen, or largest room of a Dutch or Belgian farm-house. On a long rough table was a repast, just as little in keeping with the refined kitchens of Paris as the room was with its architecture. It consisted of a large dish of meat, uncouth-looking pastry, and wine in decanters and bottles, accompanied by glasses and silver mugs, such as indicated other habits and tastes than those of modern Paris. "Do you know where we now are?" said the host to Lafayette and his companions. They paused for a few minutes in surprise. They had seen something like this before, but when and where? "Ah! the seven doors and one window," said Lafayette, "and the silver camp-goblets, such as the marshals of France used in my youth! We are at Washington's headquarters on the Hudson, fifty years ago!"

† Washington lived in a plain Dutch house at New Windsor, which has long since passed away. He occupied it first on the twenty-third of June, 1779, and again toward the close of 1780, where he remained until the summer of 1781. In that humble tenement, Mrs. Washington entertained the most distinguished officers and their ladies, as well as the most obscure, who sought her friendship. New Windsor village is about two miles below Newburgh.

‡ Washington never remained at West Point long at a time, and, properly speaking, he had no headquarters there. At this time not a single building of any

Valley Forge it is doubtful whether there exists at this time any remains of the headquarters so memorable in the history of the days of trial.*

If the headquarters at Morristown were bleak and gloomy, from being located in a mountainous region, and occupied in the depth of winter,† the soldier was cheered amid his privations by the proud and happy remembrance of his triumphs at the close of the campaign of 1776.‡

kind remains that was standing on or near the Point during the Revolution. There may be seen the mounds of Fort Clinton, and upon the mountain, westward, five hundred feet above the plateau on which the Military Academy now stands, may be seen the grey ruins of Fort Putnam, finely relieved by surrounding evergreens. Nearly opposite West Point, on the eastern shore of the Hudson, is the well-preserved mansion of Beverly Robinson, where Arnold had his quarters, and from which he fled for refuge on board the British sloop-of-war *Vulture*.

* The Potts House, the residence of Washington at Valley Forge, is well-preserved. It is at the mouth of the valley, near the banks of the Schuylkill. It is a substantial stone building. The main portion was erected by Isaac Potts (who had ironworks there), in 1770. A wing, used as a kitchen, is on the site of the log addition to which Mrs. Washington thus alluded in a letter to Mrs Mercy Warren, written in the spring of 1778 : " The general's apartment is very small ; he has had a log cabin built to dine in, which has made our quarters much more tolerable than they were at first." When I visited the house, a few years ago, I was shown a cavity in the deep east window, formed with a lid, in which the commander-in-chief kept his papers while he resided there. Mr. Potts, the Quaker who owned the house when Washington occupied it, relates that one day while the Americans were encamped at Valley Forge, he strolled up the creek, and when not far from his dam, heard a solemn voice. He walked quietly in the direction of it, and saw Washington's horse tied to a sapling. In a thicket near by was the beloved chief upon his knees in prayer, his cheeks suffused with tears. Like Moses at the bush, Isaac felt that he was upon holy ground, and withdrew unobserved. He was much agitated, and, on entering the room where his wife was, he burst into tears. On her inquiring the cause, he informed her of what he had seen, and added, " If there is any one on this earth whom the Lord will listen to, it is George Washington ; and I feel a presentiment that under such a commander there can be no doubt of our eventually establishing our independence, and that God in his providence hath willed it so."

† Morristown is in the hill-country of East Jersey, and was considered a most secure and eligible place for a winter encampment ; not easily accessible by the enemy, and surrounded by a fertile country.

‡ The brilliant achievements at Trenton and Princeton, which led to the speedy expulsion of the British from New Jersey, except at Brunswick and Amboy.

Not such were the associations that attended the headquarters at Valley Forge, at the close of the campaign of 1777. The American army, defeated in two hard-fought general engagements,* beheld its enemy comfortably housed in Philadelphia, while it was compelled at an inclement season to retire to a forest, there to erect huts for shelter, and where it afterwards endured the greatest extremities of human suffering.† But Wash-

* Brandywine and Germantown.

† The courage of the battle-field dwindles almost into insignificance when compared with that sublime heroism displayed by the American soldiery at Valley Forge, in the midst of frost and snow, disease and destitution. They had marched and countermarched, day and night, in endeavoring to baffle the designs of a powerful enemy to their country and its liberties; now they were called upon, in the midst of comparative inaction, to war with enemies more insidious, implacable, and personal. Hunger and nakedness assailed that dreary winter-camp, with all their progeny of disease and woe. Thither, as we have seen, the soldiers came with naked and bleeding feet; and there they sat down where destitution held court, and ruled with an icy sceptre. The prevalence of toryism in the vicinity, the avaricious peculations of some unprincipled commissioners, the tardy movements of Congress in supplying provisions, and the close proximity of a powerful enemy, combined to make the procurement of provisions absolutely impracticable without resort to force. But few horses were in the camp; and such was the deficiency, in this respect, for the ordinary, as well as extraordinary occasions of the army, that the men, in many instances, cheerfully yoked themselves to vehicles of their own construction, for carrying wood and provisions when procured; while others performed the duty of pack-horses, and carried heavy burdens of fuel upon their backs. — *Lossing's Field-Book of the Revolution*, ii. 129.

On the sixteenth of February, 1778, Washington wrote to Governor Clinton, "For some days past there has been little less than a famine in the camp. A part of the army has been a week without any kind of flesh, and the rest three or four days. Naked and starving as they are, we can not enough admire the incomparable patience and fidelity of the soldiery, that they have not been, ere this, excited by their sufferings to a general mutiny and desertion." — "The situation of the camp is such," wrote General Varnum to General Greene, on the twelfth of February, "that in all human probability the army must dissolve. Many of the troops are destitute of meat, and are several days in arrears. The horses are dying for want of forage. The country in the vicinity of the camp is exhausted. There can not be a moral certainty of bettering our condition while we remain here. What consequences have we rationally to expect?" — "It was with great difficulty," says Doctor Thacher, "that men enough could be found in a condition fit to discharge

ington was in the midst of his faithful companions in arms, ever employed in limiting their privations, in alleviating their miseries, and holding up to them the hopes of better fortunes. And oft in the rude wintry night, when the tempest howled among the hovels, and the shivering sentry paced his lonely round, would his eye be attracted to the taper that burned in the headquarters, where the man of mighty labors, watching while others slept, toiled in the cause of unborn millions.

At the headquarters of the Valley Forge occurred some of the most memorable incidents of the war for Independence. It was there the general received the appalling intelligence that not another ration was in store to issue to his troops. It was there that he was forced, by a stern and painful necessity, to use the high powers vested in him by Congress, to seize upon provisions for the relief of his starving soldiers.* It was there, while struggling with dangers and difficulties, while borne down with the cares and sorrows of his country's cause, that Washington was informed of the cabal† then agita-

---

the military camp duties from day to day; and for this purpose, those who were naked borrowed of those who had clothes." Unprovided with materials to raise their beds from the ground, the dampness occasioned sickness and death. "The army, indeed, was not without consolation," says Thacher, "for his excellency, the commander-in-chief, whom every soldier venerates and loves, manifested a fatherly concern and fellow-feelings, and made every exertion in his power to remedy the evil, and to administer the much-desired relief."

* The Congress, by resolution, authorized Washington to seize grain, forage, and other supplies, for the use of the army, within an area of seventy miles around his camp, the whole to be paid for. The tories were so abundant in Pennsylvania at that time, that this measure appeared necessary, for they would not sell provisions for the "rebel" camp. In February, Washington reluctantly used his power, by compelling the farmers to thrash out their grain. He condemned the system; and in a letter to the board of war, he said, "Supplies of provisions and clothing must be had in another way, or the army can not exist."

† This is known in history as *Conway's Cabal*, a French officer of Irish birth,

ting in Congress and the army, for the removal of the commander-in-chief.

But, with all these glooms, there were glories too, that shed their lustre upon the headquarters at Valley Forge. There was first proclaimed to the army the grateful tidings of the alliance with France;* and it was from

named Thomas Conway, then holding the commission of a brigadier in the American army, being one of the chief actors in the matter. Generals Gates and Mifflin of the army, and James Lovell and other New England delegates in Congress, were associated with Conway in the affair. The design of the conspirators (if blundering and not thoroughly colluding schemers may be called conspirators), was to deprive Washington of the chief command of the American armies, and give it to General Gates, or General Lee. Both of these officers had, from the beginning of the war, aspired to that honor, and Gates was fully identified with the movement to displace Washington. Conway appears to have been more the instrument of others than a voluntary and independent plotter. The whole nefarious plan was discovered, and recoiled with fearful force upon the conspirators. Washington acted with great judgment and forbearance throughout, having an eye single to the public good. "My enemies," he said, "take an ungenerous advantage of me. They know the delicacy of my situation, and that motives of policy deprive me of the defence I might otherwise make against their insidious attacks. They know I can not combat their insinuations, however injurious, without disclosing secrets which it is of the utmost moment to conceal."

* Early in the struggle, the colonists sent commissioners to Europe to solicit the aid and friendship of the continental powers. The French government evinced much sympathy for the Americans, extended some aid secretly, and promised more; but, until the capture of Burgoyne, when the Americans showed how able they were to help themselves, none of the European powers ventured to fly in the face of England, by openly aiding the revolted colonists. When that event became known, the aspect of American affairs wore a brighter hue abroad; and on the sixth of February, 1778, two treaties, one of *Alliance*, and the other of *Amity and Commerce*, were concluded and signed by the representatives of France and the United States. Intelligence of this joyful event reached Washington at Valley Forge, at midnight, on the third of May, and the sixth was set apart for a grand military *fête* and jubilee by the army. The day was fine, and the roar of artillery and shouts of the soldiery attested their great joy. Washington and his general officers, with their ladies, attended the religious services of the New Jersey brigade, and then repaired to headquarters and partook of a collation provided by the commander-in-chief. The entertainment was concluded with patriotic toasts. When the chief and his suite withdrew for a tour of inspection, there was a universal shout, "*Long live General Washington!*" This continued until they had proceeded some distance, when the

that scene of so many trials and sufferings that, on the return of the genial season, the modern Fabius marched again to grapple with his formidable and well-appointed foe, and to wrest from him, after a most gallant and hard-fought conflict, a glorious victory on the plains of Monmouth.*

The headquarters were under canvass during the siege and after the surrender of Yorktown. The marquées of the commander-in-chief were pitched in the rear of the grand battery, just out of the range of the enemy's shells.† There were two marquées attached to the headquarters during all the campaigns. The larger, or banqueting tent, would contain from forty to fifty persons; the smaller, or sleeping tent, had an inner-chamber, where, on a hard cot-bed, the chief reposed. There are most interesting reminiscences attached to the sleeping tent. The headquarters, even during the summer season, were located, in a great majority of instances, in private dwellings, the sleeping tent being pitched in the yard, or very near at hand. Within its venerable folds, Washington was in the habit of seeking privacy and seclusion, where he could commune with himself, and where he wrote the most memorable of his despatches in the Revolutionary war. He would remain in the retire-

---

general and his party turned and huzzaed several times, while a thousand hats were tossed in the air.

* See chapter on battle of Monmouth.

† The late Doctor Eneas Munson, of New Haven, who was then attached to the medical staff of the American army, informed me that while vigorous assaults upon two or three English redoubts were in progress, Washington left his marquée, and with Lincoln, Knox, and one or two other officers, disengaged at the time, stood within the grand battery, watching every movement through the embrasures. When the last redoubt was captured, Washington turned to Knox, and said, "The work is done, and *well* done;" and then called to his servant, "Billy, hand me my horse."

ment of the sleeping tent sometimes for hours, giving orders to the officer of his guard that he should on no account be disturbed, save on the arrival of an important express. The objects of his seclusion being accomplished, the chief would appear at the canvass door of the marquée, with despatches in his hand, giving which to his secretary to copy and transmit, he would either mount his charger for a tour of inspection, or return to the headquarters and enjoy social converse with his officers.

The marquées were made in Third street, Philadelphia, under the direction of Captain Moulder, of the artillery,* and were first pitched on the heights of Dorchester, in March, 1776.†

The Life-Guard was attached to the headquarters from the time of its formation till the end of the war. This chosen corps of picked men, with Gibbs and Colfax, and their gallant officers, was always in the finest order, proud of its being attached to the person of the chief, and appearing smart and soldierly, even in the worst times.

In our memoirs of the Pater Patriæ, we shall continue

---

* Captain Moulder commanded the American artillery in the battle at Princeton, on the third of January, 1777.

† Washington took command of the army before Boston, on the third of July, 1775, and, with the aid of General Gates, who was the adjutant-general, prepared the troops for a regular siege of the city. It was resolved to capture or expel the invaders, and for this purpose, a line of fortifications was built, extending from Charlestown Neck, near Bunker Hill, to Roxbury. For several months the Americans hemmed in the British army upon the little peninsula on which Boston stands. Finally, early in March, 1776, the republicans, under cover of night, proceeded to Dorchester heights with every precaution, and before morning constructed such formidable military works there, that the British commander was alarmed for the safety of his troops and shipping. The occupation of this eligible position led to a speedy evacuation of Boston by the invaders, and the recovery of that important position by the Americans.

to introduce some mention of the distinguished patriots, statesmen, and soldiers, who enjoyed his intimacy and were dear to his affections. High on this honored list appears, in bold relief, the name of Jonathan Trumbull, the patriotic governor of Connecticut during the whole of the Revolution. He was, indeed, well fitted for the times in which he flourished, and such an one as revolution alone seems capable of producing. Wise to conceive, and energetic to execute, his prudence equalled his courage in the conspicuous part he was destined to bear in those momentous concerns that eventuated in the independence of his country; yet did he " bear his high offices so meekly," that he was as deservedly beloved for the mildness of his private virtues as he was admired for the stern unyielding integrity with which he discharged his public duties. It is enough for his fame, or his epitaph, that he was a man after Washington's own heart.*

* Jonathan Trumbull was born at Lebanon, Connecticut, on the ninteenth of June, 1710. He was graduated at Harvard college in 1727, and commenced the study of theology with the Reverend Solomon Williams, of Lebanon. The death of an elder brother, who was engaged in mercantile business with his father, at Lebanon, caused him to become a merchant instead of a clergyman. At the age of twenty-three he was elected a member of the Connecticut assembly, where his business capacities raised him rapidly in public estimation. He was elected lieutenant-governor of the colony in 1766, and by virtue of that office became chief-justice of the superior court. His first bold step in opposition to Great Britain was in refusing to take the oath enjoined in 1768, which was an almost unconditional submission to all the power claimed by Parliament; nor would he be present when others, more timorous than he, took it. Because of his firmness he was elected governor of the colony in 1769, and he had the proud distinction of being the only colonial governor, at the commencement of the Revolution, who espoused the cause of the colonies. He was considered the whig leader in New England while the Adamses and Hancock were legislating in the continental Congress; and during the whole contest no man was more implicitly relied upon as a firm, consistent, and active friend of liberty, than Governor Trumbull. " General Washington relied on him," says Sparks, " as one of his main pillars of support." In 1783, when peace for the colonies returned, Governor Trumbull, then seventy-three years of age, declined a re-election to the office of gov-

When the news arrived in Connecticut of the battle of Lexington,* Putnam, who was ploughing in his field, instantly repaired to the governor for orders. "Go," said Trumbull, "to the scene of action."—"But my clothes, governor?"—"Oh, never mind your clothes," continued Trumbull, "your military experience will be of service to your countrymen."—"But my men, governor; what shall I do about my men?"—"Oh, never mind your men," continued the man for the times, "I'll send your men after you." Putnam hurried to Cambridge.†

---

ernor, which he had held fourteen consecutive years. He retired from public life, but did not live long to enjoy, in the bosom of his family, the quiet he so much coveted. He was seized with a malignant fever in August, 1785, and on the seventeenth of that month died, at the age of seventy-five years.

* When, in 1774, it became evident to the Americans that war was inevitable, unless they would consent to be slaves, they began to prepare for conflict. In Massachusetts, in particular, the republican leaders labored with great zeal to place the province in a condition to rise in open and united rebellion, when necessity should demand it. Governor Gage, in Boston, became alarmed, and commenced fortifying the Neck. The exasperated people began to collect munitions of war, and soon public affairs were like a sleeping volcano.

In April, 1775, Gage had three thousand British troops in Boston, ready to support the governor in any oppressive measure which he might choose to employ. He felt uneasy concerning some ammunition and stores which the republicans had gathered at Concord, sixteen miles from Boston, and on the night of the eighteenth of April, he sent out a secret expedition to destroy them. Vigilant patriots gave the alarm, and when the ministerial troops approached Lexington, a few miles from Concord, in the gray of early morning, they found seventy determined men standing upon the green, ready to oppose them. Pitcairn, the leader of the advanced corps, ordered them to lay down their arms and disperse. They stood firm. The British fired. A skirmish ensued, and several of the citizens were killed and wounded. The British then went on to Concord, had a fight with the Americans there, and finding the whole country rising, retreated to Boston, with great loss.

† Israel Putnam was born in Salem, Massachusetts, on the seventh of January, 1718, and at Pomfret, Connecticut, he cultivated land during many of the earlier years of his life. He was appointed to the command of some of the first troops raised in Connecticut for the French and Indian war in 1755, and during the whole of that long contest he was distinguished for bravery, in the wilds of northern New York. He distinguished himself at Bunker Hill, at the head of Connecticut troops in 1775, and

One of the most urgent appeals for assistance that ever emanated from the American headquarters was contained in a despatch to the governor of Connecticut. It was dated from the camp, near the North river, in the latter years of the war.*

Governor Trumbull was alone in his room of business; on the table were various letters and despatches, some

a few days afterward was appointed by the continental Congress one of the four major-generals of the grand army. He served his country faithfully until 1779, when partial paralysis prostrated him. His mind preserved its elasticity until his death, which occurred at Brooklyn, Connecticut, on the twenty-ninth of May, 1790, at the age of seventy-two years.

* This despatch was a circular letter, which was sent to the governors of each of the eastern states. It was dated at "New Windsor, 10th May, 1781." After stating that General Heath had consented to visit the New England states to "represent the present distresses of the army for want of provision," &c., Washington said, "From the post at Saratoga to that of Dobb's ferry inclusive, I believe there is not (by the returns and report I have received) at this moment one day's supply of meat for the army on hand. Our whole dependence for this article is on the eastern states; their resources, I am persuaded, are ample. To request and urge that they may be drawn forth regularly, and to be inforced with precision and certainty, what may absolutely be depended upon through the campaign, are the objects of this application.

"I have already made representations to the states of the want of provisions, the distress of the army, and the innumerable embarrassments we have suffered in consequence; not merely once or twice, but have reiterated them over and over again. I have struggled to the utmost of my ability to keep the army together, but it will be in vain without the effectual assistance of the states. I have now only to repeat the alternative, which has been so often urged, that supplies, particularly of beef cattle, must be speedily and regularly provided, or our posts can not be maintained, nor the army kept in the field much longer. I entreat your excellency, that this representation may be received in the serious light it is meant and deserves, or that I may stand exculpated from the dreadful consequences, which must otherwise inevitably follow in a very short time."

A few days afterward, Washington held a conference with Rochambeau, at Weathersfield, in Connecticut, and from that place he wrote another urgent circular letter. In his Diary of the twentieth of May, he wrote: "Had a good deal of private conversation with Governor Trumbull, who gave it to me as his opinion, that if any important offensive operations should be undertaken, he had little doubt of our obtaining men and provisions adequate to our wants. In this opinion Colonel Wadsworth and others concurred."

just opened and others sealed for immediate transmission; a cocked-hat, of the cut and fashion of the days of George II., the governor's sole insignia of office, was also on the table, while the chief magistrate himself was busily engaged in writing.

An aid-de-camp of the commander-in-chief was introduced, much worn and "travel stained" from the haste of his journey. The governor rose, and, while cordially welcoming Colonel ——, inquired after the health of his excellency, and what news from the army. The aid-de-camp replied that the general was well, and the news from the army of a very sombre character, and presented a letter. The letter was very short. It contained an apology from Washington for having applied for assistance where it had been so often and so liberally rendered before, but continued that the situation of the army was critical in the extreme, the country adjacent to the camp being completely exhausted, as well by the enemy's as by his own foraging parties; and concluded by lamenting that, unless supplies could be speedily obtained, he should be obliged to abandon his position, and fall back into the interior to obtain the necessary subsistence for the troops.

The governor pondered for a moment upon the contents of the letter, then rising, and cordially grasping the colonel by the hand, observed, in a firm yet cheerful tone, "When you return to camp, bear with you, my dear sir, my love and duty to his excellency, and say to him that brave old Connecticut, patriotic Connecticut, is not quite exhausted, but for every barrel of provisions she has furnished to the cause of liberty, she will furnish another, and yet another, to the same glorious cause: say further, that on such a day our teams may be looked for on the bank of the North river." The aid-de-camp departed rejoicing.

And now the patriot became "every inch" the executive officer. From his intimate acquaintance with the resources of his native state, he knew exactly where those resources were to be obtained, and their facilities for transportation, for with him everything was done by method and regularity. His orders flew in all directions. And his orders were obeyed.

Meantime, the return of the aid-de-camp to headquarters with intelligence of the promised supplies diffused a general gladness throughout the army. When the expected day arrived, many an anxious eye was turned to the road leading from the eastward to the landing on the North river.* A dust is seen in the distance, and presently are heard the cries of the teamsters, urging their fine oxen, while the heavy-laden wains groan under their generous burdens. A shout rings through the American camp, and the commander-in-chief, attended by his officers, ride to an eminence to witness the arrival of the welcome supplies.

Governor Trumbull had two sons attached to the headquarters: John, the distinguished artist, and *the last of the aids-de-camp*,† and Jonathan, military secre-

* Fishkill landing, opposite Newburgh.

† John Trumbull was born in Lebanon, Connecticut, in June, 1756. He commenced his career as a painter at the age of eighteen years. He had been graduated at Harvard college the previous year. His first historical composition, the *Battle of Cannæ*, was painted in 1774. At the breaking out of the Revolutionary war he entered the army as adjutant of the first Connecticut regiment, and went to Roxbury, near Boston. Washington heard of his talent for drawing, and employed him to sketch a draught of the enemy's works. His success commended the young painter to Washington, and in August, the commander-in-chief appointed him his aid-de-camp. In 1776 he was in the northern department, under Gates. The following year he left the army, and resumed his profession at Boston. He went first

tary to the commander-in-chief at the siege of Yorktown.*

Among the great variety of persons and character that were to be found from time to time at and about the headquarters, was the famed Captain Molly, already mentioned in the chapter on the BATTLE OF MONMOUTH. After her heroic achievements at the battle of Monmouth, the heroine was always received with a cordial welcome at headquarters, where she was employed in the duties of the household. She always wore an artilleryman's coat, with the cocked-hat and feather, the distinguishing costume of Proctor's artillery. One day the chief accosted this remarkable woman, while she was engaged in washing some clothes, pleasantly observing: "Well, Captain Molly, are you not almost tired of this quiet way of life, and longing to be once more on the field of battle?"—"Troth, your excellency," replied the heroine, "and ye may say that; for I care not how soon

---

to Paris, and then to London, in 1780, and in the latter city placed himself under the instruction of Benjamin West. The political sins of his father were visited upon his head. On suspicion of his being a secret rebel agent, he was imprisoned eight months, and then banished from the kingdom, West and Copley becoming his securities. He returned home in January, 1782, and formed a connection with the army, as aid to the chief. At the close of the war he again went to England, where he pursued his profession with zeal for several years. Finally he contemplated a series of pictures illustrative of American history. He arrived in New York in 1789, and was favored with sittings by Washington and other distinguished men of the Revolution. Having collected much material, he again went to England, as private secretary to Mr. Jay, the American embassador. He returned to America in 1804, but did not remain long. He lived in England until the close of the war of 1812–'15, and then came home. He was engaged to paint four large pictures for the rotunda of the new federal capitol. These pictures occupied him seven years, and are, *Signers of the Declaration of Independence*, the *Surrender of Burgoyne*, the *Surrender at Yorktown*, and *Washington resigning his Commission*. He died in the city of New York on the tenth of November, 1843, in the eighty-eighth year of his age.

* See note on page 174.

I have another slap at them red-coats, bad luck to them." "But what is to become of your petticoats in such an event, Captain Molly?"—"Oh, long life to your excellency, and never de ye mind them at all at all," continued this intrepid female. "Sure and it is only in the artillery your excellency knows that I would sarve, and divil a fear but the smoke of the cannon will hide my petticoats."

The name and memory of headquarters expired not with the war of the Revolution, but was preserved in the Presidoliads of New York and Philadelphia,* where hundreds of the war-worn veterans of the days of trial repaired, as they said, to *headquarters*, to pay their respects, and inquire after the health of his excellency and the good Lady Washington. All were made welcome and "kindly bid to stay;" and while they quaffed a generous glass to the health of their beloved chief, the triumphs of Trenton and Princeton, of Monmouth and Yorktown, "were freshly remembered."

And poor Pat, too, reverently with hat in hand, would approach the headquarters. "To be sure, he would say, that he well knew his excellency had no time to spare to the likes of him. He just called to inquire after his honor's health, long life to him, and the good Lady Washington, the poor soldier's friend." But, taking the steward aside, with a knowing look, would observe: "Now, my darlint, if his excellency should happen to in-

---

* The federal Congress held its first session, under the present constitution, in the city of New York, where Washington was inaugurated president of the United States, on the thirtieth of April, 1789. The seat of government was removed to Philadelphia in 1790, the Congress assembling there on the first Monday in December of that year. That city continued to be the seat of government until the year 1800, when the Congress assembled for the first time in the city of Washington.

quire who it was that called, just tell him it was one of ould Mad Anthony's boys. Hurrah for Ameriky!" And repeating the shout that so often had rang above the battle's roar, the veteran would go on his way rejoicing.

It may be, in the course of human events, that upon the places at Morristown and the Valley Forge, where the soldier of liberty erected his cheerless hut, the domes and spires of cities may arise in the splendid progress of a mighty empire, but the patriotic American of that future day, proud of the fame of the Father of his Country, and glorying in the recollections of America's heroic time, will pass by the palaces of pomp and power, to pay homage to the mouldering ruins of the HEADQUARTERS.*

* There are several other buildings, besides those already mentioned, yet standing, that were used as headquarters by Washington. The best preserved of them are located as follows: near Chad's ford on the Brandywine, and at White Marsh, fourteen miles from Philadelphia, in Pennsylvania; the Hopper house, four miles south of the Ramapo Pass, an old mansion at Rocky Hill, where his farewell address to the army was written, in New Jersey; at Tappan, in Rockland county, Quaker Hill, in Duchess county, near White Plains, and at Dobb's ferry, in Westchester county; and at No. 1 Broadway, and Madam Jumel's mansion near Fort Washington, on York or Manhattan island, in the state of New York.

CHAPTER X.

MYSTERIES OF THE REVOLUTION.*

The American Camp in New Jersey — A Night Scene — Appearance of a Stranger — A Clergyman seeks an Interview with Washington — His Admission to the Presence of the Chief — Washington Warned concerning General Charles Lee — Doctor Griffith — Conduct of General Lee at Monmouth — Rivington and Secret Service — The Quaker Loan — Rivington Faithful — Solution of the Mystery — Washington and Rivington — Secret Interview — Rivington's Manners — Amount of Secret Service Money used — Its Value to the Country.

It was Saturday night, the twenty-seventh of June, 1778, when the American army, after a toilsome march in a tropical heat, halted for rest and refreshment in the county of Monmouth, New Jersey.† The weary soldiers were gathered in groups, some preparing the evening meal, while others, exhausted by their march, threw themselves on the ground to seek repose. The short night of June was waning, the watch-fires burned dimly, and silence reigned around. Not so at headquarters.‡ There lights were seen, while the chief, seated at a table, wrote or dictated despatches, which were folded and directed by aid-de-camp and secretaries, while near at hand were expresses, seated like statues upon their drowsy horses, awaiting orders; and ever and anon an officer would approach them with the words, "This for

---

* Published in the *National Intelligencer*, on the twenty-second of February, 1856.

† See note on page 211.

‡ The American army was encamped that night upon the Manatapan creek, between Cranberry and Englishtown, a few miles from Monmouth courthouse.

Major-General ——; ride with speed and spare not the spur;" and in a moment the horseman would disappear in the surrounding gloom. Suddenly a stranger appeared on the scene. He wore no martial costume, neither had he the measured tread of the soldier; in truth his appearance was anything but *militaire*. On being challenged by the sentinel, he answered, " Doctor Griffith, chaplain and surgeon in the Virginia line, on business highly important with the commander-in-chief." The cry of "Officer of the guard!" brought forth that functionary, so necessary a personage in a night camp.* The officer shook his head, and waving his hand said, " No, sir, no; impossible; intensely engaged; my orders positive; can't be seen on any account." The reverend gentleman quailed not, but said to the officer who barred his passage, "Present, sir, my humble duty to his excellency, and say that Doctor Griffith waits upon him with secret and important intelligence, and craves an audience of only five minutes' duration."

The high respect in which the clergy of the American army was held by Washington was known to every officer and soldier in its ranks. This, together with the imposing nature of the chaplain's visit, induced the officer of the guard to enter the headquarters and report the circumstance to the general. He, quickly returning, ushered the chaplain into the presence of the commander-in-chief.

Washington, still with pen in hand, received his midnight visiter courteously, when Griffith observed; "The nature of the communication I am about to make to your excellency must be my apology for disturbing you at this hour of the night. While I am not permitted to

---

* Officer of the Life-Guard.

divulge the names of the authorities from whom I have obtained my information, I can assure you they are of the very first order, whether in point of character or attachment to the cause of American independence. I have sought this interview to warn your excellency against the conduct of Major-General Lee in to-morrow's battle. My duty is fulfilled, and I go now to pray to the God of battles for success to our arms, and that he may always have your excellency in his holy keeping." The chaplain retired, the officer of the guard (by signal from the chief) accompanying the reverend gentleman to the line of the sentinels. Doctor Griffith survived the war and became rector of a parish in which Washington worshipped. He was elected first bishop of Virginia under the new regime, but was never consecrated. He sickened and died in Philadelphia, in 1789. He was a ripe scholar, a pious minister, and an ardent enthusiast in the cause of American independence.*

---

* Reverend David Griffith was a native of the city of New York, and was educated partly there and partly in England, for the medical profession. He took his degrees in London, returned to America, and entered upon the duties of his profession in the interior of New York, about the year 1763. Having resolved to enter the ministry of the Protestant Episcopal church, he went to London in the year 1770, and there, on the nineteenth of August, was ordained by Bishop Terrick. He was a missionary in West Jersey for a while, and at the close of 1771, became rector of Shelburne parish, in Loudon county, Virginia. In 1776 he entered the military service as chaplain to the third Virginia regiment, and continued in that position until some time in the year 1780, when he became rector of Christ church, Alexandria. There he remained until his death, in 1789. During a large portion of that time Washington was his parishoner, and Doctor Griffith frequently visited Mount Vernon as a welcome guest. He was chosen bishop of Virginia in 1786, but such was the depressed state of the church in that diocese, that funds sufficient to defray his expenses to London, to receive consecration, could not be raised. He resigned all claims to the office in May, 1789, and while attending the general convention of the church at Philadelphia, a few weeks later, died at the house of Bishop White.

When the warning became known in the army it created many conjectures as to the sources from whence the chaplain acquired his information. Nothing ever transpired, and the secret died, while the mystery remains to the present time.*

The conduct of General Lee in the battle of Monmouth very fairly justified the warning of the chaplain. It is certain that that brave and skilful commander had no leaning toward the enemy, but it is thought that he expected, by throwing things into confusion, to lessen the merits of Washington in the public estimation, for he aspired to be the commander of the army.†

---

* The author of these *Recollections* received the foregoing account of the warning given to Washington by Doctor Griffith, from Colonel Nicholas, of Virginia, who was an officer of the Life-Guard at that time.

† The charity for Lee expressed by the author of these *Recollections* is not justified by recent revelations. Lee undoubtedly entertained treasonable designs at that moment. That he had held treasonable intercourse with the enemy previous to this time, his own handwriting bears testimony. That proof is in the form of a manuscript of eight foolscap pages, in Lee's own peculiar handwriting, prepared while he was a prisoner in New York, and dated the twenty-ninth day of March, 1777, in which he submits to Lord and Sir William Howe, a plan for the easy subjugation of the colonies. It is endorsed in the known handwriting of Lord Howe's secretary—"Plan of Mr. Lee, 1777." In it Lee professed to desire a cessation of bloodshed, as he considered the issue doubtful. His plan was to dissolve the system of resistance which centered in the government of Congress. He regarded that system as depending chiefly upon the people of Pennsylvania, Maryland, and Virginia; and his plan looked to the reduction or submission of Maryland, and the preventing Virginia from furnishing aid to the army then in New Jersey, and thus to dissolve the whole machinery of resistance. He proposed an expedition against New England, so as to keep the inhabitants there at home, and make it an easy matter to hold possession of New York and the Jerseys. He suggested that, simultaneously with this movement eastward, a considerable force should be sent up the Chesapeake bay, to land at and take possession of Annapolis, and march into the interior of Maryland as far as Queen Anne. Another was to be despatched up the Potomac, and take possession of Alexandria, when the two invading armies might form a junction; while a third should ascend the Delaware and capture Philadelphia. The middle states would now be in subjection, and New England and the southern states would be too wide apart to act in efficient concert. These things accomplished,

The interview between Washington and Lee, and the chivalric enthusiasm of Colonel Hamilton on that occasion, have been already described in our account of that battle.

Of all the mysteries that occurred in the American Revolution, the employment of Rivington, editor of the Royal Gazette, in the secret service of the American commander is the most astounding.*

and the system of resistance dismembered, all that would be necessary, to insure a complete subjugation of the revolted states to the crown, would be the issuing of proclamations of pardon to all who should desert the republican standard, and return to their allegiance to King George.

With such evidence of his treason, it is easy to interpret much in the conduct of Lee which has puzzled the historian and the student of our history. By the light of this evidence we may easily explain his conduct after the fall of Fort Washington, in the Autumn of 1776, until his disgraceful retreat on the field of Monmouth—his tardy movements in New Jersey, when earnestly appealed to by Washington; his repeated disobedience of orders; his capture by a small party of British light-horse in New Jersey; his provision with a suit of rooms in the City hall, New York, while a prisoner, and his great intimacy with the British officers there; his refusal at first to take the required oath of allegiance at Valley Forge; his intimations of the intended movements of the enemy (according to the suggestions of his plan), when they were about to evacuate Philadelphia; his opposition to any attack on Sir Henry Clinton; and his conduct on the field of Monmouth. The document containing the evidences of his treason was discovered at the close of 1857, among some papers said to have been brought from Nova Scotia, and offered for sale in New York. I first perused it on the second of January, 1858. It soon afterward became the possession of Professor George H. Moore, librarian of the New York Historical Society; and this, and other circumstantial evidences of Lee's treason, were first made known to the world by that gentleman in a paper read by him before that society in June following.

* James Rivington was a native of London, well educated, and of pleasing deportment. He came to America in the year 1760, and established a bookstore in Philadelphia. The following year he opened one near the foot of Wall street, in New York, where he established a paper called the *Royal Gazetteer*, in 1773. It was afterwards entitled the *Royal Gazette*. He took the ministerial side in politics when the Revolution broke out, and became very obnoxious to the republicans, whom he abused without stint. In the autumn of 1775, a company of Connecticut light-horse, led by Captain Isaac Sears of New York, entered the city at noonday, proceeded to Rivington's printing establishment, placed a guard with fixed bayonets around it, put all his types into bags, destroyed his press and other apparatus, and then in the

294 RECOLLECTIONS OF WASHINGTON.

The time that this remarkable connection took place is of course unknown. There is much probability that it may have commenced as early as the closing of the campaign of 1776, as it is known that about that period Robert Morris borrowed of a Quaker five hundred guineas in gold for the secret service of Washington's army, and that intelligence of vital and vast importance was obtained from the disbursement of the *Quaker loan.*

The worthy Quaker said to Morris: "How can I, friend Robert, who am a man of peace, lend thee money for the purposes of war? Friend George is, I believe, a good man and fighting in a good cause; but I am opposed to fighting of any sort." Morris, however, soon managed to quiet old broadbrim's scruples: the gold was dug up from his garden and handed over to the commander-in-chief, whose application of it to the secret service produced the happiest effects upon the cause of the Revolution in that critical period of our destiny.*

---

same order, cheered by the shouts of the pleased populace, and the tune of Yankee Doodle, left the city. Rivington then went to England. When, the following year, the British took possession of New York, Rivington returned. In October, 1777, he was appointed "king's printer" in that city, and resumed the publication of his paper, semi-weekly. After the war, his business declined, and he lived in comparative poverty until July 1802, when he died, at the age of seventy-eight years. A portrait of Rivington, from a painting by Stuart, may be found in *Lossing's Field-Book of the Revolution.*

* "This story," says the author of these *Recollections*, in a note, "was no mystery in Philadelphia sixty-five years ago, when the man of peace was then living, perfectly well known and deservedly esteemed, and enjoying the *peace*, liberty, and happiness which his gold had contributed to accomplish for his native land."

Another transaction of a similar character, but on a larger scale, is related upon good authority. After the capture of the Hessians at Trenton, and disposition of them in Pennsylvania, Washington resolved to recross the Delaware and occupy the field of his conquest. But the term of enlistment of many of his troops was about to expire. To retain them he offered a bounty, to be paid in specie, and he applied to Robert Morris for the metal, the credit of Congress being too low at that time to offer it as security to the lender. Morris received the application just at evening

MYSTERIES OF THE REVOLUTION. 295

Rivington proved faithful to his bargain, and often would intelligence of great importance, gleaned in convivial moments at Sir William's, or Sir Henry's table,* be in the American camp before the convivialists had slept off the effects of their wine.

The business of the secret service was so well managed that even a suspicion never arose as to the medium through which intelligence of vast importance was continually being received in the American camp from the very headquarters of the British army; and, had suspicion arose, the king's printer would probably have been the last man suspected, for during the whole of his connection with the secret service his Royal Gazette literally piled abuse of every sort upon the American general and the cause of America.†

He knew not where to apply for the money, and with a desponding spirit he left his counting-room late in the evening, musing upon the subject. He met a wealthy Quaker neighbor, and made known to him his wants. "Robert," he said, "what security canst thou give?"—"My note and my honor," replied Morris. "Thou shalt have it," was the quick response; and a few hours later, Morris wrote to Washington: "I was up early this morning to despatch a supply of fifty thousand dollars to your excellency. It gives me pleasure that you have engaged the troops to continue; and, if further occasional supplies of money are necessary, you may depend on my exertions, either in a public or private capacity." Thus strengthened, Washington turned his face toward the enemy.

The Quakers, as advocates of peace, were opposed to the war, and were among the most determined loyalists throughout the Revolution. And that loyalty to the king was not always passive, but with glaring inconsistency with their professions, some of them, in Philadelphia, aided the British troops in their efforts to crush the rebellion, so called. To such an extent did they exert an influence against the patriots, that Congress thought it advisable to recommend the several states to keep a watch upon their movements. Several leading Quakers were banished from Philadelphia in 1777; and in November, 1778, John Roberts and Abraham Carlisle, Quakers, who were found guilty of affording secret aid to the enemy, were hanged.

* Sir William Howe and Sir Henry Clinton.

† Never was an editor more unscrupulous in defaming his opponents, than Rivington. He paid no regard to truth or decency, but belabored the whigs with all his might. He was most cordially hated by the republicans, and their writers even

In 1783 this remarkable mystery was solved. When Washington entered New York a conqueror, on the evacuation by the British forces,* he said one morning to two of his officers: "Suppose, gentlemen, we walk down to Rivington's bookstore; he is said to be a very pleasant kind of a fellow." Amazed, as the officers were, at the idea of visiting such a man, they of course prepared to accompany the chief. When arrived at the bookstore, Rivington received his visiters with great politeness; for he was indeed one of the most elegant gentlemen and best bred men of the age. Escorting the party into a

after the war, never spared him when an opportunity offered to lash him. Philip Freneau, one of the bards of the Revolution, gave him many a hard hit. In a poem entitled *Rivington's Reflections*, he thus referred to the editor's mendacity when making him say, at the close of the war:—

> "For what have I done when we come to consider,
> But sold my commodities to the best bidder?
> If I offered to lie for the sake of a post,
> Was I to be blamed if the king offered most?
> The king's royal printer!—Five hundred a-year!
> Between you and me 'twas a handsome affair:
> Who would not for *that* give matters a stretch,
> And lie backward and forward, and carry and fetch."

* A preliminary treaty of peace between the United States and Great Britain, was signed at Paris on the thirtieth of November, 1782, and a definitive treaty was signed at the same place by American and English commissioners, on the third of September, 1783. In that treaty, England acknowledged the independence of the United States. By previous arrangement, the British army, which had occupied New York seven years, was to leave it on the twenty-fifth of November, 1783. On the morning of that day—a cold, frosty, but clear and brilliant morning—the American troops, under General Knox, who had come down from West Point, and encamped at Harlem, marched to the Bowery lane, and halted at the junction of the present Third avenue and Bowery. Knox was accompanied by George Clinton, the governor of the State of New York, with all the principal civil officers. There they remained until about one o'clock in the afternoon, when the British left their posts and marched to Whitehall (near the South ferry to Brooklyn) to embark. The American troops, accompanied by Washington, followed, and before three o'clock General Knox took formal possession of Fort George, amid the acclamations of thousands of emancipated freemen, and the roar of artillery upon the Battery.

parlor, he begged the officers to be seated, and then said to the chief, "Will your excellency do me the honor to step into the adjoining room for a moment that I may show you a list of the *agricultural works* I am about to order out from London for your special use?" They retired. The locks on the doors of the houses in New York more than threescore years ago were not so good as now. The door of Rivington's private room closed very imperfectly and soon became ajar, when the officers distinctly heard the chinking of two heavy purses of gold as they were successively placed on a table.*

The party soon returned from the inner-room, when Rivington pressed upon his guests a glass of Madeira, which he assured them was a prime article, having imported it himself, and it having received the approbation of Sir Henry and the most distinguished *bon vivants* of the British army.†

---

* Rivington's method of conveying intelligence to Washington was ingenious. He published books of various kinds, and by means of these he carried on his treasonable correspondence. He wrote his secret billets upon thin paper, and bound them in the cover of a book, which he always managed to sell to those spies of Washington, who were constantly visiting New York, and who, he knew, would carry the volumes directly to the headquarters of the army. The men employed in this special service were ignorant of the peculiar nature of it.

† Rivington was a high liver when his pecuniary means would allow him the indulgence. He was a fine-looking, portly man, and dressed in the extreme of fashion—curled and powdered hair, claret-colored coat, scarlet waistcoat trimmed with gold lace, buckskin breeches, and top-boots. He always kept a stock of choice wines on hand, with which to regale his friends. A good anecdote connected with his wine was related by Rivington himself. He had soundly abused Colonel Ethan Allen, while he was a prisoner, and the leader of the Green-Mountain Boys swore he would "lick Rivington the first opportunity he had." When Allen was released from the provost jail, he went directly toward Rivington's office to execute his oath. Rivington's clerk saw him coming, and went up stairs to warn his master, the loyal editor having already been informed of the irate colonel's intentions. "I was sitting," said Rivington, "after a good dinner, alone, with my bottle of Madeira before me, when I heard an unusual noise in the street, and a huzza from the boys. I was in the

The visiters now rose to depart. Rivington, on taking leave of the chief, whom he escorted to the door, said: "Your excellency may rely upon my especial attention being given to *the agricultural works,* which, on their arrival, will be immediately forwarded to Mount Vernon, where I trust they will contribute to your gratification amid the shades of domestic retirement." Rivington remained for several years in New York after the peace of 1783. It was the general opinion at that time, that if Rivington had been closely pressed on the delicate subject of the secret service, characters of greater calibre might have appeared on the tapis than the king's printer.*

---

second story, and, stepping to the window, saw a tall figure in tarnished regimentals with a large cocked hat and an enormous long sword, followed by a crowd of boys, who occasionally cheered him with huzzas, of which he seemed insensible. He came up to my door and stopped. I could see no more. My heart told me it was Ethan Allen. I shut down my window, and retired behind my table and bottle. I was certain the hour of reckoning had come. There was no retreat. Mr. Staples, my clerk, came in paler than ever, and clasping his hands, said, 'Master, he is come!' 'I know it.' 'He entered the store, and asked "if James Rivington lived there." I answered, "Yes, sir." "Is he at home?" "I will go and see, sir," I said; 'and now, master, what is to be done? There he is in the store, and the boys peeping at him from the street.' I had made up my mind. I looked at the bottle of Madeira—possibly took a glass. 'Show him up,' said I; 'and if such Madeira can not mollify him, he must be harder than adamant.' There was a fearful moment of suspense. I heard him on the stairs, his long sword clanking at every step. In he stalked. 'Is your name James Rivington?' 'It is, sir, and no man could be more happy than I am to see Colonel Ethan Allen.' 'Sir, I have come—' 'Not another word, my dear colonel, until you have taken a seat and a glass of old Madeira.' 'But sir, I don't think it proper—' 'Not another word, colonel. Taste this wine; I have had it in glass for ten years. Old wine, you know, unless it is originally sound, never improves by age.' He took the glass, swallowed the wine, smacked his lips, and shook his head approvingly. 'Sir, I come—' 'Not another word until you have taken another glass, and then, my dear colonel, we will talk of old affairs, and I have some droll events to detail.' In short, we finished two bottles of Madeira, and parted as good friends as if we never had cause to be otherwise."

* When the loyalists of New York fled to Nova Scotia, on the evacuation of the city by the British, Rivington, to the astonishment of all, remained. This fact

When the famous Rivington espionage became known there were many speculations as to the amount paid for the secret service. Some went so far as to calculate how many guineas the capacious pockets of an officer's coat made in the old fashion would contain. The general result was that, including the quaker's loan and payments made up to the final payment in full, made by the chief in person, from a thousand to fifteen hundred guineas would be a pretty fair estimate.

It was a cheap, a dog cheap bargain; for, although gold was precious in the days of the continental currency, yet the gold paid for the secret service was of inestimable value, when it is remembered how much it contributed to the safety and success of the army of independence.

puzzled those unacquainted with his career during the war. Others, not a tenth part as obnoxious to the republicans as he, were driven away. In his secret treason is the solution of the mystery. The facts above related are given by the author of these *Recollections*, he says, "on the authority of General Henry Lee, who had them from one of the officers who accompanied Washington in his visit to Rivington." I received substantially the same facts, a few years ago, from the late Senator Hunter, of Hunter's island, Westchester county, New York, who heard them from the lips of a British admiral.

CHAPTER XI.

THE INDIAN PROPHECY.*

WASHINGTON'S JOURNEY TO THE KANAWHA RIVER IN 1770 — FORMS A CAMP ON ITS BANKS — ABUNDANCE OF GAME THERE — VISITED BY A TRADER AND A PARTY OF INDIANS — FIRST INTERVIEW WITH THEM — THE INDIAN SACHEM'S MISSION — HIS GREAT REVERENCE FOR COLONEL WASHINGTON — SPEECH OF THE INDIAN SACHEM — HIS REMARKABLE PROPHECY — ITS EFFECT UPON THE COMPANY — DEPARTURE OF THE SAVAGES — DOCTOR JAMES CRAIK — HIS FAITH IN THE PROPHECY — SCENE AT THE BATTLE OF MONMOUTH — COLONEL THOMAS HARTLEY.

IT was in 1770, that Colonel Washington, accompanied by Doctor James Craik, and a considerable party of hunters, woodsmen, and others, proceeded to the Kanawha with a view to explore the country, and make surveys of extensive and valuable bodies of lands.† At that

---

* This was first published in the Philadelphia *United States Gazette*, on the twenty-seventh of May, 1826.

† The officers and soldiers who accompanied Washington in the expedition against the French, on the Ohio, in 1754, were promised grants of land in the fertile regions of the great Kanawha, where it empties into the Ohio. These lands were formally granted that year, by an order in council of the British government, and a proclamation by Governor Dinwiddie, but on account of the continuance of a state of war, they were not located, and actual possession given, until many years afterward. In 1770 a company in London solicited a grant of land within the proposed boundaries of which nearly all of the promised bounty land lay. Washington at once took the matter in hand, as the champion of the soldier about to be wronged. He first laid before Governor Botetourt a history of the claim, and entered a strong protest against the proposed grant to the English company, at the head of whom was the celebrated Horace Walpole. He was successful in his defence of the soldier's rights, and that nothing essential to their interests should be left undone, he resolved to visit the region under consideration, and select the best tracts of land for himself and his companions-in-arms; and on the fifth of October, 1770, accompanied by his friend and neighbor, Doctor Craik, with three negro attendants, he left Mount Vernon for the Ohio. His Diary, kept during this journey to the wilderness and back, which

time of day, the Kanawha was several hundred miles remote from the frontier settlements, and only accessible by Indian paths, which wound through the passes of the mountains.

In those wild and unfrequented regions, the party formed a camp on the bank of the river, consisting of rudely-constructed wigwams or shelters, from which they issued to explore and survey those alluvial tracts, now forming the most fertile and best inhabited parts of the west of Virginia.*

This romantic camp, though far removed from the homes of civilization, possessed very many advantages. The great abundance of various kinds of game, in its vicinity, afforded a sumptuous larder, while a few luxuries of foreign growth, which had been brought on the baggage horses, made the adventurers as comfortable as they could reasonably desire.†

One day when resting in camp from the fatigues attendant on so arduous an enterprise, a party of Indians led by a trader, were discovered. No recourse was had to arms, for peace in great measure reigned on the frontier; the border warfare which so long had harassed the unhappy settlers, had principally subsided, and the savage driven farther and farther back, as the settlements advanced, had sufficiently felt the power of the whites, to view them with fear, as well as hate. Again, the approach

---

occupied "nine weeks and one day," is printed entire in the appendix to the second volume of Spark's *Life and Writings of Washington*.

* These lands lay in the present counties of Kanawha, Jackson, Mason, and Cabel.

† Washington in his Diary, thus refers to one of his horses: "My portmanteau horse being unable to proceed, I left him at my brother's [Samuel, on Worthington's marsh, over the Blue Ridge], and got one of his and proceeded to Samuel Pritchard's, on Cacapehon."

of this party was anything but hostile, and the appearance of the trader, a being half savage, half civilized, made it certain that the mission was rather of peace than war.

They halted at a short distance, and the interpreter advancing, declared that he was conducting a party, which consisted of a grand sachem, and some attendant warriors; that the chief was a very great man among the northwestern tribes, and the same who commanded the Indians on the fall of Braddock, sixteen years before,* that hearing of the visit of Colonel Washington to the western country, this chief had set out on a mission, the object of which himself would make known.†

The colonel received the embassador with courtesy, and having put matters in camp in the best possible order for the reception of such distinguished visiters, which so short a notice would allow, the strangers were introduced. Among the colonists were some fine, tall, and manly figures, but so soon as the sachem approached, he in a moment pointed out the hero of the Monongahela, from among the group, although sixteen years had elapsed since he had seen him, and then only in the tumult and fury of battle. The Indian was of a lofty stature, and of a dignified and imposing appearance.

---

* See note on page 158.

† On the way, Washington and Doctor Craik were joined by several frontier men, among them Joseph Nicholson, an interpreter. Under date of October 20, he recorded in his Diary: "We embarked in a large canoe, with a sufficient store of provisions and necessaries, and the following persons, besides Dr. Craik and myself, to wit, Captain Crawford, Joseph Nicholson, Robert Bell, William Harrison, Charles Morgan, and Daniel Rendon, a boy of Captain Crawford's, and the Indians, who were in a canoe by themselves." Captain Crawford afterward suffered a horrible death at the hands of the Shawnees, in Ohio. At Fort Pitt they were joined by "Colonel Craghan, Lieutenant Hamilton, and Mr. Magee."

The usual salutations were going round, when it was observed, that the grand chief, although perfectly familiar with every other person present, preserved toward Colonel Washington the most reverential deference. It was in vain that the colonel extended his hand, the Indian drew back, with the most impressive marks of awe and respect. A last effort was made to induce an intercourse, by resorting to the delight of the savages—ardent spirit—which the colonel having tasted, offered to his guest; the Indian bowed his head in submission, but wetted not his lips. Tobacco, for the use of which Washington always had the utmost abhorrence, was next tried, the colonel taking a single puff to the great annoyance of his feelings, and then offering the calumet to the chief, who touched not the symbol of savage friendship. The banquet being now ready, the colonel did the honors of the feast, and placing the great man at his side, helped him plentifully, but the Indian fed not at the board. Amazement now possessed the company, and an intense anxiety became apparent, as to the issue of so extraordinary an adventure. The council fire was kindled, when the grand sachem addressed our Washington to the following effect:—*

"I am a chief, and the ruler over many tribes. My influence extends to the waters of the great lakes, and to to the far blue mountains. I have travelled a long and weary path, that I might see the young warrior of the great battle. It was on the day, when the white man's blood, mixed with the streams of our forest, that I first beheld this chief: I called to my young men and said, mark yon tall and daring warrior? He is not of the

---

* He addressed Washington, through Nicholson, the interpreter.

red-coat tribe—he hath an Indian's wisdom, and his warriors fight as we do—himself is alone exposed. Quick, let your aim be certain, and he dies. Our rifles were levelled, rifles which, but for him, knew not how to miss—'twas all in vain, a power mightier far than we, shielded him from harm. He can not die in battle. I am old, and soon shall be gathered to the great council-fire of my fathers, in the land of shades, but ere I go, there is a something, bids me speak, in the voice of prophecy. Listen! *The Great Spirit protects that man, and guides his destinies—he will become the chief of nations, and a people yet unborn, will hail him as the founder of a mighty empire!*"*

The savage ceased, his oracle delivered, his prophetic mission fulfilled, he retired to muse in silence, upon that wonder-working Spirit, which his dark

"Untutored mind
Saw oft in clouds, and heard Him in the wind."

Night coming on, the children of the forest spread

---

* This narrative the author of the *Recollections* received from the lips of Dr. Craik. Washington does not mention the circumstance in his Diary. It was a peculiar trait of his character to avoid everything, either in speech or writing, that had a personal relation to himself, in this manner. In his Diary he mentions a visit from an embassy of the Six Nations, led by White Mingo, who made a speech. But that occurred on the nineteenth of the month; while the incident that forms the subject of this chapter, did not occur until they had reached the mouth of the Kanawha, after the thirty-first.

The Reverend Samuel Davies, a Presbyterian minister at Hanover, in Virginia, during the earlier portions of the French and Indian war (and in 1759, was president of the college at Princeton), preached several patriotic discourses after the defeat of Braddock, to arouse his countrymen to action. In one of these, entitled "Religion and Patriotism the constituents of a good Soldier," he remarked, in allusion to the remarkable preservation of Washington on the bloody field of Monongahela, "I can not but hope Providence has hitherto preserved him in so signal a manner. for some important service to his country." It is an interesting fact, that Washington never received the slightest wound in battle.

their blankets, and were soon buried in sleep. At early dawn they bid adieu to the camp, and were seen slowly winding their way toward the distant haunts of their tribe.

The effects which this mysterious and romantic adventure had upon the provincials, were as various as the variety of character which composed the party. All eyes were turned on him, to whom the oracle had been addressed, but from his ever-serene and thoughtful countenance, nothing could be discovered: still all this was strange, "'twas passive strange." On the mind of Doctor James Craik, a most deep and lasting impression was made, and in the war of the Revolution it became a favorite theme with him, particularly after any perilous action, in which his friend and commander had been peculiarly exposed, as the battles of Princeton, Germantown, and Monmouth. On the latter occasion, as we have elsewhere observed,* Doctor Craik expressed his great faith in the Indian's prophecy. "Gentlemen," he said, to some of the officers, "recollect what I have often told you, of the old Indian's prophecy. Yes, I do believe, a Great Spirit protects that man—and that one day or other, honored and beloved, he will be the chief of our nation, as he is now our general, our father, and our friend. Never mind the enemy, they can not kill him, and while he lives, our cause will never die."

During the engagement on the following day, while Washington was speaking to a favorite officer, I think the brave and valued Colonel Hartley, of the Pennsylvania line, a cannon ball struck just at his horse's feet, throwing the dirt in his face, and over his clothes, the

* See page 222.

general continued giving his orders, without noticing the derangement of his toilette. The officers present, several of whom were of the party the preceding evening, looked at each other with anxiety. The chief of the medical staff, pleased with the proof of his prediction, and in reminiscence of what had passed the night before, pointed toward heaven, which was noticed by the others, with a gratifying smile of acknowledgment.*

Of the brave and valued Colonel Hartley, it is said, that the commander-in-chief sent for him in the heat of an engagement, and addressed him as follows: "I have sent for you, colonel, to employ you on a serious piece of service. The state of our affairs, renders it necessary, that a part of this army should be *sacrificed*, for the welfare of the whole. You command an efficient corps (a fine regiment of Germans from York and Lancaster counties). I know you well, and have, therefore, selected you to perform this important and serious duty. You will take such a position, and defend it to the last extremity." The colonel received this appointment to a forlorn hope, with a smile of exultation, and bowing, replied: "Your excellency does me too much honor; your orders shall be obeyed to the letter," and repaired to his post.

I will not be positive as to the location of this anecdote, having heard it from the old people of the Revolution many years ago, but think it occurred on the field of Monmouth—but of this I am not certain. I have a hundred times seen Colonel Hartley received in the halls of the great president, where so many Revolutionary worthies were made welcome, and to none was the hand of honored and friendly recollection more feelingly offer-

---

* The substance of this is given in the account of the battle at Monmouth.

ed; on none did the merit-discerning eye of the chief appear to beam with more pleasure, than on Hartley of York.*

* Colonel Thomas Hartley was a native of Berks county, Pennsylvania, and was born on the seventh of September, 1748. He studied law in York, and practised his profession there. He entered the army at the beginning of the Revolution, and was in several engagements. After the descent of Butler and his Indians into the Wyoming valley, in the summer of 1778, he commanded a corps in that region. Colonel Hartley was a member of Congress in 1788, and held the office twelve consecutive years. He also held several offices in his native commonwealth. He died on the twenty-first of December, 1800, at the age of fifty-two years.

CHAPTER XII.

DANIEL MORGAN.

Morgan's Narratives — His Tests of a Good Soldier — Last Survivor of his Corps — Washington and Morgan alone — Morgan sent to Reconnoitre — Special Instructions — Captain Gabriel Long — Morgan and his Party Reconnoitre — They Discover a Party of Officers — These Gather in a Groupe on a Knoll — Contrary to Instructions, Morgan and his Men Fire upon them — Death of some of the Officers — Morgan in Low Spirits — His Expectation of Disgrace for Disobedience of Orders — Interview with Colonel Hamilton — Morgan in the Presence of Washington — His Grief — Second Interview with Hamilton — Invitation to Dine at Headquarters — Generously Forgiven by Washington — Congratulations of his Fellow-Officers.

It was our good fortune, in conversations with the late General Daniel Morgan, to elicit from that distinguished veteran most interesting narratives of many of the prominent events in the Revolutionary war.*

* General Daniel Morgan was a native of New Jersey, where he was born in 1737. He emigrated to Virginia at the age of eighteen years. That was the year (1755), when Braddock went on his expedition against the French and Indians at Fort du Quesne. Morgan accompanied the army as a waggoner. During the march he replied sharply to the insults of a British officer, who then tried to run him through with his sword. Morgan well-defended himself, and succeeded in giving the officer a severe whipping. For this he was condemned to receive five hundred lashes on the bare back. Four hundred and fifty were given, when he fainted. The remainder were remitted. The officer becoming convinced that he had been in the wrong, apologized; but the memory of this indignity, no doubt, gave vigor to the arm of Daniel Morgan in the war against the British officers and soldiers twenty years later.

Morgan raised a company of riflemen and joined the continental army, at Cambridge, in 1775. During that autumn he accompanied Arnold in his famous expedition across the wilderness of the Kennebec and Chaudière to Quebec, where he was taken a prisoner at the close of the year. He was active throughout a greater portion of the war, after his exchange. He was in the army against the "Whiskey Insurgents," in 1794, and was afterward a member of Congress. His estate in Vir-

While listening to the tale of the hardships and privations of our suffering soldiery, as to a tale of wonder, we asked the general which of the men, of the various nations composing the American armies (in his excellent judgment), possessed the best natural requisites for making good soldiers?

Morgan replied: "As to the fighting part of the matter, the men of all nations are pretty much alike; they fight as much as they find necessary, and no more. But, sir, for the grand essential in the composition of the good soldier, give me the Dutchman—*he starves well.*"

It is not a little remarkable that the last survivor of the celebrated rifle corps which Morgan led across the wintry wilderness of the Kennebec in 1775, and which corps suffered an extremity of famine and hardship almost beyond belief,* is a highly respectable German, a Mr. Lauk, now resident, at a very advanced age, in Washington, Virginia.†

---

ginia, where he lived many years, he called Saratoga. He died at Berryville, in Virginia, on the sixth of July, 1802, at the age of sixty-five years.

* Colonel Benedict Arnold left Cambridge with a thousand men, in September, 1775, and, landing at the mouth of the Kennebec, marched up that stream and through the wilderness, to the St. Lawrence, by way of the Chaudière river, that flows northward from Lake Megantic, on the high water-shed in Maine. That expedition, to which reference has been made several times before, was one of the most wonderful on record. For forty days Arnold and his men traversed a gloomy wilderness without meeting a human being. Frost and snow were upon the ground, and ice was upon the surface of the marshes and the streams which they were compelled to traverse and ford sometimes armpit deep in water and mud. Yet they murmured not, and even women followed in their train. Famine beset them before they reached the French settlements on the St. Lawrence slope, and they were reduced to such extremities, that the dog of Captain Dearborn made a most acceptable meal for himself and soldiers. After incredible hardships from fatigue, intense cold, and biting hunger, they arrived at Point Levi, opposite Quebec, on the ninth of November.

† This was published in the *National Intelligencer*, on the fourteenth of December, 1835.

General Morgan related to us the substance of the following personal reminiscences; and many times during the recital his voice faltered with emotion, and his eyes filled with tears:—

The outposts of the two armies were very near to each other, when the American commander, desirous of obtaining particular information respecting the positions of his adversary, summoned the famed leader of the riflemen, Colonel Daniel Morgan, to headquarters.*

It was night, and the chief was alone. After his usual polite, yet reserved and dignified salutation, Washington remarked: "I have sent for you, Colonel Morgan, to entrust to your courage and sagacity, a small but very important enterprise. I wish you to reconnoitre the enemy's lines, with a view to your ascertaining correctly the positions of their newly-constructed redoubts; also of the encampments of the British troops that have lately arrived, and those of their Hessian auxiliaries. Select, sir, an officer, non-commissioned officer, and about twenty picked men, and under cover of the night proceed with all possible caution, get as near as you can, learn all you can, and by day-dawn retire and make your report to headquarters. But mark me, Colonel Morgan, mark me well: On no account whatever are you to bring on any skirmishing with the enemy. If discovered, make a speedy retreat; let nothing induce you to fire a single shot. I repeat, sir, that no force of circumstances will excuse the discharge of a single rifle on your part, and for the extreme preciseness of these orders, permit me to

---

* Mr. Custis has not given the locality of the events of this narrative. It is probable that it was in New Jersey, and the time a night or two before the battle of Monmouth.

say that I have my reasons." Filling two glasses of wine, the general continued, " And now, Colonel Morgan, we will drink a good night, and success to your enterprise." Morgan quaffed the wine, smacked his lips, and assuring his excellency that his orders should be punctually obeyed, left the tent of the commander-in-chief.

Charmed at being chosen the executive officer of a daring enterprise, the Leader of the Woodsmen repaired to his quarters, and calling for Gabriel Long, his favorite captain, ordered him to detail a trusty sergeant, and twenty prime fellows. When these were mustered, and ordered to lay on their arms, to be ready at a moment's warning, Morgan and Long stretched their manly forms before the watchfire, to await the going down of the moon—the signal for departure.

A little after midnight, and while the rays of the setting moon still faintly glimmered in the Western horizon, " Up sergeant," cried Long, " stir up your men!" and twenty athletic figures were upon their feet in a moment. Indian file, march, and away all sprung with the quick, yet light and stealthy step of the woodsmen. They reached the enemy's lines, crawled up so close to the pickets of the Hessians, as to inhale the odor of their pipes, and discovered, by the newly turned up earth, the position of the redoubts, and by the numerous tents that dotted the field for " many a rood around," and shone dimly amid the night haze, the encampment of the British and German reinforcements. In short they performed their perilous duty without the slightest discovery; and, pleased with themselves, and the success of their enterprise, prepared to retire, just as chanticleer from a neighboring farm-house was " bidding salutation to the morn."

The adventurous party reached a small eminence at some distance from the British camp, and commanding an extensive prospect over the adjoining country. Here Morgan halted, to give his men a little rest, before taking up his line of march for the American outposts. Scarcely had they thrown themselves on the grass, when they perceived, issuing from the enemy's advanced pickets, a body of horse, commanded by an officer, and proceeding along a road that led directly by the spot where the riflemen had halted. No spot could be better chosen for an ambuscade, for there were rocks and ravines, and also scrubby oaks, that grew thickly on the eminence by which the road we have just mentioned passed, at not exceeding a hundred yards.

"Down boys, down," cried Morgan, as the horse approached; nor did the clansmen of the Black Rhoderic disappear more promptly amid their native heather, than did Morgan's woodsmen in the present instance, each to his tree, or rock. "Lie close there, my lads, till we see what these fellows are about."

Meantime, the horsemen had gained the height, and the officer dropping his rein on his charger's neck, with a spy-glass reconnoitred the American lines. The troopers closed up their files, and were either cherishing the noble animals they rode, adjusting their equipments, or gazing upon the surrounding scenery now fast brightening in the beams of a rising sun.

Morgan looked at Long, and Long upon his superior, while the riflemen, with panting chests and sparkling eyes, were only awaiting some signal from their officers "to let the ruin fly."

At length the martial ardor of Morgan overcame his

prudence and sense of military subordination. Forgetful of consequences, reckless of everything but his enemy now within his grasp, he waved his hand, and loud and sharp rang the report of the rifles amid the surrounding echoes.

At point-blank distance, the certain and deadly aim of the Hunting Shirts of the Revolutionary army is too well known to history to need remark at this time of day. In the instance we have to record, the effects of the fire of the riflemen were tremendous. Of the horsemen, some had fallen to rise no more, while their liberated chargers rushed wildly over the adjoining plains; others, wounded, but entangled with their stirrups, were dragged by the furious animals expiringly along, while the very few who were unscathed spurred hard to regain the shelter of the British lines.

While the smoke yet canopied the scene of slaughter, and the picturesque forms of the woodsmen appeared among the foliage, as they were reloading their pieces, the colossal figure of Morgan stood apart. He seemed the very genius of war, as gloomily he contemplated the havoc his order had made. He spoke not, he moved not, but looked as one absorbed in an intensity of thought. The martial shout with which he was wont to cheer his comrades in the hour of combat was hushed; the shell[*] from which he had blown full many a note of

[*] Morgan's riflemen were generally in the advance, skirmishing with the light troops of the enemy, or annoying his flanks; the regiment was thus much divided into detachments, and dispersed over a very wide field of action. Morgan was in the habit of using a conch-shell frequently during the heat of battle, with which he would blow a loud and warlike blast. This he said was to inform his boys that he was still alive, and from many parts of the field was beholding their prowess; and, like the last signal of a celebrated sea-warrior of another hemisphere, was expecting that "every man would do his duty."—*Note by the Author.*

battle and of triumph on the fields of Saratoga, hung idly by his side; no order was given to spoil the slain. The arms and equipments for which there was always a bounty from Congress, the shirts for which there was such need in that, the sorest period of our country's privation, all, all, were abandoned, as, with an abstracted air and a voice struggling for utterance, Morgan suddenly turning to his captain, exclaimed, "Long, to the camp, march." The favorite captain obeyed, the riflemen, with trailed arms, fell into file, and Long and his party soon disappeared, but not before the hardy fellows had exchanged opinions on the strange termination of the late affair. And they agreed *nem con*, that their colonel was tricked (conjured), or assuredly, after such a fire as they had just given the enemy, such an emptying of saddles, and such a scampering of the troopers, he would not have ordered his poor rifle-boys from the field, without so much as a few shirts or pairs of stockings being divided amongst them. "Yes," said a tall, lean and swarthy-looking fellow, an Indian hunter from the frontier, as he carefully placed his moccasined feet, in the foot-prints of his file-leader, "Yes, my lads, it stands to reason our colonel is tricked."

Morgan followed slowly on the trail of his men. The full force of his military guilt had rushed upon his mind, even before the reports of his rifles had ceased to echo in the neighboring forests. He became more and more convinced of the enormity of his offence, as, with dull and measured strides, he pursued his solitary way, and thus he soliloquized:—

"Well, Daniel Morgan, you have done for yourself. Broke, sir, broke to a certainty. You may go home, sir, to the plough; your sword will be of no further use to you. Broke, sir, nothing can save you; and there is the end of Colonel Morgan. Fool, fool—by a single act of madness thus to destroy the earnings of so many toils, and many a hard-fought battle. You are broke, sir, and there is an end of Colonel Morgan."

To disturb this reverie, there suddenly appeared, at full speed, the aid-de-camp, the Mercury of the field,* who, reining up, accosted the colonel with, "I am ordered, Colonel Morgan, to ascertain whether the firing just now heard, proceeded from your detachment."—"It did, sir," replied Morgan, doggedly. "Then, colonel," continued the aid, "I am further ordered to require your immediate attendance upon his excellency, who is fast approaching." Morgan bowed, and the aid, wheeling his charger, galloped back to rejoin his chief.

The gleams of the morning sun upon the sabres of the horse-guard, announced the arrival of the dreaded commander—that being who inspired with a degree of awe every one who approached him. With a stern, yet dignified composure, Washington addressed the military culprit. "Can it be possible, Colonel Morgan, that my aid-de-camp has informed me aright? Can it be possible, after the orders you received last evening, that the firing we have heard proceeded from your detachment? Surely, sir, my orders were so explicit as not to be easily misunderstood." Morgan was brave, but it has been often and justly, too, observed, that that man never was born of woman, who could approach the great Washington, and not feel a degree of awe and veneration from his presence. Morgan quailed for a moment before the

* Colonel Alexander Hamilton.

stern, yet just displeasure of his chief, till, arousing all his energies to the effort, he uncovered, and replied: "Your excellency's orders were perfectly well understood; and, agreeably to the same, I proceeded with a select party to reconnoitre the enemy's lines by night. We succeeded even beyond our expectations, and I was returning to headquarters to make my report, when, having halted a few minutes to rest the men, we discovered a party of horse coming out from the enemy's lines. They came up immediately to the spot where we lay concealed by the brushwood. There they halted, and gathered up together like a flock of partridges, affording me so tempting an opportunity of annoying my enemy, that—that—may it please your excellency—flesh and blood could not refrain."

At this rough, yet frank, bold, and manly explanation, a smile was observed to pass over the countenances of several of the general's suite. The chief remained unmoved; when, waving his hand, he continued: "Colonel Morgan, you will retire to your quarters, there to await further orders." Morgan bowed, and the military *cortege* rode on to the inspection of the outposts.

Arrived at his quarters, Morgan threw himself upon his hard couch, and gave himself up to reflections upon the events which had so lately and so rapidly succeeded each other. He was aware that he had sinned past all hope of forgiveness. Within twenty-four hours, he had fallen from the command of a regiment, and being an especial favorite with his general, to be, what—a disgraced and broken soldier. Condemned to retire from scenes of glory, the darling passion of his heart—for ever to abandon the "fair fields of fighting, and in obscurity to drag out the remnant of a wretched existence, neglected and forgotten. And then his reputation, so nobly won, with all his "blushing honors" acquired in the march across the frozen wilderness of the Kennebec, the storming of the Lower Town, and the gallant and glorious combats of Saratoga, to be lost in a moment!

The hours dragged gloomily away. Night came, but with it no rest for the troubled spirit of poor Morgan. The drums and fifes merrily sounded the soldiers' dawn, and the sun arose, giving "promise of a goodly day." And to many within the circuit of that widely-extended camp did its genial beams give hope, and joy, and gladness, while it cheered not with a single ray the despairing leader of the Woodsmen.

About ten o'clock, the orderly on duty reported the arrival of an officer of the staff from headquarters, and Lieutenant-Colonel Hamilton, the favorite aid of the commander-in-chief, entered the marquée. "Be seated," said Morgan; "I know your errand, so be short my dear fellow, and put me out of my misery at once. I know that I am arrested, 'tis a matter of course. Well, there is my sword; but surely his excellency honors me, indeed, in these the last moments of my military existence, when he sends for my sword by his favorite aid, and my most esteemed friend. Ah, my dear Hamilton, if you knew what I have suffered since the cursed horse came out to tempt me to my ruin."

Hamilton, about whose strikingly-intelligent countenance there always lurked a playful smile, now observed, "Colonel Morgan, his excellency has ordered me to"—"I know it," interrupted Morgan, "to bid me prepare for trial, but pshaw, why a trial! Guilty, sir, guilty past all doubt. But then (recollecting himself), perhaps my services might plead—nonsense! against the disobedience of a positive order? No, no, it is all over with me, Hamilton, there is an end of your old friend, and of Colonel Morgan." The agonized spirit of our hero then mounted to a pitch of enthusiasm as he exclaimed, " But my country will remember my services, and the British and Hessians will remember me too, for though I may be far away, my brave comrades will do their duty, and Morgan's riflemen be, as they always have been, a terror to the enemy."

The noble, the generous-souled Hamilton could no longer bear to witness the struggles of the brave unfortunate, and he called out: "Hear me, my dear colonel, only promise to hear me for one moment, and I will tell you all. " Go on, sir," replied Morgan, despairingly, " go on."—" Then," continued the aid-de-camp, " you must know that the commanders of regiments dine with his excellency to-day."—" What of that," again interrupted Morgan, " what has that to do with me, a prisoner and—." " No, no," exclaimed Hamilton, no prisoner, a once-offending, but now a forgiven soldier. My orders are to invite you to dine with his excellency to-day at three o'clock precisely; yes, my brave and good friend, Colonel Morgan, you still are, and likely long to be, the valued and famed commander of the rifle regiment."

Morgan sprang from the camp-bed on which he was sitting, and seizing the hand of the little great man in his giant grasp, wrung and wrung, till the aid-de-camp literally struggled to get free, then exclaimed, " Am I in my senses? But I know you, Hamilton, you are too noble a fellow to sport with the feelings of an old brother-soldier." Hamilton assured his friend that all was true, and gayly kissing his hand as he mounted his horse, bid the now delighted colonel to remember three o'clock, and be careful not to disobey a second time, galloped to the headquarters.

Morgan entered the pavilion of the commander-in-chief, as it was fast filling with officers, all of whom, after paying their respects to the general, filed off to give a cordial squeeze of the hand to the commander of the rifle regiment, and to whisper in his ear words of congratulation. The cloth removed, Washington bid his guests fill their glasses, and gave his only, his unvarying toast, the toast of the days of trial, the toast of the evening of his "time-honored" life amid the shades of Mount Vernon—"*All our Friends.*" Then, with his usual old-fashioned politeness, he drank to each guest by name. When he came to "Colonel Morgan, your good health, sir," a thrill ran through the manly frame of the gratified and again favorite soldier, while every eye in the pavilion was turned upon him. At an early hour the company broke up, and Morgan had a perfect escort of officers accompanying him to his quarters, all anxious to congratulate him upon his happy restoration to rank and favor, all pleased to assure him of their esteem for his person and services.

And often in his after life did Morgan reason upon the events which we have transmitted to the Americans and their posterity, and he would say: "What could the unusual clemency of the commander-in-chief toward so insubordinate a soldier as I was, mean? Was it that my attacking my enemy wherever I could find him, and the attack being crowned with success, should plead in bar of the disobedience of a positive order? Certainly not. Was it that Washington well knew I loved, nay adored, him above all human beings? That knowledge would not have weighed a feather in the scale of his military justice. In short, the whole affair is explained in five words; *it was my first offence.*"

The clemency of Washington toward the *first offence* preserved to the army of the Revolution one of its most valued and effective soldiers, and had its reward in little more than two years from the date of our narrative, when Brigadier-General Morgan established his own fame, and shed an undying lustre on the arms of his country, by the glorious and ever-memorable victory of the Cowpens.*

---

* The southern states became the most important theatre of military operations in the year 1781. General Greene had been appointed commander-in-chief of the southern department, in October, 1780, and with his usual skill and energy, arranged his army for a winter campaign, in two divisions. With the main army, Greene took post at Cheraw, eastward of the Pedee, and Morgan (then promoted to brigadier-general) was sent with the remainder (about a thousand in number) to occupy the country near the junction of the Pacolet and Broad rivers. At that time, Cornwallis was preparing to invade North Carolina. He found himself in a dangerous situation, for he was placed between the two divisions of the republican army. Unwilling to leave Morgan in his rear, he sent Tarleton to capture or disperse his troops. His force was superior, and the Americans retreated northward for some distance. At length having reached a position among the Thicketty mountains, in Spartanburg district, Morgan found himself compelled to fight. Posting his men upon an eminence, he turned and faced his pursuers. This movement disconcerted Tarleton, for he expected to fall upon Morgan in the confusion of a flight. He was confident of an easy victory, however, and prepared for battle. On the morning of the seventeenth of January, 1781, a furious contest began. For more than two hours they fought desperately, when the British broke and fled. They lost almost three hundred men in killed and wounded, five hundred made prisoners, and a large quantity of arms, ammunition, and stores. It was one of the most brilliant victories achieved during the war. Congress awarded a gold medal to General Morgan, and Colonels Howard and Washington, who nobly seconded the general, each received a silver medal. Morgan pushed on across the Catawba with his prisoners, and at the Yadkin was joined by General Greene. Then commenced that remarkable retreat of Greene before Cornwallis, from the Yadkin, beyond the Dan, into Virginia, which has arrested the attention of military men.

Nearly twenty years more had rolled away, and our hero, like most of his compatriots, had beaten his sword into a ploughshare, and was enjoying, in the midst of a domestic circle, the evening of a varied and eventful life. When advanced in years, and infirm, Major-General Morgan was called to the supreme legislature of his country, as a representative of the state of Virginia.* It was at this period that the author of these Memoirs had the honor and happiness of an interview with the old general, which lasted for several days. And the veteran was most kind and communicative to one, who hailing from the immediate family of his venerated chief, found a ready and a warm welcome to the heart of Morgan. And many, and most touching reminiscences of the days of trial were related by the once famed leader of the woodsmen, to the then youthful and delighted listener, which were eagerly devoured, and carefully treasured in a memory of no ordinary power.

And it was there the unlettered Morgan, a man bred amid the scenes of danger and hardihood that distinguished the frontier warfare, with little book knowledge, but gifted by nature with a strong and discriminating mind, paid to the fame and memory of the Father of our Country a more just, more magnificent tribute than, in our humble judgment, has emanated from the thousand and one efforts of the best and brightest geniuses of the age. General Morgan spoke of the *necessity* of Washington to the army of the Revolution, and the success of the

---

* General Morgan was elected to Congress in 1797, and served two years. In July, 1799, he published an address to his constituents, in which he vindicated the administration of President Adams. Like Washington, Morgan was a federalist. The author of these *Recollections* was then about eighteen years of age.

struggle for Independence. He said we had officers of great military talents, as for instance Greene and others; we had officers of the most consummate courage and spirit of enterprize, as for instance Wayne and others. One was yet *necessary*, to guide, direct, and animate the whole, and it pleased Almighty God to send that one in the person of George Washington!

CHAPTER XIII.

ROBERT MORRIS.*

Whom did Washington most Love — Washington and Greene — Washington's Caution in Guarding against Jealousies — Intimate Acquaintances of Washington — Robert Morris — His Financial Aid to the Patriots — A chosen Guest at Washington's Table — Morris's Speculations — Washington's Advice unheeded — Washington Visits Morris in Prison — Proverbial Ingratitude of Republics.

It has often been asked, "Who were the favorites of Washington? whom did he love?" I answer, the most worthy. Washington lived for his country, and for her so much did he "live and move," and almost "have his being," that when he loved a man, that man must love his country.

In the War for Independence, Greene was his Hephæstion,† yet such was his delicacy in bestowing praise,

---

* First published in the *Philadelphia National Gazette*, on the twenty-ninth of June, 1826.

† Nathaniel Greene was born of Quaker parents, at Warwick, in Rhode Island, in 1740. He was trained to the occupation of an anchor-smith, the business of his father. He was quick and studious, and while yet a boy, had learned some Latin and collected a small library. He loved to read books on military subjects. At the age of twenty-one he was elected a member of the Rhode Island legislature; and, full of zeal for republican principles, he hesitated not a moment to take up arms for his country, contrary to the practices and traditions of his sect. He took the command of three regiments of the *Army of Observation*, which Rhode Island sent to Roxbury after the affair at Lexington. The Quakers disowned him, and the Congress made him a brigadier-general. All through the long struggle of seven years, he was the most useful of all the officers; and in genuine military genius, was in some respects superior to Washington. He retired to Rhode Island at the conclusion of the war, and soon afterward went to Georgia to look after an estate near Savannah, which that state had given him. There, in June, 1786, he was prostrated

even where most deserved, that he declined the mentioning of Greene's division, which had so gallantly covered the retreat from Brandywine, saying to that illustrious commander, who prayed that his comrades might receive their well-earned commendation: " You, sir, are considered in this army as my favorite officer; your division is composed of southrons, my more immediate countrymen. Such are my reasons."*

It has been thought that certain vivacious personages, as Gouverneur Morris, and General Henry Lee, were in the habit of taking liberties with the chief. Around the Father of his Country, his virtues and character created an atmosphere of awe and veneration, in which undue familiarity could not have existed for a moment. No men living were more ardently attached to the chief than the Revolutionary statesman and distinguished officer alluded to. They possessed brilliant talents, had rendered conspicuous services, and were the most plea-

---

by a "sun-stroke," and died on the nineteenth of that month, at the age of forty-six years.

Greene was truly to Washington what Hephæstion was to Alexander. He loved him tenderly, and from the earliest moment of their acquaintance, their attachment was warm and sincere. Alexander used to say, in speaking of the intimacy between his friend and himself, that "Craterus was the friend of the king, but Hephæstion was the friend of Alexander." Such was the relationship between Washington and Greene.

* One of the most delicate duties to which Washington was called, during the earlier years of the war particularly, was the silencing of jealousies among the officers. They all soon learned so to confide in his justice, that he seldom failed in his efforts to allay unpleasant feelings. But while he desired to avoid every appearance of favoritism, he never failed to employ, in a manner, and in a position that he deemed best for the public service, those whom his judgment approved. In Greene he discovered rare talent for every kind of military service requiring great executive ability, and he never hesitated to give him his proper position; but, as in the instance mentioned in the text, he avoided the public expression of his opinion of his superior merits, so as not to offend others unnecessarily.

surable companions of their time. These considerations, together with the absence of restraint at the private parties of the president, gave rise to the idea that there were certain characters who could approach without reserve, and even toy with the passive lion. But the lion, though passive, was the lion still. He could always be approached, and sometimes in sportive mood, but not so near as to lay hand upon his mane.*

If I am asked—" And did not Washington unbend and admit to familiarity, and social friendship, some one person, to whom age and long and interesting associations gave peculiar privilege, the privilege of the heart?"—I answer, that favored individual was Robert Morris.

The general-in-chief of the armies of Independence, in the relief afforded to the privations of his suffering soldiery, first learned the value of Robert Morris. It was he who brought order out of chaos, and whose talent and credit sustained the cause of his country in her worst of times.† Virtues and services like these endeared

---

* See note on page 175.

† Mr. Morris was one of the Pennsylvania delegates in the second continental Congress; and a few weeks after he had taken his seat, in 1775, he was placed upon the secret committee whose duty it was to contract for the importation of munitions of war. He was also on a committee for fitting out a naval armament, and specially to negotiate bills of exchange for Congress to borrow money for the marine committee, and to manage the fiscal concerns of Congress upon other occasions. From that time he was the accredited and efficient financier of the Revolutionary government. His private commercial credit was such, that all men had confidence in him as the public agent. Instances of his affording pecuniary assistance to the army have already been given in these pages. On one occasion he became personally responsible for a quantity of lead for the use of the army; at another, when the Congress was utterly without cash or credit, he supplied the army with four or five thousand barrels of flour; when the French troops came, he borrowed twenty thousand dollars in specie on his own credit from Rochambeau. After the continental money became valueless, Robert Morris's notes formed a part of the reliable circulating medium. When, in 1781, a bank for government purposes was

their possessor to the paternal chief, in whose heart the financier of the Revolution held an esteem which neither time nor misfortune could alter or impair.

Mr. Morris was ever a welcome guest at the private and select parties of the president. So much was this a matter of course, that the steward, having first placed Mr. M.'s favorite wine at the plate immediately on the right of the chief, would repair to the dwelling of Morris, and observe, "The president dines with a select party of friends to-day, and expects your company as usual."*

When Mr. Morris first engaged in those speculations which terminated so unhappily, Washington, with the privilege of sincere friendship, remonstrated, observing, "You are old, and had better retire, rather than engage in such extensive concerns." Morris replied, "Your advice is proof of that wisdom and prudence which govern all your words and actions: but, my dear general, I can never do things in the small; I must be either a *man or a mouse*."†

---

established in Philadelphia, he subscribed ten thousand pounds, and induced others to swell the amount to three hundred thousand pounds. Other instances of the manner in which, financially, he supported the cause, might be given, but these will suffice. Botta, in his History of the Revolution, says, "certainly the Americans owed, and still owe, as much acknowledgment to the financial operations of Robert Morris, as to the negotiations of Benjamin Franklin, or even the arms of George Washington."

* This was when the seat of government was in Philadelphia. Mr. Morris held the very first social position in that city. For nearly half a century, an introduction to Robert Morris was a matter in course, with all strangers who visited Philadelphia on commercial, public, or private business, and he was considered by all as a representative of the city.

† Washington was at that time quite largely, but not injudiciously, engaged in land speculations with Governor George Clinton and others, although his name did not publicly appear as such. At the time alluded to in the text, a gigantic land speculation, known as the scheme of the "North American Land Company,' had been commenced, and Mr. Morris was one of the principal partners. He soli

In 1798, when the lieutenant-general and commander-in-chief repaired to Philadelphia to superintend the organization of his last army,* unmindful of the dignity, wealth, and splendor which crowded to greet his arrival, he paid his first visit to the prison-house of Robert Morris.† The old man wrung the hand of the chief in

cited Washington to join in the speculation. He declined, and gave Morris the advice above mentioned. The chief parties in the company (which was organized in 1785), were Robert Morris, James Greenleaf, and John Nicholson. The land, for which they paid large sums of money, lay in the states of Pennsylvania, Virginia, North and South Carolina, Georgia, and Kentucky, in all six millions of acres. Their intention was to sell the lands at a handsome profit, to small speculators and actual settlers, at the average price of fifty cents an acre. Several years afterward, Mr. Morris became concerned with others in the purchase of over a million of acres in western New York, at sixteen cents an acre. This speculation, with the whole former scheme, was a failure. Morris and Nicholson were utterly ruined. The latter, who was at one time comptroller-general of the state of Pennsylvania, died, it is said, leaving unpaid debts to an immense amount. Mr. Morris was finally consigned to the debtor's apartment of the Walnut-street prison, to which was attached a small garden, in which he was permitted to exercise. There he remained a long time, and suffered much. He died in 1806; leaving a widow, a sister of Bishop White.

* John Adams was inaugurated President of the United States in March, 1797. He sought diligently to reconcile disputes that had arisen between the governments of the United States and France, but without success; and when Congress assembled in December that year, war measures were adopted. In May, 1798, quite a large standing army was authorized. Washington had expressed his approval of the measure, and in July he was appointed the commander-in-chief. He consented to accept the office, only on the condition that General Hamilton should be the *acting* commander-in-chief, for the retired president was unwilling to take the field, unless the most urgent necessity should demand it.

† The debtors' apartment of the Walnut-street prison was on Prune street. Though suffering in bodily health, Mr. Morris's mind was cheerful under the weight of his misfortunes. On one occasion he wrote the following playful note to his old partner in speculations :—

"Messrs. Henry Banks, David Allison and Robert Morris present their compliments to John Nicholson, Esq., and request the favor of his company to dine with them at the hotel with grated doors, in Prune street, at one o'clock, on Sunday next, pledging themselves most solemnly that to him the doors will be open for admission and departure on that day.

"FRIDAY MORNING, 11*th May,* 1798.

"Dear sir: I have written the above not only with the consent, but at the request

silence, while his tearful eye gave the welcome to such an home. The mouse was, indeed, in his iron-bound cage; but, in the United States of America, for Robert Morris to have been imprisoned, *in character*, the bars should *have been of gold*. How is this, Americans? Is it not the condemnation of Manlius on the Capitoline hill, a crime which the heathen Roman dared not commit? The financier of the Revolution, whose talent, whose credit sustained the cause of his country in that country's utmost need! Whatever may have been his misfortunes, say his faults, did not his generous services " plead like angels, trumpet-tongued, against the deep damnation,"

of the parties, and it is done after consulting Mr. Hoffner, who solemnly assures us that nothing can operate as a detainer but a bail-piece, and I think you have no such thing to fear; or if there is any special bail for you, it is John Baker, on whom you can safely rely. Come, therefore, my friend, as early in the forenoon as you can, that we may have some conversation before as well as after dinner. We will show you how we live here, that you may be prepared to bear your fate, should it be decided that you are to become a boarder at this hotel.

" I am your friend and servant,

" ROBERT MORRIS.

" *May* 11, 1798.
' JNO. NICHOLSON, Esq."

Mr. Nicholson afterward became a regular inmate of the same "hotel," where he edited a newspaper."

William B. Wood, the celebrated actor, was a compulsory guest at the same "hotel with grated doors," for a short time, and has left on record the following account of his interview with Robert Morris there:—

" Mr. Morris appeared cheerful, returned my salutation in the politest manner, but in silence, continuing his walk, and dropping from his hand at a given spot, a pebble on each round, until a certain number which he had in his hand was exhausted. For some mornings the same silence prevailed, until at length, observing my languid deportment, he suddenly stopped, inquired whether I was ill, and added with something like severity, ' Sir, this is but an ill place for one so sickly, and apparently *so young*.' He seemed to wait for some kind of explanation, which I found myself either unable or unwilling to give — and then passed on. From this time he spoke to me almost daily, and always with great kindness. On one occasion he unbent much more than usual, and offered some remarks which embraced much good counsel. In more than one instance he favored me with friendly notice."

of such an home for his age? And, when broken-hearted, pennyless, friendless, and forgotten, his gray hairs descended in sorrow to the grave, how was the last duty paid to him, to whom we owed so much? How many of those who had basked in the sunshine of his prosperity, fed at his ever hospitable board, and drank of his ever flowing cup, followed his hearse? Where the corporate bodies—where the long trains of youth who were led up to pay their last homage to the *republic's benefactor?**

* Unfortunately our history affords a parallel. Colonel William Barton, of Rhode Island, received a grant of land in Vermont for his Revolutionary services. By the transfer of some of this land he became entangled in the toils of the law, and was imprisoned for debt in Vermont for many years, until the visit of Lafayette to this country in 1825. That illustrious man, hearing of the incarceration of Colonel Barton and its cause, liquidated the claim against him, and restored his fellow-soldier to liberty. It was a noble act, and significantly rebuked the Shylock who held the patriot in bondage, and clamored for "the pound of flesh." This circumstance drew from Whittier his glorious poem, *The Prisoner for Debt*, in which he exclaims—

"What has the gray-haired prisoner done?
  Has murder stained his hands with gore?
Not so; his crime's a fouler one:
  God made the old man poor!
For this he shares a felon's cell,
  The fittest earthly type of hell!
For this, the boon for which he poured,
His young blood on the invader's sword,
And counted light the fearful cost—
His blood-gained liberty is lost.
*   *   *   *

Down with the law that binds him thus!
  Unworthy freemen, let it find
No refuge from the withering curse
  Of God and human kind!

Open the prisoner's living tomb,
And usher from its brooding gloom
The victims of your savage code
To the free sun and air of God!
No longer dare, as crime, to brand
The chastening of the Almighty's hand!"

CHAPTER XIV.

THOMAS NELSON.

Nelson's Ancestors — His Early Employments — A Man of Fortune — Kindling of the Revolution in Virginia — Nelson a Member of Congress in 1776 — Influence of leading Minds — Mifflin sent to Recruit for the Army — Nelson organizes a Corps of Cavalry — Elected Governor of Virginia — Arnold and Cornwallis — American Military Leaders in Virginia — Depreciation of Continental Money — The People avoid it — Nelson's Noble Example — Anecdote of his Patriotism told by Lafayette — He Borrows Money for Public Services on his own Responsibility — Public Neglect — The Familiar Friends of Washington — Nelson's Family Unrewarded.

Among the patriots, statesmen, and soldiers that Virginia contributed to the Congress and armies of the Revolution, Thomas Nelson will ever claim an elevated rank. Descended from ancient and highly respectable English ancestry, General Nelson was educated in England, and was engaged, prior to the Revolution, in mercantile concerns, upon an extensive scale, at Yorktown, in Virginia, strange to say, at that period the importing city for Philadelphia.*

Upon the breaking out of the troubles, Nelson joined the cause of the colonies. He was a man of large for-

---

* Yorktown is now an inconsiderable village, containing about three hundred inhabitants. It is still a port of entry, but commerce has deserted it, and the village is going into decay. A courthouse was built there in the year 1698; and an old church which was destroyed in 1814, had in it a bell inscribed, "County of York, Virginia, 1725." The church was built at the close of the previous century, out of the stone marl which composes the bluff on which the town stands. The water-scenery at Yorktown is very fine. The York river is there a full mile wide, and from the ruins or site of the old church, no land is visible in the direction of Chesapeake bay, into which the river flows.

tune, having many and valuable estates in different counties, particularly the county of Hanover. Greatly beloved in his native colony, he held a high and commanding influence among the people. He threw all into the scale of his country, in her struggle for the natural rights of mankind.

After the battle of Lexington, Virginia put forth all her strength in the senate and the field. The very *elite* of her statesmen had been sent to the Congress of 1774,*

---

* Failing in their efforts to obtain a redress of their grievances, by remonstrances and petitions, the colonists, in 1774, resolved to call a general congress of representatives. These were chosen in the several colonies during the spring and summer, and on the fifth of September they assembled, by appointment, in a building known as Carpenter's Hall, in Philadelphia. Some of the wisest and best men in America were there. Their sessions continued until the twenty-sixth of October; and during that time they discussed the great questions of the day in such manner that the representatives of each colony became well informed respecting the temper of the people in general, and were prepared to enter, into that union of effort for independence which was soon afterward formed. Twelve of the thirteen colonies were represented. Georgia was the exception. The delegates from Virginia were—Peyton Randolph, George Washington, Richard Henry Lee, Patrick Henry, and Richard Bland.

The author of these *Recollections* relates the following anecdote, in connection with this Congress, upon the authority of Ludwell Lee, son of Richard Henry Lee: "When the first continental congress assembled at Philadelphia, September, 1774, there had been no provision made for the maintenance of the members, while in the discharge of their public duties. A council being held to determine as to the ways and means of effecting this most just and necessary arrangement, Richard Henry Lee (the same who afterward, in '76, moved the Declaration of Independence), rose, and observed, that as he was assured that every member present was desirous of putting the country to the least possible expense, in the maintenance of the Congress, he would move, that during the session, the honorable members be fed on *wild pigeons*, that article appearing to be in very great abundance, and certainly the very cheapest food in the market.

"Now let the modern reader remember, that this Richard Henry Lee was bred in the lap of luxury, educated in Europe, and possessed the most polished and courtly manners, while his seat of Chantilly, which he had just left to obey the high and imposing call of his country, was at once the seat of the most refined and enlarged hospitality.

"This illustrious patriot and statesmen, often congratulated himself in his later life, upon his *famed motion* touching the maintenance of the members of the first Con-

while the pride of her chivalry took arms in the succeeding year. Among the illustrious names that composed the Virginia delegation to the Roman-like senate of 1776, we find the name of Thomas Nelson, junior, who affixed his signature to the Declaration of Independence on the ever-memorable fourth of July.

The state of society in the South in the olden time was very different from that of modern days, under the republic. Under the *ancien regime* there were but two orders in society—the rich and educated, and the poor. Hence, the higher classes, as they were then called, held a most material influence over those who were not so fortunately situated. Men of extensive personal influence over the minds of the people at large, were all-important to the cause of American liberty in the commencement and during the whole progress of the Revolution, with the view of diffusing and fostering the whig spirit, in opposition to the powerful and ably-directed efforts of the tories.*

It is well known to history, that the commander-in-chief spared, at a very critical period of the war, an active and valued officer (Mifflin), that he might exert his personal influence among the people of his native state, to recruit the wasted ranks of the army.†

---

gress, declaring it to have been in purity of patriotism, not secondary to even his immortal resolve in '76, ' That these united colonies are, and of right ought to be free and independent states.'—Such was a patriot of our olden time."

* The terms whig and tory had then long been used in England, as titles of political parties, and continue to be so used to the present day. The former denoted the opposers of royalty; the latter indicated its supporters. These terms were introduced into America two or three years before the Revolution broke out, and became the distinctive titles of patriots and loyalists.

† It was late in the autumn of 1776, while Washington and his little army were retreating toward the Delaware, across New Jersey. The army was rapidly melting

On his return to Virginia from serving in the continental Congress, General Nelson exerted himself in keeping alive the spirit of the Revolution, which was often flagging from the severe disasters that had attended our arms. He was also actively employed in organizing a corps of cavalry, in which young gentlemen of the first families served as volunteers. This corps he commanded up to the double invasion of 1781,* when, upon being elected governor of the state, he took the command in chief of its militia.

The invasion of Arnold was more immediately predatory, but that of Cornwallis swept like a tempest through the devoted commonwealth, already much weakened by her untiring exertions to sustain the army of Greene in the Carolinas, and to defend the many points of her territory, assailable by the attacks of the enemy's naval power.†

by desertions and the expiration of terms of enlistment. It was a most gloomy period of the contest, and few hoped for success in the field. However, Washington determined to have personal appeals made to the people for the purpose of recruiting his army, and he sent the eloquent and popular General Mifflin into Pennsylvania, "to exhort and rouse the militia to come forth in defence of their country." In Philadelphia he was very successful, and very soon he was at the head of fifteen hundred new recruits, in full march upon Trenton, to join the army under Washington.

* Early in January, 1781, Benedict Arnold, zealous in the cause of his royal purchaser, went to Virginia with about sixteen hundred British and tory troops, and a few armed vessels. He went up the James river, as far as Richmond, and destroyed much public and private property, and then returned to Portsmouth. In April, he accompanied General Philips up the same river, on a desolating expedition. They were joined at Petersburg by Cornwallis, who had invaded the state from North Carolina, and who then took the general command. Lafayette was sent into Virginia, and manœuvred skilfully against this "double invasion." He was soon followed by Wayne and Steuben.

† Toward the close of 1775, British vessels, under the general direction of Lord Dunmore, the royal governor of Virginia, who had been compelled to flee from Williamsburg, were instrumental in great ravages along the Virginia coast, especially in the

The forces under Steuben, Lafayette, and subsequently Wayne, were too limited in point of numbers, and too much straitened for supplies of every sort, to be able to check the victorious career of the enemy.* Indeed, the resources of Virginia, great as they originally were, had been sadly reduced in the previous campaign by the capture of her veteran regiments on the surrender of Charleston,† by the total discomfiture at Camden,‡ but,

vicinity of the capes. Norfolk was burned, and all along the Elizabeth river, to Hampton roads, a vast amount of property, public and private, was destroyed. In 1779, Sir George Collier, with land troops, under General Mathews, again produced great distress along the shores of the same waters; and the armed vessels under Arnold, in 1781, were no better than pirates.

* Cornwallis penetrated Virginia beyond Richmond, and destroyed an immense amount of property. He sent out marauding parties in every direction, to harass the inhabitants, and for several weeks the whole state was kept in great alarm. Tarleton and Simcoe, active officers, at the head of energetic and well-disciplined corps, were busy in all quarters, and Lafayette found it quite impossible to stem the torrent of invasion. But when Wayne, with reinforcements, was approaching from the north, Cornwallis turned his face seaward, and slowly retreated down the peninsula toward Williamsburg.

† In the spring of 1780, Sir Henry Clinton, having arrived at Charleston with a large force, borne by a fleet under Admiral Arbuthnot, invested that city. The siege went on for several weeks; the Americans within the city being under the command of General Lincoln. Finally, Cornwallis came with a reinforcement of three thousand men. On the ninth of May, a general cannonade from the ships and the land batteries commenced, and it was kept up for two days. On the night of the eleventh it was perceived that further resistance would be madness. They offered to surrender, and on the following day, the army, city, all passed into the hands of the conquerors.

‡ General Gates was appointed to the command of the southern army, after the surrender of Lincoln at Charleston. Cornwallis had been left in the chief command of the British in South Carolina, and Sir Henry Clinton had returned to New York. In order to make the subjugation of the South complete, the British army, in three divisions, marched into the interior, leaving a garrison for Charleston. One division, under Colonel Brown, marched to Augusta, in Georgia; a second, under Colonel Cruger, penetrated the country to Ninety-Six, in Western Carolina; and a third, under Lord Rawdon, took post at Camden. Toward the latter place Gates approached, early in August. He resolved to fall upon Rawdon on the night of the fifteenth of August, and marched from his camp confident of success, for that purpose. At the same time, Cornwallis (who had hastened to Camden on hearing

above all, by the enormous depreciation of the paper money; all which causes combined to elevate the hopes of the enemy, and cast a shadow over those of the friends, of American liberty. To such a wretched state of depreciation had the paper money arrived at this period, that, in numberless instances, persons were known to have concealed their horses and oxen in the woods and swamps rather than hire them to the transportation department of the army, when the hire was to be accounted for in continental bills, which had become almost valueless.*

of the approach of Gates) and Rawdon, informed of Gates's movement, marched northward to fall upon the Americans. The sand was deep, the footfalls were unheard, and the belligerents met in the dark, at Sanders' Creek. The next morning a severe battle ensued, the Americans were completely routed, and another southern army was lost.

* After the Congress had recognised the troops at Boston as a continental army, in June, 1775, it became necessary to provide money for its support. Specie sufficient could not be had, and they resorted to the issue of bills of credit. These emissions were made from time to time, as the wants of the public service demanded, and for a while all went on well. But it was soon found that it would be difficult, if not impossible, for the Congress to provide means for their redemption in specie, as promised upon their face, and they began to depreciate. The last emission was early in 1780, and at the close of that year they were almost worthless. At that time the enormous sum of two hundred millions of dollars had been issued. The following table shows the scale of depreciation:—

VALUE OF $100 IN SPECIE IN CONTINENTAL MONEY.

	1777.	1778.	1779.	1780.	1781.
January	$105	$325	$742	$2934	$7400
February	107	350	868	3322	7500
March	109	370	1000	3736	0000
April	112	400	1104	4000	—
May	115	400	1215	4600	—
June	120	400	1342	6400	—
July	125	425	1477	8900	—
August	150	450	1630	7000	—
September	175	475	1800	7100	—
October	275	500	2030	7200	—
November	300	545	2308	7300	—
December	310	634	2593	7400	—

Here the patriotic Nelson set a noble example; his crops were left to their fate, his ploughs left in the furrows, while the teams were harnessed to the cannon and munitions of war moving to the investment of Yorktown. From his personal virtues, he had the most commanding influence in the state; he exerted it in rallying her sons, when a powerful foe invaded her soil. His weight of character enabled him to unlock the coffers of avarice, and give their hoards to the aid of his country, when that country had neither a dollar in her treasury, nor credit to obtain one.

At the ever-memorable siege of Yorktown,* Governor Nelson rendered important services in blockading the enemy previous to the arrival of the combined army and the fleets of France. It was on the venerable Lafayette's last visit to Mount Vernon, in 1825, that he related to the author of these Memoirs a touching anecdote of Governor Nelson, which we shall give in the good General's own words: "I had just finished a battery," said the nation's guest, "mounted with heavy pieces; but before I opened on the town, I requested the attendance of the governor of Virginia, not only as a compliment due to the chief magistrate of the state in which I was serving, but from his accurate knowledge of the localities of a place in which he had spent the greater part of his life. 'To what particular spot would your excellency direct that we should point the cannon,' I asked. 'There,' promptly replied the noble-minded, patriotic Nelson, 'to that house; it is mine, and is, now that the secretary's is nearly knocked to pieces, the best one in the town; and there you will be almost certain to find

* See chapter vi.

Lord Cornwallis and the British headquarters. Fire upon it, my dear marquis, and never spare a particle of my property so long as it affords a comfort or a shelter to the enemies of my country.' The governor then rode away, leaving us all charmed with an instance of devotional patriotism that would have shed a lustre upon the purest ages of Grecian or Roman virtue."*

Another anecdote we will present to our readers ere we close this brief memoir. "During the campaign of 1781, when the ruined state of the finances had caused everything like hard money to have almost entirely disappeared, Nelson learned that an old Scotchman named R——, had a considerable sum in gold, which, like most other moneyed persons of that period, he kept carefully concealed. The governor waited upon the man of gold, a *rara avis* in those times, and begged and prayed for a loan on behalf of the state. R—— was inexorable, saying, 'I ken naething of your goovernment, but if ye wull ha' the siller for youself, general, de'il take me but every bawbee of it is at your service.' Nelson accepted the offer, and obtained on his own bond, and by his own personal influence, a loan for the state of Virginia, when that prominent state had neither a coin in her treasury, nor credit to obtain one. The governor received the

---

* When I visited Yorktown a few years ago, Governor Nelson's house was yet standing, and was occupied by his grandson. It was a large, two storied brick building, fronting the main street of the town, a short distance from the river bank. It bore many scars of the cannonade and bombardment alluded to in the text; and in the yard, in front, lay an unexploded bombshell, cast there at the time of the siege. A few feet from the door, was a fine laurel tree, from whose boughs a handsome civic wreath was made, on the occasion of Lafayette's visit there in 1824. The wreath was placed upon the brow of the nation's guest, when he instantly removed it, and laid it upon that of Colonel Nicholas Fish, of the Revolution, who accompanied him, remarking that no one was better entitled to wear the mark of honor than he.

gold, and quickly did its circulation give a new and cheering aspect to our destinies at that momentous period."

And now, it would be naturally asked, who paid the bond and its accumulated interest? Posterity would answer, a grateful and admiring country, surely. Say, rather, the impoverished family of the patriot. This, with other facts of equal moment, caused the author of these Memoirs to blush for his country, when, during the triumph of Lafayette, and upon his last visit to Mount Vernon, the veteran introduced the subject of Nelson, spoke in the most ardent and enthusiastic terms of his gallant services, untiring patriotism, and his unexampled and devotional sacrifices for the cause of American Independence; and presumed that a grateful and admiring nation had long since rewarded the descendants of his old companion-in-arms, his beloved and bosom friend.

It will be matter of interest to all future ages of the Republic, to learn who of the many worthies that flourished in the age of Washington were nearest to the heart of the Pater Patriæ. All tradition will agree upon Greene and Robert Morris. But if they were in the heart's core of the chief, as assuredly they were, Nelson, of Virginia, was at their side. Beloved in life, Washington showed his esteem for Nelson's memory by appointing the son, named after the sire, as one of the secretaries to the first president of the United States, on the commencement of the federal government in 1789.

Such was Nelson, of Virginia, who, in times that tried men's souls, pledged for his country in the halls of her Independence, his life, and perilled it in her battle-fields; pledged his fortune, and lavished it in his country's cause; pledged his sacred honor, and redeemed it by a life and actions honored among the most honored.*

Such was a patriot, statesman, and soldier of the American Revolution—the admired of his countrymen, the beloved of Washington and Lafayette—whose respected descendants have appealed, in the name of the services and sacrifices of their ancestor, to the justice and magnanimity of a free, powerful, and prosperous empire.

Having lived to witness the consummation of that Independence, the declaration of which his pen had signed, and achievements for which his sword had earned, he closed his eyes in peace, leaving a very numerous family, and a fortune greatly impaired, by the vast sacrifices he had made for American liberty. And will the *American* reader believe, that the widow of such a patriot and such a man, lives in Virginia—that very Virginia on which the name and character of Nelson sheds unfading lustre —that this venerable relict, now on the verge of human life, blind and poor, has yet to learn whether an emancipated country can be *just*, more than forty years not having sufficed to show them, whether it can be *grateful.*†

---

* Governor Nelson was a member of the continental Congress in 1776, and signed the Declaration of Independence. He occupied a seat in that body during the first half of the war; and in 1781, he was elected governor of Virginia. Because he exercised his prerogative, as governor of the state, in impressing men into the military service, on the occasion of the siege of Yorktown, many influential persons were offended, and many mortal enemies were created. But he outlived all the attacks of malice, and died on the fourth of January, 1789, in the fiftieth year of his age. His remains, with many others of his family, repose in the old churchyard at Yorktown.

† This sketch was first published in the *National Intelligencer,* on the third of March, 1836.

CHAPTER XV.

ALEXANDER HAMILTON.

BIRTHPLACE OF HAMILTON—HIS EARLY EDUCATION—GOES TO NEW YORK AND ENTERS KING'S COLLEGE—BECOMES A POLITICAL WRITER WHILE IN COLLEGE—PREDICTION CONCERNING THE COTTON PLANT—ESTIMATE OF HIS CHARACTER BY THE SONS OF LIBERTY—AN ARTILLERY COMPANY FORMED—HIS READY SACRIFICE—HIS VIEWS PREVIOUS TO THE BATTLE ON LONG ISLAND—ANONYMOUS LETTER—HAMILTON AT BRUNSWICK—INTERVIEW WITH WASHINGTON—HAMILTON AND LAURENS—WASHINGTON IN HIS TENT—HAMILTON AT MONMOUTH—RUPTURE BETWEEN WASHINGTON AND HAMILTON—HAMILTON AT YORKTOWN—HE STUDIES LAW—BECOMES A LEGISLATOR—MEMBER OF THE FEDERAL CONVENTION OF 1787—HIS ZEAL—HAMILTON APPOINTED SECRETARY OF THE TREASURY—MORRIS'S OPINION OF HIM—GALLATIN'S EULOGIUM—RETIREMENT TO PRIVATE LIFE—ANECDOTE—HAMILTON'S PREDICTION.

IN the illustrious Alexander Hamilton were united the patriot, the soldier, the statesman, the jurist, the orator, and philosopher, and he was great in them all. Born in the island of Nevis, the first rudiments of his education were obtained in Santa Cruz, from which, at a very early age, he came to America, and completed his studies at Columbia college, in New York.* In that city the Revolution found the young West Indian engaged in his

---

* At that time, and up to the close of the Revolution, it was called King's college, the title by which it was incorporated by George the Second. Young Hamilton came to New York in the year 1772, and soon afterward prepared for college. This preparation occupied a year, and he was about to enter the college at Princeton, when some of its rules not meeting his views, he entered King's college, in the city of New York. The Reverend Myles Cooper, D.D, was the president, having succeeded Doctor Johnson in 1763. At the very beginning, young Hamilton was marked as an extraordinary youth. He was between sixteen and seventeen years of age when he entered that institution.

collegiate studies, and he left the halls of learning for the camp.

Among the efforts then making in behalf of the royal cause in New York, were a series of able essays, published with a view to alarm the patriots as to a rupture with the mother-country, urging that, in such an event, all supplies of clothing would be withheld, and thus the most serious privations be endured by the colonists.* Young Hamilton wrote a powerful reply to these essays, in which he proved that resources abounded in the country; and then, for the first time in the world, it was left for this precocious genius to predict *that the cotton-plant could and would be grown in the southern colonies, and would yield an abundance of the raw material for the supply of our wants.*†

---

* These essays were written chiefly by clergymen of the Church of England. Among them were Doctor Cooper of the college, Samuel Seabury (afterward a New England bishop), Doctor Charles Inglis, Doctor Samuel Auchmuty, and Doctor Chandler. John Holt, who published a warm whig newspaper, had drawn upon himself the invectives of all the ministerial writers; and these, at first, Hamilton burlesqued in doggerel rhyme, with great wit and humor. But afterward, when the aspect of affairs became more serious, he replied to them with irresistible logic. Among the most able of these was his "Full Vindication of the Measures of Congress from the Calumnies of their Enemies," &c., written in December, 1774, in reply to Seabury, who wrote over the signature of "A Westchester Farmer," he being a clergyman in that county at the time.

† See Hamilton's replies to the "Westchester Farmer" (Mr. Seabury), Hamilton's works, vol. ii., first and second articles. In the second, "The Farmer Refuted," he says, "with respect to cotton, you do not pretend to deny that a sufficient quantity of that might be produced. Several of the southern colonies are so favorable to it, that with due cultivation, in a couple of years, they would afford enough to clothe the whole continent." It must be remembered that at the time this was written, the growth of cotton in the colonies was a mere experiment, and only men of far-seeing discernment, like this extraordinary young man, then dreamed of its becoming one of our great staples. It was not until twenty years afterward, when Whitney's cotton-gin produced a new epoch in our commercial history, that the annual product of cotton in all North America became a considerable item in our statistics of production. Up to that time, it was only cultivated for family use in the South. It is true that seven bags of cotton were sent to Europe from Charleston, as early

The troubles increasing, Mr. Hamilton spoke of revisiting the West Indies, with a view to recruit his finances. This the patriots of New York would not hear of for a moment; they had witnessed the powers of his pen, and wished him to try the temper of his sword. "Well, my friends," said the gallant youth, "if you are determined that I shall remain among you, and take part in your just and holy cause, you must raise for me a full company of artillery." This was done, and Captain Hamilton lost no time in enlisting the services of several veteran artillerists, and, by constant drilling, soon brought his company into a very high state of order and discipline.*

Hamilton was in New York, diligently engaged in his military duties when the *Asia*, Captain Vandeput, fired upon the city.† Retreat becoming necessary, Hamilton

---

as 1747, and two thousand pounds more in 1770, four years before Hamilton wrote. It is a remarkable fact, that when, ten years after he wrote (1784), seventy-one bags were shipped, they were seized by the British government, on the ground that America could not produce an amount so great.

* Hamilton had already joined a volunteer corps, commanded by Captain Fleming, formerly an adjutant in the British service, and an exact disciplinarian. Under his command he acquired considerable knowledge of the rudiments of a military education. They assumed the name of "Hearts of Oak," and they exercised every morning, before the hour for study or recitation at the college, in the churchyard of St. George's chapel, in Beekman street. Their uniforms were green, and on their leathern caps was the inscription "Freedom or Death." In March, 1776, Hamilton became captain of artillery in a New York regiment. In the summer following, General Greene's attention was one day arrested, as he was crossing "The Fields" (now City Hall park), by the able movements of a company of artillery, commanded by a mere youth. It was Hamilton. Greene conversed with him a few minutes, and discovered evidences of extraordinary ability. He invited him to his quarters, cultivated his acquaintance, and introduced him afterward to Washington.

† That was in August, 1775. The *Asia* was a British ship-of-war that lay in the harbor of New York to overawe the Sons of Liberty, as the whigs were called. At that time, the republican movements in New York were guided by a committee of

here displayed that noble disinterestedness and disregard of self that adorned all the subsequent actions, whether public or private, of his illustrious life. A cart, drawn by a single horse, contained the baggage of this young officer. He ordered his baggage to be abandoned, and the horse that drew it to be harnessed to the cannon.*

Hamilton's military talents were apparent in very early life. Previous to the battle of Long Island, he crossed over to Brooklyn, and thence, by examining the positions of the American forces with a military eye, he became convinced that with such materials as composed the American army, a conflict with troops which consisted of *all soldiers* would be hopeless of success. Filled with these ideas, Hamilton addressed an anonymous letter to the commander-in-chief, detailing many and forcible arguments against risking an action, and warmly recommending a retreat to the strong grounds of the main-

---

One Hundred. Governor Tryon's course was so decidedly hostile to the Sons of Liberty, and war now appeared so inevitable, that the committee of One Hundred determined to remove the cannon from the grand battery to a place of safety, for their own use. Captain John Lamb was directed to perform the act, assisted by his own artillery company, and an independent corps under Colonel Lasher; and, with a body of citizens led by Isaac Sears (better known as King Sears), he proceeded to the work on the evening of the twenty-third of August. Captain Vandeput of the *Asia* had been informed of the intended movement, and sent a barge filled with armed men to watch the patriots. These were fired upon, when Vandeput opened his ports, and hurled three round shot into the city, spreading great alarm among the inhabitants. The church bells were then rung, and soon a broadside came from the *Asia*. Terror filled the people, but the sturdy whigs removed every gun, in face of the cannonade Hamilton was among the actors, at the head of fifteen of the college students. They carried two of the six-pound cannon to the college green and buried them, in spite of the menaces of Dr. Cooper. These stood at the gateway of the college until it was demolished in 1856.

* In this the author evidently alludes to the retreat from the lines at Brooklyn, a year later, after the disastrous battle there, when the whole American army withdrew across the East river, to New York, under cover of the night and a dense fog in the morning.

land. The letter created no little surprise in the mind of the general, but it was mixed with respect for the talent displayed by the writer. The disastrous battle of Long Island is matter of history.*

Hamilton's artillery joined the American army, and took part in the memorable retreat through the Jerseys.† It was at the passage of the Raritan, near Brunswick, that Hamilton first attracted the notice of the commander-in-chief, who, while posted on the river bank, and contemplating with anxiety the passage of the troops, was charmed by the brilliant courage and admirable skill displayed by a young officer of artillery, who directed a battery against the enemy's advanced columns that pressed upon the Americans in their retreat by the ford.‡ The general ordered Lieutenant-Colonel Fitzgerald, his aid-de-camp, to ascertain who this young officer was, and bid him repair to headquarters at the first halt of the army.

At the interview that ensued, Washington quickly

* This occurred on the twenty-seventh of August, 1776. The British and Hessian troops landed from Staten Island, near the present Fort Hamilton, on Long Island, and marching up, attacked the Americans, a large portion of whom were quite strongly intrenched near Brooklyn. About five hundred Americans were killed or wounded in the engagement, and eleven hundred were made prisoners.

† A combined force of British and Hessians attacked Fort Washington toward the upper end of York island, and captured it on the sixteenth of November. More than two thousand Americans were made prisoners. Washington, with a large portion of the American army, was in the vicinity of Fort Lee, on the Jersey shore, nearly opposite. Two days afterward, Lord Cornwallis, with six thousand troops, crossed the Hudson to attack Washington. Fort Lee was abandoned, and for three weeks the Americans fled before the British across New Jersey, toward the Delaware.

‡ Washington hoped to make a successful stand at Brunswick, but his army was rapidly dissolving, and was not strong enough to risk an engagement While the broken army was retreating from the village, Hamilton, with his field-pieces planted on the highest ground there, effectually checked the advance of the enemy, and gave Washington time to get the start by several hours.

discovered in the young patriot and warrior those eminent qualities of the head and heart that shed such a renown upon the actions of his after life. From that interview Washington "marked him for his own."

The American commander-in-chief was peculiarly happy in the selection of the officers of his military family, of his guard, &c., save in a solitary instance, and in that instance the individual served but for a very short time.* The members of the military family and of the Life-Guard were gentlemen of the first order in intellect, patriotism, and all right soldierly qualities—they were attached to the chief and to each other. Hamilton and Laurens were kindred spirits, brothers alike in arms, in affection, and in accomplishments, and might be styled the *preux chevaliers* of the American army.

Lieutenant-Colonel Hamilton was at the side of the chief during the most eventful periods of the Revolutionary war. In the memorable campaigns of 1777 and 1778, the habit at the headquarters was for the general to dismiss his officers at a very late hour of the night to snatch a little repose, while he, the man of mighty labors, drawing his cloak around him, and trimming his lamp, would throw himself upon a hard couch, not to sleep, but to think. Close to his master (wrapped in a blanket, but "all accoutred" for instant service) snored the stout yet active form of *Billy*, the celebrated body-servant during the whole of the Revolutionary war.†

At this late lone hour silence reigned in the headquarters, broken only by the measured pacing of the

---

* Colonel Aaron Burr. He was in Washington's military family at the close of June, 1776, and entered that of General Putnam early in July.

† See page 157.

sentinels, and the oft-repeated cry of "all's well;" when suddenly the sound of a horse-tramp, at speed, is borne upon the night wind, then the challenging of the guard, and the passing the word of an express from the lines to the commander-in-chief. The despatches being opened and read, there would be heard in the calm deep tones of that voice, so well remembered by the good and the brave in the old days of our country's trial, the command of the chief to his now watchful attendant, "*Call Colonel Hamilton!*"

The remarkable conduct of the aid-de-camp during the exciting interview of Washington and Major-General Lee, on the field of Monmouth, as has been related in another part of this work, caused no little sensation in the army at that time. It was indeed a generous burst of enthusiasm, emanating from a noble and gallant spirit, that, pure in its own devotion to the cause of liberty, viewed with indignation and abhorrence even the suspicion of treachery in another. It is somewhat singular that there were several distinguished officers of the American army, who, judging from events at the close of the campaign of 1776, anticipated some defection on the part of Lee, on his return from captivity, and rejoining his former colors; yet it was left for a member of a different cloth from the military to give the first alarm to the commander-in-chief on this momentous subject.*

From a difficulty that occurred in 1780, Lieutenant-Colonel Hamilton retired from the headquarters and assumed his rank in the line, in the command of a battalion of light-infantry, then the crack corps of the army.†

---

* See chapter v. Also note on page 292.
† See note on page 241.

With this command he marched to the South in 1781. At the siege of Yorktown, it was determined to storm the two advanced redoubts of the enemy, and the selection of officers and men for this daring achievement was intrusted to Major-General the Marquis de Lafayette. The marquis lost no time in choosing as the officer who was to lead the assault Lieutenant-Colonel Gimat, a gallant Frenchman, who had been attached to the marquis's military family.* Hamilton, belonging to the division of light-infantry commanded by Lafayette, was about to prefer his claim, when his warmest friends and admirers dissuaded him, owing, as they said, to the vast influences in favor of the Frenchman, from the presence of a splendid French fleet and army, and the universal desire of doing every possible honor to our generous and gallant allies. Hamilton observed, "I am aware that I have mighty influences to contend with, but I feel assured that Washington is inflexibly just. I will not urge my claim on the plea of my long and faithful services, co-eval with nearly the whole war; I will only plead my rank." He accordingly repaired to headquarters. The general received his former and favorite aid-de-camp with great cordiality and kindness, listened patiently to his representations, and finally granted his claims; and Lieutenant-Colonel Hamilton, in the presence of three armies, led the assault on the redoubt on the night of the memorable fourteenth of October, with a brilliancy of courage and success that could not be surpassed.†

As the Americans mounted the works, the cry of the

---

* Colonel Gimat was Lafayette's chief aid-de-camp. He was with the marquis at the Brandywine, and helped to bear his wounded general from the field.

† See page 240.

soldiers was, "Remember New London!" alluding to the cruel massacre of the American troops at Fort Griswold the year before. When the redoubt was carried, the vanquished Britons fell on their knees, momently expecting the exterminating bayonet; but not a man was injured, when no longer resisting. For Hamilton, who commanded, and Lieutenant-Colonel Laurens, who participated as a volunteer on this brilliant occasion, courage and mercy have entwined a wreath of laurel that will never fade.*

Shortly after the surrender of Yorktown, Colonel Hamilton retired from the army, preserving his rank, but *declining all pay or emolument*, and commenced the study of the law. He was chosen to a seat in the continental Congress on the twenty-second of July, 1782, where he remained about a year. While a member of that body, he wrote a series of essays of great ability, showing the defects of the old system of government, and recommending a convention with a view to an entirely new constitution, government, and laws.† He was elected a

* This is mentioned in the text on page 241, and commented upon in a note on page 242, which see.

† This proposition for a general convention was submitted to the legislature of New York, *before* his election to the continental Congress. He had written a series of essays on public matters for Loudon's *New York Packet*, printed at Fishkill, in Duchess county, under the general title of *The Continentalist*, in which the defects of the *Articles of Confederation* were ably discussed; and finally he brought the subject before the state legislature, then in session at Poughkeepsie. That body, on Sunday, the twenty-first of July, 1782, passed a series of resolutions, in the last of which it was remarked, that "it is essential to the common welfare, that there should be as soon as possible, a conference of the whole on the subject, and that it would be advisable for this purpose to propose to Congress to recommend, and to each state to adopt, the measure of assembling a GENERAL CONVENTION OF THE STATES, specially authorized to revive and amend the CONFEDERATION, reserving the right to the respective legislatures to ratify their determination." On the following day the legislature chose James Duane, William Floyd, John Morin Scott, Ezra L'Hommedieu, and *Alexander Hamilton*, delegates to the continental Congress.

member of the convention of 1787, and was one of the brightest stars in that constellation of patriots and statesmen that formed the present happy constitution of the United States.*

Hamilton's labors by no means ended with the convention of 1787. It required all his zeal and eloquence to stem the torrent of opposition from Governor Clinton and others, up to the time of the final adoption of the constitution by the state of New York.†

In 1789, when the first president was on his way to the seat of the new government, he stopped in Philadelphia at the house of Robert Morris, and while consulting with that eminent patriot and benefactor of America, as to the members of the first cabinet, Washington observed, "The treasury, Morris, will of course be your berth. After your invaluable services as financier of the Revolution, no one can pretend to contest the office of secretary of the treasury with you." Robert Morris respectfully but firmly declined the appointment, on the ground of his private affairs, and then said, "But, my dear general, you will be no loser by my declining the

---

* The recommendation of the legislature of New York, in 1782, on Hamilton's suggestion, was finally carried out in 1787. In May of that year, delegates from all the states, except New Hampshire and Vermont, assembled at Philadelphia. Washington was a delegate from Virginia; and on motion of Robert Morris, he was chosen president of the convention. On the twelfth of September following, the present *Constitution of the United States* (except a few amendments since) was adopted.

† In the year 1788, when the Federal Constitution was before the people of the several states for consideration, it met with much opposition. This opposition, which at one time promised to prevent its ratification by a majority of the states, was ably met by a series of articles from the pens of Hamilton, Madison, and Jay, since collected under the general title of *The Federalist*. Of the eighty-five numbers which compose *The Federalist*, Hamilton wrote fifty-one, Madison twenty-nine, and Jay five.

secretaryship of the treasury, for I can recommend to you a far cleverer fellow than I am for your minister of finance, in the person of your former aid-de-camp, Colonel Hamilton." The president was amazed, and continued, "I always knew Colonel Hamilton to be a man of superior talents, but never supposed that he had any knowledge of finance." To which Morris replied, "He knows everything, sir; to a mind like his nothing comes amiss." Robert Morris, indeed, had had ample proofs of Hamilton's talents in financial matters, the financier having received from the soldier many and important suggestions, plans, and estimates touching the organization and establishment of the bank of North America, in 1780.*

Thus did Alexander Hamilton, from amid the stirring duties of a camp, devote the vast and varied powers of his mind to the organization of a system of finance, as connected with banking operations, that proved of inestimable service to the cause of the Revolution.

Washington hesitated not a moment in making the appointment of secretary of the treasury agreeably to the recommendation of Morris; for assuredly there was

---

* In May, 1781, Mr. Morris submitted to Congress a plan for a national bank, with a capital of four hundred thousand dollars. Congress approved of the plan, offered to incorporate the subscribers by the name of the *President and Directors of the Bank of North America*, and decreed that the bills should be receivable in payment of all taxes, duties, and debts due the United States. This bank, the first in the United States, went into successful operation in December, 1781. It greatly assisted in the restoration of the credit of the government, and was of efficient service in the financial affairs of the country during the remainder of the war. To secure the public confidence for the bank, there was a subscription among the citizens in the form of bonds obliging them to pay, if it should become necessary, in gold and silver, the amounts annexed to their names, to fulfil the engagements of the bank As we have elsewhere observed, Mr. Morris headed the list with fifty thousand dollars. There were ninety-six subscribers who gave their bonds. Their names may be seen in the *Pennsylvania Packet*, June, 1781.

none, no, not one of the many worthies of the Revolution who stood higher in the esteem, or approached nearer to the heart of the chief than Robert Morris, the noble and generous benefactor of America in the darkest hours of her destiny.

On the very day of the interesting event we have just related, Mr. Dallas met Hamilton in the street and addressed him with, "Well, colonel, can you tell me who will be the members of the cabinet?"—"Really, my dear sir, replied the colonel, "I can not tell you who will, but I can very readily tell you of one who will not be of the number, and that one is your humble servant." He had not, at that moment, the remotest idea that Washington had again in peace, as in war, "marked him for his own."

The very best eulogium that can be pronounced upon the fiscal department of the United States, as organized by Alexander Hamilton, is in the remarks of the Hon. Albert Gallatin, a political rival, and the most distinguished financier of the successors of the first secretary of the treasury. Mr. Gallatin has magnanimously declared that all secretaries of the treasury of the United States, since the first, enjoyed a sinecure, the genius and labors of Hamilton having created and arranged everything that was requisite and necessary for the successful operation of the department.*

In January, 1795, Hamilton resigned his seat in the

* Mr. Gallatin was a native of Geneva, Switzerland, and came to America in 1780, at the age of eighteen years. He was a relative of M. Necker, the celebrated French minister of finance. He entered the continental army, and at the close, settled in Pennsylvania. He was chosen a member of Congress in 1793, and in 1801 Mr. Jefferson called him to his cabinet as secretary of the treasury. He remained in that office until 1813, when he became a special envoy to negotiate for peace with Great Britain. He represented our government in France from 1816 until 1823. He died in 1849 at the age of more than eighty-eight years.

cabinet and retired to private life. It was our good fortune to be almost domesticated in the family of this great man, and to see and know much of him in the olden time. Among the many and imposing recollections of the great age of the Republic that are graven upon our memory, and, mellowed by time, cheer by their venerable and benign influences our evening of life, we call up with peculiar pleasure a reminiscence of the days of the first presidency embracing the resignation of Hamilton.

It was at the presidential mansion that the ex-secretary of the treasury came into the room where Mr. Lear,* Major Jackson,† and the other gentlemen of the president's family were sitting. With the usual smile upon his countenance he observed: "Congratulate me, my good friends, for I am no longer a public man; the president has at length consented to accept my resignation, and I am once more a private citizen." The gentlemen replied that they could perceive no cause for rejoicing in an event that would deprive the government and the country of the late secretary's valuable services. Hamilton continued: "*I am not worth exceeding five hundred dollars in the world; my slender fortune and the best years of my life have been devoted to the service of my adopted country; a rising family hath its claims.*" Glancing his eye upon a small book that lay on the table, he took it up and observed: "Ah, this is the constitution. Now, mark my words: *So long as we are a young and virtuous people, this instrument will bind us together in mutual interests, mutual welfare, and mutual happiness; but when we become old and corrupt it will bind us no longer.*"

* Tobias Lear, Washington's private secretary.
† Major William Jackson, one of the president's military aids.

Such were the prophetic words of Alexander Hamilton, uttered half a century ago, and in the very dawn of our existence as a nation. Let the Americans write them in their books and treasure them in their hearts. Another half century, and they may be regarded as truths.*

What a spectacle does this touching reminiscence present to the Americans and their posterity! A great man of the Revolution, the native of a foreign isle, who had employed his pen and drawn his sword in the cause of liberty before a beard had grown upon his chin; renowned alike in senates and in the field, in the halls of legislation and the "ranks of death," proudly acknowledging his honorable poverty, the result of his many and glorious services, and resigning one of the highest and most dignified offices in the government, to retire as a private citizen to labor for the support of a rising family.

Of a truth, upon the Roman model, aye, and that of the purest and palmiest days of the mistress of the ancient world, were formed the patriots, statesmen, and warriors of the American Revolution. Worthy, indeed, are they to be ranked with the purest and noblest models of ancient virtue and heroism, whom generations yet unborn will hail as the fathers of liberty and founders of an empire.

With these reminiscences, endeared to us by many venerable associations of our other days, and which we offer as an humble tribute to the fame and memory of him who was a master-spirit among the great and renowned that adorned the age of Washington, we close our brief memoir.

* This was first published in the *National Intelligencer*, on the twenty fourth of February, 1845.

CHAPTER XVI.

HENRY LEE.

Washington's Sagacity in his Selection of Officers — His Favorites — Birth of Lee — Anecdote of Lee at Princeton — His Person — He Joins the Army — His Exploit at Paulus' Hook — Commander of a Partisan Corps — His Qualifications — His Corps — His Officers — His Services under Greene — Retirement from the Army — His Marriage — His Civil Career — The Whiskey Insurrection — Pinckney's Remarks — Lee's Oration on the Death of Washington — His Speculations and Losses — His Death — His Eloquence in Speech and Readiness as a Writer.

That Washington was eminently fortunate, and showed his rare and penetrating judgment of mankind, in his selections of officers, as well for important commands, as for members of his military family, we may learn from the history of our olden times. Among many senior worthies, the illustrious names of Greene, Wayne, and Morgan, claim prominent rank, while of the young aspirants in arms, whom the chief may be said to have ushered to fame, were Lafayette, Hamilton, Pinckney, Laurens, and Lee. To these, how many more might be added, on whom the merit-discerning eye of the chief was well-known to have beamed with peculiar esteem and favor; as William Washington*—a namesake, but more related

---

* William Washington was called "the modern Marcellus," "the sword of his country," and other names indicative of his soldierly qualities. He was a son of Bailey Washington, of Stafford county, Virginia, where he was born, on the twenty-eighth of February, 1752. He was educated for the church, but was led into the field of politics at the beginning of the Revolution. He entered the army as captain under Colonel (afterward General) Hugh Mercer, and was first in battle on Long Island. He distinguished himself at Trenton, and was with Mercer when he fell at

by glory, than lineage—the gallant, gay, Otho Williams,* Watty Stewart,† Cadwalader,‡ and many, many others. Our purpose is, to attempt a brief memoir of Lee.

Princeton. He was promoted to major in Colonel Baylor's cavalry corps, and was with him when General Gray made his murderous attack upon the corps at Tappan, in 1778. The following year he joined the army under Lincoln, at the South, and was very active as commander of horse, in the vicinity of Charleston, during the siege in 1780. He became attached to the division of General Morgan, and fought bravely with him at the Cowpens. For his valor there, Congress voted him a silver medal. He accompanied Greene in his celebrated retreat, and again fought bravely at Guilford courthouse. At Hobkirk's hill and Eutaw he behaved gallantly. At the latter place he was made prisoner, and was a captive till the close of the war. While in captivity at Charleston, he became attached to a young lady there, married her, and settled in Charleston. He became conspicuous as a legislator, but declined being a candidate for governor, chiefly because he could not make a speech. General Washington, in 1798, chose Colonel Washington to be one of his staff, with the rank of brigadier. He died on the sixth of March, 1810.

* Otho Holland Williams was born in Prince George county, Maryland, in 1748. His ancestors were Welsh, and came to America soon after Lord Baltimore became proprietor of the province of Maryland. He was left an orphan at twelve years of age. He was a resident of Frederick county when the war of the Revolution began, where he entered the military service as lieutenant of a rifle corps under Colonel Michael Cresap, and with that officer he went to Boston. He was afterward promoted to the command of his company. In 1776 he was promoted to major, and fought at Fort Washington with distinction. In that engagement he was wounded and captured, and for some time experienced the horrors of the provost prison of New York. He was afterward exchanged for Major Ackland, captured at Saratoga. During his captivity, he was appointed to the command of a regiment in the Maryland line. He was Gates's adjutant-general during the campaign of 1780. When Gates collected the remnant of his army, scattered at Camden, the Marylanders were formed into two battalions, constituting one regiment. To Williams was assigned the command, with John Eager Howard as his lieutenant. When Greene assumed the command of the southern army, he perceived the value of Williams, and appointed him adjutant-general. In Greene's memorable retreat, and the subsequent battle of Guilford, Williams greatly distinguished himself; and at Eutaw Springs he led the celebrated charge which swept the field and gained the temporary victory. Congress promoted him to the rank of brigadier; and at the close of the war he received the appointment of collector of customs at Baltimore, which office he held until his death, which occurred on the sixteenth of July, 1794, while on his way to a watering-place for the benefit of his health.

† Colonel Walter Stewart was of Irish descent, had a fair and florid complexion, was vivacious, intelligent, and well educated; and, it is said, was the handsomest man in the American army.

† General John Cadwalader, of Philadelphia.

Henry Lee was born in the county of Stafford, and state of Virginia, and was educated at Nassau Hall,* in the years immediately prior to the Revolution. In very early life he showed a disposition toward manliness, as appears from a ludicrous anecdote, probably still extant in the village of Princeton. At that day, the village possessed but one knight of the strap, commonly called a barber, who mowed the chins and powdered the wigs of the "grave and reverend seigniors" of the faculty. Young Lee one day entered the shop, and pompously called to the operator, "Shave me, sir." Old Razor, though a dealer in suds, was a dry fellow, and a celebrated wag. After looking for a moment with surprise at his new customer, he seated the youthful aspirant to the honors of a beard, in a chair, and having lathered him up to the eyes, flourished the steel as if about to begin; then, laying it down, went to the door, and continued walking backward and forward in the street, as though he were looking for something which had been lost. Lee bore his situation for a while, with philosophic calmness, till his patience being exhausted, he roared out, "Why don't you come and shave me, sir?"—"Because," replied the waggish tonsor, *I am looking for your beard.*

From academic groves, Lee, then scarcely nineteen, repaired to the tented field. Of a height not exceeding the middle stature, with a form light and agile, a quick and penetrating glance, and a genius predominant toward arms, the youthful *militaire* was attached to the

---

* This is the name of the principal building of the College of New Jersey, at Princeton. It was erected in 1758, and was so named by Governor Belcher, in honor of William of Nassau, king of England, "who, under God," he said, "was the great deliverer of the British *nation* from those two monstrous furies, *popery* and *slavery.*"

cavalry service, and became distinguished in the early campaigns of the Revolution.

The affair of Paulus's Hook, in '79, in which a detachment led by Lee, succeeded in the surprise and capture of the enemy, "marked him for promotion." In reward of this brilliant achievement, Congress voted a gold medal,* and the commander-in-chief was pleased to authorize Major Lee to raise and discipline a partisan legion, to consist of three companies of horse, and as many of infantry, and to command the same, with the rank of lieutenant-colonel.† No officer in the American army could have been better fitted than Lee for the command of a partisan corps; for in the surprise of posts, in gaining intelligence, of distracting and discomfiting your enemy, without bringing him to a general action, and all the strategy which belongs to the partisan warfare, few officers in any service have been more distinguished than the subject of our memoir. The legion of Lee, under the untiring labors of its active, talented com-

---

* Paulus's Hook was the name of the point of land upon which Jersey City now stands, opposite New York. The British erected quite strong military works there, after they took possession of the city of New York and the Jerseys. Major Lee was stationed not far from that point, in the summer of 1779, and learned that Major Sutherland, the commander of the garrison, resting in fancied security, was by no means vigilant. Fired with enthusiasm at the success of Wayne at Stony Point, Lee asked permission of Washington to attack the garrison at Paulus's Hook. It was granted; and in the evening of the eighteenth of August, Lee set out in high spirits, with three hundred men, followed at helping distance by Lord Stirling with five hundred more. At three o'clock in the morning, he fell upon the little fort, killed thirty of the garrison in prosecuting the assault, and made one hundred and fifty-nine prisoners. For this exploit, the Congress honored Lee with a vote of thanks, and ordered a gold medal to be struck in commemoration of the occasion, and presented to him.

† Major Lee was promoted to lieutenant-colonel in November, 1780, and on the thirty-first of October, Congress ordered him to join Greene in the South, with his corps.

mander, became one of the most efficient corps in the American army.

The horsemen were principally recruited in the Southern and Middle states—countries proverbial for furnishing skilful riders; while the horses, under the inspection of the Virginian commander, were superior in bone and figure, and could many of them have boasted a lineal descent from the Godolphin Arabian.

Among Lee's officers, were the good and gallant names of Eggleston, Rudolph, Armstrong, O'Neil, and the surviving honored veterans Allen M‘Lane of Delaware, and Harrison of Virginia.* The arrival of the legion in the South was hailed as most auspicious to the success of our arms in that quarter; indeed, so fine a corps of horse and foot, so well disciplined, and in such gallant array, was rarely to be seen in those our days of desolation. The partisan legion did good service in the campaigns of the Carolinas, and the commander won his way to the esteem and confidence of Greene, *the well-beloved of Washington*, as he had previously done to the esteem and confidence of the great chief himself;† and, as a justice to the great military sagacity of Lee, let it be remembered, that he was mainly instrumental in advising Greene to that *return to the Carolinas*, which eventuated in the deci-

---

* This was first published in the *National Intelligencer*, on the twenty-fifth of August, 1828.

† In the early part of the war, Lee distinguished himself for skill and bravery, and Washington became very much attached to him. On one occasion while the Americans were encamped at Valley Forge, Lee performed a gallant exploit, and Washington, not content with honoring him with a public notice, wrote a private letter to him full of the warmest expressions of friendship. It is believed that Washington's friendship for Lee was partly based upon the remembrance of his early love for Lee's mother, the "lowland beauty" of which he wrote, as having won his heart when he was a lad of sixteen years.

sive and glorious combat of Eutaw,* and the virtual liberation of the South. With the close of the campaign of 1781, ended the military services of Lieutenant-Colonel Lee.† He retired on furlough to Virginia, and was happily present at the surrender of his old adversary, the formidable Cornwallis, at Yorktown, October 19th. Lee married shortly afterward, and settled in the county of Westmoreland, but was permitted, by his grateful and admiring countrymen, for a short time only, to enjoy the "*otium cum dignitate*," being successively chosen to the state legislature, the convention for ratifying the constitution, the gubernatorial chair, and the Congress of the United States.‡

On the breaking out of the western insurrection, Lee, then governor of Virginia, was appointed by the president to the command-in-chief of the forces which were marched to the seat of rebellion.§ To this appointment,

---

* In September, 1781. The British army in South Carolina had been driven toward the sea-board, and was encamped at Eutaw Springs, near the southwest bank of the Santee river, about sixty miles from Charleston. There, on the morning of the eighth of September, Greene, with a considerable force, fell upon the enemy, and a severe battle ensued. The British were driven from their camp, when Greene's troops carelessly strolled among the tents which the enemy had left. The British unexpectedly renewed the conflict, and after a bloody battle of four hours, the Americans had to give way. That night the British retreated toward Charleston, and the next morning Greene took possession of the battle-field. In that engagement, Lee and his legion were very conspicuous.

† In January, 1782, Colonel Lee sought and obtained permission to leave the army on account of his impaired health, when Greene declared that his services had been greater than those of any one man attached to the southern army.

‡ He was a delegate in Congress for Virginia, in 1786, and in 1788 he was a member of the state convention, called to ratify the federal constitution. In 1792 he was elected governor of Virginia, and in 1799 he was again elected to a seat in Congress.

§ This is known in history as the "Whiskey Insurrection," and occurred in Western Pennsylvania, in 1794. It grew out of an unpopular excise law passed in 1791, which imposed duties on domestic distilled liquors. A new act on the subject,

Major-General Morgan, who commanded the troops detailed from Virginia, at first demurred, Morgan having been a brigadier in the old service of the Revolution, while the rank of Lee was that of lieutenant-colonel; but the hero of the Cowpens soon waived his claims of rank, with the same magnanimous sentiments which afterward distinguished the estimable Charles Cotesworth Pinckney, in the difference about rank, in the army of 1798, who said, " He [the chief] should know us best; we are all his children, and he must be the best judge of our respective merits."

With the advantages of a classical education, General Lee possessed taste, and distinguished powers of eloquence; and was selected, on the demise of Washington, to deliver the oration in the funeral solemnities decreed by Congress in honor of the Pater Patriæ.* The oration having been but imperfectly committed to memory, from the very short time in which it was composed, somewhat impaired its effect upon the auditory; but, as a composition, it has only to be read to be admired, for the purity and elegance of its language, and the powerful appeal it makes to the hearts of its readers; and we will venture

---

equally unpopular, was passed by Congress in the spring of 1794; and when, soon after the session had closed, officers were sent out to the western districts of Pennsylvania to enforce the law, the inhabitants presented armed resistance. The insurrection became general throughout all that region, and in the vicinity of Pittsburgh many outrages were committed. Buildings were burned, mails were robbed, and government officers were abused. President Washington first issued two proclamations (August 7 and September 25), but without effect. All peaceable means for maintaining law being exhausted, he ordered out a large body of the militia of Virginia, Maryland, Pennsylvania, and New Jersey. These marched to the insurgent district in October, under the command of General Lee, who was then the governor of Virginia. The military argument was effectual, and the rebellion was crushed.

* An account of the congressional proceedings on that occasion will be found in another part of this work.

to affirm, that it will rank among the most celebrated performances of those highly distinguished men who mounted the rostrum on that imposing occasion of national mourning.*

With his congressional career ended the better days of this highly-gifted man. An unhappy rage for speculation caused him to embark upon that treacherous stream, which gently, and almost imperceptibly, at first, but with sure and fearful rapidity at last, hurries its victims to the vortex of destruction. It was, indeed, lamentable to behold the venerable Morris and Lee, patriots, who, in the senates of liberty, and on her battle-fields, had done the "state such service," instead of enjoying a calm and happy evening of life, to be languishing in prison and in exile. Lee, after long struggling with adversity, sought in a foreign land a refuge from his many ills, where, becoming broken in health, he returned home to die. He reached the mansion of Greene, and fortune, relenting of her frowns, lit up his few remaining days with a smile. There, amid attentions the most consoling and kindly, surrounded by recollections of his old and loved commander, the most fond and endearing, the worn and wearied spirit of the patriot, statesman, and soldier of liberty, found rest in the grave.†

In one particular, Lee may be said to have excelled his illustrious cotemporaries Marshall, Madison, Hamilton, Gouverneur Morris, and Ames. It was in a surprising

* Lee's oration is printed in the appendix of this volume.

† General Lee was severely injured by a political mob in Baltimore, in 1812, and never recovered. He went to the West Indies with the hope of improving his health, but it continually declined. Early in 1818 he returned to the United States. He stopped at the house of Mrs. Shaw, the daughter of his old friend and companion-in-arms, General Greene, on Cumberland island, off the coast of Georgia, where he died on the twenty-fifth of March, at the age of sixty-two years.

quickness of talent, a genius sudden, dazzling, and always at command, with an eloquence which seemed to flow unbidden. Seated at a convivial board, when the death of Patrick Henry was announced, Lee called for a scrap of paper, and, in a few moments, produced a striking and beautiful eulogium upon the Demosthenes of modern liberty. His powers of conversation were also fascinating in the extreme, possessing those rare and admirable qualities which seize and hold captive his hearers, delighting while they instruct. That Lee was a man of letters, a scholar who had ripened under a truly classical sun, we have only to turn to his work on the southern war, where he was, indeed, the "*magna pars fui*" of all which he relates—a work which well deserves to be ranked with the commentaries of the famed master of the Roman world, who, like our Lee, was equally renowned with the pen as the sword.* But there is a line, a single line, in the works of Lee, which would hand him over to immortality, though he had never written another. "*First in war, first in peace, and first in the hearts of his countrymen,*" will last while language lasts.† What a sublime eulogium is pronounced in this noble line! So few words, and yet how illustrative are they of the vast and matchless character of Washington! They are words which will descend with the memory of the hero they are meant to honor, to the veneration of remotest posterity, and be graven on colossal statues of the Pater Patriæ in some future age.‡

* General Lee's *Memoirs of the War in the Southern Department of the United States*, were written in 1808, and the last edition was printed in 1827. It is a work of great interest, and very reliable. It is now sought after by all collectors of works on American history, but can rarely be found, having been out print for many years

† This notable expression was used by General Lee in his oration on the character of Washington.

‡ These words were cut upon the granite pedestal of Greenough's "colossal

The attachment of Lee to Washington was like that of Hamilton, pure and enthusiastic — like that of the chivalric Laurens, devotional. It was in the praise of his "hero, his friend, and a country's preserver," that the splendid talent of Lee were often elicited, with a force and grandeur of eloquence wholly his own. The fame and memory of his chief was the fondly-cherished passion to which he clung amid the wreck of his fortunes — the hope, which gave warmth to his heart when all else around him seemed cold and desolate.

But shall the biographer's task be complete, when the faults of his subject are not taken in the account? Of faults, perhaps the subject of our memoir had many; yet how admirable is the maxim handed down to us from the ancients, "*de mortuis nil, nisi bonum.*" Let the faults of Lee be buried in his distant grave — let the turf of oblivion close over the failings of him, whose early devotion to liberty, in liberty's battles — whose eloquence in her senates, and historical memoirs of her times of trial, shed a lustre on his country in the young days of the Republic; and when the Americans of some future date shall search amid the records of their early history for the lives of illustrious men, who flourished in the age of Washington, high on a brilliant scroll will they find inscribed, Henry Lee, a son of Virginia — the patriot, soldier, and historian of the Revolution, and orator and statesman of the Republic.

statue" of Washington (now within the square, eastward of the Federal capite fifteen years after this prophecy was written.

CHAPTER XVII.

BIRTH-NIGHT BALLS AND THE THEATRE.

INSTITUTION OF THE BIRTH-NIGHT BALL—CELEBRATION OF WASHINGTON'S BIRTHDAY—WASHINGTON'S ATTENDANCE UPON THE BALLS—DECORATIONS OF THE LADIES—THE MINUET—WASHINGTON'S LAST DANCE—HIS LAST ATTENDANCE AT A BALL—WASHINGTON FOND OF THE THEATRE—RECEPTION OF THE PRESIDENT AT THE THEATRE—THE THEATRICAL COMPANY—MUSIC ON THE OCCASION OF WASHINGTON'S ATTENDANCE—DESPOTISM OF THE PIT AND GALLERY—REVOLUTIONARY SENTIMENT.

THE birth-night ball was instituted at the close of the Revolutionary war, and its first celebration, we believe, was held in Alexandria.* Celebrations of the birth-night soon became general in all the towns and cities, the twenty-second of February, like the fourth of July, being considered a national festival, while the peculiarity attending the former was, that its parade and ceremonies always closed with the birth-night ball. In the larger cities, where public balls were customary, the birth-night, in the olden time, as now, was the gala assembly of the season. It was attended by all the beauty and fashion, and at the seat of government, by the foreign ambassadors, and by strangers of distinction. The first president

* The French officers who served in America during the Revolution, appear to have celebrated the birthday of Washington immediately after the war. This fact is indicated by the following paragraph in a letter written by Washington to the Count de Rochambeau, in the spring of 1784. He says, "The flattering distinction paid to the anniversary of my birthday, is an honor for which I dare not attempt to express my gratitude. I confide in your excellency's sensibility to interpret my feelings for this, and for the obliging manner in which you are pleased to announce it."

always attended on the birth-night. The etiquette was, not to open the ball until the arrival of him in whose honor it was given; but, so remarkable was the punctuality of Washington in all his engagements, whether for business or pleasure, that he was never waited for a moment in appointments for either. Among the brilliant illustrations of a birth-night of five-and-thirty years ago,* the most unique and imposing was the groups of young and beautiful ladies, wearing in their hair bandeaux or scrolls, having embroidered thereon, in language both ancient and modern, the motto of "*Long live the president!*"†

* This was first published in the *National Intelligencer*, on the twenty-second of February, 1830.

† In a very interesting letter, dated Philadelphia, twenty-fifth May, 1859, which I received from the venerable Samuel Breck of that city, giving me a brief record of his recollections of Washington's visit to Boston in 1789, he says, after speaking of a dinner party at Governor Hancock's—" Meantime the French ships of war in the harbor were dressed in variegated lamps, and bonfires blazed in the streets. *The ladies wore bandeaux, cestuses, and ribbons, stamped and embroidered with the name of* WASHINGTON; *some in gold and silver letters, and some in pearls.*"

The birthday of Washington was early celebrated among the masses of the people. They had been accustomed to do honor to the birthday of King George, on the fourth of June; now they more delighted to do honor to a nobler George, on the twenty-second of February. Popular songs often enlivened the occasion, and expressed the sentiments of the people. One of these, written more than sixty years ago, is preserved, from which I quote some stanzas as a specimen of its spirit:—

> " Come boys, close the windows and make a good fire,
>   Wife, children, sit snug all around:
> 'Tis the day that gave birth to our country's blessed sire,
>   Then let it with pleasure be crowned.
> Dear wife, bring your wine, and, in spite of hard times,
>   On this day at least we'll be merry:
> Come, fill every glass till it pours o'er the brim,
>   If not with Madeira—then Sherry.
> *   *   *   *   *
> " May the laurels of fame that his temples enwreathed,
>   Ever flourish in gratitude's tears:
> O! ever his name with devotion be breathed—
>   That name which our country endears."

The minuet (now obsolete), for the graceful and elegant dancing of which Washington was conspicuous, in the vice-regal days of Lord Botetourt in Virginia, declined after the Revolution. The commander-in-chief danced, for his last time, a minuet, in 1781, at the ball given in Fredericksburg, in honor of the French and American officers, on their return from the triumphs at Yorktown.* The last birth-night attended by the venerable chief was in Alexandria, twenty-second February, 1798. Indeed he always appeared greatly to enjoy the gay and festive scene exhibited at the birth-night balls, and usually remained to a late hour; for, remarkable as he was for reserve, and the dignified gravity inseparable from his nature, Washington ever looked with most kind and favoring eye, upon the rational and elegant pleasures of life.†

The first president was partial to the amusements of the theatre, and attended some five or six times in a season, more especially when some public charity was to

---

* See page 144.

† The following letter from Washington, written about a month before his death, has an interest in this connection. It was in reply to an invitation from a committee of gentlemen of Alexandria to attend the dancing assemblies at that place. I copied it from the original in the Alexandria Museum, in 1848.

"*To Messrs. Jonathan Swift, George Deneale, William Newton, Robert Young, Charles Alexander, Junior, James H. Hoole, Managers.*

"Mount Vernon, 12th November, 1799.

"GENTLEMEN—Mrs. Washington and myself have been honored with your polite invitation to the assemblies of Alexandria this winter, and thank you for this mark of your attention. But, alas! our dancing days are no more. We wish, however, all those who have a relish for so agreeable and innocent an amusement all the pleasure the season will afford them; and I am, gentlemen,

"Your most obedient and obliged humble servant,

"GEO. WASHINGTON."

See letters of WASHINGTON and CUSTIS, July 1 and July 10, on pages 89 and 90 of this volume.

be benefitted by the performance. The habit was, for the manager to wait on the president, requesting him to command a play; the pieces so commanded partook of but little variety, but must be admitted to have been in excellent taste—the "School for Scandal," and "Every one has his Fault," for the plays, and for the afterpieces, there was almost a standing order for the "Poor Soldier" and "Wignell's Darby."* The old American company,

* In his diary, under date of Tuesday, November 24, 1789, Washington recorded as follows: "A good deal of company at the levee to-day. Went to the play in the evening—sent tickets to the following ladies and gentlemen, and invited them to take seats in my box, viz.: Mrs. Adams (lady of the vice-president), General Schuyler and lady, Mr. King and lady, Major Butler and lady, Colonel Hamilton and lady, Mrs. Greene—all of whom accepted and came, except Mrs. Butler, who was indisposed." What a group for our contemplation!

The theatre was in John street, north side, not far eastward from Broadway. It was a small, frail affair, and capable of holding only about three hundred persons. This was, doubtless, the occasion described by Dunlap, when Wignell performed the part of Darby, in the interlude of *Darby's Return*, a play written by that gentleman. Darby (an Irish lad) recounts his adventures in the United States and elsewhere. When he related what befell him in the city of New York, at the inauguration of the president, &c., "the interest expressed by the audience," says Dunlap, "in the looks and the changes of countenance of the great man [Washington], became intense." At the descriptive lines—

"A man who fought to free the land from woe,
Like me, had left his farm, a soldiering to go,
But having gained his point, he had, *like me*,
Returned his own potatoe-ground to see.

"But then he could not rest. With one accord,
He is called to be a kind of—not a lord—
I don't know what; he's not a *great man*, sure,
For poor men love him just as he were poor"—

the president looked serious; and when Kathleen asked,

"How looked he, Darby? Was he short or tall?"—

Washington's countenance showed embarrassment from the expectation of one of those eulogies which he had been compelled "to hear on many public occasions, and which must, doubtless, have been a severe trial to his feelings." The president was relieved by Darby's declaration that *he had not seen him*.

Mr. Dunlap, in his "History of the American Theatre," alludes thus to the fact,

comprising Hallam and Henry, Harper, Wignell, and old Morris, first played in 1789, in the theatre in John street, and nothing more truly shows our transcendant march toward refinement, than the contrast between the humble, nay, barn-like theatre, which the first president attended forty years ago, and the *now* various and magnificent temples of Thespis, which adorn the present great and splendid city of New York.

"The company moved with the government to Philadelphia, and performed in the old theatre, Southwark, in which was some scenery, said to have been painted by the interesting and unfortunate Major André, until the erection of the house in Chestnut street, where we believe the curtain fell upon the exits of the last remnants of the *old American company*.*

In New York, the play-bill was headed, "*By particular desire*," when it was announced that the president would attend. On those nights the house would be crowded from top to bottom, as many to see the hero as the play. Upon the president's entering the stage-box with his family, the orchestra would strike up *The President's March* (now *Hail Columbia*), composed by a German named Feyles, in '89, in contradistinction to the march of the Revolution,

---

that in the theatrical world particular regard was had to the birthday of Washington: "The theatre having been closed for the benefit of the managers, was reopened on the twenty-second of February [1810], with *Gustavus Vasa*, a play thought appropriate for the birthday of Washington, and frequently as such brought forward."

* Major André was chiefly instrumental in getting up theatrical performances in Philadelphia, during the occupancy of that city by the Britiish army, in the winter of 1777, '78, and tradition says that he painted nearly all the scenery that was used. Wignell, of the old American company, opened the theatre in Philadelphia (a new and splendid one), on the seventeenth of February, 1794. The last performance of the old American company was, I believe, in 1798, at about which time the Park theatre in New York was opened, with a new and strong company.

called *Washington's March.** The audience applauded on the entrance of the president, but the pit and gallery were so truly despotic in the early days of the republic, that so soon as *Hail Columbia* had ceased, *Washington's March* was called for by the deafening din of an hundred voices at once, and upon its being played, three hearty cheers would rock the building to its base. Indeed, five-and-thirty years ago there could not be gotten together any large public assembly without a considerable spice of the Revolution being among it. The soldiers and sailors of the War for Liberty abounded in all public places, and no sooner would their old chief appear, than off came each hat, and the shout of welcome resounded, pure, spontaneous, direct from the heart.

---

* The song of *Hail Columbia*, adapted in measure to the President's March, was written by Joseph Hopkinson, of Philadelphia, in 1798. At that time war with France was expected, and a patriotic feeling pervaded the community. Mr. Fox, a young singer and actor, called upon Mr. Hopkinson one morning, and said, "To-morrow evening is appointed for my benefit at the theatre. Not a single box has been taken, and I fear there will be a thin house. If you will write me some patriotic verses to the tune of the "President's March," I feel sure of a full house. Several people about the theatre have attempted it, but they have come to the conclusion that it can not be done. Yet I think you may succeed." Mr. Hopkinson retired to his study, wrote the first verse and chorus, and submitted them to Mrs. Hopkinson, who sang them to a harpsichord accompaniment. The time and the words harmonized. The song was soon finished, and that evening the young actor received it. The next morning the theatre-placards announced that Mr. Fox would sing a new patriotic song. The house was crowded—the song was sung—the audience were delighted—eight times it was called for and repeated, and when sung the ninth time, the whole audience stood up and joined in the chorus. Night after night, "*Hail Columbia*" was applauded in the theatres; and in a few days it was the universal song of the boys in the streets. Such was the original of our national song, *Hail Columbia*.

CHAPTER XVIII.

LIFE AT MOUNT VERNON.*

Washington Resigns his Commission — In Retirement at Mount Vernon — His Own Architect and Overseer — Improvement of his Estate — Enjoyment of Private Life — Two of his Aids at Mount Vernon — Bishop the Old Body-Servant — Bishop on "Braddock's Field" — His Attachment to the Fortunes of Washington — Too Old for Campaigning in the Revolution — Washington's Intercourse with him — Colonel Smith's Gallantry — Bishop's Daughter Affrighted — The Wrath of Bishop — Billy a Peacemaker — Bishop's Wrath Assuaged — Washington in the Convention of 1787 — Charles Thomson at Mount Vernon — Washington, President of the United States.

AFTER the sublime and touching event of the "resignation of the commission," at Annapolis, on the twenty-third of December, 1783, Washington hastened to his beloved retirement, hung up his sword, and prepared to enjoy the delights of rural and domestic life.†

---

* This was first published in the *National Intelligencer*, on the twenty-second of February, 1848.

† The British army evacuated the city of New York, their last resting-place on the soil of the United States, on the twenty-fifth of November, 1783. The American army was disbanded immediately afterward, and on the fourth of December, Washington bade his officers farewell, in a most touching personal interview, in New York. He then went to Philadelphia, where the fiscal officers of the government received from his hands a full statement of his receipts and expenditures during the war. The Congress were then in session at Annapolis, to which place he journeyed, and on the twenty-third of December, he resigned his commission as commander-in-chief of the armies of the United States, into the hands of Thomas Mifflin, the president of Congress. This was done at a public audience, Washington addressing the president in words appropriate for the occasion, and Mifflin replying in a most complimentary manner. "Having defended," he said, "the standard of liberty in this new world — having taught a lesson useful to those who inflict and to those who feel oppression — you retire from the great theatre of action with the blessings of your fellow-citizens. But the glory of your virtues will not terminate with your military command; it will continue to animate remotest ages."

The same exact and economical distribution of time, the same methodical and active habits of business, that had so triumphantly borne the commander of armies through the mighty labors of an eight years' war, were now destined, in the works of peace, alike to distinguish the illustrious farmer of Mount Vernon.

After so long an absence, the retired general, on returning to his home, found that there was much to create. Previous to the war, the establishment of Mount Vernon was upon a very limited scale. The mansion-house was small, having but four rooms on a floor; and there were wanting nearly all of the present outbuildings and offices.

Washington was his own architect and builder, laying off everything himself. The buildings, gardens, and grounds all rose to ornament and usefulness under his fostering hand.*

His landed estate, comprising eight thousand acres, underwent many and important changes and improvements. It was divided into farms, with suitable enclosures; hedges were planted, and excellent farm-buildings were erected, from European models. Devoting much time and attention to these various objects, Washington accomplished the most important of his improvements in the very short space of from four to five years.†

---

* In the arrangement and embellishment of his grounds, as well as in the enlargement and improvement of the mansion-house, Washington attended to the minutest details. He made drawings of every plan, made a memorandum of every relative distance of buildings, inclosures, et cetera, and designated the position of every tree that was planted. I have before me some of his original drawings, in which all these details appear, with memoranda in his neat handwriting. One of these drawings, published in "*Mount Vernon and its Associations*," shows the form of the lawn on the west front of the mansion, the flower and vegetable garden, and the name and position of every tree.

† At the close of the war, Washington commenced very extensive improvements

Nor was his time exclusively allotted to business; he had a "time for all things." He enjoyed the pleasures at Mount Vernon. The mansion was greatly enlarged, the noble piazza that adorns the river-front, the observatory and cupola upon the roof, and the kitchen and laundry, and connecting colonnades, as they now appear, were erected. In all these improvements, Washington had an eye to utility and durability. The out-buildings were made of the most substantial materials, and the floors of the piazza and the covered colonnades were paved with cut stone In this connection, the following letter to Mr. Rumney, of Alexandria (formerly an aid to General Lee), already alluded to in a note on page 171, will be found very interesting:

"General Washington presents his compliments to Mr. Rumney—would esteem it as a particular favor if Mr. Rumney would make the following enquiries as soon as convenient, after his arrival in England; and communicate the result of them by the Packet, or any other safe and expeditious conveyance to this country.

"First. The terms upon which the best kind of Whitehaven Flag stone—black & white in equal quantities—could be delivered at the Port of Alexandria by the superficial foot, workmanship, freight & every other incidental charge included.——The stone to be 2½ Inches, or thereabouts, thick; and exactly a foot square—each kind. To have a rich polished face, and good joints so as that a neat floor may be made therewith.

"2nd. Upon what terms the common Irish Marble (black & white if to be had) —same dimensions, could be delivered as above.

"3rd. As the General has been informed of a very cheap Kind of Marble, good in quality at or in the neighborhood of Ostend, he would thank Mr. Rumney, if it should fall in his way, to institute an enquiry into this also.

"On the Report of Mr. Rumney, the General will take his ultimate determination; for which reason he prays him to be precise and exact. The Piazza or Colonade for which this is wanted as a floor is ninety-two feet, eight inches, by twelve feet eight inches within the margin, or border that surrounds it. Over and above the quantity here mentioned, if the above Flags are cheap—or a cheaper kind of hard Stone could be had, he would get as much as would lay floors in the Circular Colonades, or covered ways at the wings of the House—each of which at the outer curve, is 38 feet in length by 7 feet 2 Inches in breadth, within the margin or border as aforesaid.

"The General being in want of a House Joiner & Bricklayer who understand their respective trades perfectly, would thank Mr. Rumney for enquring into the terms upon which such workmen might be Engaged for two or three years; (the time of service, to commence upon the Ship's arrival at Alexandria,) a shorter term than *two* years would not answer, because foreigners generally have a seasoning; which with other interruptions too frequently waste the greater part of the first year— more to the disadvantage of the employer than the Employed.—Bed board & Tools to be found by the former, clothing by the latter.

"If two men of the above Trades and of orderly and quiet deportment could be obtained for twenty-five or even thirty pounds sterling, per annum each (estimating

of the chase, visited his friends, and received and entertained the numerous guests who crowded to his hospitable mansion. Indeed, in the retirement at Mount Vernon, from '83 to '89, were probably passed the very happiest days of this great man's life. Glorying in the emancipation of his country from foreign thraldom; surrounded by many and dear friends; hailed with love and gratitude by his countrymen wherever he appeared among them; receiving tokens of esteem and admiration from the good, the gifted, and the great, of the most enlightened nations in the civilized world; engaged in the pursuits of agriculture—pursuits that were always most congenial to his tastes and wishes—amid so many blessings we may well believe that in the retirement at Mount Vernon Washington was happy.

On leaving Annapolis the general was accompanied by two of the officers of his former staff, Colonels Humphreys* and Smith,† who were a long time at

dollars at 4|6) the General, rather than sustain the loss of Time necessary for communication would be obliged to Mr. Rumney for entering into proper obligatory articles of agreement on his behalf with them and sending them by the first vessel bound to this Port. "GEO. WASHINGTON.

"Mount Vernon, July 5, 1784."

* David Humphreys was distinguished as a poet and soldier. He was born at Derby, Connecticut, in 1753, and was graduated at Yale college in 1771, when he went to reside with Colonel Phillipse, of Phillipse's manor, in Westchester county, New York, as tutor. He joined the continental army, and in 1778 became one of General Putnam's aids, with the rank of major. In 1780 he entered the military family of Washington, as aid to the chief, and remained in that position until the close of the war. For his valor at Yorktown, Congress presented him with a sword. In 1784 he accompanied Jefferson to Paris, as secretary of legation. In 1786 he was a member of the Connecticut legislature, and at that time he was associated with Joel Barlow in a literary enterprise. He was minister to Portugal in 1788. In 1790, he resided at Mount Vernon by invitation of Washington, and there wrote his life of Putnam. He was appointed minister to Spain in 1794. He returned to America with a wealthy wife in 1801, and devoted the remainder of his life to agriculture. He died suddenly in 1812.

† Lieutenant-Colonel William S. Smith, of New York, had been a very active

Mount Vernon, engaged in arranging the vast mass of papers and documents that had accumulated during the War for Independence. Humphreys was a man of letters and a poet, and, together with Colonel Smith, served in the staff of the commander-in-chief on some of the most important occasions of the Revolutionary war.

At a short distance from the mansion-house, in a pleasant and sheltered situation, rose the homestead of Bishop, the old body-servant. Thomas Bishop, born in England, attended General Braddock to the Continent during the seven years' war, and afterwards embarked with that brave and unfortunate commander for America, in 1775.

On the morning of the ninth of July, the day of the memorable battle of the Monongahela, Bishop was present when Colonel Washington urged upon the English general for the last time the propriety of permitting him (the colonel) to advance with the Virginia woodsmen and a band of friendly Indians, and open the way to Fort Duquesne. Braddock treated the proposal with scorn; but, turning to his faithful follower, observed: "Bishop, this young man is determined to go into action to-day, although he is really too much weakened by illness for any such purpose. Have an eye to him, and render him any assistance that may be necessary." Bishop had only time to reply, "Your honor's orders shall be obeyed,"

young officer during the war. He was acting commissary-general of prisoners for a while, and at the close of hostilities, he was an associate commissioner with Egbert Benson and Daniel Parker, to inspect and superintend the embarkation of the persons and property of the loyalists, who left the city when it was evacuated by the British army. He was at Mount Vernon for several months, assisting Colonel Humphreys in the arduous task of arranging Washington's military papers, and until the close of his life, the chief regarded him with the warmth of true friendship.

when the troops were in motion and the action soon after commenced.*

Sixty-four British officers were killed or wounded, and Washington was the only mounted officer on the field. His horse being shot, Bishop was promptly at hand to offer him a second; and so exhausted was the youthful hero from his previous illness and his great exertions in the battle, that he was with difficulty extricated from his dying charger, and was actually lifted by the strong arms of Bishop into the saddle of the second horse.

It was at this period of the combat that, in the glimpses of the smoke, the gallant colonel was seen bravely dashing amid the ranks of death, and calling on the colonial woodsmen, who alone maintained the fight, "Hold your ground, my brave fellows, and draw your sights for the honor of old Virginia!" It was at this period, too, of the battle, that the famed Indian commander, pointing to Washington, cried to his warriors: "Fire at him no more; see ye not that the Great Spirit protects that chief; he can not die in battle."†

His second horse having fallen, the provincial colonel made his way to the spot where the commanding-general, though mortally stricken, raging like a wounded lion, and yet breathing defiance to the foe, was supported in the arms of Bishop. Braddock grasped the hand of Washington, exclaiming, "Oh, my dear colonel, had I been governed by your advice, we never should have come to this!" When he found his last moments approaching, the British general called his faithful and long-tried follower and friend to his side, and said, "Bishop,

---

* See page 158.

† See chapter xi., page 300.

you are getting too old for war; I advise you to remain in America and go into the service of Colonel Washington. Be but as faithful to him as you have been to me, and rely upon it the remainder of your days will be prosperous and happy."*

Bishop took the advice of his old master, and at the close of the campaign returned with the colonel to Mount Vernon. As body-servant, Bishop attended Colonel Washington at the time of his marriage,† and was installed as chief of the stables and the equipage in Williamsburg, in the bright and palmy days of that ancient capital. Finally, the old body-servant settled on the banks of the Potomac, married, and was made overseer of one of the farms of the Mount Vernon estate.

At the commencement of the Revolutionary war Bishop was considered as too old for active service, and was left in charge of the home establishment, where the veteran soldier's rigid discipline and strict attention to everything committed to his care caused affairs immediately relating to the mansion-house to be kept in first-rate order. Upon the general's return after the peace of 1783, the ancient body-servant had passed fourscore, had been relieved from all active service, and, having lost his wife, he, with his daughter and only child, was settled down in a comfortable homestead that had been built expressly as an asylum for his age.

* Braddock was borne from the field, and carried away by his soldiers in their flight toward Fort Cumberland. The battle was fought on the ninth of July, 1755, and on the night of the fourteenth Braddock expired. At a little past midnight Washington read the impressive funeral services of the Anglican church, over his body, and it was buried in the road, so that the Indians might not discover and desecrate his grave. The place of his burial may now be seen between the fifty-third and fifty-fourth milestone, on the road from Cumberland, westward.

† See sketch of *Martha Washington*.

Although very infirm, yet, when the bright skies and balmy breath of spring renovated all nature, the veteran soldier and faithful follower of two masters would grasp his staff and wend his way to a spot by which he knew the general would pass in taking his morning ride. As Washington approached, the veteran, by aid of his staff, would draw himself up to his full height, and with a right soldierly air uncover. A few silver locks were scattered about his temples, his visage was deeply furrowed by the hand of time, while his bent and shrunken frame was but the shadow of a form once so tall and manly. The general would rein up his horse and kindly inquire, "How are you, old man; I am glad to see you abroad; is there anything you want?" The veteran would reply: "Good morning to your honor; I am proud and happy to see your honor looking so brave and hearty. I thank God I am as well as can be expected at my years. What can I want while in your honor's service? Whenever the choicest meats are killed for you honor's own table, the good lady will send to old Bishop a part. God bless your honor, the madam, and all your good family!" Washington would continue his morning ride, while the old body-servant, made happy by the interview, grasped his staff and strode manfully away to his comfortable home.

Of the two former aids-de-camp, now secretaries, in their hours of relaxation from business, Humphreys was in the habit of strolling to unfrequented places, there to recite his verses to the echoes. Smith, too, would take the air after the labors of the writing-desk.

One evening Colonel Smith in his rambles came suddenly upon the homestead of the old body-servant, whose daughter was milking at a short distance from the house. She was a slightly-built girl, and, in endeavoring to raise the pail, found it too much for her strength. Colonel Smith gallantly stepped forward, and offered his services, saying, "Do, miss, permit my strong arms to assist you." Now, the veteran's daughter had often heard from her father the most awful tales of those sad fellows, the young, and particularly the handsome British officers, and how their attentions to a maiden must inevitably result in her ruin. Filled with these ideas, Miss Bishop did not draw any line of distinction between British and American officers, and Smith, being a peculiarly fine handsome fellow, the milkmaid threw down her pail and ran screaming to the house. The colonel followed, making every possible apology, when suddenly he was brought up all standing by the appearance of the veteran, who stood, in all his terrors, at the door of his domicil. The affrighted girl ran into her father's arms, while the old body-servant rated the colonel in no measured terms upon the enormity of the attempt to insult his child. Poor Smith, well bespattered by the contents of the milk-pail, in vain endeavored to excuse himself to the enraged veteran, who declared that he would carry the affair up to his honor, aye, and to the madam, too. At the mention of the latter personage the unfortunate colonel felt something like an ague-chill pass over his frame. Smith in vain essayed to propitiate the old man by assuring him that the affair was one of the most common gallantry; that his object was to assist, and not to insult the damsel. Bishop replied, "Ah! Colonel Smith, I know what you dashing young officers are. I am an old soldier, and have seen some things in my long day. I am sure his honor, after my services, will not permit my child to be insulted; and, as to the madam, why the madam as good as brought up my girl." So saying, the old body-servant retired into his castle, and closed the door.

The unfortunate colonel wended his way to the mansion-house, aware of the scrape he had got into, and pondering as to the mode by which he might be able to get out of it. At length he bethought himself of Billy, the celebrated servant of the commander-in-chief during the whole of the War of the Revolution, and well known to all the officers of the headquarters.

A council of war was held, and Billy expressed great indignation that Bishop should attempt to carry a complaint against his friend, Colonel Smith, up to the general, and that it was perfectly monstrous that such a tale should reach the ears of the madam; "but," continued Billy, "that is a terrible old fellow, and he has been much spoiled on account of his services to the general in Braddock's war. He even says that we of the Revolutionary army are but half soldiers, compared with the soldiers which he served with, in the outlandish countries." Smith observed, "it is bad enough, Billy, for this story to get to the general's ears, but to those of the lady will never do; and then there's Humphreys, he will be out upon me in a d——d long poem, that will spread my misfortunes from Dan to Beersheba." At length the colonel determined, by the advice of his privy counsel, to despatch Billy as a special ambassador, to endeavor to propitiate the veteran, or, at any rate, to prevent his visit to the mansion-house.

Meantime the old body-servant was not idle. He ransacked a large worm-eaten trunk, and brought forth a coat that had not seen the light for many long years (it was of the cut and fashion of the days of George II); then a vest, and lastly a hat, Cumberland cocked, with a huge ribbon cockade, that had seen service in the seven years' war. His shoes underwent a polish, and were covered by large silver buckles. All these accoutrements being carefully dusted and brushed, the veteran flourished his staff and took up his line of march for the mansion-house.

Billy met the old soldier in full march, and a parley ensued. Billy harangued with great force upon the impropriety of the veteran's conduct in not receiving the colonel's apology; "for," continued the ambassador, "my friend Colonel Smith is both an officer and a gentleman; and then, old man, you have no business to have such a handsome daughter (a grim smile passing over the veteran's countenance at this compliment to the beauty of his child), for you know young fellows will be young fellows." He continued by saying, it was not to be thought of that any such matter should reach the madam's ears, and concluded by recommending to the veteran to drop the affair and return to his home.

The old body-servant, fully accoutred for his expedition, had cooled off a little during his march. A soldierly respect for an officer of Colonel Smith's rank and standing, and a fear that he might carry the matter a little too far, determined him to accept the colonel's assurance that there could be no harm where "no harm was intended," came to the right-about and retraced his steps to his home.

The ambassador returned to the anxious colonel, and informed him that he had met the old fellow, *en grand costume*, and in full march for the mansion-house, but that by a powerful display of eloquence he had brought him to a halt, and induced him to listen to reason, and drop the affair altogether. The ready guinea was quickly in the ambassador's pouch, while the gallant colonel, happy in his escape from what might have resulted in a very unpleasant affair, was careful to give the homestead of the old body-servant a good wide berth in all future rambles.

The pleasurable routine of Washington's life, in his retirement, was a little varied by his call to the convention of 1787;* but in 1788, when the constitution became ratified by the states,† letters, addresses, and memorials

* Before the close of the Revolution, many sagacious minds perceived the utter incompetency of the federal government, under the provisions of the *Articles of Confederation*, to perform the proper functions of supreme power. The doctrine of state rights was strongly impressed upon the minds of the people, and there was a growing jealousy of the assumptions of Congress, even when that body exercised its legitimate functions. To the appreciation of true statesmen such as Washington, Hamilton, Madison, Jay, and others, there appeared a necessity for a greater centralization of power, for to a great extent the people had lost all regard for the authority of Congress. The commercial and monetary affairs of the country were wretchedly deranged, and many felt serious apprehensions of a total failure of the republican scheme. Hamilton, at an early period, suggested a convention of states to consider and correct the errors of the federal system as it then existed; and finally, at the suggestion of Washington, a convention was called for the purpose, at Annapolis, in Maryland. The delegates assembled in September, 1786. Only five states were represented. These recommended the holding of another convention in May following. At that time delegates from all the states, except New Hampshire and Rhode Island, appeared. Washington was a delegate from Virginia, and was chosen to preside. Able statesmen were his associates; and on the twelfth of September, 1787, the present Constitution of the United States (except a few subsequent amendments) was adopted.

† The federal Constitution was submitted to the people for their approval or rejection. It found many able opposers. State rights, sectional interests, radical democracy, had all numerous friends, and these stood firmly in the opposition. Among its ablest supporters with pen and tongue, was Alexander Hamilton, who gave to the world most able papers on government, to which were added some by Madison and Jay. These, in collected form, bear the title of *The Federalist*. Very soon eleven of the thirteen states ratified the Constitution. The Congress then fixed the time for the new government to go into operation.

from his compatriots and old companions-in-arms poured in from all parts of the country, all praying him who had been "first in war" to become "first in peace" as the chief magistrate of the new government. These testimonials of affection made deep impression upon the retired general, as they showed him that he stood "first in the hearts of his countrymen."

In April, 1789, the doors of Mount Vernon opened to receive, and Washington hastened to embrace, the venerable Charles Thomson, the secretary to the continental Congress during fifteen consecutive years. He came charged with the important duty of announcing to the retired general his unanimous election to the office of president of the United States. The tall attenuated form, the simple yet dignified manners of Secretary Thomson, made him a most favored guest at a board where had been welcomed many of the wise, the good, the brave, and renowned.*

* On the sixth of April, 1789, John Langdon, president of the United States senate, *pro tempore*, wrote an official letter to Washington, informing him that he had been chosen first president of the United States, with John Adams as vice-president; and Charles Thomson, the secretary of the continental Congress, immediately proceeded to Mount Vernon to bear to the new officer the official announcement of his election. The president made immediate preparations for his journey to the seat of government, then at New York. He left Mount Vernon on the sixteenth, arrived at New York on the twenty-third, and there, on the thirtieth of the month, in the presence of a vast concourse of people, he took the solemn oath of office. The old continental Congress had expired on the fourth of March previously, and the federal Constitution had become the organic law of the republic.

Mr. Secretary Thomson was a native of Ireland, where he was born in 1730. He settled as a teacher in Philadelphia, and was honored with the friendship of Dr. Franklin. When the continental Congress convened in that city, in 1774, he had just married a young woman of fortune. He was chosen the secretary of that body, and held the office fifteen consecutive years. He died at Lower Merion, Montgomery country, Pennsylvania, on the sixteenth of August, 1824, at the age of ninety-four years.

The unanimous election of Washington to the chief magistracy of a new empire by a people who had hungered for an opportunity of elevating the man of their hearts to the highest gift in their power to bestow, called forth from the chief acknowledgments of profound gratitude. When he departed for the seat of the federal government, he turned a last fond lingering look upon his retired home, where he had passed so many peaceful and happy days; upon his extensive circle of friends, to whom he was attached by many and most endearing associations; upon his improvements, which he had so much delighted to rear, and which had grown up to useful and ornamental maturity under his fostering hand; he bade adieu to them all, and hastened to obey the call of his country

CHAPTER XIX.

WASHINGTON AS A SPORTSMAN.

WASHINGTON FOND OF THE CHASE—HE WAS NOT A MERE SHOOTER AND FISHERMAN—SITUATION AND CHARACTER OF HIS KENNEL—SELECTION OF HIS DOGS—HIS SPORTING FRIENDS—HIS COSTUME WHEN ENGAGED IN THE CHASE—PRESENT OF HOUNDS FROM LAFAYETTE—THEIR SAVAGE NATURE—WASHINGTON ON HORSEBACK—HIS FAVORITE HORSE FOR THE CHASE—HIS DARING—THE FAMOUS BLACK FOX—ITS SUPPOSED INFERNAL RELATIONSHIP—ROBBERY BY ONE OF THE FRENCH DOGS—WASHINGTON'S LAST HUNT—HE GIVES AWAY HIS DOGS—DEER PARK—DISPERSION OF THE DEER—POACHERS—CONSENT TO HUNT—AUTHOR OF THESE RECOLLECTIONS ON A HUNT FOR A BUCK—HIS SUCCESS—THE VENISON DINNER AT MOUNT VERNON—ANTLERS OF THE WASHINGTON STAG.

The time which Colonel Washington could spare from his building and agricultural improvements between the years 1759 and 1774, was considerably devoted to the pleasures of the chase. We have neither knowledge nor tradition of his having ever been a shooter or a fisherman: fox-hunting being of a bold and animating character, suited well with the temperament of the "lusty prime" of his age, and peculiarly well accorded with his fondness and predisposition for equestrian exercises.

His kennel was situated about a hundred yards south of the family vault in which at present repose his venerated remains.* The building was a rude structure, but afforded comfortable quarters for the hounds; with a

---

* This was first published in *The American Turf Register and Sporting Magazine*, on the twenty-ninth of September, 1829. At that time the remains of Washington were in the old vault, upon the summit of the river bank, a few rods from the lawn and about half way between the mansion and the tomb wherein they now repose. These remains were re-entombed in the autumn of 1837.

large enclosure paled in, having in the midst a spring of running water. The pack was very numerous and select, the colonel visiting and inspecting his kennel morning and evening, after the same manner as he did his stables.* It was his pride (and a proof of his skill in hunting) to have his pack so critically drafted, as to speed and bottom, that in running, if one leading dog should lose the scent, another was at hand immediately to recover it, and thus when in full cry, to use a racing phrase, you might cover the pack with a blanket.

During the season, Mount Vernon had many sporting guests from the neighborhood, from Maryland, and elsewhere. Their visits were not of days, but weeks; and they were entertained in the good old style of Virginia's ancient hospitality. Washington, always superbly mounted, in true sporting costume, of blue coat, scarlet waistcoat, buckskin breeches, top boots, velvet cap, and whip with long thong, took the field at daybreak, with his huntsman, Will Lee, his friends and neighbors; and none rode more gallantly in the chase, nor with voice more cheerily awakened echo in the woodland, than *he* who was afterwards destined, by voice and example, to cheer his countrymen in their glorious struggle for independence and empire. Such was the hunting establishment at Mount Vernon prior to the Revolution.

We come now to events of our own times. After the

---

* Washington kept a register of his horses and his hounds, in which might be found the names, ages, and marks of each; and with these, his companions of the chase, he was as punctual in his attentions as to any other business of his life. Among the names of his horses were those of Chinkling, Valiant, Ajax, Magnolia, Blueskin, et cetera. Magnolia was a full-blooded Arabian, and was used for the saddle upon the road. Among the names of his hounds were Vulcan, Ringwood, Singer, Truelove, Music, Sweetlips, Forrester, Rockwood, et cetera.

peace of 1783, the hunting establishment, which had gone down during the war, was renewed by the arrival of a pack of French hounds, sent out by the Marquis de Lafayette. These *chiens de chasse* were of great size —

> "Bred out of the Spartan kind, so flewed, so sanded,
> With ears that swept away the morning dew, dewlan'd
> Like the Salonian bulls, matched in mouth like bells"—

the bells of Moscow, and great Tom of Lincoln, we should say, and, from their strength, were fitted, not only to pull down the stately stag, but in combat to encounter the wolf or boar, or even to grapple with the lordly lion. These hounds, from their fierce dispositions, were generally kept confined, and wo to the stranger who might be passing their kennel after night-fall, should the gates be unclosed. His fate would be melancholy, unless he could climb some friendly tree, or the voice or the whip of the huntsman came "speedily to the rescue." The huntsman always presided at their meals, and it was only by the liberal application of the whip-thong that anything like order could be preserved among these savages of the chase.

The habit was to hunt three times a week, weather permitting; breakfast was served, on these mornings, at candle-light, the general always breaking his fast with an Indian-corn cake and a bowl of milk; and, ere the cock had "done salutation to the morn," the whole cavalcade would often have left the house, and the fox be frequently unkennelled before sunrise. Those who have seen *Washington on horseback* will admit that he was one of the most accomplished of cavaliers in the true sense and perfection of the character. He rode, as he did everything else, with ease, elegance, and with power.

The vicious propensities of horses were of no moment to this skilful and daring rider! He always said that he required but one good quality in a horse, *to go along*, and ridiculed the idea of its being even possible that he should be unhorsed, provided the animal kept on his legs. Indeed the perfect and sinewy frame of the admirable man gave him such a surpassing grip with his knees, that a horse might as soon disencumber itself of the saddle as of such a rider.

The general usually rode in the chase a horse called *Blueskin*, of a dark iron-gray color, approaching to blue This was a fine but fiery animal, and of great endurance in a long run. Will, the huntsman, better known in Revolutionary lore as Billy, rode a horse called *Chinkling*, a surprising leaper, and made very much like its rider, low, but sturdy, and of great bone and muscle. Will had but one order, which was to keep with the hounds; and, mounted on *Chinkling*, a French horn at his back, throwing himself almost at length on the animal, with his spur in flank, this fearless horseman would rush, at full speed, through brake or tangled wood, in a style at which modern huntsmen would stand aghast. There were roads cut through the woods in various directions, by which aged and timid hunters and *ladies* could enjoy the exhilirating cry, without risk of life or limb; but Washington rode gaily up to his dogs, through all the difficulties and dangers of the ground on which he hunted, nor spared his generous steed, as the distended nostrils of *Blueskin* often would show. He was always in at the death, and yielded to no man the honor of the brush.

The foxes hunted fifty years ago were gray foxes, with one exception; this was a famous black fox, which, differing from his brethren of "orders gray," would flourish his brush, set his pursuers at defiance, and go from ten to twenty miles an end, distancing both dogs and men; and what was truly remarkable, would return to his place of starting on the same night, so as always to be found there the ensuing morning. After seven or eight severe runs, without success, Billy recommended that the black reynard should be let alone, giving it as his opinion, that he was very near akin to another sable character, inhabiting a lower region, and as remarkable for his wiles. The advice was adopted from necessity, and ever thereafter, in throwing off the hounds, care was taken to avoid the haunt of the unconquerable *black fox.**

The chase ended, the party would return to the mansion-house, where, at the well-spread board, and with cheerful glass, the feats of the leading dog, the most gallant horse, or the boldest rider, together with the prowess of the famed black fox, were all discussed, while Washington, never permitting even his pleasures to infringe upon the order and regularity of his habits, would, after a few glasses of Madeira, retire to his bed supperless at nine o'clock. He always took a little tea and toast between six and seven in the evening.

Of the French hounds, there was one named *Vulcan*, and we bear him the better in reminiscence, from having often bestrid his ample back in the days of our juvenility. It happened that upon a large company sitting down to

---

* The red fox is supposed to have been imported from England, to the eastern shore of Maryland, by a Mr. Smith, and to have emigrated across the ice to Virginia, in the hard winter of 1779-80, when the Chesapeake was frozen over.—*Note by the Author.*

dinner at Mount Vernon one day, the lady of the mansion (my grandmother) discovered that the ham, the pride of every Virginia housewife's table, was missing from its accustomed post of honor. Upon questioning Frank, the butler, this portly, and at the same time the most polite and accomplished of all butlers, observed that a ham, yes, a very fine ham, had been prepared, agreeably to the Madam's orders, but lo and behold! who should come into the kitchen, while the savory ham was smoking in its dish, but old *Vulcan*, the hound, and without more ado fastened his fangs into it; and although they of the kitchen had stood to such arms as they could get, and had fought the old spoiler desperately, yet *Vulcan* had finally triumphed, and bore off the prize, ay, "cleanly, under the keeper's nose." The lady by no means relished the loss of a dish which formed the pride of her table, and uttered some remarks by no means favorable to old *Vulcan*, or indeed to dogs in general, while the chief, having heard the story, communicated it to his guests, and, with them, laughed heartily at the exploit of the *stag-hound*.

Washington's last hunt with his hounds, was in 1785. His private affairs and public business required too much of his time to allow him to indulge in field sports. His fondness for agricultural improvements, and the number of visiters that crowded Mount Vernon, induced him to break up his kennels, to give away his hounds, and to bid a final adieu to the pleasures of the chase. He then formed a deer-park below the mansion-house, extending to the river, and enclosing by a high paling about a hundred acres of land. The park was at first stocked with only the native deer, to which was afterwards added the

English fallow deer, from the park of Governor Ogle, of Maryland.*

The stock of deer increased very rapidly, yet, strange to say, although herding together, there never was perceptible the slightest admixture of the two races.

On the decay of the park paling, and the dispersion of the deer over the estate, as many as fifteen or twenty were often to be seen in a herd.

The general was extremely tenacious of his game, and would suffer none to be killed, till, being convinced that the poachers were abroad, that the larder of an extensive hotel in a neighboring town was abundantly supplied with plump haunches from the Mount Vernon stock, and indeed that every one seemed to be enjoying his venison but himself, he at length consented that "a stag should die."

One morning I was summoned to receive his orders for hunting. They were given as follows: "Recollect, sir, that you are to fire with ball, to use no *hounds*, and on no account to kill any but an old buck." Charmed with a permission so long coveted, and at last obtained, we prepared for the field. Determined to make a sure shot, we discarded the rifle in favor of an old British musket, of the fashion and time of George II.—a heavy, black, ill-favored looking piece, but capable of carrying two balls, each of an ounce weight, and famed for hitting hard behind as well as before. Thus equipped, and with a goodly array of drivers, and dogs of various sorts, we repaired to the haunt of a celebrated old buck, considered as the patriarch of the herd.

* Samuel Ogle was governor of Maryland at three different times, namely, in 1732, 1737, and 1747.

"Rousing him up from his lair," the woods echoed with the shouts of the huntsmen and the cries of the dogs, while the noble buck, crashing through the undergrowth, seemed to bid defiance to his pursuers. The loud report of the musket was now added to the uproar in the wood, and, it being evident from hunter's signs that the game was hit, it only remained to mount and pursue.

The "stricken deer" always seeks the water as a refuge from the dogs: in this instance, a *melee* of hunters, horses, dogs, and deer rushed into the waters of the Potomac at the same time, the huntsmen laying lustily about them to prevent the dogs from breaking up the wounded stag, that, after a gallant struggle, yielded up his life, and was carried in triumph to the mansion-house, there to await the master's inspection.

Punctual as the hand of the clock, at a quarter to three the general arrived from his morning ride. Upon his dismounting, we announced that a fine buck had been shot. "Ah, well!" he replied, "let's see," and strode along to the Locust grove, to which we led the way — ay, and manly was that stride, although he was then in the sixty-eighth year of his age. He examined the deer, that had been triced up to a tree, and observing the frosted front of the antlered monarch of the herd, he became convinced that his orders had been obeyed to the very letter; he gave a nod of approbation, and retired to his room to dress, as was his custom, before the second bell for dinner.

The carcass of the Washington Stag, after being trimmed according to hunter's fashion — that is, the neck, hocks, and offal parts removed — weighed one hundred and forty-six pounds.

The next day, several guests having assembled, the

haunch was served up in the family dining-room at Mount Vernon; and of the venison it may of a truth be said that —

"Finer or fatter
Was ne'er carved at a board, or smoked on a platter."

We have killed many a brave deer since the days of 1799, but none have left an impression on the memory or the heart like that of the Washington Stag, that was killed by Washington's special order, that was served at his board, and on which he fed in the last, the very last year of his glorious life.*

* The antlers of this famous buck may still be seen at Arlington House, where they grace the great hall, and are labelled, in the handwriting of the sportsman who killed the owner, "The Washington Stag."

CHAPTER XX.

THE FIRST YEAR OF THE PRESIDENCY.

Inauguration of Washington — His Place of Residence in New York — His Family — The Guests at the President's House — His Levees — Mrs. Washington's Drawing-Rooms — An Accident — Washington an Early Riser — His Stables in New York and Philadelphia — The Theatre in New York — Severe Illness of the President — His Recovery — His Eastern Tour — Washington's Private Secretaries — Anecdote of Humphreys — The President changes his Residence — Departure from New York — Attempt to Leave Privately — A Public Demonstration — Progress to Philadelphia — Revolutionary Veterans — The President's Reception in Philadelphia — He Visits Mount Vernon.

On the 30th of April, 1789, the Constitutional Government of the United States began, by the inauguration of George Washington as President of the United States, in the city of New York.*

---

* The president, as we have observed in a note on page 382, left his home for New York on the sixteenth, and was everywhere received on his journey with the greatest demonstrations of affection. At Trenton, where he entered New Jersey, his reception was peculiar and gratifying. It was arranged entirely by the ladies, in which, as has been already observed, Mrs. Stockton, the widow of one of the signers of the Declaration of Independence, participated. Upon Trenton bridge they caused to be erected an arch, which they adorned with laurel leaves and flowers from the forests and their hot-houses, and the first spring contributions from their gardens. Upon the crown of the arch, in large letters, formed of leaves and flowers, were the words "December 26th, 1776;" and on the sweep beneath was the sentence, also formed of flowers, "The Defender of the Mothers will be the Protector of the Daughters." Beneath this arch the president elect was obliged to pass on entering Trenton. There he was met by a troop of females. On one side a row of little girls dressed in white, and each bearing a basket of flowers, were arranged; on the other side stood a row of young ladies similarly arrayed, and behind them were the married ladies. The moment Washington and his suite approached the arch, the little girls began to strew flowers in the road, and the whole company of the fair sang the following ode, written for the occasion by Governor Howell:—

394 RECOLLECTIONS OF WASHINGTON.

In the then limited extent and improvement of the city, there was some difficulty in selecting a mansion for the residence of the chief magistrate, and a household suitable to his rank and station. Osgood's house, a mansion of very moderate extent, was at length fixed upon, situated in Cherry street.* There the president became domiciled. His domestic family consisted of Mrs. Washington, the two adopted children,† Mr. Lear,‡ as principal secretary, Colonel Humphreys,§ with Messrs. Lewis and Nelson,‖ secretaries, and Major William Jackson aid-de-camp.¶

" Welcome, mighty chief, once more
Welcome to this grateful shore.
Now no mercenary foe
Aims again the fatal blow—
Aims at Thee the fatal blow.

" Virgins fair and matrons grave,
Those thy conquering arm did save,
Build for Thee triumphal bowers.
Strew, ye fair, his way with flowers—
Strew your Hero's way with flowers!"

Washington arrived in New York on the twenty-third of April, and took the oath of office, administered to him on the balcony of the old Federal Hall, in Wall street, by Robert R. Livingston, then chancellor of the state.

* This was No. 10 Cherry street, a few doors from Franklin square. When, afterward, the houses upon Franklin square, constituting a point at the junction of Pearl and Cherry streets, were removed, the former southern side of the mansion fronted on the square, and so remained until its demolition, in 1856. Views of this house, as it appeared just before its destruction, to make way for finer buildings, may be seen in Valentine's *Manual of the Common Council of New York*, 1857.

† Eleanor Parke and George Washington Parke Custis. Mr. Custis (the author of these *Recollections*) was then eight years of age.

‡ Tobias Lear, who was a member of Washington's family at the time of that great man's death.

§ Colonel David Humphreys, a sketch of whom is given elsewhere.

‖ The former was a nephew of Washington, and the latter was a son of Governor Nelson, of Virginia.

¶ Major Jackson was a great favorite in Washington's family. He and Mr. Lear always walked out with the president; and he accompanied Washington in his eastern and southern tours, made during his presidency. His wife, a daughter of

Persons visiting the house in Cherry street at this time of day, will wonder how a building so small could contain the many and mighty spirits that thronged its halls in olden days.* Congress, cabinet, all public functionaries in the commencement of the government, were selected from the very elite of the nation. Pure patriotism, commanding talent, eminent services, were the proud and indispensable requisites for official station in the first days of the republic. The first Congress was a most enlightened and dignified body. In the senate were several of the members of the Congress of 1776, and signers of the Declaration of Independence — Richard Henry Lee, who moved the Declaration, John Adams, who seconded it, with Sherman, Morris, Carroll, etc.†

The levees of the first president were attended by these illustrious men, and by many others of the patriots, statesmen, and soldiers, who could say of the Revolution, "*magna pars fui;*" while numbers of foreigners and strangers of distinction crowded to the seat of the general government, all anxious to witness the grand experiment that was to determine how much rational liberty mankind is capable of enjoying, without that liberty degenerating into licentiousness.

Mrs. Washington's drawing-rooms, on Friday nights,

Thomas Willing, of Philadelphia, survived him a great many years, and died recently, at the age of ninety-three years.

* This was first published in the *National Intelligencer*, on the twenty-third of February, 1847.

† Roger Sherman, of Connecticut, Robert Morris of Pennsylvania, and Charles Carroll, of Maryland were all signers of the Declaration of Independence, and were members of Congress during Washington's first administration. Carroll was the last survivor of the glorious band of fifty-six who signed that great manifesto. He died in 1832, in the ninety-sixth year of his age.

were attended by the grace and beauty of New York.* On one of these occasions an incident occurred which might have been attended by serious consequences. Owing to the lowness of the ceiling in the drawing-room, the ostrich feathers in the head-dress of Miss McIvers, a belle of New York, took fire from the chandelier, to the no small alarm of the company.† Major Jackson, aid-de-camp to the president, with great presence of mind, and equal gallantry, flew to the rescue of the lady, and, by clapping the burning plumes between his hands, extinguished the flame, and the drawing-room went on as usual.

Washington preserved the habit, as well in public as in private life, of rising at four o'clock, and retiring to bed at nine. On Saturdays he rested somewhat from his labors, by either riding into the country, attended by a groom, or with his family in his coach drawn by six horses.

Fond of horses, the stables of the president were always in the finest order, and his equipage excellent, both in taste and quality. Indeed, so long ago as the days of the vice-regal court of Lord Botetourt at Williamsburg, in Virginia, we find that there existed a rivalry between the equipages of Colonel Byrd, a mag-

* Washington's levees were held on Tuesday, and Mrs. Washington's drawing-rooms on Friday evenings. In his diary, in the autumn of 1789 and the winter of 1790, Washington often makes a simple record, thus, on Fridays—"The visiters this evening to Mrs. Washington were respectable, both of gentlemen and ladies." "The visiters to Mrs. Washington this afternoon were not numerous, but respectable."—"In the evening, a *great* number of ladies and many gentlemen visited Mrs. Washington."

† This was Miss Mary M'Ivers, who was married at about that time, to the late Edward Livingston, author of the Louisiana code, and American minister at the French court.

nate of the old *regime*,* and Colonel Washington, the grays against the bays. Bishop, the celebrated body-servant of Braddock, was the master of Washington's stables. And there were what was termed *muslin horses* in those old days. At cock-crow the stable-boys were at work; at sunrise Bishop stalked into the stables, a muslin handkerchief in his hand, which he applied to the coats of the animals, and, if the slightest stain was perceptible upon the muslin, up went the luckless wights of the stable-boys, and punishment was administered instanter; for to the veteran Bishop, bred amid the iron discipline of European armies, mercy for anything like a breach of duty was altogether out of the question.

The president's stables in Philadelphia were under the direction of German John, and the grooming of the white chargers will rather surprise the moderns. The night before the horses were expected to be ridden they were covered entirely over with a paste, of which whiting was the principal component part; then the animals were swathed in body-cloths, and left to sleep upon clean straw. In the morning the composition had become hard, was well rubbed in, and curried and brushed, which process gave to the coats a beautiful, glossy, and satin-like appearance. The hoofs were then blacked and polished, the mouths washed, teeth picked and cleaned; and, the leopard-skin housings being properly adjusted, the white chargers were led out for service. Such was the grooming of ancient times.†

---

* Colonel Byrd, of Westover, son of Colonel William Byrd, some of whose letters are printed in the Memoir of Mr. Custis, in another part of this volume.

† Washington's stables in Philadelphia, were upon a narrow lane, now called Miner street, below Sixth. There he had ten fine bays and two white chargers. Samuel Breck, Esq., now [July, 1859,] eighty-eight years of age, informed me a

It was while residing in Cherry street that the president was attacked by a severe illness, that required a surgical operation. He was attended by the elder and younger Drs. Bard. The elder being somewhat doubtful of his nerves, gave the knife to his son, bidding him "cut away—deeper, deeper still; don't be afraid; you see how well he bears it." Great anxiety was felt in New York at this time, as the president's case was considered extremely dangerous. Happily, the operation proved successful, and the patient's recovery removed all cause of alarm. During the illness a chain was stretched across the street, and the sidewalks were laid with straw.* Soon after his recovery, the president set out on his intended tour through the New England states.†

few weeks since, that when a young man, he often visited those stables, with his friends from other places, to show them Washington's horses. These constituted one of the most attractive "lions" of Philadelphia. He had frequently seen Washington and his family riding in his beautiful cream-colored English coach, with six of these shining bay horses before it.

* His disease was a malignant carbuncle, which, at one time, seemed to be incurable, as mortification was continually threatened. He was attended night and day by Doctor Samuel Bard, one of the most enlightened and skilful physicians and surgeons of that day. The painful tumor was upon his thigh, and was brought on by the excitements and labors which he had undergone since his inauguration. On the third of July he wrote to his friend, James M'Henry, of Baltimore, informing him that the tumor was likely to prove beneficial to his general health, and that then he was able to exercise in his coach. To Mr. M'Henry's suggestion that Dr. Craik should be sent for, Washington replied, that it would gratify him much to have his old friend with him, but, since he could not enjoy that benefit, he thought himself "fortunate in having fallen into such good hands," as Dr. Bard's. Doctor M'Vickar, in his life of Bard, alluding to this illness of the president, relates that, on one occasion, being left alone with him, the sufferer, looking the physician steadily in the face, desired his candid opinion as to the probable termination of his disease, adding, with perfect composure—"Do not flatter me with vain hopes; I am not afraid to die, and therefore can bear the worst." Dr. Bard expressed a hope, but acknowledged his apprehensions. Washington replied, with the same coolness, "Whether to-night or twenty years hence, makes no difference; I know that I am in the hands of a good Providence."

† This tour was commenced on Thursday, the fifteenth of October, 1789, and oc-

The president's mansion was so limited in accommodation that three of the secretaries were compelled to occupy one room — Humphreys, Lewis, and Nelson. Humphreys, aid-de-camp to the commander-in-chief at Yorktown, was a most estimable man, and at the same time a poet. About this period he was composing his "Widow of Malabar."* Lewis and Nelson, both young men, were content, after the labors of the day, to enjoy a good night's repose. But this was often denied them; for Humphreys, when in the vein, would rise from his bed at any hour, and, with stentorian voice, recite his verses. The young men, roused from their slumbers, and rubbing their eyes, beheld a great burly figure, "*en chemise,*" striding across the floor, reciting with great emphasis particular passages from his poem, and calling on his room-mates for their approbation. Having in this way for a considerable time "murdered the sleep" of his associates, Humphreys at length, wearied by his exertions, would sink upon his pillow in a kind of dreamy languor. So sadly were the young secretaries annoyed by the frequent outbursts of the poet's imagination, that it was remarked of them by their friends that, from 1789, to the end of their lives, neither Robert Lewis nor Thomas Nelson were ever known to evince the slightest taste for poetry.

cupied nearly a month. Major Jackson, Mr. Lear, and six servants composed his retinue. Chief Justice Jay, and Generals Hamilton and Knox, accompanied them some distance out of the city. He returned on the thirteenth of November. In his diary of that date he says —"Between two and three o'clock arrived at my house at New York, where I found Mrs. Washington and the rest of the family all well — and it being Mrs. Washington's night to receive visits, a pretty large company of ladies and gentlemen were present."

* *The Widow of Malabar, or the Tyranny of Custom*, is a tragedy, translated from the French of M. Le Mierre. It was brought out in Philadelphia, in May, 1790, by the old American company, in which Hallam, Wignell, Harper, Biddle, Martin,

The mansion in Cherry street proving so very inconvenient, induced the French ambassador to give up his establishment—McComb's new house in Broadway—for the accommodation of the president.* It was from this house in 1790 that Washington took his final departure from New York.† It was always his habit to endeavor, as much as possible, to avoid the manifestations of affection and gratitude that met him everywhere. He strove in vain; he was closely watched, and the people would have their way. He wished to have slipped off unobserved from New York, and thus steal a march upon his old companions-in-arms. But there were too many of the dear glorious old veterans of the Revolution at that time of day in and near New York to render such an escape even possible.

The baggage had all been packed up; the horses, carriages, and servants ordered to be over the ferry to Paulus's Hook, by daybreak, and nothing was wanting

---

Henry, Mrs. Henry, and Miss Tuke, were the performers. The prologue was written by John Trumbull, the author of *M'Fingall*, and was spoken by Mr. Hallam. The epilogue was written by Mr. Humphreys, and was spoken by Mrs. Henry.

* Washington, in his diary, under date of February first, 1790, says: "Agreed on Saturday last to take Mr. M'Combs's house, lately occupied by the minister of France, for one year from and after the first day of May next. . . This day sent my secretary to examine the rooms to see how my furniture could be adapted to the respective apartments." On Wednesday, the third, he records—"Visited the apartments in the house of Mr. M'Combs; made a disposition of the rooms; fixed on some furniture of the minister's (which was to be sold, and was well adapted to particular public rooms), and directed additional stables to be built." On the twenty-second he records—"Set seriously about removing my furniture to my new house. Two of the gentlemen of the family had their beds taken there, and will sleep there to-night." This house was on Broadway, west side, a little below Trinity church. It was subsequently occupied as a hotel, and was called the *Mansion-House*, from the fact that it had been the presidential mansion.

† The seat of government was removed to Philadelphia that year, and Congress assembled in that city, on the first Monday of December following.

for departure but the dawn. The lights were yet burning, when the president came into the room where his family were assembled, evidently much pleased in the belief that all was right, when, immediately under the windows, the band of the artillery struck up Washington's March. "There!" he exclaimed, "it's all over; we are found out. Well, well, they must have their own way." New York soon after appeared as if taken by storm; troops and persons of all descriptions hurrying down Broadway toward the place of embarcation, all anxious to take a last look on him whom so many could never expect to see again.

The embarcation was delayed until all the complimentary arrangements were completed. The president, after taking leave of many dear and cherished friends, and many an old companion-in-arms, stepped into the barge that was to convey him from New York for ever. The coxswain gave the word "let fall;" the spray from the oars sparkled in the morning sunbeams; the bowman shoved off from the pier, and, as the barge swung round to the tide, Washington, rose, uncovered, in the stern, to bid adieu to the masses assembled on the shore; he waved his hat, and, in a voice tremulous from emotion, pronounced farewell. It may be supposed that Major Bauman,[*] who commanded the artillery on this interesting occasion, who was first captain of Lamb's regiment, and a favorite officer of the War of the Revolution, would, when about to pay his last respects to his beloved commander, load his pieces with something more than mere

---

[*] Major Sebastian Bauman was a meritorious artillery officer during the war. He was at West Point at the time of Arnold's treason; was at the siege of Yorktown, and was postmaster at New York thirteen consecutive years, commencing in 1790, when Washington appointed him.

blank cartridges. But ah! the thunders of the cannon were completely hushed when the mighty shout of the people arose that responded to the farewell of Washington. Pure from the heart it came; right up to Heaven it went, to call down a blessing upon the Father of his Country.

The barge had scarcely gained the middle of the Hudson when trumpets were heard at Paulus's Hook,[*] where the governor[†] and the chivalry of Jersey were in waiting to welcome the chief to those well-remembered shores. Escorts of cavalry relieved each other throughout the whole route, up to the Pennsylvania line; every village, and even hamlet, turned out its population to greet with cordial welcome the man upon whom all eyes were fixed, and in whom all hearts rejoiced.

What must have been the recollections that crowded on the mind of Washington during this triumphant progress? Newark, Brunswick, Princeton, Trenton! What a contrast between the glorious burst of sunshine that now illumined and made glad everything around these memorable spots, with the gloomy and desolate remembrances of '76! *Then* his country's champion, with the wreck of a shattered host, was flying before a victorious and well-appointed foe, while all around him was shrouded in the darkness of despair; *now*, in his glorious progress over the self-same route, his firm footstep presses upon the soil of an infant empire, reposing in the joys of peace, independence, and happiness.

Among the many who swelled his triumph, the most endeared to the heart of the chief were the old associates

---

[*] Now Jersey City, opposite New York.
[†] Governor Richard Howell, of New Jersey.

THE FIRST YEAR OF THE PRESIDENCY. 403

of his toils, his fortunes, and his fame. Many of the Revolutionary veterans were living in 1790, and, by their presence, gave a dignified tone and character to all public assemblages; and when you saw a peculiarly fine-looking soldier in those old days, and would ask, "to what corps of the American army did you belong?" drawing himself up to his full height, with a martial air, and back of the hand thrown up to his forehead, the veteran would reply, "Life-Guard, your honor."*

And proud and happy were these veterans in again beholding their own good *Lady Washington*. Greatly was she beloved in the army. Her many intercessions with the chief for the pardon of offenders, and her kindness to the sick and wounded, caused her annual arrival in camp to be hailed as an event that would serve to dissipate the gloom of the winter-quarters.

Arrived at the line, the Jersey escort was relieved by the cavalry of Pennsylvania; and when near to Philadelphia, the president was met by Governor Mifflin† and a brilliant cortege of officers, and escorted by a squadron

---

* See chapter vii.

† Thomas Mifflin was born in Philadelphia, of Quaker parents, in the year 1774. He was trained in all the strictness of the sect. He prepared for mercantile life, and at quite an early age made a voyage to Europe. In 1772, he was elected a representative in the colonial assembly of his province, and in 1774, being recognised as a warm republican, he was chosen a representative in the continental Congress. The following year he entered the military service, accompanied Washington to Cambridge, as his aid, and in the spring of 1776, was commissioned a brigadier in the continental army. He was promoted to major-general in February, 1777, and continued in service until near the close of the war. In the autumn of 1783, he was chosen president of Congress, of which he was a member, and received from Washington his commission, when he resigned it. In 1785 he was a member of the Pennsylvania legislature, and in 1787 was a member of the federal convention. He was elected governor of Pennsylvania in 1790, and held that office nine years. He retired from it in December 1799, and expired at Lancaster the following month, at the age of fifty-six years.

of horse to the city. Conspicuous among the governor's suite, as well for his martial bearing as for the manly beauty of his person, was General Walter Stewart, a son of Erin, and a gallant and distinguished officer of the Pennsylvania line. To Stewart, as to Cadwalader, Washington was most warmly attached; indeed, those officers were among the very choicest of the contributions of Pennsylvania to the army and cause of Independence. Mifflin, small in stature, was active, alert, "every inch a soldier." He was a patriot of great influence in Pennsylvania in the "times that tried men's souls," and nobly did he exert that influence in raising troops, with which to reinforce the wreck of the grand army at the close of the campaign of '76.

Arrived within the city, the crowd became intense. The president left his carriage and mounted the white charger; and, with the governor on his right, proceeded to the City Tavern in South Second street,* where quarters were prepared for him, the light-infantry, after some time, having opened a passage for the carriages. At the City Tavern the president was received by the authorities of Philadelphia, who welcomed the chief magistrate to their city as to his home for the remainder of his presidential term. A group of old and long-tried friends were also in waiting. Foremost among these, and first to grasp the hand of Washington, was one who was al-

* The City Tavern was then, and had been since its erection in 1770, the leading public-house in Philadelphia. It was in South Second, near Walnut street. It was the gathering-place for the members of the continental Congress; and from it one of the most remarkable processions ever known, was seen on the fifth of September, 1774. John Adams, in his diary, says: "At ten, the delegates all met at the City Tavern, and walked to the Carpenter's Hall." Within an hour afterward, the first Congress was organized by the appointment of Peyton Randolph as president, and Charles Thomson as secretary.

ways nearest to his heart, a patriot and public benefactor, Robert Morris.

After remaining a short time in Philadelphia, the president speeded on his journey to that home where he ever found rest from his mighty labors, and enjoyed the sweets of rural and domestic happiness amid his farms and at his fireside of Mount Vernon.

Onward, still onward, flows the tide of time. The few who yet survive that remember the father of his country, are fast fading away. A little while, and their gray heads will all have dropped into the grave. May the reminiscences of one whom Washington adopted in infancy, cherished in youth, and who grew up to manhood under his parental care, continue to find favor with the American people!

CHAPTER XXI.

WASHINGTON'S HOME AND HOUSEHOLD.*

Order — Public Days while President — Washington's Aversion to Show and Pomp — Congressional and Diplomatic Dinners — Mrs. Washington's Evening Parties — The Cincinnati — Washington's Attention to Private Concerns — His Economy — His Endeavors to Avoid Personal Attentions — His Reception everywhere — Colonel Proctor — Colonel Rogers — General Charles Scott — An Irish Soldier at the Presidential Mansion — The Wrath of Washington — His Sense of Justice — First Interview with St. Clair after his Defeat — Washington's Steward — His Extravagance Reproved — The Chief Cook of the Presidential Mansion — His Character and Habits — The Coachman — The Coach in which the President made his Tour through the Southern States — The Stables in Philadelphia — The Chargers and the Coach-Horses — Almost a Catastrophe — Washington's Punctuality — Scenes on the National Anniversaries — Reflections.

Wherever Washington established a home—whether temporary or fixed, whether amid the log huts of Morristown or the Valley Forge, the presidential mansions in New York or Philadelphia, or his own beloved Mount Vernon—everywhere order, method, punctuality, economy reigned. His household, whether civil or military, was always upon a liberal scale, and was conducted with due regard to economy and usefulness.

The public days of the first president of the United States, were two in each week. On Tuesday from three to four o'clock, a levee was held for foreign ministers, strangers, and others, who could there be presented to

---

* The earlier portion of this chapter was written in July, 1827, and published in the *Alexandria Gazette*. The latter portion, commencing with a notice of Fraunces, the steward, was written and published in a Baltimore paper, in April, 1849.

the chief magistrate, without the formality of letters of introduction. It was, indeed more an arrangement of mutual convenience to the parties, than an affair of state; still it was objected to by some, at that time of day, as savoring rather of monarchal etiquette, than of the simpler customs which should distinguish a republic.— Who thinks so now? In truth, the first president was so occupied with the multiplicity of public concerns, attendant on the outset of a new government, that it became necessary to limit the time of visiters of mere ceremony, as much as possible; and the levee enabled all such personages to pay their respects within the moderate compass of an hour. The world is always governed in a considerable degree by form and usage. There never lived a man more averse to show and pomp than Washington. Plain in his habits, there was none to whom the details of official parade and ceremony could be less desirable; but correct in all his varied stations of life, the days of the first presidency will ever appear as among the most dignified and imposing in our country's annals.*

* In a letter to Doctor Stuart, Washington gives an account of the origin of his levees. "Before the custom was established," he says, "which now accommodates foreign characters, strangers, and others, who, from motives of curiosity, respect for the chief magistrate, or any other cause, are induced to call upon me, I was unable to attend to any business whatever; for gentlemen, consulting their own convenience rather than mine, were calling after the time I rose from breakfast, and often before, until I sat down to dinner. This, as I resolved not to neglect my public duties, reduced me to the choice of one of these alternatives: either to refuse visits altogether, or to appropriate a time for the reception of them. The first would, I knew, be disgusting to many; the latter, I expected, would undergo animadversions from those who would find fault with or without cause. To please everybody was impossible. I, therefore, adopted that line of conduct which combined public advantage with private convenience, and which, in my judgment, was unexceptionable in itself.... These visits are optional; they are made without invitation; between the hours of three and four every Tuesday, I am prepared to receive them. Gentlemen,

On Thursday the president gave his congressional and diplomatic dinners; and on Friday night, Mrs. Washington received company at what was then, and is still, called the drawing-room.*

often in great numbers, come and go, chat with each other, and act as they please. A porter shows them into the room, and they retire from it when they choose, without ceremony. At their first entrance they salute me, and I them, and as many as I can I talk to."

* See note on page 396. Mr. Wansey, an English traveller, who published an account of his *Excursion in the United States*, in 1795, says, that the democrats "objected to these drawing-rooms of Mrs. Washington, as tending to give her a super-eminency, and as introductory to the paraphernalia of courts." After quoting this, Dr. Griswold, in his *Republican Court*, remarks : "With what feelings the excellent woman regarded these democrats is shown by an anecdote of the same period. She was a severe disciplinarian, and Nelly Custis was not often permitted by her to be idle, or to follow her own caprices. The young girl was compelled to practise at the harpsichord four or five hours every day, and one morning, when she should have been playing, her grandmother entered the room, remarking that she had not heard the music, and also that she had observed some person going out, whose name she would very much like to know. Nelly was silent, and suddenly her attention was arrested by a blemish on the wall, which had been newly painted a delicate cream color. 'Ah! it was no federalist,' she exclaimed, looking at the spot just above a settee; "none but a filthy democrat would mark a place with his good-for-nothing head in that manner!"

Samuel York Atlee, Esq of Washington city, called the attention of Mr. Custis to this statement, when the venerable author of these *Recollections*, in a letter to that gentleman, on the 29th of December, 1854, remarked :—

"As to the story of Nelly Custis, my sister, practising very long and very unwillingly at the harpsichord, that part of the *tale of Wansey* is true. The poor girl would play and cry, and cry and play, for long hours, under the immediate eye of her grandmother, a rigid disciplinarian in all things.

"As to the absurd details that chronicle a saying of Mrs. Washington, touching *democrats*, no one, my dear sir, who knew that venerable lady, or who had ever heard of her, will believe a word of it. As the esteemed Lady Washington of the army of Independence, or the Lady-president of later days, Mrs. Washington was remarkable for her affable and dignified manners, and her courteous and kindly demeanor to all who approached her. Again, it is notorious that the politicians and statesmen of both parties were equally well and kindly received at the presidental mansion, where were welcomed Mr. Gallatin, Mr. Giles, and others of the chiefs of the democratic party, as well as Mr. Ames, Mr. Sedgwick, and others of the federalists.

"I can, with great truth, aver that, in the whole period of the first presidency, I

The president attended Mrs. Washington's evening parties, and paid his compliments to the circle of ladies, with that ease and elegance of manners for which he was remarkable. Among the most polished and well-bred gentlemen of his time, he was always particularly polite to ladies, even in the rugged scenes of war; and, in advanced age, many were the youthful swains who sighed for those gracious smiles with which the fair always received the attentions of this old beau of sixty-five.

An interesting class of persons were to be found at the side of the chief, on both his public and private days, who gave a feeling and character to every scene, and threw a charm over very many of the associations of more than thirty years ago. We mean the patriots and heroes of the Revolution. Among the finest recollections of those gone-by days, were of the anniversary of independence, when the gray-haired brethren of the Cincinnati assembled around their illustrious president-general, many of them seamed with scars, and all bearing the badge of the most *honored association upon earth.** These

never heard Mrs. Washington engage in any political controversy, or, indeed, *touch on the subject of politics at all.*

"Another remark, and I have done.

"The sitting parlor, into which all visiters were shown, was *papered,* not " painted;" but even had it been painted *à la Griswold,* things were better ordered in the house of the first president than that a gentleman-visiter, on leaning against the wainscot, should *leave his mark behind him.*"

* The society of the Cincinnati, composed of officers of the continental army, was organized in 1783. It was conceived by General Henry Knox, and when he communicated his ideas on the subject to Washington, he heartily approved of it. A committee, consisting of Generals Knox, Hand, and Huntington, and Captain Shaw, was appointed to put the propositions of several who were interested in the matter into a proper form. This committee reported at a meeting held at the quarters of the Baron Steuben, in Fishkill, Duchess county, nearly opposite Newburgh

venerated forms are now rarely to be seen, and soon will be seen no more; but like Ossian's shadowy heroes, they will appear through the mists of time, and their heroic lives and actions will inspire the bards of liberty, while liberty exists to bless mankind.

Notwithstanding his great occupation in public affairs, the first president by no means neglected his private concerns. He was in the habit of receiving regular and lengthy reports from the agents of his estates in Virginia, and directed by letter the management of those extensive establishments, with both consummate skill and success. He also inspected the weekly accounts and disbursements of his household in Philadelphia. Indeed, nothing seemed to escape the discerning mind of this wonderful man, "who had a time for all things, and did everything in its proper time," and in order.

(the head-quarters of the army were at the latter place), and the society was duly organized.

As it was composed of officers who had served their country, and were about to resume their several domestic employments, they called themselves the CINCINNATI, in honor of that illustrious Roman, *Lucius Quintus Cincinnatus*, whose noble example they were about to follow. The chief objects of the society were to promote cordial friendship and indissoluble union among themselves; to commemorate by frequent re-unions the great struggle they had just passed through; to use their best endeavors for the promotion of human liberty; to cherish good feeling between the respective states; and to extend benevolent aid to those of the society whose circumstances might require it. They formed a general society, and elected Washington the president, and Knox the secretary. The former held his office until his death, and was succeeded by General Alexander Hamilton. For greater convenience, state societies were organized, which were auxilliary to the parent society. To perpetuate the association, it was provided in the constitution, that the eldest male descendant of an original member should be entitled to membership on the decease of such member, "in failure thereof, the collateral branches, who may be judged worthy of becoming its supporters and members." They also adopted an *Order*, to be worn whenever the society should meet. For a full account of this society, with delineations of its *Order* and certificate of membership, see Lossing's *Field-Book of the Revolution*, i. 694.

General Washington was a practical economist: while he wished that his style of living should be fully in character with his exalted station, he was utterly averse to waste or extravagance of any sort. He frequently reprimanded his first steward, Fraunces (the same at whose hotel, in New York, the general-in-chief took leave of his brother-officers), for expenditures which appeared to be both unnecessary and extravagant.*

The first president took considerable pains, and used frequent stratagems, in endeavoring to avoid the numberless manifestations of attachment and respect which awaited him wherever he went. On his journeys, he charged the courier who would precede to engage accommodations at the inns, by no means to mention the coming of the president to other than the landlord. These precautions but rarely took effect; and often when the chief would suppose that he had stolen a march upon his old companions-in-arms and fellow-citizens, a horseman would be discovered dashing off at full speed,

---

* This steward was Samuel Fraunces (commonly called *Black Sam*, because of his dark complexion), who kept a public house on the corner of Pearl and Broad streets, New York. When Washington and his army occupied the city, in the summer of 1776, the chief resided at Richmond hill, a little out of town, afterward the seat of Aaron Burr. Fraunces's daughter was Washington's housekeeper, and she saved his life on one occasion, by exposing the intentions of Hickey, one of the Life-Guard (already mentioned), who was about to murder the general, by putting poison in a dish of peas prepared for his table. In 1785, when Washington wished a good cook at Mount Vernon, he applied to Fraunces to recommend one to him. At the time he was appointed steward, the following advertisement appeared:—

"Whereas, all servants and others appointed to procure provisions or supplies for the household of the PRESIDENT OF THE UNITED STATES, will be furnished with moneys for these purposes: *Notice is therefore given*, that no accounts, for the payment of which the public might be considered responsible, are to be opened with any of them.

"May 4, 1789.   SAMUEL FRAUNCES, *Steward to the Household.*"

and soon would be heard the trumpet of the volunteer-cavalry; and the village cannon, roused from its bed of neglect, where it had lain since warlike time, would summon all within reach of its echoes, to haste and bid welcome to the man who was "first in the hearts of his countrymen." Every village and little hamlet poured forth their population to greet the arrival of him who all delighted to honor. A kind of jubilee attended everywhere the progress of the patriot chief; for even the school children, with the curiosity incident to that age of innocence, would labor hard at the daily lesson, and leave the birch to hang idly on the wall, when to *see General Washington* was the expected holyday and reward; and many of these children, now the parents of children, while recalling the golden hours of infancy, will dwell with delight on the time when they were presented to the paternal chief, and recount how they heard the kindly sounds of his voice, felt the kindlier touch of his hand, or climbed his knee, to "share the good man's smile." Pure, happy, and honored recollections! they will descend like traditionary lore from generation to generation, venerable to all future time.

In the frequent trial of generalship between the chief and his ancient comrade-in-arms—the one seeking to avoid the testimonies of respect and attachment, which the other was equally studious to offer—the late Colonel Proctor,* a gallant and distinguished officer of artillery, was several times out-generalled—the president having reached the seat of government privately and unobserved. This roused the good old colonel, who declared, "He

---

* Colonel Thomas Proctor was in the battles of Brandywine, Germantown, and Monmouth, and was with Sullivan in his famous campaign against the Indians

shall not serve me so again; I'll warrant that my matches will be found lighted next time."

At the ferry of the Susquehannah, lived a veteran worthy of the Revolutionary day, where the president always took quarters on his journeys to and from his seat in Virginia. As the boat touched the shore, punctual to the moment and true to his post, stood Colonel Rogers, prepared to hand Mrs. Washington to his house. It was his claim, his privilege; like the claims at a coronation, it had been put in and allowed, and, verily, the veteran would not have yielded it to an emperor.*

The late General Charles Scott had a most inveterate habit of swearing; whether in private or public society, on his farm, or the field of battle, every other word was an oath. On the night preceding the battle of Princeton, Scott received an order from the commander-in-chief in person to defend a bridge to the last extremity. "To the last man, your excellency," replied Scott; and, forgetting the presence of his chief, accompanied the words with tremendous oaths. The general, as may be well supposed, had but little time, on that eventful evening, to notice or chide this want of decorum in his brave and well-tried soldier. After the war, a friend of the gallant general, anxious to reform his evil habits, asked him whether it was possible that the man so much beloved, the admired Washington, ever swore? Scott reflected for a moment, and then exclaimed, "Yes, once. It was at Monmouth, and on a day that would have made any

* At the Head of Elk, was a veteran named Tommy Giles (who had served Washington as an express rider), who always claimed, and received, the same honor.

man swear. Yes, sir, he swore on that day, till the leaves shook on the trees, charming, delightful. Never have I enjoyed such swearing before, or since. Sir, on that ever-memorable day he swore like an angel from Heaven."* The reformer abandoned the general in despair.

During the first presidency, the door of the mansion gathered but little rust on its hinges, while its latch was often lifted by the "broken soldier." Scarce a day passed that some veteran of the heroic time did not present himself at *headquarters*. The most tattered of these types of the days of privation and trial were "kindly bid to stay," were offered refreshment, and a glass of something to their old general's health, and then dismissed with lighter hearts, and heavier pouches. So passed the many, but not so with one of Erin's sons. It was about the hour of the Tuesday levee, when German John, the porter, opened to a hearty rap, expecting to admit at least a dignitary of the land, or foreign ambassador, when who should march into the hall but an old fellow, whose weather-beaten countenance, and well-worn apparel, showed him to be "no carpet knight." His introduction was short, but to the purpose. He had "come to headquarters to see his honor's excellence, God bless him."

---

* Charles Scott was a native of Cumberland county, in Virginia. He raised the first company of volunteers in that state, south of the James river, that actually entered into the continental service. So much was he appreciated, that, in 1777, the shire-town of Powhatan county was named in honor of him. Congress appointed him a brigadier in the continental army on the first of April, 1777. He served with distinction during the war, and at its termination he went to Kentucky. He settled in Woodford county, in that state, in 1785. He was with St. Clair at his defeat in 1791; and in 1794 he commanded a portion of Wayne's army at the battle of the Fallen Timber. He was governor of Kentucky from 1808 to 1812. He died on the twenty-second of October, 1820, aged seventy-four years.

He was an old soldier. In vain the porter assured him that it would be impossible to see the president at that time; a great company was momentarily expected—the hall was not a fitting place—would he go to the steward's apartment and get something to drink? To all which Pat replied, that he was in no hurry; that he would wait his honor's leisure; and, taking a chair, composed and made himself comfortable. And now passed ministers of state and foreign ministers, senators, judges; the great and the gay. Meanwhile, poor Pat stoutly maintained his post, gazing on the crowd, till the levee having ended, and the president about to retire to his library, he was informed that an obstinate Irishman had taken possession of the hall, and would be satisfied with nothing short of an interview with the president himself. The chief good-naturedly turned into the hall. So soon as the veteran saw his old commander, he roared out: "Long life to your honor's excellence," at the same time hurling his hat to the floor, and erecting himself with military precision. "Your honor will not remember me, though many is the day that I have marched under your orders, and many's the hard knocks I've had, too. I belonged to Wayne's brigade—*Mad Anthony*, the British called him, and, by the power, he was always mad enough for them. I was wounded in the battle of Germantown. Hurrah for America! and it does my heart good to see your honor; and how is the dear lady and all the little ones?" Here the usually grave temperament of Washington gave way, as, with a smile, he replied, he was well, as was Mrs. Washington, but they were unfortunate in having no children; then pressing a token into the soldier's hand, he ascended the staircase to his library. The Irishman followed with his eyes the retiring general, then looked again and again upon the token, which he had received from his *honor's own hand*, pouched it, recovered his hat, which he placed with military exactness a little on one side, then took up his line of march, and as he passed the porter, called out, "There now, you Hessian fellow, you see that his honor's excellence *has not forgotten an ould soldier.*"

These anecdotes, though simple in themselves, possess no common character. They are *Tales of the Days of Washington*, and tales of the heart. We proceed to something more grave.

The president was dining, when an officer arrived from the western army with despatches, his orders requiring that he should deliver them only to the commander-in-chief. The president retired, but soon reappeared, bearing in his hand an open letter. No change was perceptible in his countenance, as addressing the company he observed that the army of St. Clair had been surprised by the Indians, and was cut to pieces.* The company

---

* For several years after the peace of 1783, British agents on the northwestern frontier of the United States, continued to tamper with the Indians, and excite them to hostilities against the people of the new republic. The Indians showed growing discontent for some time, and finally, in the spring of 1790, these developed into open hostilities. All attempts at pacific arrangements were fruitless, and a strong force, under General Harmer, was sent into the Indian country, north of the present city of Cincinnati, to desolate the Indian villages and crops, in order to impress them with terror. This accomplished, he penetrated deeper, and in two battles (October 17 and 22, 1790), near the present village of Fort Wayne, in Indiana, he was defeated, with considerable loss. The following year, General Scott led some Kentucky volunteers against the Indians on the Wabash; and another marched thither in July following, under General Wilkinson. General St. Clair was then governor of the Northwestern territory, and in September, 1791, he marched against the Indians, at the head of two thousand men. While in camp, near the northern line of the present Darke country, in Ohio, on the fourth of November, he was surprised and defeated.

soon after retired. The president repaired to his private parlor, attended by Mr. Lear, his principal secretary, and a scene ensued of which our pen can give but a feeble description.

The chief paced the room in hurried strides. In his agony, he struck his clenched hands with fearful force against his forehead, and in a paroxysm of anguish exclaimed: "That brave army, so officered—Butler, Ferguson, Kirkwood—such officers are not to be replaced in a day—that brave army cut to pieces. O God!" Then turning to the secretary, who stood amazed at a spectacle so unique, as Washington in all his terrors, he continued: "It was here, sir, in this very room, that I conversed with St. Clair, on the very eve of his departure for the West. I remarked, I shall not interfere, general, with the orders of General Knox, and the war department; they are sufficiently comprehensive and judicious; but, as an old soldier, as one whose early life was particularly engaged in Indian warfare, I feel myself competent to counsel; General St. Clair, in three words, beware of surprise; trust not the Indian; leave not your arms for a moment; and when you halt for the night, be sure to fortify your camp—again and again, general, beware of surprise. And yet that brave army surprised, and cut to pieces, with Butler, and an host of others slain, O God!" Here the struggle ended, as with mighty efforts the hero chained down the rebellious giant of passion, and Washington became "himself again." In a subdued tone of voice, he proceeded: "But he shall have justice; yes, long, faithful, and meritorious services have their claims. I repeat—he shall have justice."

Thus concluded a scene as remarkable as rare. It

served to display this great man as nature had made him, with passions fierce and impetuous, which, like the tornado of the tropics, would burst for a while in awful grandeur, and then show, in higher relief, a serene and brilliant sky.*

* The venerable Richard Rush, who died at his beautiful seat of Sydenham, near Philadelphia, while these pages were in preparation, has given in a thin volume, entitled *Washington in Domestic Life*, the following account of this matter, which corresponds with that of Mr. Custis, written thirty years before. Mr. Custis doubtless also received his information from the lips of Mr. Lear:—

"An anecdote I derived from Colonel Lear," says Mr Rush, "shortly before his death in 1816, may here be related, showing the height to which Washington's passion would rise, yet be controlled. It belongs to his domestic life, with which I am dealing, having occurred under his own roof, while it marks public feeling the most intense, and points to the moral of his life. I give it in Colonel Lear's words, as near as I can, having made a note of them at the time.

"Toward the close of a winter's day in 1791, an officer in uniform was seen to dismount in front of the president's house, in Philadelphia, and giving the bridle to his servant, knocked at the door of the mansion. Learning from the porter that the president was at dinner, he said he was on public business and had despatches for the president. A servant was sent into the dining-room to give the information to Mr. Lear, who left the table and went into the hall, where the officer repeated what he had said. Mr. Lear replied that, as the president's secretary, he would take charge of the despatches and deliver them at the proper time. The officer made answer, that he had just arrived from the western army, and his orders were to deliver them with all promptitude, and to the president in person; but that he would wait his directions. Mr. Lear returned, and in a whisper imparted to the president what had passed. General Washington rose from the table, and went to the officer. He was back in a short time, made a word of apology for his absence, but no allusion to the cause of it. He had company that day. Everything went on as usual. Dinner over, the gentlemen passed to the drawing-room of Mrs. Washington, which was open in the evening. The general spoke courteously to every lady in the room, as was his custom. His hours were early, and by ten o'clock all the company had gone. Mrs. Washington and Mr. Lear remained. Soon Mrs. Washington left the room.

"The general now walked backward and forward for some minutes without speaking. Then he sat down on a sofa by the fire, telling Mr. Lear to sit down. To this moment there had been no change in his manner since his interruption at the table. Mr. Lear now perceived emotion. This rising in him, he broke out suddenly, "It's all over—St. Clair's defeated—routed; the officers nearly all killed, the men by wholesale; the rout complete—too shocking to think of—and a surprise in the bargain!"

The first interview of the president with St. Clair, after the fatal fourth of November, was nobly impressive. The unfortunate general, worn down by age, disease, and the hardships of a frontier campaign, assailed by the press, and with the current of popular opinion setting hard against him, repaired to his chief, as to a shelter from the fury of so many elements. Washington extended his hand to one who appeared in no new character; for, during the whole of a long life, misfortune seemed " to have marked him for her own." Poor old

"He uttered all this with great vehemence. Then he paused, got up from the sofa and walked about the room several times, agitated, but saying nothing. Near the door he stopped short and stood still a few seconds, when his wrath became terrible.

"'Yes,'" he burst forth, "'HERE, on this very spot, I took leave of him; I wished him success and honor; you have your instructions, I said, from the secretary of war; I had a strict eye to them, and will add but one word—beware of a surprise. I repeat it, beware of a surprise—you know how the Indians fight us. He went off with that as my last solemn warning thrown into his ears. And yet, to suffer that army to be cut to pieces, hacked by a surprise—the very thing I guarded him against! O God, O God, he's worse than a murderer! How can he answer it to his country?—the blood of the slain is upon him—the curse of widows and orphans—the curse of Heaven!'

"This torrent came out in tone appalling. His very frame shook. It was awful, said Mr. Lear. More than once he threw his hands up as he hurled imprecations upon St. Clair. Mr. Lear remained speechless; awed into breathless silence.

"The roused chief sat down on the sofa once more. He seemed conscious of his passion, and uncomfortable. He was silent. His wrath began to subside; he at length said, in an altered voice, 'This must not go beyond this room.' Another pause followed—a longer one—when he said, in a tone quite low, 'General St. Clair shall have justice. I looked hastily through the despatches, saw the whole disaster, but not all the particulars; I will hear him without prejudice; he shall have full justice.'

"He was now, said Mr Lear, perfectly calm. Half an hour had gone by. The storm was over; and no sign of it was afterwards seen in his conduct, or heard in his conversation. The result is known. The whole case was investigated by Congress. St. Clair was exculpated and regained the confidence Washington had in him when appointing him to that command. He had put himself into the thickest of the fight and escaped unhurt, though so ill as to be carried on a litter, and unable to mount his horse without help"

St. Clair hobbled up to his chief, seized the offered hand in both of his, and gave vent to his feelings in an audible manner.* He was subsequently tried by a commission of government, and proved to have been *unfortunate*.

We have mentioned Sam. Fraunces, the president's steward. He was a rare whig in the Revolutionary day, and attached no little importance to his person and character, from the circumstance that the memorable parting of the commander-in-chief with his old and long endeared companions-in-arms had taken place at his tavern in New York.†

The steward was a man of talent and considerable taste in the line of his profession, but was at the same time ambitious, fond of display, and regardless of expense. This produced continued difficulties between the president and certainly one of the most devotedly attached to him of all his household.

The expenses of the presidential mansion were settled weekly; and, upon the bills being presented, the presi-

* Mr. Custis informed me that he happened to be present at the beginning of that interview. He was then between the tenth and eleventh year of his age, and it made an impression on his mind.

† When the British had evacuated New York, in November, 1783, and the American army was disbanded, Washington prepared to proceed to Annapolis to resign his commission. On Thursday, the fourth of December, the principal officers in the army yet remaining in the service, assembled at Fraunces', to take a final leave of their beloved chief. The scene is described as one of great tenderness. Washington entered the room where they were all waiting, and taking a glass of wine in his hand, he said, "With a heart full of love and gratitude, I now take leave of you. I most devoutly wish that your latter days may be as prosperous and happy as your former ones have been glorious and honorable." Having drank, he continued, "I can not come to each of you to take my leave, but shall be obliged to you if each will come and take me by the hand." Knox, who stood nearest to him, turned and grasped his hand, and, while the tears flowed down the cheeks of each, the commander-in-chief kissed him. This he did to each of his officers, while tears and sobs stifled utterance.

dent would rate his steward soundly upon his expensiveness, saying that, while he wished to live conformably to his high station, liberally, nay handsomely, he abhorred waste and extravagance, and insisted that his household should be conducted with due regard to economy and usefulness.

Fraunces would promise amendment, and the next week the same scene would be re-enacted in all its parts, the steward retiring in tears, and exclaiming, " Well, he may discharge me; he may kill me if he will; but while he is president of the United States, and I have the honor to be his steward, his establishment shall be supplied with the very best of everything that the whole country can afford."

Washington was remarkably fond of fish. It was the habit for New England ladies frequently to prepare the codfish in a very nice manner, and send it enveloped in cloths, so as to arrive quite warm for the president's Saturday dinner, he always eating codfish on that day in compliment to his New England recollections.

It happened that a single shad was caught in the Delaware in February, and brought to the Philadelphia market for sale. Fraunces pounced upon it with the speed of an osprey, regardless of price, but charmed that he had secured a delicacy that, above all others, he knew would be agreeable to the plate of his chief.

When the fish was served, Washington suspected a departure from his orders touching the provision to be made for his table, and said to Fraunces, who stood at his post at the sideboard, " What fish is this?"—" A shad, a very fine shad," was the reply; "I knew your excellency was particularly fond of this kind of fish, and was so fortunate as to procure this one in market—a solitary one, and the first of the season."—"The price, sir; the price!" continued Washington, in a stern commanding tone; "the price, sir?"—"Three—three—three dollars," stammered out the conscience-stricken steward. "Take it away," thundered the chief; "take it away, sir; it shall never be said that my table sets such an example of luxury and extravagance." Poor Fraunces tremblingly obeyed, and the first shad of the season was removed untouched, to be speedily discussed by the gourmands of the servants' hall.

The chief cook would have been termed in modern parlance, a celebrated *artiste*. He was named Hercules, and familiarly termed Uncle Harkless. Trained in the mysteries of his part from early youth, and in the palmy days of Virginia, when her thousand chimneys smoked to indicate the generous hospitality that reigned throughout the whole length and breadth of her wide domain, Uncle Harkless was, at the period of the first presidency, as highly accomplished a proficient in the culinary art as could be found in the United States. He was a dark-brown man, little, if any, above the usual size, yet possessed of such great muscular power as to entitle him to be compared with his namesake of fabulous history.

The chief cook gloried in the cleanliness and nicety of his kitchen. Under his iron discipline, wo to his underlings if speck or spot could be discovered on the tables or dressers, or if the utensils did not shine like polished silver. With the luckless wights who had offended in these particulars there was no arrest of punishment, for judgment and execution went hand in hand.

The steward, and indeed the whole household, treated

the chief cook with much respect, as well for his valuable services as for his general good character and pleasing manners.

It was while preparing the Thursday or Congress dinner that Uncle Harkless shone in all his splendor. During his labors upon this banquet he required some half-dozen aprons, and napkins out of number. It was surprising the order and discipline that was observed in so bustling a scene. His underlings flew in all directions to execute his orders, while he, the great master-spirit, seemed to possess the power of ubiquity, and to be everywhere at the same moment.

When the steward in snow-white apron, silk shorts and stockings, and hair in full powder, placed the first dish on the table, the clock being on the stroke of four, " the labors of Hercules" ceased.

While the masters of the republic were engaged in discussing the savory viands of the Congress dinner, the chief cook retired to make his toilet for an evening promenade. His perquisites from the slops of the kitchen were from one to two hundred dollars a year. Though homely in person, he lavished the most of these large avails upon dress. In making his toilet his linen was of unexceptionable whiteness and quality, then black silk shorts, ditto waistcoat, ditto stockings, shoes highly polished, with large buckles covering a considerable part of the foot, blue cloth coat with velvet collar and bright metal buttons, a long watch-chain dangling from his fob, a cocked-hat, and gold-headed cane completed the grand costume of the celebrated dandy (for there were dandies in those days) of the president's kitchen.

Thus arrayed, the chief cook invariably passed out at

the front door, the porter making a low bow, which was promptly returned. Joining his brother-loungers of the *pave*, he proceeded up Market street, attracting considerable attention, that street being, in the old times, the resort where fashionables "did most congregate." Many were not a little surprised on beholding so extraordinary a personage, while others who knew him would make a formal and respectful bow, that they might receive in return the salute of one of the most polished gentlemen and the veriest dandy of nearly sixty years ago.

The coachman, John Fagan, by birth a Hessian, was tall and burly in person, and an accomplished coachman in every respect. He understood the mechanism of a carriage, and could take to pieces and put together again all the parts, should he meet with any accident on his road. He drove for the president throughout his whole tour of the then southern states, from Mount Vernon to Savannah, and by Augusta and the interior of South and North Carolina, in the white chariot built by Clarke, of Philadelphia, without the slightest accident or misfortune happening in so long a journey.*

On the president's return Clarke was in attendance to learn the success of what he deemed his master-piece of coach-making. No sooner had the horses stopped at the door of the presidential mansion than the anxious coachmaker was under the body of the white chariot, examining everything with a careful and critical eye, till Fagan shouted from the box, "All right, Mr. Clarke; all right,

* Washington visited the southern states in the spring of 1791. He set out from Mount Vernon early in April, and was absent three months, during which time he performed a journey of about nineteen hundred miles, with the same span of horses. He followed the seaboard as nearly as possible to Savannah, visited Augusta, and returned by way of the interior of the Carolinas and Virginia.

sir; not a bolt or screw started in a long journey and over the devil's own roads." The delighted mechanic now found his hand grasped in that of the president, who complimented him upon his workmanship, assuring him that it been sufficiently tested in a great variety of very bad roads. Clarke, the happiest of men, repaired to his shop, in Sixth street, where he informed his people of the success of the white chariot, the account of which he had received from the president's own lips, when the day ended in a jollification at the coachmaker's.

John Kruse succeeded Fagan. He was a steady, estimable man, and having been bred in the Austrian cavalry, was perfectly conversant with horses. He was an excessive smoker, his *meerschaum* never being out of his mouth, except at meals or on the coach-box.

The stables consisted of ten coach and saddle horses, and the two white chargers, a coachman and two grooms. Of the chargers the one usually rode by the chief was named *Prescott*. He was a fine parade horse, purely white, and sixteen hands high. He was indifferent to the fire of artillery, the waving of banners, and the clang of martial instruments, but had a very bad habit of dancing about on the approach of a carriage, a habit very annoying to his rider, who although a master in horsemanship, preferred to ride as quietly as possible, especially when, during his Saturday's ride, he would meet with carriages containing ladies, it being customary with them to order their coachman to stop and let down their glasses, that the president might approach to pay his compliments.

The other charger was named *Jackson*, from the circumstance of his having run away with Major Jackson, aid-de-camp to the president, when coming into Princeton, *en route* from New York to Philadelphia, in 1790, to the sad discomfiture of the major, and the no little amusement of the chief and the brilliant *cortége* of gallant cavaliers with which he was attended. Jackson was a superb animal, purely white, with flowing main and tail. He was of a fierce and fiery temperament, and, when mounted, moved with mouth open, champing the bit, his nostrils distended, and his Arab eye flashing fire. Washington, disliking a fretful horse, rarely rode this fine but impetuous animal, while Kruse, whose duty it was to accompany the president when on horseback, had had diverse combats with the fiery charger, in several of which, it was said the old Austrian dragoon came off rather second best. When putting on the housings and caparison for the chief to ride *Jackson*, Kruse would say, " Ah, ha, my fine fellow, you'll have your match to-day, and I know you'll take care to behave yourself." In fact, the noble horse had felt the power of Washington's stalwart arm, a power that could throw a horse upon his haunches in a single moment, and the sagacious animal quailed before a force not easily resisted nor soon forgotten.

Among the coach-horses were a pair of beautiful blood bays, bred at Mount Vernon from the celebrated stallion *Magnolia*. These thorough-breds were the pets of the stables, and always drew the coach when Mrs. Washington paid her visits in Philadelphia. One day, but for the courage and presence of mind of a servant, a serious catastrophe would have occurred. Mrs. Washington and her grand-daughter* were just seated in the coach, and James Hurley (a native of Ireland) was putting up the step, when, the day being warm, and the flies trouble-

---

* Eleanor Parke Custis.

some, one of the horses rubbed off his bridle. The coachman, of course, sat powerless on his box. The affrighted animal at first stared wildly about him, and was in the act of springing forward, when Hurley, perceiving the imminent danger, with a presence of mind equalled by his courage, grappled the animal around the neck, and amid his furious and maddening plunges clung to him, and so encumbered him with the weight of a heavy man that the passengers in the street were enabled to come to the rescue, when the bridle was replaced, and the carriage drove off.

The president was much gratified when inspecting his stables at Philadelphia. They were large and roomy, and everything in and about them in the most perfect order; the grooming of the horses superb, such as the moderns can have no idea of.*

Washington, as we have elsewhere observed, was the most punctual of men. To this admirable quality, and the one equally admirable of rising at four o'clock and retiring to rest at nine at all seasons, this great man owed his being able to accomplish mighty labors during a long and illustrious life. He was punctual in everything, and made every one punctual about him.

During his memorable journey through the southern portion of the union, he had, before setting off, arranged all the stages for the whole route; the ferries, the inns, the hour of arriving at and departing from each, were all duly calculated, and punctually did the white chariot arrive at all its appointments, except when prevented by high waters or excessively bad roads.†

---

* See note on page 397.

† Thinking that the public service might require communications to be made to

His punctuality on that long journey astonished every one. The trumpet call of the cavalry had scarcely ceased its echoes when a vidette would be seen coming in at full speed, and the cry resound far and wide, "He's coming!" Scarcely would the artillery-men unlimber the cannon, when the order would be given, "Light your matches, the white chariot is in full view!"

Revolutionary veterans, hurried from all directions once more to greet their beloved chief. They called it marching to headquarters; and as the dear glorious old fellows would overtake their neighbors and friends, they would say, "Push on, my boys, if you wish to see him; for we, who ought to know, can assure you that he is never behind time, but always punctual to the moment."

It was thus that Washington performed his memorable tour of the United States—everywhere received with heartfelt homage that the love, veneration, and gratitude of a whole people could bestow; and there is no doubt yet living a gray head who can tell of the time when he gallantly rode to some village or inn on the long-remembered route to hail the arrival of the white chariot, and join in the joyous welcome to the Father of his Country.

And equally punctual in his engagements was this remarkable man nearer home. To the review, the theatre, or the ball-room he repaired precisely at the appointed

---

him during his absence, Washington wrote a letter to the head of each department, in which he designated the places that he should be at on certain days. "I shall be," he said, "on the eighth of April at Fredericksburg; the eleventh, at Richmond; the fourteenth, at Petersburgh; the sixteenth, at Halifax; the eighteenth, at Tarborough; the twentieth, at Newtown; the twenty-fourth, at Wilmington; the twenty-ninth, at Georgetown, South Carolina; on the second of May, at Charleston, halting there five days; on the eleventh, at Savannah, halting there two days. Thence leaving the line of march, I shall proceed to Augusta; and, according to the information which I may receive there, my return by an upper road will be regulated"

time. The manager of the theatre, waiting on the president to request him to command a play, was asked, "At what time, Mr. Wignell, does your curtain rise?" The manager replied, "Seven o'clock is the hour, but of course the curtain will not rise till your excellency's arrival." The president observed, "I will be punctual, sir, to the time; nobody waits a single moment for me." And, sure enough, precisely at seven, the noble form of Washington was seen to enter the stage box, amid the acclamations of the audience and the music of the President's March.

In the domestic arrangement of the presidential mansion, the private dinner was served at three o'clock, the public one at four. The drawing-room commenced at seven, and ended at a little past ten. The levee began at three and ended at four. On the public occasions the company came within a very short time of each other, and departed in the same manner. "The president is punctual," said everybody, and everybody became punctual.

On the great national days of the fourth of July and twenty-second of February, the salute from the then head of Market street (Eighth street) announced the opening of the levee. Then was seen the venerable corps of the Cincinnati marching to pay their respects to their president-general, who received them at headquarters, and in the uniform of the commander-in-chief. This veteran band of the Revolution had learned punctuality from their general in the "times that tried men's souls;" for no sooner had the thunder-peals of Colonel Proctor's twelve-pounders caused the windows to rattle in Market street than this venerable body of the Cincinnati were in full march for the headquarters. And as soon as the first gun would be heard, a venerable citizen was seen to leave his office, and moving at a more than usual pace, ascend the steps of the presidential mansion. He gave in no name—he required no ceremony of introduction—but, making his way to the family parlor, opened the general gratulation by the first welcome of Robert Morris.

A fine volunteer corps, called the light-infantry, from the famed light-infantry of the Revolutionary army, commanded by Lafayette, mounted a guard of honor at headquarters during the levee on the national days. When it was about to close, the soldiers, headed by their sergeants, marched with trailed arms and noiseless step through the hall to a spot where huge bowls of punch had been prepared for their refreshment, when, after quaffing a deep carouse, with three hearty cheers to the health of the president, they countermarched to the street, the bands struck up the favorite air, "forward" was the word, and the levee was ended.*

* In the year 1790, according to the following sketch, taken from an old number of the London *New Monthly Magazine,* an appreciating English gentleman visited the president. The sketch has been attributed to the pen of Hazlitt: "I remember my father telling me he was introduced to Washington, in 1790, by an American friend. A servant, well-looking and well-dressed, received the visitants at the door, and by him they were delivered over to an officer of the United States' service, who ushered them into the drawing-room, in which Mrs. Washington and several ladies were seated. There was nothing remarkable in the person of the lady of the president; she was matronly and kind, with perfect good-breeding; she at once entered into easy conversation, asked how long he had been in America, how he liked the country, and such other familiar, but general questions. In a few minutes the general was in the room; it was not necessary to announce his name, for his peculiar appearance, his firm forehead, Roman nose, and a projection of the lower jaw, his height and figure, could not be mistaken by any one who had seen a full-length picture of him, and yet no picture accurately resembled him in the minute traits of his person. His features, however, were so marked by prominent characteristics, which appear in all likenesses of him that a stranger could not be mistaken in the man; he was remarkably dignified in his manners, and had an air of benignity over his features which his visitant did not expect, being rather prepared for sternness of countenance.

"Old times are changed, old manners gone." True, we have become a mighty empire in extent, wealth, and

"After an introduction by Mrs. Washington, without more form than common good manners prescribes, 'he requested me, said my father, 'to be seated; and, taking a chair himself, entered at once into conversation. His manner was full of affability. He asked how I liked the country, the city of New York: talked of the infant institutions of America, and the advantages she offered, by her intercourse, for benefitting other nations. He was grave in manner, but perfectly easy. His dress was of purple satin. There was a commanding air in his appearance which excited respect, and forbade too great a freedom towards him, independently of that species of awe which is always felt in the moral influence of a great character. In every movement, too, there was a polite gracefulness equal to any met with in the most polished individuals in Europe, and his smile was extraordinarily attractive. It was observed to me that there was an expression in Washington's face that no painter had succeeded in taking. It struck me no man could be better formed for command. A stature of six feet, a robust, but well-proportioned frame, calculated to sustain fatigue, without that heaviness which generally attends great muscular strength, and abates active exertion, displayed bodily power of no mean standard A light eye and full—the very eye of genius and reflection, rather than of blind passionate impulse. His nose appeared thick, and though it befitted his other features, was too coarsely and strongly formed to be the handsomest of its class. His mouth was like no other that I ever saw; the lips firm, and the under-jaw seeming to grasp the upper with force, as if its muscles were in full action when he sat still. Neither with the general nor with Mrs. Washington was there the slightest restraint of ceremony. There was less of it than I ever recollect to have met with, where perfect good-breeding and manners were at the same time observed. To many remarks Washington assented with a smile or inclination of the head, as if he were by nature sparing in his conversation, and I am inclined to think this was the case. An allusion was made to a serious fit of illness he had recently suffered; but he took no notice of it. I could not help remarking, that America must have looked with anxiety to the termination of his indisposition. He made no reply to my compliment but by an inclination of the head. His bow at my taking leave I shall never forget. It was the last movement which I saw that illustrious character make, as my eyes took their leave of him for ever, and it hangs a perfect picture upon my recollection. The house of Washington was in the Broadway, and the street front was handsome. The drawing-room in which I sat was lofty and spacious; but the furniture was not beyond that found in dwellings of opulent Americans in general, and might be called plain for its situation. The upper end of the room had glass doors, which opened upon a balcony, commanding an extensive view of the Hudson river, interspersed with islands, and the Jersey shore on the opposite side. A grandson and daughter resided constantly in the house with the general, and a nephew of the general's, married to a niece of Mrs. Washington, resided at Mount Vernon, the general's family-seat in Virginia; his residence, as president, keeping him at the

population; but where, Americans, is the spirit of '76, the glorious and immortal spirit that dignified and adorned the early days of the republic and the age of Washington? Shall it decline and die among us? Swear on the altar of your liberty that it shall live for ever!

seat of government.' The levees held by Washington, as president, were generally crowded, and held on Tuesday, between three and four o'clock. The president stood, and received the bow of the person presented, who retired to make way for another. At the drawing-room, Mrs. Washington received the ladies, who courtesied, and passed aside without exchanging a word. Tea and coffee, with refreshments of all kinds, were laid in one part of the rooms, and before the individuals of the company retired, each lady was a second time led up to the lady-president, made her second silent obeisance, and departed. Nothing could be more simple, yet it was enough."

CHAPTER XXII.

THE RETIRED PRESIDENT.

Washington Retires from the Presidency — Inauguration of Mr. Adams — Arrangement of Washington's Letters and Papers — Albert Rawlins employed to Copy Letters — Publication of Private Memoirs of Washington Postponed — Character of some of the Letters copied — The Old Family Vault — Site for a New One selected by Washington — Disposition of Washington's Remains — The Desires of the Government — Mrs. Washington's Wish — Washington's Improvement of his Farms — A Portrait of the Farmer at Mount Vernon — His Daily Rides — Honors and Compliments — French Emigrants at Mount Vernon — G. W. Lafayette — Repairs of the Mansion — Sir John Sinclair — Marriage at Mount Vernon in 1799 — Billy — Washington's Last Visits to Alexandria — He Dines there — His Last Review — Evenings at Mount Vernon — Washington no longer a Sportsman — Father Jack — Tom Davis — Reflections.

On the fourth of March, 1797, Washington, as a private citizen, attended the dignified ceremonials of the inauguration of his successor, John Adams;* and during

* On that occasion, there was a dense crowd in the house of representatives to witness the ceremony of the inauguration of a new president. The Congress, during the residence of the federal government in Philadelphia, held their sessions in the courthouse, on the corner of Sixth and Chestnut streets; and the hall of the representatives is thus described by a cotemporary writer: "The house of representatives, in session, occupied the ground floor. There was a platform elevated three steps, plainly carpeted, and covering nearly the whole of the area, with a limited promenade for the members and privileged persons; and four narrow desks between the Sixth-street windows, for the stenographers, Lloyd, Gales, Callender, and Duane. The speaker's chair, without canopy, was of plain leather and brass nails, facing the east, at or near the centre of the western wall."

At the appointed hour, Washington entered the hall amidst the most enthusiastic cheers, and was soon followed by Mr. Adams, the president elect, who was about to take the oath of office. When they were seated, perfect silence prevailed, Washington then arose, and with great dignity introduced Mr. Adams to the audience, and proceeded to read, in a firm clear voice, a brief valedictory; not the great "Farewell Address," for that was published six months before.

the preparations for his departure from the seat of government, the ex-president enjoyed an interchange of

Mrs. Susan R. Echard, a daughter of Colonel Read, now (1859) living in Philadelphia, at the age of eighty-three years, was present on this interesting occasion, and in a letter to a kinsman, given below, has described the scene. It may be interesting to know that the memory of Mr. Rembrandt Peale, who, two years before, had painted Washington's portrait, from life, and who was also present in the gallery on that occasion, fully agrees with that of Mrs. Echard.

Mrs. Echard remarks: "When General Washington delivered his 'Farewell Address,' in the room at the southeast corner of Chestnut and Sixth streets, I sat immediately in front of him. It was in the room Congress occupied. The table of the speaker was between the two windows on Sixth street. The daughter of Dr. C., [Craik] of Alexandria, the physician and intimate friend of Washington, Mrs. H., [Harrison] whose husband was the auditor, was a very dear friend of mine. Her brother Washington was one of the secretaries of General Washington. Young Dandridge, a nephew of Mrs. Washington, was the other. I was included in Mrs. H.'s party, to witness the august, the solemn scene. Mr. H. declined going with Mrs. H., as she had determined to go early, so as to secure the front bench. It was fortunate for Miss C., [Custis] (afterwards Mrs. L) [Lewis] that she could not trust herself to be so near her honored grandfather. My dear father stood very near her. She was terribly agitated. There was a narrow passage from the door of entrance to the room, which was on the east, dividing the rows of benches. General Washington stopped at the end to let Mr. Adams pass to the chair. The latter always wore a full suit of bright drab, with lash or loose cuffs to his coat. He always wore wrist ruffles. He had not changed his fashions. He was a short man, with a good head. With his family he attended our church twice a day. General Washington's dress was a full suit of black. His military hat had the black cockade. There stood the 'Father of his Country,' acknowledged by nations—the first in war, first in peace, and first in the hearts of his countrymen. No marshals with gold-colored scarfs attended him—there was no cheering—no noise; the most profound silence greeted him, as if the great assembly desired to hear him breathe, and catch his breath in homage of their hearts. Mr. Adams covered his face with both his hands; the sleeves of his coat, and his hands, were covered with tears. Every now and then there was a suppressed sob. I can not describe Washington's appearance as I felt it—perfectly composed and self-possessed, till the close of his address: Then, when strong nervous sobs broke loose, when tears covered the faces, then the great man was shaken. I never took my eyes from his face. Large drops came from his eyes. He looked to the youthful children who were parting with their father, their friend, as if his heart was with them, and would be to the end."

In this connection, some reminiscences of Washington, and the Congress at Philadelphia, by the late Reverend Ashbel Greene, are specially interesting: "After a great deal of talking, and writing, and controversy, about the permanent seat of Congress, under the present constitution," says Mr. Greene, "it was determined that Philadelphia should be honored with its presence for ten years, and that afterwards its permanent location should be in the City of Washington where it now is. In the meantime, the federal city was in building, and the legislature of Pennsylvania voted a sum of money to build a house for the president, perhaps with some hope that this might help to keep the seat of the general government in the capital— for Philadelphia was then considered as the capital of the state. What was lately the university of Pennsylvania, was the structure erected for this purpose. But as soon as General Washington saw its dimensions, and a good while before it was finished, he let it be known that he would not occupy — that he should certainly not go to the expense of purchasing suitable furniture for such a dwelling; for it is to be understood, in those days of stern republicanism, nobody thought of Congress *furnishing* the president's house; or, if perchance such a thought did enter into some aristocratic head, it was too unpopular to be uttered.

"President Washington, therefore, rented a house of Mr. Robert Morris, in Market street, between Fifth and Sixth streets, on the south side, and furnished it handsomely, but not gorgeously. There he lived, with Mrs. Washington; Mr. Lear, his private secretary, and his wife, and Mrs. Washington's grandchildren, making a part of the family. Young Custis had a private tutor, employed by the president, who was engaged to attend on his pupil one hour in the winter mornings, before breakfast; and who, then, commonly breakfasted with the president and his family. The president ate Indian cakes for breakfast, after the Virginia fashion, although buckwheat cakes were generally on the table. Washington's dining parties were entertained in a very handsome style. His weekly dining day, for company, was Thursday, and his dining hour was always four o'clock in the afternoon. His rule was to allow five minutes for the variation of clocks and watches, and then go to the table, be present or absent, whoever might. He kept his own clock in the hall, just within the outward door, and always exactly regulated. When lagging members of Congress came in, as they often did, after the guests had sat down to dinner, the president's only apology was, 'Gentlemen (or sir), we are too punctual for you. I have a cook who never asks whether the company has come, but whether the hour has come.' The company usually assembled in the drawing-room, about fifteen or twenty minutes before dinner, and the president spoke to every guest personally on entering the room.

"He was always dressed in a suit of black, his hair powdered, and tied in a black queue behind, with a very elegant dress-sword, which he wore with inimitable grace. Mrs. Washington often, but not always, dined with the company, sat at the head of the table, and if, as was occasionally the case, there were other ladies present, they sat each side of her. The private secretary sat at the foot of the table, and was expected to be quietly attentive to all the guests. The president himself sat half-way from the head to the foot of the table, and on that side he would place Mrs. Washington, though distant from him, on his right hand. He always, unless a clergyman was present at his own table, asked a blessing, in a standing posture. If a clergyman were present, he was requested both to ask a blessing and to return thanks after dinner. The centre of the table contained five or six large silver or plated waiters, those of the ends, circular, or rather oval on one side, so as to make the

farewell visits with those in Philadelphia, whom he had known so long and loved so well.*

On Washington's resignation of the presidency, one of the first employments of his retirement as a private citizen was to arrange certain letters and papers for posthumous publication. With this view he wrote to General Spotswood, in Virginia, to select a young man of respectable family, good moral habits, and superior clerkly skill, to copy into a large book certain letters and papers that would be prepared for such purpose.

Now, these letters and papers were by no means of an official character; neither did they come within the range of recollections of the Revolution or of the constitutional

---

arrangement correspond with the oval shape of the table. The waiters between the end-pieces were in the form of parallelograms, the ends about one-third part of the length of the sides; and the whole of these waiters were filled with alabaster figures, taken from the ancient mythology, but none of them such as to offend, in the smallest degree, against delicacy. On the outside of the oval, formed by the waiters, were placed the various dishes, always without covers; and outside the dishes were the plates. A small roll of bread, enclosed in a napkin, was laid by the side of each plate. The president, it is believed, generally dined on one dish, and that of a very simple kind. If offered something, either in the first or second course, which was very rich, his usual reply was —" That is too good for me." He had a silver pint cup or mug of beer, placed by his plate, which he drank while dining. He took one glass of wine during dinner, and commonly one after. He then retired (the ladies having gone a little before him), and left his secretary to superintend the table, till the wine-bibbers of Congress had satisfied themselves with drinking. His wines were alway the best that could be obtained. Nothing could exceed the order with which his table was served. Every servant knew what he was to do, and did it in the most quiet and yet rapid manner. The dishes and plates were removed and changed, with a silence and speed that seemed like enchantment."

* On the day preceding the inauguration, Washington gave a kind of farewell dinner, to which the foreign ministers and their wives, Mr. and Mrs. Adams, Mr. Jefferson, and Mr. Morris, were invited. Bishop White, who was present, says, that when the cloth was removed, Washington filled his glass and said. "Ladies and gentlemen, this is the last time I shall drink your health as a public man; I do it with sincerity, wishing you all possible happiness." These words affected the company very much, and the wife of Mr. Linn, the British minister, wept so that the tears streamed down her cheeks.

government; they were more especially *private*, and could with propriety be termed *Passages, Personal and Explanatory, in the Life and Correspondence of George Washington.*

General Spotswood selected a young man named Albin Rawlins, of a respectable family in the county of Caroline, and well qualified for the duties he was to perform. He soon after arrived at Mount Vernon, and entered upon his employment.

The letters were delivered to Rawlins by the chief in person, were carefully returned to him when copied, and others delivered out for copying. As the duties of the clerk lasted for a considerable time, very many of the most interesting and valuable letters that Washington ever wrote or received were copied into the *Rawlins' Book*. While we repeat that these letters were not of an official character, we must observe that they were written to and received from some the most illustrious public men who flourished in the age of Washington, and shed more light upon the true character of the men and things of that distinguished period than any letters or papers that ever were written and published.

Washington postponed the arrangement for publication of his private memoirs to the last; all such matters lay dormant during the long and meritorious career of his public services. It was only when retired amid the shades of Mount Vernon that he thought of self, and determined in his latter days that nothing should be left undone to give to his country and the world a fair and just estimate of his life and actions.*

* Applications were made to Washington, soon after the war, for materials for a biography of himself, but he discouraged every attempt to write an account of his life, except as it came incidentally into the general history of the time in which he lived. He well knew that such a biography would be written at some time, and was

A portion of the letters of the Rawlins' Book were of a delicate character, seeing that they involved the reputation of the writers as consistent patriots and men of honor. *These letters are no where to be found.* But, although the veil of mystery has been drawn over the *lost letters of the Rawlins' Book* that time or circumstance can never remove, our readers may rest assured that there is not a line, nay, a word, in the lost letters that Washington wrote, that, were he living, he would wish to revoke or blot out, but would readily, fearlessly submit to the perusal and decision of his countrymen and the world.

During the agitation of the public mind that grew out of the subject of the lost letters more than fifty years ago,* it was contended that the rumors were groundless; that there were no such letters. Faithful to our purpose at the close of our labors, as the commencement of our humble work more than a quarter of a century ago, to give in these *Recollections* only of what we saw, and only of what we derived from the undoubted authority of others, we do not hesitate to declare, and from an authority that can not be questioned, that there were such letters as those described as the *Lost Letters of the Rawlins' Book.*

The ancient family vault having fallen into a state of decay, the chief surveyed and marked out a spot for a family burial-place during the last days at Mount Ver-

---

anxious to have his papers so arranged, as to be easy for reference. Perceiving also, the great value of well-arranged public papers, Washington made a contract, by authority of Congress, in May, 1781, to have all of his official papers recorded in volumes. He appointed Colonel Richard Varrick to superintend that labor, and he, with three or four assistants, were engaged in the business two years and a half.

* This chapter was first published in the *National Intelligencer* on the twenty-second of February, 1854.

non.* The new situation is peculiarly unfavorable and ill chosen, being a most unpleasant location for either the living or the dead. The executors, conceiving themselves bound by the provisions of the will to erect a burial vault on the spot marked out, proceeded to do so to the best advantage; but all their endeavors, together with the labors of skilful mechanics, have resulted in the tomb of Washington being universally condemned as unfit for and unworthy of the purpose for which it was intended, while it serves as a matter of reproach to the crowds of pilgrims who resort thither to pay homage to the fame and memory of the Father of his Country.†

It is certain that Washington never gave even a hint of his views or wishes in regard to the disposition of his remains, except what is contained in his will. He no doubt believed that his ashes would be claimed as national property, and be entombed with national honors; hence his silence on a subject that has agitated the American public for more than half a century. On the decease of

---

* The following is a clause in Washington's will: "The family vault at Mount Vernon requiring repairs, and being improperly situated besides, I desire that a new one of brick, and upon a larger scale, may be built at the foot of what is commonly called the Vineyard Enclosure, on the ground which is marked out; in which my remains, with those of my deceased relations (now in the old vault), and such others of my family as may choose to be entombed there, may be deposited. And it is my express desire, that my corpse may be interred in a private manner, without parade or funeral oration."

† The new vault is about three hundred yards southwest from the mansion, at the foot of a slope, and the head of a ravine that extends to the shore of the Potomac. The front of the tomb has an ante-chamber, built of red brick, about twelve feet in height, with a large iron gateway. This was erected for the accommodation of two marble coffins (one for Washington and the other for his wife), which stand within the enclosure, in full view of the visiter. Over the gateway, upon a marble slab, are the words: "WITHIN THIS ENCLOSURE REST THE REMAINS OF GENERAL GEORGE WASHINGTON." Over the vault door, inside, are the words. "I AM THE RESURRECTION AND THE LIFE; HE THAT BELIEVETH IN ME, THOUGH HE WERE DEAD, YET SHALL HE LIVE."

the chief, the high authorities of the nation begged his remains for public interment at the seat of the national government. They were granted by the venerable relict, conditioned that her own remains should be interred by the side of her husband in the national tomb. This memorable compact, so solemn in itself, is still in full force and binding on the nation, inasmuch as no subsequent authority could alter or annul it.

On the faith of this compact, Colonel Monroe, when president of the United States, ordered two crypts or vaults to be formed in the basement story of the centre of the capitol for the reception of the remains of the chief and his consort, agreeably to the arrangement of 1799, which vaults are untenanted to this day.

Surely it can not be denied that Mrs. Washington had the right, the only right, to the disposal of the remains of the chief, and by virtue of this right she granted them to the prayer of the nation as expressed by its highest authority.

On her deathbed the venerable lady called the author of these *Recollections*, her grandson and executor, to her side, and said, "Remember, Washington, to have my remains placed in a leaden coffin, that they may be removed with those of the general at the command of the government."*

* On the thirteenth of February, 1832, Mr. Thomas, of Louisiana, from the joint committee of the two houses, appointed to report on the subject of the Centennial anniversary of the birthday of GEORGE WASHINGTON, reported the following resolution:—

"*Resolved, by the Senate and House of Representatives of the United States of America, in Congress assembled*, That the President of the Senate and Speaker of the House of Representatives be hereby authorized to make application to John A. Washington, of Mount Vernon, for the body of GEORGE WASHINGTON to be removed and deposited in the Capitol, at Washington City, in conformity with the resolutions of Congress of the twenty-third December, 1799; and that, if they obtain the requisite consent to the removal thereof, that they be further authorized to cause it to be

> And yet we hear of the right of a state! No one state can appropriate to itself that which belongs to the whole.

removed and deposited in the Capitol, on the twenty-second day of February, 1832."
The following is a copy of the resolutions referred to —

"*Resolved, by the Senate and House of Representatives of the United States of America in Congress assembled*, That a marble monument be erected by the United States, in the Capitol, at the City of Washington, and that the family of General Washington be requested to permit his body to be deposited under it; and that the monument be so designed as to commemorate the great events of his military and political life.

"*And be it further resolved*, That the President of the United States be requested to direct a copy of these resolutions to be transmitted to Mrs. Washington, assuring her of the profound respect Congress will ever bear to her person and character; of their condolence on the late afflicting dispensation of Providence; and entreating her assent to the interment of the remains of General George Washington in the manner expressed in the first resolution."

In compliance with these resolutions, President Adams wrote a letter to Mrs. Washington on the subject, and received the following reply:—

"MOUNT VERNON, *December* 31, 1799.

"SIR: While I feel, with keenest anguish, the late dispensation of Divine Providence, I can not be insensible to the mournful tributes of respect and veneration which are paid to the memory of my dear deceased husband; and, as his best services and most anxious wishes were always devoted to the welfare and happiness of his country, to know that they were truly appreciated and gratefully remembered affords no inconsiderable consolation.

"Taught by the great example which I have so long had before me, never to oppose my private wishes to the public will, I must consent to the request made by Congress, which you have had the goodness to transmit to me; and, in doing this, I need not, I can not, say what a sacrifice of individual feeling I make to a sense of public duty.

"With grateful acknowledgments, and unfeigned thanks for the personal respect and evidences of condolence expressed by Congress and yourself, I remain, very respectfully, sir, your most obedient humble servant,

"MARTHA WASHINGTON."

President Adams transmitted her letter to Congress, accompanied by the following message:—

"*Gentlemen of the Senate, and Gentlemen of the House of Representatives*:

"In compliance with the request in one of the resolutions of Congress of the 23d of December last, I transmitted a copy of those resolutions, by my secretary, Mr. Shaw, to Mrs. Washington, assuring her of the profound respect Congress will ever bear to her person and character; of their condolence in the late afflicting dispensation of Providence; and entreating her assent to the interment of the remains of General George Washington in the manner expressed in the first resolution. As

Of the glorious Old Thirteen, little Delaware has as much right to the remains of the beloved Washington as either the sentiments of that virtuous lady, not less beloved by this nation than she is at present greatly afflicted, can never be so well expressed as in her own words, I transmit to Congress her original letter.

"It would be an attempt of too much delicacy to make any comments upon it; but there can be no doubt that the nation at large, as well as all the branches of the government, will be highly gratified by any arrangement which may diminish the sacrifices she makes of her individual feelings. JOHN ADAMS.

"*United States, January* 6, 1800."

The resolutions appended to the report submitted by Mr. Thomas, on the thirteenth of February, 1832, elicited a warm debate. Some of the members from Virginia opposed the measure. Mr. McCoy declared that such removal would be a violation of the sepulchre of the dead; and Mr. Coke desired the removal of the precious remains to Richmond, the capital of Washington's native state. In reply to these, Edward Everett, of Massachusetts, remarked:—

"But it is said, we are going to violate the repose of the dead; to break into the sepulchre, and rifle it of its precious deposite. Sir, do we do any such thing? Shall we not go to that venerated tomb with every possible warrant, both of authority and delicacy? Was not the consent of the consort of the Father of his Country obtained, at a moment when her feelings were bleeding under the recent loss of the illustrious partner of her life? Fortified with her consent, deliberately given, and at that moment, who shall question the right or the propriety of the procedure? Violate the repose of the grave! Sir, we are discharging toward that sacred depository a most imperative duty. If there is one darker spot in the history of this Union than another, it is that we have left so long unredeemed the solemn pledge, which was given by the people of America, through their representatives here, in the first moments of bereavement. Violate the repose of the dead! Sir, we are going to pay a tribute of respect to the ashes of the Father of his Country, such as the history of the world can not match with a parallel. If this resolution is adopted, and on the 22d of February the remains of our beloved hero and patriot shall be removed from Mount Vernon to this capitol, it will be a transaction of a character of extraordinary solemnity, grandeur, and interest. Such a procession as will be formed to receive these sacred remains—the multitudes of old and young—the constituted authorities of the nation, the citizens of this district, and of the neighboring region, who shall assemble to witness the awful spectacle of the remains of the Father of his Country, on their way to their resting-place beneath the foundations of this capitol—all this, sir, will constitute a transaction unexampled in the history of the world for its effects on the minds and hearts of those who may take part in it or witness it. The gentleman (Mr. Coke) was willing to open the sacred portals of that grave, and remove its deposite, not indeed to this capitol, but to Richmond. Now, sir, I cheerfully admit, that of the titles of Virginia to the respect and consideration of her sister states, it is among the first that she is the parent of our Washington. But let her not forget, that, though Washington was by birth a native of the colony of Virginia, he lived

of her larger sisters; for, though small in size, she was great in value in "the times that tried men's souls," and, in proportion to her resources, furnished as much courage, privation, and blood to the combats of liberty, as those

and died a citizen of the United States of America; united more by his labors, counsels, and sacrifices, than those of any other individual. The sacred remains are, as the gentleman well said, a treasure beyond all price, but it is a treasure of which every part of this blood-cemented Union has a right to claim its share.

"The gentleman from Virginia (Mr. McCoy) asked, if we begin in this way, where shall we end? Sir, I wish it might even become more difficult to answer that question. I wish it may even be hard to say, where shall we end with these testimonials of respect paid to a worth like that of Washington. Be it, sir, that we know not where we shall *end*. I know where we ought to *begin*, and that is, with the man who was 'first in war, first in peace, and first in the hearts of his countrymen.' Sir, I will begin with him. If, hereafter, another shall arise, who will live like Washington, when he dies, let him be laid by his side."

The resolution was adopted, and measures were immediately taken to carry it into effect on the 22d of the same month, the one hundredth anniversary of the birth of Washington, when it was shown, by records, that it was the distinct understanding between Mrs. Washington and President Adams, that her remains should accompany those of her husband, wherever the latter might lie. This reservation caused the necessity of procuring the consent of other parties, and on the sixteenth of February, on motion of Mr. Clay, the senate proceeded to the consideration of the following joint resolution from the house:—

"*Resolved, by the Senate and House of Representatives*, That the President of the Senate and Speaker of the House of Representatives be hereby authorized to make application to John A. Washington, of Mount Vernon, and to George W. P. Custis, grandson of Mrs. Washington, for the remains of MARTHA WASHINGTON, to be removed and deposited in the Capitol at Washington City, at the same time with those of her late consort, GEORGE WASHINGTON, and if leave be obtained, to take measures accordingly."

This effort to have the remains of the illustrious citizen deposited beneath the Capitol failed, and they are yet within the area marked out for them by that great man while living, and where, among his kindred, according to the words of his Will, no doubt it was his desire that they should for ever repose. Now that Mount Vernon, through the efforts of patriotic women, has become the property of the nation, every American should rejoice that the remains of Washington have not been disturbed Right glad are we that they are left alone,

―――― "To sleep for ever,
Till the trump that awakens the countless dead,
By the verdant bank of that rushing river,
Where first they pillowed his mighty head."

that were far larger than she. From Long Island to Eutaw, from the first to the last of the War for Independence, her banner was ever in the field, and ever floated mid "the bravest of the brave."

It is high time the subject of the remains, and the remains themselves, were at rest. Presuming that government should purchase Mount Vernon, and determine that the ashes of the chief should there find lasting repose, we would respectfully suggest that a sepulchre be erected on the site of the ancient family vault, a magnificent location, having an extensive view of the surrounding country and of the noble Potomac that washes its base; the massive structure to be formed of white American marble, in blocks each of a ton weight, a dome of copper, surmounted by an eagle in bronze, a bronze door, and for inscription two words only that will speak volumes to all time— *Pater Patriæ*. The key of the receptacle to be always in custody of the president of the United States for the time being. This done, and if done "'t were well it were done quickly," the Tomb of Washington would cease to be a reproach among nations. The pilgrim from distant lands, as he journeys through a mighty empire, with his heart filled with veneration of the fame and memory of America's illustrious son, when he arrives at the national Sepulchre, that casts its broad shadow over the Potomac's wave, will become awed by the solemn grandeur of the spot. The American of generations yet to come will behold, with filial reverence, the time-honored receptacle that contains the ashes of the Father of his Country; the enduring marble mellowed by age, and the inscription freshly preserved in never-dying bronze. Proud of such a monument erected by the piety of his ancestors,

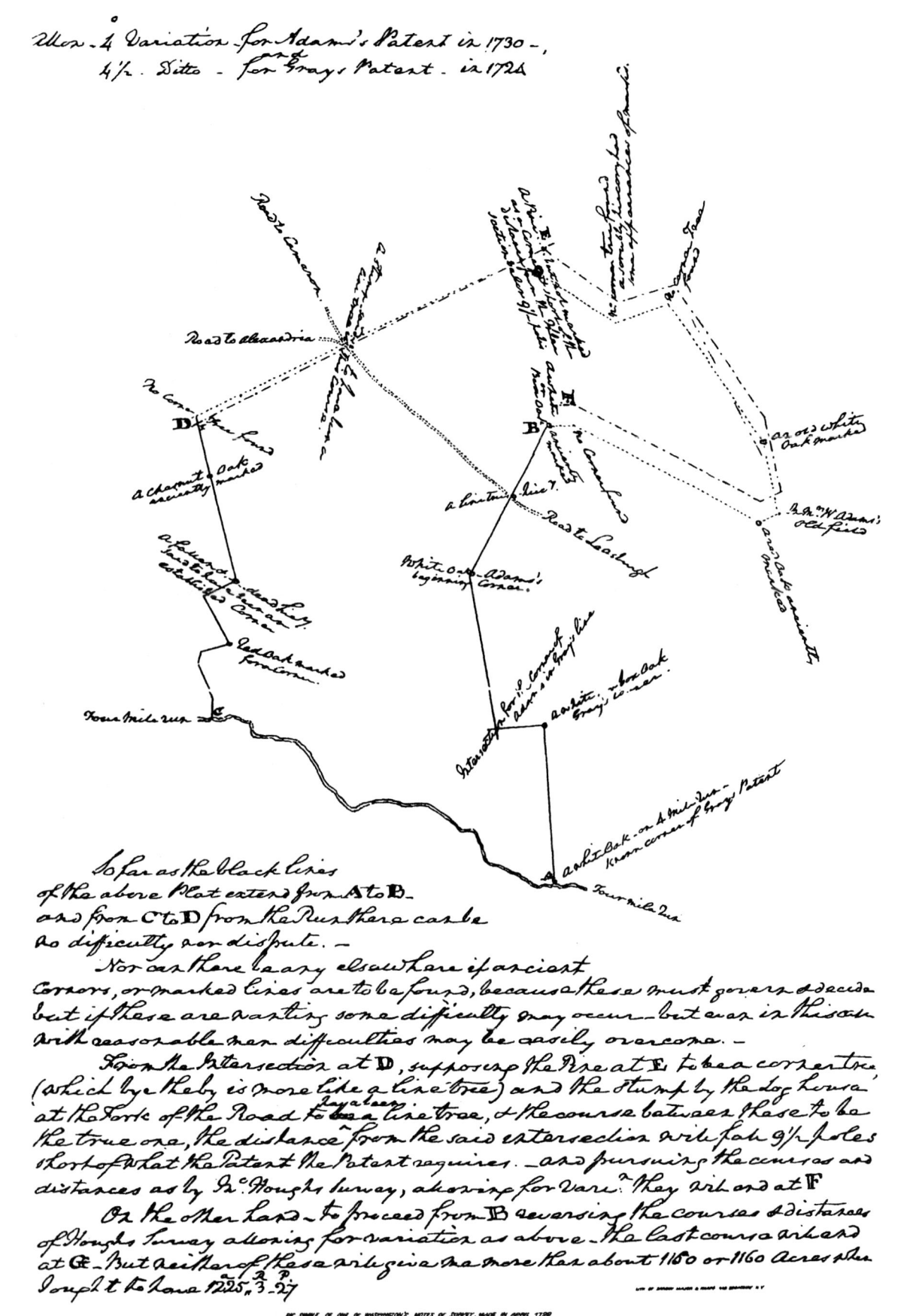

2 Mn— ¼ Variation for Adam's Patent in 1730 —
4½. Ditto — for Grays Patent. in 1724

So far as the black lines
of the above Plat extend from A to B
and from C to D from the Run there can be
no difficulty nor dispute. —

Nor can there be any elsewhere if ancient
Corners, or marked lines are to be found, because these must govern & decide
but if these are wanting some difficulty may occur — but even in this case
with reasonable men difficulties may be easily overcome. —

From the Intersection at D, supposing the Pine at E to be a corner tree,
(which bye the bye is more like a line tree) and the stump by the Log house
at the fork of the Road to Payatowny a line tree, & the course between these to be
the true one, the distance from the said intersection will fall 9½ poles
short of what the Patent the Patent requires. — And pursuing the courses and
distances as by Mr. Houghs Survey, allowing for Var.n they will end at F

On the other hand — to proceed from B reversing the courses & distances
of Houghs Survey allowing for variation as above — the last course will end
at G. — But neither of these will give me more than about 1150 or 1160 Acres when
I ought to have 1225 ″ 3 ″ 27

the future American may exclaim, in the words of the immortal bard—

"Such honors Ilion to her hero paid,
And peaceful sleeps her mighty Hector's shade."

Another object claimed the attention of the chief during the last days at Mount Vernon—the complete survey and remodelling of his farms, with a view to their improvement. These surveys he made in person, the calculations and estimates drawn out by his own hand; and, indeed, it was a rare spectacle to behold this venerable man, who had obtained the very topmost height of human greatness, carrying his own compass, the emblem of the employments of his early days.*

* Allusion has already been made, in a note on page 156, to a facsimile of a record of one of Washington's surveys, given in this volume. It was made in April, 1799, the last year of his life; and the land surveyed is that which he gave, by his Will, to the author of these *Recollections*, situated "on Four-mile-Run, in the vicinity of Alexandria, containing one thousand two hundred acres, more or less." We have on several occasions observed how methodical and careful Washington was in all his business operations. His habit of committing every bargain, even the most trivial, to writing, is well exemplified by the following curious document, which is preserved among his papers. It appears that Philip Barter was in the habit of getting intoxicated too often, and hence the execution of the following bond:—

"Articles of agreement made this twelfth day of April, Anno Domini one thousand seven hundred and eighty-seven, by and between George Washington, Esq., of the parish of Truro, in the county of Fairfax, state of Virginia, on the one part, and Philip Barter, gardener, on the other. Witness, that the said Philip Barter, for and in consideration of the covenants hereafter mentioned, doth promise and agree to serve the said George Washington for the term of one year as a gardener, and that he will during the said time, conduct himself soberly, diligently, and honestly; that he will faithfully and industriously perform all and every part of his duty as a gardener, to the best of his knowledge and abilities, and that he will not at any time suffer himself to be disguised with liquor except on times hereinafter mentioned

"In consideration of these things being well and duly performed on the part of said Philip Barter, the said George Washington doth agree to allow him (the said Philip) the same kind and quality of provisions he has heretofore had, and likewise, annually, a decent suit of clothes, befitting a man in his station; to consist of coat, vest, and breeches; a working-jacket and breeches of homespun, besides; two white

The venerable master on returning to his home, found, indeed, many things to repair, with an ample field for improvement before him. With a body and mind alike sound and vigorous in their maturity, did he bend his energies to the task, while the appearance of everything gave proofs of the taste and energy in the improvements that marked the last days at Mount Vernon.

Washington's rides on his extensive estates, would be from eight to twelve or fourteen miles; he usually moved at a moderate pace, passing through his fields and inspecting everything; but when behind time, the most punctual of men would display the horsemanship of his better days, and a hard gallop bring him up to time, so that the sound of his horse's hoofs and the first dinner-bell should be heard together at a quarter to three o'clock.

Washington's correspondence with Sir John Sinclair,* and other eminent characters in Europe, gave a great deal of information touching the improvements in agri-

---

shirts; three check, do; two linen overalls; as many pairs of shoes as are necessary for him; four dollars at Christmas, with which he may be drunk four days and four nights; two dollars at Easter to effect the same purpose; two dollars at Whitsuntide to be drunk for two days; a dram in the morning, and a drink of grog at dinner at noon.

"For the true and faithful performance of all and each part of these things, the parties have hereunto set their hands this twenty-third day of April, Anno Domini, 1787.

"Witness:
   "George A. Washington,
   "Tobias Lear."

                            his
"Philip Barter, X mark.
"George Washington.

* Sir John Sinclair was an eminent Scotch baronet, and much interested in the progress of the United States. In September, 1796, he wrote to Washington, making special and general inquiries respecting the soil and agriculture of the United States, to which Washington replied, in a lengthy and very able letter, in December following. A copy of that letter may be found in Sparks's *Life and Writings of Washington*, xii. 323.

culture and domestic economy in the Old World. This valuable information was carefully digested by the farmer of Mount Vernon, with a view to its adaptation to the climate and resources of the United States. Nothing that tended to public benefit was too vast to be undertaken by this man of mighty labors. The whole of his public as well as private career was marked by usefulness. His aim was good to his country and mankind, and to effect this desirable end, untiring were his energies and onward his course as a public benefactor.

During the maritime war with France,* the armed merchantmen that sailed from Alexandria would salute on passing Mount Vernon. On the report of the first gun, the general would leave his library, and, taking a position in the portico that fronts the river, remain there uncovered till the firing ceased.

And yet another salute awakened the echoes around the shores of Mount Vernon; another act of homage was paid to the retired chief; and this was the homage of the heart, for it was paid by an old companion-in-arms, while its echoes called up the memories of the past. A small vessel would be seen to skim along the bosom of the Potomac. Nearing the shore, the little craft furled her sails, let go her anchor, and discharged a small piece of ordnance; then a boat put off and pulled to the shore, and soon a messenger appeared, bearing a fine rock or

---

* Allusion has already been made to an expected war with France in the year 1798. There was no actual declaration of war, yet hostilities between the two countries commenced on the ocean. The United States frigate *Constellation*, captured the French frigate *L'Insurgente*, in February, 1799. That frigate had already captured the American schooner *Retaliation*. On the first of February, 1800, the *Constellation* had an action with the French frigate *La Vengeance*, but escaped capture, after a loss of one hundred and sixty men in killed and wounded.

drum fish, with the compliments of Benjamin Grymes, who resided some fifty miles down the river, and who was a gallant officer of the Life-Guard in the War of the Revolution.

Several of the most distinguished of the French emigrants, some of them bringing letters from French officers, who had served in the War for Independence, sought in vain to be received by the first president. Among these were the celebrated Talleyrand, the Duc de Liancourt, Louis Philippe, then Duc d'Orleans, and his two brothers, Montpensier and Bojolais. The first president adhered to his rule, that upon mature consideration he had laid down for his government during the wars and troubles of European nations, viz: *Respect and consideration for our own affairs, with non-intervention in the affairs of others.*

Louis Philippe and brothers visited the retired chief during the last days at Mount Vernon. The amiable Duc de Liancourt bore his reverse of fortune with great magnanimity. He used to say: "In the days of my power and affluence, under the ancient *régime* of France, I kept fifty servants, and yet my coat was never as well brushed as it is now, when I brush it myself."

George Washington Lafayette, and his tutor and friend M. Frestel, became members of the Mount Vernon family during the last days. These estimable Frenchmen, driven by persecution from their native country, found refuge in America.

While reasons of state prevented Washington, as president, from receiving *emigrés*, so soon as he became the private citizen he warmly, joyfully welcomed to his heart and his home the son of his old companion-in-arms, bidding young Lafayette to consider George Washington as a friend and father. The French gentlemen, from their superior intelligence, together with their highly-accomplished and amiable manners, endeared themselves to all who knew them during their sojourn in the United States. They remained members of the family of Mount Vernon until a change in European affairs enabled them to embark for their native land.*

Many articles, both for useful and ornamental purposes, were forwarded to Mount Vernon from Philadelphia; and that the retired chief was in full employment upon his return to his ancient and beloved mansion, may be gathered from the following extract of a letter to the author of these *Recollections*, dated April third, 1797: "We are all in the midst of litter and dirt, occasioned by joiners, masons, painters, and upholsterers, working in the house, all parts of which, as well as the out-buildings, are much out of repair." Mount Vernon, it is known, resembles a village, from there being some fourteen or fifteen buildings detached from each other; and being nearly all constructed of wood, it may well be supposed that decay had made considerable progress, more especially when the master's absence during the War of the

* Young Lafayette and M. Frestel, arrived at Boston, at the close of the summer of 1795. General Lafayette was then an exile, and in prison in Germany, having fled from his country during the storm of the French Revolution. His son came to America for refuge. He assumed the name of Motier, and resided for awhile in seclusion, with his tutor, near New York. When, in March, 1797, Washington retired from the presidency, and became a private citizen, he invited young Lafayette to make Mount Vernon his home; and the young gentleman accompanied the illustrious friend of his father to that pleasant abode on the Potomac. General Lafayette having been restored to liberty and his family, his son, with M. Frestel, sailed for France, from New York, on the twenty-sixth of October, 1797. A portrait of young Lafayette, while a resident at Mount Vernon, may be found in a work entitled, *Mount Vernon and its Associations*, New York, 1859.

Revolution and the first presidency amounted to sixteen years.

An event occurred on the twenty-second of February, 1799, that, while it created an unusual bustle in the ancient halls, shed a bright gleam of sunshine on the last days at Mount Vernon.* It was the marriage of Major Lewis, a favorite nephew, with the adopted daughter of the chief. It was the wish of the young bride that the general of the armies of the United States should appear in the splendidly embroidered uniform (the costume assigned him by the board of general officers) in honor of the bridal; but alas, even the idea of wearing a costume bedizzened with gold embroidery, had never entered the mind of the chief, he being content with the old Continental blue and buff, while the magnificent white plumes presented to him by Major-General Pinckney he gave to the bride, preferring the old Continental cocked hat, with the plain black-ribbon cockade, a type of the brave old days of '76.

Washington's great employment, and a constant stream of company, gave him but little time to go abroad; still, he occasionally visited his old and long-remembered friends in Alexandria. He attended a martial exhibition, representing an invasion by the French, which ended in an old-fashioned sham battle and the capture of the invaders. It was handsomely got up, Alexandria at that time possessing a numerous and well-appointed military; and the whole went off with great eclat.

Among many interesting relics of the past, to be found in the last days at Mount Vernon, was old Billy, the famed body-servant of the commander-in-chief during the whole

* See page 44.

of the War of the Revolution. Of a stout athletic form, he had from an accident become a cripple, and, having lost the power of motion, took up the occupation of a shoemaker for sake of employment. Billy carefully reconnoitred the visiters as they arrived, and when a military title was announced, the old body-servant would send his compliments to the soldier, requesting an interview at his quarters. It was never denied, and Billy, after receiving a warm grasp of the hand, would say, "Ah, colonel, glad to see you; we of the army don't see one another often in these peaceful times. Glad to see your honor looking so well; remember you at headquarters. The new-time people don't know what we old soldiers did and suffered for the country in the old war. Was it not cold enough at Valley Forge? Yes, was it; and I am sure you remember it was hot enough at Monmouth. Ah, colonel, I am a poor cripple; can't ride now, so I make shoes and think of the old times; the gineral often stops his horse here, to inquire if I want anything. I want for nothing, thank God, but the use of my limbs."

These interviews were frequent, as many veteran officers called to pay their respects to the retired chief, and all of them bestowed a token of remembrance upon the old body-servant of the Revolution.*

It was in November of the last days that the general visited Alexandria upon business, and dined with a few friends at the City hotel. Gadsby, the most accomplished of hosts, requested the general's orders for dinner, pre-

---

* See note on page 157. One of Washington's servants, named Cary, set free by his master's will, died in the Federal city, a few years ago, at the age of one hundred and fourteen years. He used to appear at military parades, with an old military coat, cocked hat, and huge cockade, presented to him by Washington. He was followed to the grave by a large concourse of colored people.

mising that there was good store of canvass-back ducks in the larder. "Very good, sir," replied the chief, "give us some of them, with a chafing-dish, some hommony, and a bottle of good Madeira, and we shall not complain."

No sooner was it known in town that the general would stay to dinner, than the cry was for the parade of a new company, called the Independent Blues, commanded by Captain Peircy, an officer of the Revolution. The merchant closed his books, the mechanic laid by his tools, the drum and fife went merrily round, and in the least possible time the Blues had fallen into their ranks, and were in full march for the headquarters.

Meantime the general had dined, and given his only toast of "*All our Friends*," and finished his last glass of wine, when an officer of the Blues was introduced, who requested, in the name of Captain Peircy, that the commander-in-chief would do the Blues the honor to witness a parade of the corps. The general consented, and repaired to the door of the hotel looking toward the public square, accompanied by Colonel Fitzgerald, Dr. Craik, Mr. Keith, Mr. Herbert, and several other gentlemen. The troops went through many evolutions with great spirit, and concluded by firing several volleys. When the parade was ended, the general ordered the author of these *Recollections* to go to Captain Peircy, and express to him the gratification which he, the general, experienced in the very correct and soldierly evolutions, marchings, and firings of the Independent Blues. Such commendation, from such a source, it may well be supposed, was received with no small delight by the young soldiers, who marched off in fine spirits, and were soon afterward dismissed. Thus

ing *the last military order* issued in person by the Father of his Country.

Washington ceased to be a sportsman after 1787, when he gave up the hunting establishment. True, he bred the blood horse, and a favorite colt of his, named *Magnolia*, was entered and ran for a purse; but this was more to encourage the breeding of fine horses than from any attachment to the sports of the turf. All the time that he could spare for active exercise in his latter days was devoted to riding about his farm, and inspecting his improvements. In this he was ably assisted by several of his stewards and managers, who were Europeans, and who had brought from their own countries habits of industry and a knowledge of improved agriculture and rural affairs; so that, had the Farmer of Mount Vernon been spared but a few years longer, his estate would have exhibited a series of model farms, examples to neighboring improvers and to the country at large.

Although much retired from the business world, the chief was by no means inattentive to the progress of public affairs. When the post-bag arrived, he would select the letters, and lay them by for perusal in the seclusion of his library. The journals he would peruse while taking his single cup of tea (his only supper), and would read aloud passages of peculiar interest, making remarks upon the same. These evenings with his family always ended precisely at nine o'clock, when Washington bade every one good night, and retired to rest, to rise again at four, and to renew the same routine of labor and enjoyment that distinguished his last days at Mount Vernon.

Washington's last days, like those that preceded them in the course of a long and a well-spent life, were devoted to constant and useful employment. After the active exercise of the morning, in attention to agriculture and rural affairs, in the evening came the post-bag, loaded with letters, papers, and pamphlets. His correspondence both at home and abroad was immense; yet was it promptly and fully replied to. No letter was unanswered. One of the best-bred men of his time, Washington deemed it a grave offence against the rules of good manners and propriety to leave letters unanswered. He wrote with great facility, and it would be a difficult matter to find another, who had written so much, who had written so well. His epistolary writings will descend to posterity, as models of good taste, as well as exhibiting superior powers of mind. General Henry Lee once observed to the chief, "We are amazed, sir, at the vast amount of work that you accomplish." Washington replied, "Sir, I rise at four o'clock, and a great deal of my work is done while others are asleep."

So punctual a man delighted in always having about him a good timekeeper. In Philadelphia, the first president regularly walked up to his watchmaker's (Clarke, in Second street) to compare his watch with the regulator. At Mount Vernon the active yet always punctual farmer invariably consulted the dial when returning from his morning ride and before entering his house.

The affairs of the household took order from the master's accurate and methodical arrangement of time. Even the fisherman on the river watched for the cook's signal when to pull in shore, so as to deliver his scaly products in time for dinner.

The establishment of Mount Vernon employed a perfect army of servants; yet to each one was assigned certain special duties, and these were required to be strictly performed. Upon the extensive estate there was rigid discipline, without severity. There could be no confusion where all was order; and the affairs of this vast concern, embracing thousands of acres and hundreds of dependants, were conducted with as much ease, method, and regularity, as the affairs of an ordinary homestead.

Mrs. Washington, an accomplished Virginia housewife of the olden time, gave her constant attention to all matters of her domestic household, and by her skill and superior management greatly contributed to the comfortable reception and entertainment of the crowds of guests always to be found in the hospitable mansion of Mount Vernon.

Upon Washington's first retirement, in 1783, he became convinced of the defective nature of the working animals employed in the agriculture of the southern states, and set about remedying the evil by the introduction of mules instead of horses, the mule being found to live longer, be less liable to disease, require less food, and in every respect to be more serviceable and economical than the horse in the agricultural labor of the southern states. Up to 1783, scarcely any mules were to be found in the Union; a few had been imported from the West Indies, but they were of diminutive size and of little value. So soon as the views on this subject of the illustrious farmer of Mount Vernon were known abroad, he received a present from the king of Spain of a jack and two jennies, selected from the royal stud at Madrid. The jack, called the *Royal Gift*, was sixteen hands high, of a gray color, heavily made, and of a sluggish disposition. At the same time, the Marquis de Lafayette sent out a jack and jennies from the island of Malta; this jack, called the *Knight of Malta*, was a superb animal, black color, with the form of a stag and the ferocity of a tiger. Washington availed himself of the best qualities of the two jacks by crossing the breeds, and hence obtained a favorite jack, called *Compound*, which animal united the size and strength of the *Gift* with the high courage and activity of the *Knight*. The jacks arrived at Mount Vernon, if we mistake not, early in 1788. The general bred some very superior mules from his coach mares, sending them from Philadelphia for the purpose. In a few years the estate of Mount Vernon became stocked with mules of a superior order, rising to the height of sixteen hands, and of great power and usefulness, one wagon team of four mules selling at the sale of the general's effects for eight hundred dollars.

Mount Vernon, in the olden time, was celebrated for the luxuries of the table. The fields, the forest, and the river, each in their respective seasons, furnished the most abundant resources for good living. Among the picturesque objects on the Potomac to be seen from the eastern portion of the mansion-house, was the light canoe of Father Jack, the fisherman to the establishment. Father Jack was an African negro, an hundred years of age, and, although greatly enfeebled in body by such a vast weight of years, his mind possessed uncommon vigor. And he would tell of days long past, of Afric's clime, and of Afric's wars, in which he (of course the son of a king) was made captive, and of the terrible battle in which his royal sire was slain, the village consigned to the flames, and he to the slaveship.

Father Jack possessed in an eminent degree the leading quality of all his race—somnolency. By looking through a spy-glass, you would see the canoe fastened to a stake, with the old fisherman, bent nearly double, enjoying a nap, which was only disturbed by the hard jerking of the white perch that became entangled by his hook.

But the slumbers of Father Jack were occasionally attended by some inconvenience. The domestic duties at Mount Vernon were governed by clock time. Now, the cook required that the fish should be forthcoming at a certain period, so that they might be served smoking on the board precisely at three o'clock. He would repair to the river bank, and make the accustomed signals; but, alas, there would be no response; the old fisherman was seen quietly reposing in his canoe, rocked by the gentle undulations of the stream, and dreaming, no doubt, of events "long time ago." The unfortunate *artiste* of the culinary department, grown furious by delay, would now rush down to the water's edge, and, by dint of loud shouting, would cause the canoe to turn its prow to the shore. Father Jack, indignant at its being even supposed that he was asleep upon his post, would rate those present on his landing with, "What you all meck such a debil of a noise for, hey; I wa'nt sleep, only noddin'."

Poor Father Jack! No more at early dawn will he be seen, as with withered arms he paddled his light canoe on the broad surface of the Potomac, to return with the finny spoils, and boast of famous fish taken "on his own hook." His canoe has long since rotted on the shore, his paddle hangs idly in his cabin, his "occupation's gone," and Father Jack, the old fisherman of Mount Vernon, "sleeps the sleep that knows no waking."

A hunter, too, was attached to the household establishment. Tom Davis and his great Newfoundland dog, *Gunner*, were as important characters in the department for furnishing game and wild fowl as Father Jack in that of fish. So vast were the numbers of the canvas-back duck on the Potomac in the ancient time, that a single discharge of Tom Davis's old British musket would procure as many of those delicious birds as would supply the larder for a week.

The year 1799 was in its last month. Washington had nearly completed his sixty-eighth year. The century was fast drawing to a close, and with it the great man's life. Yet the winter of his age had shed its snows so kindly upon him as to mellow without impairing his faculties, either physical or mental, and to give fair promise of additional length of days.

Nor was Washington unmindful of the sure progress of time, and of his liability to be called at any moment to "that bourne from which no traveller returns." He had for years kept a Will by him, and, after mature reflection, had so disposed of his large property as to be satisfactory to himself and to the many who were so fortunate and happy as to share in his testamentary remembrance.*

In the last days at Mount Vernon, desirous of riding pleasantly, the general procured from the North two horses of the Narraganset breed, celebrated as saddle horses. They were well to look at, and were pleasantly gaited under the saddle, but were scary, and therefore unfitted for the service of one who liked to ride quietly on his farm, occasionally dismounting and walking in his fields, to inspect his improvements. From one of these

* Washington's Will was drawn by himself, and is entirely in his own handwriting. It bears the date of July 9th, 1799, and at the bottom of each page his name is written.

horses the general sustained a heavy fall—probably the only fall he ever had from a horse in his life. It was in November, late in the evening. The general, accompanied by Major Lewis, Mr. Peake (a gentleman residing in the neighborhood), the author of these *Recollections*, and a groom, were returning from Alexandria to Mount Vernon. Having halted for a few moments, the general dismounted, and upon rising in his stirrup again, the Narraganset, alarmed at the glare from a fire near the road-side, sprang from under his rider, who came heavily to the ground. Our saddles were empty in an instant, and we rushed to give our assistance, fearing he was hurt. It was unnecessary. The vigorous old man was upon his feet again, brushing the dust from his clothes; and, after thanking us for our prompt assistance, observed that he was not hurt, that he had had a very complete tumble, and that it was owing to a cause that no horseman could well avoid or control; that he was only poised in his stirrup, and had not yet gained his saddle, when the scary animal sprang from under him. Meantime, all our horses had gone off at full speed. It was night, and over four miles were to be won ere we could reach our destination. The chief observed, that, as our horses had disappeared, it only remained for us to take it on foot, and with manly strides led the way. We had proceeded but a short distance on our march, as dismounted cavaliers, when our horses hove in sight. Happily for us, some of the servants of Mr. Peake, whose plantation was hard by, in returning home from their labor, encountered our flying steeds, captured them, and brought them to us. We were speedily remounted, and soon the lights at Mount Vernon were seen glimmering in the distance.

The sentinel placed on the watch-tower by Fate to guard the destinies of Washington, might have cried, "All's well!" during the last days at Mount Vernon. All was well. All things glided gently and prosperously down the stream of time, and all was progressive. Two blades of grass had been made to "grow where but one grew before," and a garden "bloomed where flowers had once grown wild."

The best charities of life were gathered around the *Pater Patriæ* in the last days at Mount Vernon. The love and veneration of a whole people for his illustrious services; his generous and untiring labors in the cause of public utility; his kindly demeanor to his family circle, his friends, and numerous dependants; his courteous and cordial hospitality to his guests, many of them strangers from far distant lands; these charities, all of which sprung from the heart, were the ornament of his declining years, and gave benignant radiance to his setting sun; and that scene, the most sublime in nature, where human greatness reposes on the bosom of human happiness, was to be admired on the banks of the Potomac in the last days at Mount Vernon.*

---

* A German gentleman in 1858, then eighty-four years of age, wrote as follows concerning pictures of the Washington family, which hung in his hall: "They vividly call to my mind the day — the proudest day of my life — that I passed upon the beautiful banks of the Potomac, in the family of the best and greatest personage that the world has ever produced. It was in May, 1798, now nearly sixty-one years ago. I was seated at his right hand at dinner, and I recollect as distinctly his majestic bearing as if it were yesterday. Though of mortality, his overpowering presence inspired an impression that he belonged to immortality. His stateliness, his serene face, the perfect simplicity of his manners, his modest demeanor, and the words of wisdom which he uttered, led me irresistibly to the belief that he was an emanation from the Omnipotent, for the marvellous work that he had just then consummated. It was my good fortune to contemplate him in his retirement — after he had left nothing undone that he could perform for the republic of his creation,

It pleased Providence to permit the beloved Washington to live to witness the fruition of his mighty labors in the cause of his country and mankind, while his success in the calm and honored pursuits of agriculture and rural affairs was grateful to his heart, and shed the most benign and happy influence upon the last days at Mount Vernon.

<small>and after he had quitted office for ever! What a privilege I enjoyed in being his welcome guest! Of the 240,000,000 of people in Europe, I imagine I am the only person, since the death of Lafayette, who was so favored as to break bread and take wine with Washington at his own table."</small>

CHAPTER XXIII.

OUTLINE LIFE-PICTURES.*

RECOLLECTIONS OF MOUNT VERNON — WASHINGTON GOING OUT TO THE WARS — HIS SERVICES IN THE FRENCH AND INDIAN WARS — BATTLE OF THE MONONGAHELA — WASHINGTON A BRIDEGROOM AND FARMER — GOES TO THE FIRST CONGRESS — APPOINTED TO THE CHIEF COMMAND OF THE ARMIES OF THE UNITED STATES — VISITS MOUNT VERNON IN 1781 — RETIREMENT FROM THE ARMY — VISITERS AT MOUNT VERNON — CONSTITUTIONAL CONVENTION — SECRETARY THOMSON AT MOUNT VERNON — WASHINGTON DRAWN FROM HIS RETIREMENT TO BECOME CHIEF MAGISTRATE OF THE REPUBLIC — HIS FINAL RETIREMENT TO PRIVATE LIFE — APPOINTED COMMANDER-IN-CHIEF OF THE PROVISIONAL ARMY — ANECDOTE — WASHINGTON'S CAUTION — HIS DEATH.

How many and what glorious recollections crowd upon the mind at the mention of Mount Vernon! It is a name that will be hallowed to all time, and the foot of the pilgrim journeying from all nations will continue to press the turf around the sepulchre where rest the ashes of the Father of his Country. The associations in the history of this venerated spot, with those in the history of the life and actions of its departed master, will ever cause Mount Vernon to be "freshly remembered." These associations began with the early life of Washington, and ended only with his last days on earth. Mount Vernon was the home of his youth, the retreat of his advanced age, the spot that he most loved, and to which he so often retired to find repose from the cares and anxieties of public affairs. He never left it but with regret. He always returned to it with joy. Could the old halls of

---

* First published in the *National Intelligencer*, on the fourth of July, 1850.

the ancient mansion exhibit a *tableau vivant* of the characters that have been their inmates in by-gone days, what a long and imposing list of patriots, statesmen, and warriors would appear to our admiring gaze, to adorn the scenes and memories of the past! Let us endeavor to sketch a few outlines.

Our *tableau* opens in 1753, when Washington crosses the threshold of Mount Vernon to enter upon that great theatre of life on which he was destined to play so illustrious a part. His achievement in penetrating the wilderness, and successful accomplishment of the important objects of his mission, amid dangers and difficulties the most appalling, introduced him to the favorable notice of the colonial authorities, who, in 1754, intrusted the young Virginian with the defence of the frontier of his native colony,* where, after a gallant conflict with the enemy, he resigned his commission and retired to Mount Vernon. But he was not permitted long to enjoy the pleasures of its peaceful shades; for, his martial reputation having attracted the notice of General Braddock, the provincial soldier, in 1755, was requested by the British veteran to accompany the latter in the ill-fated expedition to Fort Duquesne.

Our *tableau* now gives a perspective view of the memorable ninth of July, and the field of the Monongahela, where a youthful hero gathers his first laurels amid the fury of the fight, and where his high and chivalric daring caused "the wild untutored savage" to hail the last mounted officer on the field of Monongahela, as "the chosen of the great spirit, the warrior who could not die in battle."†

---

* See note on page 159.   † See note on page 158.

At the close of the Seven Years' War, the provincial colonel again becomes a private citizen, and returns to Mount Vernon to await the call of destiny.

It is 1759, and our *tableau* exhibits a gay and joyous scene, while the old halls ring again with the reception of a bridal party, and Washington enters Mount Vernon a prosperous and happy bridegroom. The gallant and distinguished soldier now lays aside the "pomp and circumstance of glorious war," and many years glide happily along, amid the delights of domestic felicity, the society of family and friends, and the employments of agriculture and rural affairs, when our *tableau* changes to 1774. The colonial troubles have commenced, and we behold the arrival of two distinguished personages at Mount Vernon, Patrick Henry and Edmund Pendleton. The object of their visit is to accompany Washington to the first Congress, where the soldier had been called by the voice of his country, to change the duties of the field for those of the senate-house.*

In 1775, while serving as a member of the first Congress, Washington is appointed to command in chief the armies of the colonies, then assembling to do battle for the rights and liberties of unborn generations. He obeys the call of destiny and his country; and for six eventful years, big with the fate of liberty and an empire, his home is in the tented field.†

Now, 1781, our *tableau* shows the long-deserted halls

---

* Washington was chosen delegate to represent Virginia in the First Continental Congress, which assembled at Philadelphia, on the fifth of September, 1774. He was accompanied on his journey from Mount Vernon to Philadelphia, on that occasion, by Patrick Henry and Edmund Pendleton. Richard Henry Lee expected to join them at Mount Vernon, but was detained at home.

† See note on page 134.

of Mount Vernon to be animated by the presence of the commander-in-chief of the combined armies of America and France, accompanied by the Count de Rochambeau and a brilliant suite, who halt but for a single day, *en route* for Yorktown.*

Again our *tableau* changes, and introduces us, in 1783, to happier scenes. The war has ended; its storms have passed away, and the sunshine of peace sheds its benign influences upon an infant nation, a free and independent people.† Annapolis has witnessed a sublime spectacle, and Washington, having resigned his commission, and "taken leave of the employments of public life," hastens to his beloved retirement, and never in this great man's long and glorious career did he experience so pure, so enviable a delight, as when merging the victorious general into the illustrious farmer of Mount Vernon.

Our *tableau* now teems with characters. In the old halls of Mount Vernon are assembled chosen spirits, from the wise, the good, and brave of both hemispheres, who have journeyed from distant homes, to pay the homage of their hearts to the hero of the age in the retirement of a private citizen. Conspicuous amid this honored group is the good and gallant Lafayette, who, supposing in 1784‡ that he was about to bid adieu to America for

---

* Washington arrived at Mount Vernon on the ninth of September. The next day Rochambeau and Chastelleux, with their respective suites, arrived. On the eleventh, Washington presided at a dinner-party, under his own roof, and on the twelfth, all departed for Williamsburg. Washington was accompanied by John Parke Custis, father of the author of these *Recollections*, as his aid. They arrived at Williamsburg on the evening of the fourteenth.

† See note on page 370.

‡ Lafayette came to America in the summer of 1784. After remaining a few days in New York, he hastened to Mount Vernon, where he remained almost a fortnight. He again visited the illustrious farmer on the Potomac, just before leaving America, in November following.

the last time, had hastened to Mount Vernon to pay his parting respects to the man who, of all men, he most loved and admired.

The retired chief receives his guests with that kindliness and hospitality for which Mount Vernon was always distinguished, while his early rising, his industrious and methodical habits of life, his horsemanship in the chase, his minute attention to all matters, and the improvement of his domain, elicited the warmest encomium and admiration of those who, in the old time of day, had the good fortune to visit Washington on his farm.

From the unalloyed happiness in which four years were now passed in the employments of agriculture, in social and domestic intercourse, occasionally varied by the pleasures of the chase, this period in the life of the *Pater Patriæ* may truly be said to have been the one in which all his ways were "ways of pleasantness, and all his paths were peace."

Our *tableau* changes to 1787, when his country calls upon her chosen son to leave the tranquil shades of Mount Vernon to take a prominent part in the momentous events of the times. The old confederation is ended; a new government is to be formed; confusion is to be succeeded by order. The convention assembles, and that immortal constitutional charter, that millions of freemen have since so happily enjoyed, received its first signature from the hand of George Washington.*

From this date a young and glorious empire dawned upon the world. Conceived in the purity of republican freedom, founded on the basis of equal rights and equal laws, the great and renowned of the land formed this

* See note on page 381.

masterwork of virtue; and patriotism might well expect that it would endure for centuries, till grown hoary by time, and from the decline of public virtue it should experience the fate of nations, when, from the extent and magnificence of its ruins, futurity might read the story of its rise, its grandeur, and its fall.

Our *tableau* exhibits, in 1789, important and touching events in *the history of Mount Vernon*. A special envoy arrives in the person of Mr. Secretary Thomson, a signer of the Declaration of Independence, and a genuine type of *the brave old days of* '76. Scarcely is he received with the warmest welcome, when he declares the object of his mission: That he is charged, by the Congress then assembled in New York, with the grateful duty of announcing to George Washington, a private citizen, his election to the presidency of the United States of America.*

The recipient of this highest, this proudest dignity that can ever be conferred on man, was by no means unprepared for its announcement by the venerable ambassador. From the period of the ratification of the Constitution by the states, every mail from every part of the Union brought letters to Mount Vernon, all praying the retired chief to yield to the united wishes of the people to accept the highest dignity in their power to bestow. In vain did the happy farmer of Mount Vernon plead that advanced age and long services needed repose. Many of his old and much-loved companions-in-arms gathered around him affectionately, saying, "We feel assured that you can not, that you will not, refuse the wishes of a whole people; your honored name is heard

* See note on page 383.

from every lip, while in every heart there dwells but one sentiment: *Washington, chief magistrate of the Republic.*"

The newly-chosen president was deeply affected by this generous, this universal testimonial of the love and attachment of his countrymen. The people triumphed! The man of the people yielded to the will of the people. A day or two sufficed for preparation for departure. A sigh to the fond memories of home and happy days of retirement, and the first president of the United States bade adieu to Mount Vernon. For eight years silence reigned in the ancient halls, when, in 1797, they again teem with animation. The long-absent master returns. Time has blanched his locks, and traced its furrows on his noble brow, but his manly form is still erect; ay, with lightsome step and joyous heart he once more enters the portals of his beloved Mount Vernon.

Our *tableau* having exhibited the changing events in the history of Mount Vernon for forty-six years, in its closing scene portrays the aged chief in his last retirement. His days are numbered, his glorious race is nearly run, yet, when invasion threatens, he obeys the last call of his country, and is again in arms, her general and protector.*

When Washington was appointed to his last command in the armies of his country, his acceptance was accompanied by an intimation that he should remain in his beloved retirement of Mount Vernon, till imperious circumstances should call him to the field. The commander-in-chief gave the necessary attention to military duties through his private secretary, while himself continued the occupations of rural affairs.

* See note on page 327.

A number of the principal characters in the United States were desirous that their sons should make a first essay in arms under the immediate auspices of the venerable chief. Among these was the Hon. Charles Carroll, of Carrollton, for whom Washington ever entertained the very warmest political as well as personal attachment and esteem. To Mr. Carroll's application, the general replied, that as it was his firm resolve, in case the enemy effected a landing, to meet them on the very threshold of the empire, he should, in such an event, require about his person, officers of tried knowledge and experience in war; but with a view to gratify Mr. Carroll, his son should be received as an extra aid-de-camp.

Among the applicants of a more veteran stamp, was Colonel H., of Richmond, one of that band of ardent and youthful chivalry, which Virginia sent to the War for Independence in the very dawn of the Revolution. Colonel H. was lieutenant of Morgan's famed corps of Riflemen, which performed the memorable march across the wintry wilderness of the Kennebec in 1775. During that display of almost superhuman privation and toil, and in the subsequent assault on Quebec, he displayed a hardihood of character, and heroism of heart, that won for him the admiration of his comrades, and esteem of their intrepid commander; and elicited a cognomen, that a Ney might have been proud to deserve—*"The most daring of all who dare."* Morgan, himself, bred in the hardy school of the frontier and Indian warfare, declared of Colonel H.—"He exceeds all men. During the greatest horrors of our march, when the bravest fainted and fell from exhaustion and despondency, it was he who cheered us on, for oft have I seen him *dance upon the snow, while he gnawed his moccasins for subsistence.*"

Yet even to the application of such a soldier, did the ever cautious mind of Washington pause, while he weighed in the balance not the past, but the present merits of the man. The general wrote to his nephew, then in Richmond, to this effect: "Colonel H. has applied to become a member of my military family. In the War of the Revolution I knew him well; and of a truth he was then all that could be desired in a good and gallant officer, and estimable man; but time, my dear Bushrod,* often changes men as well as things. Now, the object of this letter is to inquire whether *the habits* of Colonel H. are unaltered, and whether I shall find him *now* what I knew him to be in other days." The answer to this letter was most satisfactory. Colonel H. was the same, good, gallant, and estimable. The chief was content, and quickly marked him for promotion.

What a moral does this little private memoir impress upon those who are high in authority, upon whose knowledge and judgment of men and things, so often depend the destinies of nations! How careful should chiefs be, in the choice of their subordinates, to weigh well in the balance the present as well as the past merits of applicants for office, lest, as in the words of the venerated Washington, "Time, *which changes men as well as things,*"

---

* Bushrod Washington, son of the general's brother John Augustine. His profession was the law; and in 1798, President Adams appointed him a judge of the supreme court of the United States, an office which he held until his death. He was the first president of the American Colonization Society. On the death of General Washington he inherited the estate of Mount Vernon, and the general's books and papers. He died at Philadelphia on the twenty-sixth of November, 1829, at the age of seventy years. His remains are in the family vault at Mount Vernon, and near it is a fine white marble obelisk erected to his memory.

may have rendered them unworthy of being "marked for promotion."

After a long and unexampled career of glory in the service of his country and mankind, well stricken in years and laden with honors, in his own beloved Mount Vernon, with the fortitude and resignation befitting the Roman fame of his life and actions, the Pater Patriæ yielded up his soul to Him who gave it, calmly declaring, "I am not afraid to die."

Our *tableau vivant* closes with the grandeur and solemnity of the spectacle that bore him to his grave.

CHAPTER XXIV.

LAST HOURS OF WASHINGTON.

Last Survivor of the Death-Scene — Washington Exposed to a Storm — Symptoms of Sickness — The Succeeding Evening late in his Library — Characteristic Remark to Mrs. Washington — Sleeplessness — Alarm — Physicians sent for — Doctor Craik — Severity of the Illness — Calls for his Will — Directions about his Body — A Scriptural Custom Observed — Why no Clergyman was at the Death-bed of Washington — Mrs. Washington's Secret Prayers — The Closing Scene.

TWENTY-EIGHT years have passed since an interesting group were assembled in the death room, and witnessed the last hours of Washington.* So keen and unsparing hath been the scythe of time, that of all those who watched over the patriarch's couch, on the thirteenth and fourteenth of December, 1799, but a single personage survives.†

On the morning of the thirteenth, the general was engaged in making some improvements in the front of Mount Vernon.‡ As was usual with him, he carried his

---

* This was first published in the *National Intelligencer*, in February, 1827.

† The persons here alluded to were, Mrs. Washington, Christopher, a favorite house-servant who attended upon the master, Colonel Tobias Lear, Mrs. Forbes, the housekeeper, Mr. Albert Rawlins, Drs. Craik, Brown, and Dick, and Caroline, Molly, and Charlotte, three of the house-servants. Mrs. Lewis (Eleanor Parke Custis) was confined, by childbirth, to an upper chamber, and her husband and the author of these *Recollections*, were absent in New Kent. Who the survivor was, to whom the author alludes, can not now be determined.

‖ Colonel Tobias Lear, a talented and educated gentleman, who resided many years with Washington, first as secretary, and afterwards as superintendent of his private affairs, wrote, immediately after the death of the patriot, a circumstantial

own compass, noted his observations, and marked out the ground. The day became rainy, with sleet, and the improver remained so long exposed to the inclemency of the weather as to be considerably wetted before his return to the house. About one o'clock he was seized with chilliness and nausea, but having changed his clothes, he sat down to his in-door work—there being no moment of his time for which he had not provided an appropriate employment.

At night on joining his family circle, the general complained of a slight indisposition, and after a single cup of tea, repaired to his library, where he remained writing until between eleven and twelve o'clock.* Mrs. Washington retired about the usual family hour, but becoming alarmed at not hearing the accustomed sound of the library door as it closed for the night, and gave signal for rest in the well-regulated mansion, she rose again, and continued sitting up, in much anxiety and suspense. At length the well-known step was heard on the stair, and upon the general's entering his chamber, the lady chided him for staying up so late, knowing him to be unwell, to which Washington made this memorably reply: "I came so soon as my business was accomplished. You well

---

account of the scenes at his departure. He was present during his illness and at his death, and above all others was most competent to give a correct narrative. His account, much more minute than Mr. Custis's, agrees substantially with the more concise narrative in this chapter. It may be found in the *Life and Writings of Washington*, by Jared Sparks, i. 555.

* Mr. Lear says, "that in the evening the papers were brought from the post-office, and the family remained in the parlor until nine o'clock, when Mrs. Washington went up to Mrs. Lewis's room. After that he and the general read. Washington was quite hoarse; and when he left, as Lear supposed, for the night, the latter observed to the general, that he had better take something for his cold. Washington replied, "No; you know I never take anything for a cold—let it go as it came."

know that through a long life, it has been my unvaried rule, never to put off till the morrow the duties which should be performed to-day."

Having first covered the fire with care, the man of mighty labors sought repose; but it came not, as it long had been wont to do, to comfort and restore after the many and earnest occupations of the well-spent day. The night was passed in feverish restlessness and pain. "Tired nature's sweet restorer, balmy sleep," was destined no more to visit his couch; yet the manly sufferer uttered no complaint, would permit no one to be disturbed in their rest, on his account, and it was only at daybreak he would consent that the overseer might be called in, and bleeding resorted to. A vein was opened, but no relief afforded. Couriers were despatched to Dr. Craik,*

---

* Doctor James Craik was born at Abigland, near Dumfries, Scotland, in 1730, and at about that time, John Paul, the father of John Paul Jones, was the gardener of Dr. Craik's father. Dr. Craik came to America in 1750. He had practised his profession a short time in the West Indies. He settled in Virginia; and on the seventh of March, 1754, he was commissioned a surgeon in Colonel Fry's regiment, which was commanded by Washington on the death of that officer. He served in the provincial army during a greater portion of the French and Indian war. At that time his home was in Winchester, Virginia. He was married in December, 1760. In 1770 he accompanied Washington to the Ohio, and then it was that the scene of the Indian Prophecy occurred, which is cited in chapter xi. of this work. He afterwards settled near Port Tobacco, Charles county, Maryland, where he built a fine house, but by the persuasion of Washington, he removed to Alexandria. In 1777, Dr. Craik was appointed assistant director-general in the hospital department of the continental army. He continued to reside in Alexandria, until old age caused him to relinquish the practice of his profession, when he retired to Vaucluse, a part of the Ravensworth estate, where he died in February, 1814, at the age of eighty-four years. His wife died a few months afterward, at the age of seventy-four. Dr. Craik had nine children—six sons and three daughters. His eldest son, William, was a representative in Congress from 1796 to 1801, when he was appointed judge of the federal court. He and the author of these *Recollections* married sisters, the daughters of William Fitzhugh, of Chatham, Virginia. His younger son, George Washington, born in 1774, was President Washington's private secretary.

Dr. Craik was vigorous and active until the last. His grandson, Rev. James

the family,* and Drs. Dick and Brown,† the consulting physicians, all of whom came with speed. The proper remedies were administered, but without producing their healing effects; while the patient, yielding to the anxious looks of all around him, waived his usual objections to medicines, and took those which were prescribed without hesitation or remark. The medical gentlemen spared not their skill, and all the resources of their art were exhausted in unwearied endeavors to preserve this noblest work of nature.

The night approached—the last night of Washington. The weather became severely cold while the group gathered nearer to the couch of the sufferer, watching with intense anxiety for the slightest dawning of hope. He spoke but little. To the respectful and affectionate inquiries of an old family servant, as she smoothed down his pillow, how he felt himself, he answered, "I am very ill." To Dr. Craik, his earliest companion-in-arms, longest tried and bosom friend, he observed, "I am dying, sir—but am not afraid to die." To Mrs. Washington he said, "Go to my desk, and in the private drawer you will find two papers—bring them to me." They were brought.

Craik, of Louisville, Kentucky, from whom I received the foregoing facts, says: "He was a stout, thick-set man, perfectly erect, no stoop of the shoulders, and no appearance of debility in his carriage. Not long before his death he ran a race with me (then about eight years old), in the front yard of the house, at Vaucluse, before the assembled family." A profile of Dr. Craik, in Silhoutte, may be found in a work, by the author of these notes, entitled *Mount Vernon and its Associations*.

* These were Mrs. Law and Mrs. Peter, and their husbands, the grandchildren of Mrs. Washington; also her daughter-in-law, Mrs. Stuart. None of them arrived before Washington's death.

† These were neighboring physicians. Dr. Craik had advised Washington to send for Dr. Brown, of Port Tobacco, in the event of severe illness in his family during the absence of Dr. Craik. Dr. Elisha C. Dick was generally the consulting physician with Dr. Craik.

He continued—"These are my Wills—preserve this one and burn the other," which was accordingly done. Calling to Colonel Lear, he directed—"Let my corpse be kept for the usual period of three days."*

The custom of keeping the dead for the scriptural period of three days, is derived from remote antiquity, and arose, not from fear of premature interment, as in more modern times, but from motives of veneration toward the deceased; for the better enabling the relatives and friends to assemble from a distance, to perform the funeral rites; for the pious watchings of the corpse; and for many sad, yet endearing ceremonies with which we delight to pay our last duties to the remains of those we loved.

The patient bore his acute sufferings with fortitude and perfect resignation to the Divine will, while as the night advanced it became evident that he was sinking, and he seemed fully aware that "his hour was nigh." He inquired the time, and was answered a few minutes to ten. He spoke no more—the hand of death was upon him, and he was conscious that "his hour was come." With surprising self-possession he prepared to die. Composing his form at length, and folding his arms on his bosom, without a sigh, without a groan, the Father of his Country died. No pang or struggle told when the noble spirit took its noiseless flight;† while so tranquil

---

* "At length," he said, "I am just going. Have me decently buried; and do not let my body be put into the vault in less than three days after I am dead."—*Mr. Lear's statement.*

† "Dr. Craik," says Mr. Lear, "put his hands over his eyes, and he expired without a struggle or a sigh. While we were fixed in silent grief," he continues, "Mrs. Washington, who was sitting at the foot of the bed, asked, with a firm and collected voice, 'Is he gone?' I could not speak, but held up my hand as a signal,

appeared the manly features in the repose of death, that some moments had passed ere those around could believe that the patriarch was no more.

It may be asked, Why was the ministry of religion wanting to shed its peaceful and benign lustre upon the last hours of Washington? Why was he, to whom the observances of sacred things were ever primary duties throughout life, without their consolations in his last moments? We answer, circumstances did not permit. It was but for a little while that the disease assumed so threatening a character as to forbid the encouragement of hope; yet, to stay that summons which none may refuse, to give still farther length of days to him whose "time-honored life" was so dear to mankind, prayer was not wanting to the throne of Grace. Close to the couch of the sufferer, resting her head upon that ancient book, with which she had been wont to hold pious communion a portion of every day, for more than half a century, was the venerable consort, absorbed in silent prayer, and from which she only arose when the mourning group prepared to lead her from the chamber of the dead. Such were the last hours of Washington.*

that he was no more. "'Tis well,' said she, in the same voice, 'all is now over; 1 shall soon follow him; I have no more trials to pass through.'"

* Washington died on Saturday night, the fourteenth of December, 1799, between the hours of ten and eleven. On Sunday a coffin was procured from Alexandria, and on the same day several of the family arrived. The coffin was made of mahogany, lined with lead, and upon it was placed at the head, an ornament inscribed SURGE AD JUDICIUM; about the middle of the coffin, GLORIA DEO; and on a small silver plate, in the form of the American shield, were the words:

GEORGE WASHINGTON,
BORN FEB. 22, 1732.
DIED DECEMBER 14, 1799.

The time for the funeral was fixed on Wednesday the eighteenth, at twelve o'clock, and the Rev. Mr. Davis was invited to perform the funeral services, according to the ritual of the Protestant Episcopal church. The family having been informed that the military and Freemasons of Alexandria desired to participate in the ceremonies, arrangements were made accordingly. People began to collect at Mount Vernon at eleven o'clock; but as a great part of the troops did not get down from Alexandria in time, the ceremonies were postponed until three. Eleven pieces of artillery were brought down from Alexandria; and a schooner belonging to Mr. Robert Hamilton, of that city, lay off Mount Vernon, and fired minute-guns.

The arrangements of the procession were made by Colonels Little, Simms, Deneale, and Dr. Dick. It moved at three o'clock. The pall-bearers were Colonels Little, Simms, Payne, Gilpin, Ramsay, and Marsleter. Colonel Blackburn preceded the corpse. Colonel Deneale marched with the military. The procession moved out through the gate at the left wing of the house, and proceeded round in front of the lawn, and down to the vault on the right wing of the house. The following was the composition and order of the procession:—

The troops, horse and foot.
The clergy, namely, the Rev. Messrs. Davis, Muir, Moffat, and Addison.
The general's horse, with his saddle, holsters, and pistols, led by two grooms,
Cyrus, and Wilson, in black.
The body, borne by the Freemasons and officers.
Principal mourners, namely,
Mrs. Stuart and Mrs. Law.
Misses Nancy and Sally Stuart.
Miss Fairfax and Miss Dennison.
Mr. Law and Mr. Peter.
Mr. Lear and Dr. Craik.
Lord Fairfax and Ferdinando Fairfax.
Lodge, No. 23.
Corporation of Alexandria.
All other persons, preceded by Mr. Anderson and the overseer.

When the body arrived at the vault, the Rev. Mr. Davis read the service, and pronounced a short address. The Masons then performed their ceremonies, and the body was deposited in the vault. Three general discharges of musketry were given by the infantry; and eleven pieces of artillery, which were ranged back of the vault, and simultaneously discharged, "paid the last tribute to the entombed commander-in-chief of the armies of the United States." The vault was the old one, on the brow of the hill, now in ruins. The new tomb, directed by Washington, in his Will, to be constructed, was not made until many years afterward.

The Congress, then sitting in Philadelphia, received information of the death of Washington on the eighteenth, and on the following day the announcement was formally made on the floor of the house of representatives, by the Honorable John Marshall, of Virginia (afterward chief-justice of the United States), and the house, after some appropriate action, adjourned. On the twenty-third, the Congress adopted joint resolutions—*first*, that a marble monument should be erected at the capitol, already mentioned in the preceding chapter; *secondly*, that there should be "a funeral procession from Congress hall to the German Lutheran church, in memory of

General George Washington, on Thursday the twenty-sixth instant, and that an oration be prepared at the request of Congress, to be delivered before both houses that day; and that the president of the senate, and the speaker of the house of representatives, be desired to request one of the members of Congress to perform and deliver the same; *thirdly*, that the people of the United States should be recommended to wear crape on their left arm as mourning for thirty days; *fourthly*, that the president of the United States should direct a copy of the resolutions to Mrs. Washington, with words of condolence, and a request that his remains might be interred at the capitol of the Republic.

On the thirtieth of December, Congress further resolved that it should be recommended to the people of the Union, to assemble on the succeeding twenty-second of February, "to testify their grief by suitable eulogies, orations, and discourses, or by public prayers."

Pursuant to one of the foregoing resolutions, General Henry Lee, then a member of Congress, was invited to pronounce a funeral oration. He consented, and the Lutheran church in Fourth street, above Arch, Philadelphia, the largest in the city, was crowded on the occasion. The M'Pherson Blues, a corps of three hundred men, composed of the *elite* of the city, were a guard of honor on that occasion. There are now [July, 1859] only six survivors of that corps, who were present on the occasion, namely, Samuel Breck, aged eighty-eight, S. Palmer, aged seventy-nine, S. F. Smith, aged seventy-nine, C. N. Bancker, aged eighty-three, Quinton Campbell, aged eighty-three, and John F. Watson (the annalist of Philadelphia and New York), aged eighty. These names were given me by Mr. Breck, at a recent interview. General Lee's oration on that occasion will be found in the Appendix to this volume.

CHAPTER XXV.

PERSONAL APPEARANCE OF WASHINGTON.

Common Likeness of Portraits — Failure in the Delineation of Washington's Figure — His Form and Weight — Trumbull's Equestrian Statue of Washington — Washington's Height — His Limbs — Power of his Arm displayed — Illustration given by Charles Willson Peale — Easy Exercise of His Powers — Wrestling — Anecdote of His Early Life — His Large Hand — His Resemblance to Ralph Izard — Washington's Features — His Equestrian Accomplishments — Marked for His Martial Elegance in New York — Anecdote.

All of the many portraits which have been given of Washington, possess a resemblance, from the drawings on a signboard to the galleries of taste.* He was so unique, so unlike any one else, his whole appearance so striking and impressive, that it was almost impossible to make a total failure, in forming a likeness of him, "on whom every God appeared to have set his seal, to give the world assurance of a man."

While several original pictures and sculptures are excellent likenesses of his physiognomy, in various stages of life, there has been a general failure in the delineation of his figure. His manliness has been misrepresented by bulkiness, while his vigorous, elastic frame, in which so many graces combined, has been drawn from the model

---

* John B. Moreau, Esquire, of New York, has a large collection of engraved portraits of Washington, American and foreign. Among them are one hundred and five different engravings, all dissimilar. Yet, with a few exceptions, all present some resemblance to Washington, as delineated by the best artists.

of Ajax, when its true personification should be that of Achilles.

With all its developments of muscular power, the form of Washington had no appearance of bulkiness, and so harmonious were its proportions that he did not appear so passing tall as his portraits have represented. He was rather spare than full during his whole life; this is readily ascertained from his weight. The last time he weighed was in the summer of 1799, when having made the tour of his farms, accompanied by an English gentleman, he called at his mill and was weighed. The writer placed the weight in the scales. The Englishman, not so tall, but stout, square built, and fleshy, weighed heavily, and expressed much surprise that the general had not outweighed him, when Washington observed, that the best weight of his best days never exceeded from two hundred and ten to two hundred and twenty pounds. In the instance alluded to he weighed a little rising two hundred and ten.

Of the portraits of Washington, the most of them give to his person a fullness that it did not possess, together with an abdominal enlargement greater than in the life, while his matchless limbs have in but two instances been faithfully portrayed—in the equestrian portrait by Trumbull, of 1790, a copy of which is in the city hall of New York, and in an engraving by Loisier, from a painting by Cogniet, French artists of distinguished merit. The latter is not an original painting, the head being from Stuart, but the delineation of the limbs is the most perfect extant.*

General Washington, in the prime of life, stood six

* See the next chapter.

feet two inches, and measured precisely six feet when attired for the grave. From the period of the Revolution, there was an evident bending in that frame so passing straight before, but the stoop is attributable rather to the care and toils of that arduous contest than to age: for his step was firm, and his carriage noble and commanding, long after the time when the physical properties of man are supposed to be in the wane.

To a majestic height, was added correspondent breadth and firmness, and his whole person was so cast in nature's finest mould as to resemble the classic remains of ancient statuary, where all the parts contribute to the purity and perfection of the whole.

The power of Washington's arm was displayed in several memorable instances; in his throwing a stone from the bed of the stream to the top of the Natural Bridge; another over the Palisades into the Hudson, and yet another across the Rappahannock, at Fredericksburg. Of the article with which he spanned this bold and navigable stream, there are various accounts. We are assured that it was a piece of slate, fashioned to about the size and shape of a dollar, and which, sent by an arm so strong, not only spanned the river, but took the ground at least thirty yards on the other side. Numbers have since tried this feat, but none have cleared the water. 'Tis the "Douglas cast," made in the days when Virginia's men were strong, as her maids are fair; when the hardy sports of the gymnasium prepared the body to answer the "trumpet call to war," and gave vigor and elevation to the mind, while our modern habits would rather fit the youth "to caper nimbly in a lady's chamber."

While the late and venerable Charles Willson Peale was at Mount Vernon, in 1772, engaged in painting the portrait of the provincial colonel, some young men were contending in the exercise of pitching the bar. Washington looked on for a time, then grasping the missile in his master hand, whirled the iron through the air, which took the ground far, very far, beyond any of its former limits—the colonel observing, with a smile, "You perceive, young gentlemen, that my arm yet retains some portion of the vigor of my earlier days." He was then in his fortieth year, and probably in the full meridian of his physical powers; but those powers became rather mellowed than decayed by time, for "his age was like a lusty winter, frosty yet kindly," and, up to his sixty-eighth year, he mounted a horse with surprising agility, and rode with the ease and gracefulness of his better days. His personal prowess that elicited the admiration of a people who have nearly all passed from the stage of life, still serves as a model for the manhood of modern times.

In the various exhibitions of Washington's great physical powers, they were apparently attended by scarcely any effort. When he overthrew the strong man of Virginia in wrestling, while many of the finest of the young athletæ of the times were engaged in the manly games, Washington had retired to the shade of a tree, intent upon the perusal of a favorite volume; and it was only when the champion of the games strode through the ring, calling for nobler competitors, and taunting the student with the reproach that it was the fear of encountering so redoubted an antagonist that kept him from the ring, that Washington closed his book, and, without divesting himself of his coat, calmly walked into the arena, observing, that fear formed no part of his being; then grappling with the champion, the struggle was fierce but momentary, for, said the vanquished hero of the arena, in Washington's lion-like grasp, I became powerless, and was hurled to the ground with a force that seemed to jar the very marrow in my bones; while the victor, regardless of the shouts that proclaimed his triumph, leisurely retired to his shade, and the enjoyment of his favorite volume.

Washington's powers were chiefly in his limbs: they were long, large, and sinewy. His frame was of equal breadth from the shoulders to the hips. His chest, though broad and expansive, was not prominent, but rather hollowed in the centre. He had suffered from a pulmonary affection in early life, from which he never entirely recovered. His frame showed an extraordinary development of bone and muscle; his joints were large, as were his feet; and could a cast have been preserved of his hand, to be exhibited in these degenerate days, it would be said to have belonged to the being of a fabulous age. During Lafayette's visit to Mount Vernon in 1825, he said to the writer, "I never saw so large a hand on any human being, as the general's. It was in this portico, in 1784, that you were introduced to me by the general. You were a very little gentleman, with a feather in your hat, and holding fast to *one finger* of the good general's remarkable hand, which was all you could do, my dear sir, at that time."

To a question that we have been asked a thousand and one times, viz.—to what individual, known to any who are yet living, did the person of Washington bear the nearest resemblance?—we answer, to Ralph Izard, senator from South Carolina, in the first Congress under the Constitution. The form of Izard was cast in nature's manliest mould, while his air and manner were both dignified and imposing. He acquired great distinction while pursuing his studies in England, for his remarkable prowess in the athletic exercises of that distant period.*

An officer of the Life-Guard has been often heard to observe, that the commander-in-chief was thought to be the strongest man in the army, and yet what thews and sinews were to be found in the army of the Revolution. In 1781, a company of riflemen from the county of Augusta, in Virginia, reinforced the troops of Lafayette. As the stalwart band of mountaineers, defiled before the general, the astonished and admiring Frenchman exclaimed, "Mon Dieu! what a people are these Americans; they have reinforced me with a band of giants!"

Washington's physiognomy was decidedly Roman—not in its type expressing the reckless ambition of the "broad-fronted Cæsar," or the luxurious indulgence of the "curled Anthony," but rather of the better age of Rome—the Fabius Maximus, Marcellus, or the Scipios.

An equestrian portraiture is particularly well suited to him who rode so well, and who was much attached to the noble animal which so oft and so gallantly had borne him in the chase, in war, and in the perilous service of the frontier. Rickets, the celebrated equestrian, used to

* Ralph Izard represented South Carolina in the United States senate, from 1789 to 1795. He was distinguished as an eloquent statesman, and was loved by Washington for his integrity and purity of character. In the senate he had the confidence of all parties. Mr. Izard was wealthy, and held a high social distinction. His wife was a daughter of Peter Delancey, of New York. Mr Izard died in May, 1804, at the age of sixty-six years.

say, "I delight to see the general ride, and make it a point to fall in with him when I hear that he is abroad on horseback—his seat is so firm, his management so easy and graceful, that I, who am a professor of horsemanship, would go to him and *learn to ride.*"

Bred in the vigorous school of the frontier warfare "the earth his bed, his canopy the heavens," he excelled the hunter and woodsman in their athletic habits, and in those trials of manhood which distinguished the hardy days of his early life. He was amazingly swift of foot, and could climb the mountain steep, and "not a sob confess his toil."

So long ago as the days of the vice-regal court at Williamsburg, in the time of Lord Botetourt, Colonel Washington was remarkable for his splendid person. The air with which he wore a small sword, and his peculiar walk, that had the light elastic tread acquired by his long service on the frontier, and a matter of much observation, especially to foreigners.

While Colonel Washington was on a visit to New York, in 1773,* it was boasted at the table of the British governor that a regiment, just landed from England, contained among its officers some of the finest specimens of martial elegance in his Majesty's service—in fact, the most superb looking fellows ever landed upon the shores of the New World. "I wager your excellency a pair of gloves," said Mrs. Morris, an American lady, "that I will show you a finer man in the procession to-morrow, than your excellency can select

* Washington visited New York, on that occasion, for the purpose of placing Mrs. Washington's son, John Parke Curtis, in King's (now Columbia) college. He arrived there on the thirty-first of May, and remained until after the king's birthday, the fourth of June.

from your famous regiment?"—"Done, madam!" replied the governor. The morrow came (the fourth of June), and the procession, in honor of the birthday of the king, advanced through Broadway to the strains of military music. As the troops defiled before the governor, he pointed out to the lady several officers by name, claiming her admiration for their superior persons and brilliant equipments. In rear of the troops came a band of officers not on duty—colonial officers—and strangers of distinction. Immediately, on their approach, the attention of the governor was seen to be directed toward a tall and martial figure, that marched with grave and measured tread, apparently indifferent to the scene around him. The lady now archly observed, "I perceive that your excellency's eyes are turned to the right object; what say you to your wager now, sir?" "Lost, madam," replied the gallant governor; "when I laid my wager, I was not aware that Colonel Washington was in New York."*

* The following interesting sketch of the personal appearance of Washington is from an anonymous hand:—

"I saw this remarkable man four times. It was in the month of November, 1798, I first beheld the Father of his Country. It was very cold, the northwest wind blowing hard down the Potomac, at Georgetown, D. C. A troop of light-horse from Alexandria escorted him to the western bank of the river. The waves ran high, and the boat which brought him over seemed to labor considerably. Several thousand people greeted his arrival with swelling hearts and joyful countenances; the military were drawn up in a long line to receive him; the officers, dressed in regimentals, did him homage. I was so fortunate as to walk by his side, and had a full view of him. Although only about ten years of age, the impression his person and manner then made on me is now perfectly revived. He was six feet and one inch high, broad and athletic, with very large limbs, entirely erect, and without the slightest tendency to stooping; his hair was white, and tied with a silk string, his countenance lofty, masculine, and contemplative; his eye light gray. He was dressed in the clothes of a citizen, and over these a blue surtout of the finest cloth. His weight must have been two hundred and thirty pounds, with no superfluous flesh, all was bone and sinew, and he walked like a soldier. Whoever has seen, in

In person, Washington, as we have said, was unique. He looked like no one else. To a stature lofty and the patent-office at Washington, the dress he wore when resigning his commission as commander-in-chief, in December, 1783, at once perceives how large and magnificent was his frame. During the parade, something at a distance suddenly attracted his attention; his eye was instantaneously lighted up as with the lightning's flash. At this moment I see its marvellous animation, its glowing fire, exhibiting strong passion, controlled by deliberate reason.

"In the summer of 1799 I again saw the chief. He rode a purely white horse, seventeen hands high, well proportioned, of high spirit: he almost seemed conscious that he bore on his back the Father of his Country. He reminded me of the war-horse whose neck is clothed with thunder. I have seen some highly-accomplished riders, but not one of them approached Washington; he was perfect in this respect. Behind him, at the distance of perhaps forty yards, came Billy Lee, his body-servant, who had perilled his life in many a field, beginning on the heights of Boston, in 1775, and ending in 1781, when Cornwallis surrendered, and the captive army, with unexpressible chagrin, laid down their arms at Yorktown. Billy rode a cream-colored horse, of the finest form, and his old Revolutionary cocked hat indicated that its owner had often heard the roar of cannon and small arms, and had encountered many trying scenes. Billy was a dark mulatto. His master speaks highly of him in his will, and provides for his support.

"Sometime during this year, perhaps, I saw him at Seeme's tavern, in Georgetown; the steps, porch, and street, were crowded with persons desirous of beholding the man.

"I viewed him through a window. The most venerable, dignified, and wealthy men of the town were there, some conversing with him. Washington seemed almost a different being from any of them, and, indeed, from any other person ever reared in this country. His countenance was not so animated as when I first saw him, for then his complexion was as ruddy as if he were only twenty years old.

"A few months before his death, I beheld this extraordinary man for the last time. He stopped at the tavern opposite the Presbyterian church, in Bridge street, Georgetown. At that time, a regiment of soldiers was stationed in their tents, on the banks of Rock creek, and frequently attended Dr. Balch's church, dressed in their costume, and powdered after the Revolutionary fashion. I attended their parade almost every day, and, on one of these occasions, I recognised Washington riding on horseback, unaccompanied by any one. He was going out to see his houses on Capitol hill, as I supposed. They were burnt by the British, in 1814. My youthful eye was riveted on him until he disappeared, and that for ever. I was surprised, that he did not once look at the parade; so far as I could discover, on the contrary, he appeared indifferent to the whole scene.

"It has been my privilege to see the best likenesses of the chief. The one of all others most resembling him, is that prefixed to the first volume of 'Irving's Life of Washington.' All the rest wanted the animation which I perceived in his features.

commanding, he united a form of the manliest proportions, limbs cast in Nature's finest mould, and a carriage the most dignified, graceful, and imposing. No one ever approached the Pater Patriæ that did not feel his presence.

Of the remarkable degree of awe and reverence that the presence of Washington always inspired, we shall give one out of a thousand instances. During the cantonment of the American army at the Valley Forge, some officers of the fourth Pennsylvania regiment were engaged in a game of fives. In the midst of their sport, they discovered the commander-in-chief leaning upon the enclosure, and beholding the game with evident satisfaction. In a moment all things were changed. The ball was suffered to roll idly away; the gay laugh and joyous shout of excitement were hushed into a profound silence, and the officers were gravely grouped together. It was in vain the chief begged of the players that they would proceed with their game, declared the pleasure he had experienced from witnessing their skill, spoke of a proficiency in the manly exercise that he himself could have boasted of in other days. All would not do. Not a man could be induced to move, till the general, finding that his presence hindered the officers from continuing the amusement, bowed, and, wishing them good sport, retired.*

"In personal appearance, Washington has never been equalled by any man in the United States. I agree with Lord Erskine, when he said that the Father of his Country was the only man he ever saw whose character he could not contemplate without awe and wonder. B."

* A part of this chapter was published in the *National Intelligencer* in 1826, a part in 1842, and a part in 1857. As each communication was upon the same subject, and in some paragraphs quite similar in fact and expression, I have combined the three parts in one. In February, 1847, the following article on the *Character and*

Personal Appearance of Washington, appeared in the *National Intelligencer*, over the signature of *Sigma*, and appears to have an appropriate place here:—

"The description given by 'R.' [a correspondent of the *Intelligencer*] of Washington's approach to the hall of Congress in Philadelphia, has freshly awakened my own reminiscences of the same scene. Its vivid truth can not be surpassed. I stood with him on that same stone platform, before the door of the hall, elevated by a few steps from the pavement, when the carriage of the president drew up. It was, as he describes it, white, or rather of a light cream color, painted on the panels with beautiful groups, by Cipriani, representing the four seasons. The horses, according to my recollection, were white, in unison with the carriage. R. says they were bays; perhaps he is more correct. As he alighted, and, ascending the steps, paused upon the platform, looking over his shoulder, in an attitude that would have furnished an admirable subject for the pencil, he was preceded by two gentlemen bearing long white wands, who kept back the eager crowd that pressed on every side to get a nearer view. At that moment I stood so near that I might have touched his clothes; but I should as soon have thought of touching an electric battery. I was penetrated with a veneration amounting to the deepest awe. Nor was this the feeling of a school-boy only; it pervaded, I believe, every human being that approached Washington; and I have been told that, even in his social and convivial hours, this feeling in those who were honored to share them never suffered intermission. I saw him a hundred times afterward, but never with any other than that same feeling. The Almighty, who raised up for our hour of need a man so peculiarly prepared for its whole dread responsibility, seems to have put an impress of sacredness upon his own instrument. The first sight of the man struck the heart with involuntary homage, and prepared everything around him to obey. When he 'addressed himself to speak' there was an unconscious suspension of the breath, while every eye was raised in expectation.

"At the time I speak of he stood in profound silence, and had that statue-like air which mental greatness alone can bestow. As he turned to enter the building, and was ascending the staircase leading to the Congressional hall, I glided along unperceived, almost under cover of the skirts of his dress, and entered instantly after him into the lobby of the house, which was of course in session to receive him. On either hand, from the entrance, stood a large cast-iron stove; and, resolved to secure the unhoped-for privilege I had so unexpectedly obtained, I clambered, boy-like, on this stove (fortunately then not much heated), and from that favorable elevation, enjoyed, for the first time (what I have since so many thousands of times witnessed with comparative indifference), an uninterrupted view of the American Congress in full session, every member in his place. Shall I be pardoned for saying its aspect was very different from what we now witness? There was an air of decorum, of composure, of reflection, of gentlemanly and polished dignity, which has fled, or lingers only with here and there a 'relic of the olden time.'

"The house seemed then as composed as the senate now is when an impressive speech is in the act of delivery. On Washington's entrance the most profound and death-like stillness prevailed. House, lobbies, gallery, all were wrapped in the deepest attention; and the souls of that entire assemblage seemed peering from their eyes on the noble figure which deliberately, and with an unaffected but surpassing majesty, advanced up the broad aisle of the hall between ranks of standing senators and members, and slowly ascended the steps leading to the speaker's chair. I well remember, standing at the head of the senate, the tall, square, somewhat gaunt form of Mr. Jefferson; conspicuous from his scarlet waistcoat, bright blue coat, with broad bright buttons, as well as by his quick and penetrating air, and high-boned Scottish cast of features. There, too, stood General Knox, then secretary of war, in all the sleek rotundity of his low stature, with a bold and florid face, open, firm, and manly in its expression. But I recollect that my boyish eye was caught by the appearance of De Yrujo, the Spanish ambassador. He stood in the rear of the chair, a little on one side, covered with a splendid diplomatic dress, decorated with orders, and carrying under his arm an immense *chapeau-bras*, edged with white ostrich feathers. He was a man, totally different in his air and manner from all around him, and the very antipode especially of the man on whom all eyes but his seemed fixed as by a spell. I saw many other very striking figures grouped about and behind the speaker's chair, but I did not know their names, and had no one to ask: besides, I dared not open my lips.

"The president, having seated himself, remained in silence, serenely contemplating the legislature before him, whose members now resumed their seats, waiting for the speech. No house of worship, in the most solemn pauses of devotion, was ever more profoundly still than that large and crowded chamber.

"Washington was dressed precisely as Stuart has painted him in Lord Landsdowne's full-length portrait — in a full suit of the richest black velvet, with diamond knee-buckles, and square silver buckles set upon shoes japanned with the most scrupulous neatness, black silk stockings, his shirt ruffled at the breast and wrists, a light dress sword, his hair profusely powdered, fully dressed, so as to project at the sides, and gathered behind in a silk bag, ornamented with a large rose of black riband. He held his cocked hat, which had a large black cockade on one side of it, in his hand, as he advanced toward the chair, and, when seated, laid it on the table.

"At length, thrusting his hand within the side of his coat, he drew forth a roll of manuscript, which he opened, and rising, held it in his hand, while in a rich, deep, full, sonorous voice, he read his opening address to Congress. His enunciation was deliberate, justly emphasized, very distinct, and accompanied with an air of deep solemnity, as being the utterance of a mind profoundly impressed with the dignity of the act in which it was occupied, conscious of the whole responsibility of its position and action, but not oppressed by it. There was ever about the man something which impressed the observer with a conviction that he was exactly and fully equal to what he had to do. He was never hurried; never negligent; but seemed ever prepared for the occasion, be it what it might. If I could express his character in one word, it would be appropriateness. In his study, in his parlor, at a levee, before Congress, at the head of the army, he seemed ever to be just what the situation required him to be. He possessed, in a degree never equalled by any human being I ever saw, the strongest, most ever-present sense of propriety. It never forsook him, and deeply and involuntarily impressed itself upon every beholder.

"His address was of moderate length: the topics I have of course forgotten; indeed I was not of an age to appreciate them; but the air, the manner, the tones, have never left my mental vision, and even now seem to vibrate on my ear.

"A scene like this, once beheld, though in earliest youth, is never to be forgotten. It must be now fifty years ago, but I could this moment sit down and sketch the chamber, the assembly, and *the* man.

"Having closed the reading, he laid down the scroll, and, after a brief pause, retired as he had entered: when the manuscript was handed, for a second reading, to Mr. Beckley, then clerk of the house, whose gentlemanly manner, clear and silver voice, and sharp articulation I shall ever associate with the scene. When shall we again behold such a Congress and such a President?"

To make the picture of the personal appearance of Washington more complete, I add the following from *Sullivan's Familiar Letters*:—

"The following are recollections of Washington, derived from repeated opportunities of seeing him during the last three years of his public life. He was over six feet in stature; of strong, bony, muscular frame, without fulness of covering, well formed and straight. He was a man of most extraordinary physical strength. In his own house his action was calm, deliberate, and dignified, without pretension to gracefulness, or peculiar manner, but merely natural, and such as one would think it should be in such a man. His habitual motions had been formed before he took command of the American armies, in the wars of the interior, and in the surveying of wilderness lands, employments in which grace and elegance were not likely to be acquired. At the age of sixty-five, time had done nothing toward bending him out of his natural erectness. His deportment was invariably grave; it was sobriety that stopped short of sadness. His presence inspired a veneration and a feeling of awe rarely experienced in the presence of any man. His mode of speaking was slow and deliberate, not as though he was in search of fine words, but that he might utter those only adapted to his purpose. It was the usage of all persons in good society to attend Mrs. Washington's levee every Friday evening. He was always present. The young ladies used to throng around him, and engage him in conversation. There were some of the well-remembered *belles* of that day who imagined themselves to be favorites with him. As these were the only opportunities which they had of conversing with him, they were disposed to use them. One would think that a gentleman and a gallant soldier, if he could ever laugh or dress his countenance in smiles, would do so when surrounded by young and admiring beauties. But this was never so; the countenance of Washington never softened; nor changed its habitual gravity. One who had lived always in his family said, that his manner in public life was always the same. Being asked whether Washington *could* laugh, this person said this was a rare occurrence, but one instance was remembered when he laughed most heartily at her narration of an incident in which she was a party concerned; and in which he applauded her agency. The late General Cobb, who was long a member of his family during the war, and who enjoyed a laugh as much as any man could, said that he never saw Washington laugh, excepting when Colonel Scammel (if this was the person) came to dine at headquarters. Scammel had a fund of ludicrous anecdotes, and a manner of telling them, which relaxed even the gravity of the commander-in-chief.

"General Cobb also said that the forms of proceeding at headquarters were exact and precise; orderly and punctual. At the appointed moment, Washington appeared at the breakfast-table. He expected to find all the members of his family (Cobb, Hamilton, Humphreys were among them) awaiting him. He came dressed for the day, and brought with him the letters and despatches of the preceding day, and a short memoranda of the answers to be made; also the substance of orders to be issued When breakfast was over, these papers were distributed among his aids, to be pu into form. Soon afterward he mounted his horse to visit the troops, and expected to find on his return before noon, all the papers prepared for his inspection and signature. There was no familiarity in his presence; it was all sobriety and business. His mode of life was abstemious and temperate. He had a decided preference for certain sorts of food, probably from early associations. Throughout the war, as it was understood in his military family, he gave a part of every day to private prayer and devotion.

"While he lived in Philadelphia, as president, he rose at four in the morning; and the general rule of his house was, that the fires should be covered, and the lights extinguished at a certain hour; whether this was nine or ten is not recollected.

"In the early part of his administration, great complaints were made by the opposition of the aristocratic and royal demeanor of the president. Mr. Jefferson makes some commentaries on this subject, which do no credit to his heart or his head. These are too *little* to be transcribed from the works of this '*great and good man.*' Dr. Stuart, of Virginia, wrote to him of the dissatisfaction which prevailed on this subject in Virginia. In the fifth volume of Marshall, page 164, will be found an extract of Washington's vindication of his conduct, and a most satisfactory one, which shows the proper character of Mr. Jefferson's 'Anas.' These complaints related, in particular, to the manner of receiving such visiters as came from respect or from curiosity, of which there were multitudes. The purpose of Washington was, that such visiters should accomplish their objects without a sacrifice of time, which he considered indispensable to the performance of his public duties.

"He devoted one hour every other Tuesday, from three to four, to these visits. He understood himself to be visited as the *president* of the United States, and not on his own account. He was then to be seen by anybody and everybody; but required that every one who came should be introduced by his secretary, or by some gentleman whom he knew himself. He lived on the south side of Chestnut street, just below Sixth. The place of reception was the dining-room in the rear, twenty-five or thirty feet in length, including the bow projecting into the garden. Mrs. Washington received visiters in the two rooms on the second floor, from front to rear.

"At three o'clock, or at any time within a quarter of an hour afterward, the visiter was conducted to this dining-room, from which all seats had been removed for the time. On entering, he saw the tall figure of Washington clad in black velvet; his hair in full dress, powdered and gathered behind in a large silk bag; yellow gloves on his hands; holding a cocked hat, with a cockade in it, and the edges adorned with a black feather about an inch deep. He wore knee and shoe buckles; and a long sword, with a finely-wrought and polished steel hilt, which appeared at the left hip; the coat worn over the blade, and appearing from under the folds behind. The scabbard was white polished leather.

"He stood always in front of the fireplace, with his face toward the door of entrance. The visiter was conducted to him, and he required to have the name so distinctly pronounced that he could hear it. He had the very uncommon faculty of associating a man's name, and personal appearance, so durably in his memory as to be able to call any one by name who made him a second visit. He received his visiter with a dignified bow, while his hands were so disposed as to indicate that the salutation was not to be accompanied with shaking hands. This ceremony never occurred in these visits, even with the most near friends, that no distinctions might be made.

"As visiters came in, they formed a circle around the room. At a quarter past three the door was closed, and the circle was formed for that day. He then began on the right, and spoke to each visiter, calling him by name, and exchanging a few words with him. When he had completed his circuit, he resumed his first position, and the visiters approached him in succession, bowed, and retired. By four o'clock this ceremony was over.

"On the evenings when Mrs. Washington received visiters, he did not consider *himself* as visited. He was then as a private gentleman, dressed usually in some colored coat (the only one recollected was brown, with bright buttons), and black on his lower limbs. He had then neither hat nor sword; he moved about among the company, conversing with one and another. He had once a fortnight an official dinner, and select companies on other days. He sat, it is said, at the side, in a central position; Mrs. Washington opposite; the two ends were occupied by members of his family, or by his personal friends."

m. Washington

CHAPTER XXVI.

MARTHA WASHINGTON.*

Mrs. Washington's Lineage — Her Early Life — Her Marriage to Daniel Parke Custis — His Father's Ambitious Views — Death of Mr. Custis — Anecdote — A Money-lender in want of a Customer — First Interview between Washington and Mrs. Custis — Virginia Hospitality — Washington in Love — The Marriage of Washington and Mrs. Custis — Date of the Marriage — Mrs. Washington in Camp — Her Escort — Death of her Son — The Home at Mount Vernon — Washington made President of the United States — Mrs. Washington at the Head of the Presidential Mansion — Family Habits there — Scenes on the National Anniversaries — Attendance upon Divine Service — Old Soldiers at the President's House — Retirement to Mount Vernon — Visiters there — Mrs. Washington's Domestic Habits — Washington's Death — Disposition of his Remains — Mount Vernon after his Death — Sickness and Death of Mrs. Washington.

MARTHA DANDRIDGE was descended from an ancient family, which first migrated to the colony of Virginia, in the person of the Reverend Orlando Jones, a clergyman of Wales. She was born in the county of New Kent, colony of Virginia, in May, 1732. The education of females in the early days of the colonial settlements, was almost exclusively of a domestic character, and by instructors who were entertained in the principal families, that were too few and too "far between" to admit of the establishment of public schools.

Of the early life of Miss Dandridge, we are only able to record, that the young lady excelled in personal charms, which, with pleasing manners, and a general amiability of demeanor, caused her to be distinguished

---

* This was first written for, and published in, the *American Portrait Gallery*.

amid the fair ones who usually assembled at the court of Williamsburg, then held by the royal governors of Virginia.

At seventeen years of age (in 1749), Miss Dandridge was married to Colonel Daniel Parke Custis, of the White House, county of New Kent. This was a match of affection. The father of the bridegroom, the Honorable John Custis, of Arlington, a king's counsellor, had matrimonial views of a more ambitious character for his only son and heir, and was desirous of a connection with the Byrd family, of Westover, Colonel Byrd being, at that time, from his influence and vast possessions, almost a count palatine of Virginia.*

The counsellor having at length given his consent to the marriage of his son with Miss Dandridge, they were married. They settled at the White House, on the banks of the Paumunkey river, where Colonel Custis became an eminently successful planter. The fruits of this marriage were, a girl, who died in infancy, and Daniel, Martha, and John. Daniel was a child of much promise, and it was generally believed, that his untimely death hastened his father to the grave. Martha arrived at womanhood, and died at Mount Vernon, in 1773;† and John, the father of the biographer, perished while in the service of his country, and the suite of the commander-

---

* See page 18.

† See page 21. We have observed that this daughter was very delicate in health, from early childhood. Everything that affection and ample means could afford for the preservation of her health, were employed. Among Washington's accounts of expenditures in her behalf, is one on a single half-sheet of foolscap, which shows how carefully he made his memoranda. We give a *facsimile* of it. It will be seen that Washington took none of the responsibility of incurring the expense of a journey to the medicinal springs and back. He notes in the preface to the account, that the journey was undertaken by the advice of the physician.

Miss Custis — to — George Washington — Dr.

1769	To the Expences of a Journey to the Fredk. Springs in Augt. 1769 — Undertaken solely on her Acct. to try (by the advice of her Physician) the effect of the Waters on her Complaint — viz.			
July	To a Cot			15 —
Journey 1st to 6th of Augt.	To Travelling Expens. up, to wit	£ s d		
	At Wm. Carr Lanes	£0 . 7 . 9		
	Lodging &ca. at Chs. Wests	14 . 4½		
	Dinner &ca. at Snicker's	7 —		
	Ditto &ca. on Opechon	6 . 9		
	Lodging &ca. at Hedges	11 —		
	Dinner &ca. at Harrefords	8 —	2 . 14 . 10½	
From the 6th Aug. to 9th Sept.	To Cash pd. for Sundries while there viz.			
	For Repairg. Houses & Buildg. an Arbr.	15 —		
	Butcher's Meat	4 . 15 . 11		
	Poultry Eggs & Milk	1 . 0 . 9		
	Butter 34½ lb	1 . 6 . 5½		
	Roots, Green's & Fruit	1 . 18 . 7½		
	Baker for Bread & Flour	4 . 6 . 8		
	Washing	1 . 18 . 1½		
	Smith	3 . 1½		
	Paid the Bath keeper	1 . 10 —		
	Oats & Pasturage for 7 Horses	8 . 4 . 1		
		26 . 3 . 5		
	Deduct 25 pr Ct. to reduce it to Virga. Currency	5 . 4 . 8	20 . 18 . 9	
Journey 9th Sepr. to 12th Sepr.	To Exps. in Travelg. down viz.			
	Dinner, Oats, &ca. at Morgans	8 . 6		
	Lodgings &c. at Hedges	12 —		
	Feeding &c. on the Road	8 . 6		
	Oats &c. under the Ridge	8 . 9		
	Lodging &ca. at Chas. Wests	14 . 6		
	Dinner &c. at Wm. Carr Lanes	6 . 7½	2 . 18 . 10½	
	To Waggonage of our Necess. up & down	9 —		
	Exps. of the Servants with the Waggon	6 . 9		
			£36 . 14 . 3	

Excepted pr.

Septr. 13th. 1769.   G: Washington

in-chief, at the siege of Yorktown, 1781, aged twenty-seven.

On the decease of her husband, which happened at about middle age, Mrs. Custis found herself at once a very young, and among the very wealthiest widows in the colony. Independently of extensive and valuable landed estates, the colonel left thirty thousand pounds sterling in money, with half that amount to his only daughter, Martha. It is related of this amiable gentleman, that, when on his death-bed, he sent for a tenant, to whom, in settling an account, he was due one shilling. The tenant begged that the colonel, who had ever been most kind to his tenantry, would not trouble himself at all about such a trifle, as he, the tenant, had forgotten it long ago. "But I have not," rejoined the just and conscientious landlord, and bidding his creditor take up the coin, which had been purposely placed on his pillow, exclaimed, "Now, my accounts are all closed with this world," and shortly after expired. Mrs. Custis, as sole executrix, managed the extensive landed and pecuniary concerns of the estates with surprising ability, making loans, on mortgage, of moneys, and, through her stewards and agents, conducting the sales or exportation of the crops, to the best possible advantage.*

---

* On the death of her husband, Mrs. Custis employed her young friend, of James City, Robert Carter Nicholas, as legal adviser in the settlement of the estate. Mr. Nicholas was then just rising in his profession, and soon became one of the brightest lawyers in a galaxy, such as Virginia has never since possessed. Afterward, as a legislator and true patriot, he took a foremost part in the concerns of his native commonwealth, and was particularly conspicuous in the Virginia convention of 1775. The following letters, from Mr. Nicholas and Mr. Waller, relate to the business of Mrs. Custis's estate:—

"WILLIAMSBURG, 7th August, 1757.

"MADAM: It gave me no small pleasure to hear with how great Christian patience and resignation you submitted to your late misfortune; the example is rare,

While on the subject of the moneyed concerns of seventy years ago, we hope to be pardoned for a brief digression. The orchard of fine apple-trees is yet standing near Bladensburg, that was presented to Mr. Ross, by

though a duty incumbent upon us all; and therefore I can not help esteeming it a peculiar happiness whenever I meet with it. My late worthy friend, from a very short acquaintance with him, had gained a great share of my esteem, which would have naturally continued towards his family, had I been an utter stranger to them. How greatly this is increased by the pleasure of even a slight acquaintance with you, I shall leave it to time to evince, as it might savor of flattery, were I to attempt the expression of it. When your brother was with me, I was indisposed, and therefore could not conveniently comply with your request, in writing my opinion upon the several matters he proposed. As it will be absolutely necessary that some person should administer upon the estate, and no one appears so proper as yourself, I would recommend it to you, and that so soon as it may be done with convenience. I dare say your friends will endeavor to ease you of as much trouble as they can; and since you seem to place some confidence in me, I do sincerely profess myself to be of that number. I imagine you will find it necessary to employ a trusty steward; and as the estate is large and very extensive, it is Mr. Waller's and my own opinion, that you had better not engage with any but a very able man, though he should require large wages. Nothing appears to us very material to be done immediately, except what relates to your tobacco; if is not already done, it will be necessary that letters should be wrote for insurance, and that we, or some other of your friends, should be acquainted with the quantities of tobacco put on board each ship, that we may get the proper bills of lading. If you desire it, we will cheerfully go up to assist in sorting your papers, forming invoices, etc., and in any other instance that you think I can serve you, I beg that you will freely and without any reserve command me. I congratulate you upon your little boy's late recovery, and am, madam,
"Your hearty well-wisher and obedient humble servant,
'ROBERT C. NICHOLAS."

Three weeks later, Mr. Waller, mentioned by Mr. Nicholas, wrote to Mrs. Custis as follows:—

"MADAM. I am at a loss in drawing your power of attorney for receiving the interest or dividends of your bank stock. I had formerly a printed form which I am pretty sure I gave to Mr. Power, to draw one by for the late colonel. Mr. Lyons says he remembers it, and that he believes Mr. Power gave it to the colonel; and so amongst us it is lost. I send you a general power of attorney, which you may execute before some persons going to Great Britain, and send it by this fleet; it may possibly be of service till they send you a letter. It will be proper for you to get letters of administration from your clerk, to send them here for the governor's name, and seal of the colony (all of which you may have for the fees already charged you), and to send them with the power to Messrs Carey and Co.; and desire them to send you, in proper forms and directions, what to do concerning the

the father of the late venerated Charles Carroll, of Carrollton, as a recompense for Mr. Ross having introduced to Mr. Carroll a good borrower of his money. A Colonel T., one of the ancient dons of Maryland, being observed riding over the race-course of Annapolis in a very disturbed and anxious manner, was accosted by his friends with a "What's the matter, colonel? Are you alarmed for the success of your filly, about to start?" "Oh, no," replied T., "but I have a thousand pounds by me to loan, and here have I been riding about the course the whole morning, and not a single borrower can I get for my money." We opine that the same anxieties would not be long suffered now.

It was in 1758, that an officer, attired in a military undress, and attended by a body-servant, tall and *militaire* as his chief, crossed the ferry called Williams's, over the Pamunkey, a branch of the York river. On the boat touching the southern or New Kent side, the soldier's progress was arrested by one of those personages, who give the beau ideal of the Virginia gentleman of the old *régime*, the very soul of kindliness and hospitality. It was in vain the soldier urged his business at Williamsburg, important communications to the governor, etc. Mr. Chamberlayne, on whose domain the *militaire* had just landed, would hear of no excuse. Colonel Washington (for the soldier was he) was a name and character so

---

bank stock another year. I return the letters relating to Dunbar's appeal, which very probably received a determination before the colonel's death. I know not what further you can do than advise Mr. Cary and Mr. Hanbury of the time he died, to desire them to continue their case in that affair, and to instruct you what your solicitor thinks needful for you to do. In all these cases they will preserve their own forms and methods. My wife tenders you her best respects, and I am, madam,
"Your most obedient servant,
"WILLIAMSBURG, August 30th, 1757." "BEN. WALLER."

dear to all the Virginians, that his passing by one of the old castles of the commonwealth, without calling and partaking of the hospitalities of the host, was entirely out of the question. The colonel, however, did not surrender at discretion, but stoutly maintained his ground, till Chamberlayne bringing up his reserve, in the intimation than he would introduce his friend to a young and charming widow, then beneath his roof, the soldier capitulated, on condition that he should dine, "only dine," and then, by pressing his charger and borrowing of the night, he would reach Williamsburg before his excellency could shake off his morning slumbers. Orders were accordingly issued to Bishop, the colonel's body-servant and faithful follower, who, together with the fine English charger, had been bequeathed by the dying Braddock to Major Washington, on the famed and fatal field of the Monongahela. Bishop, bred in the school of European discipline, raised his hand to his cap, as much as to say, "your honor's orders shall be obeyed."

The colonel now proceeded to the mansion, and was introduced to various guests (for when was a Virginian domicil of the olden time without guests?), and above all, to the charming widow. Tradition relates that they were mutually pleased on this their first interview, nor is it remarkable; they were of an age when impressions are strongest. The lady was fair to behold, of fascinating manners, and splendidly endowed with worldly benefits. The hero, fresh from his early fields, redolent of fame, and with a form on which "every god did seem to set his seal, to give the world assurance of a man."

The morning passed pleasantly away. Evening came, with Bishop, true to his orders and firm at his post, held-ing his favorite charger with one hand, while the other was waiting to offer the ready stirrup. The sun sank in the horizon, and yet the colonel appeared not. And then the old soldier marvelled at his chief's delay. "'Twas strange, 'twas passing strange"—surely he was not wont to be a single moment behind his appointments, for he was the most punctual of all men. Meantime, the host enjoyed the scene of the veteran on duty at the gate, while the colonel was so agreeably employed in the parlor; and proclaiming that no guest ever left his house after sunset, his military visiter was, without much difficulty, persuaded to order Bishop to put up the horses for the night. The sun rode high in the heavens the ensuing day, when the enamored soldier pressed with his spur his charger's side, and speeded on his way to the seat of government, where, having despatched his public business, he retraced his steps, and, at the White House, the engagement took place, with preparations for the marriage.

And much hath the biographer heard of that marriage, from gray-haired domestics, who waited at the board where love made the feast and Washington was the guest. And rare and high was the revelry, at that palmy period of Virginia's festal age; for many were gathered to that marriage, of the good, the great, the gifted, and the gay, while Virginia, with joyous acclamation hailed in her youthful hero a prosperous and happy bridegroom.

"And so you remember when Colonel Washington came a courting of your mistress?" said the biographer to old Cully, in his hundredth year. "Ay, master, that I do," replied this ancient family servant, who had lived to see five generations; "great times, sir, great times! Shall never see the like again!"—"And Washington looked something like a man, a proper man; hey, Cully?"—"Never see'd the like, sir; never the likes of him, tho' I have seen many in my day; so tall, so straight! and then he sat a horse and rode with such an air! Ah, sir; he was like no one else! Many of the grandest gentlemen, in their gold lace, were at the wedding, but none looked like the man himself!" Strong, indeed, must have been the impressions which the person and manner of Washington made upon the rude, "untutored mind" of this poor negro, since the lapse of three quarters of a century had not sufficed to efface them.

The precise date of the marriage the biographer has been unable to discover, having in vain searched among the records of the vestry of St. Peter's church, New Kent, of which the Reverend Mr. Mossom, a Cambridge scholar, was the rector, and performed the ceremony, it is believed, about 1759.* A short time after their mar-

* Mr. Sparks, whose sources of information have been more ample than all others, says the marriage took place on the *sixth* of January, 1759. Mrs. Bache, daughter of Doctor Franklin, in a letter to her father, written in January, 1779, says, "I have lately been several times invited abroad with the general and Mrs. Washington. He always inquires after you, in the most affectionate manner, and speaks of you highly. We danced at Mrs. Powell's on your birthday, or night, I should say, in company together, and he told me it was the anniversary of his marriage; it was just twenty years that night."

Franklin's birthday was the *seventeenth* of January. The apparent discrepancy in the statements of Mrs. Bache and Mr. Sparks, is easily reconcilable, by supposing the date given by the latter to be Old Style. There being eleven days difference between the two styles, so called, the *sixth*, Old Style, would be the *seventeenth*, New Style.

Reverend David Mossom was rector of New Kent parish for forty years. Bishop Meade, in illustration of the condition of church matters in that parish, during the earlier years of Mr. Mossom's rectorship, says that, on one occasion, the rector and

riage, Colonel and Mrs. Washington removed to Mount Vernon, on the Potomac, and permanently settled there.

The mansion of Mount Vernon, more than seventy years ago, was a very small building, compared with its present extent, and the numerous out-buildings attached to it. The mansion-house consisted of four rooms on a floor, forming the centre of the present building, and remained pretty much in that state up to 1774, when Colonel Washington repaired to the first Congress, in Philadelphia, and from thence to the command-in-chief of the armies of his country, assembled before Cambridge, July, 1775. The commander-in-chief returned no more to reside at Mount Vernon till after the peace of 1783. Mrs., or Lady Washington, as we shall now call her (such being the appellation she always bore in the army), accompanied the general to the lines before Boston, and witnessed its siege and evacuation. She then returned to Virginia, the subsequent campaigns being of too momentous a character to allow of her accompanying the army.*

At the close of each campaign, an aid-de-camp

---

his clerk had a quarrel, and the former assailed the latter in a sermon. In those days, it was the duty of the clerk to "give out" the psalm. On the occasion in question the clerk, after receiving the pulpit assault from Mr. Mossom, read, in revenge, the psalm, in which occurs the following verse:—

"With restless and ungoverned rage,
    Why do the heathen storm?
Why in such rash attempts engage,
    As they can ne'er perform?"

Mr. Mossom was married four times. His last nuptials were celebrated in January, 1755, in his own church. His bride was Elizabeth Masters, a widow.

* Mrs. Washington did not return to Virginia until the close of August, 1776. A letter, written by her to her sister, Mrs. Bassett, of Eltham, and dated at Philadelphia, on the twentieth of that month, is published in the *Historical Magazine*, volume ii., page 135; 1858.

repaired to Mount Vernon, to escort the lady to headquarters. The arrival of Lady Washington at camp was an event much anticipated, and was always the signal for the ladies of the general officers to repair to the bosoms of their lords. The arrival of the aid-de-camp, escorting the plain chariot, with the neat postillions, in their scarlet and white liveries, was deemed an epoch in the army, and served to diffuse a cheering influence amid the gloom which hung over our destinies at Valley Forge, Morristown, and West Point. Lady Washington always remained at the headquarters till the opening of the campaign; and she often remarked, in after life, that it had been her fortune to hear the first cannon at the opening, and the last at the closing, of all the campaigns of the Revolutionary war.

During the whole of that mighty period, when we struggled for independence, Lady Washington preserved her equanimity, together with a degree of cheerfulness that inspired all around her with the brightest hopes for our ultimate success. To her, alone, a heavy cloud of sorrow hung over the conclusion of the glorious campaign of 1781. Her only child,* while attending to his duties, as aid-de-camp to the general-in-chief, during the siege of Yorktown, was seized with an attack of the camp-fever, then raging to a frightful extent within the enemy's intrenchments. Ardently attached to the cause of his country, having witnessed many of the most important events of the Revolutionary contest, from the siege of Boston, in 1775-6, to the virtual termination of the war, in 1781, the sufferer beheld the surrender of the British army, on the memorable nineteenth of Octo-

---

* John Parke Custis.

ber, and was thence removed to Eltham, in New Kent, where he was attended by Doctor Craik, chief of the medical staff.

Washington, learning the extreme danger of his stepson, to whom he was greatly attached, privately left the camp before Yorktown, while yet it rang with the shouts of victory, and, attended by a single officer, rode with all speed to Eltham. It was just day-dawn when the commander-in-chief sprang from his panting charger, and, summoning Doctor Craik to his presence, inquired if there was any hope. Craik shook his head, when the chief, being shown into a private room, threw himself upon a bed, absorbed in grief. The poor sufferer, being in his last agonies, soon after expired. The general remained for some time closeted with his lady, then remounted and returned to the camp.

It was after the peace of 1783, that General Washington set in earnest about the improvements in building and laying off the gardens and grounds that now adorn Mount Vernon. He continued in these gratifying employments, occasionally diversified by the pleasures of the chase, till 1787, when he was called to preside in the convention that formed the present federal constitution; and in 1789 he left his beloved retirement to assume the duties of the chief magistracy of the Union.

During the residence of General and Mrs. Washington at Mount Vernon, after the peace of 1783, the ancient mansion, always the seat of hospitality, was crowded with guests. The officers of the French and American armies, with many strangers of distinction, hastened to pay their respects to the victorious general, now merged into the illustrious farmer of Mount Vernon. During these stirring times, Mrs. Washington performed the duties of a Virginia housewife, and presided at her well-spread board, with that ease and elegance of manners which always distinguished her. At length the period arrived when General and Mrs. Washington were to leave the delights of retirement, and to enter upon new and elevated scenes of life. The unanimous voice of his country hailed the hero who had so lately led her armies to victory, as the chief magistrate of the young empire about to dawn upon the world.

The president and his lady bade adieu with extreme regret to the tranquil and happy shades, where a few years of repose had, in a great measure, effaced the effects of the toils and anxieties of war; where a little Eden had bloomed and flourished under their fostering hands; and where a numerous circle of friends and relatives would sensibly feel the privation of their departure. They departed, and hastened to where duty called the MAN of his country.

The journey to New York, in 1789, was a continued triumph. The august spectacle at the bridge of Trenton brought tears to the eyes of the chief, and forms one of the most brilliant recollections of the age of Washington.*

Arrived at the seat of the federal government, the president and Mrs. Washington found their establishment upon a scale that, while it partook of all the attributes of our republican institutions, possessed at the same time that degree of dignity and regard for appearances, so necessary to give to our infant republic, respect in the eyes of the world. The house was handsomely furnished; the equipages neat, with horses of the first order;

* See note on page 393.

the servants wore the family liveries; and, with the exception of a steward and housekeeper, the whole establishment differed but little from that of a private gentlemen. On Tuesdays, from three to four o'clock, the president received the foreign ambassadors and strangers who wished to be introduced to him. On these occasions, and when opening the sessions of Congress, the president wore a dress-sword. His personal apparel was always remarkable for its being old-fashioned, and exceedingly plain and neat. On Thursdays were the congressional dinners, and on Friday nights, Mrs. Washington's drawing-room. The company usually assembled about seven, and rarely staid after ten o'clock. The ladies were seated, and the president passed around the circle, paying his compliments to each. At the drawing-rooms, Mrs. Morris always sat at the right of the lady-president, and at all the dinners, public or private, at which Robert Morris was a guest, that venerable man was placed at the right of Mrs. Washington. When ladies called at the president's mansion, the habit was for the secretaries and gentlemen of the president's household to hand them to and from their carriages; but when the honored relicts of Greene and Montgomery came to the presidoliad, the president himself performed these complimentary duties.

On the anniversaries of the great national festivals of the fourth of July and twenty-second of February, the sages of the Revolutionary Congress and the officers of the Revolutionary army renewed their acquaintance with Mrs. Washington. Many and kindly greetings then took place, with many a recollection of the days of trial. The Cincinnati, after paying their respects to their chief, were seen to file off toward the parlor, where Lady Washington was in waiting to receive them, and where Wayne, and Mifflin, and Dickenson, and Stewart, and Moylan, and Hartley, and a host of veterans, were cordially welcomed as old friends, and where many an interesting reminiscence was called up, of the headquarters and the "times of the Revolution."

On Sundays, unless the weather was uncommonly severe, the president and Mrs. Washington attended divine service at Christ church;* and in the evenings, the president read to Mrs. Washington, in her chamber, a sermon, or some portion from the sacred writings. No visiters, with the exception of Mr. Speaker Trumbull, were admitted to the presidoliad on Sundays.

There was one description of visiters, however, to be found about the first president's mansion on all days. The old soldiers repaired, as they said, to headquarters, just to inquire after the health of his excellency and Lady Washington. They knew his excellency was of course much engaged; but they would like to see the good lady. One had been a soldier of the Life-Guard; another had been on duty when the British threatened to surprise the headquarters; a third had witnessed that terrible fellow, Cornwallis, surrender his sword; each one had some touching appeal, with which to introduce himself to the peaceful headquarters of the presidoliad. All were "kindly bid to stay," were conducted to the stew-

---

* In Philadelphia. They attended St. Paul's church, when in New York, in which two pews were expressly prepared, one for the president and his family, and the other for the governor of the state of New York and his family — the city of New York then being the state capital. The pews have since been changed, but the old paintings over each still remain. Washington, according to his diary, attended divine service in the morning, and occupied the afternoon in writing private letters.

ard's apartments, and refreshments set before them; and after receiving some little token from the lady, with her best wishes for the health and happiness of an old soldier, they went their ways, while blessings upon their revered commander and the good Lady Washington, were uttered by many a war-worn veteran of the Revolution.

In the spring of 1797, General and Mrs. Washington, bidding adieu to public life, took their leave of the seat of government and journeyed to the South, prepared in good earnest to spend the remnant of their days in their beloved retirement of Mount Vernon. The general resumed with delight his agricultural employments, while the lady bustled again amid her domestic concerns, showing that neither time nor her late elevated station had in any wise impaired her qualifications for a Virginia housewife; and she was now verging upon threescore and ten.

But for Washington to be retired at Mount Vernon, or anywhere else, was out of the question. Crowds which had hailed the victorious general as the deliverer of his country, and called him with acclamation to the chief magistracy of the infant empire, now pressed to his retirement, to offer their love and admiration to the illustrious farmer of Mount Vernon.

Mrs. Washington was an uncommon early riser, leaving her pillow at day-dawn at all seasons of the year, and becoming at once actively engaged in her household duties. After breakfast she retired for an hour to her chamber, which hour was spent in prayer and reading the Holy Scriptures, a practice that she never omitted during half a century of her varied life.*

---

* Mrs. Carrington, wife of Colonel Edward Carrington, who, with her husband, visited the family at Mount Vernon a little while before General Washington's

Two years had passed happily at Mount Vernon; for although the general, yielding to the claims of his country, had again accepted the command-in-chief of her armies, yet he had stipulated with government that he should not leave his retirement, unless upon the actual invasion of an enemy. It was while engaged in projecting new and ornamental improvements in his grounds, that the fiat of the Almighty went forth, calling the being, the measure of whose earthly fame was filled to overflowing, to his great reward in a higher and better world. The illness was short and severe. Mrs. Washington left not the chamber of the sufferer, but was seen kneeling at the bedside, her head resting upon her Bible, which had been her solace in the many and heavy afflictions she had undergone. Dr. Craik, the early friend and companion-in-arms of the chief, replaced the hand, which was almost pulseless, upon the pillow, while he turned away to conceal the tears that fast chased each other down his furrowed cheeks. The last effort of the expiring Washington was worthy of the Roman fame of his life and character. He raised himself up, and casting a look of benignity on all around him, as if to thank

death, wrote to her sister as follows, concerning Mrs. Washington: "Let us repair to the old lady's room, which is precisely in the style of our good old aunt's — that is to say, nicely fixed for all sorts of work. On one side sits the chambermaid, with her knitting; on the other, a little colored pet, learning to sew. An old decent woman is there, with her table and shears, cutting out the negroes' winter clothes, while the good old lady directs them all, incessantly knitting herself. She points out to me several pair of nice colored stockings and gloves she had just finished, and presents me with a pair half done, which she begs I will finish and wear for her sake."—See Bishop Meade's *Old Churches and Families of Virginia*, i. 98. Such is the picture of the wealthy and honored wife of Washington in the privacy of her home. What an example of industry and economy for the wives and daughters of America! Mrs. Washington always spoke of the days of her public life at New York and Philadelphia, as her "lost days."

them for their kindly attentions, he composed his limbs, closed his eyes, and folding his arms upon his bosom, the Father of his Country expired, gentle as though an infant died!

The afflicted relict could with difficulty be removed from the chamber of death, to which she returned no more, but occupied other apartments for the residue of her days.

By an arrangement with government, Mrs. Washington consented to yield the remains of the chief to the prayer of the nation, as expressed through its representatives in Congress, conditioning that at her decease, her own remains should accompany those of her husband to the capitol.

When the burst of grief which followed the death of the *Pater Patriæ* had a little subsided, visits of condolence to the bereaved lady were made by the first personages of the land. The president of the United States with many other distinguished individuals, repaired to Mount Vernon; while letters, addresses, funeral orations, and all the tokens of sorrow and respect, loaded the mails from every quarter of the country, offering the sublime tribute of a nation's mourning for a nation's benefactor.*

---

* The following letter to Mrs. Washington, from the Earl of Buchan, brother of Lord Erskine, was found among that lady's papers, after her death, by her granddaughter, Mrs. Lawrence Lewis:—

"Dryburgh Abbey, *January 28th*, 1800.

"Madam: I have this day received from my brother in London the afflicting tidings of the death of your admired husband, my revered kinsman and friend. I am not afraid, even under this sudden and unexpected stroke of Divine Providence, to give vent to the immediate reflections excited by it, because my attachment to your illustrious consort was the pure result of reason, reflection, and congeniality of sentiment. He was one of those whom the Almighty in successive ages has chosen or raised up to promote the ultimate designs of his goodness and mercy, in the gradual melioration of his creatures, and the coming of his kingdom which is in heaven. It may be said of that great and good man who has been taken from

Although the great sun of attraction had sunk in the west, still the radiance shed by his illustrious life and among us, what was written by Tacitus concerning his father-in-law, Agricola: 'Though he was snatched away whilst his age was unbroken by infirmity or dimmed by bodily decay, so that if his life be measured by his glory, he attained a mighty length of days: forming true felicity, namely, such as arise from virtue, he had already enjoyed to the full. As he had likewise held the supreme authority of the state, with the confidence and applause of all wise and good men from every part of the world, as well as among those he governed, and had enjoyed triumphal honors in a war undertaken for the defense of the unalienable rights of mankind, what more, humanly speaking, could fortune add to his lustre and renown.'

"After enormous wealth he sought not; an honorable share he possessed. His course he finished in the peaceful retreat of his own election, in the arms of a dutiful and affectionate wife, and bedewed with the tears of surrounding relatives and friends with the unspeakably superior advantage to that of the Roman general, in the hopes afforded by the gospel of pardoning peace. He therefore, madam, to continue my parallel, may be accounted singularly happy, since by dying, according to his own Christian and humble wish, expressed on many occasions, whilst his credit was nowise impaired, his fame in its full splendor, his relations and friends, not only in a state of comfort and security, but of honor, he has escaped many evils incident to declining years. Moreover, he saw the government of his country in hands conformable with our joint wishes, and to the safety of the nations, and a contingent succession opening not less favorable to the liberties and happiness of the people.

"Considering my uniform regard for the American states manifested long before their forming a separate nation, I may be classed, as it were, among their citizens, especially as I have come of a worthy ancestor, Lord Cardross, who found refuge there in the last century, and had large property in Carolina, where Port Royal is now situated. I hope it will not be thought impertinent or officious, if I recommend to that country and nation at large, the constant remembrance of the moral and political maxims conveyed to its citizens by the Father and founder of the United States, in his Farewell Address, and in that speech which he made to the senate and house of representatives, when the last hand was put to the formation of the Federal Constitution; *and may it be perpetual*. It seems to me that such maxims and such advice ought to be engraven on every forum or place of common assembly among the people, and read by parents, teachers, and guardians to their children and pupils, so that true religion and virtue, its inseparable attendant, may be imbibed by the rising generation to remotest ages, and the foundations of national policy be laid and continued in the superstructure, in the pure and immutable principles of private moralitity; since there is no truth more thoroughly established than that there exists in the economy and course of Nature, an indissoluble union between virtue and happiness, between duty and happiness, between duty and advantage, between the genuine maxims of an honest and magnanimous people, and the solid rewards of public prosperity and felicity; since we ought to be no less persuaded that the propitious smiles of Heaven can never be expected on a nation that dis-

actions drew crowds of pilgrims to his tomb. The establishment of Mount Vernon was kept up to its former standard, and the lady presided with her wonted ease and dignity of manner, at her hospitable board. She relaxed not in her attentions to her domestic concerns, performing the arduous duties of the mistress of so extensive an establishment, although in the sixty-ninth year of her age, and evidently suffering in her spirits, from the heavy bereavement she had so lately sustained.

In little more than two years from the demise of the chief, Mrs. Washington became alarmingly ill from an attack of bilious fever. From her advanced age, the sorrow that had preyed upon her spirits, and the severity of the attack, the family physicians gave but little hope of a favorable issue. The lady herself was perfectly aware that her hour was nigh; she assembled her grandchildren at her bedside, discoursed to them on their respective duties through life, spoke of the happy influences of religion upon the affairs of this world, of the consolations they had afforded her in many and trying afflictions, and of the hopes they held out of a blessed immortality; and then surrounded by her weeping relatives, friends, and domestics, the venerable relict of Washington resigned her life into the hands of her Creator, in the seventy-first year of her age.*

---

regards the eternal rules of order and right which Heaven itself has ordained; and since the preservation of the sacred fire of liberty and the destiny of the republican model of government are justly considered as deeply, perhaps finally, staked on the experiment entrusted to the hands of the American people.

"Lady Buchan joins with me in the most sincerely respectful good wishes. I am, madam, with sincere esteem, your obedient and faithful humble servant.

"BUCHAN."

* The following notice of the death of Mrs. Washington appeared in the *Port Folio*, June 5, 1802:—

Agreeably to her directions her remains were placed in a leaden coffin, and entombed by the side of those of the chief, to await the pleasure of the government.

In person, Mrs. Washington was well-formed, and somewhat below the middle size. To judge from her portrait at Arlington House, painted by Woolaston, in 1757, when she was in the bloom of life, she must at that period have been eminently handsome. In her dress, though plain, she was so scrupulously neat, that ladies have often wondered how Mrs. Washington could wear a gown for a week, go through her kitchen and laundries, and all the varieties of places in the routine of domestic management, and yet the gown retained its snow-like whiteness, unsullied by even a single speck. In her conduct to her servants, her discipline was prompt, yet humane, and her household was remarkable for the excellence of its domestics.

Our filial task is done. Few females have ever figured in the great drama of life, amid scenes so varied and imposing, with so few faults and so many virtues, as the subject of this brief memoir. Identified with the Father of his Country, in the great events which led to the establishment of a nation's independence, Mrs. Washington necessarily partook much of his thoughts, his councils, and his views. Often at his side, in that awful period that "tried men's souls," her cheerfulness soothed his anxieties, her firmness inspired confidence, while her devotional piety toward the Supreme Being

"Died at Mount Vernon, on Saturday evening, the 22d of May, 1802, Mrs. Martha Washington, widow of the late illustrious General George Washington. To those amiable and Christian virtues which adorn the female character, she added dignity of manners, superiority of understanding, a mind intelligent and elevated. The silence of respectful grief is our best eulogy."

enabled her to discern the beautiful form of hope, amid the darkness occasioned by the greatest earthly grief.

After a long life abounding in vicissitudes, having a full measure of sorrows, but with many and high enjoyments, the venerable MARTHA WASHINGTON descended to the grave, cheered by the prospect of a blessed immortality, and mourned by the millions of a mighty empire.

CHAPTER XXVII.

PORTRAITS OF WASHINGTON.*

A GOOD PORTRAIT OF WASHINGTON DESIRABLE — AMERICAN ARTISTS COMPETENT TO PERFORM THE TASK — FOUR ORIGINAL PICTURES AT ARLINGTON HOUSE — PORTRAITS BY PEALE, HOUDON, MARCHIONESS DE BRIENNE, AND SHARPLESS — THE EARLIEST PICTURE — CHARLES WILLSON PEALE — PORTRAIT OF GREENE AT VALLEY FORGE — WASHINGTON'S GREAT STRENGTH — TRUMBULL'S EQUESTRIAN PORTRAIT — WASHINGTON'S TEETH — STUART AND HIS PORTRAITS — CRAYON BY WILLIAMS — PORTRAITS BY CHARLES WILLSON PEALE AND HIS SON REMBRANDT — THE SHARPLESS PICTURE AT ARLINGTON HOUSE — CERRACCHI'S BUST — WASHINGTON'S FIGURE — WESTMULLER'S PICTURE — WASHINGTON'S SIZE AND WEIGHT — PECULIAR FORM OF HIS TRUNK — LAFAYETTE TO TRUMBULL — WHAT SHALL THE STANDARD PORTRAIT BE.

IT is assuredly both desirable and proper that there should belong to the American people, and descend to their posterity, a faithful portraiture of their Washington. They have in their own country all the materials requisite and necessary for such a work; nor need they to go abroad to ensure its most happy execution — they having artistic genius and skill of the highest order at home.

Of original pictures, there are four at Arlington House. The most ancient, and the only one extant of the hero at that time of day, is the work of the elder Peale.† It was painted in 1772, full size and three-quarter length; representing the provincial colonel in the colonial uniform — blue, with scarlet facings, silver lace, and scarlet

---

* This chapter is composed of two, the last published in the *National Intelligencer* in 1855.

† Charles Willson Peale. He was at Mount Vernon in May, 1772, at which time he also painted a portrait, in miniature, of Mrs. Washington, for her son, John Parke Custis.

under-clothes, with sash and gorget, and the hat usually called the Wolfe hat, which, from its size and shape, must have been better suited for service in a forest warfare than would be the *chapeaux* of modern times. This is a fine, expressive picture, and said by his contemporaries, to be the Washington in the prime of life—the countenance open and manly, the mild blue eye, the whole bespeaking intelligence, the dominion of lofty feelings, and the passions at rest.

It will be remembered that 1772 was the year of the remarkable Indian prophecy.*

This splendid and most interesting picture formed the principal ornament of the parlor at Mount Vernon for twenty-seven years, and for the truth of its resemblance to the Washington of colonial times, Dr. James Craik was frequently applied to, who pronounced it to be a faithful likeness of the provincial colonel in the prime of life. The venerable James Craik, it is well known, was the associate and bosom friend of the chief, from 1754 to the last days at Mount Vernon.†

Next in the order of originals, at Arlington House, is a half bust, by Houdon, after the manner of the antique, full size, and was taken soon after the war of the Revolution.‡

3d. A beautiful cabinet picture, in relief, by Madame de Brienne, representing the heads of Washington and Lafayette, about the time of Houdon.§

4th. The profile likeness in crayon, by Sharpless, in

---

* See Chapter xi.

† See page 474.

‡ Houdon was at Mount Vernon in the autumn of 1785.

§ The Marchioness de Brienne had her first and only sitting from Washington, in October, 1789. See note in the Appendix.

1797, an admirable likeness, the profile taken by an instrument, and critically correct.

Next in the order of succession we have a full-length of the commander-in-chief, painted by Peale in 1779, during the Revolution.* This Peale may be very properly styled the soldier-artist; for in spring-time he would lay aside his palette, and, commanding a company, fight a campaign, and on going into winter-quarters, take up his palette again, and paint the portraits of the great men of the army of Independence. The soldier-artist gave a most graphic and amusing account of his painting the portrait of General Greene at Valley Forge. He said: "The wretched hut that formed my studio had but two articles of furniture—an old bedstead and a three-legged chair! The general being a heavy man, I placed him upon the bedstead, while I steadied myself as

---

* Charles Willson Peale was born at Chestertown, in Maryland, in 1741, and was apprenticed to a saddler in Annapolis. He became also a silversmith, watchmaker, and carver. He offered a handsome saddle to Hesselius, a portrait-painter, living in his neighborhood, if he would explain to him the mystery of putting colors upon canvass. Hesselius complied, and from that day Peale's artist-life began. He went to England, where he studied under Benjamin West, from 1767 to 1769. He returned to America, and for fifteen years was the only portrait painter of excellence in this country. By close application he became a good naturalist and preserver of animals. He practised dentistry, and invented several machines. During the war he conceived the grand design of forming a portrait gallery, and for that purpose he painted a great number of likenesses of the leading men of the Revolution, American and foreign. Many were of life size, and others in miniature. A large number of the former are now in the possession of the American Museum in New York, and grace the gallery of that establishment; and others cover the walls of Independence Hall, in Philadelphia.

Mr. Peale opened a picture gallery in Philadelphia, and also commenced a museum, which, in time, became extensive. He delivered a course of lectures on natural history, and was very efficient in the establishment and support of the Philadelphia Academy of Fine Arts. He lived temperately, worked assiduously, and was greatly esteemed by all who knew him. He died in February, 1827, aged eighty-six years. His son, Rembrandt, is now [July 1859] practising his art in Philadelphia, at the age of eighty-two years.

well as I could upon the rickety chair; it was awfully cold, and I had every few moments to thrust my hands into the fire to enable me to hold my pencil." In such a studio, and with such appliances, was painted the only reliable likeness that we have of the illustrious soldier who was the hero of the South, and second only to him who was first of all.

Peale delighted to relate incidents that occurred during his intercourse at various times with Washington, particularly the display of the vast physical prowess of the chief in 1772. He said: "One afternoon several young gentlemen, visiters at Mount Vernon, and myself were engaged in pitching the bar, one of the athletic sports common in those days, when suddenly the colonel appeared among us. He requested to be shown the pegs that marked the bounds of our efforts; then, smiling, and without putting off his coat, held out his hand for the missile. No sooner," observed the narrator, with emphasis, " did the heavy iron bar feel the grasp of his mighty hand than it lost the power of gravitation, and whizzed through the air, striking the ground far, very far, beyond our utmost limits. We were indeed amazed, as we stood around, all stripped to the buff, with shirt sleeves rolled up, and having thought ourselves very clever fellows, while the colonel, on retiring, pleasantly observed, 'When you beat my pitch, young gentlemen, I'll try again.'"*

In 1790 appeared the equestrian portrait of the chief by Colonel Trumbull. In the execution of this fine work of art, the painter had *standings* as well as sittings—the white charger, fully caparisoned, having been led out and held by a groom, while the chief was placed by the

* See page 483.

artist by the side of the horse, the right arm resting on the saddle. In this novel mode the relative positions of the man and horse were sketched out and afterwards transferred to the canvass.* There is a copy, size of life, of the equestrian portrait by Trumbull, in the City-hall of New York. The figure of Washington, as delineated by Colonel Trumbull, is the most perfect extant. So is the costume, the uniform of the staff in the war for Independence, being the ancient *whig colors*, blue and buff—a very splendid performance throughout, and the objection to the face as being too florid, not a correct one. He was both fair and florid.

In 1789 the first president lost his teeth, and, the artificial ones with which he was furnished answering very imperfectly the purpose for which they were intended, a marked change occurred in the appearance of his face, more especially in the projection of the under lip, which forms so distinguishing a feature in the works of Stuart and others who painted portraits of the great man subsequent to 1789.†

We come now to a brilliant era in the history of the fine arts in the United States, in the return of Gilbert Stuart to his native land from a long sojourn in Europe, where his great fame as a portrait painter obtained for him the title of the modern Vandyke.‡ The distinguish-

* There must be some error in this account. See remarks on the subject in Note vii. in the Appendix.

† Washington, at the time Stuart painted his portrait, had a set of sea-horse ivory teeth. These, just made, were too large and clumsy, and gave that peculiar appearance of the mouth seen in Stuart's picture. He very soon rejected them. Stuart's mouth is a caricature, in a small degree.

‡ Gilbert Charles Stuart was a native of Rhode Island, and son of a Scotch snuff-maker. He was born in 1754, and at an early age manifested a genius for art. He commenced a course of instruction in painting at the age of eighteen years, with an

ing excellence of Stuart, as a portrait painter, consisted in his giving the expression of character to his portraits, a novelty in portrait painting in the United States more than half a century ago. Stuart's object and ambition, on returning to America, were to paint the great man of his country. He gave to this work all his genius, all his skill, and the best feelings of his heart. The first portrait of Washington by Stuart created a great sensation on its appearance in Philadelphia. It was soon followed by the celebrated full-length for the marquis of Lansdowne. In this splendid picture Stuart has failed in the figure of the chief, unapproachable as he was, in painting the head.* The great artist had never made the human figure his peculiar study or practice. Hence, *for the correct figure of Washington we must refer, in all cases, to the works of Trumbull.* It was our good fortune to see much of Gilbert Stuart in his studios of Philadelphia and

amateur artist named Alexander. They made a tour of the Southern States together, and, finally, the preceptor invited the pupil to go to Scotland with him. He remained there sometime, and returned to New York quite a competent portrait painter. There he, and the late Doctor Benjamin Waterhouse, commenced drawing from life together. In 1775 Stuart went to England, and being a skilful musician, he employed music and painting in gaining a livelihood. He was eccentric and did not succeed well. In West he found a friend and benefactor, and in the studio of that great artist, he first became acquainted with Trumbull. He rapidly improved in his art, and might have become the first portrait painter in England, had not intemperate habits thwarted the aspirations of his genius. He went to Dublin, and then to New York. His fame had preceded him to America, and his studio was filled with sitters. But his habits of intemperance increased. He went to Philadelphia to paint President Washington. He resided there and at Germantown for some time, and went to Washington city, when the federal government was removed to that place. From 1805 until his death, he practised his profession in Boston. His death occurred in July, 1828, when he was about seventy-four years of age.

* A small man named Smith, with whom Stuart boarded in Philadelphia, stood for the figure of Stuart's full-lengths of Washington. He had a cast of his arm and hand made from a model of that of Washington seen upon the extended arm of the picture. His hand was much smaller than that of the chief.

Washington city, and to hear him say, "I do not pretend to have painted Washington as the general of the armies of Independence; I knew him not as such; I have painted the first president of the United States." And again, upon his being asked, "Whom did Washington most resemble?" he replied, "No one but himself." Stuart complained bitterly of his painting for the marquis of Lansdowne having been pirated by Heath, the engraver to his Britannic majesty. He showed us a copper-plate prepared in England for him by the celebrated Sharpe, the first engraver in Europe, who, although retired from the burin, had consented to execute a farewell engraving of Stuart's Washington. The copper-plate, was large, thick, and heavy, and polished like a mirror; while Stuart, laying his hand upon the plate, observed with much feeling, "The profits, my young friend, of this copper-plate engraved by Sharpe were all the fortune I expected to leave to my family." Heath made a fortune from his engraving of the work of Stuart, which engraving is a superb specimen of the art.

Washington was a bad sitter. It annoyed him exceedingly to sit at all; and, after every sitting, he was wont to declare this must be the last. Stuart, once finding the chief very dull, bethought himself to introduce the subject of horses. This roused up the sitter, and the artist obtained the desired expression.

The works of Stuart have acquired such extensive and deserved celebrity, that a *critique* from us would be almost superfluous. Of the great president, the head (that is, the head only) of Stuart is certainly a *chef d'œuvre*. There are three originals by this distinguished master: the head and bust, from which many copies have been taken, the full length for the marquis of Landsdowne, and an original intended for Mrs. Washington.* The artist has been particularly happy in delineating that graceful fall of the shoulders, for which the chief was remarkable, and which is said to constitute among the finest lines in the portraiture of manly excellence. The defects of the full length are in the limbs. There is too much of roundness and finish, according to the rules of art and the most approved models of taste and celebrity; whereas the original was in himself a model for the arts. Stuart once observed, "My impressions of his superior size considerably abated on trying on his coat, and finding that the span of his body was not greater than was to be found in some other men." True. We repeat, that his remarkable conformation was exclusively in the limbs; and the great artist, and truly pleasant gentleman, might have continued his trials, and worn out the coat in trying, ere he would have found a man whose arms should have filled the sleeves, or who possessed that breadth of wrists and those hands which, in the chief, almost "exceeded nature's law."

A Mr. Williams, a painter in crayons, had sittings about 1794, and made a strong likeness; but we have no further knowledge of him or his works.†

In 1795, both the elder and younger Peale had sittings. It was the fortune of the venerable Charles Willson Peale to have painted the provincial colonel of his Britannic majesty's service in 1772, and the same individual, as

* This is in the possession of the Boston Athenæum.

† Of this artist I find no record. Dunlap mentions a Williams who painted thirty years before the Revolution, and lent West books on the subject of art; also, a Williams, "a painter both in oil and miniature," who flourished in Boston about forty years ago.

chief magistrate of a great empire, in 1795. The Revolutionary recollections of the Peale family embrace James Peale, who was one of that gallant band of Philadelphians who joined the wreck of the grand army in '76, and was engaged in the battles of Trenton and Princeton. The collection of portraits, made by the patriotic founder of the first American museum, are of inestimable value to our posterity, being the only likenesses extant of some of the most distinguished worthies of the days of trial. This collection, and the museum entire, should be government property, and attached to a national university.*

Mr. Rembrandt Peale, with a laudable desire to give a genuine portrait of the Father of his Country, has devoted much time and talent to his Washington. His fine performance has received commendation from such high authorities that we deem it unnecessary to add anything to our certificate, which will be found in the publications on that subject.† The equestrian picture, by Rembrandt Peale, is a spirited work, and entitled to praise, as well for its able delineation of the person of the hero, as for the other characters which are introduced, particularly Hamilton, which is to the life. The white charger is rather too small, and the face of the general-in-chief older than he must have appeared in 1781. The execution of this large work is highly creditable to the artist, and the school of American arts.‡

---

* These were sold a few years ago, and a large proportion of them now adorn the walls of Independence Hall, Philadelphia.

† This picture was purchased by the United States government for $2,000, and now adorns the senate chamber in the federal capitol.

‡ This equestrian portrait is now (1859) in the rotunda of the federal capitol, awaiting the action of Congress upon a proposition to purchase it for the government.

The last original (profile in crayons) was by Sharpless, 1796, and, as we have said, is now at Arlington House. So much was this performance admired for the exquisite likeness and uncommon truthfulness of expression, that the chief ordered portraits by the same artist of every member of his domestic family, including George W. Lafayette.*

Cerracchi, the celebrated sculptor and enthusiast for liberty, came to this country about 1793 or 1794, and executed two busts, in marble, of the president and of Hamilton, the last said to be the best. Cerracchi was a singularly-looking man — very short, full of action, brilliant eyes, emitting the sparks of genius, and wore two watches. He afterward perished at Paris, as author of the "infernal machine." Cerracchi's bust of the chief is a failure; his bust of Hamilton, magnificent.†

We have thus enumerated most of the reliable originals of the Pater Patriæ from 1772 to 1796, with remarks upon each. These, with the statue by Houdon in 1788, constitute, in our humble opinion, all the resemblances in paintings and sculpture of the beloved Washington that will descend, venerated and admired, to posterity.

We believe that we have gone through the best originals, and we hope with equal candor and justice to all. We come now to the beautiful statue, by Canova, which long will "enchant our western world."‡

If the drawings which we have seen are correct, Canova, too, has mistaken the figure of the Pater Patriæ.

---

* This portrait, with one of the author of these *Recollections*, made in 1797, are now at Arlington House.

† See Note vii. in the Appendix.

‡ This statue is at Raleigh, North Carolina. The head is from Cerracchi's bust.

The illustrious artist, seated in the Eternal City, amid the classic remains of Roman grandeur, has had in his mind's eye the stout, square figure of those heroes whose patient endurance of hardships, whose valor and discipline, rendered thèm masters of the ancient world. But the great American can not be modelled, from coin or statue, by the force of genius or the illustrations of art. The graces of his person, like the virtues of his soul, owed their perfections to the master-hand, the hand of Nature.

Of the painting, said to be an original, by Wertmuller, and executed about 1795, we literally know nothing;* yet, in 1795, we were not absent from the presidential mansion in Philadelphia a single day. Again, through whose influence was the sitting obtained for a picture said to be for a Swedish nobleman? It is notorious that it was only by hard begging that Mrs. Bingham obtained the sittings for the marquis of Lansdowne's picture. And, again, we knew little or nothing of Sweden in the olden days, while we had, and still preserve, a most honored recollection of Denmark in the memory of a gallant Dane, Colonel Febiger, a distinguished officer of our Revolutionary army. And, lastly, if the Wertmuller was painted about 1795, where is the distinguishing feature in the physiognomy of the chief at that period — the projection of the under lip?

In giving a description of the stature and form of Washington, we give not only the result of our personal observation and experience of many years, but information derived from the highest authority — a favorite nephew.

---

* A well-engraved copy of this portrait is published in the first volume of Irving's *Life of Washington*. See Note vii. in the Appendix.

Major Lawrence Lewis asked his uncle what was his height in the prime of life? He replied, "In my best days, Lawrence, I stood six feet and two inches in ordinary shoes." We know that he measured, by a standard, precisely six feet when laid out in death. Of his weight we are an evidence, having heard him say to Crawford, governor of Canada, in 1799, "My weight, in my best days, sir, never exceeded from two hundred and ten to twenty." His form was unique. Unlike most athletic frames that expand at the shoulders and then gather in at the hips, the form of Washington deviated from the general rule, since it descended from the shoulders to the hips in perpendicular lines, the breadth of the trunk being nearly as great at the one end as at the other. His limbs were long, large, and sinewy; in his lower limbs, he was what is usually called straight-limbed. His joints, feet, and hands, were large; and, could a cast have been made from his right hand (so far did its dimensions exceed nature's model), it would have been preserved in museums for ages as the anatomical wonder of the eighteenth century.

The eyes of the chief were a light-grayish blue, deep sunken in their sockets, giving the expression of gravity and thought. Stuart painted those eyes of a deeper blue, saying, "In a hundred years they will have faded to the right color." His hair was of a hazel brown, and very thin in his latter days. In his movements, he preserved, in a remarkable degree and to an advanced age, the elastic step that he had acquired in his service on the frontier.

Being ordered one morning very early into the library at Mount Vernon (a place that none entered without orders), the weather being warm, we found the chief very much undressed, and, while looking on his manly frame, we discovered that the centre of his chest was indented. This is an exception to the general rule laid down by anatomists, that, where the human frame possesses great muscular power, the chest should rather be rounded out and protuberant than indented.* We were equally surprised to find how thin he was in person, being, with the absence of flesh, literally a man of "thews and sinews." He wore around his neck the miniature-portrait of his wife. This he had worn through all the vicissitudes of his eventful career, from the period of his marriage to the last days at Mount Vernon.†

In the appearance of Washington, there was nothing of bulkiness; but there was united all that was dignified and graceful, while his air and manner were at once noble and commanding. No one approached him that did not feel for him, as Lord Erskine observed, "a degree of awful reverence."‡ He wore a sword with a peculiar grace. The Viscomte de Noailles said it was because "the man was made for the sword, and not the sword for the man."

---

* Washington, as we have observed elsewhere, was much affected by a pulmonary disease in 1757 and 1758, which threatened, at one time, to become a consumption.

† This miniature could not have been painted earlier than the visit of C. W. Peale to Mount Vernon, in 1772, by whom it was probably executed. We have no account of any painter in miniature in the colonies previous to that time, except Taylor, who painted small heads in water-colors, in Philadelphia, in 1760.

‡ On the 15th of March, 1797, Lord Erskine wrote to Washington from London, saying, "I have taken the liberty to introduce your august and immortal name in a short sentence, which is to be found in a book I send you. I have a large acquaintance among the most valuable and exalted classes of men; but you are the only human being for whom I have ever felt an awful reverence. I sincerely pray God to grant you a long and serene evening to a life so gloriously devoted to the universal happiness of the world."

Lafayette, not long after the war of the Revolution, wrote a letter to Colonel Trumbull, urging him to paint an equestrian portrait of the chief as he appeared on the field at Monmouth. The illustrious Frenchman, America's great benefactor, said to us, "I was a very young major-general on that memorable day, and had a great deal to do, but took time, amid the heat and fury of the fight, to gaze upon and admire Washington, as, mounted on a splendid charger covered with foam, he rallied our line with words never to be forgotten: 'Stand fast, my boys, and receive your enemy; the southern troops are advancing to support you!' I thought then, as I do now," continued the good Lafayette, "that never have I seen so superb a man."*

Our readers may ask, Shall the *standard portraiture* be equestrian? We reply, to the portrait of one so accomplished a cavalier as Washington was, the white charger, with the leopard-skin housings, &c., would be an embellishment, the chief to be dismounted, with arm resting on the saddle, after the manner of Trumbull.

But, whether equestrian or not, the Americans have the materials for the standard before them in *the head from Stuart*, with some slight modifications from the original of 1772, and *the figure from Trumbull entire*. They have only to choose their artist, and let the work be done.

We have been thus minute in describing the portraiture of Washington, because posterity always inquires, "How looked the great of the olden time?" Should these *Recollections* meet the eye of posterity, we can only say that our portrait, though humbly, is faithfully drawn.

* See page 220.

Those who may portray the chief in latter life, should lay on their tints of age full lightly, for his was an age of action and of untiring labors in the cause of public utility, and for the good of mankind; and, although he had nearly reached the scriptural duration of man, time had so gently ushered him into the "vale of years" as to have left its usual infirmities behind, while his "lusty winter" had shed its "frosts so kindly" that he seemed rather as a full ripened autumn, for no desolation was there.

When this noble empire shall have achieved its high destiny, and, embracing a continent, attained a power and grandeur unexampled in the history of nations, the future American from the topmost height of his greatness, will look back upon the early days of his country, and call up the "time-honored" memories of the heroic era and the age of Washington; and, when contemplating the image of the *Pater Patriæ*, perpetuated by the mellowed tints of the canvass and the freshness of time-enduring bronze, with honest pride of ancestry he will exclaim, "My forefather was the associate of that great man in the perils and glories of the struggle for American independence. Let there be undying honor to the memory of Washington; ever green be the laurels that deck his trophied tomb; ever living be the homage in the hearts of his countrymen and mankind for the patriot, the hero, and the sage, who, under Providence, with humble means, so much contributed to raise his native land from the depths of dependence, and to place her in the rank of nations; who presided over her civic destinies in the dawn of the great experiment of self-government; and who, after an illustrious life spent in the service of liberty and mankind, and without a cloud to dim the lustre of his fame, descended to the grave with the august title of the FATHER OF HIS COUNTRY.*

* In Note vii. in the Appendix, I have given a brief account of several original portraits of Washington, not mentioned by Mr. Curtis.

APPENDIX.

NOTE I.—PAGE 34.

ORIGINAL CORRESPONDENCE BETWEEN GENERAL WASHINGTON AND JOHN PARKE CUSTIS.

THE following letters, never before published, passed between General Washington and his step-son, John Parke Custis, during the Revolution. They serve to exhibit, in a strong light, that characteristic of the great leader's mind, which enabled him to abstract himself from the most important public concerns, and to attend to the consideration of the minute details of private life. These letters also have an intrinsic interest, because they contain much information of a public character, having a bearing upon the current events of the time. One of them reveals a fact, not generally known, namely, that officers of the continental army—even Washington himself—speculated in the chances of profits arising from the success of privateering.

It will be seen by the dates of these letters, and the allusions in them to current events, that some of them were written by Washington at times when the weightiest public affairs must have occupied his mind.

[WASHINGTON TO CUSTIS.]

PHILADELPHIA, *June* 19, 1775.

DEAR JACK: I have been called upon by the unanimous voice of the colonies to take the command of the continental army. It is an honor I neither sought after, or was by any means fond of accepting, from a consciousness of my own inexperience and inability to discharge the duties of so important a trust. However, as the partiality of the Congress has placed me in this distinguished point of view, I can make them no other return but what will flow from close attention and an upright intention—for the rest I can say nothing. My great concern upon this occasion is, the thought of leaving your mother under the uneasiness which I fear this affair will throw her into; I therefore hope, expect, and indeed have no doubt, of your using every means in your power to keep up her spirits, by doing everything in your power to promote her quiet. I have, I must confess, very uneasy feelings on her account, but as it has been a kind of unavoidable necessity which has led me into this appointment, I shall more readily hope that success will attend it and crown our meetings with happiness.

At any time, I hope it is unnecessary for me to say, that I am always pleased with yours and Nelly's abidance at Mount Vernon, much less upon this occasion, when I think it absolutely necessary for the peace and satisfaction of your mother; a consideration which I have no doubt will have due weight with you both, and require no arguments to enforce.

As the public gazettes will convey every article of intelligence that I could communicate in this letter, I shall not repeat them, but with love to Nelly, and sincere regard for yourself, I remain,

Your most affectionate,

GEO. WASHINGTON.

P. S.—Since writing the foregoing, I have received your letter of the fifteenth instant. I am obliged to you for the intelligence therein contained, and am glad you directed about the tobacco, for I had really forgot it. You must now take upon yourself the entire management of your own estate, it will no longer be in my power to assist you, nor is there any occasion for it, as you have never discovered a disposition to put it to a bad use.

The Congress, for I am at liberty to say as much, are about to strike two million of dollars as a continental currency, for the support of the war, as Great Britain seems determined to enforce us into—and there will be at least fifteen thousand raised as a continental army. As I am exceedingly hurried, I can add no more at present than that I am, &c. G. W.

[WASHINGTON TO CUSTIS]

NEW YORK, *July* 24, 1776.

DEAR SIR: I wrote to you two or three posts ago, since which your letter of the tenth instant is come to hand. With respect to the proposed exchange of lands with Colonel Thomas Moore, I have not a competent knowledge of either tract to give an opinion with any degree of precision; but from the situation of Moore's land, and its contiguity to a large part of your estate, and where you will probably make your residence, I should, were I in your place, be very fond of the exchange; especially, as the land you hold in Hanover is but a small tract, and totally detached from the rest of your estate. What local advantages it may have I know not. These ought to be inquired into, because a valuable mill seat often gives great value to a poor piece of land (as I understand that of yours in Hanover is). I have no doubt myself, but that middling land under a man's own eye, is more profitable than rich land at a distance, for which reason I should, were I in your place, be for drawing as many of my slaves to the lands in King William and King and Queen as could work on them to advantage, and I should also be for adding to those tracts if it could be done upon reasonable terms.

I am very sorry to hear by your account that General Lewis* stands so unfavorably with his officers. I always had a good opinion of him, and should have hoped that he had been possessed of too much good sense to maltreat his officers, and thereby render himself obnoxious to them.

We have a powerful fleet in full view of us—at the watering-place of Staten island. General Howe and his army are landed thereon, and it is thought will make no attempt upon this city till his re-enforcements, which are hourly expected, arrive. When this happens it is to be presumed that there will be some pretty warm work. Give my love to Nelly, and compliments to Mr. Calvert and family, and to others who may inquire after, dear sir,

Your affectionate,   GEO. WASHINGTON.

* General Andrew Lewis, an excellent Virginian officer who commanded at Point Pleasant, in the battle with the Indians there, in 1774.

[CUSTIS TO WASHINGTON.]

MOUNT AIRY, *August* 8, 1776.

HONORED SIR: Your letters of the eighth and twenty-fourth ultimo came safely to hand, and I should certainly have answered them before now, if I had not been in hopes of collecting something worth relating. I feel the sincerest pleasure that my professions of gratitude were received in the light I would wish them to be. I can only express it in words at this time. I fervently wish to have an opportunity of fulfilling them by my actions; I need no more words to convince you of my sincerity, for I flatter myself you are satisfied that deceit makes no part of my character. I am happy to find my ideas of land coincide with yours. Hill informed me that a good part of Colonel Moore's land was as finely timbered as he ever saw, and the soil very proper for farming: these circumstances, added to its situation, render it in my opinion a very desirable purchase. I desired Hill to contract for it on the best terms he could, with the advice of Uncles Bassett and Dandridge, who were kind enough to promise all their assistance. My land in Hanover, as far as I can learn, is very indifferent, and is valuable only for its timber.

You have no doubt heard of the men-of-war coming up Potowmack as far as Mr. Brent's, whose house they burnt with several outhouses and some stacks of wheat. A Captain James with sixty militia were stationed there who all got drunk, and kept challenging the men-of-war to come ashore, and upbraiding them with cowardice. Hammond sent one hundred and fifty men, who landed about ten o'clock under cover of a gondola and tender. The militia were asleep after their drinking frolic, and did not discover the enemy until they landed and their vessels began to fire. Captain James desired his men to shift for themselves, and ran off without firing a gun. A young man by name of Combs stayed until he killed three of the enemy. Colonel Grayson appearing with thirty Prince William volunteers, the enemy thought proper to retire to their ships. Captain James is to be tried for cowardice. The fleet, after performing this exploit, returned down the river to George's island, from whence they have been drove off by Major Price with some loss. They are gone down the bay in a most sickly condition. I have not heard where they have stopped. Before they left the island they burned several vessels, and I hear that two sloops belonging to them have fallen into Captain Boucher's hands.

This province has been thrown into much confusion lately, on account of elections. In several counties it has been determined contrary to an express order of convention, that every man who bears arms is entitled to vote. This, in my opinion, is a dangerous procedure, and tends to introduce anarchy and confusion as much as anything I know. The latter it has already introduced in the counties where it has been practised; men who are by no means qualified having been chosen, and proper men left out.

I have the pleasure to inform you that a majority of the counties have obeyed the order of convention. Your old friend Colonel Fitzhugh is elected for the county he lives in. His military knowledge will be very useful in council, where such knowledge is much wanting. T. Johnson is left out of every office at present. He was appointed a brigadier-general. The county he lived in petitioned him to resign his commission, that they might elect him a burgess. He granted their request, and they deceived him. You will, I doubt not, regret with me that so proper a man should be left out of office.

I received by last post a letter from Dr. Attwood, containing an account against me of two dollars, for bleeding and sundry medicines. I well remember when at King's college to have received them, but I am much at a loss to account for Doctor Cooper's extravagant charge, and leaving so many accounts unpaid. I shall be obliged to you to order him to be paid. I enclose you his letter which you sent under cover last post.* The family here and at Milwood join in compliments. Nelly presents her love. I am, honored sir,

    Your most affectionate,
      JOHN PARKE CUSTIS.

---

* Mr. Custis was in Kings (now Columbia) college in 1773.

[WASHINGTON TO CUSTIS.]

MORRIS TOWN, *January* 22, 1777.

DEAR SIR: Your letter of the seventh came to my hands a few days ago, and brought with it the pleasing reflection of your still holding me in remembrance.

The misfortune of short enlistments, and an unhappy dependance upon militia, have shown their baneful influence at every period, and almost upon every occasion, throughout the whole course of this war. At no time, nor upon no occasion, were they ever more exemplified than since Christmas; for if we could but have got in the militia in time, or prevailed upon those troops whose times expired (as they generally did) on the first of this instant, to have continued (not more than a thousand or twelve hundred agreeing to stay) we might, I am persuaded, have cleared the Jerseys entirely of the enemy. Instead of this, all our movements have been made with inferior numbers, and with a mixed, motley crew, who were here to-day, gone to-morrow, without assigning a reason, or even apprizing you of it. In a word, I believe I may with truth add, that I do not think that any officer since the creation ever had such a variety of difficulties and perplexities to encounter as I have. How we shall be able to rub along till the new army is raised, I know not. Providence has heretofore saved us in a remarkable manner, and on this we must principally rely. Every person in every state should exert himself to facilitate the raising and marching the new regiments to the army with all possible expedition.

I have never seen (but heard of) the resolve you mentioned, nor do I get a paper of Purdie's* once a month. Those who want faith to believe the account of the shocking wastes committed by Howe's army—of their ravaging, plundering, and abuse of women—may be convinced, to their sorrow, perhaps, if a check can not be put to their progress.

It is painful to me to hear of such illiberal reflections upon the eastern troops as you say prevails in Virginia. I always have, and always shall say, that I do not believe that any of the

* *Virginia Gazette*, published at Williamsburg, Virginia.

states produce better men, or persons capable of making better soldiers, but it is to be acknowledged that they are (generally speaking) most wretchedly officered. To this, and this only, is to be attributed their demerits. The policy of those states has been, to level men as much as possible to one standard. The distinction, therefore, between officers and soldiers * * * and that hunger and thirst after glory which* * * *
This is the true secret, and we have found, that wherever a regiment is well-officered, their men have behaved well—when otherwise, ill—the misconduct or cowardly behaviour always originating with the officers who have set the example. Equal injustice is done them, in depriving them of merit in other respects; for no people fly to arms readier than they do, or come better equipped, or with more regularity into the field than they.

With respect to your inquiries about payments made Mr. —— I can not answer them with precision, but I am exceedingly mistaken if I have not made him two, for both you and myself. Indeed I am as sure of it as I can be of anything from the badness of my memory. I think I made him one payment myself, and the treasurer, or Hill, made him the other. The book, however, in which I keep your accounts will show it (the parchment-covered quarto one†) as you will, I suppose, find yourself charged by me, with the payments made.

In my letter to Lund Washington, I have given the late occurrences, and to avoid repetition, I refer you to him. My love to Nelly, and compliments to Mr. Calvert's family, and all other inquiring friends, leaving me nothing else to add, than that

I am, your affectionate, GEO. WASHINGTON.

[CUSTIS TO WASHINGTON.]

WILLIAMSBURGH, *August* 8, 1777.

HONORED SIR: I do with the most unfeigned pleasure congratulate you and your success in the Jerseys over our enemy.

---

* Some modern pen has blotted out several words in the four or five lines succeeding this portion of the sentence, and entirely destroyed the connection.

† This account-book is now at Arlington House.

We are now anxious to know where these disturbers of our peace will next bend their course; but rest satisfied that at your approach, the plunderers will quit any part of the country they may have seized upon, with the same disgrace they left the Jerseys.

You will, no doubt, be surprised to hear of the acquital of Davis and his accomplices. It has indeed astonished every one here, except the judges, and the lawyers who defended the criminals. I was present at the trial, and was clearly satisfied from the evidence that Davis was guilty—the jury brought in their verdict to that purpose. But the attorney having omitted to mention who the enemies of America were, although he accused Davis of adhering to the enemies of America, the lawyers took hold of the quibble, and persuaded the judges to overset the verdict. It is now determined that releasing prisoners of war from their place of confinement, is not treason against the state. This judgment, in my opinion, does not reflect much honor on the talents of our judges, and indeed it is much to be lamented, that our assembly might have made a much better appointment and did not do it. Their decision, I am afraid, will be productive of much injury, for no tory or prisoner of war can be kept in this state, as those who set them at liberty are subject to no penalty. Davis was not admitted as an evidence, on account of his having been a convict, and not having served his seven years, for the lawyers made this quibble, that no man can be an evidence unless he served the whole time of his conviction. Your kindness to Davis in giving him two years of his time, had well nigh cost him his life in this instance, and prevented him from bearing testimony against two as great villains as himself.

I have the pleasure to acquaint you that the test is generally taken through the country, few or none hesitating to take it. I wish our assembly had laid a tax at the same time they made the test. I am convinced there would have been as little objection to the one as the other; but unfortunately for us our rulers, like other men, can not divest themselves of their attachment to their private gain, many of them being guilty of the crime they ought to punish in others, their whole aim being to get immense fortunes, which some have succeeded in.

When at Philadelphia, I thought nothing could exceed the price of goods at that place, but I am sorry that I have found good reason to change my opinion. Our country is crowded with harpies from Maryland and Pennsylvania, who buy up every article, and retail them out again at the most intolerable prices, distressing the poor at a cruel degree. Our assembly provided nothing against this evil, which we must submit to, without any hopes of redress, until October, unless the people fall upon means to redress themselves, which, I fear, they will, from the great want of salt which these devils have engrossed.

I am happy to inform you that your people at Davenport's are recovered from their sickness. They have had a dreadful fever among them, which has at last subsided. You have a prospect of a very plentiful crop this year, which is the same through the country. I have heard some old gentlemen say they do not remember such prospects of a crop these twenty years past. There has been more rain since harvest then I remember to have seen fall at this season of the year. We shall have Plenty if not Peace this year, but I hope to enjoy both before this time twelvemonths.

I shall always acknowledge with pleasure the many favors and kindnesses I have received at your hands, and shall always gladly do everything to make you some return. I must now beg of you, sir, to accept, as an instance of gratitude in me, a horse colt, which was got by Delany's horse, out of a very fine high-bred mare, given me by Mr. Calvert. I wish the colt was older, as he would be more acceptable. He was foaled only in June. He is a dark bay with a blaze in his face, and, as I am informed, is a very fine made colt, and large. I must beg of you not to be scrupulous about accepting the colt, as by doing it, you will much oblige me.

Nelly joins me in wishing you health and victory over the enemy, and I am,   Honored sir, your most affectionate,

J. P. CUSTIS.

[EXTRACT OF A LETTER FROM JOHN PARKE CUSTIS TO GENERAL WASHINGTON.]

ELTHAM, *September* 11, 1777.

I AM sorry that I have nothing to inform you of by the way of news, except that the militia have turned out to the number of five thousand very fine men. General Nelson parades twice a week, and they fire away an amazing quantity of powder, I think to very little purpose, when we are not overstocked, and the militia to continue but a short time. The cry against the eastern troops was beginning to break out with double vigor. Your letter that I published last winter had the desired effect for some time, but the enemies to the eastern states concluded that it was generally forgot in the country. A member of Congress from this state, wrote to his son, that General Stark had, on account of some disgust, drawn himself off from the army with two thousand men. The gentleman asked me in a very large company, if I knew a General Stark, formerly Colonel Stark. I told him, yes, and he was looked upon as a brave and good officer. He replied he knew him to be a damned rascal, and produced this letter, when the whole company agreed with him. This letter was greedily circulated about the town, and every one was abusing the eastern troops as cowards. General Stark has given a good contradiction to Colonel H———n's* letter. It is to be lamented that the gentlemen of Congress can not divest themselves of their private animosities, and give fair and impartial accounts. I have seen several of his letters filled with the most bitter invectives against the eastern men; such conduct tends only to breed divisions among us, and weaken our glorious cause.

I was prevailed upon yesterday at court to offer myself as a delegate at the next election in New Kent. The gentlemen gave me every reason to expect success should they honor me with the appointment. I am determined to serve them on true independent principles to the best of my abilities.

Nelly joins me in love, and wishing you a glorious victory over our enemy, believe me sincerely and affectionately,

J. P. CUSTIS.

* Colonel Harrison.

[WASHINGTON TO CUSTIS.]

{ PERKIOMY CREEK IN PHILADELPHIA, N. Y.
September 28, 1777.

DEAR SIR: Your letter of the eleventh instant came to my hands yesterday.

It was always my intention, if agreeable to your mother, to give you the offer of renting her dower-estate in King William during my interest therein, so soon as you come of age to act for yourself. On two accounts I resolved to do this — first, because I was desirous of contracting my own business into as narrow a compass as possible; and, secondly, because I thought an estate, so capable of improvement as that is (in the hands of a person who had a permanent interest in it, and the means withal) ought not to be neglected till an unfortunate event, and perhaps a distant one, might put you in possession.

The little attention I have been able to pay to any part of my own private business for three years last past is the cause why this among other matters has escaped me, but since you have mentioned it yourself, I have only to add, that it will be quite agreeable to me that you should have the land, and everything thereon except breeding mares, if any, and fillies.

To regulate the rent by the rule you have mentioned, I could not consent, because, if the plantation had been under good management, it would have fixed it higher than you ought to give. If, under bad management, which I believe to be the case, it would fix it too low, and might settle it at nothing. The only true criterion is to determine what so much land, with so much marsh, in such a part of the country, would rent for; and then the annual value of so many slaves, estimating them at their present worth, at the same time having respect to the advantages and disadvantages of the old and the young, as the one is declining and the other improving.

As you are desirous of having the matter fixed as speedily as possible—as the distance between us is too great — the season far advanced—and letters too apt to miscarry to negotiate a business of this kind, in that way, and as I wish for no more than impartial gentlemen, unconnected with both of us, shall say I ought to have; I am content to leave the valuation of the whole to General Nelson, Colonel Braxton, and George Webb, Esq. I mention these gentlemen because they are persons of character, and because no time may be lost in the appointment.

Whatever rent they shall fix upon the land, and whatever hire for the negroes, I contentedly will take. The stock of every kind (except mares and fillies), and plantation utensils and working tools may also be valued; at which you may take them; by which means the whole business may be finished at once.

That these gentlemen (if you approve the method of ascertaining the rent) may know it is with my approbation, the request is made to them you will show them this letter, and at the same time apologize in my name for the trouble it will give them if they are obliging enough to undertake it.

My extreme hurry, especially at this juncture, only allows me time to give my love to Nelly, and to assure you that I am, with sincere regard and affection, dear sir, yours,

GEO. WASHINGTON.

P. S. In the present fluctuating state of things, there is one thing which justice to myself and your mother requires me to condition for, and that is that the rent stipulated shall have some relative value, to secure an equivalent for the land and slaves; otherwise, as the lease will be an absolute conveyance of the estate from your mother and me, we may at the end of a few years, if paper money continues to depreciate, get nothing for it. I do not mean by this to insinuate that I am unwilling to receive paper money — on the contrary, I shall, with cheerfulness receive payment in anything that has a currency at the time, but of equal value then to the intrinsic worth at the time of fixing the rent. In a word, that I may really, and not nominally, get what was intended as a rent. Yours, &c.

G. W——N.

JOHN PARKE CUSTIS, ESQ.

[CUSTIS TO WASHINGTON.]

HONORED SIR: I have intended for several letters past, but as often forgot it, to ask whether it would be agreeable to you, to admit Colonel Baylor a partner in the share we have of the privateer. He was very desirous to become an adventurer, and I promised to acquaint you of it, but forgot it until now. The share I own is divided into four parts, Mr. Lund Washington has one fourth, the remaining three-fourths are divided between you and myself. If you have no objections, I am willing to oblige Colonel Baylor with a fourth part of the share. I would not be understood by this, that I think I have a bad bargain. On the contrary, I think we have every reason to expect great success. I propose it altogether to oblige Colonel Baylor, as he was very desirous of being concerned in the ship. If it is agreeable to you, you will please to acquaint Colonel Baylor that we shall look upon him as a partner, and that I should be glad to know on whom I shall draw for his proportion of the expense. You will, I hope, sir, excuse this liberty, and believe me, honored,

Your ever affectionate,

J. P. CUSTIS.

[WASHINGTON TO CUSTIS]

WHITEMARSH, 12 miles from Philadelphia,
November 14, 1777.

DEAR SIR: Your letter of the twenty-sixth ultimo came to my hands in due course of post. I observe what you say respecting the renting of Claibornes. It is not my wish to let it for any longer term than your mamma inclines to, and at no rate, for her life, unless it is perfectly agreeable to her. This I did conceive would have been the case (as I think she informed me) to you; but if it is not, I am equally well pleased. I am very well convinced that I can, when time will permit me to attend to my own business, readily rent the place for my own interest in it, as there are many that wish for it. If there is but tolerable good grounds to suspect that the distemper will get among my cattle at Claibornes, I shall be glad if you would desire Mr. Hill, when you next write to him, to dispose of them if he can (provided he also coincides with you in opinion).

It is much to be wished that a remedy could be applied to the depreciation of our currency. I know of no person better qualified to do this than Colonel Mason, and shall be very happy to hear that he has taken it in hand. Long have I been persuaded of the indispensable necessity of a tax for the purpose of sinking the paper money, and why it has been delayed better politicians than I must account for. What plan Colonel Mason may have in contemplation for filling up the Virginia regiments I know not, but certain I am that this is a measure that can not be dispensed with, nor ought not under any pretext whatsoever. I hope Colonel Mason's health will admit his attendance on the assembly, and no other plea should be offered, much less received by his constituents.

It is perfectly agreeable, too, that Colonel Baylor should share part of the privateer. I have spoken to him on the subject; he still continues in the same mind, and will write to you on the subject. I shall therefore consider myself as possessing one fourth of your full share, and that yourself, Baylor, L. Washington, and I, are equally concerned in the share you at first held.

The only articles of intelligence worth communicating I have written to your mamma, and refer you to that letter. We have an account, indeed, which seems to gain credit, that Weeks, with a squadron of ships fitted out of the French ports, under continental colors, had taken fifty-three homeward-bound West-Indiamen (chiefly from Jamaica) in the English channel; that Lord Stormont was recalled from the court of France; and war expected every moment between France and Britain. God send it.

Give my love to Nelly, and be assured that with sincere regard I remain, dear sir,   Your most affectionate,

GEO. WASHINGTON.

[WASHINGTON TO CUSTIS.]

VALLEY FORGE, *February* 1, 1778.

DEAR SIR: I will just write you a few lines in acknowledgment of your letter of the fourteenth ultimo, which was detained by the posts, not being able to cross Susquehanna, till the evening before last. I congratulate you upon the birth of another daughter, and Nelly's good health; and heartily wish the last may continue, and the other be a blessing to you.

The money received for your land was, I think, well applied, unless you could have laid it out for other lands more convenient; which method I should have preferred, as land is the most permanent estate we can hold, and most likely to increase in its value. Your mamma is not yet arrived, but if she left Mount Vernon on the twenty-sixth ultimo, as intended, may, I think, be expected every hour. Mead set off yesterday (as soon as I got notice of her intention) to meet her. We are in a dreary kind of place, and uncomfortably provided; for other matters I shall refer you to the bearer, Colonel Fitzgerald, who can give you the occurrences of the camp, &c., better than can be related in a letter. My best wishes attend Nelly and the little ones, and with sincere regard I am and shall ever remain, dear sir,

Your most affectionate,

GEO. WASHINGTON.

[MRS. WASHINGTON TO CUSTIS AND WIFE.]

MIDDLEBROOK, *March the* 19th, 1778.

MY DEAR CHILDREN: Not having received any letters from you the two last posts, I have only to tell you that the general and myself are well. All is quiet in this quarter. It is from the southward that we expect to hear news. We are very anxious to know how our affairs are going in that quarter. Colonel Harrison is not yet arrived at camp. We have heard that he is in Philadelphia several days ago.

I hear so very seldom from you, that I don't know where you are, or whether you intend to come to Alexandria to live this spring, or when. The last letter from Nelly she says both the children have been very ill: they were, she hoped, getting better.

If you do not write to me I will not write to you again, or till I get letters from you. Let me know how all friends below are; they have forgot to write to me, I believe.

Remember me to all inquiring friends. Give the dear little girls a kiss for me, and tell Bett I have got a pretty new doll for her, but don't know how to send it to her. The general joins me in love to you both, and begs to be remembered to all our friends that inquire after us. I am, with sincere love,

Your truly affectionate mother,

MARTHA WASHINGTON.

[CUSTIS TO WASHINGTON.]

MOUNT VERNON, *June* 17, 1778.

HONORED SIR: When I last did myself the pleasure of writing you, I was in so great a hurry that I believe my letter was scarcely legible. I must, therefore, in this, beg an excuse, and likewise make an apology for not giving you an account of the acts passed in the last assembly. I herewith transmit you the titles of the acts, and wish I could send you the acts themselves; they might afford you some satisfaction. But through laziness or some other default the printer has not got them ready; I will transmit them as soon as I can get them. The bill for recruiting the army holds out every inducement to the men to enlist. We found the method of drafting men, though the best, was the most disagreeable; we therefore determined to give them every inducement to enlist, and if that fails, we shall adopt some kind of draft.

I am sorry to inform you that, great as the advantages are, I am afraid they will not have the desired effect. Our countrymen appear to be totally changed. The military ardor, which displayed itself in Virginia in the beginning of this dispute in a distinguished manner, appears to be almost extinguished. This little paltry trade among us has engrossed the attention of all orders of men, and has increased the price of labor to such an exorbitant degree that a soldier can not be enlisted. It may appear extraordinary, but is very true, that officers are as difficult to get as men; I mean good ones. The governor has been obliged to advertise for officers to fill up our state troops, and from the few applications has been obliged to make a very indifferent choice. There was a bill brought into the house for regulating trade, which, I am confident, would have been productive of good consequences; but it had too many friends in the house to let it be injured. The bill was thrown out.

Our delegation to Congress, I am sorry to say, is not so good as I could wish, or as we might have had, if the act for preventing members of Congress sitting in the assembly had been repealed. A bill for that purpose was brought in and shared the same fate with the other. I have often wished my colleague had been present; we might have prevented this evil. He is most inexcusable in staying away. He got as far as Colonel Blackburn's and heard the house had broken up. If that act had been repealed, our delegation would have been very respectable.

I mentioned in my last the arrival of a fifty-gun ship from France. She has brought the most valuable cargo that ever arrived in one ship. The governor had made a very advantageous bargain with the captain; but some scoundrels persuaded the captain he had sold his goods too cheap, and he was off the bargain. I have since heard the governor has made a second bargain. The cloth on board alone cost 80,000 pounds sterling. There are 4,000 suits ready made; 20,000 pairs of stockings; 15,000 pairs of shoes; 7 or 8,000 hats; several thousand shirts ready made; besides, a great quantity of linen. She has a great deal of Burgundy and claret, first quality, and other wines. Her cargo, the governor told me, cost five millions of livres. The ship goes out a letter-of-marque, if war should be declared between France and England, with fifteen thousand hogsheads of tobacco on board. The state has more than that number on hand, which was chiefly bought at twenty-five shillings. The tobacco is to be delivered along side the ship at four pounds per hundred. We shall, by this means, get the goods on good terms. This cargo is sufficient to clothe our quota without purchasing any more, and will prevent the emission of more money for this purchase.

I was so unlucky as not to receive your letter in answer to mine by Mr. Washington; and I intended to write you fully my plan in selling my land, by this post; but, as I have already exceeded the bounds of moderation in the length of my letter, I must defer it to the next post, and remain, as I have ever been, your most affectionate, J. P. CUSTIS.

[WASHINGTON TO CUSTIS.]

I THANK you for your cordial and affectionate congratulations on our late success at Monmouth, and the arrival of the French fleet at the Hook. The first might, I think, have been a glorious day, if matters had begun well in the morning; but, as the court-martial, which has been sitting upward of a month for the trial of General Lee, is not yet over, I do not choose to say anything on the subject, further than that there evidently appeared a capital blunder, or something else, somewhere. The truth, it is to be hoped, will come out after so long an investigation of it. If it had not been for the long passage of the French fleet, which prevented their arrival till after the evacuation of Philadelphia — or the shallowness of the water at the entrance of the harbor at New York, which prevented their getting in there — one of the greatest strokes might have been aimed that ever was; and, if successful, which I think would have been reduced to a moral certainty, the ruin of Great Britain must have followed, as both army and fleet must, undoubtedly, have fallen. Count D'Estaing, with his squadron, are now at Rhode Island, to which place I have detached troops, and hope soon to hear of some favorable adventure there, as an attempt will be made upon the enemy at that place.

After the battle of Monmouth, I marched for this place, where I have been encamped more than a fortnight. We cut off, by the present position of the army, all land supplies to the city of New York, and had the best reasons to believe that the troops there were suffering greatly for want of provisions, but the French fleet, leaving the Hook, opens a door to the sea, through which, no doubt, they will endeavor to avail themselves.

Give my love to Nelly, Colonel Bassett, and the rest of our friends, and be assured that I am, with sincere regard and affection, Yours, GEO. WASHINGTON.

[WASHINGTON TO CUSTIS.]
{ FREDERICKSBURG, IN THE STATE OF NEW YORK,
October 12, 1778.

DEAR SIR: I have now, at your request, given my full consent to the sale of the lands which I hold, in right of dower, in a tract in the county of York; to a water grist-mill thereon; to lots in the city of Williamsburg, and others in Jamestown; as also to your renting, or otherwise disposing of the other dower land and slaves which I am possessed of in the county of King William, upon the terms which have been specifically agreed and subscribed to. But I should think myself wanting in that friendship and regard which I have ever professed for and endeavored to evince toward you, were I to withhold my advice from you with respect to the disposal of them.

A moment's reflection must convince you of two things: first, that lands are of permanent value; that there is scarcely a possibilty of their falling in price, but almost a moral certainty of their rising exceedingly in value. And, secondly, that our paper currency is fluctuating, that it has depreciated considerably, and that no human foresight can, with precision, tell how low it may get, as the rise or fall of it depends upon contingencies which the utmost stretch of human sagacity can neither foresee nor prevent. These positions being granted (and no one can gainsay the justice of them), it follows that, by parting from your lands, you give a certainty for an uncertainty, because it is not the nominal price—it is not ten, fifteen, or twenty pounds an acre— but the relative value of this sum to specie, or something of substantial worth, that is to constitute a good price. The inference, therefore, I mean to draw, and the advice I shall give in consequence of it, is this, that you do not convert the lands you now hold into cash faster than your present contract with the Alexanders, and a certain prospect of again vesting it in other lands more convenient, requires of you. This will be treading upon sure ground. It will enable you to discharge contracts already entered into, and, in effect, exchange land for land; for it is a matter of moonshine to you, considered in that point of view simply, how much the money depreciates, if you can discharge one pound with another, and get land of equal value to that you sell. But far different from this is the case of those who sell for cash and keep that cash by them, put it to interest, or receive it in annual payments; for, in either of these cases, if our currency should unfortunately continue to depreciate in the manner it has done in the course of the last two years, a pound may not, in the space of two years more, be worth a shilling, the difference of which becomes a clear loss to the possessor, and evinces, in a clear point of view, the force and efficacy of my advice to you to pay debts, and vest it in something that will retain its primitive value; or rather, in your case, not to part with that thing of value for money, unless it be with a view to the investing it in something of equal value; and it accounts, at the same time, for the principle upon which I act with respect to my own interest in the dower-lands; for I should be wanting to myself, and guilty of an inexcusable act of remissness and criminal injustice to your mother not to secure an equivalent for her releasement of dower; and this might be the case of a nominal sum that had no relative value to the thing in question, and which, eventually, might be a means of giving away the estate; for it is not the number of pounds, but the worth and what these pounds will fetch, that is to stamp the value of them. Four hundred pounds in paper dollars now is, and, I suppose, at the time of parting with this dower, may be worth one hundred pounds in specie; but, two years hence, one hundred pounds in specie may be worth, and will fetch, one thousand pounds of paper. It can not be reasonable or just, therefore, to expect that I, or your mother (if she should be the survivor), should lose this, when no person, I believe, will undertake to give it as an opinion that the value of the dower will decrease, but the direct contrary, as lands are increasing in their price every day. This, if you will follow the advice here given, can not be the case with you, let money depreciate as it will, because with a pound you pay a pound in discharge of a purchase already made, and for those to be made you can regulate your sales by your purchases.

It may be said that our money may receive a proper tone again, and in that case it would be an advantage to turn lands, &c., into cash for the benefit of the rise. In answer to this, I shall only observe that this is a lottery; that it may, or may not, happen; that, if it should happen, you have lost nothing; if it should not, you have saved your estate, which, in the other case, might have been sunk. Hence it appears that you may play a good and sure game, so far as it relates to yourself, and, as far as it respects me, the advantage is wholly on your side; for instance, if the difference between specie and paper at this time is as four to one, and next year is eight to one, it makes no difference to you, because the presumption is that tobacco, corn, and other produce, will rise in proportion to the fall of the money, and fetch in quantity what it lacks in quality. But, on the other hand, if the interest was to be fixed at the present difference of four to one, and should hereafter become as one to one (that is equal), I should get four times as much as I am content to receive, and you would lose it; from hence, as before, you may gain, and can not lose, while I get the simple value of the estate, and can neither gain nor lose, which is all I aim at by fixing the value of the dower in specie, to be discharged in any money current in the country at the time of payment, at the prevailing exchange or difference between specie and paper. It may possibly be said that this is setting up a distinction between specie and paper, and will contribute to its depreciation. I ask if there is a man in the United States that does not make a distinction when four to one is the difference, and whether it is in the power of an individual to check this evil when Congress, and the several assemblies, are found unequal to the task? Not to require, or contract for, the actual payment in specie, but to keep this as much out of sight as possible, in common cases that are to have an immediate operation, is all that can be expected; but, in a bargain that may exist for twenty years, there should be something to insure mutual advantage, which advantage, though every man can judge of in the transactions of a day, no one can do it when it is to be extended to years, under the present fluctuating state of our paper bills of credit.

My design in being thus particular with you, is to answer two purposes: first, to show my ideas of the impropriety of parting with your own lands faster than you can invest the money in other lands (comprehending those already purchased); and, secondly, to evince to you the propriety of my own conduct in securing to myself and your mother the intrinsic value, neither more nor less, of the dower-estate. I have only one piece of advice more to give, and that is, to aim rather at the exchange than sale of your lands; and I think, among those gentlemen mentioned in a former letter, you may find chapmen. I am with very sincere regard,

Your affectionate friend and servant,

GEO. WASHINGTON.

To PARKE CUSTIS, ESQ.

[WASHINGTON TO CUSTIS.]

FREDERICKSBURG, NEW YORK, *October* 26, 1778.

DEAR JACK: If my brother, to whom the enclosed is addressed, should not be a member of assembly, and in Williamsburg, I should be glad if you would continue it to him by a safe hand.

The enemy still continue to keep us in suspense and baffle all conjecture — they have five or six thousand men at this time actually on board transports, lying in New York bay; and a fleet of more than a hundred sail left the Hook on the twentieth instant for England; said to contain invalids, officers of the reduced corps, &c.

This fleet comprehended empty provision ships, merchant ships, and private adventurers, taking the benefit of a convoy; at the same time Admiral Byron with fourteen or fifteen sail of the line, and some frigates, sailed from the Hook, with the design, as is supposed, to blockade the French squadron at Boston, and keep them shut in there till the transports can get advanced to their respective places of destination.

It still remains a matter of great uncertainty, whether the enemy mean to evacuate New York or not. I do not myself think they will, but can give no better reason for their staying than that they ought to go—their uniform practice is to run counter to all expectation. I am, therefore, justified in my conclusion in the present instance.

I forgot when you were here to desire that you would let your vessel bring up to Mount Vernon all the nails and other stores which had been imported for the use of my plantation at Claiborne's, and not delivered out. These I shall want myself. The nails are of great importance to me.

My love to Nelly, if with you, and compliments to all friends. Sincerely and affectionately, I am yours,

GEO. WASHINGTON.

P. S.—When you come, or send to Mount Vernon, let my mare be brought.

[WASHINGTON TO CUSTIS.]

FREDERICKSBURG, *October* 30, 1778.

DEAR SIR: The letter herewith sent for Mr. Hill is left open for your perusal; after reading which, seal and cause it to be safely delivered. He will find my sentiments fully expressed, and I hope will make no further appeals to me on the subject of his wages.

You had better take the whole crop of corn, fodder, &c., so soon as measured, at such a price as Colonel Bassett shall fix, and if the same thing was done respecting the wheat, it would be best also to avoid a divided interest, and distracting the attention of the overseer between your property and mine, in order to keep it separate on the plantation, and in the sale of it. The tobacco I expect, and hope you will positively direct Davenport to carry to the warehouse as soon as possible, that it may not be wasted, or in any degree be injured by keeping it on hand.

When it is inspected, it is my wish that his share be immediately given to him, and my part put into the hands of Colonel Bassett, to be sold at such times, and for such prices as his judgment shall direct. If you do not incline to take the corn and wheat upon the terms mentioned before, I beg that it be immediately sold, so soon as it is out of the shuck and straw; as I would not wish to have it lay in barns or corn-houses five days my property, in expectation of a good market, if it can be tolerably well sold at the time and in the manner I have mentioned, having little expectation that Davenport, after his connection with me ceases, will give that attention to my property as he would to those on whom he immediately depended for his place and employment. The cotton, I presume, your mother will want; it should therefore be got in order to come round when you shall find occasion to send your vessel to Potomac.

We are yet in a state of suspense respecting the enemy's intentions of evacuating New York wholly, or in part; circumstances daily arising to justify one in the adoption of either opinion. A considerable embarkment of troops has actually taken place, and is still continuing. One hundred and fifty transports are now at the Hook ready for sea. A few days, therefore, must, I should think, develop Sir Harry's designs. I have no doubt, as I have mentioned in my former letter, that the West Indies is their object. My love to Nelly, and compliments to all friends. I am yours, affectionately.

GEO. WASHINGTON.

[WASHINGTON TO CUSTIS.]

PHILADELPHIA, *January 2*, 1779.

DEAR SIR: Your letter of the twelfth of last month from Williamsburg is got safe to hand, and I am obliged to you for the deed which you have got from the secretary's office in Richmond, and purposed bringing to Lund Washington.

You say, I shall be surprised at the slow progress made by your assembly in the passage of the bills through both houses. I really am not, nor shall I, I believe, be again surprised at anything; for it appears to me that idleness and dissipation seems to have taken such fast hold of every body, that I shall not be at all surprised if there should be a general wreck of everything.

From my former knowledge of Finney, and what you said (when at camp) of his conduct respecting a contract for corn, I could not help mentioning the matter to the quartermaster-general, who wishes to know the precise circumstances of the case, that he may take measures accordingly. If my memory has not failed me, you said that Finney agreed to give Mr. Geo. Webb 40s. a barrel for some certain quantity, or all that he could purchase, and that Webb immediately sent, or rode up York river himself and purchased the corn at 25s. or 30s. a barrel.

If this is a fact, and if I recollect right, you spoke of it without reserve, it is such a violent imposition upon the public, and such a proof of his indolence, to say no worse of it, and unfitness for such a place of trust as to remove him from office. I would not have you say more of him than you know can be proved, lest it should recoil. I think you mentioned some other circumstance relative to a contract of Finney with Mr. Braxton. Let me hear from you by the first post on this subject. My love to Nelly and the children. Your mother will, I expect, write to you, as she is with me here, and well. Yours, affectionately,

GEO. WASHINGTON.

[WASHINGTON TO CUSTIS.]

WEST POINT, *November* 10, 1779.

DEAR SIR: Your letter of the seventh of last month came duly to hand, and should have been acknowledged sooner, but for the load of business which has pressed upon me of late.

With respect to the valuation of the cattle (by Colonel Bassett), you had of me last fall, I do not conceive there will be real occasion for any dispute. I want nothing but justice, and as you declare your willingness to do this, we can not disagree; but, as the matter was confided to Colonel Bassett, it will, in point of respect, if nothing more, be necessary to know upon what principle he made the valuation, which, when obtained, I shall be able to give you a decisive answer; and as you are now together, you can request him to favor me with the reasons that governed him in this business. However you may have understood it, I do not conceive that it ever was my promise or intention that you should have picked and culled the cattle; and if it was done, you surely can not wish to fix the valuation of the *refuse*, as a criterion for the appraisement of the *chosen;* consequently, the prices annexed to those which were left on the plantation can be no just rule for estimating the value of those of better quality which were brought off. The remainder of a small stock of cattle, after selecting forty-eight head of the best, may be of little worth, while the number chosen may be very valuable, and is so much opposed to the separation of them, that I think there must have been a misunderstanding if you conceive that I agreed to your culling the stock. My idea of the matter, as far as recollection can carry me, is, that you were to take the whole at an appraised value, or the whole was to be sold at public auction. The whole would have invited purchasers and competitors, but a few of the refuse must have brought on derision and resentment if people had been assembled at a sale of them. When you can get Colonel Bassett to state his sense of the matter to me, I shall be able to determine finally and without delay.

We have waited so long in anxious expectation of the French fleet at the Hook, without hearing anything from it, or of it, since its first arrival at Georgia, that we begin to fear that some great convulsion in the earth has caused a chasm between this and that state that can not be passed; or why, if nothing is done, or doing, are we not informed of it? There seems to be the strangest fatality, and the most unaccountable silence attending the operations to the southward that can be conceived—every measure in this quarter is hung in the most disagreeable state of suspense—and despair of doing anything, advanced as the season is, and uncertainty of the count's co-operating to any extent, if he should come, is succeeding fast to the flattering ideas we but lately possessed.

Nothing new has taken place since the evacuation of Rhode

Island, excepting a preparation of transports at New York, sufficient for the embarkation of about four thousand men, which, it is said, Lord Cornwallis is to command. The destination of them is at present unknown, but conjectured to be for the West Indies.

Remember me affectionately to your uncles Bassett and Dandridge, and our other friends in that quarter, and be assured that I am, with great regard and much truth, yours affectionately.

GEO. WASHINGTON.

[WASHINGTON TO CUSTIS]

WEST POINT, *August* 24, 1779.

DEAR SIR: In answer to your letter of the 11th inst., I candidly acknowledge I am at a loss what advice to give you, with precision, respecting the sale of your estate upon the eastern shore; but, upon the whole, in the present uncertain state of things, should, were I in your place, postpone the measure a while longer.

Your own observation must have convinced you of the rapid depreciation of the paper currency in the course of the last ten months, and this it will continue to do till there is a stop put to further emissions, and till some vigorous measures are adopted by the states respectively and collectively to lessen the circulating medium. You must be sensible that it is not forty thousand pounds, nor four hundred thousand, nor any nominal sum whatever, that would give you the value of the land in Northampton. Instance your unfortunate sale of the York estate to Colonél Braxton for twenty thousand pounds, which, I suppose, would now fetch one hundred thousand pounds, and, unless for the purpose of speculating in that or some other article, this sum, I am persuaded, would be refused by that gentleman. The present profit of your land on the Eastern shore may be trifling—nay, I will admit that, at this time, it is an encumbrance to you—but still it retains in itself an intrinsic and real value, which rises nominally in proportion to the depreciation, and will always be valuable, if (admitting the worst) the money should cease to pass. But, though the event is not probable, I will suppose that to be the case, or that it should continue to depreciate, as it has done, for the last ten months, where are you then? Bereft of your land, and in possession of a large sum of money that will neither buy victuals nor clothes.

There are but two motives which ought, and, I trust, can, induce you to sell: the one is to invest the money in the purchase of something else of equal value immediately; the other, to place it in the public funds. If the first is your object, I have no hesitation in giving my opinion in favor of the sale; because lands at so great a distance from you never will be profitable, and your only consideration is to be careful in your bargains elsewhere, making the prices of the thing sold and the things bought correspond with respect to times and places. In fact, this is but another name for barter or exchange; but, when the other is your inducement, the whole matter turns upon the credit and appreciation of the money, and these again upon financing, loans, taxes, war, peace, good success, bad success, the arts of designing men, mode of redemption, and other contingent events, which, in my judgment, very few men see far enough into to justify a capital risk; consequently you would be playing a hazardous, and possibly, in the issue, a ruinous game, for the chance of having sold at the turn of the tide, as it were, when there is not much fear of foregoing this advantage by any sudden appreciation of our money. In a word, by holding your land a few months longer, you can only loose the taxes; by selling, to place the money in the fund, you may lose considerably. Selling to buy, as I have before said, I consider as an exchange only; but then both bargains should be made at the same time. This was my advice to you before, and I now repeat it; otherwise the purchases you have in contemplation may rise fifty per cent. between your sale and the final accomplishment of them.

I observe what you say also respecting payment of your old bonds, and have less scruple in giving it to you as my opinion that you are not bound, in honor or by any principle of reason or love to your country, to accept payment of such as are upon demand, and were given previous to the contest and to the depreciation of the money at the present nominal value of it, by which a just debt, and where great indulgences have been shown the creditor in forbearance, is discharged at the rate of a shilling in the pound. Every man who is a friend to the cause is to receive the money in all payments, and to give it a circulation as free as the air he breathes in; but it is absurd and repugnant to every principle of honor, honesty, and common sense, to say that one man shall receive a shilling in the pound of another for a just debt when that other is well able to pay twenty shillings, and the same means which enabled him to pay the one formerly will enable him, with as much ease, to pay the other now.

It is necessary for me to premise that I am totally unacquainted with your laws on this head, and the consequences of a refusal. I am only arguing, therefore, in behalf of the reason and justice of my opinion, and on the presumption that all law is founded in equity. The end and design, therefore, of this (if there is such a one as compels payment under certain penalties and forfeitures) could only be to give credit and circulation to the bills in all payments, not to enrich one man at the ruin of another, which is most manifestly the case at present, and is such a glaring abuse of common justice that I can not but wonder at the practice obtaining.

Our affairs, at present, put on a pleasing aspect, especially in Europe and the West Indies, and bids us, I think, hope for the certain and final accomplishment of our independence. But, as peace depends upon our allies equally with ourselves, and Great Britain has refused the mediation of Spain, it will puzzle, I conceive, the best politicians to point out with certainty the limitation of our warfare.

Experience, which is the best rule to walk by, has, I am told, clearly proved the utility of having the ditch for draining of sunken grounds on the inside, and at a considerable distance (for instance, two shovels' throw) from the bank, consequently is a better criterion to judge from than the simple opinion of your ditcher, who may govern himself by the practice of other countries that will not apply to the circumstance of this, when there may be enemies to our banks unknown, perhaps, to them.

We have given the enemy another little stroke in the surprise of Powles-hook* (within cannon-shot of New York), and bringing off seven officers and one hundred and fifty-one men, commissioned officers and privates. This was a brilliant transaction, and performed by a detachment of Virginians and Marylanders, under the command of Major Lee,† of the light dragoons, with the loss of not more than ten or a dozen men. The colors of the garrison were also brought off.

Remember me affectionately to Nelly and the children; give my compliments to any inquiring friends, and be assured that, with the truest regard, I am yours,

GEO. WASHINGTON.

[CUSTIS TO WASHINGTON.]

MOUNT VERNON, *October 26, 1779*

HONORED SIR: Your two letters, of the 20th ult., were handed to me by Colonel Hooe, on my way from Eltham. I am much obliged to you for your kind advice respecting the sale of my land in King and Queen. My principal reason for wanting to sell it soon, is this: the houses are now in good repair, and will sell better on that account; the land is too mean to make it worth my while to keep negroes there with a prospect of making a crop, when I could employ them otherwise to more advantage. It would not do for me to leave the house and plantation without some one to take care of them. They would, in that case, be soon in such a situation that would make them sell for less than they would now do. I have fixed upon three pounds per acre as my lowest price, which I believe I shall get, and perhaps more. I am in hopes to purchase F. Foster's land for the money I sell my land for, which will be the greatest addition to my estate in N. Kent. My being so unlucky in not receiving your letter before I left Williamsburg, prevented my

---

* Paulus's Hook, now Jersey City.
† Major Henry Lee; afterward governor of Virginia.

applying to Mr. Wythe about drawing the deed between us; but, as a delay in this matter will not be productive of bad consequences, and from the favorable reports circulating among us, I am in hopes shortly to hear that Howe is in the same situation with Burgoyne, which I pray God may happen, I shall once more have the pleasure of seeing you at Mount Vernon, when we shall have leisure to settle this matter. But if this desirable event should not happen, I intend myself the pleasure of visiting camp shortly, and we may then have an opportunity of doing this business.

I believe I shall be obliged to postpone settling the rent of your plantation in King William until that wished-for period, as mamma seems to have some objections to renting it during her life, and it would not answer my purpose to rent it on any other terms. When I first wrote to you, I thought she had no objections; but, since I received your letter, I have talked to her on that subject, and it does not appear to be perfectly agreeable to her to part with the place altogether during life. When I wrote to you, I was at some loss how to employ those hands that now work on the King and Queen land to advantage; but, since that time, I have fallen on a plan of employing them in making meadows, which, I think, will turn out to as much advantage as anything I can set them about. I am very sorry to inform you that I am afraid your stock can not possibly escape the distemper another summer; indeed, I am so thoroughly convinced of it that I am determined, as the most prudent method, to sell all my cattle that have not had the distemper, and get those that have had it, both in N. Kent and King and William. The distemper has killed fifty odd head for Mr. Dandridge, and several for Mr. Braxton. It is a miracle we escaped this summer; we can hardly expect to do it another, as the malady is on each side of us.

Our neighbor, Colonel Mason is preparing a remedy against the depreciation of our money, which I think will do him great credit. He is preparing a bill for a general assessment on all property, by which he will draw in £5,000,000 per annum. His valuation of property is very low, which will render his plan very agreeable to the people. He has, likewise, a plan for recruiting our army, which I think a very good one; but I am fearful they will not succeed, by his not attending the assembly which met last Monday. He proposed to set off this day; but, as it is a rainy day, he will be disappointed. I wish he may set off when the weather will permit; his attendance in assembly is of the greatest importance to this state, as it was never so badly represented as at present.

Nelly joins me in wishing you health, victory, and every blessing in this world, and believe me, honored sir,

Your most affectionate,
I. P. CUSTIS.

[WASHINGTON TO CUSTIS.]

MORRISTOWN, *January* 20, 1780.

DEAR CUSTIS: I should have acknowledged the receipt of your letter of the twelfth ult. long since, but for the many important matters which have claimed my attention.

My letter which missed you on its passage to Williamsburg, will acquaint you (as there is little doubt of its having got to hand long ere this) of the footing I proposed to put the valuation of the cattle upon that you had of me. I only wished to hear upon what principle Colonel Bassett acted, as I thought it ungenteel to give a gentleman the trouble of performing a service and disregard it so much afterwards as not even to inquire upon what grounds he went—as I want nothing but justice, and this being your aim, it is scarce possible for us to disagree—but there is one thing which ought to be held in remembrance, and I mention it accordingly, and that is, that I should get no more *real* value for my cattle at £40 apiece, payable in the fall of 1779, than I should have got at £10 the preceding fall, provided the money had been then paid. For example—you could have got two barrels of corn in 1778 for £10, and I can get no more now for £40. With respect to other things it is the same. It would be very hard, therefore, by keeping me out of the use of the money a year, to reduce the debt three-fourths of the original value—which is evidently the case, because the difference between specie and paper, in the fall of 1778, was about four for one only—now the difference is upwards of thirty, consequently, ten pounds paid at that period was equal to 50s. good money; but paid at this day, is not worth, nor will it fetch more than a dollar. Had the money been paid and put into the loan office at the time you say the cattle ought to have been valued, I should have received a proportionate interest—that is, as the money depreciated the nominal sum for the interest would, by a resolve of Congress, have increased, and I should have got the real value in the interest; whereas, if you pay me £10 in loan-office certificates of this date for my cattle, I shall received for every £10 or 50s., which is the relative worth of it, according to the then difference of exchange, one dollar and no more.

These are self-evident truths; and nothing, in my opinion, is more just and reasonable, if you can come at, and do fix the value of the cattle at what they were worth in the fall of 1778, and would then have been appraised at, that you should pay loan-office certificates of that date; for had you paid me the money at that time, I should have lent it to the public, if there had been no other use for it, as it is not a custom with me to keep money to look at.

This reasoning may, in part, be considered as an answer to so much of your letter of the twelfth of December, as relates to the payment of the annuity for the dower-estate. You do not seem disposed to make the just and proper distinction between real and nominal sums. A dollar is but a dollar, whether it passes in silver at 6s., or paper at £6, or sixty pounds. The nominal value, or the name, is but an empty sound, and you might as well attempt to pay me in oak leaves, with which I can purchase nothing, as to give me paper money that has not a relative value to the rent agreed on.

If you have been unfortunate in your crops, or in the means of raising money from your estate, I am sorry for it, and do not by any means wish to put you to an inconveniency in paying the rent at this time which became due the first of this month. It may lie till my wants, or your convenience is greater, but as it was certainly the expectation of us both that this annuity was to be raised and paid out of the produce of your crops, a moment's reflection and calculation must convince you that it is full as easy to do it at this day (if you have those crops) as at any period before or since the war began, because the difference between the old and present prices of every article raised upon a plantation or farm, bears at least an equal proportion to the difference between specie and paper. It is a matter of little consequence then, whether you pay £30 in paper or 20s. in specie, when the same quantity of corn, wheat, tobacco, or any other article you possess will fetch the former with more ease now, than it would the latter in the best of times.

The fact is, that the real difference between the prices of all kinds of country produce now and before the war, is greater than between specie and paper. The latter, in Philadelphia, being about thirty, when it is well known that the former, in many things, is at least a hundred, and in scarce any article less than forty. Witness flour, wheat, Indian corn, &c., which are the great articles of produce of every Virginia estate. It is the unusualness of the idea, and high sound which alarms you in this business; for supposing the difference to be thirty prices, and in consequence you pay £15,750, I neither get nor do you pay a farthing more that £525, because, as I have already observed, less corn, wheat, &c. will enable you to pay the former now, than it would take to pay the latter while they were at their old and accustomed prices—calling the sum, therefore, which you pay to me £15,750 or £525, is a matter of moonshine, as it is the thing, not the name, that is to be regarded.

I have wrote to Mr. Lund Washington concerning Sheredine's point, but am in some doubt whether the strip of land will compensate the expense of the bank which must be lengthy. I have left it to him, however, to determine this matter, and to apply for the ditchers (who were about to leave you) if he should want them. If your banks are not properly executed, it is to be feared you will find more plague from the muskrats and other vermin than you seem to apprehend, when the warm weather returns.

I am glad to hear that your assembly are disposed to exert themselves in the great work of appreciation. I heartily wish them success in the attempt. We have nothing new in this quarter. The weather has been, and now is intensely cold, and we are beginning to emerge from the greatest distress on account of the want of provisions.

My love to Nelly and the children, and I am sincerely and affectionately yours,

GEO. WASHINGTON.

JOHN P. CUSTIS, ESQ.

[WASHINGTON TO CUSTIS]

PEEKSKILL, *August* 6, 1780.

DEAR CUSTIS: Your letter of the 26th of July came to my hands yesterday, and I thank you for the account given of the proceedings of the assembly. If you had not adopted the finance scheme, I should have thought the omission unpardonable, as it must, in a manner, have set our money afloat again, when every measure which human policy is capable of devising ought to be adopted to give it a fixed and permanent value. I much fear your act for raising three thousand men will rather fall short than exceed that number, because it is our fortune to have such kind of laws (though most important) badly executed, and such men as are raised dissipated and lost before they join the army. Your scheme for association I must approve; it is certainly high time to retrench in all kinds of extravagance, and to adopt the most economical plans, that, by a return to virtue, we may be the better able to support the war and bring it to a happy issue.* In consequence of General Clinton's embarking a considerable part of the force at New York, and sailing down the sound for Rhode Island, I put my troops in motion and crossed at King's ferry, where, assembling my whole force, was determined to

---

* Mr. Custis was now a member of the Virginia house of burgesses.

make a vigorous effort to possess myself of the city. This brought him back again, and, though I am disappointed by it, has answered the end of relief to the French troops at Rhode Island, which was the object of his destination. I am now, for the sake of shortening our transportation of provisions and forage, recrossing the river, and shall move down toward Dobbs' ferry till our reinforcements (not a fourth of which are yet come in) arrive, and the supplies which are to enable us to commence the operations of the campaign.

My love to Nelly and the children, and compliments to inquiring friends. I am, with much truth and sincerity,

Your affectionate friend and servant,

GEO. WASHINGTON.

[WASHINGTON TO CUSTIS.]

CAMP, near Dobbs' ferry, *July* 25, 1781.

DEAR CUSTIS: Your letter of the 11th, covering certain proposals which were made by you to Mr. Robert Alexander, came safe by the last post. I read the letter with attention, and, as far as I can form a judgment without seeing the mortgage, or having recourse to the original agreement, and the missives which may have passed, think they are founded on principles of liberality and justice.

How far the purchase on your part, and the sale on Alexander's, was a matter of speculation at the time of bargaining, yourselves and the nature of the agreement can alone determine If, from the tenor of your contract, you were to pay paper money — if this paper money was at that time in a depreciated state, and the difference between it and specie fixed and proved — and if, moreover, Alexander, like many others, entertained an opinion that it would again appreciate, so as that a paper dollar would be of equal value with a silver one — it might be more just than generous (when we consider that paper is, in fact, worth little or nothing) to let him abide the consequences of his opinion by paying him in depreciated paper; because the presumption is that he would have made no allowance for appreciation, though the former should be of equal value with the latter, pound for pound. But this, as I have before observed, depends upon the nature of the bargain, and the light in which the matter was understood at the time it was made by both parties.

If the bargain was unaccompanied by particular circumstances, and had no explanatory meaning, but simply imported that so much money was to be given for so much land, to be paid on or before a certain period, it is certainly optional in you to discharge it at any time you please short of that period. But I conceive that this can only be done by an actual tender of the money, and that there is no legal obligation upon Alexander to take your bond (with any security whatever), and that the only chance you have of his doing it, is the fear of losing the original debt, or the interest of it, by refusing the tender you propose to make him of £48,000 at this time; for I lay it down as a maxim that no man can be compelled to change the nature of his debt, or alter the security of it, without his own consent.

I have before said, that, for want of the mortgage, or a better knowledge of all the circumstances attending your bargain, it is impossible for me to give a decided opinion. Your proposals appear to me to be fair and equitable; but what views Alexander may have had, and how far he is prepared to obtain those views, by written or other valid proof, I am unable to say. As an honest man, he ought to be content with justice, and justice I think you have offered him.

You may recollect that I disliked the terms of your bargain when they were first communicated to me, and wished then that you might not find them perplexing and disadvantageous in the issue, as I now do, that you may settle the matter with honor and satisfaction to yourself.

It gave me pain to hear that your people had been so much afflicted with sickness, and that you thought your son in danger. It would give me equal pleasure to learn that he and the rest of your family were restored to perfect health. That so few of our countrymen have joined the enemy, is a circumstance as pleasing to me as it must be mortifyingly decisive to them of the fallacy of their assertion, that two-thirds of the people were in their interest, and ready to join them when opportunity offered. Had this been the case, the marquis's forces, and the other one-third, must have abandoned the country.*

I am much pleased with your choice of a governor.† He is an honest man — active, spirited, and decided, and will, I am persuaded, suit the times as well as any person in the state. You were lucky, considering the route by which the enemy retreated to Williamsburg, to sustain so little damage. I am of opinion that Lord Cornwallis will establish a post at Portsmouth, detach part of his force to New York, and go with the residue to South Carolina.

I returned yesterday from (with Count de Rochambeau and the engineers of both armies) the enemy's work near Kingsbridge; we lay close by them two days and a night, without any attempt on their part to prevent it. They begun and continued a random kind of cannonade, but to very little effect. I am waiting impatiently for the men the states (this way) have been called upon for, that I may determine my plan and commence my operations.

My best wishes attend Nelly (who I hope is perfectly recovered) and the little girls. My compliments await inquiring friends, and I am,

Sincerely and affectionately, yours,

GEO. WASHINGTON.

JNO. P. CUSTIS, ESQ.

---

* The Marquis de Lafayette, then in command in Virginia, opposing the invasion of Cornwallis.

† Thomas Nelson.

NOTE II.—PAGE 61.

GENERAL JAMES M. LINGAN.

A FUNERAL ORATION BY GEORGE WASHINGTON PARKE CUSTIS.*

AND is it left for the stranger, my friends, to speak your HERO'S praise? I never fed at his board, I never drank of his cup, nor did the cheering smile of welcome, ever meet me at his

---

* This oration, in connection with an account of the funeral solemnities at Georgetown, was published in pamphlet form at Washington city, soon after its delivery. The explanatory notes accompanying this oration were written by the editor of the pamphlet at the period of its publication; and, though deeply infused with strong partisan sentiments, they are valuable at this time as illustrative of the intense excitement and party rancor which culminated in the political mob at Baltimore, in which General Lingan and others lost their lives. These notes were originally inserted at the end of the oration; for the convenience of the reader, they are herein given at the bottom of the pages to which they have reference.

The editor in his preface says: "On Tuesday the first of September, 1812, funeral honors were paid to the memory of General JAMES M. LINGAN. While his mangled body, which had been *vouchsafed* by his murderers to one mourning relative for *secret burial*, slept in some obscure, neglected grave, the citizens of Columbia and part of the states of Maryland and Virginia, impressed with a just admiration of his worth, convened at Georgetown to perform the duteous offices of piety and affection, and hallow the memory of the illustrious dead. The notice of the projected solemnities had barely extended to the nearer counties, but such was the eagerness testified, wherever the notice reached, to do honor to the obsequies of the departed hero, that, had it extended further, we may fairly believe the funeral train would have been worthy of an emperor. So numerous were the mourners, that it was found necessary to substitute for a church, which had been originally selected, a shady eminence in the neighborhood of the city."

The procession moved from the Union hotel in the following order: "Marshals on horseback; four clergymen of different denominations; the committee of arrangement; Mr. Custis, of Arlington, the orator of the day; music; Captain Stull's rifle corps, commanded by Lieutenant Kurtz; the hearse, with the horses clad in mourning, and eight venerable pall-bearers, with white scarfs; Mr. George Lingan, the general's son, as chief mourner; the general's horse in mourning, led by a groom; family and relatives of the deceased in coaches; the wounded veteran, Major Musgrove, who survived the midnight massacre in which his brother-soldier fell, bearing the general's sword, and supported by two heroes of the Revolution; Mr. Hanson, and other survivors of the band who defended liberty and the press; veteran band of the Revolution; strangers of distinction; citizens from the counties of Montgomery, Baltimore, Frederick, Charles, Prince George's, and St. Mary's, and from

hospitable threshold. Sure then, no partial motives can influence the sentiments which I am about to utter. Yet as the brave man who fought the battles of my country's liberty, is to

the cities of Georgetown, Washington, and Alexandria; Captain Peter's troop of horse, commanded by Lieutenant John S. Williams; marshals on horseback.

"The train moved to the music of a funeral dirge. During its march minute-guns were fired from the first ship ever built in Georgetown, which was this day decorated with mourning flags, and named *The General Lingan*. Many of the stores were hung with black. A solemn stillness pervaded the streets. When the procession reached the ground, the troops opened to receive it. Gray-headed men, who had long bid adieu to the bustle of public life, and whose pursuits, with their years, had 'dwindled to a narrow span,' ennobled with their presence this interesting scene. The effects produced by the appearance of the military — of the aged Revolutionary heroes, who came from all quarters to mourn for their departed brother-in arms — of the weeping family of the deceased — and of those who, though covered with wounds, survived the tremendous massacre in which Lingan fell, was indescribable.

"We do not regret that circumstances rendered it necessary to perform the ceremonies in the open air. The platform overhung by lofty oaks, among whose branches the venerable tent of Washington — 'The Pretorium of Virtue,' — was suspended for a canopy, exhibited a patriarchial simplicity which carried back the mind to the earlier ages of the world. Here sat clergymen of different denominations, officers of the procession, and the orator of the day. Immediately around it were placed the veteran band of the Revolution. The venerable Major Musgrove, pale and disfigured by wounds received in the massacre, took the centre, supported by Colonel Stuart and Major Stoddart, who had shed their best blood and devoted their best days in the battles of their country. The front benches were occupied by the family of Lingan, together with Mr. Hanson and surviving members of the band who had gallantly defended the rights of freemen and the liberty of the press. Near them, shaded by trees, an immense and brilliant assemblage of ladies and gentlemen from all parts of the adjacent country. The ceremonies commenced with introductory prayers from the Reverend Mr. Addison, and concluded with appropriate prayers from the Reverend Mr. Balch. The oration of Mr. Custis was extemporaneous. It riveted the attention of the audience; the solemn stillness which reigned was only interrupted by sighs and tears."

The tent of Washington that overhung the platform, was at that time "in good preservation, though bearing the marks of six-and-thirty years' service. It should be remembered that the same canvass which now enjoys the calm, braved the storms of the Revolution, from the disastrous battle of Long island, to the glorious victory of Yorktown — that within this tent, the captured Cornwallis surrendered the sword which had wasted America, and became a guest where he had expected to have been a conqueror."

"The venerable and pious widow of the general, from a special request of Mr Custis, had arrived at Georgetown to attend the obsequies of her martyred husband On the morning of the first of September, a ruffian paraded, as if to insult the sorrows of this excellent lady, before the hotel, with a bloody spear and military cap stained with blood, and inscribed, 'Federal Republican.' Mrs. Lingan, who had hitherto borne up against her griefs, now dissolved in tears, and became so overpowered as to be unable to leave the hotel, although many ladies offered to support her in the train. All her family, however, attended.

"Toward the base and unmanly insults offered on this day of mourning. federal-

be the subject of my praise; as the illustrious citizen who died in defence of one of the dearest rights which freemen can boast, is to be the hero of my tale; I can only say, my friends, that were my powers commensurate with my zeal, I would hope on this day to do honor to his memory.

By what standard of patriotism shall we try your LINGAN? Shall we try him by the standard of modern patriots; mushrooms of yesterday, who have grown up from the soil, first fattened by the blood of heroes? or rather, shall we try him by the illustrious standard of 'seventy-six? Look to the mighty period which tried men's souls; look into the embattled ranks of liberty's host, and there will you find your Lingan! Witness the dreadful combat of Long Island, where the famous Maryland regiment, after bearing the brunt of the day, were nearly annihilated and cut to pieces. Again behold him at the storming of Fort Washington, and then you may change the scene.* You

ists, with calm dignity, declared, 'Our work, is the work of piety and peace; but if a dagger is raised against us, there are men, and good men enough here, to walk over the body of the assassin.' When told that bayonets were glittering in their neighborhood, it was observed, 'We are going to the tent of Washington — let it be the winding-sheet of his children!'"

"Colonel Philip Stuart of Charles," who occupied a seat on the platform beside Major Musgrove, was "the gallant officer who led the forlorn hope of Washington's horse in the memorable battle of the Eutaws. The order came from Greene to break the British line. Stuart, with only sixteen men, advanced to obey the general's command, and fell, covered with wounds, almost within his enemies, ranks Lieutenant-Colonel Washington too, pressing on, fell under his dying charger, and was made prisoner of war.

"On the day of the oration, Colonel Stuart, Major Stoddard, and others of the veteran Revolutionary band, were placed very near the orator. In Stuart it was plainly to be perceived that the firmness of the hero was struggling with the feelings of the man, till at length the hero surrendered; and the manly tear 'which filled the furrow in the veteran's cheek,' proclaimed the triumph of virtuous sympathy.

"In the course of the day Colonel Stuart observed to Mr. Custis — 'After the sufferings which I have borne in my country's cause, I never expected to have wept again, but this mighty day has quite unmanned me.' Americans! sure virtue triumphs when the brave man weeps!"

* It is uncertain whether General Lingan belonged to Smallwood's or Rawling's regiments. The first was raised exclusively in Maryland, consisted of the flower of her youth, and might be compared with Cæsar's Tenth Legion. Though overpowered by superior numbers, these heroes disdained to fly, and were nearly annihilated on the memorable twenty-seventh of August, '76. Rawling's rifle regiment, raised partly in Maryland and partly in Virginia, opposed the Hessians at the storming of Fort Washington, and with unerring weapons did great execution. Lingan,

have yet only viewed your friend, the gallant soldier in the tented field. You must now behold him the wretched prisoner in the dungeons of the prison-ship!* There while listening to the groans of expiring humanity; there while beholding his brave brethren dying by inches in all the horrors of captivity and want, well might your Lingan say—" Sweet, O my country! should be thy liberties, when they are purchased at this monstrous price!"†

Yes, my friends, of that very prison-ship was your Lingan a sufferer, which, even at this late time of day, excites the warmest sensibilities in the American bosom. You have seen our brethren perform a pious pilgrimage to the spot where the victims were slain—you have seen them rake up the bones which six-and-thirty years had bleached, and inter them with all the pomp and solemnity of woe.‡ Ay, and I trust that my country will yet find a tear to hallow the memory of the brave old man,

---

at the battle of Long Island, finding his corps giving way, displayed the noblest intrepidity and finally succeeded in bringing them to the charge.

* The horrors of the prison-ship need not be told at this time of day. It was indeed "the bourne from whence" scarce "traveller returned." Lingan, with many of his brave associates-in-arms, were removed to the Jersey shortly after the surrender of Fort Washington. Faint from his wounds, and almost perishing under the magnitude of his many sufferings, the generous soldier yet felt for others; and when, on the death of one of his companions a coffin being brought which proved too short, the guard proposed to cut off the head of the deceased and put it in with the body, Lingan, fired at the indignity offered to a deceased fellow-prisoner, rose from his couch of pain, and laying his hand upon the lifeless corpse of the departed soldier, swore he would destroy the first man who dared to mutilate the body of his friend.

† The venerable relict of Lingan has often said, since his lamented death—"Lingan loved liberty. He would often point to the picture of the benign goddess of freedom which adorns his house, and in admiring the shadow would remember the sufferings which he had borne to procure the substance. He considered liberty as his child, and in fighting for liberty, felt as if he fought in defence of his own offspring."

‡ In New York, three or four years since, the bones of thousands of Americans who had perished on board the Jersey prison-ship, were collected from the beach; appropriate orations were delivered, and the bones were attended to a previously prepared monument by an immense procession. The health of Lingan, one of the few who survived these unfortunate soldiers, was so much injured by his sufferings on board the Jersey, that he was reduced by a dreadful rheumatism for many months subsequent to a state of entire helplessness. And yet, the very party by which Lingan is now called a "Tory,' erected a monument and proclaimed the virtues of his companions in persecution. "*Tempora mutantur et nos mutamur in illis.*"

who died in defence of one of the dearest rights those immortal sufferings have procured!

When the war had ended, your Lingan retired to the shades of domestic life; happy in the conscientious reflection, that his services and sufferings had contributed to rear the temple of rational freedom, to found the glorious empire of laws. There, in the relative duties of a father, a master, a neighbor, and a friend, was the gallant veteran most nobly distinguished. Say, ye who best can tell, was he not the kind indulgent parent? the good husband? the faithful friend? the upright honorable man? "If there be any one in this assembly who will deny this praise, now let him speak, for him have I offended;" and if it were further necessary to inquire into the merits of this excellent man, know that they were stamped with a seal which bore the name of Washington! Yes, my friends, your Lingan and your Williams were each appointed in the early formation of the government, to offices of honor and trust, by that immortal chief, whose unerring judgment was never deceived, when the soldier was the object!* Williams, did I say? the gallant, gay Williams of Guildford and the Eutaws? Peace be to his ashes! happy that he is gone! for sure it would have rent his manly heart to have witnessed the melancholy end of his old brother-soldier! †

It has been said by some, my friends, and supposed by others, that the venerable Lingan was induced to engage in the enterprise which terminated his life, by the arts and intrigues of de-

---

* In the early periods of the government, offices were not only few in number, but small in value. The collectorship of such a port as Georgetown, was bestowed upon Lingan, not as a mean of extensive emolument, but as a testimonial of due remembrance and consideration.

† General Otho Holland Williams —This distinguished soldier was not more remarkable for his heroism in the field than for his elegant and manly accomplishments. Williams was taken with Lingan at Fort Washington, and, though wounded, was carried as a spectacle about the streets of New York by the tories, for the special amusement of his majesty's loyal subjects, and then consigned to the miseries of the prison-ship. Strange, that six-and-thirty years after, his venerable companion, grown gray in the same country's service, should, for defending "the very liberties" those mighty sufferings had procured, be martyred with every species of horrific cruelty, and his aged body left, dishonored, on the cold ground, to glut the vengeance of exclusive republicans!

signing men, contrary to the dictates of his better judgment. In the face of his family, his country, and the world, I deny the assertion! No, my friends, the whole heart of the veteran was in this thing. He had seen the laws of his country prostrated at the feet of tyrannic power, and the liberty of the press violated, and usurped! And when he saw a band of youth prepare to defend their rights, or perish in the breach, the soul of the veteran rejoiced.—" I admire these boys," he said, " their heroic ardor reminds me of my other days — I will join their gallant calling — age and experience will be useful to temper their valor, to moderate their zeal, to direct their energies. I will be the Nestor to the young Achilles."

When, after a brave defence, our brethren had laid down their arms, and submitted to the constituted authorities of their country, mercy and generosity should have been shown to submission. They are the privileges of the brave, in every age and condition of society.

Who were these prisoners? Were they the rakings of kennels; were their shoes yet new, since they landed on our shores?[*]

[*] Major-general Henry Lee commanded the party. Lee, at the early age of nineteen, was devoted to liberty in liberty's battles. Greene considered him as a man whom nature had formed for war; and his achievements as commander of the partisan corps in the southern army, were eminent and deserving. Since the Revolution he has filled high civil and military stations. He has distinguished himself as governor of the state of Virginia, and as a member of the national legislature. His misfortunes are those of the man, while his public services derive a lustre from his public integrity.

The grandfather of Mr. Hanson, was appointed by the Maryland legislature a member of the Revolutionary Congress, and afterward became president of Congress, then the first magistrate of the country; being the third elected under the old confederation. Mr. Hanson's father was high in the confidence of Washington, resided a long time in his family, was for several years his private secretary, and was afterward chosen by the general as one of his aids; but sickness prevented him from accepting the offer, although the place was several months kept open for him. When the war ended, the father of Mr. Hanson was appointed judge of the general court, and afterward chancellor of Maryland, which situation he retained until his decease. The father of Dr. Warfield was the first citizen of Maryland who openly proposed a separation from the parent-country. He also directed the celebrated burning of the tea in 1775, at Annapolis. Captain R. I. Crabb is the son of General Crabb, one of the heroes of the Revolution. The other gentlemen are worthy to be ranked with the patrician youth of ancient republics. They are men of the first respectability; and two of them have recently been proposed as candidates for the Maryland legislature.

or were they sons of the sires, who had fought the battles, and labored in the councils of their country's glory; generous scions, sprang from the oak which had borne the hardest blasts of liberty's storm; yeomen of our land, who had grown up with the growth, and with the strength of freedom? Their cause was holy. They knew they had done no wrong—for people of America remember that when the laws of a community can no longer protect the citizen, the great law of nature commands him to protect himself! Yet, that the ends of justice might be subserved—that their accusers might obtain the full measure of justice denied to them; these gallant heroes, consented to be carried, like malefactors, to the prison-house! There they received the most solemn assurances, which honor and religion could give, of perfect safety and protection. Who will then believe, that in a few short hours, the asylum of justice—the asylum in which even the condemned criminal is safe—should be converted into the chamber of death!

Hide, hide my country, thy diminished head! Thou, an empire of laws, and yet this monstrous outrage within thy bosom! Thou, the seat of justice, and yet the asylum of justice with innocent blood profaned!* The weeping genius of my country, seeks to draw a veil before the dreadful spectacle, but an higher power commands that no veil shall screen this work of darkness from the light of truth!

The murder of prisoners! Why 'tis abhorrent to nature—my soul sickens at the thought. Sure such hideous sin was once foreign to the American character! Say, ye gray-headed men, veterans of liberty, and fathers of my country, when was the time, during our arduous struggle, that the soldier of freedom

* It is the standard principle of our common law that a man is always innocent till he is proved to be guilty. When the prison-house is forced, and even those who are indicted for the grossest crimes, slaughtered without trial or condemnation, may not the asylum of justice be said to be "profaned with innocent blood?" But in the present case there was no indictment, not even a commitment! All parties acknowledge that the Spartan band were conveyed to prison for "safety," not as prisoners, but guests of those who induced them to surrender. Some hours after their arrival a commitment was informally procured, and they were detained contrary not only to the rules of law, but the laws of hospitality.

stained his laurels with his prisoner's blood! While storming the redoubts at Yorktown, the cry of the soldiers was, "Remember New London;" yet, no sooner had the foe submitted, than mercy, divine mercy, sat triumphant on my country's colors — Ay, my friends, Hamilton and Laurens commanded then!*

The murder of prisoners! Even sanguinary France now cowers to our superior genius in iniquity. She is no longer supreme in sin. If we contemplate the tremendous scenes of her revolution, so widely different is the state of our society, they appear but as Christmas gambols to this hellish tragedy.† There the tiger had long been confined within the bars of oppression. For centuries had he gnawed his galling chain, and thirsted for the blood of his oppressors; but here, in the mild land of liberty, in the wise and good government, whose laws provide the punishment of crimes, great indeed must be that injury which requires an extra vengeance!

The murder of prisoners! 'Tis true, Napoleon, the chosen monster of crime, first set this horrid example at Jaffa; but even under his authority, the poor victims, met a speedy and merciful death! The battalion, which was drawn up against them, soon

* When the garrison at New London had surrendered to the British troops, the gallant Colonel Ledyard presented his sword, according to custom, to the victorious commander, who inhumanly returned it through his captive's body. This was the signal for general massacre, and many of our soldiers who had surrendered as prisoners of war were immediately bayoneted on the spot. When victory next leaned to the American side, orders were given by the Marquis de Lafayette to retaliate this cruelty, and the American soldiers mounted the redoubts of Yorktown shouting, "Remember New London." Hamilton commanded in the light-infantry. Lieut-colonel Laurens, the Bayard of the age, personally took Major Smith, the English commandant, a prisoner of war. The conquered Britons momently expected the exterminating bayonet. Our countrymen, flushed with triumph, pressed on, while their trembling victims fell in despair and agony at their feet. The youthful chiefs threw themselves between the vanquished and destruction. The victors were ordered to spare the prostrate enemy. Hamilton and Laurens, bred in the tent of Washington, disdained the savage privilege of destroying a defenceless foe, and showed to their country and an admiring world, that mercy is the noblest attribute of the brave!

† At the time of the French revolutionary massacres, France had, in fact, no government; one day a faction wielding the power; the next day cut off, and another succeeding. But even in this horrible state of society, though death speedily overtook the proscribed, promises of protection were still held sacred.

put a period to their sufferings by an immediate passport to eternity.

The murder of prisoners! Even when the Indian savage a prisoner takes, if he promises him protection, the poor captive is safe.* Nay, go further. Look to the Arab robber of the desert. When he meets the wandering pilgrim in the sands, if he conducts him within his tent, the robber will die at its door in defence of his guest!† Such are the examples of mercy, fidelity and honor which adorn even the savage life; and yet, my countrymen, it has been left to the enlightened republic of America, to show more horrid examples of cruelty than ever distinguished the inquisition or the rack.

Let us attend the venerable Lingan in the last moments of his life. When he found the inevitable fate which awaited him, that fortitude which had distinguished the gallant veteran in the direful fields of the Revolution, while fighting for the liberties of his country, did not desert him in the closing hour. And yet, sure he thought, that if Americans were his foes, the sight of his venerable figure, bent with age, must touch their hearts! Ah, Lingan! thou hadst indeed survived thy country's better days. There was a time when thy venerable presence would have arrested the falling dagger, had it been grasped by an American hand! What did I say? Sure there was a time when a thousand sabres would have gleamed to defend the gray head of an aged soldier, sinking at the feet of an assassin!‡ Alas! those days are gone! The glory of my country hath sunk into the grave of her chief!

Attend the closing scene. The old man falls; yet feebly raising his wounded head, on which threescore winters had shed

* This is notorious. The Indian never betrays after promising protection. His offered hand contains his plighted honor.

† Pilgrims, and even caravans, have been known to seek the protection of professed robbers in the desert, and never have had cause to repent their confidence even in a robber's word.

‡ Yes! before America (who, in opening her arms to afford an asylum to suffering humanity, hath opened them too wide) became gorged with filth from all the kennels in Europe! The ancient republics were corrupted by the extraneous streams which brought pollution to the pure fountain of their liberties.

their snows, he appeals to his murderers—" Spare the old man, whose years are few to live! Spare the father, whose orphans will want! Spare the old soldier, whose faithful services, and whose hard sufferings have earned his country's liberties! Spare! Here, as if it were necessary to cap the climax of horror, to render the catastrophe of hell complete—know, Americans, that James Lingan, the soldier of your Washington, the patriot, the hero, and the friend; the man of charity who felt for others' woes; the noble example to youth; the man of virtue, religion, and honor, with the foul epithet of " Tory," ringing in his ears —expired! The defender of liberty disgraced by the epithet of " Tory?" " That was the unkindest cut of all!"

Are there men in this assembly who can feel! Now let them feel!

O, Maryland! Would that the waters of thy Chesapeake could wash this foul stain from thy character. O, Maryland! Would that the recording angel who carries thy black deed to heaven's chancery on high, could drop a tear upon it, and blot it out for ever! But no! A voice cries from the tomb of the brave. It rises to the God of nature and humanity, and demands a vengeance on the murderer!

Can Montgomery boast no band of youthful patriots, who will redeem the remains of their venerable friend, and give them the rights of sepulture near his own home?* Sure it would soothe the widow's sorrowing heart—sure it would soothe the orphans' woes! Then go—perform the pious task, and the applause of all good men speed you on your way! Mark well my words. 'Tis not that I would sharpen your swords to vengeance—vengeance belongs to the laws; but I would open your hearts to gratitude—gratitude belongs to man!

Shade of the venerable Lingan! Farewell! Accept the feeble

* The mangled body of Lingan was exposed on the bare earth until noon on the day following the murder, and then, with difficulty, obtained by a relative for secret burial. It now "sleeps in some obscure, neglected grave," in Baltimore. Would not the youth of Montgomery, the county of Lingan's former residence, perform a pious office in transferring the remains of their venerable friend to the sepulchre of his fathers?

tribute of a stranger's praise; although thy sun hath sunk in the horizon, still, its last parting gleam sheds a benign lustre on thy fame. The laurel that covers thy hoary head, old man! shall ever bloom with youthful verdure! Thy illustrious services in liberty's cause, shall rear for thee a cenotaph in each freeman's bosom, while thy endearing virtues will cause the ready tear of affection to freshen the turf on thy humble grave!

Soldier of my country! Defender of her liberties! Farewell!

Permit me, my friends, to offer you a few remarks, on the present state of our republic. People of America! The liberty of the press is one of the noblest rights a freeman can boast. When the right of opinion, the liberty of speech, and the liberty of the press, are prostrated at the feet of lawless power, the citadel of of freedom must soon surrender. Yes, my friends, and that power which destroys these attributes of liberty, is the pioneer which precedes the march of despotism!

I well remember the good old federal times, when the Father of his Country, blest with his virtues our rising empire. Then was the majesty of the laws supreme; then was the liberty of the press inviolate; and sure, if ever there was a time, when its licentiousness required a curb, it was, when its slanders were aimed at the reputation of the first of men! The modern Archimedes of malice and ambition had upreared his mighty engines of calumny, to assail our chieftain's virtue!* But the great, the god-like Washington, had only to oppose the ægis of his integrity, and their shafts fell harmless to the ground.†

---

* The first engines of calumny levelled against the chief were reared in the press of Philip Freneau, then a clerk in the department of state. They received great improvement from the scientific labors of Bache and his principal engineer, Duane, and were brought to perfection by James T. Callender, who betraying his employers the machines have since fallen into common hands.

† Among the monstrous calumnies circulated at that time, certain letters, said to have been written during the Revolution and addressed by the general to members of his own family, were published under pretence of their having been taken with the baggage and servant of the commander-in-chief at Fort Lee, in 1776. These letters contained sentiments unfriendly to the cause of liberty. The forgery was apparent to all those who had served in the war, since it was notorious that the servant and baggage of the commander-in-chief were never taken. Washington disdained to notice these incendiary attacks during his term of chief magistracy, but

Yes, people of America! and wretched indeed is that man's cause, which can not be defended by his integrity!

Why are federalists a persecuted race? Must they leave their Egypt, and under the conduct of another Moses, seek a new Canaan? Can they boast of no virtues, no services, to entitle them to the joys of liberty's land?

Who reared the temple of national freedom? Who kindled the sacred flame on its altars? Whose virtues, whose services, have contributed to nourish that flame? Go! untie the scroll fame! Peruse the list of American worthies, and tell me if any federalists are there! Go to the hard-fought fields of the Revolution — kneel on their sacred earth, which tells no lies, and ask her, if, on the memorable days when we fought for liberty, no federal blood moistened her bosom? Nay, persecuted as we are, perhaps at this moment some fearless sailor climbs the shattered mast to nail the flag of my country to its stump — my life on it that fellow is a federalist!* Perhaps some gallant soldier may yet scale the heights of Abraham, to wreathe liberty's standard around Montgomery's tomb — I tell you the first foot, which presses that classic ground, will be a federalist's! For ever live the glorious name our Washington bore! For ever let his example inspire his children!

The spirit of federalism rises from the tomb of Mount Vernon: — and when my country shall bend under the storms of adversity, the children of Washington will show "their generous nature;" but should those storms rock Liberty's temple to its base, then will the Sampson of federalism grasp the pillars, and in his expiring struggles, perish with Liberty in liberty's ruins.

Yes, Americans! the power which made you great and free, independent and happy, still opens its arms to receive the prodigal returned. When my country shall have been deeply stricken by misfortune, may she — grown wise by her experience — deter-

---

when he had retired to the walks of domestic life, the illustrious citizen gave full proof of his innocence by exposing, not only the malice, but the absolute impossibility of the tale. The original letters written by the general at that period, are now in the possession of Mr. Custis of Arlington.

* Two days afterward, the prophecy was fulfilled! Hull and the constitution!

mine to restore the age of Washington — to render the last of republics immortal!

Did I speak of the age of Washington! The golden age of my country! when peace, prosperity, and protection blessed our land! Great is the contrast now. Attend me, friends, to the house of a federalist at this portentious period. I open you the door, and that too of a man who can look his country in the face, and say I have been thy benefactor.* Near the cradle of my sleeping child stands the musket and bayonet; near the pillow of my innocent wife the sharpened sabre! and why? Because I will enjoy the right of opinion, the freedom of speech, and the liberty of the press — these sacred privileges I inhaled with my first breath, and will only lose them with my last. When my parent

---

* Mr. Custis has established an annual convention for the promotion of agriculture and domestic manufactures, known throughout the country by the title of "Arlington sheep-shearing." Its motto, "*pro patria semper.*" At Arlington House, under the tent of Washington, a numerous concourse of the most exalted characters in our republic, besides strangers of distinction, assemble on every thirtieth of April, to witness the distribution of the first prizes ever thus given in America, for the best specimens of sheep and domestic manufactures. After the prizes are assigned, Mr. Custis collects his friends at a splendid repast under the tent of his illustrious relative, and when the cloth is removed, commonly addresses them in strains of eloquence and feeling worthy of the sacred canvass which canopies his head. After appropriate toasts and other convivialities, the company disperse. The prizes offered by Mr. Custis are all at his own individual expense, and, together with the cost of entertaining so great a concourse, subject him to a very heavy annual disbursement. Besides the better part of nine years, since the first "Arlington sheep-shearing," employed in the promotion of agriculture and domestic economy, Mr. Custis has devoted considerable pecuniary resources to the same noble enterprize. This purpose has been steadfastly pursued, and, notwithstanding the great political changes which have taken place since the thirtieth of April, 1803, it has kindled a fondness for the great objects which it was meant to promote, and convinced Americans that they may indeed be independent. The sheep-shearing speeches, which are before the public, will prove that no party motives have prompted the conduct of Mr. Custis. In one of these he remarks, "America shall be great and free, and minister to her own wants, by the employment of her own resources." In another, "The citizen of my country will proudly appear, when clothed in the produce of his native soil." By the disinterested devotion of Mr. Custis to the public good, he has illustrated the motto "*Pro patria semper.*" May not such a man "look his country in the face," and exultingly exclaim, "I have been thy benefactor!" "My life on it this fellow is a federalist"

Mr. Custis had the satisfaction of being able to say, at a recent sheep-shearing, "My humble institution, which first taught my country to hail the sound of industry with independence, is growing old in its usefulness, and, as the happy parent, beholds a numerous progeny arising to support its age."

was perishing at Yorktown, he bequeathed this invaluable legacy to his child, and damned be the man who would relinquish the rights obtained by a parent's sufferings!*

O, Washington! discerning man! well indeed didst thou foresee thy country's fallen destiny! As a father didst thou warn thy children of the precipiece to which they were approaching. Yes, as thy country's guardian angel didst thou stand on the brink and point to the abyss below.† Thy sun hath sunk in the west, but may its last parting gleam still serve to light us in our darksome course, till the sun of another Washington shall arise, and give to America a glorious day!

Weep not my brethren, that our chief is gone. Dry up your tears; and thank the Author of divine mercies for having so long preserved our benefactor for our happiness, and at last only to have taken him from us when the degeneracy of his country had began to sorrow his declining years.‡ Methinks I hear his mighty spirit sigh in the breeze; methinks I see his venerated form enshrined in glory — his opened arms receive the shade of Lingan! Listen to his awful words:

"Welcome to thy chief, thou good and faithful soldier! Twice hast thou bled in liberty's cause! Here shalt thou enjoy the recompense of the brave!"

* Mr. Custis's father, then a member of the military staff of Washington, died near Yorktown, in 1781, from an infectious disorder received in the British camp. Mr. Custis, at that time an infant, was adopted into the family of Mount Vernon.

† The discerning mind of Washington "looked quite through the deeds of men,' and early perceived the dangerous precipice to which the principles and conduct of certain persons were hurrying his devoted country. Like a guardian genius, he warned her of her fate, and, placing the majesty of his exalted character and example on the brink, sought to preserve the nation his virtues and services had rendered illustrious; but all in vain! Urged by her untoward destiny, she falls from her envied height and sinks into "the abyss below!"

‡ It was about the year 1798 that Washington, being visited by Judge Marshall, Judge Washington, and General H. Lee, observed to these gentlemen on their departure, while standing at the western door of Mount Vernon (emblematic of the decline of his setting sun)—"Gentlemen, you must come forward in the nation's councils. The exigencies of her affairs require your good services. The most unhappy consequences will ensue should the principles of the party now rising into power ever predominate in our country. *I* may not live to witness these things — *you* may!" Marshall and Lee obeyed the patriarch's summons; Bushrod Washington, from peculiar circumstances, was prevented. It soon after became the melancholy duty of Marshall to announce his death, and the pride of Lee to proclaim his eulogy!

NOTE III.—PAGE 61.

CELEBRATION OF THE RUSSIAN VICTORIES.

AN ORATION BY MR. CUSTIS, OF ARLINGTON, DELIVERED JUNE 5, 1813.

Though feeble in health, yet being honored as your choice, I will humbly endeavor to execute the task which your too partial favor has assigned me.

The purpose of this association is at once novel and interesting. It has heretofore been deemed a full measure of duty for nations to celebrate events which may have had immediate relation to themselves; but generous America will set to the world a nobler example, and, forgetting for a moment that selfish impulse which directs our feelings to our own immediate welfare, let us evince a laudable sympathy in the welfare of others.

When we fought for liberty, many were the foreign bosoms which beat in unison with our cause. Perhaps, under the fur-garment of the distant Russian, America and her efforts may have excited that cheering warmth which virtuous bosoms nourish. Then reciprocate the generous feeling, and show to the world that, grateful for our own liberties, we deem it a bounden duty to rejoice in the liberties of others.

Sure Americans should feel an interest in the successes of those who war for the right of self-government, whatever may be the clime they inhabit, and wish strength to the arm which strikes for national liberty, whether it wield the lance of the Cossack or the Highlander's claymore.

Amid those great events, which of late years have so convulsed the civilized world, the invasion of Russia forms a most grand and predominant feature. It seems as if the last energies of Europe were aroused to this consummate struggle. Napo leon, mighty in genius and vast in resources, like a Colossus, had long bestrode the European world, and, fired with the rage of conquest, sought to plant his standard on the banks of the Neva. His march is like the sirocco of the desert, spreading ruin and desolation around him; his course is known by the smoke of villages cooling in human blood; his triumphs are heard in the lamentations of human misery. The host of Prussia retires — all seems his prey, until, urged by high destiny, he seeks to rest from his labors in the palace of the czars, and finds in the flames of Moscow a funeral pyre for his ambition. Immortal Moscow! Magnanimous people! who, rather than their ancient capital should afford to the tyrant a domicil, seize the torch and fire at once the altars of their God, the temples of their saints, and the sepulchre of their kings. And are these the people whom the world has been pleased to denominate *barbarians?* True, the sun of science hath, as yet, but feebly twinkled in their frozen clime; but, by heaven, this late act of theirs would have done honor to the most splendid era of ancient virtue — ay, it would have immortalized old Rome even in her Fabian age, or Lacedæmon in the time of Leonidas.

Though Moscow remains but a heap of blackened ruins, still from its ashes may be raked a gem of purest, brightest value. I mean its great example, which tells to the nations of the world that, when a people are resolved to serve their own rulers and obey their own laws, among that people corruption can never enter, nor can tyrants subdue them. Had the Austrians, the Italians, or the Swiss, fired his Vienna, his Milan, or his Berne, Europe might have long since been saved. Their misfortunes have taught them a useful lesson; but now, if, after the wisdom which burning Moscow has thrown upon surrounding nations, they are again enslaved, a long night of tyranny must overshadow a despairing world.

From the history of these events, let nations learn to place a firm reliance on the all-wise Disposer of human affairs, who, even in her darkest day, raised up for Russia, the avenger of his country's wrongs, the aged, the illustrious Koutusoff. This venerable chief had been the soldier of other wars; his spring of youth first budded in the fields of honor; his meridian summer blazed high on the walls of Oczatchoff, and, though age may fade the leaf of his autumn, stern winter can never wither a leaf of the laurel which binds his silvery brow — it must bloom even amid his native snows.

Russia, go on! Thine own chains broken, break thou the the chains of others. Gray warrior of the North! if thine aged frame can bear more honors, go whet thy avenging sword on the tomb of Suwarrow, and again thunder on the plains of Italy— climb the glacier steeps, where the descendants of Tell pine in ignominious bondage and sigh for their native liberty. Burst that confederation, linked only by the tyrant's power, nor furl thy conquering banner till it shall feel the breezes of the Rhine. Then pause; give to each nation the government it may choose, and, retiring to the polar forests, the blessings of millions will cheer thy declining days, and a brilliant halo of glory encircle thy immortal fame. The name of Koutusoff will not be ranked with the destroyers of nations, but will proudly swell the list of virtuous heroes, with Vasa, with Tell, with Wallace, with Washington, deliverers of their country and benefactors of man. Ere we leave the field of fame, let us pay due homage to the memory of the brave. Bagration, the prince of Russian chivalry, the patriot, the hero, now sleeps in the bed of honor! But not unremembered hath he fallen; for, whenever the roving Cossack shall gallop over Borodino's plain, his wild and warlike eye will rest with delight on the tumulus which contains Bagration's ashes.

Russia, farewell! So long as thou shalt wield the sword of justice — the deliverance of nations mark the progress of thy march — may the eagle of victory perch on thy standard, and the prayers of rescued humanity speed the triumph of thine arms.

Americans! let the events which have lately distinguished the theatre of Europe, be held up as a mirror, in which you may view the fate of nations, and learn to protect your own from those evils which have befallen so many others. Think not because a vast ocean intervenes, the frantic ambition which has desolated the fairest portion of the Old World will look unconcerned toward the New. It was customary with chieftains of other days to pause in the high career of ambition. Rome's great Julius, when arrived at the rubicon, debated with himself whether he should pass those limits prescribed by the laws, and infringe on those liberties which his illustrious family had founded, and himself sworn to protect; and " Philip's warlike son," when in the midst of submissive nations, listened to counsel and retraced his conquering steps. But what limits, what barriers, shall ever curb Napoleon's ambition? Think you that he who hath scaled the Alps would not attempt the Andes? And that mighty genius, which scared the chamois from the snowy heights of St. Bernard, would start the lonely condor on the cloud-capped summits of the Chimborazo.

Returning from abroad, the delighted American beholds rich triumphs at home. They seem like an elysian dream, from which we fear to awaken; but the vision hath passed away — the glorious truth bursts like the morning light upon our ravished senses — and we hail with ecstacy the rising of our naval sun.

Twelve months ago, could a man have been found hardy enough to assert that America should meet in equal combat with the mistress of the main, and that, too, upon her usurped element, and there should deal her a harder measure of battle than she hath dealt even to her meanest foe, that man would have been called a fool. But now, my friends, the experiment has been so oft repeated that we have proved to our country and an admiring world the glorious fact, that we, too, can "march upon the mountain wave"— we, too, can share " in the empire of the deep."

Our noble sailors have so well employed their time, that already are they teachers of that very science in which their enemy has always claimed the mastership, and American seamen deserve a patent-right for the destruction of armed vessels on principles and practice wholly their own.

Nay, even were great Nelson living, whose last sigh still dwells in glory on Trafalgar's wave, his generous soul would have given to his enemy the just meed of praise.

On the outermost cliff, which overlooks the main, we should erect a naval trophy, adorned with the busts of our heroes, that, when the future sailor-boy should thither roam, his delighted eye may rest on the monument of our early fame, and his youthful heart be fired with a generous emulation.

And who have achieved these glories? The nurslings who have long fed at the bosom of public bounty, and gambolled in the sunshine of public patronage and protection? Say, rather, it is the neglected children of our Washington — they who, for a long, long time, have endured their country's scorn, and been deemed unworthy of her confidence or esteem. Yet, when dangers assail and misfortunes press hard on their native land, see them, mindful of the example of their chief, forget their wrongs and show their generous nature. And are these the men who but the other day bore the hard names of traitors and of tories?—and has it been left for traitors and tories to strike Britannia's flag upon the ocean? My country, for shame! Will you never know your friends? So when your old soldier died, the brave, the virtuous Lingan, these tender epithets were the cruel comforts of his parting hour; they were the tender mercies offered to soothe a hero at the end of a blameless life; they were the pious blessings with which he closed his eyes for ever! Americans, have you forgot this old man's wrongs? There is a God of justice and humanity who may forget *you*. Let us go back for a moment to that gloomy, yet interesting, period when, in pious assemblage, we paid our last duties to the memory of the brave. You must all remember that, while I feebly breathed my poor tribute of praise to the manes of the martyred Lingan, I dared to say that the *hand* which should "nail the flag of my country to the mast" would belong to one of those who then bore their country's odium and persecution. I thought I knew my brethren — knew those fellows to be of no mongrel breed, but the true, legitimate children of our chief, and such most worthily have their deeds proved them to be.

Encouraged by success in one prophecy, I prophesy again, and now will say that the *heart* which shall direct the energies of this great nation to the accomplishment of that high destiny the meritorious life of her Washington founded, must feel the principles and be warned by the virtues of that immortal man.

How doth every day more and more bring to our view that wisdom and foresight which distinguished the Father of our Country — he to whose humble grave this ungrateful nation hath not yet rolled even one poor stone! He first laid those keels which now triumphant plough the main; he first hoisted that flag which now flies victorious on our conquering decks.

How acceptable to the shade of our parent must be the glorious deeds of his children! They rise like grateful incense to his departed spirit in the realms of bliss!

Go on, my brethren — the eye of the chief still rests on his beloved country; his affections are coincident with his glory. However she may have forgotten her duties to you, forget not the high duties which you owe to the land of your birth. If she deny you her honors and rewards, there is left you the sweet consolation of having deserved them. It behooves not to say whether our rulers are wicked or unwise. If so, we but share in the common fate of nations, all of whom at some time or other have been unfortunate in these respects. An enemy's anchor now clings to our soil. Be firm, my friends — be mindful of the heroic fame of your fathers; hug to your hearts your recent triumphs, and show to posterity and the world that, in the hour of danger, Americans will venerate their laws and give their lives to the liberties of their country.

NOTE IV.—PAGE 67.

LAFAYETTE AT THE TOMB OF WASHINGTON.

The solemn and imposing scene of the visit of Lafayette to the tomb of Washington took place on Sunday, the 17th of October, 1826. About one o'clock, the general left the steamboat *Petersburg* at anchor, off Mount Vernon, and was received into a barge manned and steered by captains of vessels from Alexandria, who had handsomely volunteered their services for this interesting occasion. He was accompanied in the barge by his family and suite, and Mr. Secretary John C. Calhoun. On reaching the shores, he was received by Mr. Lawrence Lewis, the nephew of Washington, and by the gentlemen of the family of Judge Bushrod Washington (the judge himself being absent on official duties), and conducted to the ancient mansion, where, forty years before, Lafayette took the last leave of his " hero, his friend, and our country's preserver."

After remaining a few minutes in the house, the general proceeded to the vault,* supported by Mr. Lewis and the gentlemen relatives of the judge, and accompanied by G. W. Lafayette and G. W. P. Custis, the *children of Mount Vernon*, both having shared the paternal care of the great chief. Mr. Custis wore the *ring*† suspended from a Cincinnati ribbon. Arrived at the sepulchre, after a pause, Mr. Custis addressed the general as follows:—

* The old vault, now in ruins.
† See page 67. The following description of the ring is from the *National Intelligencer*, October 9, 1824:—

"We have had an opportunity of inspecting the ring made by Mr. Greenbury Gaither, enclosing a lock of the hair of General Washington, which Mr. Custis had prepared to be presented by him to General Lafayette. It will remain at Mr.

"Last of the generals of the army of independence! at this awful and impressive moment, when, forgetting the splendor of a triumph greater than Roman consul ever had, you bend with reverence over the remains of Washington, the child of Mount Vernon presents you with this token, containing the hair of *him* whom, while living, you loved, and to whose honored grave you now pay the manly and affecting tribute of a patriot's and a soldier's tear.

"The ring has ever been an emblem of the union of hearts from the earliest ages of the world, and *this* will unite the affections of all the Americans to the person and posterity of Lafayette now and hereafter; and, when your descendants of a distant day shall behold this valued relic, it will remind them of the heroic virtues of their illustrious sire who received it, not in the palaces or amid the pomp and vanities of life, but the laurelled grave of Washington. Do you ask, Is this the Mausoleum befitting the ashes of Marcus Aurelius or the good Antonius? I tell you that the Father of his Country lies buried in the hearts of his countrymen, and in those of the brave, the good, the free, of all ages and nations. Do you seek for the tablets which are to convey his fame to immortality? They have long been written in the freedom and happiness of his country. These are the monumental trophies of Washington the Great, and will endure when the proudest works of art have 'dissolved and left not a wreck behind.'

"Venerable man! will you never tire in the cause of freedom

Gaither's to-day, subject to public inspection. The ring is of solid gold, and perfectly plain, but neat workmanship. On the inner surface of it is the following inscription beautifully engraved:

'LAFAYETTE.
1777.
Pro novi orbis liberate
decerbatat Juvenis,
stabilitam Senex
Invenit.
1824.'

On the face of the ring, surrounding the hair, are the words 'Pater Patriæ;' and on another side the words 'Mount Vernon.' This is an appropriate, and must be a highly acceptable gift."

and human happiness? Is it not time that you should rest from your generous labors, and repose on the bosom of a country which delights to love and honor you, and will her children's children to bless your name and memory? Sure where liberty dwells there must be the country of Lafayette!

"Our fathers witnessed the dawn of your glory, partook of its meridian splendor, and O! let their children enjoy the benign radiance of your setting sun, and, when it shall sink in the horizon of nature, *here*, here, with pious duty, we will form your sepulchre, and, united in death as in life by the side of the great chief, you will rest in peace, till the last trump awakes the slumbering world and calls your virtues to their great reward.

"The joyous shouts of millions of freemen hailed your returned foot-prints on our sands; the arms of millions are opened wide to hug you to their grateful hearts, and the prayers of millions ascend to the throne of Almighty power, and implore that the choicest blessings of Heaven will cheer the latter days of Lafayette!"

The general, having received the ring, pressed it to his bosom and replied:—

"The feelings which, at this awful moment, oppress my heart do not leave the power of utterance. I can only thank you, my dear Custis, for your precious gift, and pay a silent homage to the tomb of the greatest and best of men, my paternal friend!"

The general affectionately embraced the donor and the other three gentlemen, and, gazing intently on the receptacle of departed greatness, fervently pressed his lips to the door of the vault, while tears filled the furrows of the veteran's cheeks. The key was now applied to the lock — the door flew open and discovered the coffins strewed with flowers and evergreens. The general descended the steps and kissed the leaden cells which contained the ashes of the great chief and his venerable consort, and then retired in an excess of feeling which language is too poor to describe. After partaking of refreshments at the house, and making a slight tour in the grounds, the general returned to to the shore. In descending the hill to the river, the horses became restive. Some spirited young men rushed forward, removed the horses, and would have drawn the carriage themselves; but this the general would not permit, and, alighting, walked to the shore, a distance of nearly a quarter of a mile. Previous to re-embarkation, Mr. Custis presented the Cincinnati ribbon, which had borne the ring to the vault, to Major Ewell, a veteran of the Revolution, requesting him to take a part of it and divide the remainder among the young men present, which was done, and a general struggle ensued for the smallest portion of it.

The same barge conveyed the general to the *Petersburg*, the marine band playing, as before, a strain of solemn music. The vessel immediately proceeded on her voyage to Yorktown.

Not a soul intruded upon the privacy of the visit to the tomb. Nothing occurred to disturb its reverential solemnity. The old oaks which grew around the sepulchre, touched with the mellowed lustre of autumn, appeared rich and ripe as the autumnal honors of Lafayette. Not a murmur was heard, save the strains of solemn music and the deep and measured sound of artillery, which awoke the echoes around the hallowed heights of Mount Vernon.

'Tis done! the greatest, the most affecting scene of the grand drama has closed, and the pilgrim who now repairs to the tomb of the Father of his Country will find its laurels moistened by the tears of Lafayette.*

* This was communicated to the *National Intelligencer* immediately after the occurrence, and was published in that paper on the 26th of October, 1824.

NOTE V.

AGRICULTURAL DIRECTIONS, BY WASHINGTON.*

Having given very full and ample details of the intended crops, and my ideas of the modes of managing them at the sevral plantations, little, if these are observed, needs be added on this subject. But, as the profit of every farm is greater or less, in proportion to the quantity of manure which is made thereon, or can be obtained by keeping the fields in good condition, these two important requisites ought never to be lost sight of.

To effect the former, besides the ordinary means of farm-yards, cow-pens, sheep-folds, stables, &c., it would be of essential use, if a certain proportion of the force of each plantation could be appropriated, in the summer or early part of autumn, to the purpose of getting up mud to be ameliorated by the frosts of winter for the spring-crops, which are to follow. And, to accomplish the latter, the gullies in these fields, previous to their being sown with grain and grass-seeds, ought invariably to be filled up. By so doing, and a small sprinkling of manure there, they will acquire a green sward and strength of soil sufficient to preserve them. These are the only means I know of by which exhausted lands can be recovered, and an estate rescued from destruction.

Although a precise number of tobacco hills is, by my general

---

* On several occasions, the author of the *Recollections* has referred to the extreme care and method which Washington always exercised in the management of his estate. The following "directions respecting the management of the plantations and other affairs at Mount Vernon," given to his nephew, George A. Washington, to whom he committed the superintendence of his private concerns when he assumed the office of President of the United States, will give the reader a fair specimen of that care and method. The paper is dated March 31, 1789, a little more than a fortnight before he left Mount Vernon for New York.

directions, allotted to each plantation, yet my real intention is, that no more ground shall be appropriated to this crop than what is either naturally *very* good (for which purpose small spots may be chosen), or what can be made strong by manure of some kind or other; for my object is to labor for profit, and therefore to regard quality instead of quantity, there being, except in the article of manuring, no difference between attending a good plant and an indifferent one. But, in any event, let the precise number of hills be ascertained, that an estimate may be formed of their yield to the thousand.

Being thoroughly convinced, from experience, that embezzlement and waste of crops (to say nothing of the various accidents to which they are liable by delays) are increased proportionably to the time they are suffered to remain on hand, my wish is, as soon as circumstances will permit after the grain is harvested, that it may be got out of the straw, especially at the plantations where there are no barns, and either disposed of in proper deposites, or sold, if it is wheat, and the price is tolerable, after it has been converted into flour. When this work is set about as the sole or as a serious business, it will be executed properly; but when a little is done now and a little then, there is more waste, even if there should be no embezzlement, than can well be conceived.

One or two other matters I beg may be invariably attended to. The first is to begin harvest as soon as the grain can be cut with safety; and the next, to get it in the ground in due season. Wheat should be sown by the last of August; at any rate by the 10th of September; and other fall grain as soon after as possible. Spring grain and grass-seeds should be sown as soon as the ground can possibly, with propriety, be prepared for their reception.

For such essential purposes as may absolutely require the aid of the ditchers, they may be taken from that work. At all other times they must proceed in the manner which has been directed formerly, and in making the new roads from the ferry to the mill, and from the tumbling dam across the neck, till it communicates with the Alexandria road, as has been pointed out on the spot. The ditch from the ferry to the mill along this road may be a common four-feet one; but from the mill to the tumbling dam, and thence across to the head of the old field by Muddy-Hole fence, it must be five feet wide at the top, but no deeper than the four-feet one, and the same width at bottom as the latter.

After the carpenters have given security to the old barn in the neck, they must proceed to the completion of the new one at the ferry, according to the plan and the explanations which have been given. Gunner and Davis should get bricks made for this purpose; and, if John Knowles could be spared (his work, not only with respect to time, but quantity and quality, to be amply returned) to examine the bilged walls, and the security of them, and to level and lay the foundations of the other work when the bricks are ready, it would be rendering me an essential service; and, as the work might be returned in proper season, would be no detriment to your building.

When the brick work is executed at the ferry barn, Gunner and Davis must repair to Dogue Run, and make bricks there, at the place and in the manner which have been directed, that I may have no salmon bricks in that building.

Oyster-shells should be bought whenever they are offered for sale, if good and on reasonable terms.

Such moneys as you may receive for flour, barley, fish, as also for other things, which can be spared and sold; and for rents, the use of the jacks, &c.; and for book debts, which may be tried, though little is expected from the justice of those who have been long indulged; may be applied to the payment of workmen's wages as they arise, Fairfax, and the taxes, and likewise to the payment of any just debts which I may be owing in small sums, and have not been able to discharge previous to my leaving the state. The residue may await further orders.

As I shall want shingles, plank, nails, rum for harvest, scantling, and such like things, which would cost me money at another time, fish may be bartered for them. The scantling, if any is taken, must be such as will suit for the barn now about to be built, or that at Dogue Run, without waste and of good quality.

I find it is indispensably necessary, for two reasons, to save my own clover and timothy-seed; first, because it is the only certain means of having it good and in due season; and, secondly, because I find it is a heavy article to purchase.

Save all the honey-locusts you can of those which belong to me; if more could be obtained, the better; and, in the fall, plant them on the ditches where they are to remain about six inches apart, one seed from another.

The seeds, which are on the case in my study, ought, without loss of time, to be sown and planted in my botanical garden, and proper memoranda kept of the times and places.

You will use your best endeavors to obtain the means for support of G. and L. Washington, who, I expect, will board, till something further can be decided on, with Dr. Craik, who must be requested to see that they are decently and properly provided with clothes from Mr. Porter's store. He will give them a credit on my becoming answerable to him for the payment; and, as I know of no resource that H. has for supplies but from me, Fanny will, from time to time, as occasion may require, have such things got for her, on my account, as she shall judge necessary. Mrs. Washington will, I expect, leave her tolerably well provided with common articles for the present.

My memorandum books, which will be left in my study, will inform you of the times and places, when, and where, different kinds of wheat, grass-seeds, &c., were sown. Let particular attention be paid to the quality and quantity of each sort that a proper judgment of them may be formed. To do this, great care must be taken to prevent mixture of the several sorts, as they are so contiguous to each other.

The general superintendence of my affairs is all I require of you; for it is neither my desire nor wish that you should become a drudge to it, or that you should refrain from any amusements or visitings which may be agreeable either to Fanny or yourself to make or receive. If Fairfax, the farmer, and Thomas Green, on each of whom I have endeavored to impress a proper sense of their duty, will act their part with propriety and fidelity, nothing more will be necessary for you to do than would comport with amusement and that exercise which is conducive to health. Nor is it my wish that you should live in too parsimonious a manner. Frugality and economy are undoubtedly commendable, and all that is required. Happily for this country, these virtues prevail more and more every day among all classes of citizens. I have heard of, and I have seen with pleasure, a remarkable change in the mode of living from what it was a year or two ago; and nothing but the event, which I dreaded would take place soon, has prevented my following the example. Indeed, necessity, if this had not happened, would have forced me into the measure, as my means are not adequate to the expense at which I have lived since my retirement to what is called private life. Sincerely wishing you health and happiness, I am ever your warm friend and affectionate uncle.

A VIEW OF THE WORK AT THE SEVERAL PLANTATIONS AT MOUNT VERNON, IN THE YEAR 1789, AND GENERAL DIRECTIONS FOR THE EXECUTION OF IT.

From the plans of the plantations, from the courses of the crops, which are annexed to these plans, and from the mode of managing them as there prescribed, may be derived a full and comprehensive view of my designs, after the rotation is once perfectly established in the succession that is proposed. But, as this cannot, at all the plantations, be adopted this year, everything in the meantime must be made to tend to it, against the next, as far as circumstances will admit.

MUDDY-HOLE FARM.

The ploughs belonging to this plantation, together with those from Dogue Run, are to continue without interruption or delay, when not prevented by frost or rain, to break up field No. 5 for Indian corn. And, when this is accomplished, next to break up No. 4 for buckwheat, which is to be sewed in April, and ploughed in before harvest, as a manure for the crop of wheat, which is to be sown therein in the month of August next, after these ploughings are performed.

Then, as there is no field at this plantation which can with convenience be appropriated for spring grain, or for the crop of sundries this year, and as the ploughs at Dogue Run, especially if the winter should prove hard and unfavorable, will not be able, of themselves, to break up fields No. 4 and No. 6 at their own plantation, and at the same time prepare those of No. 3 for barley and oats, and No. 7 for Indian corn, in due season, the whole may go to Dogue Run, till the corn at Muddy-Hole shall want them, and work in No. 6, if the condition of it is such as to admit thereof — or in No. 4 at the same place, if it is not — for the respective crops which are designed for them.

The fence on the ferry road, from the division between the fields No. 4 and No. 5 to the lane on the mill road, must be repaired with new rails; but from thence to the gate leading to the barn from the overseer's house it should be made tolerably secure with rails, which may be taken from the opposite side.

As the days are short, walking bad, and the different kinds of stock will require careful attendance, it may, perhaps, be best to relinquish the idea of the people of this place having anything further to do with the new ground at the Mansion House; and when not employed, in open weather, with their fencing, to be threshing out grain. But there is a work of great importance, if the weather and other circumstances would concur for the execution of it in season. I mean that of getting up rich mud from the most convenient part of the creek, and laying it in small heaps, for amelioration, to be carried over the poor parts of No. 5, which will be in corn. If this last-mentioned work can be accomplished (and it must be done soon, if any effect is expected from it this year, in order that the frost may have time to operate), the cart may be employed in hauling it to the ground.

Another piece of work to be done here (as I propose to make a small quantity of tobacco at this as well as my other plantations), is to hill the ground that is marked off for it in time. But, previous to hilling, it must be laid off with the plough into three-feet squares, that the hills may be made directly on the cross; so that, in the early stages of the growth of the tobacco, it may be tended with a plough each way.

If these several kinds of work should not afford sufficient employment for the hoe people, with the cultivation of the ground, which will be marked out for potatoes and carrots, and which ought to be ploughed up immediately, they may be preparing field No. 6, on the creek, for corn in 1790. In the execution of this work, the cedar-trees are not to be cut down, but trimmed only, and other trees left here and there for shades. The brush and rubbish, of all sorts, are to be be thrown into the gullies and covered over, so as to admit the ploughs to pass.

Both parts of field No. 1 should from this time be withheld from stock of all kinds, that there may be, in the spring, early food for the ewes, lambs, and calves. Field No. 3, now in wheat and rye, must be sown with clover and timothy on the first snow that falls, six pints of the first and two of the latter per acre.

DOGUE-RUN FARM.

The ploughs belonging to this plantation, when they have performed what has already been directed for them at Muddy Hole, together with those of the latter, are to begin, if the ground will admit of it, to break up No. 6 for buckwheat, to be sown in April. But if this, on account of the levelness of the field and the water which may stand on it, can not be done, then plough No. 4 for the crop of sundries. But, as it is of essential importance that the oats and barley should be sown early, and the working of the fields for Indian corn not so much delayed as to endanger the prospect for that crop, the ploughings of both No. 6 and No. 4 must be delayed, at least, till the oats and barley are in, if they can not be broken up in season for the above purposes. The oats ought to be sown in February, next the post-and-rail fence; and the barley as soon after as possible on the other side adjoining the corn. With both, clover and timothy, in the proportions already mentioned, are to be sown.

After the above work is accomplished, it will be time to cross-plough and sow such parts of No. 4 as are intended for carrots, and this is to be done in drills four feet asunder; and, if the ground is dry enough, in the month of March, and for flax, which should be sown in April.

By the time these are done, possibly before it, the fields for corn will want listing. This corn, in the south part of the field, next to the woods, may be planted at five feet each way, with two stalks in a hill, and in the north part, next to Colonel Mason's, at four feet each way, with one stalk in a hill. The ploughings and harrowings necessary for which, without going into detail with respect to the manner and times, must be given when wanted.

The sowing of buckwheat in April for manure seems to be the next thing which calls for the ploughs, because it ought to be in the ground as soon as all danger of frost is over, that it may be in the proper state (full bloom) for ploughing in before harvest.

After buckwheat, pease will come next, and the ground for these, as for the tobacco, must be laid off in squares for hilling, that they may, before they begin to run and spread, be ploughed each way. They ought to be planted in May.

Pumpkins, potatoes, turnips, and buckwheat for a crop, in the order they are mentioned, will next claim the assistance of the ploughs. The first should be planted in May, in hills eight feet apart and well manured; the second in June, in drills four feet apart and a foot asunder in the rows, with a large handful of manure on each potato, which should be uncut and of the largest sort; the third — that is, turnips — to be sown partly in June and partly in July; and the fourth, buckwheat, as near as may be to the 10th of July.

This field of sundries may be thus apportioned: Carrots, five acres; potatoes, five; pumpkins, one; turnips, one; pease, fifteen; flax, three; tobacco, five; buckwheat, thirty-five; being seventy acres in all.

That it may be ascertained, by repeated experiments, whether carrots or potatoes are the most productive and valuable root, I would have the ten acres allotted for them in one square, and the rows for each alternate through the whole square, and each to have the same quantity of manure allowed to it.

The work which has been mentioned for the ploughs, together with the ploughing in of the buckwheat before harvest, the wheat after harvest, with the workings of the several species of crops during their growth, is all the employment that can be recollected at present for this part of the force of the plantation, until the autumn ploughing for the next year's crop commences. But as these — till the system is brought more into practice, and the preceding crop is a better preparation of the ground for the succeeding one than is the case at present — will require much exertion and an addition of ploughs, one may be added to the number at Dogue Run, which will make five there; and another at Muddy Hole, which will make four there.

Much fencing is necessary at this plantation before it can be said to be advantageously laid off, and in good order. That which requires to be first done, is the one which divides field No. 4 from the meadow; but, as the rails which are about the stacks will be most convenient for this work, it may be delayed until they can be spared. In the meantime, no heavy stock must run in that field to trample and poach the meadow.

The next that requires doing, is the line from the head of the meadow to the new road, which is to be laid off thence with the road to the tumbling dam, and thence round field No. 7, agreeably to the ploughing, and the rails which have been laid there.

Next after these, the cross-fence between field No. 5 and the wood should be done; and then the fence, which was begun last year, but not finished, between fields No. 2 and No. 3. The fence which divides the first of these — that is, No. 2 — from the great meadow, requires doing also. All these are essential; as it also is to strengthen the post-and-rail fence which divides No. 1 from No. 2 and No. 3; but, as this never can be made a good one until the whole is taken down and both posts and rails shortened, it must be postponed till there is time to do this — righting up in such a manner as to make it answer for the present, being all that can be attempted this year.

Lastly, when time will admit, after the posting and railing from the tumbling dam to the mill is completed, the rails, which at present run upon that line, may serve to separate the great meadow into three divisions, as will be marked out.

Everything that the hoe people can do in the course of the winter toward getting the old crop off hand, and preparing for the new one, ought to be the first object of consideration, and must be closely attended to. Carrying out manure, when the cart can be spared and the ground is in order for its reception, either for carrots, potatoes, tobacco, or other things, is not to be neglected. Grubbing and filling up gullies, in the fields which are to receive crops this year, is also essential; and, if these should not afford sufficient employment, the overplus time may be spent in clearing swamps, or the sides of them, so that they may hereafter, when drained effectually, be tended in tobacco previous to their being laid down in grass.

At this place I propose to plant about thirty thousand tobacco-plants, in field No. 4, round the houses and stacks, where they will be most convenient to the manure; and, where the ground is not very rich, I would join a gallon or a large double handful of manure to each hill. The ground for the crop ought to be broken up early, either with the ploughs or hoes, that the green sward may have time to rot. If thirty thousand hills can not be got here, the deficiency may be made up by the gate that goes into field No. 5.

RIVER FARM.

Early and good ploughing at this place is indispensably necessary. The field No. 7, intended for spring grain — that is, barley and oats — would, if justice were done to it, call for a second or cross ploughing by the time the ploughs will begin to break it up. Consequently, field No. 1, designed for corn, will hardly get more than a listing; and the field No. 4 which ought to have received a crop of sundries, must go altogether uncultivated this year.

After field No. 7 is sown with barley, oats, and grass-seed — the latter in the proportion mentioned in the other places, if the preparation of No. 1 for corn can not be postponed, without involving injurious consequences to that crop — the ploughs must go there next, and do all that is necessary for getting it planted in time, and in good order.

But, as I do not mean to plant potatoes or carrots among corn this year, as was the case last year, inclining to allot separate spots for this purpose, these spots, and that which is intended for tobacco, ought to be immediately ploughed; that the weeds and grass, where there are any, may have time to rot, and the ground be in order to receive manure. The spot which I would principally appropriate for carrots and potatoes, is that whereon the flax grew last year; but if more can be conveniently obtained elsewhere, it ought to be had, as that spot is insufficient. The ground for tobacco (forty thousand plants) I mean to lay off in a long square, from the farm-pen up to field No. 2, which, when ploughed and checkered, will be ready to receive manure at times when the carts can with convenience carry it out.

All the ploughings, which are here enumerated, being accomplished, the season probably will have arrived when No. 8 will require to be cross-ploughed, and sowed with buckwheat for manure in April. This is, in all respects, to be managed as has been directed for Dogue Run, and after harvest is to receive wheat, in August, as there mentioned.

These, with the necessary workings of the several species of crops, which must not be neglected, will, it is presumed, give sufficient employment for the ploughs. If not, there can be no difficulty in finding work for them.

Much fencing is wanting on this plantation before it can be in the order I wish to see it; but, among the most essential of these, is the fence which is to enclose field No. 1 for corn; that which runs from the second gate, going into the plantation, to the creek, dividing my land from Colonel Mason's; and that which is to form the lane, which is to lead from the barn into the lane which now goes to Johnson's, and which must continue the other way, so as to open a communication with the fields No 1, No. 2, No. 3, and No. 4. As timber is very scarce on this tract, it must, in fencing as well as in other things, be made to go as far as possible; consequently, posts and rails, of a good and substantial kind, must be substituted instead of the usual kind of worm-fences.

To point out all the work for the hoe people of this plantation, is unnecessary. To finish the old, and to prepare for the new crop; to put up fences; to heap up manure early, that it may get well and soon rotted; to carry it out, and to lay it in the furrows intended for carrots and potatoes, and on the ground intended for tobacco; making hills for the tobacco; grubbing and filling gullies in the fields, which are to receive crops this year, with old rails, old stumps, old trees, and such other rubbish as can be had conveniently; levelling the bank on which a fence formerly ran through field No. 8—will, with the cultivation of the crops that will be planted and sown, and gathering them in, compose the greater part, if not all, of their labor. But, if there should, notwithstanding, be time for other things, I know of nothing in which they could be more advantageously employed than in getting up rich mud from the branches in field No. 8, to spread over the poor and washed parts of that field, before it is sown in wheat next August.

MANSION-HOUSE FARM.

The ditchers, after the post-and-rail fence, which they are now about, to the tumbling dam is completed, and a strong one put up across the mill run, as will be marked off, may continue on to the mill by the line of stakes which will be set up; but they are not to use for this purpose those posts which were got by Marley's house, as they will be more convenient for the lane which is to form the new road from the ferry by the mill, as authorized by the court. After this work is performed, it will be time enough to point out more.

To say what the other part of the force at this place shall be employed about, is next to impossible, since there is such a variety of jobs for them to attend to, besides fishing, hay-making, and the grain-harvest in their respective seasons, which must unavoidably employ them while they last.

But, as it is designed to raise tobacco, and to tend in corn that part, at least, of the new ground in front of the house, which was cleared last year, in order that it may be laid down in the fall in wheat and orchard grass, they must prepare for them accordingly, and, under the circumstances above-mentioned, attempt as much of the first — that is, tobacco — as there is a moral certainty of their tending well. The men may be employed in getting posts and rails of a good kind for the purpose of enclosing this tobacco. But it is essential, if any labor is expected from the girls and boys who are about this house, to keep some person with them, who will not only make them work, but who will see that the work is well executed, and that the idleness which they appear every day in the practice of may be avoided.

608 APPENDIX.

FIRST STATEMENT OF THE CROPS IN 1789.

	Acres	Acres	Harrowed

Corn; 375 acres   1 ploughing in the fall of 1788 375
        Listing the field in March, about ¼ of the above work . 94
        Opening the furrows in April, ⅓ of the last work . . 31
        Breaking up the balks in May, ¾ of the whole . . 281
        Ploughing   do.   in June, do. do. . . . 281
        Do.   do.   in July, do. do. . . . 281
                                                           1343
        Three times harrowed   do do. each 281 .   843
Rye; 375 acres.   Once ploughed for seeding in September .   281
        Once harrowed   do. . .   281
Buckwheat; 375 acres.   One ploughing after Rye comes off . 375
        One   do.   in April . . . 375
                                                            750
        Three harrowings, 1 before, and 2 after sowing .   1125
Wheat; 375 acres.   Ploughing in Buckwheat in June . 375
        Do.   seeding ground with Wheat in August 375
                                                           750
        One harrowing after sowing . .   375
Sundries; 375 acres.   One ploughing in the fall of 1788 . . 375
  75 do.   in Pease ploughed into three-feet ridges in April 75
        Checkered, about ¼ of above work in April 19
234 do.   in Buckwheat for a crop, ploughed in April . 234
                           Do.   1st July 234
        Three times harrowed 1st of July . .   702
  8 do.   Scarcity ploughed in March . . . 8
        do.   May . . . 8
        do.   July . . . 8
  8 do.   Pumpkins, ploughed in March . . 8
        do.   May . . 8
        do.   July . . 8
20 do.   Flax, ploughed in March 20
        do.   April . . . 20
                                                            1025
        Three times harrowed . .   60
Barley; 375 acres.   First ploughing January or February . . 375
        Second   do.   February or March . . 375   750
        Three times harrowed   1125
                                                            4899   4511

Of the above Work,

Between the 1st of October and Christmas, Corn amounts to . . 375
                                Buckwheat " " . 375
                                Sundries " " . 375
                                                        1125
In January and February, Barley, first ploughing . . . 375
February and May   do.   second " 375   1125
March, listing for Corn as above 94
        Ploughing first time for Root of Scarcity . . . 8
        Do.   do.   Flax 20
        Do.   do.   Pumpkins 8
                                                             130
                                            Carried over,   2005   1125

	Acres	Acres	Harrowed
Brought over,		2005	1125
April, second ploughing for Flax	20		60
Do. Pease, in three-feet ridges	75		
Do. checkered	19		
Opening Corn lists for planting	31		
Buckwheat for manure	375	520	1125
May, Do. for seed	234		
Pumpkins, second ploughing, 8; Root of Scarcity, 8	16		
Breaking balks between Corn	281	531	281
June, ploughing Corn second time	281		281
Do. Buckwheat for manure	375	656	
July, Buckwheat for seed	234		702
Third ploughing of Corn	281		281
Third do. Root of Scarcity, 8; Pumpkins, 8	16	531	
August, Wheat		375	375
September, Rye		281	281
		4899	4511

Results of the First Statement.

DR.   **CR.**

	£	s.	d.		£	s.	d.
For 375 bushels Rye for seed, at 3s.	56	5	0	By 5625 bushels Corn, at 3s.	843	0	0
375 bushels Buckwheat for seed, at 2s.	37	10	0	5625 do. Rye, 3s.	843	0	0
375 do. Wheat, do. 5s.	93	15	0	5625 do. Potatoes, 1s.	281	5	0
750 do. Barley, do. 3s. 6d.	131	5	0	4500 do. Barley, 3s. 6d.	787	0	0
Sundries, viz:				3750 do. Wheat, 5s.	937	10	0
75 bush. Pease for seed, at 4s.	15	0	0	Sundries, viz.:			
234 do. Buckwheat, 2s.	23	8	0	1404 bushels Buckwheat, at 2s.	140	8	0
30 do. Flax, 3s. 6d.	5	5	0	375 do. Pease, 4s.	75	0	0
3750 lbs. Clover-seed, 8d.	125	0	0	100 do. Flax-seed, 3s. 6d.	17	10	0
3120 bushels of Corn for negroes, at 3s.	468	0	0	Dressed Flax. Buckwheat, 375 acres for manure			
2750 bushels of Rye for horses, 3s.	412	10	0		3924	13	0
100 do. Salt, 2s. 6d.	12	10	0	375 acres Clover 20s.	375		
330 gallons Rum, 2s.	33	00	0		4299	13	0
750 bushels of potatoes, for seed, 1s.	37	10	0	100 thousand Tobacco hills, 20 hhds. £7 10s.	150		
	£1450	18	0		£4449	13	0

SECOND STATEMENT OF CROPS IN 1789.

	Acres	Acres	Harrowed
Corn; 375 acres. Same in all respects as No. 1		1343	843
Buckwheat; 375 acres. First ploughing in April	375		
Second do. last of June	375	750	
Three harrowings			1125
Wheat; 375 acres. One ploughing after the Buckwheat is cut		375	
Two harrowings			750
Sundries; 375 acres. The same as No. 1		1025	762
Barley; 375 acres. The same as No. 1		750	1125
		4243	4605

Of the above Work,

	Acres	Acres	Harrowed.
One ploughing for Corn, 1788		375	
Fall, one ploughing for Sundries, do.		375	
January and February, first ploughing for Barley	375		
February and March, second do. do.	375		
		750	1125
March, listing for Corn	94		
ploughing first time for Root of Scarcity	8		
Do. do. Flax	20		
Do. do. Pumpkins	8		
		130	
April, second ploughing for Flax	20		60
Do. Pease, in three-feet ridges	75		
Do. checkered	19		
Opening Corn lists	31		
First ploughing for Buckwheat for a crop	375		
		520	
May, first ploughing of Buckwheat among the sundries	234		
Pumpkins, second ploughing, 8 acres; Scarcity, 8 do.	16		
ploughing balks between Corn, first time	281		
		531	281
June, ploughing Corn second time	281		281
second do. of Buckwheat	375		
		656	1125
July, the same	234		702
Corn third time	281		281
third ploughing for Scarcity, 8; for Pumpkins, 8	16		
		531	
August, ploughing for Wheat		375	750
		4243	4605

Results of the Second Statement.

Dr.	£	s.	d.	Cr.	£	s.	d.
For 375 bushels of Buckwheat for seed, 2s.	37	10	0	By 5625 bushels of Corn, 3s.	843	0	0
375 do. seed Wheat, 5s.	93	15	0	5625 do. Potatoes, 1s.	281	5	0
Sundries, viz.:				Buckwheat ploughed in for manure.			
75 bushels Pease, 4s.	15	0	0	3750 bushels Wheat, 5s.	937	10	0
234 do. Buckwheat, 2s.	23	8	0	Sundries, viz.:			
30 do. Flax-seed, 3s. 6d.	5	5	0	375 bushels of Pease, 4s.	75	0	0
750 do. Barley, 3s. 6d.	131	5	0	1404 do. Buckwheat, 2s.	140	8	0
3750 lbs. Clover-seed, 8d.	125	0	0	4500 do. Barley, 3s. 6d.	787	0	0
3120 bushels of Corn, 3s.	468	0	0	100 do. Flax-seed, 3s. 6d.	17	10	0
2750 do. Rye, 3s.	412	10	0		£3081	13	0
100 do. Salt, 2s. 6d.	12	10	0	Dressed Flax.			
330 gallons Rum, 2s.	33	0	0	375 acres Clover, 20s.	375	0	0
750 bushels Potatoes for seed, 1s.	37	10	0	375 do. do. do.	375	0	0
	£1394	13	0		£3831	13	0

THIRD STATEMENT OF CROPS IN 1789.

	Acres	Harrowed
Corn; 375 acres. The same as No. 1 and No. 2	1343	843
Barley; 375 acres. do. do. do.	750	1125
Buckwheat; 375 acres. Ploughed in fall, in March and April,	1125	1125
Wheat; 375 acres. Ploughed in June, to cover Buckwheat and Corn in August	750	375
Flax; 20 acres. Ploughed twice — harrowed three times	40	60
	4008	3528

Of the above Work,

	Acres	Acres	Harrowed
Fall, one ploughing for Corn, 1788	375		
Do. Buckwheat, do.	375		
		750	
January and February, first ploughing for Barley	375		
February and March, second do. do.	375		
		750	1125
March, listing for Corn	94		
Second ploughing for Buckwheat	375		
First do. Flax	20		
		489	
April, second do. do.	20		60
Third do. Buckwheat	375		750
Opening Corn lists	31		
		426	
May, breaking up the balks between Corn		281	281
June, second ploughing of Corn	281		281
Ploughing in Buckwheat	375		
		656	
July, ploughing Corn the third time	281		281
Ploughing for Wheat or Buckwheat	375		
		656	750
		4008	3528

Results of Third Statement.

DR.

	£	s.	d.
For 750 bushels of Barley for seed, at 3s. 6d.	131	15	0
375 do. Buckwheat, 2s.	37	10	0
375 do. Wheat, 5s.	93	15	0
3750 lbs. Clover-seed, 8d.	125	0	0
30 bushels of Flax-seed	5	5	0
3120 do. Corn, 3s.	468	0	0
2750 do. Rye for horses	412	10	0
100 do. Salt, 2s. 6d.	12	10	0
330 gallons of Rum, 2s.	33	10	0
750 bushels Potatoes for seed, 1s.	37	10	0
£1357	5	0	

CR.

	£	s.	d.
By 5625 bushels of Corn, 3s.	843	0	0
5625 do. Potatoes, 1s.	281	5	0
4500 do. Barley, 3s. 6d.	787	0	0
3750 do. Wheat, 5s.	937	10	0
Buckwheat for manure.			
100 bush. Flax-seed, 3s. 6d.	17	10	0
	£2866	5	0
375 acres Clover, 20s.	375		
375 do. do. do.	375		
375 do. do. do.	375		
	£3091	5	0

MANAGER'S WEEKLY REPORT.*

APRIL 14, 1792.

Meteorological Table.

	Morning.	Noon.	Night.
April 8th	E. Clear.	S. E. Cloudy.	S. E. Rain.
" 9th	S. E. Rain.	S. E. Cloudy.	S. E. Cloudy.
" 10th	S. W. Cloudy.	S. W. Rain.	60 S. E. Rain.
" 11th	58 E. Rain.	S. E. Rain.	58 S. E. Rain.
" 12th	57 N. E. Rain.	56 N. E. Hard Rain.	54 N. E. Cloudy.
" 13th	52 N. E. Cloudy.	56 N. E Rain.	58 N. E. Rain.
" 14th	54 N.W. Cloudy.	58 N. W. Cloudy.	52 N.W. Clear.

DR.

	Days
MANSION-HOUSE FARM for the work of 12 men, 6 boys, and 4 girls, amounting per week to	132

CR.

By a wagon hauling posts and rails to Ferry-Barn lane	1
By do. hauling hay 1, stocks 1, timber for shafts for carts and moving park rails 1	3
By hauling 6 barrels salt to Major Washington's landing, and bringing home straw	1
By carts hauling manure from Ferry Barn to No. 2 French's	6
By cleaning loose manure about stables, and hauling it to lot intended for lucerne	5
By hauling corn from Ferry, and bran and meal from Mill wood to Mansion	2
By hauling stones to repair the crossing-place of Muddy-Hole Swamp, at the head of French's meadow	2
By Old Jack in care of granary 6, Old Frank in care of stock 6	12
By Peter, in care of mares, mules, and jacks	6
By Gunner digging brick-earth 3, cutting poles to build a brick house 2	5
By putting up post-and-rail fence leading to Ferry Barn	5
By hauling seine, cleaning, striking, and packing fish	41
By Easter Monday	22
By sickness Boatswain 6, Mima 3, Richmond 3, Postilion Joe 3, Lynna 3, Sam 3	21
Total	132

---

* While Washington was absent from home, in discharging the duties of President of the United States, it was his custom to exact from the manager at Mount Vernon, once in each week, a full report of the proceedings on all the farms. This paper is a sample of those reports. In the meteorological table, the figures denote the state of the thermometer, and the initial letters the direction of the wind. The design of this table was to communicate a knowledge of the weather, by which a more correct judgment could be formed of the amount of time that the laborers could properly be employed at their work. Each report was accompanied with an explanatory letter from the manager, containing other particulars. These were regularly answered once a week by the President, and sometimes oftener. His letters frequently filled two or three sheets, closely written. The importance he attached to these letters, and his diligence in preparing them, may be understood from the fact that he first made rough drafts, which were copied out by himself in a fair hand before they were sent off. Press-copies were then taken, which he preserved. This habit was pursued, without intermission, from the beginning to the end of the presidency.—*Sparks.*

Increase 2 Calves and 2 mules. Received from Mill, 22 bushels of Meal, and 29 bushels of Bran; from Ferry, 3 barrels of Corn. Stock, 11 head of Cattle, 4 Calves, 60 Sheep, 28 Lambs, 4 working Mares, 4 do. Horses, 5 Colts, 4 spring do., 2 Jacks, 2 old Jennies, 1 do. three years old, 1 do. two years old, 1 do. one year old, 15 Mules, 10 one year old, 2 spring do.; and 11 Mares.

DR.	Days
Ditchers, for the work of 6 men, amounting per week to	36

CR.

By Baths and Paschal mortising posts 1, fencing Ferry-Barn new lane 4	10
By Boatswain and Robin mauling rails 1, and fencing as above 4	10
By Charles hauling seine	5
By Dundee sawing trunnels with Dogue-Run hands	5
By Easter Monday	6
Total	36

N. B. There has been almost one day and part of another lost by rain this week.

DR.	Days
MUDDY-HOLE FARM for the work of 3 men and 9 women, amounting per week to	72

CR.

By listing in No. 2	4
By a cart hauling stakes and trunnels to the fence between Nos. 1 and 7	3
By hauling rails to No. 1 Lane fence	1
By raising the bank with a plough and hoes between No. 1 and No. 7	11
By putting up fences on said bank 19, cutting stakes and trunnels for do. 7	26
By taking down and new setting the Lane fence of No. 1	7
By Easter Monday	12
By sickness, Kate 3, Amy 2, Molly 3	8
Total	72

Received from Mill 6 bushels of Meal, and 6 bushels of Rye Meal. — Stock, 37 head of cattle, 5 Calves, 30 Sheep, 8 working Horses, and 1 Mule.

DR.	Days.
FERRY AND FRENCH'S FARMS for the work of 7 men, 16 women, and 4 boys, amounting per week to	162

CR.

By listing new ground in French's meadow	16
By carts hauling stakes, rails, and trunnels to different fences	6
By hauling manure to No. 2 French's 3; hauling corn to Mill 1	4
By repairing fences, 34; burning logs and brush in the swamp 30	64
By heaping manure 4, beating out corn 4, cutting and mauling stakes and trunnels 4	12
By spinning 3, hauling seine 5, French's Tom at Mansion-House 5	13
By Easter Monday	27
By sickness, Doll 6, Old Daph 5, Betty 4, Rose 3, Delia 2	20
Total	162

Increase, 2 Calves and 5 Lambs. Received from Mill, $12\frac{1}{4}$ bushels of Meal, sent do. 53 bushels of Corn. To Mansion-House 3 barrels of do., feed to Horses 1 barrel of do. — Stock, 83 head of Cattle, 5 Calves, 136 Sheep, 60 Lambs, 16 working Horses, and 2 Mules.

DR.	Days.
RIVER FARM for the work of 9 men, 18 women, and 1 girl, amounting per week to	168

CR.

By listing in No. 6	10
By carts hauling manure on do.	6

	Days
By hauling rails 2, going to Mill 1	3
By loading carts with manure 6, cutting straw 3	9
By plashing thorn-hedge 4, repairing the bank of Lane fence No. 6, 2	6
By stopping hog-hole in do. 6, putting up new fence next to the woods of do. 18	24
By cutting corn-stalks, and getting them off	56
Lost by rain, or very little done	20
By Easter Monday	28
By Cornelia in childbed	6
Total	168

Increase, 2 Calves. Received from Mill, 9¾ bushels of Meal, and 10 bushels of Rye Meal. — Stock, 83 head of Cattle, 5 Calves, 221 Sheep, 45 Lambs, 4 working Mares, 13 working Horses, and 1 Mule

Dr.

	Days
Dogue-Run Farm for the work of 6 men, 8 women, and 2 girls, amounting per week to	96

Cr.

By listing in No. 2, 5, by ploughing in Mill meadow 2	7
By raising a bank with a plough and hoes in Mill meadow for the fence	19
By sawing trunnels 5, mauling do. 5, cutting in Mill meadow 2	12
By repairing fence around the middle meadow	10
By repairing fence around No. 2, 7, by spinning 2	9
By hauling post and rails to Ferry-Barn, new lane	5
By hauling rails to Mill meadow fence	3
By hauling rails to the middle meadow fence	2
By Easter Monday	16
By sickness, Grace 3, Molly 3, Sall 3, Cicely 4	13
Total	96

Received from Mill, 6¾ bushels of Meal. — Stock, 57 head of Cattle, 1 Calf, 124 Sheep, 9 working Horses, and 1 Mule.

Dr.

	Days
Joiners and Carpenters for the work of 6 men and 2 boys, amounting per week to	48

Cr.

By Thomas Green making sashes for the new quarter	5
By Mahony putting up the berths in do.	5
By Isaac making and mending ploughs 4, getting ash for rake-handles 1	5
By Jam making a new cart and shafts, and getting beach stocks for planes	5
By Sambo and David sawing gate-stuff 2, getting stocks and ash for rake-handles 6	8
By Sambo ripping plank on account of rain	1
By David with Isaac on account of do.	1
By Joe planing plank	5
By Christopher at do. 4, and 1 day with the wagon	5
By Easter Monday	8
Total	48

Dr.   Mill for Sundries.   Cr.

	Corn.		Meal	Bran	Rye Meal
Ferry and French's	53	By Dogue-Run Plantation	6¾		
Toll Corn received	9½	By River Plantation	9¾		10
		By Muddy Hole	6		6
Total received	62½	By Ferry and French's	12¼		
		By Mansion-House	22	29	
Toll Corn ground	56	Total delivered	56¾	29	16
		By Coopers and Miller	1		

NOTE VI.—PAGE 361.

ORATION ON THE DEATH OF GENERAL WASHINGTON,

PRONOUNCED BEFORE BOTH HOUSES OF CONGRESS, ON DECEMBER 16, 1799 BY MAJOR-GENERAL HENRY LEE.

IN obedience to your will, I rise, your humble organ, with the hope of executing a part of the system of public mourning which you have been pleased to adopt, commemorative of the death of the most illustrious and most beloved personage this country has ever produced; and which, while it transmits to posterity your sense of the awful event, faintly represents your knowledge of the consummate excellence you so cordially honor.

Desperate, indeed, is any attempt on earth to meet correspondently this dispensation of Heaven; for while, with pious resignation, we submit to the will of an all-gracious Providence, we can never cease lamenting, in our finite view of Omnipotent Wisdom, the heart-rending privation for which our nation weeps. When the civilized world shakes to its centre—when every moment gives birth to strange and momentous changes—when our peaceful quarter of the globe, exempt, as it happily has been, from any share in the slaughter of the human race, may yet be compelled to abandon her pacific policy, and to risk the doleful casualties of war—what limit is there to the extent of our loss? None within the reach of my words to express—none which your feelings will not disavow.

The founder of our federate republic, our bulwark in war, our guide in peace, is no more! O that this were but questionable! Hope, the comforter of the wretched, would pour into our agonizing hearts its balmy dew; but, alas! there is no hope for us,

Our Washington is removed for ever! Possessing the stoutest frame and purest mind, he had passed nearly to his sixty-eighth year, in the enjoyment of high health, when, habituated by his care of us to neglect himself, a slight cold, disregarded, became inconvenient on Friday, oppressive on Saturday, and, defying every medical interposition, before the morning of Sunday, put an end to the best of men. An end did I say? His fame survives! bounded only by the limits of the earth and by the extent of the human mind. He survives in our hearts, in the growing knowledge of our children, in the affections of the good throughout the world; and, when our monuments shall be done away — when nations now existing shall be no more — when even our young and far-spreading empire shall have perished — still will our Washington's glory unfaded shine, and die not, until love of virtue cease on earth, or earth itself sink into chaos.

How, my fellow-citizens, shall I single to your grateful hearts his pre-eminent worth? Where shall I begin in opening to your view a character throughout sublime? Shall I speak of his warlike achievements, all springing from obedience to his country's will — all directed to his country's good?

Will you go with me to the banks of the Monongahela to see your youthful Washington supporting, in the dismal hour of Indian victory, the ill-fated Braddock, and saving, by his judgment and by his valor, the remains of a defeated army, pressed by the conquering savage foe? Or, when oppressed America, nobly resolving to risk her all in defence of her violated rights, he was elevated by the unanimous voice of Congress to the command of her armies, will you follow him to the high grounds of Boston, where, to an undisciplined, courageous, and virtuous yeomanry, his presence gave the stability of system, and infused the invincibility of love of country? Or shall I carry you to the painful scenes of Long Island, York Island, and New Jersey, when, combating superior and gallant armies, aided by powerful fleets, and led by chiefs high in the roll of fame, he stood the bulwark of our safety, undismayed by disaster — unchanged by change of fortune? Or will you view him in the precarious fields of Trenton, where deep glooms, unnerving every arm, reigned triumphant through our thinned, worn down, unaided ranks, himself unmoved? Dreadful was the night! It was about this time of winter. The storm raged; the Delaware, rolling furiously with floating ice, forbade the approach of man. Washington, self-collected, viewed the tremendous scene; his country called. Unappalled by surrounding dangers, he passed to the hostile shore; he fought — he conquered! The morning sun cheered the American world. Our country rose on the event, and her dauntless chief, pursuing his blow, completed, on the lawns of Princeton, what his vast soul had conceived on the shores of Delaware.

Thence to the strong grounds of Morristown he led his small but gallant band, and through an eventful winter, by the high efforts of his genius, whose matchless force was measurable only by the growth of difficulties, he held in check formidable hostile legions, conducted by a chief experienced in the art of war, and famed for his valor on the ever-memorable heights of Abraham, where fell Wolfe, Montcalm, and, since, our much lamented Montgomery, all covered with glory. In this fortunate interval, produced by his masterly conduct, our fathers, ourselves, animated by his resistless example, rallied around our country's standard, and continued to follow her beloved chief through the various and trying scenes to which the destinies of our Union led.

Who is there that has forgotten the vales of Brandywine, the fields of Germantown, or the plains of Monmouth? Everywhere present, wants of every kind obstructing, numerous and valiant armies encountering, himself a host, he assuaged our sufferings, limited our privations, and upheld our tottering republic. Shall I display to you the spread of the fire of his soul by rehearsing the praises of the hero of Saratoga and his much-loved compeer of the Carolina? No, our Washington wears not borrowed glory. To Gates — to Green — he gave, without reserve, the applause due to their eminent merit; and long may the chiefs of Saratoga and of Eutaws receive the grateful respect of a grateful people.

Moving in his own orbit, he imparted heat and light to his most distant satellites; and, combining the physical and moral force of all within his sphere, with irresistible weight he took his course, commiserating folly, disdaining vice, dismaying treason, and invigorating despondency, until the auspicious hour arrived, when, united with the intrepid forces of a potent and magnanimous ally, he brought to submission the since conqueror of India; thus finishing his long career of military glory with a lustre corresponding with his great name, and in this, his last act of war, affixing the seal of fate to our nation's birth.

To the horrid din of war sweet peace succeeded; and our virtuous chief, mindful only of the public good, in a moment tempting personal aggrandizement, hushed the discontents of growing sedition, and, surrendering his power into the hands from which he had received it, converted his sword into a ploughshare, teaching an admiring world that, to be truly great, you must be truly good.

Was I to stop here, the picture would be incomplete and the task imposed unfinished. Great as was our Washington in war, and much as did that greatness contribute to produce the American republic, it is not in war alone his pre-eminence stands conspicuous; his various talents combining all the capacities of a statesman with those of a soldier, fitted him alike to guide the councils and the armies of our nation. Scarcely had he rested from his martial toils, while his invaluable parental advice was still sounding in our ears, when he who had been our shield and our sword was called forth to act a less splendid, but more important, part.

Possessing a clear and penetrating mind, a strong and sound judgment, calmness and temper for deliberation, with invincible firmness and perseverance in resolutions maturely formed, drawing information from all, acting from himself, with incorruptible integrity and unvarying patriotism, his own superiority and the public confidence alike marked him as the man designed by Heaven to lead in the great political, as well as military, events, which have distinguished the area of his life.

The finger of an overruling Providence pointing at Washington was neither mistaken nor unobserved; when, to realize the vast hopes to which our Revolution had given birth, a change of political system became indispensable.

How novel, how grand, the spectacle — independent states stretched over an immense territory, and known only by common difficulty, clinging to their Union as the rock of their safety, deciding by frank comparison of their relative condition to rear on that rock, under the guidance of reason, a common government, through whose commanding protection liberty and order, with their long train of blessings, should be safe to themselves and the sure inheritance of their posterity!

This arduous task devolved on citizens selected by the people, from a knowledge of their wisdom and confidence in their virtue. In this august assembly of sages and of patriots, Washington, of course, was found; and, as if acknowledged to be most wise where all were wise, with one voice he was declared their chief. How well he merited this rare distinction — how faithful were the labors of himself and his compatriots, the work of their hands and our union, strength, and prosperity — the fruits of that work best attest.

But to have essentially aided in presenting to his country this consummation of her hopes, neither satisfied the claims of his fellow-citizens on his talents, nor those duties which the possession of those talents imposed. Heaven had not infused into his mind such an uncommon share of its etherial spirit to remain unemployed, nor bestowed on him his genius unaccompanied by the corresponding duty of devoting it to the common good. To have framed a constitution, was showing only, without realizing, the general happiness. This great work remained to be done; and America, steadfast in her preference, with one voice summoned her beloved Washington, unpractised as he was in the duties of civil administration, to execute this last act in the completion of the national felicity. Obedient to her call, he assumed the high office with that self-distrust peculiar to his innate modesty, the constant attendant of pre-eminent virtue. What was the burst of joy through our anxious land on this exhilirating event, is known to us all. The aged, the young, the brave, the fair, rivalled each other in demonstrations of their gratitude; and this high-wrought, delightful scene was heightened in its effect by the singular contest between the zeal of the bestowers and the avoidance of the receiver of the honors bestowed. Commencing his administration, what heart is not charmed with the recollection of the pure and wise principles announced by himself as the basis of his political life? He best understood the indissoluble union between virtue and happiness, between duty and advantage, between the genuine maxims of an honest and magnanimous policy, and the solid rewards of public prosperity and individual felicity. Watching with an equal and comprehensive eye over this great assemblage of communities and interests, he laid the foundations of our national policy in the unerring, immutable principles of morality, based on religion; exemplifying the pre-eminence of free government by all the attributes which win the affections of its citizens or command the respect of the world.

"O fortunatos dimium sua sibona norint!"

Leading through the complicated difficulties produced by previous obligations and conflicting interests, seconded by succeeding houses of Congress, enlightened and patriotic, he surmounted all original obstructions and brightened the path of our national felicity.

The presidential term expiring, his solicitude to exchange exaltation for humility returned with a force increased with increase of age; and he had prepared his farewell address to his countrymen, proclaiming his intention, when the united interposition of all around him, enforced by the eventful prospects of the epoch, produced a further sacrifice of inclination to duty. The election of president followed, and Washington, by the unanimous vote of the nation, was called to resume the chief magistracy. What a wonderful fixture of confidence! Which attracts most our admiration—a people so correct or a citizen combining an assemblage of talents forbidding rivalry, and stifling even envy itself? Such a nation deserves to be happy — such a chief must be for ever revered.

War, long menaced by the Indian tribes, now broke out; and the terrible conflict, deluging Europe with blood, began to shed its baneful influence over our happy land. To the first-outstretching his invincible arm, under the orders of the gallant Wayne, the American eagle soared triumphant through distant forests. Peace followed victory, and the melioration of the condition of the enemy followed peace. Godlike virtue, which uplifts even the subdued savage!

To the second he opposed himself. New and delicate was the conjuncture, and great was the stake. Soon did his penetrating mind discern and seize the only course continuing to us all the blessings enjoyed. He issued his proclamation of neutrality. This index to his whole subsequent conduct was sanctioned by the approbation of both houses of Congress, and by the approving voice of the people.

To this sublime policy he invariably adhered, unmoved by foreign intrusion — unshaken by domestic turbulence.

> "Justum et tenacem propositi virum,
> Non civium ardor prava jubentium,
> Non vultus instantis tyranni
> Mente quatit solida."

Maintaining his pacific system at the expense of no duty, America, faithful to herself and unstained in her honor, continued to enjoy the delights of peace, while afflicted Europe mourns in every quarter under the accumulated miseries of an unexampled war — miseries in which our happy country must have shared had not our pre-eminent Washington been as firm in council as he was brave in the field.

Pursuing steadfastly his course, he held safe the public happiness, preventing foreign war and quelling internal disorder, till the revolving period of a third election approached, when he executed his interrupted, but inextinguishable, desire of returning to the humble walks of private life.

The promulgation of his fixed resolution stopped the anxious wishes of an affectionate people from adding a third unanimous testimonial of their unabated confidence in the man so long enthroned in their hearts. When, before, was affection like this exhibited on earth? Turn over the records of Greece — review the annals of mighty Rome — examine the volumes of modern Europe — you search in vain. America and her Washington only affords the dignified exemplification.

The illustrious personage, called by the national voice in succession to the arduous office of guiding a free people, had no difficulties to encounter. The amicable effort of settling our difficulties with France, begun by Washington and pursued by his successor in virtue as in station, proving abortive, America took measures of self-defence. No sooner was the public mind roused by a prospect of danger than every eye was turned to the friend of all, though secluded from public view and gray in public service. The virtuous veteran, following his plough,* received the unexpected summons with mingled emotions of indignation at the unmerited ill-treatment of his country, and of a determination once more to risk his all in her defence.

The annunciation of these feelings in his affecting letter to the president, accepting the command of the army, concludes his official conduct.

First in war, first in peace, and first in the hearts of his countrymen, he was second to none in the humble and endearing scenes of private life; uniform, dignified, and commanding, his example was as edifying to all around him as were the effects of that example lasting.

To his equals he was condescending; to his inferiors, kind; and to the dear object of his affections, exemplarily tender; correct throughout, vice shuddered in his presence, and virtue always felt his fostering hand; the purity of his private character gave effulgence to his public virtues.

His last scene comported with the whole tenor of his life. Although in extreme pain, not a sigh, not a groan escaped him;

---

* General Washington, though opulent, gave much of his time and attention to practical agriculture.

and with undisturbed serenity he closed his well-spent life. Such was the man America has lost—such was the man for whom our nation mourns.

Methinks I see his august image, and hear falling from his venerable lips these deep-sinking words:—

"Cease, sons of America, lamenting our separation. Go on and confirm, by your wisdom, the fruits of our joint councils, joint efforts, and common dangers; reverence religion; diffuse knowledge throughout your lands; patronize the arts and sciences; let liberty and order be inseparable companions. Control party spirit, the bane of free government; observe good faith to, and cultivate peace with, all nations; shut up every avenue to foreign influence; contract rather than extend national connections; rely on yourselves only; be Americans in thought, word, and deed. Thus will you give immortality to that union which was the constant object of my terrestrial labors; thus will you preserve undisturbed, to the latest posterity, the felicity of a people to me most dear; and thus will you supply (if my happiness is now ought to you) the only vacancy in the round of pure bliss high Heaven bestows."

NOTE VII.—PAGE 516.

ORIGINAL PORTRAITS OF WASHINGTON.

As Mr. Custis, in his chapter on the *Portraits of Washington*, has omitted several originals, it is proposed, in as brief space as possible in the following article, to notice all that are well authenticated, and in the order in which they were painted.

I. Charles Willson Peale painted the first portrait of Washington, in May, 1772. It was done at Mount Vernon; and, at the same time, he painted portraits in miniature of all the rest of the family. The original study of Washington was made of small size. The finished picture, full size, now at Arlington House, is a copy of it. It is a three-quarter length, and represents Washington in the costume of a Virginia colonel. The study was afterward arranged in the continental costume, and is now in possession of Charles S. Ogden, Esq. of Philadelphia.

II. Peale painted a half-length portrait of General and Mrs. Washington, in the summer of 1776, for John Hancock; also a miniature of Mrs. Washington.

III. In December, 1777, Peale completed a miniature of the general for Mrs. Washington. It was begun at the close of October. While sitting for it, in a farm-house near Skippack Creek, in Pennsylvania, the general (who occupied the side of a bed, and the artist the only chair in the room) received despatches, advising him of the capture of Burgoyne. He glanced at them, and then remained, apparently unconcerned, until the sitting was finished. That miniature is published in Irving's Life of Washington, under the erroneous impression that it is a portrait of Washington at the age of twenty-five years. Of this picture, Peale made several copies.

IV. Peale painted a whole-length miniature of Washington, in 1778, for Lafayette; also,

V. A whole length, full size, for the state of Maryland; also,

VI. A whole length, full size for the state of Pennsylvania. A copy of the one painted for Maryland, is in the patent-office at Washington city.

VII. In 1782, Peale painted a full-size head of Washington, and,

VIII. At Rocky Hill, near Princeton, in New Jersey, in the autumn of 1783, he painted a full length for the College of New Jersey, to occupy a frame that had contained a portrait of George the Second. The picture of the king was destroyed by an American cannon-ball that passed through one of the college buildings in which the portrait hung, during the battle of Princeton, in 1777. That portrait of Washington yet occupies the frame that surrounded the king's portrait. It is in Nassau Hall at Princeton.

IX. Joseph Wright, a young painter, made a half-length portrait of Washington at Rocky Hill, in the autumn of 1783. He carried a letter of introduction to the commander-in-chief, from Doctor Franklin. That portrait is in the possession of the Powell family, near Philadelphia. It was presented to Mrs. Elizabeth Powell, by General Washington, she being his particular friend. Wright also painted,

X. A portrait of Washington for the Count de Solms. It was finished in 1784.

XI. William Dunlap also painted a portrait of Washington in the autumn of 1783, at Rocky Hill. He had only one sitting. It was a failure. That picture is in the possession of Doctor Ellis, of New York city.

XII. Robert Edge Pine, an English artist, painted Washington at Mount Vernon, in 1785. That picture is in the possession of J. Carson Brevoort, Esq., of Bedford, Long Island.

XIII. In the autumn of the same year, Houdon, a celebrated portrait sculptor, from France, modelled a bust of Washington in clay, at Mount Vernon, and afterward executed a full-length statue of him, for the state capitol, at Richmond, Virginia, by order of the legislature of that commonwealth.

XIV. In 1786, Peale painted a head of Washington, from life, for his own gallery. His brother, James, copied it on a larger canvass, and added the figure in military costume, and an attendant and horse in the background. It is in the possession of James Lennox, Esq., of New York city.

XV. On the first of October, 1789, Washington gave John Ramage, an Irish artist, a sitting of two hours. Ramage made a portrait of him in miniature for Mrs. Washington.

XVI. Three days afterward, he gave one sitting to the Marchioness de Brienne, sister of the Count de Moustier, the French minister, to complete a miniature profile of him, " which," he says, in his diary, " she had begun from memory, and had made exceedingly like the original." This was afterward engraved in Paris. She also painted a miniature profile of Washington and Lafayette, together, in medallion form, on copper, and presented the picture to Washington. It is now at Arlington House.

XVII. On the third of November, 1789, while on his eastern tour, Washington sat two hours to Mr. Gulligher, a Boston painter, who had a commission from Mr. Samuel Breck, of that city. Washington was then at Portsmouth, New Hampshire. Gulligher had followed him, and first made a sketch of him by stealth, while the general was in the chapel of Mr. Buckminster. He then obtained a sitting, and destroyed his stolen sketch. That portrait is in the possession of Edward Belknap, Esq., of New York.

XVIII. On the twenty first of December, 1789, Washington sat three hours to Edward Savage, an English painter, who had been commissioned to execute a portrait of him, for Harvard college, at Cambridge, in Massachusetts. Savage was then a resident of New York. On the twenty-eighth, Washington recorded in his diary, " Sat all the forenoon for Mr. Savage, who was taking my portrait." On the sixth of January, he gave him the last sitting. That portrait is now at Harvard.

XIX. In February, 1790, Colonel John Trumbull painted Washington's portrait. His object was to make an equestrian picture. He also was preparing to paint his historical pictures of the battles of Trenton and Princeton, in which Washington was engaged. Washington rode out with Trumbull once or twice, that the painter might catch his appearance on horseback. Trumbull, who was near-sighted, always painted his studies small. In that way he portrayed Washington on this occasion, and afterward painted the full length, standing by a horse, which is now in the governor's room, in the City Hall, New York. In 1792, Trumbull painted several full lengths of Washington. For his first and second pictures only did he procure a sitting. All the others were copies.

XX. Early in 1791, Archibald Robertson, a Scotchman, painted Washington and his wife, in miniature, and then painted a larger portrait for the Earl of Buchan, Robertson having been commissioned by the earl to procure one for his collection at Dryburgh Abbey.

XXI. In 1792, Joseph Cerracchi, an Italian sculptor, modelled a bust of Washington, from life, and repeated it in colossal size. These he took to Europe, and executed in marble. One, of the colossal size, was brought to this country by Richard W. Meade, of Philadelphia. Congress purchased it for four thousand dollars. It was destroyed when the Congress library was burnt, in December, 1851. A copy of it is in the gallery of the Pennsylvania Academy of Fine Arts; another is in the private gallery of Gouveneur Kemble, Esq., of Cold Spring, New York.

XXII. In 1795, Washington sat to Adolph Ulric Wirtmuler, a Swede, and native of Stockholm. It is believed that he had only one sitting; and as a likeness, the picture is considered, in many respects, a failure. Washington is represented with a lace-frilled shirt bosom, an article he never wore. His ruffles were always fine, but plain. The picture it is believed, was purchased by Washington, and presented by him to the late Mr. Cazenove, who took it to Switzerland. It is now in possession of Charles Augustus Davis, Esq., of New York city. An engraving of it appears in the first volume of Irving's Life of Washington.

XXIII. In September, 1795, Rembrandt Peale, son of Charles Willson Peale, obtained from Washington three sittings, of three hours each, and completed a study, from which, in connection with a portrait of his father, and Houdon's bust, he painted a portrait which was pronounced by the relatives and intimate friends of Washington, the best likeness of the first president that was ever painted. Congress purchased it for two thousand dollars, and it now occupies a place over the vice-president's chair, in the senate chamber at Washington city. Mr. Peale (who is yet [1859] living at the age of nearly eighty-two years) was then very young, and his father, to keep him in countenance, painted a portrait of the president at the same time.

XXIV. That portrait, by the elder Peale, is now in the Bryan Gallery, New York city.

XXV. At the same time, James Peale, a brother of Charles Willson Peale, painted a miniature of him, and

XXVI. Another member of the family, made a pencil sketch of the president, in profile.

XXVII. Washington sat to Gilbert Stuart, the eminent portrait painter, on the same days when he sat to Rembrandt Peale. Stuart was not well satisfied with his own performance. He made five copies, and finally sold the original to Winstanley, an English landscape painter, for two hundred dollars. Winstanley took it to England. It was there bought by Mr. John Vaughan, who brought it to Philadelphia, and it is now in possession of Joseph Harrison, Esq., of that city.

XXVIII. Stuart then procured other sittings, that he might paint a portrait for Mrs. Washington. The head only was finished in the winter of 1795-'96, and so the picture yet remains. It belongs to the Boston Athenæum, and is the so-called *standard head* of Washington when president.

XXIX. Stuart's full-length portrait of Washington, painted for the Marquis of Lansdowne, in the spring of 1796, can hardly be classed among originals, for Washington gave him only one sitting. The head was copied from his second picture; and a small man named W. R. Smith, with whom Stuart boarded in Philadelphia, stood for the figure. The extended hand of Washington, was painted from a wax cast of Stuart's own hand, which was much smaller than Washington's.

XXX. The last sitting Washington ever gave to a painter, was in 1796, when James Sharpless, an English artist, then in Philadelphia, made an admirable profile likeness of him, in crayon. Sharpless also painted a profile, in crayon, of Mrs. Washington, of these he made several copies. His wife also copied that of Washington, in water-color. The originals are at Arlington House. They have been pronounced by those of the Washington family competent to judge, admirable likenesses. Engravings from them are published in a work by the writer, entitled *Mount Vernon and its Associations*.

ANALYTICAL INDEX.

ADAMS, John, appoints Washington to the chief command of the army 327
inauguration of, as president..... 433
Adlum, Major, his account of Smallwood's regiment.............. 264
Agnew, General James, killed at Germantown 204
Agriculture, Washington on....... 595
Alexandria, Washington's visit to .. 450
martial exhibition at............ 450
Allen, Colonel Ethan, and Rivington 297
Allied armies, Chevalier de Barras sends vessels for 240
Allies prepare to attack New York . 230
march for the South............ 230
move against the British at Yorktown 240
Amoskeag Veterans, visit of, to Mount Vernon 62
Ancestors of Washington......125, 129
Anderson, Mrs., nurse of Eleanor Parke Custis 39
André, Major, theatrical preparations of 368
Anecdote of Annapolis race-course. 499
Bishop, body-servant of Washington.................. 377
Custis, Daniel Parke........... 497
Hartley, Colonel................ 305
hunting-shirt fellows............ 268
Lafayette 248
Lee, Henry, when at college..... 356
Lee, Richard Henry............ 331
Mossom, Rev. David............ 503
Tarleton, Colonel............. 253
Vulcan, a French hound........ 388
Washington and his mother's blooded horse 132
Annapolis, old capital of Maryland. 154
anecdote of race-course at....... 499
Arlington Spring, annual gatherings at 64
Armies, allied, prepare to attack New York 230
leave the Hudson for the South... 232
Army, British, at Germantown, ready to retreat 207
lay down their arms at Yorktown 247

Arnold, Benedict, expedition of, across the wilderness to Quebec 267, 309
his invasion of Virginia 232, 333
Asia, British ship-of-war, at New York 342
Asses, presented to Washington by the king of Spain and by Lafayette.................. 455
Atlee, Samuel Y., Custis's letter to. 408

Bacon, rebellion of............... 13
Ball, Colonel William, ancestor of Washington's mother......... 129
Balls, birth-night, and the theatre... 364
Bank of North America 350
Bard, Doctor, attends President Washington 398
Barfleur, battle of, with the Ville de Paris 238
Hood, Sir Samuel, commander of the 238
Barras, Chevalier de, arrival of, in the Chesapeake.............. 239
sends vessels for the allied armies 240
Barren Hill, affair at 260
Allen McLane, at.............. 260
retreat of Life-Guard from 261
Barton, Colonel William, in debtors' prison 329
Barter, Philip, agreement of, with Washington to abstain from liquor 445
Battle of the Brandywine 170
Eutaw Springs 359
Germantown 193
King's Mountain................ 272
Long Island................265, 344
Monmouth 211
Princeton 179
Battles of Saratoga and Germantown, effects of 217
Bauman, Major................. 401
Baylor, Lieutenant-Colonel, massacre of corps of.............. 259
seeks an interest in a privateer... 545
Billy, Washington's huntsman and favorite servant.............. 157
in danger at Monmouth..... . 224

	PAGE
Billy, a diplomat	379
Biographical sketch of Cadwalader, General John	212
Carroll, Right Rev. John	173
Craik, Dr. James	474
De Grasse	233
Gallatin, Albert	351
Greene, General	323
Griffith, Rev. David	291
Hartley, Colonel Thomas	307
Haslet, Colonel	186
Humphreys, Colonel	373
Izard, Ralph	485
Knapp, Uzal	262
Lamb, Colonel John	242
Lee, Henry	356
Mercer, General	183
Mifflin, Thomas	403
Molly, Captain	225
Morgan, Daniel	308
Nash, General	204
Nelson, Governor	339
Peale, Charles Willson	518
Pulaski, Count Casimir	195
Putnam, Israel	282
Rivington, James	293
Rush, Dr. Benjamin	186
Rush, Hon. Richard	184
Scott, General Charles	414
Smith, Samuel Stanhope	77
Stockton, Richard	177
Stuart, Gilbert Charles	520
Tarleton, Colonel	252
Thomson, Charles	382
Trumbull, Governor	281
Trumbull, John, the painter	285
Trumbull, Jonathan	174
Washington, Bushrod	470
Washington, William	354
White, Right Rev. William	173
Williams, Otho Holland	355
Bird, Lieutenant, killed at Germantown	204
Birth of George Washington Parke Custis	33
Birth-night balls and the theatre	364
Birth-night ball, last one attended by Washington	366
Birth-night ode	365
Bishop, Washington's oldest body-servant	158
too old for service in war	161
his character	161
in the battle of the Monongahela	374
commended to Washington	375
at Mount Vernon and in the Revolution	376
anecdote of	377
Blenheim, news of the battle of, carried to Queen Anne by Colonel Parke	23

	PAGE
Blooded horse belonging to Washington's mother, anecdote respecting	132
Blueskin, Washington's hunting horse	387
Boquet, Colonel	267
Boston, siege of	280
Botetourt, governor of Virginia	154, 396
Botta, Charles, his estimate of Washington's achievements	190
Braddock, General, at the battle of the Monongahela	374
commends Bishop to Washington	375
death of	376
Brandywine, battle of	170
Breck, Samuel, letter of, concerning a dinner-party in Boston	365
Brienne, Madame de, profiles of Washington and Lafayette by	517
Brown, Doctor, called to see Washington	475
Burnaby, Rev. Andrew, account of his travels in Virginia	166
Burr, Colonel Aaron	345
Busts of Washington and Hamilton	525
Byrd, Colonel William	15
letters of	26–33
son of, Washington's rival in horses	396
Cabal, Conway's	277
Cadwalader, General John	212
Calvert, Eleanor, wife of John Parke Custis	33
Calvert family, Hope Park the residence of	114
Cambridge, headquarters at	273
Campbell, Major, British officer at Yorktown	241
Camp, Mrs. Washington in	138
Cannon, French, in the arsenal at Richmond	239
Canova, statue of Washington by	525
Carrington, Mrs., letter of, respecting the domestic life of Mrs. Washington	510
Carroll, Right Rev. John, D.D.	173
Cary, one of Washington's servants, death of	451
Cerracchi, busts of Washington and Hamilton, by	525
Chamberlayne, Colonel, introduces Washington to Mrs Custis	499
Charleston, siege and surrender of	334
Chesapeake, arrival of the Chevalier de Barras in the	239
Chew's house at Germantown	198
Church, Washington a communicant of the Protestant Episcopal	173
Cincinnati, society of the	409
on national anniversaries	429
City Tavern, at Philadelphia	404

INDEX.

	PAGE
Clarke, the maker of Washington's coach	424
Clarke, Washington's watch-maker, in Philadelphia	454
Clinton, General Sir Henry, successor of General Howe	211
orders of, to Cornwallis	231
Coachmen of Washington, John Fagan and John Kruse	424, 426
Cobb, Colonel, at Yorktown	242
Cochran, Colonel, British officer at Yorktown	244
daring exploits of, and death	245
Colfax, William, commandant of Washington's Life-Guard	259
College (Columbia), King's	340
Colors, delivery of British, to Americans at Yorktown	249
Confederation, Articles of	381
Congress, Continental, first one in 1774	331
anecdote of R. H. Lee in connection with	331
Congress, Federal, its first session in New York, the seat of government	287
thanks of, to Washington and his soldiers for conduct at Monmouth	227
proceedings of, in relation to Washington's death	478
Constitution, federal, formation of	349
Convention of states proposed, to amend Articles of Confederation	348
adopt a federal constitution	349
Conway's cabal	277
Cook, Hercules, Washington's chief	422
Cornwallis, Earl	189
at Williamsburg, Jamestown, and Yorktown	232
earth-retreat of, at Yorktown	244
contemplates flight from Yorktown	245
surrender of, at Yorktown	247
with Washington at Yorktown	249
entertained at dinner by Washington	250
in Virginia	334
in chief command in the Carolinas	334
Correspondence between Washington and George Washington Parke Custis	73
Correspondence between Washington and John Parke Custis	533–570
Cotton-plant, views of Alexander Hamilton respecting the	341
Councils of war, held at Valley Forge and at Hopewell, New Jersey	212
Cowpens, Morgan at the	320
Craik, Dr. James, attends General Nash at Germantown	203

	PAGE
Craik, Dr. James, refers to Indian prophecy, at Monmouth	223
accompanied Washington to the Ohio in 1770	300
effect of the Indian prophecy on the mind of	305
"Crisis," by Thomas Paine	220
Cropper, Colonel, anecdote of	170
Cully, his recollections of Washington's marriage	501
Custis, Daniel Parke, and Evelyn Byrd	18
loves Martha Dandridge	19
marriage of	19
death of	20, 496
anecdote of	497
children of	496
Custis, Eleanor Parke, and George Washington Parke	394
Custis, Fanny Parke, marriage of	18
Custis, George Washington Parke, birth of	33
adopted by Washington	38
indulged by his grandmother	38
appointed Cornet	51
made aid-de-camp to General Pinckney	51
residence of, at Mount Vernon after Washington's death	52
marriage of	52
remembrance of, in Washington's will	52
children of	56
employment of leisure hours of	58
drama written by	59
letters to his wife	58–60
his talent for oratory	60
oration of, on the occasion of the death of General Lingan	61, 571
oration of, on the Russian victories	61, 585
letter to, from the Russian minister	61
speech of, at Washington's tomb, before the Amoskeag Veterans	64
interest of, in agricultural affairs	66
a volunteer in 1812	66
with Lafayette in 1824, '25	66
presents a ring to Lafayette at Washington's tomb	67, 591
his "Conversations with Lafayette"	68
painting by	68
death and funeral of	69
notice of in the National Intelligencer	71
personal appearance of	72
letter of, respecting Mrs Washington	408
Custis, Major-General John, collector of customs	13
his will	14
his children	14

INDEX.

Custis, Major-General John, marriage of, to Fanny Parke 15
   love-letter of, to Fanny Parke.... 16
   inscription on the tomb of....... 17
Custis, John Parke, marriage of, to Eleanor Calvert 33, 37
   at college in New York........... 37
   children of 37
   sickens at Yorktown, in camp.254, 504
   dies at Eltham 38, 255, 505
Custis, Mrs., character of, delineated 53
   death of 56
Custis, Mrs. Martha, marriage of, with Washington............. 21
   death of the daughter of 21

Dandridge, Miss Martha.......... 19
   marriage of, to Daniel Parke Custis 20, 496
   children of 20
"Darby's Return," performed before Washington 367
Davies, Rev. Samuel, his prophetic allusion to Washington....... 304
Davis, Tom, Washington's huntsman 457
   canvass-back ducks shot by...... 458
Death of Braddock............... 376
   Cary, one of Washington's servants, at the age of one hundred and fourteen years........... 451
   Cochran, Colonel, at Yorktown.. 245
   Custis, Daniel Parke.........20, 496
   Custis, George Washington Parke 69
   Custis, John Parke, at Eltham..................38, 255, 505
   Custis, Mrs. G. W. P........... 56
   Fauntleroy, Captain, at Monmouth 221
   Leslie, Captain, son of the earl of Levin 187
   Mercer, General Hugh... 183
   Monckton, Colonel.............. 221
   Nash, General 203
   Parke, Colonel Daniel.......... 25
   Washington, Lear's narration of . 472
   Henry Lee's oration on 360, 479, 615
   proceedings of Congress in relation to...................... 479
Death-room, Washington's, group in 472
Debtors' prison, Robert Morris in.. 327
   Washington visits Morris in...... 327
   Colonel William Barton in 329
De Chastellux, Marquis, Mount Vernon spoken of, in Travels of, in America 167
   with Washington in Virginia 235
Declaration of Independence, notice of some signers of............ 395
Deer-park at Mount Vernon....... 389
De Grasse, Count, expected in Chesapeake bay 231
   sketch of...................... 233
   fleet of, in Chesapeake bay 233

De Grasse, Count, Washington's reception of 236
Despatch, important, to Governor Trumbull 283
D'Estaing, Count, commands a French fleet on the American coast 213
Dick, Doctor, called to see Washington.......................... 475
Domestic life of Washington, from 1759 to 1775 464
   of Mrs. Washington 510
Drama written by John Parke Custis 59
Drawing-rooms of Mrs. Washington 395, 408
Dunlap, William, quoted from..... 367
Dunmore, Lord, marauding expeditions of..................... 333
Dutchmen as soldiers, Morgan's opinion of................... 309

Echard, Mrs Susan R, description of the scene at Washington's valedictory 434
Eden, Sir Robert, governor of Maryland......................... 154
Elk, Head of, combined armies at.. 239
Eltham, death of John Parke Custis at.....................38, 255, 505
Emigrants, distinguished French, sought the protection of the president 448
Erskine, Lord, letter of, to Washington........................... 528
Essays, political, by churchmen, answered by Hamilton.......... 341
Ethan Allen and Rivington 297
Eutaw Springs, battle at.......... 359
Everett, Edward, his remarks on the removal of Washington's remains 442
Eyes of Washington, color of the.. 527

Facsimile of surveys by Washington............................ 445
Fagan, John, Washington's coachman.......................... 424
Father Jack, Washington's fisherman.......................... 456
Fauntleroy, Captain, death of, at Monmouth 221
Federal Congress, notice of 287, 395
Federal constitution, adoption of ... 349
"Federalist," writers of the........ 349
Ferguson, Major Patrick, killed at King's mountain.............. 272
Fifer-boy, informs Washington of the retreat of Lee............ 217
Fish, Major, at Yorktown... 241
Fish, Nicholas, his account of a dinner in Paris 274

INDEX.

Fitzgerald, Colonel, his account of Washington in the field at Princeton 190
  on the battle-field at Princeton... 192
  at Alexandria 452
Forts Mercer and Mifflin.......... 194
"Forty-five," rebellion of 270
"Forty-twa," Highland regiment, called the 270
Fox, kind of, hunted in Virginia... 387
  the famous black................ 388
  the red 388
France, expected war with........ 447
  naval war with................. 447
Frederick the Great, his opinion of Washington's exploits........ 190
French and Indian war, origin of... 158
French fleet and army come to America 229
Frestel, M., young Lafayette's tutor, at Mount Vernon 448
Fraunces, Samuel, Washington's steward 411
  keeps tavern in New York....... 420
  extravagance of, rebuked by Washington 421

Gallatin, Albert, his eulogy of Hamilton 351
  biographical sketch of 351
Gates, General, his praise of Morgan's corps................... 268
Germantown, battle of............ 193
  arrangement of attack upon..... 197
  Americans defeated at.......... 206
  effect of battle of.............. 206
  Washington and soldiers commended by Congress for conduct at 206
Gibbs, Caleb, commandant of Life-Guard 256
  Washington's letters to 258
Giles, Tommy.................... 413
Gordon, Doctor, relates what Washington said of bloody foot-prints of soldiers 210
Graves, Admiral, off the Capes of Virginia 238
Gray, General, at the battle of Germantown 203
Great Meadows, conflict at........ 159
Greene, General, at Germantown... 201
  biographical sketch of 323
  Washington's favorite officer..... 324
  Peale's picture of, at Valley Forge......................... 518
Greene, Rev. Ashbel, his recollections of Washington.......... 434
Griffith, Rev. David, warning of, given to Washington 290
  biographical sketch of 291
Griswold, Fort, massacre at 242

Grymes, Lieutenant, on the field at Germantown 196
Gurley, R. R., letter of, to Mrs. Lee concerning Mr. Custis........ 10

"Hail Columbia"................. 363
  its origin...................... 369
Hale, Sir Matthew, writings of, at Mount Vernon 171
Hamilton, Alexander, at Germantown 200
  at the battle of Monmouth...... 219
  at Yorktown.................... 240
  birthplace of.................... 340
  his arrival in New York......... 340
  views of, respecting the cotton-plant 341
  political essays by churchmen answered by................... 341
  thought of returning to the West Indies 342
  persuaded to stay in New York.. 342
  joins a volunteer corps.......... 342
  letter of, to Washington, before the battle of Long Island 343
  company of artillery of, join the continental army............. 344
  at the passage of the Raritan.... 344
  interview of, with Washington... 344
  with Washington 345
  dependence of Washington upon. 346
  retirement of, from Washington's family 346
  at the siege of Yorktown.... 240, 347
  retires from the army........... 348
  proposes a convention of the states to amend the Articles of Confederation.................... 348
  efforts of, in favor of the federal constitution 349
  recommended for secretary of the treasury 349
  his appointment 350
  eulogy of, by Gallatin 351
  his resignation of the office of secretary of the treasury......... 352
  his prediction respecting the constitution 352
Hampton, Washington and other officers at 235
Hands of Washington very large 523, 527
Hartley, Colonel, anecdote of...... 305
  notice of 307
Haslet, Colonel, death of.......... 186
  sketch of...................... 186
Hazlitt, sketch of Washington from the pen of.................... 430
Head of Elk, combined armies at.......................... 239
Headquarters of Washington, notice of remains of................. 273
  at Cambridge and Morristown... 273

	PAGE
Headquarters of Washington at Newburgh, West Point, and New Windsor	274
joy at, on seeing supplies coming from Connecticut	285
several of the buildings yet standing	288
Hercules, Washington's chief cook	422
Hessians at Yorktown	248
afraid of Morgan's riflemen	269
how they came to be in America	269
Holidays, national, salutes on	429
Home and household of Washington	400
Hood, Sir Samuel, commander of the Barfleur	238
Hope Park, residence of the Calvert family	114
Horses, Washington's	385
Houdon, his half bust of Washington	517
Hounds, Washington's	384
present of, to Washington from Lafayette	386
Howe, Sir William, army of, quartered at Germantown	194
Humphreys, Colonel, biographical sketch of	373
at Mount Vernon	373
one of Washington's secretaries	394
recites his poetry at night	399
Hunt at Mount Vernon	390
Hunting-shirt, the	264
Custis's remarks on	266
Washington's advocacy of it	266
"Hunting-shirt fellows," anecdote of	268
Huntsman, Tom Davis, Washington's	457
Inauguration of President Adams	433
Independent Blues of Alexandria, reviewed by Washington	452
Indian prophecy	223, 300
related by Dr. Craik	304
Indian war in the West	416
Intelligencer, National, Custis's "Recollections" printed in	9
Izard, Ralph, resemblance of, to Washington	485
notice of	485
Jackson, Major, Washington's aid-de-camp	394
Jackson, one of Washington's chargers	425
Jefferson, Thomas, his opinion of Washington	214
Jersey prison-ship, General Lingan among the sufferers in the	574
Kanawha, Washington's visit to the, in 1770	300
King's Mountain, battle of	272
Major Patrick Ferguson killed at	272

	PAGE
King of Spain, asses presented to Washington by	455
Knapp, Uzal, last survivor of Washington's Life-Guard	262
sketch of	262
Knowlton, Colonel, his military corps	256
Knox, General, at Germantown	200
opposed to leaving Chew's house in the rear	200
proposes the society of the Cincinnati	409
Kruse, John, Washington's coachman	425
Lady Washington's dragoons, Baylor's corps	259
Lafayette, Marquis de, visit of, to the United States	67
at the tomb of Washington	67, 591
visit of, to Washington's mother	144
at Mount Vernon	144
in council of war, near Monmouth	212
in Virginia	232, 334
refuses the honor of capturing Cornwallis	234
influence of, with De Grasse	237
wife of	237
anecdote of	248
at Barren Hill	260
imprisonment and exile of	449
asses presented to Washington by	455
astonishment of, at the size of his Virginia recruits	485
urged Trumbull to paint an equestrian portrait of Washington	529
ring presented to, by Custis	591
Lafayette, George Washington, letter of, to Mr. Custis	67
residence of, at Mount Vernon	96, 448
his departure from the United States	449
Lamb, Colonel John, sketch of	242
Lansdowne, Marquis of, portrait of Washington painted for	522, 624
Land speculation, career of Robert Morris and others in	326
Last hours of Washington	472
Lauk, Mr., last survivor of Morgan's rifle corps	309
Laurens, Colonel John, at the battle of Germantown	199
sketch of	241
at Yorktown	241, 348
Lear, Tobias	394
his account of Washington's reception of the news of St. Clair's defeat	418
Washington's secretary	472
his narrative of Washington's death	472
Ledyard, Colonel, death of	578

INDEX

	PAGE
Lee, General Charles, against proposed attack on Clinton	212
his misconduct at the battle of Monmouth	219
his interview with Washington at Monmouth	293
Lee, Henry, letter of, to young Custis	57
sketch of	356
anecdote of, when at college	356
exploit of, at Paulus's Hook	357, 562
legion of, in the South	358
officers of	358
exploit of, near Valley Forge	358
at Eutaw Springs	359
retires from the army	359
commander of troops to put down the "Whiskey Insurrection"	359
a delegate in Congress	359
his oration on the occasion of the death of Washington	360, 479, 615
misfortunes of	361
death of	361
character of	361
his impromptu eulogium of Patrick Henry	362
his words concerning Washington	362
attachment of, to Washington	363
Lee, Mrs. Mary Custis, wife of Colonel R. E. Lee	56
Lee, Richard Henry, and the Continental Congress	331
Leslie, Captain, son of the earl of Levin, death of	187
Letter to author of "Recollections" concerning an officer killed at Germantown	205
Letters of Byrd, Colonel William	27–33
Baron von Washington respecting his family	126
Custis, Daniel Parke, to his wife	58–60
respecting Mrs Washington	408
Custis, G W. P., to Gideon Snow	40
to Washington	73–116
Custis, John Parke and Washington	533–570
Custis, Major-General John, to Fanny Parke	16
Earl of Buchan to Mrs Washington	511
Gurley, R R., to Mrs Lee respecting Mr G. W. P. Custis	10
Hamilton to Washington, before the battle of Long Island	343
Lafayette, George Washington to Mr G. W. P. Custis	67
Lee, Henry, to young Custis	57
Lord Erskine to Washington	528
M'Henry, James, to G W. P. Custis	51
Madison to Mrs. G. W. P. Custis	65, 66
Letters of Parke, Colonel Daniel, to his daughter	15, 23
Potter, Colonel, respecting speech of Mr. Custis	64
Russian minister to G. W. P. Custis	61
Snow, Gideon, to G. W. P. Custis	39
Waller, Benjamin, to Mrs. Martha Custis	498
Washington to Benedict Calvert	34
Nelly Custis	41
Lawrence Lewis	45, 46, 49
G. W. P. Custis	73–116
Mr M'Dowell, president of college at Annapolis	98
deceptive	233
Caleb Gibbs	258
respecting a dancing assembly at Alexandria	366
Mr. Rumney	372
copied by Rawlins, not to be found	438
John Parke Custis	533–570
Washington, Mrs, respecting the remains of her husband	441
to J. P Custis and his wife	547
Levees, kind of persons who attended the	409
Lewis, Lawrence, Washington's letters to	45, 46, 49
Washington's secretary	394
marriage of, to Nelly Custis, at Mount Vernon	450
Lewis, Mrs. Eleanor Parke Custis	39
her beauty and character	40
Lexington, news of battle of	282
events connected with battle of	282
Life at Mount Vernon	370
Life-Guard, Washington's	256
how organized	256
historical sketch of	257
uniform of	257
reorganization of	258
William Colfax, commandant of	259
at Monmouth	261
in the retreat from Barren Hill	261
Uzal Knapp, last survivor of	262
Life-pictures, outline	462
Lingan, General James M., Custis's oration on the death of	571
Liquor, agreement of Philip Barter with Washington, to abstain from	445
Long, Captain Gabriel, at Monmouth	262
captain in Morgan's regiment	311
Long Island, reference to battle of	247
battle of	265, 344
prisoners at	266
Louis Philippe, visit of, at Mount Vernon	418

	PAGE
M'Comb, Washington occupies the house of	400
M'Dowell, Mr., president of college at Annapolis, Washington's letter to	98
M'Fingal, quotation from	227
M'Henry, James, letter of, to G. W. P. Custis	51
M'Ivers, Mrs, accident to, at Mrs. Washington's reception	396
M'Lane, Allen, at Barren Hill	260
M'Pherson Blues, a guard of honor	479
only survivors of	479
Madison, President, letters of, to Mr. G. W. P. Custis	65, 66
Magnolia	426
Marbois, M., dinner given by, to Americans in Paris	274
Marquées, Washington's description of	279
where made, and by whom	280
Marriage, Cully's recollections of Washington's	501
Custis, Fanny Parke	18
Custis, John Parke, to Eleanor Calvert	33, 37
Custis, Major-General John, to Fanny Parke	16
Custis, Mrs. Martha, with Washington	21, 502
Dandridge, Miss Martha, to Daniel Parke Custis	20, 496
Maryland, Annapolis, the old capital of	154
Massacre of corps of Lieutenant-Colonel Baylor	259
Mathews, Colonel, at Germantown	202
Matson's Ford	261
Mawhood, Colonel, regiment of, at Princeton	187
in battle at Princeton	191
Memoirs, Washington declines affording materials for his	437
Memoir of George Washington Parke Custis	172
Mercer, General Hugh, death of	180
monument to, ordered by Congress	182
son of, educated by the public	182
particulars of death of	184
monument in memory of	184
funeral ceremonies of	185
Merchantmen, armed, salutes of, before Mount Vernon	447
Mifflin, Thomas, on recruiting service	332
biographical sketch of	403
Militia, Washington's opinion of.	187, 538
Minuet, danced by Washington	366
Molly, Captain, at Monmouth	224
sketch of	225
exploits of	286

	PAGE
Monckton, Colonel, death of, at Monmouth	221
Monmouth courthouse, American army approach to	211
Monmouth, battle of	211
Monmouth, events on the field of	218
retreat of Americans at, checked	221
retreat of British from	226
Congress thanks Washington and soldiers for conduct at	227
night-scene in the commander-in-chief's tent, near	289
Monongahela, Braddock at the battle of the	374
Moore's house, at Yorktown, place where capitulation was agreed upon	253
Moreau, John B., his collection of Washington's portraits	480
Morgan, Daniel	308
his corps at Monmouth	262
his laugh at the Life-Guard	262
corps of, with Arnold at Quebec	267
riflemen of, made prisoners at Quebec	267
description of riflemen of	267
General Gates's praise of corps of	268
rifle corps of, how formed	270
biographical sketch of	308
accompanies Arnold across the wilderness	309
his opinion of "Dutchmen" as soldiers	309
personal reminiscence of	310
disobeys orders	313
interview of, with Washington	315
anticipating disgrace	317
Washington's forgiveness of	319
congratulated by officers	319
at the Cowpens	320
member of Congress	321
his opinion of Washington	322
demurs at General Lee's appointment	359
Morris, Robert	328
in Washington's camp at Dobb's Ferry	231
loans money of a Quaker	294
his financial aid to the colonies	325
one of Washington's best-loved friends	325
his services in the cause of his country	325
Washington's favorite guest	326
his inclination to speculate	326
in prison, visited by Washington	327
how treated by his countrymen	328
appearance of, in prison	328
recommends Hamilton for secretary of the treasury	349
establishes Bank of North America	350

INDEX.

Morris, Robert, Washington's welcome guest.................... 430
Morristown, camp at, alarmed..... 139
   headquarters at............... 273
   location of headquarters at...... 275
Mossom, Rev. David, officiated at Washington's marriage....... 502
   anecdote of.................... 503
Mother of Washington, memoir of. 125
   ancestors of................... 129
   character of................... 130
   recollections of, by Lawrence Washington.................. 131
   residence of, during the war...... 135
   her patriotism.................. 137
   example of..................... 139
   foreign officers astonished at simple manners of............... 143
   her fear of lightning............ 141
   Washington's last visit to her.... 141
   visited by Lafayette............. 144
   personal appearance of.......... 146
   resemblance of daughter of, to the general..................... 147
   grave of, and monument to...... 148
Moulder, Captain, commands artillery at Princeton............. 191
   maker of Washington's tents.... 280
Mount Vernon, visit of Amoskeag Veterans to.................. 62
   Washington at................. 151
Mount Vernon, origin of the name of........................... 152
   spoken of by De Chastellux in his Travels..................... 167
   life at........................ 370
   improvements at............371, 449
   visit of Louis Philippe at....... 448
   visit of a German gentleman at.. 460
   associations of................. 462
   mansion of, described........... 503
   guests at...................... 505
Mules, extraordinary, raised by Washington................... 456
Munson, Dr. Eneas, his account of Washington at Yorktown..... 279
Musgrave, Lieutenant-Colonel, at battle of Germantown........ 198
Mysteries of the Revolution....... 289

Narraganset pony at Mount Vernon......................... 458
Nash, General, mortally wounded at Germantown................. 202
   death of...................... 203
   burial-place of................. 204
   monument to................... 204
Naval, engagement between English and French off Capes of Virginia....................... 239
Neely, Matthew, child of, in Ireland, named George Washington...... 172

Nelson, Mr., Washington's secretary 394
Nelson, Secretary, house of, at Yorktown, injured................ 244
Nelson, Thomas, notice of......... 330
   signer of the Declaration of Independence..................... 332
   active as a military officer....... 333
   sacrifices of, for his country..... 336
   at the siege of Yorktown........ 336
   patriotism of.................243, 336
   obtains money on his own security for public use................. 337
   house of...................... 337
   losses of, never made up by the government................... 338
   beloved by Washington......... 338
   his son made Washington's private secretary................ 338
   family of, left in poverty........ 339
   official career of................ 339
Nelson, war-horse of Washington at Yorktown.................... 249
   at Mount Vernon.............. 249
Newburgh, headquarters at, described...................... 274
   representation of, in Paris....... 274
New Windsor, headquarters at..... 274
Nicholas, Colonel John, of the Life-Guard....................... 262
Nicholas, Robert C., legal adviser of Mrs. Custis.................. 497
Nicholson John, in Walnut street prison....................... 328
Norfolk, ravages of British in neighborhood of.................... 334
North Lord, his reception of the news of Cornwallis's defeat.... 250

Ode, birth-night................. 365
Ogle, Governor, Washington procured deer from.............. 389
O'Hara, General, delivers Cornwallis's sword to Lincoln......... 248
Old Point Comfort, Washington and other officers at.............. 235
Oration of G. W. P. Custis on occasion of the death of Lingan.... 571
   in celebration of the Russian victories over Napoleon.......... 585
   of General Lee on the death of Washington.................. 615
Original portraits of Washington 516, 624
Outline life-pictures.............. 462

Paine, Thomas, author of "The Crisis"......................... 220
Paper-money, issues of, by Congress 335
   depreciation of................. 335
Parke, Colonel Daniel, letters of, to his daughter.................15, 23
   bearer of news of battle of Blenheim to Queen Anne.......... 23

	PAGE
Parke, Colonel Daniel, account of..	22
governor of Leeward Islands....	24
death of........................	25
will of.........................	26
Parliament, British, debates in, concerning cessation of the war...	250
Paulus's Hook, position of and events at 357,	562
Washington at	402
Peale, Charles Willson, description of his first portrait of Washington........................	516
Washington's full-length portrait by	518
biographical sketch of..........	518
his account of Washington's strength	519
Peale, James......................	524
Peale, Rembrandt, his recollections of Washington's valedictory...	434
portrait of Washington, by......	524
equestrian portrait of Washington, by	524
Piercy, Captain, commands Independent Blues at Alexandria..	452
Pepper, Mrs, letter of Colonel Custis to....................	18
Personal appearance of Washington	480
Peters, Richard, in Washington's camp at Dobbs's Ferry	231
Pinckney, Colonel, at Germantown.	200
his opinion of Washington's judgment	360
Poellnitz, Baron de, thrashing machine of.....................	167
Portraits of Washington, Moreau's collection of.................	480
general resemblance among the..	480
originals at Arlington House.....	516
an equestrian, by Trumbull......	519
by Charles Willson Peale.......	516
by Gilbert Charles Stuart	520
painted for Marquis of Lansdowne	522
by Wertmuller	526
notice of all the original........	624
Potter, Colonel, letter of, to Mr Lossing, concerning Mr. Custis's speech	64
Prescott, one of Washington's chargers....................	425
Presidency, first year of the.......	393
"President's March"	368
Presidential mansion, visiters at....	414
Pretender, Scotch, notice of	270
Princeton, battle of	179
Prison, Walnut street, Morris and his friends in	327
Prisoner for Debt, poem, by J. G. Whittier, extract from........	329
Prisoners, deposition of, taken at Yorktown...................	250

	PAGE
Privateering, Washington a speculator in the profits of 533,	545
Proctor, Colonel.............412,	429
Prophecy, Indian	300
Dr. Craik refers to, at Monmouth	223
Pulaski, Count, at battle of Germantown.........................	195
sketch of.......................	195
Putnam, Israel, hears of the battle of Lexington	282
biographical sketch of	282
Quakers opposed to the Revolution.	295
Quebec, Benedict Arnold's expedition to.................. 267,	309
Ramsay, Lieutenant-Colonel, at Monmouth.........	219
Rawlins, Albert, employed to copy Washington's letters...........	437
Recollections and private memoirs of Washington, author's preface to	121
Redoubt, British at Yorktown, taken by storm.....................	241
Reed, Colonel, at Germantown	200
Remains of Washington, remarks of Edward Everett respecting removal of.....................	442
final action of Congress respecting...........................	443
Retreat of American army at Monmouth	217
from Barren Hill................	261
Revolution, crowning event of.....	247
mysteries of the.........	289
Ricketts's opinion of Washington as a horseman	485
Rivington, James, biographical sketch of.....................	293
hated by the whigs.............	295
his secret service for Washington......................296,	299
Freneau's satire on.............	296
Rochambeau, Count, with Washington in Virginia............231,	235
Robert Morris....................	323
Rodney, Admiral, in West Indies ..	238
Rogers, Colonel	413
Ross, Mr, rewarded for finding a money-borrower	498
Rumney, Mr., letter of Washington to.....................171,	372
Rush, Dr. Benjamin, attends Captain Leslie	186
sketch of......................186	
Rush, Richard............178,	418
Russian minister, letter of, to G. W. P Custis...................	61
Russian victories, oration on, by G W. P. Custis	585

INDEX.

	PAGE
Sachem, Indian, meets Washington in the Ohio country and prophesies	302
St. Clair, General, defeat of	416
Washington's anger on hearing of defeat of	417
first interview of, with Washington after his defeat	419
St. Simon, Marquis de, at head of troops on De Grasse's fleet	233
Saratoga, influence in Europe of the victory at	208
Scott, General Charles	413
biographical sketch of	414
Servant, Billy, Washington's favorite	157, 224, 379
Bishop, Thomas, Washington's oldest	158, 161, 374, 377
Sharpless, profile likeness of Washington and G. W. Lafayette, by	517, 525
Sheep-shearing, annual, at Arlington House	583
Sherman, Roger	395
Siege of Boston	280
Charleston	334
Sigourney, Mrs, poem of, on the tomb of Washington's mother	149
Simcoe, Lieutenant-Colonel	201
Sinclair, Sir John, Washington's correspondence with	446
Sister of Washington (Mrs. Fielding Lewis), resemblance of, to her brother	147
Smallwood, Colonel, regiment of	189, 264
at battle of Long Island	265
Smith, Lieutenant-Colonel William S.	373
adventure of, with Bishop	377
Smith, Samuel Stanhope, president of college at Princeton	77
Smith, Stuart's manikin when painting the figure of Washington	521
Snow, Gideon, Custis's letter to	40
letter of, to Custis	39
Sportsman, Washington as a	384
Stable, Washington's, in Philadelphia	397
Stag, carcass of the Washington	391
Statue of Washington, by Canova	525
Stephen, General Adam, conduct of, at Germantown	196
Steuben, Baron, at Monmouth	223
in Virginia	334
Stewart, Colonel, at Monmouth	219
Stewart, General Walter	355, 404
Stockton, Richard, wife of	177
biographical sketch of	177
Strength of arm of Washington	519
Stuart, Dr. David, husband of Mr. Custis's mother	86

	PAGE
Stuart, Dr. David, Washington's letter to, concerning reception days	407
Stuart, Gilbert Charles, portraits of Washington by	520, 628
biographical sketch of	520
Sullivan, General, at Germantown	199
Surrender of Charleston	334
Surrender of Cornwallis's army at Yorktown	229, 247
Tarleton, Colonel, slighted at Yorktown	251
humiliated in the street at Yorktown	253
anecdote of	253
sketch of	253
Teeth, Washington lost his, in 1789	520
Theatre in New York, Washington's attendance at	367
Theatrical company, old American	367, 368
The retired president	433
Thomson, Charles, at Mount Vernon	382
sketch of	382
Tilghman, Lieutenant-Colonel, carries news of capture of Cornwallis to Congress	246
Tomb of Major-General John Custis, inscription on	17
of Washington, speech of G. W. P. Custis at	64, 591
Lafayette at the	591
Tomb for Washington, proposed	444
Tory, term of, how derived	332
Tour, Washington's, to the eastern states	398
Treason of General Lee	292
Treaty with France proclaimed at Valley Forge	278
Trenton, Washington's reception at	393
Trumbull, Governor, important despatch to	283
Trumbull, John, the artist	285
his equestrian portrait of Washington and its faithfulness	519, 520
Trumbull, Jonathan, admitted to president's house on Sunday evenings	174
important despatch to, from Washington	283
Welcome supplies from, at camp of Washington	285
Valedictory of President Washington, Mrs Echard's description of	434
Rembrandt Peale's recollections of	434
Valley Forge, American winter-quarters there	208
march of Americans to	209
headquarters at	275
sufferings of the American army at	276

INDEX.

Valley Forge, how the army at, obtained supplies................ 277
Vandeput, Captain, at New York.. 342
Vaults, old and new, at Mount Vernon...................... 439
Vergennes, Count de, feelings of, on hearing of the battle at Germantown...................... 208
Vessels, English, burned at Yorktown...................... 240
Ville de Paris 235
 battle of, with British ship Barfleur 238
Virginia, Benedict Arnold's invasion of......................232, 233
Vulcan, a French hound, anecdote of 388

Waller, Benjamin, letter of, to Mrs. Martha Custis................ 498
Walnut-street prison, John Nicholson in 328
Wansey, visit of, to Washington ... 408
War-tent, Washington's, at Arlington Spring 65
War-sword, Washington's......... 160
Washington, Baron Von, letter of, concerning his family......... 126
Washington, Bushrod 470
Washington, Fort, captured by the British and Hessians 344
Washington Lawrence............. 152
Washington, George, letter of, to Benedict Calvert, concerning the marriage of J. P. Custis...... 34
 adopts two of the children of J. P. Custis....................38, 255
 letter of, to Nelly Custis, concerning love and coquetry......... 41
 letter of, to Lawrence Lewis..... 45
 orders marriage license for Lawrence Lewis and Nelly Custis.. 45
 appointed commander-in-chief of the army in 1797.............. 46
 correspondence of....73, 467, 533, 570
 ancestors of 125
 birth-place of, marked 127
 displayed..................... 133
 appointment of, as commander-in-chief of American army in 1775. 134
 wife of, in camp................ 138
 anecdote of, respecting an alarm . 138
 visit of, to his mother........... 141
 dances a minuet 143
 last visit of, to his mother....... 145
 at Mount Vernon 151
 letter of, to his wife, announcing his appointment to the command of the army in 1775..... 151
 member of Virginia assembly.... 153
 his election expenses............ 153
 his personal appearance ..... { 155, 164, 385, 430 / 485, 487, 492

Washington, George, member of Continental Congress......... 155
 habits of, at Mount Vernon 156
 a surveyor..................... 156
 as a master of slaves 157
 aversion of, to medicine......... 162
 an early riser.................. 162
 ill health of, in French war...... 162
 his great labors 163
 his importations from London ... 163
 his appearance on horseback when abroad................. 164, 385
 his dress....................... 165
 his inspection of his stables 165
 called to command independent companies in 1774............ 165
 diet of........................ 166
 his agricultural improvements.... 167
 products of his estate........... 167
 Nelson, the favorite charger of. 166, 249
 on his farm 168
 dining hour of 169
 habits of, at dinner............. 169
 his invariable "Toast"..169, 250, 452
 habits of, in his family.......... 171
 child in Ireland named after him . 172
 an observer of the Sabbath...... 173
 a communicant of the Protestant Episcopal church............. 173
 his moral power and his sympathies 175
 Gouverneur Morris rebuked by... 175
 journey of, to seat of government a continued scene of triumph.. 176
 his opinion of militia........187, 538
 made dictator.................. 188
 in battle at Princeton........... 190
 approaching Germantown....... 194
 exposure of, at Germantown..... 201
 letter of, to Congress, concerning the battle of Germantown..... 207
 on the march to Valley Forge ... 209
 determines to attack Clinton..... 213
 summary of exploits of 215
 on the field of Monmouth 220
 exposure of, at Monmouth 222
 sends deceptive letters 233
 visits De Grasse's flag-ship 235
 at Williamsburg 240
 has domestic affliction 254
 at the death-bed of J. P. Custis. 255, 505
 journey of, to the Ohio in 1770 .. 300
 his defence of the soldiers' rights to land 300
 company with, in the Ohio country 302
 meets an Indian sachem in the Ohio country................. 302
 speech of Indian sachem respecting...................... 303
 clemency of................319, 320
 refuses to go into a land speculation with Robert Morris....... 326

INDEX. 643

	PAGE
Washington, George, advice of, to Robert Morris	326
commander-in-chief of the provisional army in 1798	327
visits Robert Morris in prison	327
happy in the selection of his officers	345
letter of, respecting a dancing assembly at Alexandria	366
his love of theatrical performances	366
at the theatre in New York	367
in retirement at Mount Vernon	370, 453, 464
resignation of commission of	370
life of, at Mount Vernon	371
drawings by	371
letter of, to Mr. Rumney, respecting paving-stone	372
at the battle of the Monongahela	375
called to convention of 1787	381
announcement to, of his election to the presidency of the United States	382, 467
as a sportsman	384
kennel of	384
horses and hounds of	385
appearance of, when hunting	385
hunting habits of	386
on horseback	386
last hunt of	389
reception of, at Trenton	393
inaugurated first president of the United States	393
residence of, in New York	394
levees of	396
severe illness of, in New York	398
attempted stealthy departure of, from New York in 1790	400
embarkation of, from New York in 1790	401
journey of, from New York to Mount Vernon in 1790	402
in Philadelphia and Mount Vernon	405
home and household of	406
public days of	406
exacts weekly reports from his agents	410
endeavors of, to avoid notoriety	411
anger of, on learning St. Clair's defeat	417
parting of, with his officers at New York in 1783	420
tour of, to southern states in 1791	424
punctuality of	427
personal description of	430, 487
private papers of	436
his farewell dinner	436
remains of, asked by government for interment under the capital	440
final action of Congress respecting remains of	443
surveys made by	445
facsimile of	445

	PAGE
Washington, George, rides of, over his estate	446
dines at Alexandria	451
reviews troops at Alexandria	452
habits of, respecting correspondence	454
once thrown from a horse	459
in the old French and Indian war	463
from 1759 till 1775 in domestic life and in continental Congress	464
as commander-in-chief of armies	464
his return from victory	464
in retirement	464
visited by Lafayette	465
in convention of states	466
president of the United States	468
last military command of	469
last employment of, at Mount Vernon	472
commencement of illness of	473
Lear's account of illness of	473
last night of the life of	475
calls for his wills	476
his death	476, 497, 510
interment of	477, 478
weight, size, form, and features of	481, 527
Trumbull's equestrian portrait of	481
examples of his power of arm	482, 483
power of the limbs and size of hands of	484
physiognomy of	485
personal appearance of, admired in New York in 1773	486
sketch of personal appearance of, by an unknown hand	487–490
awe and reverence inspired by	489
personal recollections of, by Sullivan	492
journey of, toward Williamsburg	499
first acquaintance of, with Mrs Custis	500
courtship and marriage of	500–502
call of, into public life in 1787	505
portraits of	516, 624
loss of the teeth of	520
anecdote of his sitting to Stuart	522
directions of, respecting management of his farms	595
Funeral oration, by General Lee, before Congress	615
Washington, Mrs., at headquarters	287
drawing-rooms of	395, 408
accident at drawing-room of	396
beloved in the army	403
Griswold statement respecting	408
narrow escape of, in a carriage	426
letter of, concerning the remains of her husband	441
an accomplished Virginian housewife	455

INDEX.

Washington, Mrs., grandchildren of, sent for on occasion of Washington's illness.............. 475
at the death-bed of her husband.. 477
ancestry and birth of............ 496
first marriage of................ 496
children of..................... 496
death of children of............ 496
death of husband of 497, 510
legal advisers of................ 497
first acquaintance of, with Washington..................... 499
in continental camp........ 503, 504
leaves home for public life in New York........................ 506
establishment of, in New York... 506
in public life in New York....... 507
renewals of acquaintance with... 507
attendance of, on religious services...................... 508
visits of old soldiers to.......... 508
retirement of, to domestic life.... 509
devotional practices of.......... 509
description of, in domestic life.... 510
yields the remains of her husband to the federal government..... 511
letter of condolence to, from the Earl of Buchan.............. 511
mode of life of, after her husband's death...................... 513
death of....................... 513
personal appearance of.......... 514
neatness of.................... 514
miniature of, worn by her husband 528
Washington, Mrs. Lund........... 39
Washington, William, sketch of.... 354
"Washington's March".......... 369
Watson, John F., erects monuments to Generals Nash and Agnew, and Lieutenant Bird.......... 204
Wayne, General Anthony......... 212
Wertmuller, portrait of Washington by.......................... 526
Westford, resident at Mount Vernon....................... 157

West Point, Washington at........ 274
Whig, term of, how derived....... 332
Whiskey insurrection, account of the........................ 359
White, Major, killed at Germantown...................... 199
White, Right Rev. William, D.D... 173
"*Widow of Malabar*," translation of, by Colonel Humphreys....... 399
Will, Washington's 439, 458
Williams, Otho Holland, biographical sketch of................ 355
Williams, artist in crayon, likeness of Washington by............ 523
Williamsburg, old capital of Virginia........................ 154
Wood, William B., in Walnut-street prison...................... 328

Yorktown, surrender at 229, 247
preparations for the siege of...... 230
attack upon, by the allies........ 240
effect of cannonade upon the defences of.................... 240
constant exposure of Washington at the siege of................ 242
patriotism of Governor Nelson at. 243
headquarters of Cornwallis at.... 444
letter from Clinton, received by Cornwallis, urging him to hold out to the last extremity...... 244
death of Colonel Cochran at..... 245
details of the surrender at....... 247
total numbers of the army surrendered at.................... 247
delivery of British colors at...... 249
Cornwallis, the guest of Washington after the surrender of..... 249
how Lord North received the news of the surrender of........... 250
Colonel Tarleton at............. 251
small-pox and camp-fever at, after the surrender................ 253
at the present time an inconsiderable village................... 330

THE END.

Printed in the United States
23428LVS00001B/12

9 780766 137578